Challenges for Rural America
in the Twenty-First Century

Challenges for Rural America in the Twenty-First Century

edited by David L. Brown and Louis E. Swanson

with assistance from Alan W. Barton

The Pennsylvania State University Press
University Park, Pennsylvania

Library of Congress Cataloging-in-Publication Data

Challenges for rural America in the 21st century/
    edited by David L. Brown and Louis E. Swanson
    with assistance from Alan W. Barton.
        p.   cm.
(Rural studies series of the Rural Sociological Society)
"Sponsored by the Rural Sociological Society"—Ack.
ISBN 0-271-02241-8 (cloth : alk. paper)
ISBN 0-271-02242-6 (pbk. : alk. paper)
1. United States—Rural conditions.
2. Sociology, Rural—United States.
3. Rural development—United States.
I. Title: Challenges for rural America in the twenty-first century.
II. Brown, David L. (David Louis), 1945- .
III. Swanson, Louis E.
IV. Barton, Alan W.
V. Rural Sociological Society.
VI. Series.

HN59 .2 .C435 2003
307.72'0973—dc21

                                                    2003009910

For rural America and its continuing struggle
to achieve the American dream.

CONTENTS

Part I: Who Lives in Rural America Today?

New Directions in Population Change and Diversity

Reshuffling and Remaking Rural Families

Part II: A Transformed Rural Economy

Part III: The Rural Community: Is It Local? Is It a Community?

Perspectives on Community

The Social Institutions That Maintain and Reproduce Community

Part IV: People and the Environment: Tough Tradeoffs in an Era with Vanishing Buffers

Part V: Changing National and International Policies: New Uncertainties and New Challenges

FIGURES

TABLES

ACKNOWLEDGMENTS

This book is sponsored by the Rural Sociological Society (RSS). The sustained support and enthusiasm of the RSS Council and membership is warmly appreciated. We received financial assistance from the Rural Sociological Society, the Polson Institute for Global Development in Cornell University's Department of Development Sociology, and the Department of Sociology at Colorado State University. Alan W. Barton copyedited the entire manuscript and deserves a warm thank you for helping to knit together thirty-two chapters from over fifty authors into an integrated whole. Mary Wright helped produce the manuscript. We also wish to acknowledge Peter J. Potter, our editor at Penn State University Press, for his good advice, continuing support, and patience.

Introduction

Rural America Enters the New Millennium
\

David L. Brown and Louis E. Swanson

Why Do Rural People and Areas Merit Special Attention in the Twenty-First Century?

America is a predominantly urban society, yet rural people and communities continue to play important social, economic, and political roles in the nation's life. While the 2000 census showed that eight out of every ten Americans live in urban areas, over fifty-six million persons reside in rural communities (Johnson, Chapter 1). According to the Population Reference Bureau (2000), this exceeds the total population of all but twenty-two of the world's two hundred nation-states. So while rural people make up a minority of the U.S. population, they are a very large minority indeed.

In contrast to its population, most of the nation's land area is located in rural areas. In fact, nearly three-fourths of U.S. counties are classified as nonmetropolitan areas. This means that most of the nation's natural resources are rural. Energy, metals, water, soil, timber, wildlife habitat, open space, and attractive viewscapes are all primarily rural resources. America's future depends on the prudent use and conservation of this rural-based natural endowment. Suffice it to say, society and natural resources are mutually interrelated. The long-term sustainability of the nation's natural resource base affects and is affected by its institutions and social organization.

Rural people and communities merit special attention because Americans generally accord them a value that far exceeds their material contribution to the nation's growth and well-being. The American public tends to see its rural population as a repository of almost sacred values and a stable anchor during times of rapid social change. Attitudes about rural people and communities are a complex mix of pro-rural and anti-urban

(Rowley 1996). Some Americans value rural people and communities for what they perceive to be intrinsic attributes. For others, rurality is an oppositional attitude, a way of criticizing the urban/industrial system (Berry 1977; Jackson 1980). Regardless of the content of their attitudes, most Americans form their opinions about rural people and communities from a distance—through literature, art, and music, but not through direct experience. The true nature of rurality—the worldviews of rural people and the conditions of their lives—is often at variance with the typical perception of most Americans (Logan 1996).

Equity is a final reason for being concerned about rural people and communities during the new millennium. The rural/urban gap in quality of life, by most measures, has diminished significantly in recent decades, but rural areas still lag behind their urban counterparts. For example, the rural poverty rate exceeded the urban rate by over five percentage points during most of the 1980s; today, the gap has declined to about half that (Jensen, McLaughlin, and Slack, Chapter 9).

Nonetheless, rural people have a higher likelihood of being poor than urban residents, and some of the nation's most chronically depressed areas are rural. In fact, over five hundred rural counties have consistently had poverty rates in excess of 20 percent over the last four decades (Whitener, Weber, and Duncan 2002).

What Is Rural in Contemporary American Society?

The social and economic organization of community life has been thoroughly transformed by institutional and technological changes that have occurred since the mid-twentieth century. Accordingly, many of the notions about what differentiates rural and urban communities that grew out of the industrial era no longer provide a reliable lens for viewing such differences. Some measures, such as population size and density, are still arguably valid indicators of urbanization and rurality; however, others, such as economic dependence on agriculture and natural resources or physical isolation, have diminished in importance as markers of rurality. Other conventional measures of rural/urban differentiation, such as the completeness and capacity of local institutional structures and generally conservative attitudes on social and political issues, may still delimit rural from urban communities, but systematic research on these questions is lacking. The classical notion that rural society is more likely to be characterized by primary group relationships while urban areas are distinguished by work- and organization-based social interaction may never have been true;

certainly, research has shown that it is not the case in contemporary American society (Hummon 1990).

This discussion indicates that urbanity and rurality are multidimensional concepts that incorporate economic, social, and institutional aspects. Unfortunately, the rural/urban classification in most national statistical systems is based on one or two key demographic indicators such as population size and/or density. The issue is not that government statisticians fail to understand that urbanization is a multidimensional process; rather, political realities make it unrealistic to expect statistical agencies to adopt a complex delineation, as budget constraints and competition between stakeholder groups determine which items are included on surveys and how tabulations and data products are organized. In addition, most scholars and statisticians recognize that rural and urban categorizations are variables, not discrete categories, and copious evidence shows that both urban and rural areas are highly diverse and differentiated. Nevertheless, conventional statistical practice privileges urban areas over rural (Brown and Cromartie 2003).

United States government statisticians use two separate methods to delineate urban and rural areas—urban versus rural and metropolitan versus nonmetropolitan. In both instances, the categories are dichotomous, with urban/metropolitan areas defined first, leaving rural/nonmetropolitan areas as residuals. The urban/rural delineation is a nodal concept based almost entirely on satisfying a population size threshold. Places with less than 2,500 residents and open country residents outside of *urbanized areas* are the rural residual. The metropolitan/nonmetropolitan distinction embodies the concept of a large metropolitan city and its interdependent hinterland. Metropolitan areas consist of entire counties that contain one or more central cities that meet minimum size criteria plus outlying counties that are integrated with the center via commuting. Until recently the nonmetropolitan residual was completely undifferentiated, despite a large body of research that showed this to be untrue (Hines, Brown, and Zimmer 1975; Cook and Mizer 1994). Beginning with the 2000 census, the U.S. Office of Management and Budget (OMB) has modified its official geocoding scheme to recognize diversity within nonmetropolitan America. The OMB has instituted a "core-based statistical area classification system" that recognizes that both metropolitan and nonmetropolitan territory can be integrated with a population center. The new system establishes *micropolitan areas* as a means of distinguishing between nonmetropolitan areas that are integrated with centers with populations of 10,000 to 49,999, and nonmetropolitan territories that are not integrated with a center having that minimum size (U.S. Office of Management and Budget 2000).

While we recognize that each of these classification systems gives a somewhat different picture of what is urban and what is rural, we also acknowledge that both classification systems are valid ways of differentiating rural and urban areas; thus, *we have permitted contributors to use either delineation in this book.* In all instances, however, they have been asked to identify data sources so that readers can determine how figures were produced. Readers should note that contributors are more likely to use the urban/rural terminology, as it is more frequent in common usage, and as the metropolitan/nonmetropolitan terminology is awkward.

Why Have We Written This Book?

This book continues a tradition of decennial volumes co-edited by presidents of the Rural Sociological Society, and published in the Society's *Rural Studies Series.* The first volume, entitled *Rural Society in the U.S.: Issues for the 1980s,* was published in 1982 and co-edited by Don Dillman and Daryl Hobbs. *Rural Policies for the 1990s* followed nine years later and was co-edited by Cornelia Flora and James Christenson. The present volume comes at a particularly opportune time because we are entering not only a new decade, but a new century and millennium as well. Hence it is an appropriate time to examine what sociologists have learned about rural life during the previous ten years, to identify high-priority knowledge needs that remain unfulfilled, and to suggest how sociological knowledge about rural people and communities might be brought to bear on the nation's critical policy decisions. We have taken a broad-brush approach in this volume, including major sections on people, economies, communities, institutions, and natural environments. Our goal is to integrate knowledge across these domains to identify fundamental issues of interest to both social scientists and policy-makers.

This book showcases both the disciplinary and policy-oriented work of rural sociologists. About half of the book's contributors were established scholars when the Society published its previous volume in 1991; however, twenty-one have joined our ranks since then. Accordingly, we feature contributions from established researchers and we introduce a new generation of rural sociological scholars.

As we mentioned, this book has an explicit policy focus. Each author was asked to synthesize recent research about a particular aspect of rural society, to identify gaps in knowledge, and to explain how this knowledge helps to justify special attention in public policy for rural people, places, and environments. One of the Society's goals in publishing this book is to use it to build a bridge between rural sociological researchers and the public policy process. This concern for policy is appropriate given rural sociology's applied tradition, and its predominant institutional location in Land Grant Universities.

Overview: Authors and Chapters

Each of this book's six sections focuses attention on a major dimension of rural life in contemporary American society. Organizing the material into sections is a convenient expository device; however, the sections are not mutually exclusive domains of knowledge. In many ways, people, economies, natural environments, and community institutions are interdependent, and aspects of each are embedded in the others. Convenient but nonetheless false pigeon-holing obscures the need to understand how demographic change affects and is affected by the natural environment, how economic development and community development are interrelated, and how changes in family organization influence and are influenced by economic opportunities, among myriad other interrelations. The following discussion describes each of the book's sections in turn, but it is truly *the integration across these substantive domains that constitutes rural America in the new millennium.*

Who Lives in Rural America?

Part I surveys diversity and change among rural people and families. One key theme focuses on the demographic and social trends that are transforming the ethnic makeup and climate in rural America—including awareness of and attitudes toward an increasingly multicultural rural population. A second important theme concerns the changing structure of rural families, and vulnerabilities faced by different types of families and family members, given emerging structural and economic changes.

As Kenneth Johnson points out in Chapter 1, demographic change is both a determinant and a consequence of social structural change in rural America, and the direction of rural/urban migration, the principal determinant of contemporary rural population change, has been extremely unpredictable during recent decades. *Hence adapting to unpredictable fluctuations in population change is the first challenge identified for rural America.*

The next three chapters indicate that *changes in rural America's racial and ethnic composition and the continuing impoverishment of a disproportionate share of rural African Americans, American Indians, and Latinos poses the second major challenge for rural America.*[1] In Chapter 2, Rosalind Harris and Dreamal Worthen show that 95 percent of rural African Americans continue to live in the South, and they contend that the current situation for rural African Americans is a legacy of past racial, class, and political inequalities and intrigues. They emphasize that economic restructuring has proceeded in tandem with the restructuring of the welfare state in ways that expose rural African Americans to high levels of economic and social insecurity. Angela Gonzales, in Chapter 3, demonstrates that American Indians are the nation's most rural minority population. She examines the complex dynamics of American Indian identity, and concludes that answering the question of "who is an American Indian" depends on a number of social, political, and legal considerations. Many American Indian groups have turned to gaming as an economic development strategy to alleviate the population's extreme poverty. Gonzales looks at the pros and cons of this strategy and concludes that the benefits of gaming have been unevenly spread, and that it may have unanticipated negative social consequences. In Chapter 4, Rogelio Saenz and Cruz Torres emphasize that Latinos are the nation's fastest growing rural minority. Moreover, they show that rural Latinos are experiencing a significant regional redistribution from an almost complete concentration in the Southwest to the South and Midwest. This relocation is associated with economic opportunities in a number of low-wage, low-skill industries such as meat packing. Saenz and Torres emphasize the critical role of education as a vehicle for social mobility and a brighter social and economic future.

Trends and changes in family organization have elevated concern about family viability in the United States today. Yet most social scientists believe that the family is a lasting institution, albeit one with a changing configuration. Katherine MacTavish and Sonya Salamon begin Chapter 5, and the next subsection of the book, by comparing family changes occurring in rural and urban communities. They suggest that rural and urban families are changing in similar ways, and are facing similar challenges—ones not faced by previous generations. For example, they indicate that the separation of home and work has fragmented rural, urban, and suburban families alike. They conclude that *commuting to nonlocal jobs has strained intergenerational and other relationships, posing critical challenges for socialization and child rearing.*

The next three chapters focus on aspects of family life in contemporary rural society. Each highlights a segment of the rural population—the elderly, youth, and women—at risk of disadvantage in a society that is experiencing

---

1. We have chosen to use the terms African American, American Indian, and Latino to identify race/ethnic groups. We recognize that there is no consensus on this issue, and that all of these terms are contested to some extent.

economic restructuring and a fundamental reconsideration of the social contract, particularly with respect to vulnerable persons. Nina Glasgow, in Chapter 6, establishes that population aging is a society-wide phenomenon, and that aging will accelerate in both rural and urban areas when the first members of the baby boom generation reach older age. In fact, more than one in five Americans in both urban and rural areas will be sixty-five or older by the year 2030. Glasgow identifies *caregiving for elders as a major challenge facing rural America*. She contends that older people in rural areas have less immediate access to their adult children than their urban counterparts, a worrisome condition because after spouses, children are most likely to provide care to older persons. In Chapter 7, Daniel Lichter, Vincent Roscigno, and Dennis Condron contend that rural children have not shared equally in America's abundance. They indicate that unless we as a society do a better job of educating and socializing rural youth, and protecting them from drug and alcohol abuse, violence, victimization, and unintended teen pregnancy, a large share of rural "at risk" children will be ill-prepared for good jobs in the information-based economy, for a healthy family life, and for active civic engagement. *The challenge is to make sure that rural children are not left behind in our rapidly changing economy and society.* In Chapter 8, Ann Tickamyer and Debra Henderson indicate that women's broad-scale entrance into the paid labor force is both a determinant and a consequence of the economic restructuring that occurred in both rural and urban America during the last third of the twentieth century. With the increase in single parent households, many women now must simultaneously fulfill two roles: primary earner and family caregiver. Moreover, even among married mothers, paid employment has not been accompanied by other family members sharing household labor. Accordingly, *a challenge for rural society is to move toward a more egalitarian family model in which economic and familial roles as well as decision-making are shared equally among adult members.*

Our discussion of rural families is capped off by Leif Jensen, Diane McLaughlin, and Tim Slack's examination of the persisting challenge presented by rural poverty in Chapter 9. They demonstrate that rural people are at a higher risk of being poor than their urban counterparts, but that rural poverty is often hidden or camouflaged, and therefore unrecognized. They indicate that poor rural families who live in depressed areas are doubly disadvantaged. Moreover, they show that rural persons who follow society's prescriptions to work and stay married obtain less protection from poverty than is the case in urban America. *Recognizing the severity, complexity, and persistence of rural poverty, and leveling the playing field for the rural poor, are major challenges for American society.*

A Transformed Rural Economy

Part II focuses on a transformed rural economy. Here, the differential effects of economic restructuring are the key theme. David McGranahan initiates the discussion in Chapter 10 by describing both long- and shorter-term trends and changes in the ways rural Americans make a living. He shows that while agriculture and natural resources have declined as sources of employment, they continue to dominate economic life in some regions. Similarly, manufacturing has declined as a share of rural employment, but it still accounts for nearly one-fifth of rural jobs, a much higher level of dependence than in urban economies. In contrast, dependence on services is much lower in rural than in urban America, and rural services are more likely to involve low-wage, low-skill, seasonal, and/or involuntarily part-time employment.

William Falk and Linda Lobao, in Chapter 11, elaborate on the topic of restructuring by examining who this process benefits and who it harms. Their approach reminds us why it is important to recognize that diversity characterizes rural America, as policies, programs, and social processes have different effects in different types of areas. They conclude that economic restructuring has contributed to polarization within rural America, noting that rural areas close to metropolitan centers are able to benefit from the expansion of urban influence, while more remote rural places are unable to replace their traditional industries. Leanne Tigges and Glenn Fuguitt pick up on the topic of rural-urban proximity in Chapter 12, showing that commuting is an important aspect of urban/rural interdependence and that it also facilitates urban deconcentration. They indicate that commuting permits individuals to have access to a wider range of economic opportunities, and may serve as a substitute for rural/urban migration. Echoing the polarization theme introduced by Falk and Lobao, Tigges and Fuguitt indicate that communities with high out-commuting rates face higher levels of economic and social risk. Chapters 10 through 12 indicate that *attracting and retaining an adequate supply of high-quality jobs is one of rural America's foremost challenges in the new millennium.*

Chapters 13 and 14 are concerned with the future of two traditional economic activities in rural areas—agriculture and tourism. In Chapter 13, Frederick Buttel considers the ramifications of trends suggesting that farming is being abandoned as a household livelihood strategy in rural America. He indicates that seven simultaneous trends are transforming the agro-food system at the turn of the century, and that their coincidence has made the abandonment of family farming irreversible. While employment opportunities in farming are waning in rural areas, tourism is on the increase;

however, Richard Krannich and Peggy Petrzelka caution, in Chapter 14, that tourism is not a panacea for rural underdevelopment. First, not every rural place has natural features or other amenities that would attract tourists. Second, tourism can have both positive and negative consequences for the people and places concerned. While tourism is a path to successful development in some places, more commonly it is an inadequate substitute for the higher-paying and more secure jobs it often replaces. *A challenge for rural America is to secure well-paying, secure jobs in more remote areas, including areas that previously depended on family farming.*

The Rural Community

Rural communities, like the society in which they are embedded, are composed of much more than jobs and income. While individuals are more likely to choose to live where jobs pay well and are plentiful, entrepreneurs are not likely to locate their firms in areas that lack effective institutions and social organization. The classic question "which came first, jobs or community institutions?" is best answered by noting that the two are mutually interrelated. Neither can occur without the other. Accordingly, Part III focuses on different aspects of rural social organization. We ask why some localities are more successful at development than others, and consider the vital role that various institutions play in creating and reproducing the important characteristics and ties that define communities and enhance development. We also address how processes of local social organization are embedded within, influenced by, and constituent of processes of global integration.

In Chapter 15, A. E. Luloff and Jeffrey Bridger contend that a community arises naturally out of the social interaction that occurs in its locality. They indicate, however, that the possibilities for community mobilization are reduced by the social inequality that separates people and interests. Yet these possibilities are enhanced when populations develop relationships and lines of communication that span interest group boundaries. They argue that local capacity to address important interests depends on a population's ability to identify and articulate common ground and work together. They call this capacity for collective action *community agency,* and contend that it is a key element in successful development.

Cornelia Butler Flora and Jan Flora present a different perspective on community in Chapter 16, yet they also focus on the importance of local social relationships. They develop the concept of *entrepreneurial social infrastructure* as a characteristic that facilitates community action. For the Floras, entrepreneurial social infrastructure involves two types of *aggregate level social capital*—bonding, which involves connections among homogeneous individuals, and bridging, which connects heterogeneous groups within a community to each other and to groups outside of the community. They suggest that entrepreneurial social capital can be enhanced through collective effort.

In Chapter 17, Thomas Lyson and Charles Tolbert offer a third perspective on rural community. They share a vision of civic community that involves small, locally owned enterprises, an economically independent middle class, and a high degree of participation in local governance, religious groups, and social organizations. Such communities have civic foundations that perpetuate community-oriented institutions, effective problem solving, and cultural attachment to locality. They believe that civic communities have less social inequality and higher social welfare. These three chapters taken together, then, indicate that *strengthening local social relationships that contribute to communities' abilities to secure collective goals is a challenge for rural America.*

Turning to the question of social institutions in rural communities, Alessandro Bonanno and Douglas Constance examine external influences on rural community life in Chapter 18. They argue that the nation-state is no longer the central unit of reference in international relations, but that increasingly, transnational corporations and other global actors directly influence localities. New technology has facilitated new forms of global interaction with political, economic, and social dimensions, which limit the autonomy of local communities and economies. While Bonanno and Constance believe that power imbalances between global and local entities inevitably disadvantage local ones, it should be mentioned that other scholars, such as those who subscribe to notions of bridging social capital, envision situations where effective external relationships can enhance local well-being (Young and Lyson 1993).

Communities may be thought of as structured ways in which human beings satisfy their daily needs on a continuing basis. A variety of specific institutions maintain and reproduce communities and make the satisfaction of daily needs possible. While not exhausting all institutional realms, our treatment of community institutions includes the "usual suspects": governance, religion, education, and health care. In Chapter 19, Mildred Warner indicates that privatization and decentralization—in this case, from higher to lower levels of government—are reducing local governments' ability to produce and deliver services, administer municipal functions, and plan and execute strategies for future development. Moreover, she contends that privatization and decentralization are producing inequality among areas because decentralization typically requires local governments to "do more with less," so that areas with more limited fiscal capacity are likely to scale back or eliminate services altogether. She promotes interlocal cooperation between governments, nongovernmental organizations, and the private sector as a way for local rural governments to enhance their managerial, functional, and administrative capacity. Accordingly, *a challenge for rural America is for local government to find a new role within the decentralized and privatized environment.* Warner believes that this role might emphasize facilitation and networking, rather than the traditional role of providing services.

Leland Glenna, in Chapter 20, characterizes religion as a body of beliefs and rituals that connect people to society rather than as a commitment to a religious organization. He contends that in general, rural people are both more strongly religious and more conservative than urban people, and consequently that rural-based religions are more resistant to change. Regardless of this conservatism, however, Glenna suggests that the rural church has not been immune to twenty-first-century worldviews. He contends that portraying religion as a set of quaint but dying beliefs and values misses its complex function in modern rural society. Religions persist and flourish, according to Lester (2002), because they provide a sense of social connectedness that helps people deal with new social realities.

Next, in Chapter 21, Lionel Beaulieu, Glenn Israel, and Ronald Wimberley begin from the observation that rural educational attainment, especially completing college, lags behind urban attainment. Rather than blaming rural schools and educational systems for this lamentable situation, however, the authors indicate that rural educational attainment is contingent on a complex interaction between the school, the home, and the community. Their chapter is a "wake-up call" to educational policy-makers, encouraging them to look beyond the schools when considering how human capital is produced in rural America.

Lois Wright Morton indicates that rural people have poorer health than their urban counterparts, and that there are rural/urban gaps in access to and availability of hospitals, health care professionals, and public health services. She argues in Chapter 22 that while these gaps have been a chronic problem for rural America, they are exacerbated by recent policy changes and by the competitive-market model of health care provision. She underscores that policies emphasizing cost containment diverge from national health goals, which stress the need to eliminate disparities and increase longevity and quality of life for all Americans. Rural/urban disparities in health and education undermine the nation's current and future stock of human capital, and hence its economic and social development. Accordingly, *ensuring equality of access to health and education is a challenge for rural America in the new millennium.*

People and the Environment

Rural America contains 79 percent of the nation's land area, and hence the majority of its water, minerals, energy, soil, and other resources. The inter-relationships between society and natural resources are explored in Part IV. The salient theme is expressed in this section's subtitle: "Tough Trade-offs in an Era of Vanishing Buffers."

In Chapter 23, Douglas Jackson-Smith focuses on land use change in rural America, and contends that the predominant concern with urban sprawl has obscured land use issues in rural areas farther from the city. While sprawl is clearly a problem of national proportions, so is the less intense development experienced by rural communities located outside of the urban periphery. Moreover, Jackson-Smith suggests that rural land use change is further complicated by the fact that most rural areas have little experience with planning and land management, and have few land use ordinances in place. Accordingly, rural land use change is often chaotic and haphazard.

In Chapter 24, Lynn England and Ralph Brown compare agricultural- and extractive-based rural communities, arguing that people live in harmony with nature in the former but in conflict with nature in the latter. They suggest that the roots of conflict in extractive communities do not stem from the loggers, miners, and oil riggers, however. Rather, external forces such as multinational corporations and the federal government are largely responsible for the environmental damage done in extractive communities. Overspecialization in an exhaustible commodity, especially when the extraction process is controlled from outside, puts communities at risk of resource depletion, environmental damage, and boom and bust cycles. The authors promote a long-term vision of sustainable development for extractive communities, and they indicate that an increasing number of such areas are showing a greater ability to exercise local control over the future of their landscapes.

Steven Daniels and Joan Brehm argue in Chapter 25 that the nation's current positive view of wildlife is at risk, because more and more people are experiencing negative interactions with wildlife, such as Lyme disease, crop and garden damage from deer browsing, and encounters with coyotes and other predators. These negative interactions are becoming more frequent because people are moving into natural settings, not vice versa. The Endangered Species Act, designed to protect the habitat of threatened and endangered species, has brought public land managers into direct conflict with ranchers, woodsmen, and others with a more utilitarian view of rural land use. Daniels and Brehm recommend that future wildlife protection laws should incorporate more equity between competing uses.

Taken together, the three chapters of Part IV demonstrate the complex, and at times contentious, interactions between society and the natural environment. Thus, we are *challenged to design and implement enlightened management strategies that mediate competing claims on the environment, ensure equity of access, and protect the resource base and landscape for future generations.*

Changing National and International Policies

The final section examines changing policy trends that affect rural people and communities. Chapters 26 through 30 present a vision of rural communities that are linked in both overt and subtle ways to larger-scale policy environments, including public policy at the national level and an increasingly important set of global economic policies and institutions. A key theme is the tension between policies that promote concentration and centralization and those that promote devolution and local control.

Addressing this tension in Chapter 26, Gary Paul Green outlines a debate regarding the autonomy of local leaders: are they constrained by external forces and/or by local political and economic interests, or do they have sufficient agency to choose development options that benefit the community widely? His response favors local agency, although he suggests that local economic development is most likely to occur in places that have effective institutions and organizations and an active process of public participation. Green contends that development decisions that arise through a democratic process will be shaped by other than strictly economic goals, and will spread benefits more widely than strategies that reflect the needs of one or several dominant economic interests.

Devolution, the shifting balance in authority, accountability, and functional responsibility between levels of government, is the latest chapter in our nation's continuing debate over federalism and the appropriate balance of power between the central government and states and localities. The pendulum has now swung back in the direction of greater powers to states and localities, the rationale being that public decisions are best made where people live and work. In Chapter 27, Jeffrey Sharp and Domenico Parisi confirm Warner's earlier concern (Chapter 19) that devolution may create inequality between those places with sufficient capacity to manage their own affairs and other areas that lack the means to manage and administer public functions.

Welfare reform represents an important contemporary example of devolution in practice. As Julie Zimmerman and Thomas Hirschl indicate in Chapter 28, the Personal Responsibility and Work Opportunities Reconciliation

Act (PRWORA) of 1996 furnishes a block grant to states, which then administer the provision of funds to low-income citizens for income maintenance, within certain federal guidelines. The large number of working poor and underemployed in rural America led most analysts to fear that rural low-income families would fare worse than urban families under PRWORA; however, Zimmerman and Hirschl found so much variability among states in the way the program is administered that it is difficult to determine whether rural people have fared better or worse than their urban counterparts. What is clear, however, is that rural America's special circumstances—limited access to child care, inadequate public transportation, and high underemployment—were not considered when PRWORA was designed. *Rural advocates have a special challenge to ensure that the rural poor are not disadvantaged merely by place of residence where income maintenance is concerned.*

Policies of economic liberalization encourage firms to seek the lowest production costs, relocating if necessary to gain cost advantages. This pits localities against each other in a destructive "beggar thy neighbor" competition. In Chapter 29, Phillip McMichael shows that agriculture is no more immune from the negative effects of this economic restructuring than other industrial sectors. He indicates that globalization has undermined national systems of agriculture, replacing them with systems dominated by transnational corporations. The result is that farmers are brought into competition with each other in the global system, and smaller firms, especially those in developing countries, are being forced out of business. McMichael concludes that food security is diminished by this global arrangement in which the supply and character of food is dictated by relatively few global actors.

The book's final chapter focuses on the practice of rural community development. Kenneth Pigg and Ted Bradshaw promote a new bottom-up view of community development praxis in which the community developer is a resource coordinator and network facilitator rather than an expert technician. They suggest that this model encourages cooperation among all stakeholders and widespread citizen participation. Pigg and Bradshaw's *catalytic development model* differs from conventional top-down practice, in which success depends on technical assistance provided by the community developer and other experts. The catalytic development approach is consistent with the views of community put forth by Luloff and Bridger and the Floras, as well as Warner's vision of interlocal cooperation among rural governments. *The overall challenge raised by these diverse policy-oriented chapters is that rural areas will not succeed if they employ "go it alone" strategies. Only through cooperation between communities, among interests within communities, and between local governments, NGOs, and the private sector will rural areas be able to prosper in the new millennium.*

Conclusion

This book provides a comprehensive view of rural America as our nation enters the twenty-first century. We have emphasized that while each chapter focuses on a particular aspect of rural life, these issues are highly interdependent. Rural development is about the interrelationships among the various aspects of rural life; about how population, employment, environment, politics, institutions, and national and international policies affect and are affected by each other. We have also stressed that while the authors here, as a practical matter, discuss the rural community, the rural population, and rural policy, in reality there is no one rural America. Rural Americans and rural communities are extremely diverse—demographically, economically, environmentally, culturally. Like rural research, rural policy must be sensitive to this diversity so that particular types of persons and areas are not marginalized in the new century.

PART I

Who Lives in Rural America Today?

New Directions in Population Change and Diversity

1

Unpredictable Directions of Rural Population Growth and Migration

Kenneth M. Johnson

Rural America enters the new century with a turbulent history of demographic change. Through most of the twentieth century, nonmetropolitan areas experienced modest population growth because the excess of births over deaths was sufficient to offset migration losses. The magnitude of the migration loss varied from decade to decade, but the pattern was quite consistent; more people left rural areas than came to them. This changed abruptly in the 1970s when rural America experienced a remarkable demographic turnaround, as population gains in nonmetropolitan areas exceeded those in metropolitan areas for the first time in at least 150 years. Not only were these rural population gains substantial, they were also fueled primarily by net in-migration. Nonmetropolitan areas actually gained more than 3.1 million people in migration exchanges with metropolitan areas during the 1970s. The rural turnaround appeared to wane in the 1980s as widespread out-migration and population decline reemerged; however, as we shall see, rural demographic trends rebounded in the 1990s, adding yet another twist to the complex patterns of population changes in nonmetropolitan America.

Understanding the population redistribution trends that have swept nonmetropolitan America is critical to addressing the challenges rural America faces in the twenty-first century. Demographic change does not occur in a vacuum. It is a direct response to prior organizational, technological, and environmental changes that interact in complex ways with individual and household decision-making to produce overall demographic change (Brown 2002). Nor is demographic change merely a response to

The research for this chapter was supported by grants from the Economic Research Service (43-3AEM-9-80118) and from the North Central Research Station of the U.S. Forest Service (01-JV-11231300-038).

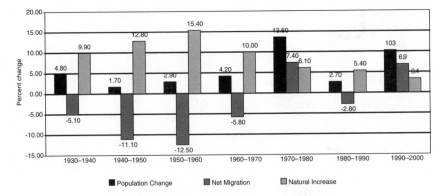

Fig. 1.1 Nonmetropolitan demographic change, 1930–2000

these forces; it is also a causal agent fostering future changes in the social, economic, and political landscapes of rural America. For rural areas with histories of population loss that have recently rebounded to growth, an influx of new people presents communities with both challenges and opportunities. Recent arrivals may differ from the existing population along multiple dimensions of race and ethnicity, socioeconomic status, life cycle, and work experience and knowledge. They may also have different life experiences, networks of acquaintances, and social and business contacts. Finally, their expectations for the future of the community may differ from those of long-term residents. Integrating such a diverse population into the existing community structure and balancing the differing expectations and aspirations of these various constituencies represents a significant challenge to local institutions. Not all of rural America is growing; large segments of the nation's heartland continue to lose people and institutions. Areas like these face a different set of challenges—how to maintain the social, economic, and political fabric of the community with diminishing human and economic capital. The ensuing chapters address the myriad challenges facing rural America in the twenty-first century. The task of this chapter is to provide a demographic context for these essays.

Recent Nonmetropolitan Demographic Change

Data from the 2000 census confirm earlier reports that a rural demographic rebound did occur during the 1990s. Demographically, the 1990s were more similar to the 1970s than any other recent decade (Fig. 1.1). Nearly 74 percent of the 2,303 counties classified as nonmetropolitan in 1993 gained population between 1990 and 2000 (Fig. 1.2). The nonmetropolitan

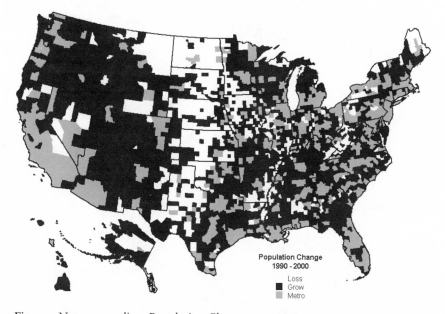

Fig. 1.2 Nonmetropolitan Population Change, 1990–2000

Analysis K.M. Johnson, Loyola University Chicago
Data: U.S. Census Bureau

population was 56.1 million in April 2000, a gain of 5.2 million (10.3 percent) since April 1990.[1] In contrast, nonmetropolitan areas grew by fewer than 1.3 million during the 1980s. The nonmetropolitan population still grew at a slower pace (10.3 percent) than did the metropolitan population (13.8 percent) during the 1990s, but the gap was much narrower than during the previous decade. Gains were prevalent in the Mountain West, Upper Great Lakes, Ozarks, parts of the South, and in rural areas of the Northeast. Widespread losses occurred in the Great Plains, western Corn Belt, and Mississippi Delta (Table 1.1).

A striking characteristic of nonmetropolitan demographic trends during the 1990s is the substantial number of counties that rebounded from population loss during the 1980s to population gain during the 1990s. Some 716 nonmetropolitan counties followed this trend. In contrast, only

1. Most research on nonmetropolitan demographic trends in the 1990s relied on population estimates. Such estimates proved to be considerably lower than the enumerated nonmetropolitan population in the 2000 census. The census revealed 1.2 million (2.3 percent) more nonmetropolitan residents in April 2000 than were suggested by estimates. This difference is attributed to net migration, because it is treated as a residual of population change minus natural increase. The percentage of counties with population gain and net in-migration also increases when 2000 census data are used. Thus, conclusions based on the 2000 census suggest considerably greater population and net migration gains in nonmetropolitan areas.

Table 1.1 Population change, net migration, and natural increase, by adjacency and metropolitan status, 1970–2000

	Number of Cases	Initial Population	Population Change			Net Migration			Natural Increase		
			Absolute Change	Percent Change	Percent Growing	Absolute Change	Percent Change	Percent Growing	Absolute Change	Percent Change	Percent Growing
1970–1980											
All nonmetropolitan	2,276	43,345	5,805	13.4	80.0	3,159	7.3	66.9	2,630	6.1	88.1
Nonadjacent	1,274	19,772	2,477	12.5	72.1	1,223	6.2	60.5	1,249	6.3	85.9
Adjacent	1,002	23,573	3,328	14.1	89.1	1,936	8.2	75.1	1,381	6.3	90.8
Metropolitan	834	158,884	17,146	10.8	88.6	5,948	3.7	73.4	11,198	7.0	97.8
Total	3,110	202,229	22,937	11.3	82.0	9,107	4.5	68.7	13,830	6.8	90.7
1980–1990											
All nonmetropolitan	2,305	49,578	1,320	2.7	45.1	-1370	-2.8	27.3	2,690	5.4	89.6
Nonadjacent	1,298	22,612	134	0.6	36.4	-1175	-5.2	20.7	1,309	5.8	87.0
Adjacent	1,007	26,966	1,186	4.4	56.3	-194	-0.7	35.8	1,382	5.1	92.9
Metropolitan	836	176,965	20,848	11.8	81.0	6575	3.7	57.7	14,271	8.1	97.7
Total	3,141	226,543	22,168	9.8	54.7	5206	2.3	35.4	16,962	7.5	91.8
1990–2000											
All nonmetropolitan	2,303	50,824	5,249	10.3	73.9	3,509	6.9	68.3	1,740	3.4	71.4
Nonadjacent	1,297	22,671	1,848	8.2	64.4	1,079	4.8	59.8	769	3.4	64.1
Adjacent	1,006	28,154	3,400	12.1	86.1	2,430	8.6	79.2	971	3.4	80.9
Metropolitan	837	197,963	27,383	13.8	90.1	12,044	6.1	77.5	15,338	7.7	95.2
Total	3,140	248,787	32,631	13.1	78.2	15,553	6.3	70.7	17,078	6.9	77.8

Notes: 1993 metropolitan status used for all periods.
Natural increase 1990–1999 from FSCPE. Natural increase projected to 4/2000 from FSCPE.
Source: Census 2000 PL-94 data 1970–1990 Census and Federal-State Cooperative Population Estimates.

fifty-five counties that gained population during the 1980s lost population during the 1990s. Consistent population loss during the 1980s and 1990s occurred in 547 nonmetropolitan counties, whereas 983 counties grew consistently through both decades. In all, six hundred more nonmetropolitan counties gained population during the 1990s than in the 1980s.

Migration gains accounted for 67 percent of the total population increase in nonmetropolitan areas. Rural areas had a net inflow of 3.5 million people during the 1990s compared to a net outflow of 1.4 million during the 1980s. The nonmetropolitan net migration gain (6.9 percent) between 1990 and 2000 was greater than that in metropolitan areas (6.1 percent). This is a sharp contrast to the 1980s, when metropolitan areas had net in-migration, whereas nonmetropolitan areas had a net outflow. Such migration gains were widely distributed geographically, though they were least prevalent in the Great Plains, western Texas, and the Mississippi Delta.

Natural increase accounted for only 33 percent of the nonmetropolitan population increase between 1990 and 2000. In all, births exceeded deaths by an estimated 1.7 million in nonmetropolitan areas. The gain through natural increase in nonmetropolitan areas diminished during the 1990s compared to the rate of the 1980s. Diminished natural increase in nonmetropolitan areas is also reflected in a sharp increase in the incidence of natural decrease in these regions since 1990 (Johnson and Beale 1992; Johnson 1993; Johnson 2000).

Selective Deconcentration

Population trends over the past several decades suggest a gradual deconcentration of the population. This deconcentration has been selective (Frey and Johnson 1998), and has been affected by a variety of cyclical forces, but the overall trend reflects a general flow from more to less densely settled areas (Vining and Strauss 1977; Long and Nucci 1997; Boyle and Halfacree 1998). Evidence of population deconcentration in nonmetropolitan America is greatest in areas near metropolitan centers. It has long been recognized that the spillover of population from proximate metropolitan areas has contributed to growth in adjacent nonmetropolitan counties (Fuguitt 1985). The population residing in nonmetropolitan counties that are adjacent to metropolitan ones was 28.2 million in 2000 (see Table 1.1). Population growth is extremely widespread in adjacent areas. More than 86 percent of these counties gained population between 1990 and 2000. The population gain is also substantial—3.4 million (12.1 percent) since

1990. Most of the growth in these counties is from net in-migration. Adjacent counties gained 2.4 million from net in-migration between 1990 and 2000, compared to a gain of 971,000 from natural increase, and more than 79 percent of these areas had net in-migration. Population growth in nonmetropolitan areas was not restricted to counties near metropolitan centers. Even among more remote nonmetropolitan counties, recent population gains were significantly greater than during the 1980s. Growth occurred in 64.4 percent of counties not adjacent to metropolitan areas in the 1990s, compared to 36 percent during the 1980s. Such nonadjacent counties had net in-migration (4.8 percent) between 1990 and 2000, compared to a net migration loss (−5.2 percent) in the 1980s.

Nonmetropolitan counties with significant amenities or quality of life advantages have been particularly prone to rapid growth. The population in the 190 retirement-destination counties, located in the Sunbelt, coastal regions, portions of the West, and in the Upper Great Lakes (Cook and Mizer 1994), grew by 28.4 percent between 1990 and 2000. Virtually all this growth was due to net in-migration. Population and migration gains were also substantial in nonmetropolitan recreational counties (Beale and Johnson 1998; Johnson 1999; Johnson and Beale 1994; McGranahan 1999b). Such counties were prominent growth nodes during the 1970s and 1980s, a trend that has persisted in the 1990s. Counties where much of the land is federally owned also had substantial growth in the 1990s. Most of these counties are concentrated in the western United States and many have experienced significant net in-migration in recent years with migrants attracted by the scenic and recreational amenities.

Counties with a large proportion of their workforce commuting to jobs in other counties and those with economies dominated by service-sector jobs also grew rapidly because of net migration gains. Nonmetropolitan population gains were also widespread, though more modest, in manufacturing- and government-dependent counties. The gains in these latter two types of counties were more evenly balanced between natural increase and net migration.

Counties dependent on farming and mining were the least likely to gain population during the 1990s. The population gain was only 6.6 percent in farming-dependent counties, only 49 percent of which had net in-migration. Natural decrease was also common in these counties. Population gains were even smaller (2.3 percent) in mining counties, the only identifiable group that had net out-migration. The smaller than average population gains and widespread out-migration from mining- and farming-dependent counties during the 1990s represent a continuation of the trends of the 1980s; however, even among these counties the population and migration trends were more moderate in the 1990s than in the 1980s. Counties with histories of persistent poverty also had modest growth rates during the 1990s, with natural increase and net migration contributing roughly equally to the growth.

Increasing Rural Diversity

Most discussions of diversity focus on metropolitan populations. Minorities (African Americans, Latinos, Asians, and others) made up 40 percent of the population residing in metropolitan counties containing a central city in 2000 (Murdock and Johnson 2001). In metropolitan counties that are entirely suburban, nearly 22 percent of the population is minority. The increasing diversity of metropolitan areas may contribute to rural growth as well. Frey (1996) suggested that the influx of immigrants to some larger metropolitan areas may be stimulating an outflow of domestic migrants (including some to nonmetropolitan areas), especially among those who might compete directly with immigrants in the urban labor market; however, some questions remain about the extent of this phenomenon (Kritz and Gurak 2001). In contrast, only 17 percent of the nonmetropolitan population is minority, although the nonmetropolitan population is becoming more diverse. Between 1990 and 2000, minorities accounted for nearly 39 percent of the population increase in nonmetropolitan counties that were adjacent to metropolitan areas. In nonmetropolitan counties that were not adjacent to metropolitan areas, minorities accounted for 48 percent of the population increase. Latinos were prominent in the growth of both adjacent and nonadjacent areas. There was significant regional variation in the proportion of nonmetropolitan growth attributable to minorities, but in no region did minorities constitute less than 40 percent of the overall growth (Murdock and Johnson 2001).

Are Demographic Trends Shifting Yet Again?

Although 2000 census data are not yet available to support this, recent research suggests that there may have been a change in the age-specific character of migration to and from nonmetropolitan areas during the 1990s. Net migration to nonmetropolitan areas has always been age selective (Fuguitt and Heaton 1995). Historically, young adults have left nonmetropolitan areas in substantial numbers, while the net flow of individuals at other ages from nonmetropolitan areas has been less consistent. Regarding net migration exchanges with metropolitan areas, in some periods (notably the 1970s), nonmetropolitan areas gained individuals at all ages except young adult. In other periods, these areas experienced net migration losses at virtually every age. Researchers examining migration patterns in the 1990s report a puzzling finding with significant implications: between 1990 and 1995, the net influx of those under the age of sixty-five to nonmetropolitan areas has been much higher than would have been expected given historical trends (Fuguitt et al. 1998; Johnson and Fuguitt 2000). In contrast, the influx of adults sixty-five and over to such areas has been considerably less than expected. To be sure, retirement destination counties have received a significant influx of older migrants, but many other nonmetropolitan areas have not. Fuguitt et al. (1998) document the consistency of this pattern across regional groupings and county socioeconomic categories. This is surprising given the historical propensity of older Americans to move to and remain in nonmetropolitan areas. If data from the 2000 census substantiate this finding, it suggests that those under sixty-five account for a considerable majority of the migration gain fueling the rural rebound of the 1990s. Given the looming presence of the baby boom on the retirement front, any change in the pattern of age-specific migration trends has significant implications for rural America.

Population estimates for the 1990s suggest that the amount of net migration into nonmetropolitan areas has varied from year to year during the 1990s. The net inflow peaked in 1994–95 and has diminished since then (Johnson 2000; Beale 2000; Cromartie 2001). Data from the Current Population Survey show a similar trend, though the two series are collected independently and cannot be directly compared. Year to year variation in nonmetropolitan migration has been common, with the migration slowdown in the late 1990s closely resembling the migration pattern of the 1970s. Little is known about why net migration to nonmetropolitan areas slowed in the late 1990s; however, given the importance of migration to nonmetropolitan demographic change, a continuation of this pattern for an extended period will dramatically slow the rate of population increase in such areas.

Topics for Additional Research

Migration now drives demographic change in rural America. The once substantial excess of births over deaths in rural areas has dwindled, and the age structure of nonmetropolitan America is no longer conducive to substantial natural increase. Thus, a primary focus of future research must be on a better understanding of migration.[2] Most research on rural migration has focused on net migration. Such analysis yields good information about the overall patterns of population redistribution underway; however, there are limits to what can be learned from this type of analysis. At least three opportunities exist to enhance our knowledge beyond what a general study of net migration affords us—disaggregating migration patterns, studying migration streams, and enriching our understanding of individual- and family-level migration decision-making.

Disaggregating Migration

Net migration data can be disaggregated, a good example of which is the analysis of age-specific net migration. Such an analysis now spans several decades (Fuguitt and Heaton 1995; Johnson and Fuguitt 2000) and provides detailed information about age structure shifts and the linkage between county characteristics and migration. The smaller than expected contribution of the over-sixty-five population to the rural rebound exemplifies how disaggregating migration can be useful. Demographers need to know which of the under-sixty-five age groups are fueling this growth. Is it the leading edge of the baby boom? If so, it may indicate that they are disengaging from the labor force early, resulting in a significant stream of amenity migrants into recreational and retirement areas. Or are rural areas now attracting and retaining more of their young adult population? If this is the case, it may alter the future potential for human capital retention, social structural change, and natural increase in rural America.

Examining Migration Streams

More information on migration would be provided by the analysis of migration streams. Often substantial amounts of in- and out-migration underlie a modest net change. In addition, the streams of in- and out-migrants often differ, as, for example, when an outflow of young adults is offset by an influx of retirement-age migrants. Aside from the differing character of the two streams, the fact that there has been considerable turnover in the population also has significant implications for the demographic social, economic, and political fabric of the community.

The nonmetropolitan turnaround of the 1970s demonstrated that economic forces alone could not account for rural migration trends; however,

2. Some of the ideas offered here are not new. John Wardwell (1982) addressed several of the same points in a chapter prepared for the 1980 predecessor of this volume. David Brown (2002) underscored the need to examine microlevel migration data in his Rural Sociological Society Presidential Address.

it is equally clear that economic factors certainly contributed to the pattern of migration to and from nonmetropolitan areas. The recession of the early 1980s had a greater impact and longer effects in nonmetropolitan areas, while the farm crisis of that decade also hurt many agricultural counties badly, resulting in widespread out-migration. In contrast, the economic recession of 1990–92 had a greater impact on urban areas, undercutting the economic attraction of cities, particularly to rural young people.

During the late 1990s, nonmetropolitan net migration gains diminished as the economy boomed. Recent data suggest that the wage gap between rural and urban workers widened during the late 1990s, particularly for college educated workers (Gibbs and Parker 2001). At the same time, the difference between the stream of college graduates moving in and that moving out has shifted from a significant surplus for rural areas to a nearly even balance (Cromartie 2001). Is there a connection? Is it possible that the stream of migrants out of nonmetropolitan areas is smaller and the incoming stream is greater when the economic situation in rural and urban areas converges, and that the opposite occurs when economic trends diverge? This hypothesis needs to be tested with data on migration streams because only the working-age population is likely to be sensitive to it. The relevance of this issue to understanding rural/urban migration streams is particularly acute when the economy weakens.

Migration of Individuals and Households

David Brown (2002) makes a compelling case for bringing individuals and households into the study of migration. Rural researchers have learned a great deal from aggregate level analysis, but there are limits to what we can learn from such data. Qualitative analysis together with the new generation of analytical tools that facilitate the use of multi-level data provide a promising opportunity to integrate information about individuals and households into migration research. How individuals and households make decisions about whether or not to migrate also deserves considerably more attention in migration research. How do economic and noneconomic factors (i.e., life course stage, attachment to place, family ties, lifestyle, etc.) balance in such decisions?

If the turnaround and rebound have taught us anything, it is that noneconomic factors must also be considered in any explanation of nonmetropolitan demographic trends. Concern about urban problems such as crime, pollution, and schools of poor quality may also have attracted urban residents to rural areas and discouraged rural residents from moving to cities. Recent survey data suggest that many residents of the nation's largest cities would rather live in smaller places, whereas a substantial majority of rural residents are happy where they are (Brown et al. 1997). Although these findings are consistent with earlier surveys, the diminished friction of distance—facilitated by technological innovations in transportation and communications—probably allowed more households to act upon their preferences in the 1990s. But exactly how this process operates and how much impact noneconomic factors have on households and individuals at different life stages is still not well understood.

Migration research focuses on the relatively small number of people who migrate, but it is also important to investigate nonmigrants. This is of particular relevance to rural researchers given the long-standing preference of most rural residents to remain in their current area. Places able to retain a larger share of their existing population are at a distinct advantage in migration exchanges with other areas (Irwin et al. 1999). It is easy to forget that the stream and net data are the result of myriad individual and household decisions about whether or not to migrate. As demographers integrate information about individual and household decision-making into migration models, the future direction of demographic change in rural America may become more predictable.

Implications

The population deconcentration underway underscores the fact that discussions of "urban sprawl" and "smart growth" have significance to nonmetropolitan as well as metropolitan areas. Sprawl is usually characterized as peripheral growth on the outer edge of metropolitan areas; however, such growth often spills over metropolitan boundaries and need not be contiguous to existing buildup areas. With telecommunications, computer, and transportation innovations diminishing the "friction of distance," location decisions for both firms and individuals now encompass a wider geographic sphere. Yet much current discussion of smart growth might better be characterized as suburban sprawl abatement. It is dominated by city and suburban interests maneuvering to protect turf and access to resources. From this point of view, the deconcentration of the population represents a loss of people, power, resources, and votes.

For rural communities that have coped with declining populations and resources for years, managing an influx of people and businesses represents a serious challenge many are not fully prepared to deal with. Prior population loss together with the decline in intergovernmental revenues associated with devolution leave many of these local governments in fiscal stress

(Johnson et al. 1995). If growth is to be managed in such areas, local governments need the staff, training, legal framework, and resources to produce and enforce plans that allow growth, but protect the environment, public access, open space, and farmland. These special needs associated with rural growth must be considered in developing national and regional growth plans. Thus, any serious discussion of smart growth or sprawl must recognize nonmetropolitan governments, communities, and organizations as viable partners in the policy-making process.

The Impact on the Natural and Social Environment

People who subsisted, and sometimes flourished, by extracting food, fiber, and minerals from the environment originally settled rural America. Though agriculture no longer dominates rural America as it once did, it remains an extremely important element of the local economy and psyche in broad swaths of the country. The deconcentration of the population has a significant impact on both the natural and social environment in these areas. Development can consume thousands of acres of prime farmland at an alarming rate. Aside from taking the land out of production, development so fragments the remaining agricultural land that farmers have difficulty continuing to raise crops on it. Development also pushes up land prices, which places an enormous financial burden on young farmers getting started, and makes it difficult for older farmers to pass on their land to the next generation. And rapid development quickly makes farmers a minority despite their centrality to the character and appeal of the area. To be sure, many agricultural areas with long histories of population decline welcome new residents, but such growth presents significant challenges as well.

Rural America was settled by people who built lives and communities by extracting sustenance from the bountiful natural resources of the area. Originally it was the soil, forests, and minerals that attracted people. Those industries are now mature and consistently produce more food, fiber, and minerals with fewer people. Rural areas have other natural resources including lakes, rivers, forests, and scenic viewscapes that attract millions of visitors and a significant number of migrants. The implications of continuing growth in recreational and natural amenity areas are particularly significant because they contain many environmentally sensitive areas. Population growth is likely to increase the population density along the forest edge, put additional pressure on riparian and environmentally sensitive areas, increase recreational facilities usage, and complicate forest management and fire suppression (Radeloff et al. 2001; Wear and Bolstad 1998; Wear, Turner, and Naiman 1998).

Rural population growth presents a challenge for the social as well as the natural environment. Many nonmetropolitan areas need and welcome additional population. But rural residents are concerned about how the influx of people and businesses might influence the area. Will the newcomers alter the style and pace of life that originally made these areas appealing? People who move to rural areas often want to escape problems associated with urban life, yet they expect services available in urban places. But newcomers bring more than expectations for better services—they also bring new talents, ideas, and ways of doing things. Such an influx of new people and ideas is both threatening and exciting. The excitement comes from the infusion of new human capital into communities that have lost much through the years. Newcomers bring expertise and skills that may reinvigorate existing institutions and create new ones. Yet the influx of newcomers is threatening because it challenges long-established social networks and ways of doing things. Integrating new arrivals without destroying the sense of community that make smaller places appealing to many is no less daunting a task than protecting the natural environment.

Nonmetropolitan America has experienced a remarkable range of demographic changes over the past several decades. And with migration now the dominant force influencing population redistribution, the future could be even more turbulent. Demography is not destiny, but a researcher ignores it at his or her peril. Rural America's demographic future, like its past, is closely intertwined with the social, economic, and political changes under way in the nation and the world beyond. The following chapters illustrate how the people and institutions of rural America are responding to these changes.

2

African Americans in Rural America

Rosalind P. Harris and Dreamal Worthen

The past is very much alive in the present, when the life circumstances of African Americans in rural America are considered. Fully 91 percent of African Americans living in rural America reside in the South, where patterns of education, income, employment, and poverty give testament to the persistence of significant inequalities resulting from slavery and its aftermath. Slave narratives and oral histories of plantation life in the American South after slavery suggest that marriage, the nuclear and extended family, and kin arrangements were adaptive strategies for assuring subsistence and for nurturing opportunities for social mobility (Tolnay 1999). These arrangements continued until a number of forces converged to both push and pull African Americans out of farming and out of the rural South in large numbers. With neither land ownership nor opportunities for the development of economic and political means for nurturing economically sustainable and civically engaged communities, African Americans experienced intensified disruptions to family and community cohesion, exacerbated by policies such as the share-tenancy systems and the inequitable brokering of New Deal policies at the local level, and trends such as the mechanization of agriculture.

The current Southern political and economic structure has been shaped by historical policies and trends that have intensified inequalities for African Americans. As a result, the economic security of African American families in the region has been particularly compromised by outside changes, such as the restructuring global economy of the twentieth and twenty-first centuries. Moreover, economic restructuring has proceeded in tandem with the restructuring of the welfare state. Welfare reform and the dynamics of general policies of devolution require states to absorb a substantial portion of the costs of social entitlement programs formerly paid for by the federal government. This has major implications for how the rural South responds to the needs of vulnerable populations.

Although the dynamics of the Southern economy remain a dominant force in structuring and restricting livelihood opportunities and options for African Americans, centuries-old patterns of class, race, and political practice intersect with local and global economic forces to continue long-standing patterns of racial discrimination. Such patterns can only further compromise the status and well-being of African Americans. Moreover, given the changing racial composition of the regional workforce, such patterns will surely further undermine the potential of the regional economy to provide economic security for all.

We use this brief overview as a point of departure to describe some of the more pressing issues facing African Americans in the rural South. It also shapes the agenda for those who carry out research and enact policy affecting this population. We begin with a discussion of the key conceptual and theoretical issues that have (and have not) been raised by prior research in this area, in order to identify the strengths and limitations of current scholarship, and particularly its relevance in clarifying and addressing key policy issues. We then move through a historically informed review of major trends and policies that have had an impact on the structure of rural African American families and communities. Finally, we discuss current problems in relation to research and policy considerations, offering guidance for more fully understanding and responding to the needs and concerns of African Americans in rural America.

Conceptual and Theoretical Issues

Much of the research on rural African Americans reflects what has been most salient in scholarship on rural America more generally—comparative analyses of spatial inequality such as the rural/urban divide and the consequences of economic and social restructuring for rural communities and people (Rural Sociological Society Task Force on Persistent Rural Poverty 1993). This work is important because it provides rich descriptive data on the status of Black farmers and workers, particularly in relation to white farmers and workers; however, the almost exclusive focus on market processes, farm structure change, labor market dynamics, and the economic consequences for African American farmers and workers obscures the consideration of other factors that combine with the dynamics of the economy in continuing the marginalization and impoverishment of rural African American communities and families. As noted by the Rural Sociological

Society Task Force on Persistent Rural Poverty, "rural sociologists have never shown much interest in these [rural minority] communities, have never been too interested in studies of racism and its consequences, nor of thinking about poverty as more than a matter of income" (1993, 198). Notable exceptions include Thompson (1995), Brown et al. (1995), Wimberley and Morris (1997), Swanson et al. (1995), Tolnay (1999), Stack (1996), and Duncan (1999).

These studies depart from the economy-centered approach by using historical analyses to understand the dynamics and legacies of racism and plantation agriculture, and by explaining the dramatic restructuring of African American families and communities in the rural South. They draw attention to the intertwined nature of racism and political economy, and offer contexts for understanding such disturbing trends as the disappearance of Black farmers and farms, the disproportionate number of toxic waste repositories located in Southern rural communities with large African American populations and the health problems residents suffer as a result, and the rapid rise in mother-only families and the impoverishment of African American children.

Strictly economic analyses of rural African American life circumstances and conditions fail to examine assumptions about the causes and nature of long-standing patterns of rural African American unemployment, under-employment, poverty, and dependence on government transfer payments. Moreover, they have the potential to represent rural African Americans in ways that reinforce stereotypical notions of powerlessness and dependence. The following discussion will incorporate these concerns in examining the historical background shaping the current issues and challenges facing African Americans in the rural South.

Poverty of Place: Poverty of People

Scholars and policy-makers face challenges in understanding and responding to the chronic poverty that characterizes the area that comprises the old plantation South. This is because conventional conceptual formulations preclude "understanding the historical dynamics that create poor people and poor places" (Billings and Blee 2000, 51). The post–Civil War South witnessed the impressive emergence of stable and prospering African American communities and the growth in numbers of African American educators, politicians, and land owners (DuBois 1967). After Rutherford B. Hayes was elected President in 1876, federal protections for African Americans were dismantled and Southern planters were able to reassert their political control in the South. The interests of share-tenants and the African American population generally were not recognized in political decision-making (Mandle 1992). What remained and dominated in the wake of the post-Reconstruction compromise were well-entrenched norms and patterns of social and political interaction between whites and Blacks that were deeply rooted in the dynamics of the plantation/slave economy. Egregious and insidious forms of intimidation and social control, such as debt peonage, rape, lynching, patronage, and the containment of any kind of civic culture, effectively closed off social mobility, economic self-sufficiency, and participation in the larger society for African Americans.

Restructuring and Racism

These well entrenched norms and patterns persist today, as witnessed by African Americans "returning" to the rural South (Stack 1996). Returnees have faced difficulties finding work, although they clearly possess the training and skills required for available jobs. They have also found it difficult to find safe, quality daycare and schools for their children. For the majority of African Americans in their new home communities, perhaps most painful to bear are the ongoing consequences of these well-entrenched norms and patterns that deny them many entitlements that most Americans take for granted. These include access to land, an adequate livelihood, a quality education, health care, child care, and environmental health and safety, among others.

The interrelationship between racism, diminished African American economic power, low social mobility, constricted civic culture, and underdevelopment of the plantation South forms mutually reinforcing feedback loops that are apparent, but largely unacknowledged in policy discussions. Currently, 255 of the 500 counties classified as "persistent poverty counties" by the USDA stretch across the heart of the old plantation South (Beale 1996). The majority of these counties make up the "Black Belt," the largest expanse of rural poverty within the nation. The Black Belt spreads from eastern Texas to Virginia, covering portions of Louisiana, Arkansas, Mississippi, West Tennessee, Alabama, North and South Carolina, Georgia, and North Florida. It contains 79 percent of the nonmetropolitan African American population and 45 percent of all African Americans (Wimberley and Morris 1997). The Black Belt contains 35 percent of the nation's poor, 43 percent of the rural poor, and 90 percent of poor rural African Americans.

Within the Black Belt the deeply rooted connection between poverty of place and poverty of people is clear. Racism exaggerates the effects of historically weak investments in basic education and skills training. Also, like other areas that have been historically dependent on agriculture, the slow move to economic diversification within the Black Belt has rendered the economy rigid and weak. Combining these factors with significant pools of poorly educated, low-skill workers in a severely constricted economy, the result is the lowest wage scale in the country, and high rates of unemployment and underemployment (Jensen 1995). Moreover, these historically embedded structures conditioned by racism have exacerbated the problems in African American communities in the South, making them especially vulnerable to the global economic changes of the twentieth and twenty-first centuries. Manufacturing gains made nationwide in the 1970s have been lost to the urban South because better educated urban work forces are better positioned to respond to the shifting high tech information needs of industries (MDC Research Committee 2000). The urban South has attracted both more jobs and better quality jobs, offering higher wages, greater prestige and more lucrative fringe benefits (Lyson 1989). The dynamics of globalization have also continued the movement of lower end jobs out of the rural South to low-cost labor sites overseas (MDC Research Committee 2000). The loss of low-skill production activities in the rural South has undermined economic opportunities for rural African Americans whose skill sets are not well matched to high tech, information intensive occupations.

African Americans in Agriculture

The protracted disenfranchisement of descendants of former slaves is also reflected in the dramatic decline in the number of African American farms. This has had tremendous economic and political significance for African Americans in the region. Although share-tenant arrangements predominated after the Civil War,[1] a significant number of African Americans owned farms. The number of African American farms peaked in 1920 at 926,000 and remained at about 800,000 until 1935 (Beale 1966). Except during the 1940s, the number of African American farm operations declined dramatically between 1910 and 1990 (Fig. 2.1); if current trends continue it is predicted that by the year 2010 there will no longer be any African American farm operations in existence. Farm ownership declined for both Blacks and whites, but the more rapid decline among Blacks is attributed both to entrenched norms and patterns of racism that discouraged African American

---

1. Under this system, African American farmers rented a portion of land usually owned by white landowners and paid for the land in labor and/or with a portion of the harvested crop.

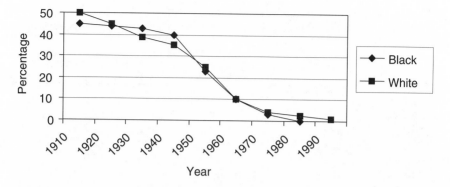

Fig. 2.1 Comparison of Black and white Southern farm households, 1910–1990

Source: 1910 and 1940–90 Integrated Public Use Microdata Series, Social Science Research Laboratory, University of Minnesota.
Note: Percentages for 1920 and 1930 are interpolated.

land ownership and to the systematic practices of the USDA's Farmer's Home Administration (currently the Farm Service Agency), which discriminated against African Americans in the provision of loans and failed to enforce fair and equitable terms for loans when they were provided. Recent research indicates that African Americans are attempting to reenter farming (Wood and Gilbert 1998). While returnees are people who have not been officially defined as "farmers" by the census, they still own land and want to farm. These farmers are younger, better educated, and wealthier than the traditional African American farmers, on average, but they still need federal loans from the Farm Service Agency to finance farm operations.

This historical overview has emphasized that the legacy inherited by rural African Americans endures and forms the context for understanding the current challenges facing African Americans in the rural South. The following discussion highlights the trends and patterns associated with these challenges.

Contemporary Patterns of Inequality

Education

As Table 2.1 illustrates, low levels of education continue to plague rural African Americans. Contemporary Black/white differences in educational attainment are rooted in historical inequalities, which in turn have shaped basic access to opportunities to obtain an education. Most scholars are aware of the restrictions placed on education during slavery, but many incorrectly assume that these constraints ended with Emancipation. In

Table 2.1 Educational attainment of persons 25 years and over, by metropolitan/nonmetropolitan residence and Black/white racial identification, 2000

	Nonmetropolitan		Metropolitan	
	Black	White	Black	White
None–8th grade	12.6	8.3	5.9	6.6
9th grade–11th grade	20.8	10.9	13.5	8.5
High school graduate	39.5	40.2	34.7	31.5
Some college, no degree	13.7	16.0	21.0	17.9
Associate's degree	6.0	8.3	7.0	7.7
Bachelor's degree, professional degree, or more	7.3	16.3	18.0	27.8

Data: U.S. Census Bureau, Current Population Survey, March 2000 (Percentage)
Source: U.S. Department of Commerce, *Educational Attainment in the United States,*
Current Population Reports, series P20-536, issued December 2000.

many Southern localities throughout the 1930s and 1940s, it was illegal for Black children to attend junior high and high school. Due to the demands of the sharecropping system and Jim Crow separate-but-equal laws, the education that was available to African Americans was inferior and available only for a few months each year.

Over the last thirty years, rural/urban differences in the quality of school infrastructure and curricula have narrowed, as have differences in standardized test scores; however, schools in the rural South continue to fall below the regional and national averages on a wide variety of measures. For example, test scores for the rural South are significantly lower than for other regions, teacher salaries are lower, and learning resources much more limited (Gibbs et al. 1998).

When educational attainment rates are analyzed by region and race (Table 2.1), it is clear that race is a major contributor to the low educational levels in rural areas. Blacks are less likely than whites to complete high school in both metropolitan and nonmetropolitan areas, and college attainment rates are much lower for Blacks than whites in both rural and urban areas as well. These data suggest that the South's poor educational performance, in general, can be best understood within the context of the region's historical restrictions on providing equitable opportunities for African American education.

Work and Income

Educational deficiencies consistently translate into economic disadvantages for African American men and women. Table 2.2 illustrates the relatively

Table 2.2 Poverty rates and median income for the southern region, by metropolitan/ nonmetropolitan residence and Black/white racial identification, 2000

	Nonmetropolitan		Metropolitan	
	Black	White	Black	White
Persons				
Poverty rate (all persons)	27.7	12.7	20.1	9.3
65 years and over	31.3	14.1	24.9	9.0
6–17 years	36.7	16.2	26.0	11.3
Families				
Poverty rate (all persons)	24.6	9.5	17.2	6.9
Married couple families	7.0	6.5	6.1	4.8
Female householder with children	49.9	37.5	36.4	25.1
Median income (per family)	$23,816	$42,597	$35,860	$57,220

Data: U.S. Census Bureau, Current Population Survey, March 2001. (Percentage)
Source: Joseph Dalaker, U.S. Census Bureau, *Poverty in the United States: 2000,* Current Population Reports, series P60-214, issued September 2001.

low income and high poverty rates for African Americans regardless of where they live; however, these data also show that rural African Americans have the lowest incomes and highest poverty rates of the population groups under consideration.

McGranahan and Kassel (1996) demonstrated that the earnings disadvantage resulting from low education increased for rural African Americans between 1980 and 1990, as median earnings declined for all except those with a college degree. During this period unemployment rates were also higher for all rural African Americans, but were particularly high for those with lower levels of education. With restricted access to adequate education, training, and living wages, African Americans confront a range of difficulties that further compromise well-being for themselves and the region as a whole.

Women, Children, and Poverty

The poverty rate for African American children in the rural South is 41 percent. This compares to a rate of 34.6 percent for African American children in Southern cities and 21 percent for rural Southern white children (Rogers 2001). Increasing poverty rates for rural African American children correspond to the sharp rise in families headed solely by women in the region. Children experience high rates of poverty as a reflection of their parent or parents' diminished capacity to earn a living wage.

This trend is not surprising, as African American women have been historically disadvantaged as wage earners within the Southern rural economy. Weaker links to the labor market stemming from unemployment, underemployment, and concentrations in the lowest paying jobs within a notably weak economy have roots in the gendered work structures of the plantation economy, and in the segmented industrial structures that compounded gender and racial discrimination after slavery (Jones 1985). This historical vulnerability to poverty due to relative exclusion from the paid workforce has forced rural African American women to become much more dependent on government transfer payments to provide for themselves and their children.

With the implementation of the 1996 Personal Responsibility and Work Opportunity Reconciliation Act (PRWORA), the rate of decline in welfare recipients within persistent-poverty counties, where the majority of rural African Americans live, has outpaced the national average (Henry and Lewis 2001). The rate will drop much more with the imposition of term limits. Breaking the cycle of poverty will be a much greater challenge under these conditions for African American families.

The Consequences of the Cycle of Poverty for Rural African American Families

For children whose parents face ongoing challenges to economic security, growing up poor means they are more likely to live in environments ridden by conflict and stress. Moreover, poor children face considerable obstacles to meeting their educational needs, as learning opportunities are limited at home or in less-than-adequate child care centers. When these factors combine with the poor nutrition, poor health, and poor health care typically experienced by rural African American children and their families, educational setbacks such as poor school performance or school dropout are almost assured. Over the course of a lifetime, these setbacks will prevent children from developing the knowledge and skills necessary to obtain and keep adequate jobs and livelihoods, thereby continuing the cycle of poverty by perpetuating the social structures and norms that reinforce it.

The legacy of the social and power structures typical of plantation economies conditions the immediate context in which African American children in the rural South come to define themselves vis-à-vis the broader society and come to understand their potential and options. Within their home communities, poor African American children in the rural South are often enmeshed within networks of kin and friends who have also had their dreams and ambitions blocked. Powerful institutions, families, and individuals have historically restricted African American social mobility and economic and civic viability. Given these patterns, these communities are characterized by large numbers of people who have been prevented from developing the skills, habits, and worldviews that will allow them to negotiate pathways out of poverty and oppression (Duncan 1999). This gives children few models to follow in developing alternative coping strategies and strategies for social mobility. Moreover, the communities as a whole inherit the collective vulnerabilities that make it virtually impossible to change the context within which these children's lives unfold.

Research and "Policy as Usual"?

The return migration of African Americans to the rural South and the reentry of African Americans into farming signal, perhaps, a willingness on their part to give rural life and farming in the South another chance. Recent research suggests, however, that the repressive race and class relationships that encouraged Blacks to leave the South in the first place endure. Moreover, it is clear from both anecdotal and statistical evidence that the communities to which many are returning reflect the worst consequences of "American apartheid," including high levels of joblessness, poverty, and dislocated families.

Research and policy have not played neutral roles in shaping the vulnerabilities that plague African American communities in the rural South. Therefore when "policy as usual" recommendations such as human-capital-enhancing strategies or firm-attraction strategies are prescribed, they should be viewed warily, no matter how well intentioned they are. Decades of experience have shown that "policy as usual" is not an adequate approach for addressing the peculiar case of Southern rural underdevelopment.

The federal government must address Southern rural underdevelopment as a priority. This does not mean that regional, state, and local initiatives are less urgent or less significant; rather, the federal government plays an essential role not only in mitigating the well-entrenched social and political inequalities persisting from the plantation system, but also in moderating aspects of current economic policies that have intensified inequalities nationwide. Growing poverty, a function of increasing inequality within the United States, parallels the shift in government policies from the late 1970s to the present. These policies have significantly weakened the state's role in moderating the effects of the skewed accumulation and concentration of wealth (O'Connor 2001). Cross-national studies indicate that governments that have been more interventionist, especially in addressing the wealth concentration produced by globalization, have been more successful at keeping poverty and inequality to a minimum (Navarro 2000). The "race to the bottom," a phenomenon that some argue is inevitable with globalization, is countered by evidence that proactive state policies do produce positive effects. Policies developed in this vein provide for investments in a broad range of universal social provisions to support families. They also provide for an array of public work strategies to strengthen local infrastructures and provide work to counter poverty.

Scholars such as Theda Skocpol (1991) and Robert Reich (1991) have called on the state to invest in such policies, as an important role of the state is to equalize opportunity. These policies would address the increasing race and class polarization that has diminished the potential to develop strong civic cultures in poorer communities. For poor and low-income African Americans in the rural South, such policies could provide the impetus for the development of a political base. They could also strengthen the social fabric that nurtures civically engaged African American communities. By their very nature, such policies challenge the oppressive character of the Southern rural political economy that has systematically discouraged the emergence of a strong Black civic culture over time.

In addition, further support from middle-class African Americans from both within and outside of the region could be encouraged. These individuals have a stake in preserving African American culture and heritage (Rural Sociological Society Task Force on Persistent Rural Poverty 1993). Ultimately, through purposive investment and restoration, an increasing number of middle-class African Americans may find Southern rural communities more appealing places to live. This would further strengthen the political bases and civic cultures of these communities.

With the federal government providing the essential policy scaffolding, a multifaceted approach that takes the Southern region as a whole as the unit of concern can be shaped. A regional commission, along the lines of the Appalachian and Delta Commissions, could examine and make explicit the ties between alleviating the poverty of individual families, the inequality between genders, races, and classes, and the potential for resilience within the region overall. These strategies must be sensitive to the peculiar history and dynamics of the Southern political economy. Such an approach would be a striking departure from approaches of the past that either ignore history and political economy altogether or subordinate it to individual-oriented, behaviorist approaches. Based on the analysis we have presented, the dismantling of the repressive structures of Southern rural apartheid is realistic and desirable, not just for African Americans, but for the overall good of the whole region.

3

American Indians

Their Contemporary Reality and Future Trajectory

Angela A. Gonzales

Historically, American Indians have been one of the most economically deprived segments of American society.[1] According to nearly every social indicator—such as income, employment, educational attainment, quality of health care, and life expectancy—American Indians are well below the national averages. On most rural Indian reservations, persistent poverty, unemployment, and overcrowded and inadequate housing are similar to conditions found in many underdeveloped nations. Still, American Indians have shown phenomenal resilience in the face of overwhelming economic adversity and cultural change. Today, hundreds of Indian tribes, each with its unique history, culture, language, and traditions, persevere despite

1. Unlike the practice of using the terms "American Indian" and "Native American" interchangeably, I limit my use to the terms "American Indian" and "Indian" when referring to the descendants of the aboriginal inhabitants of North America resident within the political boundaries of the United States. I do this for several reasons. First, the terms "American Indian" and "Indian" are standard within the field of federal Indian law and are the terms most often used by individuals to identify themselves. Second, the term "Native American" creates confusion that may suggest that anyone born in America is *Native* American. Third, the term "Native American," like African American, Asian American, or Italian American, implies that persons so described stand in the same relationship to the federal government as a "race," "ethnic," or "minority" group; however, unlike these other groups, American Indians occupy a unique and distinct position within United States polity vis-à-vis their political status and relationship to the federal government. Likewise, my use of the terms "Indian tribe" and "tribe" follows standard practice in the field of federal Indian law and is consistent with the many Indian communities who designate "tribe" as part of their official name. Although my preference would be to use tribal names when referring to specific tribal groups, for the purposes of this chapter, some term must be used to describe the various tribal entities as a whole. For despite their many differences, they share certain common features, at least by virtue of their place within the American legal system.

predictions that they would vanish in the face of Western expansion and development.

This chapter examines some of the challenges and opportunities facing American Indians in the twenty-first century. To the extent that American Indians make up a part of the ethnic mosaic of rural America, it is their collective organization and unique political status as tribes that will provide the substantive focus of this chapter. The first part of the chapter begins with a brief discussion of tribal sovereignty, the government-to-government relationship between Indian tribes and the federal government, and the importance of this relationship for understanding the contemporary reality and future trajectory of Indian tribes. This is followed by a demographic profile of the population, highlighting important trends and characteristics of the American Indian population residing in rural America. On the basis of this interpretive context, the remainder of the chapter examines two of the most salient challenges that Indian tribes face in the coming century: (1) challenges to the legal tenets of tribal sovereignty in light of the proliferation of tribal gaming, and (2) resistance to the reacquisition, consolidation, and expansion of tribal trust land.

Tribal Sovereignty

Unlike other ethnic or racial groups in the United States, American Indians occupy a unique position in the U.S. polity vis-à-vis their political status and relationship to the federal government as sovereign nations. This is a legacy of an earlier period when colonial powers, including France, Britain, and Denmark, recognized Indian tribes as sovereign political entities with the inherent, rather than delegated, power of self-government. Subsequent treaties negotiated and signed between the U.S. government and Indian tribes acknowledged the separate political status of Indian tribes as sovereign nations.

Today, the sovereignty of the more than 560 Indian tribes formally recognized by the U.S. has been limited by Congress.[2] In 1831, Chief Justice John Marshall qualified tribal sovereignty when he wrote in *Cherokee Nation v. Georgia* that while Indian tribes were indeed "distinct political communities, having territorial boundaries, within which their authority is exclusive," under U.S. domination, they were no longer foreign nations,

2. In the vernacular of Indian affairs and federal Indian law, the terms "federally recognized Indian tribe" and "federally acknowledged tribal entity" are used to identify the various indigenous groups that are legally recognized as having a government-to-government relationship with the United States.

but rather "domestic dependent nations" whose relationship to the federal government was that of a "ward to his guardian." From this was born the trust relationship and responsibility of the federal government to protect and preserve the interests of Indian tribes and their members (Deloria 1985; Wilkins 1997; Wilkinson 1987).[3]

Although Congress has plenary (near absolute) power to limit tribal sovereignty, two principle attributes of tribal sovereignty remain: the inherent power over internal affairs and the preclusion of state intervention in tribal affairs and self-government (Canby 1988). From these early-established tenets of tribal sovereignty emerged a distinction that has a significant bearing on contemporary Indian affairs, namely, that the basis of different treatment of Indian tribes is not racial but legal difference based on the tribes' continuing legal existence as sovereign, albeit domestic and dependent, nations. This distinction has been confirmed and reiterated not only by the courts, but by scholars as well (see Cohen 1942; Deloria 1984; Wilkins 1997; Wilkinson 1987).

Trends in Population and Socioeconomic Conditions

Demographic Profile

The number of American Indians in the United States has grown considerably during the twentieth century. U.S. Census data show that between 1900 and 1950, the American Indian population increased by roughly 46 percent from 237,000 to 357,000 (Snipp 1989). Between 1950 and 2000, the number increased by about 700 percent to just under 2.5 million (see Table 3.1).

Several factors account for the growth in the American Indian population, namely improved access to health care, lower infant mortality, increased longevity, and procedural changes in census enumeration. Much of the increase, however, has been attributed to changing patterns of self-identification, i.e., people previously self-identifying as non-Indians changing their

3. In 1977, the American Indian Policy Review Commission outlined the concept of the trust relationship in its final report to Congress: "The scope of the trust responsibility extends beyond real or personal property which is held in trust. The United States has the obligation to provide services, and to take other appropriate action necessary to protect tribal self-government. The doctrine may also include a duty to provide a level of services equal to those services provided by the states to their citizens. These conclusions flow from the basic notion that the trust responsibility is a general obligation which is not limited to specific provision in treaties, executive orders, or statutes; once the trust has been assumed, administrative action is governed by the same high duty which is imposed on a private trustee" (American Indian Policy Review Commission 1977, 130).

Table 3.1 Comparative census enumeration, American Indians and total U.S. population, 1950–2000

Date	American Indian		Total United States	
	Population	Percent change	Population	Percent change
1950	357,499		151,325,798	
1960	523,591	46.5	179,323,175	18.5
1970	792,730	51.4	203,302,031	13.4
1980	1,366,676	72.4	226,545,805	11.4
1990	1,959,234	43.3	246,750,639	8.9
2000	2,475,956	26.4	281,421,906	14.1

Note: Figures for 2000 are for those who racially self-identified as American Indian alone.

identification to American Indian (Eschbach 1993, 1995; Harris 1994; Nagel 1996; Passel 1976, 1996; Passel and Berman 1986; Snipp 1989). For example, between 1970 and 1980, it has been estimated that nearly three-fifths of the American Indian population growth can be attributed to increases in self-identification. Declining social discrimination, changes in the use and meaning of "race" as a signifier of personal identity, and the resurgence in ethnic pride and identification have all been cited as possible explanations for "ethnic switching" (Gonzales 1998; Nagel 1996).

In 2000, the U.S. Census Bureau's "snapshot of the nation" showed between 2.5 and 4.1 million American Indians (Ogunwole 2002). This minimum/maximum range reflects recent changes in census enumeration that, for the first time in 2000, permitted Americans to identify themselves as belonging to more than one race. For example, using the 2.5 million figure for American Indians in the United States identifying by single race alone results in a 26 percent increase in the population over the previous decade. When compared to both those identifying as American Indian alone and those in combination with at least one other race, however, the American Indian population of 4.1 million suggests a 110 percent increase since 1990. Because of this change, it is imperative for those studying American Indian demography to distinguish between those reporting their race as American Indian alone, and those who reported themselves to be American Indian in combination with one or more other races.

Population Distribution and Migration

Until the onset of World War II, more than 90 percent of American Indians lived in rural environs. In the years that followed, federal policies and postwar migration streams urbanized the population (Fixico 1986; Bernstein 1991). Between 1952 and 1972, the Bureau of Indian Affairs Direct

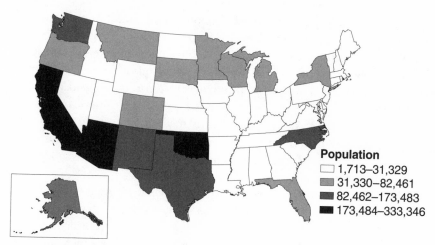

Fig. 3.1 American Indian population, 2000

Source: United States Bureau of the Census, 2000 Summary File 1, American Indian and Alaskan Native Alone

Employment Program relocated approximately 100,000 American Indians from their rural reservations to preselected urban centers in cities such as Los Angeles, Denver, Minneapolis, and San Francisco (Sorkin 1978). Nevertheless, unlike other minority groups such as Latinos, Blacks, and Asians who are concentrated in cities at rates of 90 percent or higher, roughly 50 percent of all American Indians continue to reside outside of census-defined metropolitan areas (see Fig. 3.1).

In 2000, of all respondents who self-identified as American Indian in the U.S. Census, either alone or in combination with at least one other race, about 43 percent lived in the West, 31 percent in the South, 17 percent in the Midwest, and 9 percent in the Northeast.[4] Of the ten states with the largest American Indian populations, seven (including Alaska) are in the West (Ogunwole 2002). California has the largest American Indian population (333,346), followed by Oklahoma (273,230), Arizona (255,879), New Mexico (173,483), Texas (118,362), Alaska (98,043), and Washington (93,301).

Socioeconomic Status

In recent years, while economic conditions for American Indians have generally improved, the population continues to lag behind the rest of the

4. The distribution of the American Indian population is not coincidental. It reflects nearly two centuries of federal policies and governmental actions that have either displaced American Indians from their homelands east of the Mississippi River to Indian Territory in what is now the state of Oklahoma or resettled them onto remote reservations.

United States with respect to social, economic, and educational attainment levels. According to nearly any measure American Indians have less income, lower educational attainment, higher unemployment, and higher poverty rates than non-Indians. For those living on or near rural reservations, the situation is even more pronounced. According to statistics compiled by the Indian Health Service (2001), in 1989, American Indians residing on or near reservations had a median household income of $19,897, compared to the national average of $30,056. During this same period, 31.6 percent of American Indians lived below the poverty level, in contrast to the national average of 13.1 percent.

The effects of persistent poverty on morbidity and mortality for the population are staggering. American Indians suffer from diabetes at 2.5 times the national rate; Indian children suffer the effects of fetal alcohol syndrome at rates thirty-three times greater than for all other Americans; and tuberculosis among American Indians is 533 percent greater than for all other Americans (Rhoades 2000). Perhaps most shocking of all is that one in six Indian adolescents has attempted suicide. For Indian youth between five and fourteen years old, the suicide rate is twice the national rate, and for those between the ages of fifteen and twenty-four, the suicide rate is nearly three times the national average (Indian Health Service 2001).

The geographic isolation of most Indian reservations has had an adverse effect on infrastructure development in rural reservation communities as well. Indians on rural reservations lag far behind their non-Indian counterparts in access to basic infrastructure such as roads, utilities, housing, and telecommunications. In a study commissioned by the U.S. Department of Commerce (Riley et al. 1999) researchers found that for American Indians living in rural areas on or near reservations, only 39 percent of households had telephones, compared to 94 percent for their non-Native counterparts, 12 percent are without electricity, and another 23 percent without natural gas. The digital divide separating American Indians from non-Indians is even greater. Only 22 percent of rural Indian households have cable television, 9 percent have personal computers, and less than 1 percent have Internet access.

The historical legacy of dispossession and displacement has had and continues to have an enormous impact on the lives and livelihoods of American Indians. For those living on or near rural reservations, the effects are even more pronounced. Lack of economic opportunity, limited access to quality health care, persistent poverty, and unemployment rates near 80 percent on some reservations have led to increased violence and drug and alcohol abuse among reservation residents. Although persistent poverty and geographic isolation are ubiquitous to many Indian reservations, it can also be argued that as tribal "homelands," reservations are vital to the perpetuation of tribal culture, traditions, and identity.

Issues and Challenges for the Twenty-First Century

The challenges confronting American Indian tribes in the twenty-first century are numerous. Issues ranging from water rights to repatriation and from religious freedom to criminal jurisdiction occupy places of equal importance on tribal agendas. In light of the recent economic success and proliferation of Indian gaming in the past decade, however, the issue of greatest challenge and consequence to the future of American Indian tribes will be increased political opposition to the legal tenets of tribal sovereignty. While the opposition to tribal sovereignty is registered on many fronts, the two specific instances to be examined here are the organized opposition to the development and expansion of Indian gaming by elected officials, citizens groups, and business organizations, and opposition to the reacquisition, consolidation, and expansion of tribal trust lands.

Tribal Gaming

Tribal gaming is a relatively new phenomenon in Indian Country. In the 1970s, as state-sponsored lotteries proliferated, several tribes introduced gaming enterprises in an effort to alleviate persistent poverty and dependence on federal resources. In 1979, the Seminole Tribe of Florida opened the first high-stakes bingo hall, and in California, the Cabazon Band of Mission Indians opened a similar facility near San Diego. When Florida and California threatened to close these tribal gaming operations, the tribes sued in federal court. In 1987, the U.S. Supreme Court ruled that once a state has legalized any form of gambling, Indian tribes within that state have the right to offer the same form of gambling without the state imposing governmental restrictions (*California v. Cabazon Band of Mission Indians* 480 U.S. 202 [1987]).

In response to the *Cabazon* decision, state officials and gaming interests from Nevada and New Jersey lobbied Congress to limit tribal gaming operations. In an effort to balance American Indian legal rights with the interests of the states and the gambling industry, Congress enacted the Indian Gaming Regulatory Act (IGRA) in 1988.[5] Although the IGRA upholds the sovereign

---

5. The IRGA provides for three classes of tribal gaming. Class I consists of social games for prizes of nominal value or traditional forms of Indian gaming as a part of tribal ceremonies or

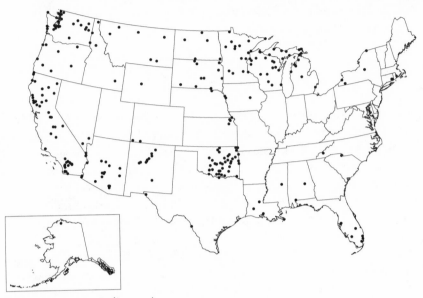

Fig. 3.2 American Indian casinos, 2000
Source: The National Indian Gaming Association

right of tribes to run gaming operations, it limits casino operations to tribal trust land and requires a tribe to enter an agreement with the state in question stipulating the kinds of games offered, the size of the facility, the number of gaming devices permitted, betting limits, security, and other parameters.

Today, there are more than 300 tribal gaming facilities found in twenty-nine states (see Fig. 3.2). Between 1989 and 2001, revenues from tribal gaming grew from $212 million to $12.7 billion, more than 20 percent of total gaming revenues in the United States. Among proponents, tribal gaming development has been hailed as the "new buffalo" for American Indians, credited with elevating once destitute Indian reservations from the grips of poverty, unemployment, welfare dependency, and social despair.

Under IGRA provisions, all tribal gaming revenue is to be used exclusively for tribal government operations, the general welfare of the tribe and its members, support of economic development, charitable contributions, and local government agencies. However, as sovereign political entities,

---

celebrations, which are subject solely to tribal regulations. Class II gaming consists of bingo, lotto, and other similar manual card games not prohibited under state law. Finally, Class III consists of all other games including slot machines, horse and dog racing, pari-mutuel wagering, blackjack, baccarat, and jai alai. This class is permitted only in those states in which these forms of gaming are legal, provided that the tribe has entered into a compact with the state for their operations (Anders 1998).

tribal governments determine how to allocate the proceeds among these purposes. Some tribes have used gaming profits to build houses, schools, day-care centers, clinics, and hospitals; to support social service programs, drug and alcohol treatment programs, roads, and sewer systems; and to fund retirement programs for their tribal elders as well as college scholarships for tribal youth. In a study conducted by the American Indian Economic Development Program at Harvard University, Cornell et al. (1998) found that prior to the signing of any state/tribe casino compacts under the auspices of the IGRA, the average unemployment rate for the 214 tribes studied was 38 percent. Six years later, the rate of unemployment had fallen to 13 percent for tribes that had opened casinos in the interim, while the unemployment rate for tribes without casinos remained unchanged.

The economic benefits of tribal gaming accrue to the non-Indian community as well. The direct effects of tribal gaming on an annual or cumulative basis include the wages paid to full- and part-time employees, health and other benefits paid to employees, payroll related taxes, goods and services purchased for ongoing operations from local suppliers, and tourist dollars from day and overnight visitors. According to the National Indian Gaming Association (2002), in 2001 tribal casinos generated over 300,000 jobs, with 75 percent of these jobs going to non-Indians.

In 1992 in Wisconsin, Indian tribes operated fifteen Class III gaming facilities, with a total payroll of about $68 million (Murray 1993). In a study of the impact of tribal casinos on the state, Murray found that half of the state's 4,500 casino employees were previously unemployed or underemployed, and 18 percent of these were both unemployed and receiving some form of public assistance. The same study found that welfare costs in eleven rural counties with Indian casinos dropped 26 percent over three years, saving taxpayers $470,000 per month and removing an estimated 820 people from welfare. Another study (Thompson, Gazel, and Rickman 1995) found that Indian gaming generated a net gain of more than $400 million in 1994 for local areas within a thirty-five mile radius of Indian gaming establishments. On the Oneida reservation, for example, the tribe employed 3,350 people, making it the largest single employer in metropolitan Green Bay. Unemployment, at around 40 percent a few years ago, has declined precipitously to about 15 percent (Alesch 1997). In addition to providing employment to Oneida Indians, other Indians, and non-Indians, gaming serves as the means for the tribe to generate investment capital for land acquisition, diversified business enterprises, and development of human capital.

In Connecticut, the success of the Mashantucket Pequot's Foxwoods Casino has had an overwhelming economic impact on the state and the immediate region. Prior to its opening in 1992, eastern Connecticut was primarily a rural area with little economic activity except in several pockets that supported large industries, including defense. In 1999, the tribe's casino and other businesses employed nearly 20,000 full- and part-time employees with an annual payroll of nearly $480 million (Carstensen et al. 2000). One study found that every Foxwoods job supports 1.107 additional noncasino jobs elsewhere in New London County, plus 0.74 new jobs in the rest of Connecticut (Wright et al. 1993).

Even though tribal gaming enterprises have had a positive economic impact on both the Indian and non-Indian communities in which they are located, they have also engendered much controversy. In many states, elected officials, citizens groups, and business organizations oppose the development and expansion of tribal gaming. Concerns range from social problems associated with gambling, such as compulsive gambling, increased crime, and domestic violence, to those over the regulation and expansion of tribal gaming facilities. These and other concerns have raised the unpleasant specter of racism and the organization and mobilization of anti-Indian opposition in a number of states, including New York, Wisconsin, and Washington.

At the same time that external opposition to tribal gaming continues to grow, internal disputes and disagreements have created or exacerbated existing cleavages between tribal members over power and control of tribal resources. The revenues generated from tribal gaming have raised the issue of the accountability of Indian leadership and its responsibility to inform tribal members about how these revenues are spent (Mezey 1996). In some cases, tribes have become internally divided over the question of whether to distribute casino profits to individual tribal members in per capita payments or to reinvest revenues in tribal education and infrastructure (Gonzales 2003).

From the standpoint of economic development, the revenue from casinos has dramatically improved the living standards of many tribes and their members. Overall, in the majority of cases, the economic gains are considered by many to greatly outweigh the negative factors, at least in the short run. From a cultural standpoint, however, the question that many tribes will confront in the twenty-first century is whether this rapid increase in wealth will create long-term problems for Indian tribes and their members (Mika 1995). Many have begun to express the concern that the materialism that gaming fosters is inherently antithetical to tribal culture and poses a threat to cultural values, practices, and traditions. Because tribal gaming is a relatively recent phenomenon, its long-term ramifications for the social relations and cultural traditions of Indian tribes remain uncertain.

Despite the abundantly clear positive economic impact that tribal gaming has had on the communities in which tribal casinos are located, the future of tribal gaming remains uncertain. Since the IGRA was enacted, Congress has attempted to introduce amendments to the act to give greater leverage to states. In 1992, the federal Supreme Court held in *Seminole Tribe v. Florida* that the IGRA's enforcement clause, which allows states to be sued in federal court for failure to "bargain in good faith," violated states' sovereign immunity under the Eleventh Amendment of the U.S. Constitution. It is not clear to policy-makers and tribal governments what effect this decision will have on the IGRA. It is likely that negotiations between tribes and states for gaming compacts will be a continued requirement; however, if states refuse to negotiate, tribes may either petition the Secretary of the Interior directly or act on the basis of the *Cabazon* rule and simply establish gaming activities not prohibited by state legislation. Given the financial and political stakes involved, it is clear that the conflict between states and tribes over tribal gaming will persist into the twenty-first century.

Tribal Trust Land

In addition to the expected opposition to tribal gaming that tribes will confront in the twenty-first century, they will also face opposition to the efforts to reacquire, consolidate, and expand tribal trust land. Just as sovereignty accords to tribes the legal right to own and operate casinos, lands held in trust by the United States for Indian tribes confer similar protections. Indian reservations—areas of land held in trust by the United States for one or more Indian tribes, nations, bands, or villages—are exempt from most federal and state taxation and regulation.

In the United States today, there are 310 federal Indian reservations located in thirty-three states. Many of these reservations were created through treaties signed between the U.S. government and Indian tribes, in which the latter were recognized to have prior rights of ownership to the land, or what is referred to as "Indian title," "rights of occupancy," or "aboriginal rights." In exchange for ceding the right, title, and interest to huge tracts of land, Indian tribes held back and "reserved" a portion of land, usually within their former original land holding, for their exclusive use and occupancy.

Following the end of treaty-making in 1871, Indian reservations continued to be created through legislative agreements negotiated with Indian tribes, by specific legislative designations and acts of Congress, by executive orders of the President, and by congressionally authorized actions of the Secretary of the Interior (Canby 1988). While some reservations were created within former Indian land holdings, others were established for tribes displaced from their ancestral homelands. In some cases a single tribe occupied a reservation, while in others two or three ethnologically distinct tribes were placed together onto a single reservation. In still other cases, single tribes were broken up and placed on separate reservations.

Today, federal Indian reservation trust lands total nearly fifty-five million acres and range in size from the one acre Sheep Rancheria in California to the more than sixteen million acre Navajo Reservation in Arizona, New Mexico, and Utah. Excluding Alaska, twenty-one of the twenty-four states west of the Mississippi River have at least one Indian reservation within their boundaries (see Fig. 3.3). The highest concentration of Indian reservation trust land is in Arizona, where approximately 27 percent (about twenty million acres) of the state's seventy-three million acres lies within the boundaries of some twenty reservations. Approximately 98 percent of tribal trust land is in the lower forty-eight states.

An interesting paradox of reservation lands is that while they are Indian owned, title is held in trust by the United States. Essentially, this means that "ownership" of the land is divided between the federal government, which holds "bare legal title," and the tribe or individual Indian who holds full equitable title (Canby 1988; Kalt and Cornell 1994). Moreover, while a great majority of trust land is reservation land, not all reservation land is trust land. While forty-four million acres of reservation land are Indian owned and held in trust by the federal government, the remaining eleven million acres are allotted lands owned and occupied by non-Indians (U.S. Bureau of Indian Affairs 1997). This is not coincidental. It reflects the legacy of federal government efforts to assimilate American Indians into the mainstream of American society, the most notable of which was the General Allotment Act of 1887 calling for the dissolution and dissipation of collectively owned tribal lands into individual parcels deeded to tribal members (Prucha 1984). Land within reservation boundaries not allotted to tribal members was made available for white settlement and sold (see McDonnell 1991).[6] This has resulted in a "checkerboard" pattern of land ownership common on many reservations, where some parcels of land are privately owned while others are Indian-owned trust land.

Since 1934, the total amount of tribal trust land nationwide has increased by approximately twelve million acres, which is roughly 10 percent of the total amount of Indian land lost through allotment and other administrative actions prior to 1934. Congress or the Secretary of the Interior reacquired

6. As a result of the General Allotment Act, between 1887 and 1932 the aggregate tribal land base within the United States was reduced from roughly 139 million acres to less than 48 million acres.

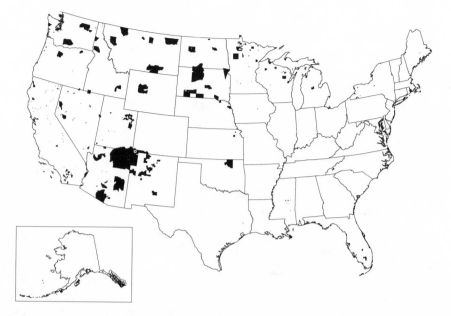

Fig. 3.3 American Indian reservations, 2000

Source: United States Bureau of Indian Affairs

much of this land through legislative action, but some lands were obtained through direct tribal acquisition. Although the vast majority of the reacquired land has been within existing or historic reservation boundaries, some of it has been outside of reservation boundaries.

The consolidation and expansion of tribal trust land, particularly for reservations with checkerboard land ownership, poses both a challenge and an opportunity for Indian tribes in the twenty-first century. Significant nonrenewable resources such as coal, oil, gas, and uranium lie beneath Indian reservation land. As population and development pressures in the West have increased demand for these and other natural resources, and increased competition from outside interests over their use and development, the battle over ownership and control of tribal trust land has intensified (Snipp 1986).

Opposition from elected officials, citizens groups, and business organizations against the consolidation and expansion of tribal trust land has grown in recent decades following a number of successful Indian land claim settlement cases.[7] Because tribal trust land falls under tribal government authority, it is exempt from most state and local laws, regulations, and taxation. At the same time that tribes face opposition from state,

7. For example, following a claim filed by the Passamaquoddy tribe to two-thirds of the state of Maine, Congress passed the Maine Indian Settlement Act in 1980 in which the tribe retained rights to 120,000 acres and a $40 million settlement (White 1990, 291).

county, and local municipalities that fear the loss of property tax revenues, they also confront landowners who fear that intervention by the federal government in the adjudication of Indian land claims will drive property values down should the tribes successfully have the land placed into trust.

Perhaps the most daunting challenge to the consolidation and expansion of tribal trust land is the capital needed by tribes to purchase land from non-Indian landowners. While tribal gaming has proved a boon to some tribes, not all tribes own and operate tribal casinos, and of those that do, only a handful have been enormously successful. Far more have experienced only moderate success. Moreover, even if the necessary capital is available, tribes face the additional challenge of transferring the land into government trust, no easy feat in light of the media fervor and opposition to tribal gaming.

Conclusion

Since Christopher Columbus made landfall in 1492, American Indians have faced successive waves of disease, warfare, and governmental policies that have threatened their survival as sovereign nations and peoples with unique cultures and traditions. Although American Indians living on or near reservations continue to lag behind the rest of the United States in terms of employment, education, and other socioeconomic indicators, there have been marked improvements on many reservations in recent years. One reason for this improvement has been largely due to gaming revenues. But caution must be taken not to overestimate the impact of Indian gaming on tribal communities. Less than half of the 562 Indian tribes formally recognized by the federal government operate tribal casinos.

For Indian tribes, the struggle for survival is far from over. In the past decade, with the proliferation and success of Indian gaming, challenges to the legal tenets of tribal sovereignty have intensified. In some cases, revenues from tribal gaming have elevated American Indians from the poorest and least powerful segment of a community to one of the wealthiest, altering social relations, political power, and control of resources in some regions. Indian tribes have also faced opposition to their efforts to reacquire, consolidate, and expand tribal trust lands. The effects of these and other challenges facing Indian tribes can only be judged at some point in the future, but given the enormous political and economic stakes involved, opposition from federal, state, and local governments will no doubt continue to pose a threat to the legal tenets of tribal sovereignty. Apart from these challenges to tribal sovereignty, perhaps the greatest challenge facing American Indian tribes and peoples in the twenty-first century will be the struggle to protect, preserve, and revitalize their unique cultures, languages, and traditions for future generations.

4

Latinos in Rural America

Rogelio Saenz and Cruz C. Torres

The Latino population is one of the fastest growing racial or ethnic populations in the United States. This group increased by about 58 percent between 1990 and 2000, a rate that was 4.4 times faster than growth for the nation's overall population, more than ten times faster than the non-Hispanic white population, and about three times faster than the African American population. It is often assumed that Latinos are clustered exclusively in large urban centers, with sparse, isolated pockets of Latinos living in rural areas. Moreover, it is commonly assumed that it is only a matter of time before most rural Latinos will move to urban areas.

However, many Latinos have deep rural roots. Many non-U.S.-born Latinos, especially those of Mexican origin, can trace their roots to rural areas. Indeed, the initial incorporation of Mexicans into the United States occurred in rural settings. Furthermore, throughout the twentieth century, the agricultural industry in the United States has relied on Latinos for hired labor. More recently, we have seen a tremendous growth of Latinos in rural areas, especially outside of traditional Latino enclaves, and Latino immigrants are increasingly settling in rural areas. Thus, rural communities are experiencing significant growth in their Latino populations. Yet we continue to have a dearth of information about rural Latinos.

In this chapter we seek to assess existing knowledge about the rural Latino population. First, we describe recent population changes and demographic and socioeconomic patterns involving rural Latinos. Second, we offer an overview of the existing research and literature on rural Latinos. Third, we identify the major research areas and issues that need to be addressed to better understand this population. Finally, we close the chapter with a discussion about the importance of addressing the needs of

Address all correspondence to Rogelio Saenz, Texas A&M University, Department of Sociology, College Station, TX 77843-4351. E-mail: rsaenz@tamu.edu.

Latinos and including them in plans for sustaining and developing rural communities.

Recent Population Changes Among Latinos in Nonmetropolitan Areas

We draw on data from the 1990 and 2000 censuses to assess major population trends involving rural Latinos. Specifically, we use data from the Inter-University Program for Latino Research (2001) based on Census 2000 Redistricting Data (P.L. 94-171) Summary File and the 1990 Summary Tape File (STF1).[1] Using these data, we compare Latino demographics in nonmetropolitan and metropolitan counties.

Metropolitan areas have typically expanded their populations at a faster pace than nonmetropolitan areas. For instance, at the national level the metropolitan population grew by 13.9 percent between 1990 and 2000, while the nonmetropolitan population grew by 10.2 percent during the same period (see Chapter 1). In contrast, Latino population growth was actually higher in nonmetropolitan areas during the 1990s, increasing by 67 percent (from nearly 1.9 million in 1990 to slightly more than 3.1 million in 2000), compared to 57 percent in metropolitan areas. Latino growth in nonmetropolitan areas made up about one-tenth of the nearly 13 million Latinos added to the U.S. population by international migration or natural increase between 1990 and 2000.

A closer view of the data, however, reveals significant variation across regions. We divided the fifty states and the District of Columbia into five regions, grouping states in the Southwest together to capture the unique geographic clustering of Latinos. As defined here, the Southwest includes Texas, Arizona, California, Colorado, and New Mexico. The nonmetropolitan Latino population rose faster than the metropolitan Latino population in three regions (Northeast, Midwest, and South) (Table 4.1). Yet the Latino nonmetropolitan population grew especially fast in the southern and midwestern regions, with the group tripling in the South and doubling in the Midwest between 1990 and 2000. The other three regions experienced comparatively slower growth rates in the nonmetropolitan Latino population.

As a result of these variable growth rates during the decade, the regional distribution of the Latino nonmetropolitan population shifted significantly between 1990 and 2000. While the Southwest saw its share of the nation's nonmetropolitan Latino population decrease from 66 percent in 1990 to

---

1. See http://www.nd.edu/~iuplr/cic/4St_county.html.

Table 4.1 Percentage of change in Latino population, by region and metropolitan/nonmetropolitan residence, 1990–2000

	Nonmetropolitan	Metropolitan
United States	67.1	57.9
Midwest	112.8	77.0
Northeast	71.2	39.4
South	202.6	93.6
Southwest	35.3	50.3
West	81.7	130.3

Source: U.S. Census of Population.

53 percent in 2000, the South increased its share from 11 percent to 19 percent and the Midwest from 10 percent to 13 percent between 1990 and 2000.

The growth of the Latino population in nonmetropolitan areas contributed significantly to the overall Latino population growth in three regions between 1990 and 2000. Nonmetropolitan Latinos made up nearly one-fifth of the overall Latino growth in the West during this decade, and about one-sixth of the growth in the South and Midwest. By 2000, one in five Latino residents in the western region lived in nonmetropolitan areas, as did one in eight inhabitants of the midwestern and southern regions.

As noted, the fastest Latino growth in nonmetropolitan areas has taken place in the South and Midwest, regions that have traditionally had relatively few Latinos. What has driven this unprecedented population growth? Employment opportunities in the meat processing industry have attracted many Latinos to nonmetropolitan areas of the South and Midwest. This industry underwent major restructuring in the 1980s, leading to the displacement of high-wage beef and pork processing workers in the Midwest and poultry plant workers in the South, and the movement of meat packing plants from urban to rural areas (see Stull et al. 1995). The industry has actively recruited Latinos directly from Mexico and from other U.S. locations (e.g., California and Texas) to work in jobs that offer low wages and benefits and hazardous work conditions. As a result, Latinos have had a major impact on the population dynamics of rural communities in the South and Midwest.

Demographic and Socioeconomic Profile of Nonmetropolitan Latinos

We used data from the 2000 census to create an age profile of nonmetropolitan Latinos, which shows that this population is quite young. Nearly

37 percent of nonmetropolitan Latinos in the country were less than eighteen years of age in 2000, compared to only 27 percent of all nonmetropolitan residents. Additionally, only 5 percent of nonmetropolitan Latinos were aged sixty-five or older, compared to approximately 15 percent of all nonmetropolitan people in the nation. These data demonstrate the youthful nature of nonmetropolitan Latinos.

Data from the March 2000 Current Population Survey (CPS)[2] were the basis for assessing other demographic and socioeconomic patterns of nonmetropolitan Latinos. Our analysis is based on Latinos sixteen years and older living in nonmetropolitan areas, and uses the five regions delineated above. Overall, 40 percent of nonmetropolitan Latinos in the United States were foreign-born; in the West, this figure rises to about two-thirds (Table 4.2).

Nationwide, half of nonmetropolitan Latinos aged twenty-five and older were high school graduates, with close to 70 percent of those in the Northeast holding a high school diploma. About 6 percent of nonmetropolitan Latinos in the civilian labor force were unemployed, with those in the South and West most likely to be jobless. Around 45 percent of nonmetropolitan Latino workers in the nation were employed in three occupational sectors: precision production, craft, and repair; service (excluding protective/household service); and farming, forestry, and fishing. Latino workers in the West had the most occupational concentration, with two-thirds of this population working in three sectors: farming, forestry, and fishing; transportation and material moving; and machine operators, assemblers, and inspectors. About two in five Latino workers in the West worked in farming, forestry, and fishing occupations, while only about one in eight held such jobs in the South. Finally, nonmetropolitan Latino workers earned an average hourly wage of $8.20, ranging from $7.79 in the West to $8.96 in the Northeast.

What Do We Know About Rural Latinos?

Our overview of recent demographic and socioeconomic patterns provides insight into broad trends involving rural Latinos. The following literature review assesses what sort of research has been conducted focusing on this growing population. Overall, studies on rural Latinos have been sparse. Among the more than 250,000 articles published between 1975 and 2001 listed in *Sociological Abstracts,* only forty-two focused on rural Latinos. Although this set of articles does not incorporate all of the existing literature

2 See http://www.bls.census.gov/cps/cpsmain.htm.

Table 4.2 Selected demographic and socioeconomic characteristics of rural Latinos, by region, 2000.

Socioeconomic characteristic	Total	Midwest	Northeast	South	Southwest	West
Foreign-born	39.7%	52.9%	58.9%	59.0%	27.5%	67.4%
Foreign-born, immigration 1990–2000	16.4%	21.8%	33.3%	23.3%	9.3%	39.0%
Age 25 and older, with high school diploma	50.1%	55.9%	69.2%	49.7%	47.6%	54.7%
Unemployed	5.9%	3.9%	6.8%	8.8%	5.3%	8.4%
Selected occupation						
Primary	PPCR 19.5%	MOAI 18.8%	SERV 30.0%	MOAI 20.4%	PPCR 26.2%	FFF 41.6%
Secondary	SERV 15.2%	PPCR 16.2%	MOAI 17.3%	SERV 15.4%	SERV 18.3%	TRMM 14.3%
Tertiary	FFF 10.7%	ADMSP 13.0%	PRTSRV 14.7%	FFF 12.3%	HECHL 9.4%	MOAI 10.3%
Average hourly wage	$8.20	$8.68	$8.96	$8.28	$8.15	$7.79
Weighted N	1,804,302	235,018	48,517	218,415	1,110,501	191,850

Note: The following are the occupations for the abbreviations shown in the table: ADMSP (administrative support, including clerical); FFF (farming, forestry, and fishing); HECHL (handlers, equipment cleaners, helpers, and laborers); MOAI (machine operators, assemblers, and inspectors); PPCR (precision production, craft, and repair); PRTSRV (protective service); SERV (service, excluding protective and household service); TRMM (transportation and material moving).

Source: Based on data for Latinos 16 years of age and older in the March 2000 Current Population Survey.

on rural Latinos, we believe that it approximates our existing knowledge of this group.

Among these forty-two articles, the most common substantive areas of research are social inequality, education, health and aging, and substance abuse and violence. Research on social inequality is the most likely to appear in mainstream rural sociology publications. This research has shown that rural Latinos lag behind a variety of comparison groups with respect to poverty, income, and employment. To explain the lagging socioeconomic position of rural Latinos, researchers have studied the role of spatial inequality in limiting economic opportunities, the unique types of jobs available in rural areas, the presence of discrimination in rural labor markets, and the limited human capital of rural minorities.

A second line of research has focused on education. Here, studies show that Latino children are active learners with unique interaction styles, that participation in high school athletics is related to positive social and economic outcomes especially among females, and that Latino parents rate stronger in the social, as opposed to academic, aspects associated with the scholastic development of their children.

Research on health and aging has produced findings along two lines. One strand has observed positive outcomes related to the health and aging of rural Latinos, noting the important role that family and kin play in the care of sick and elderly family members, and the favorable birth outcomes of infants of Mexican-born versus U.S.-born Mexican mothers. A second strand has noted negative outcomes related to health and aging, citing the underutilization of health services, the unfavorable birth outcomes for infants of U.S.-born Mexican American women, the low prevalence of prenatal care, the low level of health insurance coverage, the stresses and coping problems that more acculturated rural Latina caregivers experience, and the lack of information that migrant farmworker Latino men have about AIDS and their low level of condom use.

Another common area of research involving rural Latinos concerns substance abuse and violence. This research paints a grim portrait of conditions for rural Latino youth and women. Findings show disconnected youth who abuse drugs and alcohol, and females in traditional positions abused by their male partners.

Overall, the forty-two articles that we reviewed provide a glimpse of the conditions that shape the lives of rural Latinos; however, our stock of knowledge is woefully inadequate. This literature is limited to a few studies that are poorly integrated theoretically and methodologically; hence we lack a concise and succinct understanding of rural Latinos. Much more research is necessary to understand this group and to address the unique challenges that this population brings to the table of rural community leaders and policy-makers. We now turn our attention to some of the major research needs, and to issues that must be addressed to improve our understanding of this group.

What Do We Still Need to Know About Rural Latinos?

This section highlights several key areas that need to be addressed to help us better understand and improve the conditions of rural Latinos, at a time when this group is undergoing tremendous growth and change. Unique characteristics of the rural Latino population underscore the fact that we cannot assume they share the same needs and face the same problems as urban Latinos or other racial and ethnic groups in rural areas. Rural Latinos live in a specific context that sets limits on the extent to which they have access to the resources of the larger society.

Education and Human Capital Formation

The most significant challenge facing the Latino community today is education. Latinos, especially Mexican Americans, lag significantly behind other racial and ethnic groups in academic performance and educational attainment. Current demographic trends suggest that today's Latino youth will increasingly be called upon in the coming decades to generate the revenues required to sustain national and local economies. The extent to which they can succeed in the job market will depend on two things: the degree to which structural barriers that have long blocked Latino upward mobility are removed, and the degree to which they gain access to education and other societal resources.

Latino students face a series of problems in the educational arena. Broadly, these include high levels of school segregation, high dropout rates, and pervasive inequities in school funding. More narrowly, Latino students are underrepresented in pre-kindergarten, gifted-and-talented, advanced placement, and college-prep programs, and overrepresented in remedial courses. In addition, Limited English Proficiency Latino students are underenrolled in bilingual education programs.

In addressing these problems, administrators need to be aware of the diverse nature of the Latino population. For instance, many Latino immigrant children arrive in this country with large gaps in their schooling, leading to academic needs that differ from their U.S.-born peers. Many are not fully literate in their native language, and thus require basic language and literacy skills along with remedial and English-language instruction. Educators often grapple with the grade-level placement of older immigrant children who are not academically prepared to be placed with their age peers.

Many rural communities that have experienced unprecedented growth in the Latino population are poorly equipped to educate Latino children, especially immigrants, and administrators have little understanding of the unique needs of Latino children. Yet there are success stories that can be instructive for communities that find themselves in such situations. The case of Dalton, Georgia, provides an illustration of an innovative and proactive approach to educating Latino students (Hernandez-Leon and Zuniga 2002; Zuniga et al. 2002). In the early 1990s, Dalton experienced a rapid growth in its Latino population, as large numbers of Latino immigrant students entered the local schools. Concerned with these students' special needs, school officials and community leaders established the Georgia Project in collaboration with faculty at the Universidad de Monterrey in Mexico to meet the educational needs of its Latino students. The Project set up four collaborative initiatives: "a bilingual teacher program to bring graduates from the university to Dalton, the design of a bilingual education curriculum, a Latino adult education and leadership initiative, and a summer institute for local teachers to learn Spanish and Mexican history and culture in Monterrey" (Hernandez-Leon and Zuniga 2002, 10–11).

Much research has documented the more favorable educational outcomes for the children of immigrants as opposed to U.S.-born minority groups (Valenzuela 1999). This work demonstrates the positive aspects of immigrant cultures that may help children succeed academically. Such research has suggested that U.S.-born minorities, including Latinos, may exhibit lower educational achievement because they adhere to oppositional cultures that shun mainstream goals, values, and aspirations. Unfortunately, this research has been limited to urban students. There is an important need to assess the role of place of birth and oppositional cultures on the academic outcomes for rural Latino youth.

The Labor Force and Social Mobility

The growing presence of Latinos in rural areas suggests that they will make up an increasingly important portion of the rural workforce in the near future. Latino males aged sixteen and older already have the highest civilian labor force participation rate among racial and ethnic groups (80 percent versus 74 percent for whites) (U.S. Bureau of the Census 2001b). We need more information on how Latinos are integrated into different sectors of rural labor markets, and how their experiences may vary by gender and place of birth. This is especially important from an equity standpoint, as Latino workers have traditionally been concentrated in low-wage industries such as agriculture that offer few opportunities for upward mobility.

While we often focus on rural Latino workers that lag behind, a small but significant number of Latinos experiences economic success. This can be seen in the development of businesses and the formation of a middle and professional class in rural areas. We need information about Latinos who have "made it," especially those who did so despite the odds, in order to understand and encourage routes to success for other rural Latinos who may not understand how they can take advantage of opportunity structures.

Finally, we do not have the information to assess intergenerational mobility among rural Latinos. Our understanding of the economic experience of rural Latinos has been limited to cross-sectional secondary data. Unfortunately, national longitudinal data sets include few rural Latinos, so it is difficult to undertake serious research in this area. To this end, we need to develop longitudinal data sets that follow individuals over time, so that we can assess social mobility across time and space and identify any variation that may be related to gender and birthplace. Such data could spawn a line of research that explores the degree to which there are short- and long-term costs for Latinos for being raised in a rural environment.

Health

Addressing health care issues facing rural Latinos is imperative given the significant growth of this group and its changing sociodemographic profile. Research indicates that Latinos tend to be more traditional in their health care behaviors and to underutilize formal health services. Aside from the obvious problem involving the inadequate provision of comprehensive health care services in nonmetropolitan communities, Latinos face multiple barriers to adequate health care. These include financial limitations, lack of health insurance, lack of transportation, language barriers, and cultural differences. There is often a wide chasm between white health care providers and Latino patients, especially women, that stems from differences in language, social class, and cultural constructions of gender. These impede communication and health care delivery. In addition, recent dramatic changes in the health care system have compounded access problems for an already seriously underserved rural Latino population.

The focus of concern for rural Latinos today remains access to health care, health promotion, and disease prevention. Yet there is a paucity of knowledge about the health status of rural Latinos, and about how current policies affect this population's health outcomes. We also have little specific knowledge about health-care-seeking behaviors among rural Latinos. Without such information, it is difficult to plan for the future health care needs of this group. Lack of adequate data creates the risk of introducing policies that are based on stereotypes rather than on real needs and problems.

Moreover, we need a better understanding of the role of nativity and acculturation on the health of rural Latinos. Research has shown more favorable health outcomes for Latino immigrants that their U.S.-born peers. For instance, Forbes et al. (2000) found an "epidemiological paradox" in which Latino immigrants have relatively low mortality rates. It has been suggested that traditional Mexican culture encourages healthier lifestyles that result in better overall health among these populations. It could also be explained by the "salmon bias" in which sicker persons return to their countries of origin. Unfortunately, research has not adequately assessed the role of nativity and acculturation on health outcomes for Latinos in rural settings. A better understanding of these factors would increase not only our awareness of the health patterns of rural Latinos, but also our ability to craft functional programs that respond to these needs.

Aging

Because of the youthful age structure of the Latino population, aging issues are largely invisible in the larger Latino and aging policy contexts. Not only are Latino elderly a relatively small part of the Latino population, they also represent a small share of the overall elderly population. Moreover, on the assumption that people of similar ages share similar experiences, basic factors that decide life chances (race, ethnicity, gender, nativity, and social class) receive relatively limited attention; however, the life experiences of rural Latino elderly are vastly different than those of their peers from other racial and ethnic groups. Historically, Latinos have disproportionately worked in occupations such as farm work characterized by higher health risks, early retirement, and inadequate retirement and health plans. Thus, Latino elderly are likely to have significant and unique needs compared to majority-group or other minority elderly.

We know that as people age, their social networks tend to decrease. Loss of social networks is especially critical in the case of elderly persons living alone. Unfortunately, there is an erroneous assumption that Latino elderly do not live alone (see Chapter 6 in this volume). The persistent belief that cultural familism dictates that Latinos provide for and take care of their elders encourages formal institutions to underestimate their responsibility to meet the needs of Latino elderly. In reality, it is unclear whether this phenomenon is a cultural attribute or an adaptive strategy emerging from economic necessity. Numerous questions related to rural Latino seniors remain unanswered.

New Settlements

As shown earlier, one of the most significant trends for the Latino population over the past decade has been their increased settlement in rural areas that traditionally have not had Latino populations. Unfortunately, we have little information about the experiences of Latino newcomers in these areas. While the 2000 census will provide valuable data to fill this gap, we will need to supplement these data with ethnographies and other qualitative studies that capture the underlying dynamics related to intergroup relations involving newcomers and established residents. How readily do Latino newcomers gain access to the different dimensions of social and economic life in their new communities? How well do community institutions meet the unique needs of Latino newcomers? How will the influx of Latino newcomers change the community profile (see Torres 2000)? Will these new settlement areas become ghettoes where Latinos are isolated from opportunity structures or will they become ethnic enclaves where coethnics flourish socially and economically? These are important questions that will allow us to gauge the degree to which rural Latino newcomers experience a receptive environment. This information is useful in that successful cases can be identified and used as models for other communities that experience Latino population growth.

Intragroup Diversity

Changes within Latino populations in rural areas signal greater degrees of social and economic differentiation within this group. Even though Mexicans represent the largest Latino group in the United States, followed by Puerto Ricans and Cubans, their predominance has decreased somewhat over the last decade. "Other Hispanic or Latino" populations, composed largely of Dominicans and different groups from Central America, have grown significantly. In addition, the continual flow of immigrants has produced increasing diversity with respect to generational status, language use, and economic standing within the Latino population. It will be important in the coming years to assess the results of this diversity for the social and economic standing of this group.

Immigration

Latino immigrants, particularly Mexicans, are increasingly settling in rural areas. Immigration is a crosscutting issue that provides a window for understanding the Latino experience in the United States across various dimensions. Unfortunately, most of our knowledge about Latino immigrants is based on those who end up in urban areas. We need to develop a research agenda to monitor the experiences of rural Latino immigrants.[3] Moreover, we need a better understanding of transnational movements involving Latinos in rural areas. This form of migration has important implications for the integration of Latinos into their communities of destination and origin.

Special Rural Latino Populations

In contrast to immigrants who are newcomers in rural areas, farmworkers and *colonia* residents, commonly seen as "the poorest of the poor," are established and recognized groups in rural America. Many of the problems associated with other Latino groups are especially acute among these two groups. Latino farmworkers continue to be a significant part of the rural work force. In addition, many Latinos continue to follow crops as migrant farmworkers, frequently traveling long distances across regions. It is estimated that California and Texas together have more than 928,000 farmworkers, including nearly 471,000 migrant farmworkers (Larson 2000a, 2000b). Farmworkers typically have low wages, unstable employment patterns, high levels of unemployment, and high rates of poverty. Moreover, because of the hazardous working and living conditions and the lack of access to health care, they experience elevated health problems. The National Center for Farmworker Health's Migrant Health Monograph Series presents an informative overview of high priority health issues involving farmworkers (see National Center for Farmworker Health 2001).

Colonias are unincorporated areas located in rural settings along the United States–Mexican border. Typically, *colonia* residents do not enjoy many of the basic services that most Americans take for granted (e.g., sanitary water supply, sewage systems, paved roads, and other services typically provided by municipal or county governments). It is estimated that in 1996, 392,188 people lived in 1,495 designated economically distressed areas (EDAs) in Texas alone, along that state's border with Mexico (Texas Water Development Board 1997). An EDA is defined as "one in which

3. The Mexican Migration Project is a useful starting point (see http://lexis.pop.upenn.edu/mexmig/welcome.html).

water supply or wastewater systems do not meet minimal state standards, financial resources are inadequate to provide services to meet those needs, and 80 percent of dwellings in the area were occupied on June 1, 1989" (Texas Water Development Board 1997, 1). *Colonia* residents, many of whom are farmworkers, face economic and health conditions similar to those of farmworkers in general.

There is a tremendous need to develop primary data to monitor the economic and health conditions of Latino farmworkers and *colonia* residents. We need research that examines the degree to which members of these groups are trapped in a cycle of poverty or have access to upward social mobility. In addition, we need an inventory of programs and policies intended to improve the plight of these groups in order to identify programs that have been effective in the past, and under what conditions. Finally, we need data about the health status of Latino farmworkers and *colonia* residents. Members of these groups continue to live and toil in hazardous conditions, typically without access to health care. Especially important are data to assess links between environmental conditions and health and mortality outcomes among farmworkers and *colonia* inhabitants.

In sum, this section has highlighted some of the areas that need to be addressed in order to increase our understanding and improve the conditions of rural Latinos. Rural Latinos continue to be an invisible population, too often overlooked in discussions and debates concerning rural policy. We believe that the absence of research on rural Latinos has contributed to this neglect. We need to develop a research and policy agenda to place rural Latinos in a more central position in the formation of rural social and economic development policy. The development of a knowledge base for this group is crucial for improving the social and economic conditions of rural Latinos in the future.

Conclusion

Based on our assessment, we know that the rural Latino population is growing quite rapidly, that it is a youthful population, and that it endures major socioeconomic and health disadvantages. Under these conditions, what does the future hold for rural Latinos? Will they remain in rural areas or will they eventually make their way into urban areas? Will they have access to opportunity structures or will they continue occupying a subordinate position in the stratification system?

Latinos have a long and well-established presence in rural areas of the country, extending back to the nineteenth century. More recently, we have seen significant growth of the Latino population in new rural settlements outside of the traditional southwestern enclaves. These trends suggest that Latinos will remain a part of the American rural landscape. Rural communities continue to recruit, attract, and depend heavily on the Latino workforce. Without the presence of Latinos, many of these communities would continue to face population declines. Yet while Latinos have much to offer their communities, they also have numerous needs that require attention in order for them to contribute to the development and sustainability of rural communities.

In the end, we conclude that education is the primary vehicle through which rural Latinos can gain access to opportunity structures and successfully meet the challenges and opportunities that await them in the coming decades. Given demographic trends, many rural communities will depend on their Latino inhabitants to provide the workforce needed to generate adequate revenues to sustain them and support increasingly aging populations. The extent to which Latinos will be able to answer that call will depend heavily on how well they have been educated and trained today.

However, the extent to which Latinos will become a productive part of the development equation of rural communities also depends heavily on the dismantling of the structural barriers and discrimination that have traditionally kept them and other members of minority groups from gaining access to opportunity structures. Rural community leaders need to view their Latino residents as assets rather than liabilities and to invest in the development of their human capital in order for Latinos to help sustain their communities.

We have shown that our existing knowledge about rural Latinos is woefully inadequate and have outlined some of the key issues that need to be addressed to improve the conditions of this population. This information is crucial for developing solutions to help rural Latinos face a brighter future and contribute to the sustainability and development of their communities.

Reshuffling and Remaking Rural Families

5

What Do Rural Families Look Like Today?

Katherine MacTavish and Sonya Salamon

For much of the last century rural families were distinctively larger, more stable, and younger than urban families. Yet in the last quarter of the twentieth century rural families, like all U.S. families, have experienced critical changes. Increasing rates of marital instability and unwed parenthood have reshaped family structures. Changing work patterns that moved an increasing proportion of mothers with young children into the formal work force have shifted role behavior within the household. Greater geographic mobility and the restructuring of the economic sector have rewoven the social fabric of local places. Thus, at the dawn of the twenty-first century families across the United States look and function differently than did the families of their parents' and grandparents' generations.

Much attention has been focused on the implications such changes have for family well-being and child development. While most scholars hesitate to label the family an endangered institution, there is widespread agreement that the challenges now faced by families are daunting. Evidence is mounting that the fragmented structure and hectic pace of modern family life strain even the capacity of middle-class families to effectively nurture children and other dependent family members such as the elderly (Elkind 1994; Bronfenbrenner 1992).

This chapter locates the transformation of U.S. families in the context of rural America—a place where families are seemingly buffered from the changes and challenges facing families in suburban or urban places. Yet already by the late 1980s, demographic trends emerging among rural populations called into question the distinctiveness of rural families (Fuguitt, Brown, and Beale 1989). It is thus important as we enter a new century to reconsider the nature of rural families and rural family life. We begin by examining how rural families look, the daily rhythms of their lives, and what challenges they face in this new century. We then turn to the potential implications these features have for rural family well-being. Finally, we suggest a means for supporting American rural families as they enter the twenty-first century. Rural families represent a historically valuable yet overlooked resource that has contributed significantly to the rich diversity of family forms fundamental to our nation's vitality.

Rural Families in an Era of Change

Historically, rural people shared an ideology that marked their family structure and way of life as distinctive and, in their minds, often superior to that of urban or suburban families. Rural people could draw on a common pioneering heritage, strong intergenerational bonds, and a stable, cohesive small community to construct a way of life that valued family self-reliance. The rural community was a place where residents knew one another, shared values and history, and felt a sense of trust. They also were integrated by effective social norms. In truth, not all rural families benefited from this ideal way of life. Still, notions about the richness of social supports linked to a small town persist in symbolizing what is unique about family life in rural America.

For generations, these ideals validated and rationalized how many rural families went about their lives and raised their children. That is, rural families remained in the countryside, often despite economic hard times, because they believed in the intrinsic worth of a rural way of life. When communities came close to the ideal, growing up in a rural family made it likely that a child forged rich cross-age ties outside the immediate kin group. In such an ideal community context, dedicated elders mentored children and youth as a collective responsibility. That is, a childhood spent in such a cohesive small town brought those integrated into the social structure access to a level of security and collective nurturance not easily approximated in more residentially fluid places like cities and suburbs. Generation after generation of rural families who had access to this ideal rural life, or something similar to it, obtained a level of social support that fostered the successful development of their children and youth and provided for the care of their elderly (Elder and Conger 2000; White Riley and Uhlenberg 2000).

Today, however, despite an enduring commitment to a rural way of life, family experiences more often diverge from the ideal of an intact family embedded in supportive kin and community networks. The same changes experienced by U.S. families in general—altered family and household

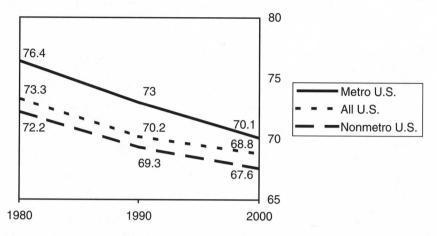

Fig. 5.1 Comparison of the proportion of family households among all households, by location, 1980–2000

structures, shifting work patterns, and emerging community forms—now exist throughout rural America. Such changes challenge rural families in ways unknown to past generations.

Changing Rural Family Structure

Today, the structure of rural families resembles their urban and suburban counterparts (see Figs. 5.1–3). Demographic trends evident in the wider society, including higher divorce rates and more single parents, are clearly emerging in rural places. Just two decades ago married couples represented a firm majority (86.1 percent) of nonmetropolitan family households. Today, married-couple households are less common, representing only 79.1 percent of nonmetropolitan households. The rising rate of divorce in

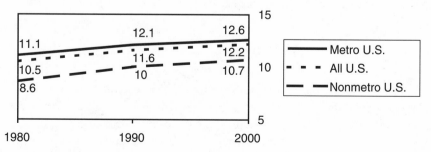

Fig. 5.2 Comparison of the proportion of female-headed households, by location, 1980–2000

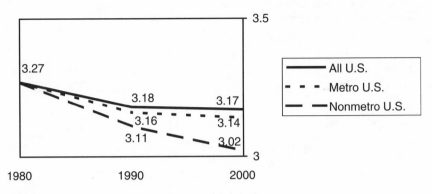

Fig. 5.3 Comparison of mean family size, by location, 1980–2000

rural America in part explains the climbing proportion of single-parent rural family households. Single mothers now head 10.7 percent of non-metropolitan family households, compared to 8.6 percent two decades ago (see Fig. 5.2). These shifts in rural household structure parallel trends in household structure across the wider U.S. population.

Rural families currently diverge from past trends when it comes to family size as well (see Fig. 5.3). Historically, rural households have been larger than urban ones. Yet by 1980, for the first time the mean family size of 3.27 persons was similar across the metropolitan and nonmetropolitan United States. Since then, rural families have grown smaller at a more rapid rate than their urban counterparts. Where once it was common for rural households to include six or more members, today they average only 3.02 persons, making them smaller than the average urban household (U.S. Bureau of the Census 2000). The drop likely reflects the aging population in rural places as much as it does rural parents having fewer children. Thus, the structural distinctiveness of rural families has faded in recent decades. Today, rural families are more likely to resemble the demographic profile and structure of the median American family (Teachman, Tedrow, and Crowder 2000).

Changing Patterns of Rural Work

As changes in the basic household structure have emerged, work patterns among rural adults have shifted as well. Involvement in agriculture, once the dominant rural family way of life, has declined dramatically. As agriculture restructured between 1950 and 1999, the number of family farms lost averaged 60 percent nationally. First small farms disappeared, while later medium- to large-sized farms showed the greater reductions

(U.S. Bureau of the Census 2001a). Today, fewer than one in ten rural families earn their primary livelihood from the land (Lasley 1997). Thus, although the rural American landscape is still dominated by agriculture, a postagrarian way of life—where few are involved or connected with agriculture—now shapes rural community priorities.

The transition to a postagrarian era has had a ripple effect on rural family and community life. With fewer farm families to shop locally or to send children to local schools, main street businesses have declined, schools have consolidated, and local jobs have almost vanished. The decline in farm families has indirectly spurred more adults in rural places, including those never in agriculture, to seek employment away from their hometown, commuting to find work in nearby metropolitan centers (see Chapter 12). Commuting alters the daily schedule of rural families to one that more closely resembles suburban families. Dealing with such circumstances means that many rural families need not only more cars but also more nonfamily child care, as both parents as well as extended family members (including even grandparents) enter the labor force (Perry-Jenkins and Salamon 2002). Cohesive small communities, even where families have maintained intergenerational residential stability, are fragmented by the demands of commuting, as adults have less time available for community engagement.

Historically, for less educated rural workers, "bad jobs"—jobs that pay low wages, offer variable or part-time schedules, and lack benefits—were the standard (Nelson and Smith 1999). Yet in the recent past, such jobs at least had the advantage of being local, reducing travel and child care costs. Now, compounded by longer commutes, "bad jobs" stretch even middle-income rural family finances and sap energy. Today, even for the better educated, "good jobs"—jobs that pay a fair wage, provide predictable and steady work, and include benefits—have moved away from hometowns. Those rural parents fortunate enough to secure these better jobs must share with other rural workers the social and financial costs of traveling long distances and obtaining child care.

Even for rural children, weekdays often include a commute. Due to widespread consolidation, rural schools in many regions may now serve an entire county rather than a single community. Bus rides of over an hour each way are not uncommon for many rural children (Howley 2001). In addition, younger children now spend many hours in child care, while older children may find themselves in latchkey situations, leaving little time during weekdays to engage in shared family time, intergenerational activities, or even the daily chores so central to the ideals of a rural childhood.

While rural families maintain a preference for living in the countryside, their daily lives are fragmented by the necessity of frequently traveling between the various dispersed places—home, work, child care, school, shops, and services—necessary to sustain domestic life. Rural families have developed a lifestyle that more closely resembles suburban families than those of their ancestors from the agrarian, locally centered community of just fifty years ago.

The Changing Social Contexts of Rural Community

Significant alterations are taking place in the social fabric of rural places, with implications for rural family well-being. Rural communities in many areas have been transformed by upscale real estate development, typically in the form of subdivisions built on the edge of small towns. Increasingly, these house newly arrived urban families looking for a rural location in order to be closer to nature and experience small-town life. In small towns with rapid suburbanization, the population reaches a tipping point when new residents come to make up a critical mass of the local population. Social structure then changes dramatically. In the past, family reputation influenced rural social hierarchy and served as a fundamental basis for social control in a community. Acts such as ostentatious consumption were generally frowned upon, and community members at least paid lip service to the notion of egalitarian relations among local residents. Yet when mobile urbanites arrive with unknown family histories and a lack of awareness for the reputation of local families, personal wealth and conspicuous consumption often become the measures of household worth, altering the social hierarchy and mechanisms for social control (Duncan 1999; Salamon 2003). Furthermore, as formerly agrarian communities become suburbanized, priorities attached to a suburban lifestyle such as child enrichment activities have emerged to dominate the rural family schedule. Small town and rural youth, like their suburban counterparts, are now overscheduled with music lessons, dance lessons, skill classes, competitive sports, or other activities. Rural parents complain of suburbanite-style demands such as chauffeuring their children to these classes, and the negative effect this has on the family as it shares less time together, foregoing shared evening meals or simply time to talk (Doherty 1997).

In regions where upscale development occurs, poorer rural families become clustered geographically in towns unlikely to attract wealthy newcomers. These are communities with a depressed economy and little to hold younger, local families. Such physically and economically deteriorating towns concentrate poor families in what are emerging as rural slums. In these poor towns, a rural version of inner-city impoverishment or "ghettoization" could incur a high social cost to family well-being (Fitchen 1992; Salamon 2003; Wilson 1996).

In their struggle to remain vital places, other rural communities employ economic development efforts to attract industry—often any industry. Such efforts have brought an influx of lower-income and ethnically diverse families to fill low-skill industrialized agriculture jobs in large-scale production, canning, meatpacking, or dairy operations. In some regions these new rural residents, whether migrant workers or recent immigrants, enter a community historically composed of European American and middle- to lower-middle-class residents (see Chapter 4). Changes in the ethnic diversity of a small town have tended to sharpen differentiation by ethnic and economic status (Stull, Broadway, and Griffith 1995). Such changes, however, can be confounded as class distinctions blend with ethnic differences. For example, some rural towns have recruited Indian or Filipino doctors and dentists. Likewise, Indians commonly own local motels in many rural American towns. International professionais may differ by race, yet according to income and work may together rank among a town's elite. Both lower-income and upper-income ethnically different families raise new issues of tolerance, especially pertaining to the community's youth and their friendships, dating practices, and marriage experiences. More than in the past, rural families are facing dilemmas encountered more commonly in urban settings (Salamon 2003). In these and many other ways, rural small towns increasingly resemble suburban or urban places in terms of demographic diversity and the complexity of the social structure.

The Challenge of Change for Rural Families

We have established that rural families, to a greater extent than previously recognized, have changed and now resemble suburban and urban families in structure and daily routine. Yet rural families have remained distinctive in several ways, and this uniquely defines the challenges such changes bring forth. First, although they are decreasing, the dependency ratio—the number of children and elderly per one hundred working-age adults (Rogers 1996)—remains higher among rural populations than among other U.S. populations (see Fig. 5.4). While the child dependency ratio—the number of children per one hundred working age adults—has fallen due to smaller family size, the elderly dependency ratio has risen across rural areas (see Fig. 5.5), and has risen at a rate more rapid than in other contexts. Thus, rural households are comparatively pressed to provide care for more dependents, both children and elderly (see Chapter 6 in this volume). Further, unlike suburban and

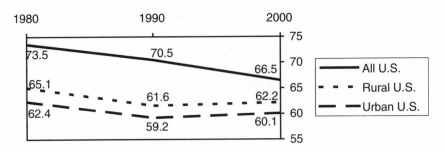

Fig. 5.4 Comparative dependency ratios, by location, 1980–2000

urban places, rural families must provide for a higher ratio of dependents in a context that does not readily offer formal support services such as center-based child or elder care or medical services for even those who can afford them.

Despite these added challenges, rural families in general continue to believe in the ideals and benefits of a rural way of life. Yet while rural families persist at "working hard and making do," fewer and fewer are able to do so in ways that have been traditionally valued (Nelson and Smith 1999). Even the most fundamental family acts of putting food on the table, keeping a roof overhead, and, in particular, caring for and effectively socializing children have been altered and now take new forms for rural families, especially the rural poor.

Putting Food on the Table

Rural households are stereotypically regarded as having the potential for self-provisioning through fruit and vegetable gardening, hunting, fishing, wood gathering, self-employment, or bartering for goods and services (Jensen et al. 1945). As work moves farther from where rural people reside, patterns of daily life change and time diminishes for engaging in activities capable of stretching modest incomes. Access to areas once used for hunting and fishing are increasingly denied as exurban sprawl creates physical and legal barriers to old-timers' customary use. Those rural families who can least afford it are drawn more into the cash economy; dependent on supermarkets, convenience stores, and stores such as Wal-Mart for the goods their immediate ancestors produced for themselves. As dependence on markets for basic necessities grows, skills for self-provisioning a family by gardening or food processing are rapidly lost. While some rural families continue self-provisioning practices, many others today may not know how to garden, cook, or preserve foods, another feature making them indistinguishable from suburban and urban households.

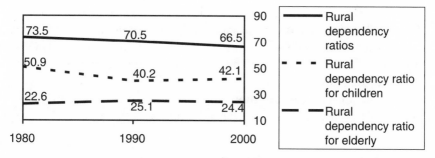

Fig. 5.5 Comparative rural dependency ratios over time

Keeping a Roof Overhead

Decades of suburban growth and commuting changes have tightened housing markets in many regions across rural America by driving up property values (Ziebarth, Prochaska-Cue, and Shrewsbury 1997). Rising housing costs, particularly in suburbanized small towns, challenge lower-income rural families to obtain the basic necessity of shelter. Suitable and sufficient housing, both in terms of availability and quality, is often hard to find within such areas. Newer housing stock takes the form of high-end construction meant to attract urbanites. Older rural housing stock has deteriorated as elderly owners find themselves unable to maintain a home, or as absentee heirs abandoned their worthless inheritance. Landlords then purchase these repossessed shabby houses from county sales for back taxes, and sell the units on contract to lower-income rural families (Salamon 2003).

As an alternative, manufactured or mobile homes represent a seemingly viable option for lower-income rural households seeking affordable housing. This type of housing now represents one in five new homes and one in eight existing homes in nonmetropolitan America. Over half of these homes are sited in mobile home parks, three-quarters of which are found in rural areas. Thus, mobile home parks have become a community form characteristic of rural areas. Historically marginalized to the outskirts of rural communities, mobile home parks have long been viewed disparagingly, and thus have been subject to formal and informal stigmatization. As they are likely to be home to a highly concentrated population of younger, poorer, less educated residents, mobile home parks have the potential to become a type of rural ghetto, with resident families and children considered a burden by both town residents and public officials (Fitchen 1991). Residence in a rural trailer park has been shown to bring with it a level of social stigmatization based on place of residence that compromises integration into the social structure of place, particularly for youth (MacTavish

2001). Further, the very nature of a trailer park—a place where residence is seen as temporary and where the land on which a home sits is rented rather than owned—can erode any sense of community among its residents (Mac-Tavish and Salamon 2001). While a mobile home may appear to be a viable housing option for lower-income rural families, the potential costs—both in the form of stigmatization and compromised pride in home owner-ship—might outweigh benefits for rural families.

Caring For and Socializing Children

As rural families grow more dependent on the urban economy, less support is accessible for the care and socialization of children from traditional local sources. Economic trends that pull rural women and men toward distant labor markets have the unintended consequence of weakening kinship bonds and the type of community embeddedness that historically consti-tuted a safety net for rural families. Strong intergenerational bonds hinge on the availability of extended kin. Residential stability once accounted for the multi-strand kin support available for young or elderly family mem-bers. Recent changes for rural families now test such bonds. Time and energy are in limited supply in both single-parent and dual-earner rural households. Work patterns strain parents' capacity to preserve basic family routines and extended kin traditions. Elements vital to a rural way of life, such as shared meals, frequent visits with grandparents, and family involvement in church and school, are often elbowed out of the family schedule by the demands of parents commuting to nonlocal jobs (Perry-Jenkins and Salamon 2002).

Rural residents most frequently prefer to place young children in the care of kin (Beach 1995). Yet with these kin now less available, untrained nonkin adults are often the only option in small towns. Older, school-aged children come home alone to a latchkey situation without adult supervi-sion or are left to hang out unsupervised with siblings and peers. Given the extended commuter workday of rural parents, child care situations may include long hours in inadequate or unsupervised situations. Furthermore, such settings are by and large age-segregated, thus denying children and youth the opportunity to form the kind of cross-age ties that in the past proved vital to successful youth development in agrarian communities even in the worst of times (Elder and Conger 2000; White Riley and Uhlenberg 2000).

For older rural youth, the social world outside of the home is often structured by experiences shaped by the professional staff at local educa-tional and recreational institutions. When school personnel, for instance, view children as a collective community resource, they are inclined to make an extra effort to mentor youth toward success. Children and youth with access to such supportive resources are more resilient in overcoming serious family traumas than are those with less access (Elder and Conger 2000; Schwartz 1987). Small-town police once typically showed tolerance for youth, allowing adolescents to cruise town streets and hang out in public spaces. Such tolerance is fundamental for young people to establish a sense of worth and attachment to the community. Yet given the greater social and economic stratification emerging in postagrarian towns, and the transformation of social life by suburbanizing forces, the potential capacity for local adults to act collectively in support of youth may be declining (Salamon 2003).

It is clear that rural families today are markedly different from generations past. What is not yet clear are the specific consequences for family well-being and child development as rural customs are altered. We have indicators—the explosion of methamphetamine use among rural youth, rising crime rates in small towns, and less tolerance by small-town authorities toward rural youth—that suggest an association between community change and family social costs (see Chapter 7). Yet much research remains to be done in this area.

Supporting Rural Families Through the Next Century

Change has deeply penetrated rural households and rural places, creating new challenges for sustaining family well-being and rural ideals. We have argued in favor of maintaining a rural way of life and the small town structure of generations past; however, it is unlikely that such resources will be revived to recreate past support systems. Instead, we need to find innovative ways to support both long-standing and newly arrived rural families. As rural families and family ways of life have come to resemble their suburban counterparts, it is plausible that solutions that meet challenges among suburban families would also hold promise as rural solutions. Along these lines we propose initiatives around two areas—work and dependent care.

Recent innovations have emerged in suburban areas with the goal of reducing work/family strains. First, workplaces have moved to suburbs to reduce daily commute times. Intel plants and Microsoft campuses, for example, have purposely relocated to the suburban areas where their workers reside. Concentrated efforts to bring the workplace closer to home, whether through the creation of local jobs or the development of telecommuting in rural places, could possibly benefit rural families as well. In the absence of such measures, the implementation of family-friendly work policies such as flextime—which is more likely in the context of "good jobs"—and, at a minimum, fixed rather than variable work schedules for "bad jobs," would lend some support to rural parents juggling work and family responsibilities. Changes in such policies came about in suburban areas because workers pushed for them. Rural workers need to voice their needs to employers collectively if such changes are to happen. Realistically, however, such changes are unlikely to happen in a weak economy.

Suburban areas have instituted various formal mechanisms to provide care and socialization for children during the daily absence of working parents. For example, before- and after-school child care programs have existed for decades in suburban areas. Formal provision of these resources is a critical need in rural places. School-based initiatives, such as the U.S. Department of Education's "Twenty-First Century Community Learning Centers," have begun to tackle expanding quality child care in rural places. Yet large numbers of rural children lack access to the kind of quality programs readily available to their suburban and urban counterparts. This is a significant need for rural policy-makers to address.

We have learned that successful formal supports for families in urban and suburban contexts hinge on having a well-integrated system of services to strengthen families and neighborhoods (Schorr 1997). Initiating the proposals described above in isolation is unlikely to ameliorate the daily struggles that rural families face; rather, a comprehensive system that bolsters the availability of both formal and informal supports for families is needed. Whether such efforts will be effective among rural populations remains an open question. Rural people, as previously discussed, traditionally depended on kin and neighbors for support services. Furthermore, by virtue of their size and organization, rural communities are not as well suited as urban places to deliver formal supports. The long distances between homes and amenities inherent in rural places present barriers to service provision. Low population density makes it imperative that adjacent towns collaborate to achieve economies of scale in providing services such as care for children and elders. Yet neighboring rural communities historically have had rivalries that complicate cooperative efforts. As a result, even if service and program provisions were to equal those provided in suburban and urban settings, many rural families would be less likely to seek help due to customary ideals about self-reliance. For the rural elderly, self-reliance is more deeply ingrained, making this population even harder to integrate into a system of formal support.

There never has been, nor will there ever be, a single rural family type. Families in rural America include nuclear, extended, communal, intergenerational, blended, and single-parent, as well as ethnic, generational, and class variations. Likewise, rural families do not experience a uniform way of life, and in many places they are becoming more diverse. Families in the countryside have historically had lives both tied to and independent of the land. A rural way of life has offered to some financial security and residential stability, but to others it has meant struggle and an itinerant existence. Despite moving toward a demographic profile that more closely resembles the U.S. mainstream, intuitive and empirical knowledge both suggest that rural families remain somewhat distinct from their urban and suburban counterparts. What is becoming more problematic is whether the aspects of the rural way of life that we know to be beneficial to child, family, and community development will endure the changes brought about by recent trends of suburbanization, fragmentation, and marginalization.

6

Older Rural Families

Nina Glasgow

The aim of this chapter is to examine changes over time in the structure of older rural families, the causes of these changes, and their implications for the well-being of rural elders. The United States at the beginning of the twenty-first century is an urbanized society, with approximately three-fourths of both older and younger age groups living in metropolitan counties. Older people are somewhat more concentrated in rural and small town areas, however, than are younger age groups. Only 22 percent of the total population of the United States resides in nonmetropolitan counties, but 26 percent of people aged sixty-five and older are nonmetropolitan residents (Glasgow 2000; McLaughlin and Jensen 1998). Moreover, almost 15 percent of the nonmetropolitan population are older than sixty-five, compared to less than 12 percent of the metropolitan population. This higher than average concentration of older people in rural and small town areas has implications for family and household composition and family relationships, adding to the importance of studying older rural families.

The rapid aging of the U.S. population, and of other developed countries' populations as well, poses significant challenges and opportunities for families. In 1900, the population of the United States aged sixty-five and older made up only 4 percent of the total population; today this group is approximately 13 percent of the population. By 2030, when all members of the Baby Boom generation will be aged sixty-five or older, the older population is projected to be 21.1 percent of the total population (Siegel 1993).

This work was partially supported by a grant from the National Institute on Aging (AG11711-05) and by USDA Hatch grant NY159440 from the Cornell University Agricultural Experiment Station. I thank Alan Barton for analyzing the data reported in this chapter.

Policy-makers express concerns about the health, economic well-being, access to services, and social support of older families. Questions that emerge include the following: Who will care for older people? Will older families care for themselves? Will younger family members care for older members? Will government programs provide formal care for older families? Or will a combination of sources provide the care that older families may need? Questions about the ability of informal sources and communities to meet the needs of older families are important in an aging society, as are questions of how older families can and do assist younger members of the broader family system.

With improvements over time in Social Security benefit levels, older people generally are not more impoverished than younger age groups (Preston 1984). However, nonmetropolitan older people have lower incomes and higher poverty rates than their metropolitan counterparts (Glasgow 1988; Glasgow and Brown 1998; Glasgow et al. 1993; McLaughlin and Jensen 1993). The lower socioeconomic status of nonmetropolitan older families has implications for intergenerational exchanges and family relationships. Due significantly to the receipt of Social Security benefits, however, the majority of both rural and urban older people do not rely on adult children for their economic support. Today, intergenerational family relationships focus instead on the social support and caregiving each generation offers to the other.

Older persons' informal caregivers may include a spouse, adult children, other relatives, friends, neighbors, or paid helpers, and caregiving may consist of social and/or "instrumental" support (Coward, Lee, and Dwyer 1993). Instrumental caregiving includes informal services and financial support. Through modern communication technologies, social and financial support can be provided from a distance. Informal services, however, often must be provided on a face-to-face basis. Assisting someone with grocery shopping, transportation, or meal preparation involves personal contact. Coresidence with, or geographic proximity to, kin is crucial if older family members are to receive informal services from kin caregivers. The popular image is that older rural families are embedded in extended family networks that provide strong support to their older members. Whether the image and the reality actually coincide is an important part of this discussion.

A Life Course Perspective on Older Rural Families

A life course perspective—which emphasizes the ways in which people's location in the social system, the historical period of their lives, and their

personal characteristics influence their family experiences (Stoller 1998)—
is used here to investigate older rural families. For example, older members
of farm families may value filial responsibility and thereby expect caregiving support from their adult children. Their adult children, on the other
hand, may have been influenced by a wider culture that holds less traditional values regarding who is responsible for caring for older family members. In such situations, younger family members may not meet the
expectations of older family members.

A life course perspective also emphasizes people's embeddedness in the
institution of the family throughout their lives, although the roles of individual family members change across the life course. For example, middle-
aged and older family members may assume the role of grandparent, and
older members may become great-grandparents. Families consisting of
older individuals are most likely to face marital disruption due to the death
of a spouse rather than through divorce, which is more typical among
younger families. Across the life course, family roles are patterned, but the
roles and the content of these roles change over time. Older families cannot
be viewed in isolation from the broader family system.

The context of individual and family life is an important component of
a life course perspective, and residence is a crucial aspect of this context.
Rural and urban areas differ, as do various rural areas, on such dimensions
as population density, proximity to metropolitan areas, economic base,
regional culture, and migration patterns. Older families residing in a rural
area characterized by out-migration of younger adults may have few adult
offspring living nearby to provide informal caregiving. In high retirement
in-migration areas, older newcomers are also unlikely to have adult children living nearby (Siegel 1993). In both situations, the nature of intergenerational family relationships leads to questions about who will care for
older family members with health problems or disabilities. Older long-term
rural residents may have social support networks of friends and neighbors
that provide a variety of informal services to substitute for distant adult
children. The friend and neighbor networks of older rural newcomers may
be too weak for such substitution. To date, however, researchers have paid
little attention to nonmetropolitan retirement in-migrants' family relationships and their caregiving support.

Changing Family Structure

Declining fertility, which characterized all but the Baby Boom era of the
twentieth century, and increasing longevity have resulted in what some

have described as a "beanpole" family structure (e.g., Bengtson, Rosenthal, and Burton 1996). With people having fewer children and with increased life expectancy, families have become smaller, but members across the different generations of a family know each other longer. Today, it is common for three or four generations of a family to be alive at the same time, perhaps resulting in closer family relationships.

This relatively new family structure characterizes both rural and urban families, but not to the same degree. Marriage, fertility, divorce, and other family trends have been similar and parallel over time across rural and urban areas of the United States, although family structure has remained somewhat more traditional in rural areas (Fuguitt, Brown, and Beale 1989). Different conditions, such as fewer formal services, prevail in rural areas. Thus, strong family networks are especially important for older rural residents who must rely more on informally provided services.

Older Rural Families

Conventional wisdom holds that older rural residents have stronger family support networks than older urbanites, but relatively few studies have investigated rural/urban differences. To address this issue, I examine demographic data to determine whether the availability of kin varies by place of residence, discuss general trends for the United States and trends in the marital status and living arrangements of metropolitan versus nonmetropolitan older residents, and review past studies on this issue.

Marital Status

Census data for the United States show sharp increases between 1950 and 1990 in the proportions of married men aged sixty-five and older and aged eighty-five and older (Pillemer and Glasgow 2000). By 1998, the proportion of older married men declined slightly from the 1990 peak, though still three-quarters of men aged sixty-five and above were married. Between 1950 and 1998 older married women experienced smaller increases in their numbers than men, but each time-point showed an increase over the previous in the proportion of married older women aged sixty-five and older and aged eighty-five and older (Pillemer and Glasgow 2000). However, in 1998, almost 50 percent of women aged sixty-five and older and almost 80 percent of women aged eighty-five and older were widows.

The historical increase in the proportion of older married people is explained by increased joint survivorship of married couples into old age and by fewer older people who remained single over the life course (Siegel 1993). Women's greater longevity, their tendency to marry men somewhat older than themselves, and men's higher remarriage rates after divorce or widowhood explain most of the gender differences in marital status. Older women who become widowed have little chance of remarrying.

Place of residence differences in older people's marital status have converged. According to the 1990 Current Population Survey (CPS), somewhat higher proportions of nonmetropolitan men and women in the sixty-five and older and eighty-five and older age groups were married than were their metropolitan counterparts. By 2001, however, the CPS data showed that the proportions of married people in these age groups differed only slightly by place of residence. Rural older people no longer have an "advantage" over urban older residents in the availability of a spouse as a potential caregiver. The proportion of divorced older men and women increased in both metropolitan and nonmetropolitan areas between 1990 and 2001, but divorce is uncommon among today's older population, and does not vary by place of residence.

Living Arrangements

The living arrangements of older people are closely linked to their marital status. Related to women's greater likelihood of being widowed, women are more likely than men to live alone during old age. U.S. census data show that the most striking change between 1960 and 1998 in the living arrangements of older people was the increased proportion of older women living alone (Pillemer and Glasgow 2000). This occurred, despite the fact that older women are somewhat more likely today to live with a spouse than in earlier decades, because of a proportional decline in living with nonspousal relatives, primarily adult offspring. Between 1960 and 1985, the proportion of older women living with "other relatives" declined from 33.9 to 18.4 percent, and has since continued to decline by small percentages (Pillemer and Glasgow 2000). Major changes in the living arrangements of older men were the increased number living with a spouse (especially between 1960 and 1985) and the decreased number living with nonspousal relatives. Older men, too, became somewhat more likely over time to live alone. If available, a spouse is usually an older person's primary caregiver (Hess and Soldo 1985).

Historically, intergenerational coresidence in the later stages of life was common, particularly in the case of widows and the infirm (Hareven 1996; Ruggles 1996), but coresidence between adult children and older parents is uncommon today. Today, both adult offspring and their parents are most satisfied when they live in separate households but near each other (Chevan and Korson 1972; Climo 1992; Sauer and Coward 1985). Nonetheless, older persons who live alone risk not having their caregiving needs met, and older people of today are more at risk than were previous older generations. Among older people's informal caregivers, adult children are second in importance to spouses in providing the highest levels of care over the longest periods of time (Coward et al. 1993; Hanson and Sauer 1985).

Data from the 1990 and 1998 Current Population Surveys reveal that nonmetropolitan older residents are slightly more likely to live alone or to live with a spouse than are their metropolitan counterparts. Metropolitan older males and females, on the other hand, are somewhat more likely than their nonmetropolitan counterparts to live with nonspousal relatives. These findings suggest that coresidence with adult children is lower among nonmetropolitan than metropolitan older residents. Even though they are more likely to be impoverished, older people living in smaller places appear less likely to coreside with adult children. Differences over time in the living arrangements of metropolitan and nonmetropolitan older residents are small, however, with little change in the distributions between 1990 and 1998.

The somewhat greater likelihood of coresidence between metropolitan older parents and their adult children probably relates to the higher concentration of Latinos and Asians in urban than rural areas, as these groups, and perhaps other minorities concentrated in urban areas, have a stronger tradition of intergenerational coresidence.

Nonmetropolitan older women have a higher average number of children born than metropolitan older women (Glasgow 1988), but they appear to have less access to those children. Less access implies less face-to-face informal caregiving from adult children for nonmetropolitan than metropolitan older residents, as geographic mobility affects access.

Migration and Geographic Proximity

Geographic proximity is the strongest predictor of frequency of contact with and informal caregiving for older parents from noncoresident children (Dewit, Wister, and Burch 1988; Krout 1988; Rossi and Rossi 1990; Spitze and Logan 1991). Increasing geographic mobility among either younger or older age groups is an important factor in reducing kin proximity and support of older families. Contrary to popular perceptions about geographic mobility, however, Siegel (1993) and Uhlenberg (1993) have demonstrated that geographic mobility in the United States among both younger and older age groups has declined during the last few decades.

Using data from the 1987 National Survey of Families and Households, Uhlenberg (1993) estimated that 74 percent of older people have an adult child living within a twenty-five-mile radius.

Few studies have examined rural/urban differences in geographic proximity between older parents and their noncoresident adult children. In Wisconsin, however, Bultena (1969) found that older urban parents were more likely to have an adult child living in their community than were older rural parents, and that urban older parents were more likely to see a child at least weekly than were their rural counterparts. Likewise, Krout (1984) found older urban parents in western New York were more likely than older rural parents to live near their adult children. Using a national level sample of impaired older people, Lee, Dwyer, and Coward (1990) found that large city and farm residents (a small percent of older rural residents) were more likely than older residents of small towns and suburban places to live near their adult children. The few studies that have examined place of residence differences in geographic proximity of older parents and noncoresident adult children suggest that older urban parents are more likely to live near their adult children.

Even with diminishing rates of geographic mobility over time in the United States, when migration occurs, it tends to be channeled to certain types of areas. Migration among working-age people is often motivated by a search for job opportunities, which has resulted in the historic out-migration of young adults from many rural areas, especially the farming areas of the Plains states (see Chapter 1). A large number of nonmetropolitan counties in the Plains states have especially high concentrations of older people (Glasgow 1988), showing that in a sense, older people have been left behind in this area. Greater geographic distance between older rural families and their adult children thus appears to vary by region of the country.

Migration of older people occurs primarily among "young-old" (usually defined as aged sixty to seventy-four years) individuals and primarily to amenity destinations, many of which are located in nonmetropolitan counties (Glasgow 1988). Amenity destinations are scenic areas that provide opportunities for outdoor recreation. These areas are distinguished by large numbers of older persons who have low probabilities of frequent contact with adult children (Siegel 1993). In a study of amenity migration in the nonmetropolitan Midwest, Glasgow (1980) found that only 17 percent of older in-migrants had children living in or within thirty miles of destination communities, a sharp contrast to the 74 percent of older parents Uhlenberg estimated had an adult child living within a twenty-five-mile radius. In England, Harper (1987) similarly found that older people who had in-migrated to rural communities had fewer available kin than indigenous older rural residents. After age seventy-five, net migration of older people is from nonmetropolitan to metropolitan counties, presumably to be nearer children or better health care services because of mounting frailties (Glasgow 1988; Longino 1990). But due to both chronic out-migration of younger people from some rural areas and in-migration of older people to nonmetropolitan retirement destinations, geographic proximity appears somewhat lower among rural older people and their noncoresident children than among their urban counterparts.

Intergenerational Family Relationships

Historical research has demonstrated that intergenerational coresidence in the later stages of life was common in earlier periods. The large decline in this trend, which began at the turn of the twentieth century, is a major demographic shift (Ruggles 1996). This decline is somewhat more pronounced in rural and small town areas than in metropolitan areas of the United States. Living with an adult child does not ensure a quality relationship, but the continual presence of a child in the household of an older parent provides a source of caregiving assistance that older persons living alone are not guaranteed.

The unprecedented gains in average life expectancy during the twentieth century (Siegel 1993) have also altered family relationships. Family members now spend more time than ever occupying family roles, which may positively affect bonds of affection and obligation. The implications of longer shared lifetimes between older parents and their adult offspring, and in particular the differential effects of rural versus urban older residents, lead to a set of interesting empirical questions for researchers to address.

For example, morbidity and disability differentials may have implications for the development of intergenerational relationships. Morbidity and disability rates are somewhat higher among rural than urban older people (Glasgow and Beale 1985; Krause and Stoddard 1989), although mortality rates do not differ significantly by place of residence (Wallace and Wallace 1998). Older rural residents' disadvantage in terms of morbidity and disability suggests they have greater need for caregiving support than do urban older people.

Middle-aged adults provide more care to other age groups than they receive in return, including that provided to young children and to a lesser extent to older family members (Hofferth and Iceland 1998; Sauer and

Coward 1985). Middle-aged family members have been referred to as the "sandwich" generation (e.g., Bengtson et al. 1996) because some care for children and elderly parents simultaneously.

Exchange and reciprocity characterize intergenerational family relationships. Older people both receive care from and provide support to their middle-aged children, and older people may be a source of caregiving to or receivers of care from grandchildren. It is more common for financial resources to flow from older to younger generations within families (e.g., Coward et al. 1993). With increases in single parenthood, the grandparent role has taken on added importance in recent decades, and greater numbers of grandparents have become the primary parental figures for their grandchildren, particularly in cases where parents abuse drugs or alcohol (Bengtson et al. 1996; Hill 2002).

Hofferth and Iceland's (1998) examination of rural/urban differences found that rural families were more likely than urban families to exchange care exclusively with kin. Rural families (whether by origin or current residence) were also more likely than urban families to provide financial support to older kin. Both greater economic need and rural norms of filial responsibility may explain this finding. Rural families, however, did not expend more time caring for older family members.

Regarding norms and expectations of filial responsibility, research has shown that rural-origin older individuals are more likely than urban-origin persons to expect assistance from their adult children and other kin (Lee, Coward, and Netzer 1994). Given that rural older people appear less likely than urban older people to coreside with or live in geographical proximity to adult children, rural older individuals may be particularly at risk of having their expectations for filial responsibility go unmet. Powers and Kivett (1992) found that among rural North Carolinians, older parents' expectations for assistance from their adult children were high in proportion to the amount of assistance received, but their research did not provide a rural/urban comparison.

The Future of Intergenerational Relationships

The parents of Baby Boomers—the currently elderly—have on average three children surviving until age forty for each woman ever married (Easterlin 1996). The Baby Boom generation, which will reach old age during the first quarter of the twenty-first century, is projected to have under two children per ever-married woman. This implies that Baby Boomers will have fewer adult children upon whom they can depend for caregiving during their old age, and with rural and urban trends converging, both rural and urban Baby Boomers are likely to have relatively few informal kin caregivers during old age.

Marriage trends will affect the availability of spouses and parent-child relations. Marriage rates are lower among Baby Boomers than previous generations (Siegel 1993). Among Baby Boomers who do marry, divorce rates are high in comparison to the divorce rates of their parents (Easterlin 1996): approximately half of the marriages of Baby Boomers will end in divorce. Divorce rates have increased among the currently old as well (Pillemer and Glasgow 2000), but the majority of parents of Baby Boomers are either married or widowed, and the number of those divorced is small.

The high divorce rates of Baby Boomers may impair relationships with their offspring before and during old age. Older men and women who have divorced report a decline in the strength of intergenerational ties, including lower contact with and less emotional support from their adult children (Uhlenberg and Miner 1996). Most people who divorce eventually remarry, and in that way some lost ties are replaced. But divorce and remarriage negatively affect intergenerational exchanges, and reduce the likelihood that caregiving will be provided to older biological parents (Pezzin and Schone 1999).

Baby Boomers generally share characteristics predicting that a large proportion will live alone during old age, such as their lower numbers of adult children and high marital dissolution rates. The children of Baby Boomers also have fewer siblings with whom to share caregiving during their parents' old age. Easterlin (1996) has estimated that among the first cohorts of the Baby Boom generation, one-third will live alone by age sixty-five, compared to between one-fifth and one-quarter of their parents. With family and household structures among rural and urban older residents becoming more similar over time, both groups are expected to be more likely to live alone.

Societal preparations for the Baby Boom generation as it enters old age must take changing circumstances into account: larger numbers of persons living alone without the benefits conferred by a spouse, with fewer adult offspring, and with few siblings. Given the projected increase in the older population, shortages in both formal and informal caregiving may result.

Conclusion

The evidence is mixed regarding the supply of kin to provide caregiving services among rural versus urban older families. Nonmetropolitan older residents are somewhat more likely to live with a spouse and to have a larger average number of children. But urban older people are more likely to coreside with adult children, or have them living nearby. The geographic distance between older parents and adult children is greatest for the older rural residents of the Plains states and for the "young-old" amenity-destination in-migrants in nonmetropolitan as well as metropolitan communities. But trends in marital status and living arrangements among metropolitan and nonmetropolitan older people have largely converged.

The anticipated future problems of Baby Boomers are likely to be shared by both rural and urban older families, with neither group having a clear advantage over the other. Older families and individuals in the twenty-first century are likely to need more formal care options. Rural older families have less access to and less availability of formal care options, and older rural Baby Boomers will be disadvantaged unless policy-makers address issues related to formal service deficits in rural communities.

An important topic for future research is how the informal caregiving that older Baby Boomers receive varies among the never married, married, divorced, widowed, and remarried according to place of residence. Those who are not married and/or do not have adult children are especially likely to need to plan for formal care options. To the extent that older rural residents continue to be economically disadvantaged compared to their urban counterparts, this group will have greater difficulty purchasing formal care, provided these options are available in rural communities.

A life course perspective, which encourages examination of the impacts of historical changes for current situations, shows that the structures of older rural and urban families are becoming more similar. An aging society means not only fewer middle-aged adults to care for the older generation but also fewer workers to support Social Security and other government programs that benefit older people. It will be important to understand how both informal and formal caregiving networks can be constructed to bolster each other when challenged by an increasingly aged society.

7

Rural Children and Youth at Risk

Daniel T. Lichter, Vincent J. Roscigno, and Dennis J. Condron

Children are a public good and a key to America's future—they will become tomorrow's political and civic leaders, entrepreneurs and workers, and spouses, parents, and caretakers. America's future, however, is threatened by increasing numbers of children "at risk" because of family disruption, school dropout, drug abuse, delinquency, and teen pregnancy (Lichter 1997; Teachman, Tedrow, and Crowder 2000; Bryson 1997). Perhaps nostalgically, we cling to the belief that these problems have largely bypassed rural areas, affecting mostly disadvantaged children and minority youth living in inner-city neighborhoods. We assume that strong families, informal community social networks, small and participatory local schools, and faith-based institutions and traditions will steer a positive developmental trajectory for rural children and youth. Geographic isolation also presumably buffers negative urban influences.

Unfortunately, these persistent stereotypes have diverted scholarly attention away from rural children and their healthy psychosocial development. Indeed, America's rural children are often overlooked. They are literally and figuratively out of public view, thinly dispersed throughout the countryside or hidden away in isolated and economically depressed rural areas in Appalachia and the Mississippi Delta and on Indian reservations (Save the Children 2002). A generation ago, the lives of more Americans were inextricably bound to rural communities. Many of our parents and grandparents grew up on farms or lived in small towns. The replacement of successive generations—death followed by the birth of a new generation—means that with each passing year more adults experience rural America only obliquely, if at all. Most of us now come to know rural America only through stereotypical media portrayals (Logan 1996), through exposure to rural vacation spots (i.e., ski or outdoor resorts), or by traversing the rural countryside from city to city by automobile. All the while, rapid urbanization has meant that fewer Americans have reason to travel through the nation's mostly forgotten rural regions or to make them their final destinations. The implications are clear: the problems of disadvantaged rural youth are often ignored, unrecognized, or poorly understood.

Our goals here are straightforward: to reexamine persistent rural problems that shape children's healthy development and that call for serious research and policy attention. We aim to make visible the changing social and economic circumstances of America's rural children and youth. We also identify emerging demographic trends that will surely shape the life course of today's rural children and their successful transition into productive adult roles.

Rural Children in an Urban Society

Rural America is at a crossroads. The boom economy of the late 1990s, along with welfare reform, brought new job growth and unprecedented declines in welfare caseloads throughout America (Lichter and Crowley 2002). More recently, increasing unemployment rates, slowing job growth, and sliding stock prices have eroded public confidence in America's economic future, raising concerns about the implications for America's families and children. How rural communities, families, and especially children have fared in this changing social and economic environment is uncertain (Weber, Duncan, and Whitner 2002).

Poverty and Welfare Dependence

Innumerable studies show that the incidence, duration, and chronic nature of poverty adversely affect children's positive cognitive and emotional development (e.g., Duncan and Brooks-Gunn 1997; McLeod and Shanahan 1996). Rural children are especially vulnerable, as poverty rates for them have been historically higher than for their metropolitan counterparts (Rogers 2001; Swanson and Dacquel 1996). Indeed, in 2000 the poverty rate was 20.8 percent for nonmetropolitan children, compared to 16.9 percent in metropolitan areas (see Fig. 7.1).

A hopeful sign is that poverty rates among rural children have declined unexpectedly since the mid-1990s, paralleling the declines recorded nationwide. Rural poverty rates among single-parent, female-headed families also have declined, and average income of these families with children

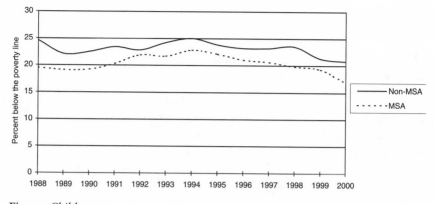

Fig 7.1 Child poverty rates, 1988–2000

improved throughout the late 1990s (Lichter and Jensen 2002). More rural single mothers today are earning a living rather than relying on public assistance income. There is little evidence that the 1996 welfare reform bill imposed a special hardship on impoverished rural families (Lichter and Jayakody 2002; Weber et al. 2002). Indeed, the scenario for rural minorities is generally positive. For example, poverty rates for rural African American children, although still unacceptably high, declined very rapidly, from 57 percent to 36.4 percent, between 1988 and 2000 (U.S. Bureau of the Census 2002).

Child poverty in rural America manifests itself differently than it does in metropolitan areas (Lichter and Eggebeen 1992; Jensen and Eggebeen 1994). Rural hardship historically has been more likely than metropolitan poverty to involve children of married couples rather than children of single-parent families. Rural poverty is more likely to involve families with adult workers (i.e., a working "head") and families that experience underemployment or "working poverty" (Findeis, Jensen, and Wang 2000). The rural poor are less likely to receive cash public assistance or welfare, but more likely to receive child support income from noncustodial fathers (Bartfeld and Meyer 2001). Rural poverty is less likely to be linked to residential or neighborhood segregation by race, but more likely to be associated with physical isolation in remote and culturally distinct rural regions (i.e., Appalachia or the Central Valley of California). It is also more likely to be chronic and of longer duration.

For the sake of America's rural children and youth, we can and should endeavor to reduce poverty, or at least eliminate its most pernicious effects. Unfortunately, we know surprisingly little about the short- and long-term developmental consequences of poverty for rural children, especially for their emotional and cognitive development (see Duncan and Brooks-Gunn

1997; Guo 1998). We need to revisit the commonplace assumption that small-town living mitigates the negative effects of childhood poverty.

Children and the Changing Rural Family

The growing consensus is that children fare best, on balance, when they grow up with two biological parents who are married (Corcoran 1995; Guo and Harris 2000). Policy concerns about family decline are buttressed by the statistical evidence. Between 1970 and 2000, for example, the share of America's children living with two parents declined from 85 percent to 69 percent, and a sizeable share of two-parent families includes a stepparent. The children of divorce often have little contact with their nonresidential biological parents. At the same time, the percentage of families with children headed by single parents grew substantially over the same period, from 11 percent to 27 percent. Growing shares of out-of-wedlock births, high divorce rates, declines in marital fertility, and the continuing "retreat from marriage" (i.e., nonmarriage or delayed marriage) have fundamentally altered the life circumstances of America's children (Teachman et al. 2000).

Just how recent trends associated with marriage have affected rural children is unclear (Cready, Fossett, and Kiecolt 1997; McLaughlin, Gardner, and Lichter 1999). Indeed, the federal government's National Center for Health Statistics, which collects and reports on the nation's marriage and divorce patterns, does not routinely report vital statistics for rural or nonmetropolitan areas. The March demographic supplement of the Current Population Survey, however, does provide important data on this topic, revealing that the share of rural children residing with both parents was 72.4 percent in 2000, only slightly higher than the national average. Clearly, the common assumption that rural children are less susceptible to recent family trends is at odds with the statistical reality (see Chapter 5 in this volume).

Over the past five years, growth in single-parent, female-headed families has slowed—perhaps in response to a strong economy, and perhaps because welfare reform has led to new family adaptations, including marriage and lower nonmarital fertility among at-risk groups (Bramlett and Mosher 2001; Dupree and Primus 2001). The challenge today is to provide a better understanding of family change in rural areas—how it is different from and how it is similar to the rest of the country. The decline in two-parent families and family fragmentation affects the economic and social well-being of children, and rural children are no exception (Swanson and

Dacquel 1996; Lichter and Eggebeen 1992). Increasing shares of children are residing with other relatives—especially grandparents—rather than living with economically independent single mothers. Nationally, unmarried cohabitation now precedes the majority of marriages, increasingly providing a context for childbearing and childrearing (Bumpass and Lu 2000; Graefe and Lichter 1999). But we do not yet understand whether such trends have diffused to the countryside, or whether small-town life engenders the stigmatization of unconventional living arrangements.

Strong families are an important aspect of rural human resource development. We must therefore balance discussions of rural economic development with attention to family structure and functioning. Do rural parents provide a nurturing family environment for children? Or are rural children, on balance, exposed in greater proportions to parents who suffer from mental health problems such as depression, who are neglectful, or who are physically or emotionally abusive? We currently lack the data necessary to better understand the risk and protective factors now influencing the development of America's rural children (DeHaan and Deal 2001).

Rural Deficits in Schooling and Educational Achievement

Rural children's developmental trajectories are also shaped by the elementary and secondary schools they attend. Indeed, a good education is essential for making a successful transition to productive adult roles and to good citizenship. For the most part, however, policy dialogues have centered on urban issues such as school segregation, busing, and funding disparities between inner cities and affluent suburban enclaves. Concerns for rural school-aged children often go unheeded (McGrath et al. 2001; Hobbs 1991). This is troubling. Rural educational achievement lags behind national norms, and dropout rates are pronounced (Roscigno and Crowley 2001; U.S. Department of Education 1997). Data from the National Education Longitudinal Survey show large rural/urban achievement gaps for a nationally representative sample of U.S. eighth graders (see Fig. 7.2).

Low income and family instability undoubtedly play a part in rural children's cognitive development, achievement aspirations, and academic attainment (Lichter, Cornwell, and Eggebeen 1993; Israel, Beaulieu, and Hartless 2001; Roscigno and Ainsworth-Darnell 1999). And investments in schooling reflect the low economic returns to education in depressed rural labor markets—a high school or college education is less likely to be rewarded with a decent job in America's small towns and rural areas. To make matters worse, rural schools suffer disproportionately from inadequate funding, dilapidated

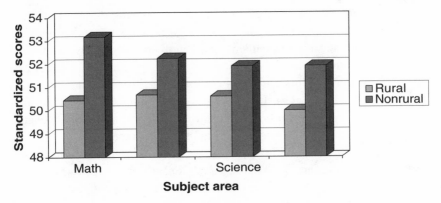

Fig. 7.2 Differences in rural/nonrural educational achievement

buildings, and less experienced and less qualified teachers. Inadequate air ventilation, poor noise control, and the lack of physical security in rural schools rival conditions in large inner city schools and can undermine children's capacity to learn (U.S. Department of Education 1999).

Efforts to improve rural schools are often thwarted by funding formulas that depend heavily on local property taxes. The difficulty in attracting and keeping qualified teachers in rural areas is exacerbated by low salaries and obsolete facilities, lab equipment, and textbooks (U.S. Department of Education 1996). For some rural schools, the curriculum has shifted toward specialized, vocational training and away from college preparatory coursework that can provide broad-based skills for lifelong learning. Consequently, rural adolescents are often poorly prepared for a successful postsecondary education. Many more are simply steered into marginal jobs (assuming they are not unemployed after high school) that offer low wages, few fringe benefits, and little job security (Ainsworth-Darnell and Roscigno 2001). For many rural children and youth, poorly funded schools reinforce low educational aspirations and achievement rather than providing a route to upward mobility.

Delinquency and Drug Use Among Rural Youth

Delinquency and drug use among America's teenagers are typically viewed as inner-city problems. Recent events, including school shootings in small rural towns, have seriously challenged this common assumption (Edwards 1992; Puzzanchera 2000; Osgood and Chambers 2000). Rural youth are less likely to use hard drugs like cocaine, heroine, and even marijuana. Yet they are much more likely than their urban and suburban counterparts to use and abuse alcohol, and they do so at very young ages (U.S. Department of Education 1996). Roughly one-third of rural youth have used alcohol by the age of twelve (Felton et al. 1996). By the twelfth grade, this figure jumps to 78 percent (U.S. Department of Education 1992). Four-fifths of rural school teachers report that alcohol use by their students is a serious problem at school, compared to 61 percent in inner-city areas of the United States (Metropolitan Life 1996).

Alcohol abuse affects academic achievement and healthy development for adolescents. Moreover, alcohol is a "pipeline" drug that is often linked to experimentation with "hard drugs" (Donnermeyer 1993), and is associated with delinquency, violence, and victimization (Komro et al. 1999). Over 30 percent of rural adolescents report being a victim of theft at school, 11 percent have engaged in fights, and 14 percent have been threatened with physical assault (U.S. Department of Education 1992). Thirty percent of rural school teachers report that violence in and around their schools is a major problem, while one-third report that students carrying handguns, knives, and weapons is a major concern (Metropolitan Life 1996). Clearly, rural adolescents are not immune to broader social problems linked to drug use, victimization, and violence.

Early intervention programs can be effective, but many rural schools lack sufficient staff and financial resources to implement effective school-based programs (Fahs et al. 1999). To complicate matters, gang activity has spilled over into many rural communities. As recently as 1989, only 8 percent of rural adolescents reported gangs as a problem at their schools. Only six years later, in 1995, this figure more than doubled to approximately 20 percent (Evans et al. 1999; U.S. Department of Justice 1996). To some observers, rural poverty, family instability, and ineffective schools breed increased gang activity, violence, drug use, and delinquency. Perhaps a more important lesson is that rural children and youth are no longer shielded from what have been thought of as urban problems. Furthermore, the institutional capacity of many rural communities and schools to fully address the urban cultural assault on rural youth remains weak.

Adolescent Sexuality, Pregnancy, and Childbearing

Premature or unplanned childbearing fundamentally alters the life course trajectories of America's adolescents (Wu and Wolfe 2001). It cuts education short, reduces the likelihood of forming marriages that last, and is associated with higher rates of adult poverty and welfare receipt. The children of unwed mothers, especially teenage unwed mothers, also fare poorly in comparison with children born to older married parents. Clearly, the personal costs to adolescent girls and their children—and to society—are immense.

Today, the share of all U.S. births to unmarried women is roughly 33 percent, and nonmarital birth rates are remarkably similar in rural and urban areas (Frenzen 1997; Skatrud, Bennett, and Loda 1998; Ventura et al. 2001). Significantly, though, teenagers in rural areas account for a larger proportion of all nonmarital births than in urban areas (36.2 percent versus 29.2 percent). The late 1990s brought substantial changes in America's teenage sexual behavior and childbearing practices, including delaying the age of first sexual intercourse and adopting safer sexual and contraceptive practices. Since the mid-1990s, teenage pregnancy rates and abortion rates have dropped significantly. Unwed childbearing among teenagers declined 20 percent among fifteen- to seventeen-year-olds and 10 percent among eighteen- and nineteen-year-olds between 1994 and 1999 (Ventura et al. 2001).

Whether these trends have been observed among rural adolescents is unclear. What we do know, however, is that the intergenerational transmission of rural poverty is linked to early and unintended adolescent childbearing (Duncan 1999). Still, we usually view this as an urban problem. Policy discussions about effective community- and school-based sex education and abstinence programs are aimed at discouraging early sexual activity and pregnancy among urban teens. The welfare reform bill, in fact, targeted such programs for urban areas while ignoring issues of sexual and reproductive health relevant to rural adolescents.

Narrowly targeting urban areas is shortsighted. Economic constraints, poor transportation, social stigma, and privacy concerns affect the physical and legal access of rural youth to reproductive health clinics (as well as contraception and pregnancy planning). To illustrate this point, in the largely urban state of New Jersey, 51 percent of nonmarital teen pregnancies are terminated by abortion (Allan Guttmacher Institute 1999), while only 37 percent end in a live birth. In contrast, in the rural state of Mississippi only 15 percent of pregnancies are aborted and 70 percent result in a live birth. Not surprisingly, 45 percent of all births in Mississippi are to unmarried women, compared to only 28 percent in New Jersey. Clearly, sexual and reproductive health are important issues for isolated and impoverished rural communities that fail to receive appropriate federal and state programmatic responses.

Early and unwanted pregnancy is, in the end, a rural human resource development problem that cannot be ignored. Teenage pregnancy and childbearing undermine the capacity of rural adolescents to achieve their educational goals and occupational aspirations. The children of adolescent mothers are at risk for developmental delays and economic deprivation. At the very least, teen childbearing reinforces the intergenerational cycle of poverty in rural areas.

Emerging Youth Issues

The issues facing America's rural children and youth are ever-changing. Our interest in the persistent rural youth problems discussed above should not deflect attention from other evolving policy issues, such as rural racial and ethnic diversity, increasing spatial inequality, and positive youth development.

Racial and Ethnic Diversity in Rural America

America's most impoverished rural areas are populated disproportionately by minorities (Swanson 1996; Mather 2002). The historical legacy of slavery (i.e., in the South's rural "Black Belt") and the effects of government policies on Indian affairs (i.e., on reservations) are deeply imprinted on the political economy of rural America (see Chapters 2, 3, and 4 in this volume). One often unnoticed trend is that many rural areas are now experiencing new in-migration of racial and ethnic minorities, especially Latinos (Voss 2001). Mexican-born Latinos have moved in large numbers into rural communities of the Midwest and South, often to towns with meat-packing or food-processing plants, and have spread throughout the rural Southwest, the central valley of California, and the Pacific Northwest.

Policy concerns about Latino children have centered for the most part on migrant laborers and their families. But indigenous Latino families and children face different but equally important issues—those related to community economic development, schooling (i.e., bilingual and culturally sensitive education), and race relations are critical but largely unstudied. Between 1989 and 1997, only twelve of the one hundred poorest nonmetropolitan counties experienced increases in child poverty. Most were counties with large percentages of Latinos (U.S. Bureau of the Census 2001d).

As in urban neighborhoods, small rural towns will be reshaped in uncertain ways by these population shifts. What will be the response of majority white children and the community as a whole? Will the new and culturally distinct in-migrants be accepted or will they face indifference or even hostility by their peers? What will be the institutional and community responses to diversity? Will first- and second-generation rural immigrant children assimilate? How will social service programs and schools accommodate the needs of the new immigrant children? These are increasingly salient questions for the well-being of minority children and youth as they spread widely throughout rural America.

Rural Economic Balkanization

Not all rural children have shared in America's economic largess, or have been helped rather than hurt by rural economic restructuring and welfare reform (see Chapters 11 and 28 in this volume). Between 1989 and 1997, for example, over 40 percent of nonmetropolitan counties experienced increases in child poverty (U.S. Bureau of the Census 2001d). Some counties had poverty rates over 50 percent in 1999, such as Buffalo and Shannon Counties in South Dakota and Starr County in Texas (Mather 2002). The challenge today is clear: identifying rural children, especially those in geographic "pockets of poverty," who have fallen by the wayside. More than ever before, statistical averages can hide substantial inter- and intra-county inequality in rural children's economic well-being and life circumstances (Friedman and Lichter 1998; Lobao 1996). The 1990s and beyond have ushered in growing income and wealth inequality in America—inequality that both reflects and reinforces growing spatial differences in economic opportunity and well-being for rural children and youth.

Indeed, concepts like "rural" and "urban" may be rendered increasingly obsolete. Affluent rural areas (i.e., exurban areas of major cities or high-amenity recreational and retirement areas) may hide the continuing economic stagnation found in other more isolated rural counties and regions. We know little about how spatial inequality has translated into inequality in the developmental trajectories of rural children. Has economic and geographic inequality exacerbated spatial differences in academic test scores, rates of teen pregnancy and childbearing, and substance abuse? Clearly, we must be ever vigilant to the concerns of rural children left behind by an increasingly fractured rural (and global) economy.

Positive Youth Development

Young adults of the late 1990s and early 2000s represent the first full generation in which large percentages grew up with single parents (as the result of out-of-wedlock childbearing), lived in poverty, experienced first-hand the divorce and remarriage of their parents, or some combination of these circumstances. Understandably, scholars have carefully documented the deleterious effects of family instability and poverty on children's developmental trajectories—diminished cognitive development, early sexual activity, teen pregnancy, delinquency, and substance abuse. More recently, however, interest has shifted to prosocial behaviors—investigating whether a disadvantaged childhood leads inexorably to a socially disengaged and politically disaffected citizenry (Moore and Glei 1995; Lichter, Shanahan, and Gardner 2002). Simply put, risk factors during childhood may be better revealed in the absence of prosocial or civic behaviors than in antisocial or pathological behaviors.

This reorientation toward positive child outcomes is reflected less in scholarly research than in ongoing policy and practices already "on the ground." School-based programs that emphasize civic learning, moral education, and volunteerism are clear cases in point. But good citizenry has always been emphasized in rural areas through youth development programs. Scouts, Future Farmers of America, 4-H Clubs, and other community- and school-based programs reflect the traditional values of good citizenry and communalism in rural America. The challenge today is to learn more about whether or not rural economic and social dislocations have undermined the enduring strengths of rural communities: good citizenship and strong community ties (see Chapter 21 in this volume).

Robert Putnam's *Bowling Alone* (2000) is an indictment of eroding social capital in America—the erosion of interpersonal networks of support and trust. Whether these concerns apply to rural areas is unknown but worthy of additional attention, in part because any solution to rural problems, including the problems of rural youth, will require an active and committed citizenry concerned about the common good. Are rural youth today engaging in local civic and communal life and preparing for future leadership roles? Will they be part of the solution or part of the problem?

Conclusion

Urbanization and urbanism continue to grow in America. We easily forget that rural children have not shared fully in America's economic abundance, but we do so at our peril. Historically, the problems of rural America have become problems for all Americans. The urban migration of impoverished Appalachian families and displaced rural black sharecroppers from the South during the mid-1900s are obvious historical cases in point. Today, a large share of rural "at risk" children may be ill-prepared for good jobs in a rapidly changing urban and bicoastal economy. Though many stay in depressed rural communities, others move on to cities, adding to the problems of urban joblessness, poverty, family disruption, and crime, while taxing the institutional capacity of urban centers to adequately respond. Both scenarios pose challenges for current and future rural youth.

If history is our guide, the problems of rural youth ultimately affect us all. We need to redouble efforts to identify, better understand, and address the critical developmental issues facing rural youth that, as we now know, often parallel those of disadvantaged inner-city minority youth. Unless we do, rural America's next generation of adults may be poorly prepared for success in the workplace, for a healthy family life, and for active community engagement, participation, and civic leadership. Unfortunately, rural areas arguably are less likely today than in the past to be safe harbors for America's children and youth.

8

Rural Women

New Roles for the New Century?

Ann R. Tickamyer and Debra A. Henderson

At the beginning of a new century and millennium, one of the most note-worthy developments in both rural society and its scholarship is the growing prominence of gender issues. A burgeoning literature on women and gender applies feminist theories and perspectives to rural sociology and rural life. This represents the culmination of developments spanning at least three decades. The products of this interest are a legacy of women's entry into and growing representation in academic and policy circles, as well as numerous changes in the social, economic, and cultural life of rural America.

An expanding body of research examines rural women and men as gendered actors. Areas of study range from scrutiny of women (and less frequently men) in specific settings to overviews and analyses of feminist theories, methods, policy applications, and agenda-setting pieces (Feldman and Welsh 1995; Naples and Sachs 2000; Tickamyer 1996; Whatmore et al. 1994). The results of these studies, however, show less change in women's actual work and activity than in how scholars have come to view these women. Women's roles in the twenty-first century and the dilemmas they face look very similar to those confronting women throughout the previous century. What has changed is the scholarly interest in these issues: the recognition of the diversity that exists spatially and culturally, in the intersections with other social locations, and in the choices and constraints available to women in their allocation to various roles. In this chapter, we examine the roles of rural women with specific emphasis on the related issues of continuity and change, similarity and diversity that mark women's experience in twenty-first-century rural America.

The More Things Change...: Old Roles in New Guises

Women in rural America today juggle the same roles in household and workplace, family and community, domestic and public domains that they have managed throughout the second half of the twentieth century and that occupy women in other locations. Rural women have always worked hard—as agricultural workers engaged in food and fiber production; as waged labor in ever-growing numbers in manufacturing, retail, and service industries; and in the informal sector in industrial home work, cottage industry, and informal exchanges of goods, services, and labor. They have provided paid and unpaid caretaking for family, friends, and neighbors, and have staffed community and volunteer agencies. Both historical and contemporary accounts and case studies document the wide array of responsibilities and roles women assume in rural families, communities, and enterprises (Fink 1986; Fitchen 1991; Gringeri 1994; Lobao and Meyer 2001; Nelson and Smith 1999; Salamon 1992).

Rural women have made small gains in obtaining entry into and recognition in nontraditional positions that had eluded them previously because of particularly strong gender norms—for example, in mining (Tallichet 2000), as farm operators (Lobao and Meyer 2001), as union organizers (Maggard 1998), or as agricultural scientists (Buttel and Goldberger 2002). However, many of these changes involved very small numbers, were short-lived, or were more symbolic than far-reaching. They demonstrate the breakdown of old taboos and legal barriers or the public acknowledgment of long established but little recognized social facts, rather than heralding systematic change in the majority of women's lives.

More substantial changes have mirrored larger economic, demographic, and social trends. The restructuring of the rural economy has both spurred and responded to the growth of rural women's entry into the paid labor force, even if most of this growth has been in jobs traditionally allocated to women. The growing numbers of women in single and single-parent households reflect family and household restructuring throughout society (see Chapter 5 in this volume). Rural women, like women everywhere, continue to face the quandary of a double or triple day as they engage in both paid and unpaid labor, including income-earning activities in formal and informal sectors, household and family maintenance and reproduction, and community-sustaining activities.

What has changed most for rural women are the demands on their time and their understanding of their choices as they confront old issues. Social and economic transformations have pressured women to diversify their efforts further. Thus few women expect to pursue only traditional roles in the household, even among communities and groups most firmly adherent to patriarchal norms and rigid gender roles. For example, in farm families, in spite of women's substantial labor contributions to both household and enterprise, a traditional gender division of labor has been most resistant to change (Whatmore 1991). However, the survival of both the family and the farm has increasingly depended on women's waged labor. During the farm crisis of the 1980s, women were more likely to move into off-farm work than men, and the continuing pressure of agricultural transformation has consolidated this strategy as typical for the majority of family farms (Lobao and Meyer 2001). Similarly, women in coal field communities that historically preserved a male monopoly over family wage jobs in coal production increasingly have moved into the labor market, as capital-intensive production methods replace men's jobs. This occurs despite the lack of stable, good-paying jobs for women workers in these labor markets. Deepening labor attachment is equally evident among rural households and communities regardless of the specific social forms and cultural practices or the economic opportunities available. The irony is that rural women's labor has increased, including their waged labor, at the same time that their communities have suffered from economic contraction, deindustrialization, or restructuring, making their labor both more necessary and less rewarding (see Chapter 11 in this volume). Similarly, the apparent greater array of choices has often meant, in reality, more constraint, as women are forced to find ways to support their households.

The result is that currently more women work in the paid labor market, regardless of where they live in rural America, whether they are located in distressed economies or in new growth areas of an expanding metropolitan fringe. These increases have occurred both because of and in spite of the restructuring of rural labor markets and the decline of traditional rural industries in agriculture, natural resource extraction, and manufacturing that has diminished income and economic opportunities for rural communities. As men's jobs disappear and the number of female-headed households increases in rural areas, women are taking on the role of primary earners in addition to their traditional role as family caregivers (McLaughlin et al. 1999).

Rural women and their families also continue to have disproportionately high rates of poverty (Tickamyer et al. 1993). However, their access to and use of public assistance, always lagging behind urban areas, decreases further as welfare reform legislation restructures the safety net and human service provision and delivery, pushing yet more women into the labor force despite limited opportunities for jobs that provide a living wage, benefits, and quality child care (Tickamyer et al. 2000). The majority of rural women, regardless of race, class, or spatial location, face the obstacles of limited opportunities, unstable labor markets, inaccessible or nonexistent public services, and crumbling infrastructure that characterize many remote rural areas.

Rural communities are often perceived as wholesome, family-friendly environments that promote overall well-being (Seebach 1992). However, transitions in labor market participation coupled with inadequate structural support have resulted in rural areas that are deficient in basic services and opportunities, lacking jobs, child care, transportation, health care, educational facilities, and places to shop. These inadequacies have profound impacts on the lives of rural women who struggle to make ends meet and care for their families without the necessary economic and social resources. Yet, based on the belief that rural communities offer safety, security, and quality of life for their families, many women make conscious decisions to continue living in rural areas even when other options may be available (Stack 1996; Tickamyer et al. 2000).

Similarity and Diversity in Rural Communities

Case Studies of Responses to Economic Restructuring

Common themes emerge from broader-based case studies of regionally distinct rural poverty, communities, and livelihoods. Evaluation of women's roles in these studies suggests that even though their geographic location may differ, rural women share similar life experiences. Many rural women face the dilemma of balancing a response to economic transition and hardship with deep-seated local affiliations and loyalties. Comparison of women's experiences in three distinct rural regions that have experienced large-scale economic restructuring—Appalachia, the Pacific Northwest, and the agrarian Midwest—illustrate these similarities.

APPALACHIA

Massive layoffs and job loss in the coal mines of rural Appalachia have forced many traditional women homemakers to assume the role of sole breadwinner (Oberhauser and Turnage 1999). As they try to deal effectively with financial crisis by entering the labor market, these women also struggle with the difficulty of providing for their families with limited resources. Lack of child care constrains many women in isolated rural areas where both organized child care facilities and independent providers are sparse.

As a result of restricted opportunities in the formal labor market and the lack of child care, rural women in Appalachia often resort to home-based occupations that allow them to provide financially for their families while still carrying out household responsibilities (Oberhauser and Turnage 1999). Even when opportunities exist in larger urban areas, many women indicate that extended family and environmental security make them unwilling to leave their homes in rural Appalachia (Tickamyer et al. 2000).

PACIFIC NORTHWEST

Women in the rural Pacific Northwest experience circumstances similar to those of women in rural Appalachia. The area has become known as the "new Appalachia," the result of economic and structural instability arising from the rapid deterioration of the logging industry due to the decline in timber supply and battles over environmental issues (Carroll 1995). Women in rural logging communities also find themselves dealing with the pressure of trying to maintain the traditional role of homemaker and child care provider along with the added role of employee in the paid labor market. Negotiating these roles effectively is complicated by the economic strain created by the loss of jobs in the community and the stress of trying to maintain the emotional stability of the family unit.

While many women in rural Appalachia have attempted to deal with limited job and child care opportunities by creating home-based businesses, the majority of the women living in rural logging communities attempt to successfully integrate outside employment into their daily home routine. Similar to women in Appalachian coal towns, women in logging communities are fearful that in order to make ends meet they may be forced to relocate to urban areas. They too are bound by family and community ties and a commitment to the land that make relocation an undesirable option (Carroll 1995).

THE AGRARIAN MIDWEST

The farm crisis of the 1980s affected rural Midwestern farm communities, creating an economic trauma analogous to the decline of extractive industries. Increasing debt or loss of land and livelihood destabilized families and communities. Economic instability and a declining standard of living resulted in what some have labeled the "rural ghetto" (Lasley 1994). Families' attempts to keep their farms placed a formidable burden on rural women who added the responsibility for reducing family consumption and increasing family income with off-farm employment to their previous full-time tasks of farm hand and homemaker (Elder et al. 1992).

The displacement that resulted from actual loss of farms forced farm women to enter the formal labor market in low-wage, low-skill occupations. Although some women reported positive outcomes from opportunities to develop new job skills and experience personal growth, few saw this as a substitute for the land and the lifestyle they shared with their families on the farm. Women caught in the farm crisis exhibited extremely high and long-lasting levels of emotional distress as they renegotiated their changing roles and responsibilities (Elder et al. 1994).

Race and Ethnic Diversity

Common responses to spatial, structural, and economic similarities must be tempered by recognition of the diversity that exists among rural women and the unique circumstances that different groups face. Especially significant are the racial boundaries found in rural communities. The loss of economic and social support disproportionately affects women of color. Like most rural women, minority women also must maintain families on limited resources, yet they must do so in the context of a distinct cultural history and a frequently inhospitable climate due to their race.

AFRICAN AMERICAN WOMEN

Once again case studies provide insight, in this case to the intersections of race and class, particularly for African American women in the rural South. For example, studies of the Carolinas (Stack 1996) and the Mississippi Delta (Dill and Williams 1992; Duncan 1999) suggest that an obvious class and race hierarchy has a strong impact on minority women who raise families in the midst of extreme rural poverty. While jobs are scarce in these areas, racially motivated hiring practices further limit the opportunities for African Americans to the worst jobs in the low-wage secondary labor market.

In contrast to other rural women whose entry into the labor market often is a more recent response to economic crisis, African American women historically have been considered both the economic and emotional foundation of the family, with a long history of simultaneously managing the responsibilities of economic provider, homemaker, and caretaker of children. Although they may lack adequate resources, they often have strong support systems that allow them to survive via an underground economy, and that also may discourage efforts to migrate to seek better opportunities (Dill and Williams 1992). Loyalty to the extended family and the land itself often keeps African American women in rural communities, or in some cases encourages return to their rural roots, even though better employment opportunities may be available in urban areas.

LATINO WOMEN

Latino groups represent large and growing segments of rural residents. Although by no means the majority of the Latino population, migrant workers constitute another overlooked yet vital group of rural minority women. The manual labor of these women and their families is integral to the success of the agricultural industry. As transients, they do not have the ideological connection to rural communities that other women may possess. Yet migrant Latino women are tied to rural lands for their own survival and they, of all rural women, experience some of the most deleterious conditions in which to raise a family (Valle 1994).

Like African American women, migrant Latino women have always combined productive and reproductive labor. Seasonal labor for migrant workers is scarce and unstable. Latino women spend long hours in the fields working alongside men where they are treated as equals; however, their position in the home is extremely traditional, with sole responsibility for household labor and care-taking (Valle 1994). They provide sustenance for their families as well as economic and emotional support. Yet, due to the transient nature of their lives and racially motivated inequality, they often must carry out these roles in the context of extreme poverty resulting in a limited food supply, a lack of housing and transportation, no medical care, and no consistent social support system.

Similar to other women in rural settings, African American women and migrant Latino women experience high levels of emotional distress as they try to successfully negotiate the varied roles for which they are responsible. However, unlike other rural women who have experienced a significant structural and/or economic crisis in their communities, much of the distress for these minority women is the result of the contextual complexities of their lives as women of color and the effects of specific stressors on their quality of life (McLaughlin and Sachs 1988; Stack 1996). There is little evidence that this will change in the foreseeable future.

New Activism

One realm where women's efforts have gained new prominence is in the area of political mobilization and activism, perhaps a reflection of the ties that bind women to rural communities. In political realms, rural women mirror larger national and global trends. Although women remain greatly underrepresented in formal political office, they have gained ground at the local level, and it is projected that these gains will increasingly push women into higher office. Whether rural women lead or lag in this slow evolution remains to be seen. What impact increasing participation will have on specific political issues and public policies also is speculative. While women are clearly not monolithic in their political affiliations, there is reason to think that gender-gap politics also hold in rural America. Suggestive evidence comes from research on women's political attitudes during the 1980s farm crisis, where they expressed greater support than men for state intervention to support family farms and farm families (Meyer and Lobao 1994).

The primary opportunities for and targets of women's activism often are in grassroots responses to the realities of their communities and livelihoods. Women's mobilization in sustainable agriculture, conservation, and environmental movements evoke attention and debate among rural sociologists, social movement analysts, and feminist theorists, who argue about the strength and sources of women's interest and participation (Sachs 1994). Women have been active in these new social movements, composing a strong cadre of grassroots organizers and workers. Their activism stems from situated knowledge of environmental, health, and livelihood hazards generated by their own experience (Sachs 1996). Similarly, women have mobilized around livelihood issues—either their own, through efforts to organize their work places, or as support for jobs and work places of male relatives and family enterprises (Anderson and Schulman 1999; Maggard 1999). Finally, their contributions have always been central to local issue-based activism in small towns and rural communities. The particular issues and forms of mobilization vary by place, time, and group, and new forms emerge under new social pressures. For example, the return migration of African American women to small Southern towns from northern cities has been a source of new activism on the part of these women and for their communities (Mele 2000; Stack 1996).

Research and Policy Needs

In spite of the growing literature on women and the recognition of diversity in these studies, research remains restricted to specific groups, locales, and topics. Case studies provide insight into the experiences of rural women, but are difficult to generalize beyond the level of anecdote. Currently, there is no systematic way to determine the similarities and differences between these women, or how specific circumstances and differential effects by location, race, and class affect their lives. In order to broaden our understanding of gender issues and rural women, there is a pressing need for systematic evaluation of the intersections of race, class, economic sector, and location. This requires more research using national samples of rural women; more attention to gender, spatial inequality, and diversity; and more case-comparative approaches to locality-based research. It is especially important to provide a basis for comparative work by using both broadly representative national samples and a variety of specific case studies to expand knowledge of gender issues beyond the traditional arenas of farm families and distressed places and populations, in order to encompass new rural growth areas that include emerging labor markets and industries.

Additionally, new research needs to examine the complexities of linked roles and embedded social relations, which raise questions about the intersections of seemingly diverse social processes. Research on the household division of labor and women's labor force participation in some cases has given way to complex studies of family and household livelihood strategies in different types of rural communities under different social and economic conditions. Separate research traditions focusing either on household reproduction and domestic labor or on wage labor and formal labor market participation have been reconfigured and broadened to consider the embedded nature of formal and informal labor, and public and private sectors (Falk, Schulman, and Tickamyer 2003). Similarly, such basic issues as the factors that encourage women to remain in or return to rural communities versus the factors that encourage out-migration can be more fruitfully investigated by research that combines different theoretical and methodological traditions such as the recent call for linking demography and community studies (Brown 2002). These trends must be encouraged and accelerated.

Finally, current research clearly demonstrates the need for new policies that address the needs of rural women and their families more directly. International traditions concerned with women in development, or gender and development, combine interest in research and policy needs, yet the domestic literature idiosyncratically documents the needs women have for better services and opportunities in rural areas while doing little to systematically examine ways to address those needs. Policy analysis is buried in scattered research on gender and rural poverty, community development, or environmental issues and activism. Program development and evaluation is even rarer. These deficits can be lessened by focused research in the areas outlined above. The women of rural America have pressing needs in the twenty-first century that require new attention to prevent a continuation of old problems.

9

Rural Poverty

The Persisting Challenge

Leif Jensen, Diane K. McLaughlin, and Tim Slack

In 1966, amidst America's emerging War on Poverty, President Johnson appointed the National Advisory Commission on Rural Poverty to draw attention to this comparatively hidden problem, explore its unique causes and consequences, and offer possible solutions. In its report, *The People Left Behind,* the Commission boldly concluded that "[we are] convinced that the abolition of rural poverty in the United States, perhaps for the first time in any nation, is completely feasible" (National Advisory Commission on Rural Poverty 1967, xi). A generation later, that vision remains as elusive as ever. The enigma of poverty amidst plenty persists in both rural and urban America. Rural poverty continues to be of equal if not greater severity than urban poverty, yet remains much more hidden from view. In this chapter, we discuss prevailing definitions of poverty, provide a statistical portrait of rural poverty in the United States today, review theory and evidence regarding the etiology of poverty, discuss household and community strategies to cope with rural poverty, and consider policy options.

Defining Poverty

Poverty is commonly measured using total income for an individual or family as a gauge of economic well-being. Developed in the early 1960s, the official definition sets the poverty threshold at three times the cost of a minimally adequate diet. Multiple thresholds were specified to adjust for family size, number of children, gender and age of family head, and farm residence. Farm families were assigned lower thresholds under the assumption that they had lower food and housing costs; however, this distinction is no longer made. The thresholds are adjusted annually to account for inflation. In 2001, a family of four with two adults and two children was defined as poor if their total money income before taxes was less than $17,960.

The official definition of poverty has been criticized over the years (see Ruggles 1990; Citro and Michael 1995). One critique that bears directly on rural/urban differences is that while thresholds are sensitive to differences in family size and structure, they are insensitive to cost of living differences between places. A popular perception is that it costs less to live in rural areas, and that the rural poverty rate may not be as high as official statistics indicate. While some reject the view that it is cheaper to live in the countryside (Summers 2000), others feel the question is at least arguable (Nord 2000). In the end, any quibbling at the margins deflects attention from the persisting problem of rural poverty, which is unacceptably high by any measure.

Rural Poverty: Trends and Correlates

Figure 9.1 shows the trend in poverty rates (the percentage who are poor) for nonmetropolitan and metropolitan residents during the period 1959 to 2001. Three things stand out. First, poverty rates declined precipitously in

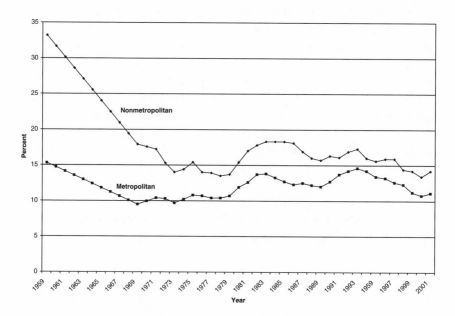

Fig 9.1 Poverty rates, by residence, 1959–2001

the 1960s. Second, the trend is clearly countercyclical—poverty rates are higher when the economy struggles, as it did during the early 1980s and early 1990s. Finally, poverty rates are always higher in nonmetropolitan than metropolitan areas, a gap that has widened somewhat in recent years.

Based on an analysis of data from the March 2001 U.S. Current Population Survey, Table 9.1 shows poverty rates within categories of selected variables, as well as the percentage distribution of the poor across categories of these same variables. Following the lengthy expansion of the national economy in the latter half of the 1990s, the poverty rate fell to a twenty-five-year low of 11.5 percent in 2001. The nonmetropolitan poverty rate (13.6 percent) exceeds that of metropolitan areas (11 percent); however, the metropolitan aggregation masks the vastly different circumstances in central cities (15.9 percent) versus suburbs (7.7 percent).

Children suffer the highest rates of poverty (16.8 percent) of any age group, especially in central cities and nonmetropolitan areas, where nearly one-quarter and one-fifth of those under eighteen are poor, respectively (see Chapter 7 in this volume). Poverty rates fall substantially as people enter their prime working years, and climb slightly among those sixty-five and older. Research suggests the oldest of the elderly have particularly high poverty rates (McLaughlin and Jensen 1993) and constitute a greater proportion of the poor population in nonmetropolitan areas.

Stark racial and ethnic differences exist. Poverty rates among Blacks and Latinos are nearly three times those of whites. White poverty is highest in nonmetropolitan areas (10.9 percent), where this group constitutes a much greater share of the poor (66.6 percent) compared to other residential settings. Likewise, poverty rates are higher among nonmetropolitan Blacks, Latinos, and other non-whites than their central city counterparts. This reflects a historical legacy that has left rural areas with concentrated minority populations (e.g., the Mississippi Delta and American Indian reservations) among the nation's most economically depressed locales (Summers 1991). That overall poverty rates are higher in central cities than nonmetropolitan areas reflects the residential concentration of minorities in the inner city. We stress that examining racial and ethnic groups separately shows that nonmetropolitan residents are at the greatest risk of poverty.

Poverty rates drop sharply with greater educational attainment. Those with less than a high school education suffer far higher rates of poverty (22.2 percent) than do those with a high school degree (9.2 percent), some postsecondary education (6.5 percent), or a bachelor's degree or more (3.5 percent).[1] Poverty rates are far higher among those who have never

---

1. Educational attainment data were restricted to those twenty-five years and older.

been married, those who have been separated or divorced, and those who have been widowed than among those who are married. For those who have been separated, divorced, or widowed, poverty rates are highest in nonmetropolitan areas. Finally, employment is understandably a major factor shaping the incidence of poverty.[2] Those with full-time work realize lower poverty rates (3.5 percent) than those with part-time work (10 percent), those unemployed (21.5 percent), or those not in the labor force (23.3 percent). Working poverty (poverty rates among full- and part-time workers) is somewhat more prevalent in nonmetropolitan than metropolitan areas, and correspondingly the nonmetropolitan poor are slightly more likely than the metropolitan poor to be working full time.

The Causes of Poverty: Theory and Evidence

Studies and theories of the causes of poverty can be very roughly subdivided into those that emphasize the social, demographic, and economic characteristics of poor individuals and families themselves, and those that point to more macrostructural characteristics of communities, labor markets, and regions. Though empirical studies have increasingly used individual and structural variables in the same analysis (e.g., Brown and Hirschl 1995), we use this dichotomy to structure our discussion.

Individual-Level Explanations

As reflected in Table 9.1, individual-level factors that influence poverty operate similarly in rural and urban areas. Whether one lives in the city or countryside, having little education, being Black or Latino, or being an unmarried adult increases the likelihood of poverty. Researchers have attempted to explain the disadvantage of rural residence by examining residential differences in population composition and the impact of specific variables on poverty.

An important theoretical approach to poverty is grounded in the notion of human capital—the bundle of skills that workers bring to the labor market and exchange for steady employment and wages (Lin 2001). Those with limited human capital—with low education and labor force experience—will be at greater risk of poverty. As noted, nonmetropolitan adults have lower average levels of education compared to their metropolitan counterparts, which contributes to higher poverty rates in rural areas (Summers 1995).

---

2. Employment status data were restricted to those twenty-five to sixty-four years of age.

Table 9.1 Poverty rates and distribution of poverty, by selected characteristics and place of residence, 2001

| | Poverty Rate (percent poor) | | | | | Distribution of Poverty (percent) | | | | |
| | National | Nonmetro | Metropolitan | | | National | Nonmetro | Metropolitan | | |
			Total	Central City	Suburb			Total	Central City	Suburb
Total	12.0	14.6	11.4	16.6	8.3					
Age										
Under 18	17.6	20.8	16.9	25.8	11.8	38.7	37.1	39.1	40.6	37.9
18–34	13.3	15.3	13.0	17.1	9.7	26.1	22.0	27.3	28.3	26.3
35–64	8.0	11.1	7.3	11.0	5.4	25.6	29.6	24.4	23.4	25.4
65 and over	9.7	11.7	9.1	12.0	7.6	9.6	11.3	9.1	7.7	10.5
Race/ethnicity										
White	7.8	11.9	6.7	8.5	5.7	46.2	67.9	39.7	24.9	51.3
Black	23.9	29.1	23.2	26.0	17.7	25.0	16.1	27.7	37.8	18.9
Latino	23.1	26.2	22.8	26.4	18.6	23.1	9.7	27.1	30.3	25.3
Other	14.2	29.8	12.1	14.8	8.1	5.7	6.3	5.5	7.0	4.5
Education										
Less than high school	22.4	24.0	22.0	26.7	17.8	40.2	40.0	40.3	42.8	35.4
High school	9.2	11.2	8.7	12.7	7.0	34.5	38.8	33.0	31.6	36.0
Some college	6.4	8.7	5.9	8.4	4.5	12.7	12.0	12.9	12.7	12.9
Bachelor's degree or more	3.4	4.3	3.2	4.3	2.7	12.7	9.2	13.9	12.9	15.8

Table 9.1 (continued) Poverty rates and distribution of poverty, by selected characteristics and place of residence, 2001

	Poverty Rate (percent poor)					Distribution of Poverty (percent)				
				Metropolitan					Metropolitan	
	National	Nonmetro	Total	Central City	Suburb	National	Nonmetro	Total	Central City	Suburb
Marital status										
Married	5.2	7.1	4.8	7.3	3.6	18.5	22.5	17.3	15.2	19.3
Never married	17.0	20.6	16.3	22.5	11.8	62.3	56.2	64.1	67.8	60.5
Separated/divorced	16.9	23.4	15.5	18.2	13.3	12.5	13.2	12.3	11.4	13.3
Widowed	16.1	21.1	14.8	18.3	12.3	6.7	8.2	6.3	5.6	6.9
Employment status										
Full-time	3.5	4.9	3.2	4.5	2.5	24.7	24.6	24.7	23.5	26.0
Part-time	6.2	8.5	5.6	7.7	3.9	5.1	5.6	5.0	4.4	4.7
Unemployed	11.0	14.3	10.3	15.6	7.6Å	10.7	10.6	10.7	10.2	11.0

Source: 2001 Current Population Survey.

Racial and ethnic minorities suffer well-known economic disadvantages in the United States, and rural poverty rates would be even higher were it not for the fact that rural populations are disproportionately non-Latino white (Snipp et al. 1993). As indicated in Table 9.1, rural minorities are especially vulnerable to poverty (Jensen and Tienda 1989). Listing race and ethnicity under individual causes of poverty belies the fact that to a large degree, poverty among rural minorities is rooted in societal-level forces that work against those of lower class origins and non-whites (Summers 1995). For example, drawing on intensive ethnographic research, Cynthia Duncan (1999) finds that the dire circumstances of Blacks in the Mississippi Delta can be traced to a rigid class system—itself an echo of slave plantation economy—that denies employment and other opportunities to rural Blacks in the region. Indeed, a defining feature of rural minority poverty is its clustering in places proximate to areas like the Delta, the four corners region in the Southwest, and American Indian reservations, in which these groups were subjugated historically (Snipp et al. 1993).

Migration patterns associated with transformations in production agriculture also contribute to poverty. Low-wage job opportunities in large-scale fruit and vegetable operations and meat packing constitute a draw for immigrant workers (especially Latino and Southeast Asian workers), increasing poverty rates and race or ethnic diversity in rural communities near these operations (Fitchen 1995). Currently, about two-thirds of America's 2.5 million farm workers are foreign born (Martin and Midgley 1999), and many more immigrants are employed in meat, poultry, and other food-processing industries (Stull et al. 1995).

Poverty rates are higher among the youngest and oldest Americans. That about one-fifth of nonmetropolitan children are poor is troubling given the detrimental effects of disadvantaged origins on child outcomes (Mayer 1997). Perhaps less well appreciated is the plight of the nonmetropolitan elderly who, compared to their metropolitan counterparts, have a higher risk of poverty, are more likely to slide into poverty from one year to the next, and are less likely to move out of poverty (Glasgow et al. 1993; McLaughlin and Jensen 1993, 1995; Jensen and McLaughlin 1997). Disadvantaged occupational histories, lower lifelong earnings, and less access to pensions among rural elders are partly to blame (Glasgow and Brown 1998; McLaughlin and Jensen 2000).

Relative to other marital status categories, those who are married have a lower prevalence of poverty (Table 9.1). Compositional differences in marital status have historically benefited rural residents where proportionately more adults are married. Nonetheless, the rise in single-female-headed families that has characterized urban areas also has been witnessed in the countryside, and with the same effect—a rise in measured poverty (Lichter and McLaughlin 1995; Albrecht, et al. 2000). A similar rural/urban convergence can be seen in the related patterns of teenage pregnancy and out-of-wedlock birth (see Chapters 5 and 7 in this volume).

An explanation for poverty that straddles the individual/structural dichotomy is the "culture of poverty" approach. This theory holds that poverty is perpetuated across generations through particular cultural characteristics, including lack of integration with formal institutions and society in general, early initiation into sex and consensual unions, feelings of dependence and inferiority, and a present-time orientation and sense of fatalism that hinders people from seeing and seizing opportunities and planning for the future (Lewis 1966). Many social scientists have been averse to adopting culture as an explanation for poverty since it appears to blame the victim. Nonetheless, scholars of rural poverty (Fitchen 1981; Billings and Blee 2000) and urban poverty (Wilson 1987; MacLeod 1987) have invoked both positive and negative aspects of culture, effectively avoiding appearances of blaming the victim (Summers 1995). They point out that while some cultural traits may indeed serve to perpetuate poverty over time, others may offer support and subsistence that enable the poor to survive (Billings and Blee 2000).

Several individual-level factors associated with poverty hint at explanations rooted in social institutions and structure. We now turn to these explanations.

Structural Explanations

Structural explanations of poverty stress the importance of local opportunity structures rather than individual characteristics as central to understanding poverty. They address how social structures affect the allocation of people to job opportunities, the quality and quantity of locally available jobs, the availability of job training and education, and the ability of local communities to influence their own opportunity structures.

Poverty is clearly associated with the quality and quantity of jobs available. Individuals with good jobs are less likely to be poor, and areas with a larger share of good jobs have a lower prevalence of poverty among residents. Areas with low unemployment, low underemployment, and high labor force participation rates provide adequate jobs for local residents, resulting in lower poverty. While there is discussion about which industries and occupations offer "good" or "adequate jobs" and how that has changed over time (Dickens and Lang 1985; Doeringer and Piore 1971; Hodson 1983, 1984; Tolbert et al. 1980), most would agree that good jobs offer higher earnings, job stability, opportunities for advancement, and benefits. Those who study rural opportunity structures note that good jobs make up a smaller share of rural than urban jobs (Galston and Baehler 1995).

One predicament facing many rural areas is whether and how much to invest in training workers. The availability of job training programs or other educational opportunities can increase the human capital and economic prospects of residents, but this is only beneficial to the local area if suitable jobs are available for those newly trained. Lacking access to suitable local jobs, they may look elsewhere for employment, taking the local investment in education and training with them. While there is evidence that areas that invest in job training and education are better able to attract new, higher quality jobs, such investment remains a risky strategy to decrease poverty locally. Also, those communities that would gain the most from offering job training (those with the least educated and skilled workforces) are often least able to afford such programs, and often have the lowest quality employment when jobs are available.

As indicated earlier, social structures within local labor markets can operate to channel certain types of people to "good," "bad," or no jobs. Employers may identify female workers or minorities as less desirable employees, paying them lower wages or offering them part-time positions if they hire them at all (Doeringer and Piore 1971; Gordon et al. 1982). Such practices would reinforce higher poverty among certain subgroups of the population. Paternalism in rural labor markets may give individuals from particular families the inside track to jobs, while those from other families are excluded regardless of their credentials and capabilities (Doeringer 1984; Duncan 1999). While such practices do not necessarily increase rural poverty rates, they do help explain patterns of higher poverty among some segments of the rural population, and may attenuate the links between human capital and economic well-being.

There are some characteristics of rural labor markets that may result in higher poverty and lower earnings among rural residents. Empirical analyses of earnings and poverty suggest that even when a rural person has the same human capital and the same job as an urban person, the rural person has lower earnings (McLaughlin and Perman 1991). Typically, rural labor markets are smaller in number of workers and jobs, have few large employers, and are more likely to be dominated by a single industry. Such conditions are likely to combine so that workers have limited choice in the labor market and limited power to demand higher wages or benefits (Doeringer 1984). This would be especially true in labor markets with high levels of unemployment and underemployment, and a large share of discouraged workers, where employers have a relatively large pool of replacement workers from which to choose (McLaughlin and Perman 1991; Tomaskovic-Devey 1988). In addition, local labor markets dominated by extractive industries have long been associated with high and persistent poverty (Nord 1994), due in part to industry dominance and control of local labor markets and to the geographic isolation of areas where extractive industries tend to dominate. Few alternative employers are apt to locate in such areas.

The nature of job quality and the human capital of nonmetropolitan (compared to metropolitan) residents have been well-documented. Various perspectives on uneven development provide plausible explanations for why poorer jobs and human capital are concentrated in nonmetropolitan areas, and why there is variation across rural areas. Core/periphery explanations, such as central place theory (Berry 1973), argue that rural areas supply raw materials and labor to larger urban centers, where better-paying jobs are found. Such spatial allocation of activities and jobs is an unintentional result of market processes. Other theorists suggest that rural areas are intentionally underdeveloped so that raw materials can be extracted more cheaply and rural workers remain a viable source of cheap labor should they be needed (Colclough 1988; Lobao 1990; Lobao et al. 1999; Lyson and Falk 1993; Markusen 1987; Storper and Walker 1989; Walker 1978). Another explanation is that high-end research and development in manufacturing and business services tend to cluster together in larger metropolitan areas, while routine production processes in manufacturing seek low labor and land costs (Lonsdale and Seyler 1979). Smaller rural areas are less able to attract and support business services, and so end up with a higher share of "low-end" service sector jobs in personal services and retail trade (Galston and Baehler 1995; Smith 1993). Underdeveloped rural economic systems reflect the operation of markets for labor, land, and other inputs to production and the demand for services in rural areas.

Whichever explanation one prefers—intentional exploitation or market forces—these processes have become problematic for rural communities. As firms that were formerly locally owned are purchased by multinational corporations, the U.S. economy has become more integrated into the world economy. Rural workers and places must now compete in global as well as national labor and product markets (Erickson 1981; Galston and Baehler 1995; McMichael 1996a).[3]

---

3. It is important to recognize that the nature of community structure (e.g., degree of pluralism) can influence whether the local-level effects of globalization will be negative or positive (Young and Lyson 1993).

More recent efforts have gone beyond examining labor market opportunities to consider other structural forces that enable (or prevent) the poor to improve their circumstances. History, the physical environment, and local power structures (Billings and Blee 2000; Green and Haines 2002; Schulman and Anderson 1999) contribute to the development of social contexts that assist the poor in leaving poverty (Duncan 1999; Kusel 1996; Flora 1998; Gittell and Vidal 1998; Woolcock 1998; Couto and Guthrie 1999) or that support rigid stratification systems that keep the poor "in their place." The social context in the local community affects opportunities and willingness to both enhance human capital and offer social and human services for the poor.

Finally, a good argument can be made that there is a link between the human capital of residents and the ability of communities to successfully organize to attract or retain good jobs, or to meet other goals such as assisting their poorer members. Communities that lack human, social, and financial resources face severe deficits in competition with other communities for jobs and external investment. The poorest communities, and the people in them, tend to remain that way. Future researchers can make an important contribution by identifying successful strategies that poor places and people can use to build the capacity of local residents to work for change and attract external investments for infrastructure, services, and economic development.

Coping Strategies and Implications for Policy

Rural social scientists have become increasingly interested in the ways in which low-income families piece together a living. Research on "household economic survival strategies" describes the complex array of means by which the rural poor make ends meet. This research has been motivated by important economic trends and policy shifts, including continued industrial restructuring and globalization of production, which have reduced manufacturing employment, increased low-paying service sector employment (e.g., in tourism) (Fitchen 1995; Galston and Baehler 1995), and contributed to the emergence of "temps" and other contingent labor arrangements (Barker and Christensen 1998). On the political side, interest in livelihood strategies has been heightened by legislated increases in the Earned Income Tax Credit and minimum wage during the 1990s, and most notably by the major overhaul of the welfare system in 1996, which drastically reduced the long-term availability of public assistance and increased the necessity of employment as survival strategies (see Chapter 28 in this volume).

One method by which researchers have sought to understand economic coping strategies among the poor, including how these differ between rural and urban areas, is to examine sources of household or family income (Jensen and Eggebeen 1994; Lichter and Jensen 2002). Two conclusions stand out. First, historically and today, earnings have made up a larger share of the income of nonmetropolitan than metropolitan poor families. Conversely, nonmetropolitan poor families are less likely to rely on public assistance income when compared to their metropolitan counterparts. Second, the 1990s witnessed a very dramatic shift in this so-called income packaging, such that in both rural and urban areas poor families came to rely much less on public assistance and much more on earnings to make ends meet (Lichter and Jensen 2002). This reflects both the strong economy of the mid- to late 1990s and welfare reform legislation.

The increasing importance of employment for the economic well-being of the poor in both rural and urban areas raises important questions about the quality of jobs available. One possibility that needs greater study is that those with good jobs (versus bad jobs, as discussed above) are doubly advantaged in the effort to prosper economically. In a study of rural Vermont, Nelson and Smith (1999) conclude that "good-job households," by virtue of their greater security, stability, social connections, and other advantages that come with a good job, are better positioned than "bad-job households" to engage in other economic pursuits that benefit the household. These might include such things as having a small business on the side, placing additional family members into the labor market, or engaging in substantial self-provisioning. These alternative livelihood strategies are either out of reach or differ in ways that make them less beneficial in bad-job households, contributing to their higher risk of impoverishment.

Other recent research has focused specifically on informal or underground economic activities as household survival strategies both among the general population (Tickamyer and Wood 1998) and among the poor (Jensen et al. 1995). The informal economy consists of unregulated economic activities that generate real or in-kind income. Such activities include, for example, under-the-table work for cash or other things of value, selling rummaged goods, and selling home-produced food or crafts. Several studies have shown that informal work is common in rural areas, and can be critical for helping poor rural families survive through difficult periods.

Community strategies for coping with poverty fall into two broad categories. The first dovetails with the ideas of household survival strategies by focusing on providing assistance of various forms to poor residents. These would include community efforts to offer job training programs, worker placement programs with local employers, literacy education, child care services, food banks, goodwill stores for clothing and furniture, and social support for those needing such services. In some areas, drug treatment, domestic violence, and mental health services assist some poor residents in finding a better quality of life. Of course, these services can also benefit residents of all social classes.

One of the hallmarks of the recent welfare reform is the emphasis on communities taking more responsibility for helping individuals to move off of welfare to become self-sufficient, refocusing attention to local efforts to assist those in need. The implementation of locally initiated education and job training programs designed to meet the needs of local employers is one strategy being used in some communities to assist poor and low-income individuals. Economic development efforts could be identified as a community strategy to help poor residents cope with poverty, but only if job training and other skills development programs needed for new jobs are made available to the poor. Unfortunately, rural communities are less likely to have these types of services available (Weber and Duncan 2001) and, even when available, the greater stigma and/or lack of confidentiality in their use may make rural residents more hesitant to use them.

As indicated, communities, like individuals and families, have different resources that can be brought to bear to provide services to their disadvantaged members. The wealth of communities is going to affect the type and quantity of assistance that can be provided to the poor, with more wealthy communities (and those with a smaller share of poor residents needing help) having access to substantial resources for poverty alleviation. Poorer communities—those with higher proportions of residents who are poor—are much less likely to have such resources. *Thus, the poor in poor communities are doubly disadvantaged.*

While substantial rural poverty exists in places that are not persistently poor, the situation of persistently poor communities raises the second category of community strategies for coping with poverty (Nord 1997). How do poor communities cope not only with the poverty of residents, but with the limited community resources this entails? Many of the perspectives on economic development ultimately suggest that those communities that have local resources and the ability to leverage them by accessing state or federal funds are the most likely to be successful. Such findings leave little room for determining how poor communities might achieve success in improving their well-being. Possible coping strategies may include multicommunity collaboration, whereby poor communities and neighboring communities (whether poor or not) pool resources and knowledge to try to improve their situation. Often poor communities, especially many natural-resource-dependent or minority communities, have little infrastructure (e.g., adequate highways, telecommunications, educational systems, and water and sewer systems) that would enable them to attract new employers or assist local employers in expanding their markets. The geographic isolation of these communities makes these problems even more difficult and expensive to resolve. These persistent poverty communities do not have the resources to solve their multiple problems alone.

The new federalism's emphasis on devolution and local solutions places these poor communities at even greater risk of being left behind (see Chapter 19 in this volume). If they are to improve their situation and that of their poor and nonpoor residents, multiple outside resources need to be available and utilized. These would include financial resources to support infrastructure, educational, and economic development. Support also needs to be provided for training, information, and assistance in building human capital and skills for local action and the involvement of local residents (especially the poor and disadvantaged) in the social, institutional, and power networks of the community. This would amplify the voice of the poor, and enhance their ability to shape the future of their own community. Such resources also would assist poor communities in reaching their social and economic goals.

PART II

A Transformed Rural Economy

10

How People Make a Living in Rural America

David A. McGranahan

People originally moved into rural America to take advantage of its natural resources, whether through hunting, fishing, gathering, farming, mining, or forestry. Employment in these activities peaked in the early 1900s, however. Farm employment has since dropped by about 70 percent, and employment in the other resource industries by half (Freudenberg 1992). Yet in all but a few states, rural (nonmetropolitan) areas now have larger populations than they had in 1920. Some areas have attracted manufacturers seeking to escape the high costs of urban labor and land. Other areas, favored by mild climates, lakes, or mountains, have developed into recreation centers for urban vacationers and retirees. But some areas have retained their dependence on agriculture or mining, which has often meant declining jobs and population. The result is a wide diversity of local rural economies that have in common the limitations and advantages of sparse settlement. This situation is not static. Like other social sciences, rural sociology has been concerned recently with the continued economic viability of rural areas in the context of market globalization and technological change. Rural sociology stands out, however, in its concern with the impact of these changes on the well-being of people who make a living in rural America.

This review of recent research on making a living in rural areas is divided into four major sections. The first draws on an ecological perspective to examine the rural role in the broader economy and factors accounting for differences across rural areas. At issue are the ways that rurality, local education, and natural resources shape the types of jobs available to rural residents. The second section looks at some of the broader forces affecting rural areas, including globalization and technological change. Many rural areas have attracted manufacturers because of their low labor costs. Can these areas thrive as the relevant cost comparison increasingly becomes overseas regions rather than the urban United States? The third section focuses on the literature concerned with marginal local economies, with high rates of poverty or population decline. Well-being, both economic and social, has been a central issue in rural sociology. It is affected not only by broad national and international trends, but also by structure and change in the local economy. The final section covers research on household strategies for making a living, including work in the "informal sector." Research on household strategies—often involving case studies—gives us a much fuller sense of rural life and its complexity than we get from formal employment surveys.

Underlying this review is a conceptual distinction between sustenance and maintenance activities in human systems. Sustenance activities bring money or goods into a household or community, while maintenance activities keep it circulating within the community. Both are necessary for survival. At the household level, we typically distinguish between work outside the home that brings in money or goods and household tasks such as home repair, child care, and the purchase or making of clothes and meals. Similarly, at the community or area level, we can distinguish between what economists call "economic base" activities (agriculture, mining, manufacturing, and services for people or businesses outside the community), which bring money or goods into the community, and services that support the community and its members. These support activities include not only the maintenance of "social institutions" such as health care, education, churches, and local government, and civic activities (see the chapters in Part III of this volume), but also services for local businesses and households. Paid work in these areas is sustenance activity for households, but maintenance activity at the community level. A community cannot survive on services alone, unless outsiders such as tourists are making the purchases and/or residents have considerable transfer income (e.g., welfare, social security, pension income). These distinctions make clear that the question of how rural communities and regions are sustained is quite different from the question of how rural households make a living.

The Spatial Division of Labor: The Influences of Rurality and Human and Natural Resources

The major industrial shift in the nonmetropolitan United States in the past thirty years, at least as measured by earnings, has been from agriculture to support services (Fig. 10.1).[1] In contrast, metropolitan areas as a whole

---

1. There is no completely satisfactory way to divide local economies into economic base and support/maintenance activities using the available data. Many businesses such as banks are active both locally and more broadly. Moreover, the extent of broader involvement varies. Rural North Dakota banks probably serve mostly local markets, while New York banks are

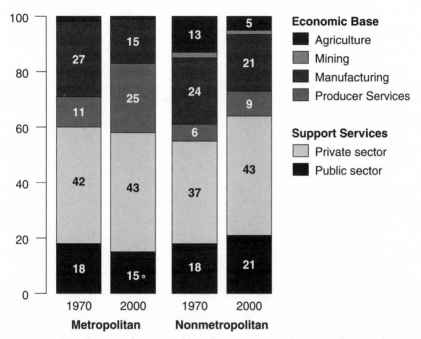

Fig. 10.1 Distribution of earnings by industry sector and metropolitan and nonmetropolitan areas, 1970 and 2000

Source: Based on Bureau of Economic Analysis REIS data files

have seen a major shift out of manufacturing to producer services. If rural areas are no longer simply providers of raw materials for urban producers and food for urban consumers, how can we conceptualize their economic role? Rural human ecology has conceptualized rural areas not as contrasts to urban areas but as the low end of an urban/rural continuum. Briefly, the more complex an activity, the more concentrated it will be at the high (urban) end of the continuum. The complexity approach draws chiefly on central place theory, as developed by Christaller (1966) and others (see Berry and Kasarda 1977), and on Thompson's (1965) "filtering down" hypothesis, which has many variants (see Malecki 1997). Christaller saw places organized in a hierarchy, with larger places having both a greater variety of types of businesses and a greater centrality in communications networks. The filtering down thesis posits that young, highly innovative industries face a great deal of uncertainty—in inputs, technology, product demand, and financing. They locate in major urban locations, where access

---

often international in scope. In Figure 10.1, producer services (financial, insurance, legal, accounting, consulting, and business services; communications) are included as sustenance activities as these activities often serve outside markets. All other service-sector activities, including transportation and utilities, are assumed to be local.

to specialized knowledge, skills, and services are most available. When industries are older and technologies and markets are well-established, competition is based less on innovative products than on product costs, and industries move to where labor and land are cheaper.

Analyses drawing on these concepts found sharp differences across the urban/rural continuum, or at least between metropolitan and nonmetropolitan areas. High tech industries are disproportionately urban, while low-tech industries are disproportionately rural (Bloomquist 1988), a difference that seems particularly strong in the South (Falk and Lyson 1988). More generally, for manufacturing and producer services, the larger the proportion of managerial, professional, and technical jobs in an industry, the greater its concentration in urban areas (McGranahan 1988). Moreover, within production-sector industries, managerial and professional jobs are more concentrated in urban areas than blue collar jobs. When high tech industries do locate in rural areas they tend to locate near large cities (Glasmeier 1991). The concentration of high-end, production-sector jobs in urban areas has become more accentuated over time (McGranahan and Ghelfi 1998).

These rural/urban patterns are considerably weaker in the consumer services industries. These industries tend to be organized on a local rather than national or international level, so there is considerably less division of labor across areas (McGranahan 1988). Thus, while schools, for example, tend to be larger and offer more specialized services in more urban areas, their occupational structures are basically the same whether the location is urban or rural.

Despite these results, rurality may not be the only or even the strongest constraint on the location of industrial activity involving complex tasks and thus high skill requirements. There are considerable differences among rural areas in population education levels. The rural South, particularly in the Black Belt and Appalachia, tends to have much lower high school completion rates than the Corn Belt or upper Midwest, for instance. The same type of argument that has been made for the urban/rural continuum may be made with respect to work force education levels, namely, that more routine types of activities are likely to be concentrated in low-education areas. In 1990, low-education counties—the bottom quarter of nonmetropolitan counties in young adult (ages twenty-five to forty-four) high school completion—had the highest proportion of employment in routine manufacturing of all education quarters. This reflects the low-wage/low-skill strategies of many manufacturers moving to rural areas; however, it is also likely that the availability of manufacturing jobs for people without high school degrees may have discouraged high school completion, as did the presence of mining jobs in Appalachia (see Stallmann et al. 1995).

Markusen (1985) has criticized the filtering down approach for ignoring economic organization. Industries dominated by a few major corporations have relatively little incentive to reduce labor costs, since these costs can be passed on to consumers. Consequently, labor is relatively well paid in these industries compared to industries in highly competitive markets. Another consequence is that the oligopolistic industries, lacking competitive pressures, tend to remain where they originated and not to diffuse to other locations. This certainly would characterize the automotive and steel industries twenty years ago.

The final attribute to be considered here is natural resource endowment. There have been several analyses that identify rural areas dependent on natural resource extraction (e.g., Weber, Castle, and Shriver 1988; Elo and Beale 1984), sometimes as parts of overall economic classifications of counties (Cook and Mizer 1994). But endowment and economic dependence are different concepts, as the latter involves importance relative to other activities. Many counties with extensive cropland, for instance, are not very dependent on farming because they also have another industry such as an autoparts plant that brings money into the county.

Freudenberg (1992), focusing on mining and timber industries, points out that capitalizing on natural resource endowment depends largely on markets and technology. A seam of coal does not create jobs unless coal prices are high enough and the available technology is efficient enough to make extraction worthwhile. Prices vary over time with both discoveries of new deposits (now usually overseas) and discoveries of substitute materials. New extraction technologies may suddenly make old deposits worth mining. Employment in mining has been characterized by booms and busts. For socioeconomic analyses, it is thus not feasible to rate rural areas according to their generic natural resource endowments, only by some measure of actual extractive activity.

With the growth of recreation and tourism and the decline of traditional rural resource-based activities, natural amenities—mountains, lakes, pleasant climate—have become major natural resource endowments. Galston and Baehler (1995) argue that recreation is perhaps the major rural "competitive advantage." McGranahan (1999b) found that both population and employment change in nonmetropolitan areas have been highly correlated with a natural amenities scale combining climate, topography, and water area measures. One of the problems facing agricultural communities is that conditions that create the best agriculture—flat, unbroken terrain;

warm, humid summers; and cold, wet winters—are the conditions least attractive for recreation, tourism, and retirement living. Beale and Johnson (1998) have identified recreation counties, very few of which are in areas with extensive cropland.

Industrial Transformation

The nature of U.S. industry has changed considerably in the past twenty-five years, and rural sociology has spent considerable effort to identify the consequences for rural people. Briefly, four aspects of this transformation have been identified, each of which raises serious questions about the future of rural jobs.

The Globalization of Production and Markets

Lowered costs of transportation, better communications systems, greater capital mobility, and lower trade barriers have led to an internationalization of the U.S. economy. Exports and imports of goods and services, taken together, rose from about 13 percent of GDP in 1973 to about 26 percent of the GDP in 2000. In general, the United States has been an exporter of high-end services (e.g., banking, computer software) and high tech manufacturing (e.g., airplanes, military hardware, electronic equipment) and an importer of low-tech manufactured goods (e.g., apparel), and oil and other primary products.

Globalization threatens the rural competitive advantage in low-cost labor and land, as both are considerably less expensive in overseas locations. Falk and Lyson (1988) suggest that the rural South, with development policies based largely on attracting low-wage/low-skill manufacturing, is in danger of being beaten at its own game. Singelmann (1996) notes, however, that globalization has not meant a wholesale shift to overseas locations. Multinational firms tend to spread production, in order to gain flexibility in dealing with changes in exchange rates, market barriers, and other factors. Thus, while domestic auto companies have shifted production abroad, foreign companies have built plants in the United States, with many of the suppliers going to rural areas in the Midwest and the South. At the end of the 1990s, U.S. auto industry employment was nearly back to its earlier peak in the late 1970s.

As a whole, rural areas have not experienced "deindustrialization." Manufacturing's share of nonmetropolitan earnings was slightly lower in 2000 than in 1970 (Fig. 10.1), but this is only because other sectors have had greater growth. Real employment earnings in 2000 were up by 20 percent over 1970. However, industrial growth and decline have been uneven over space and time. As noted below, some rural areas have experienced a loss in jobs and earnings even as others have gained.

Shifts in Competitive Strategies

In what has been called "post-Fordism" (Lobao 1996), many producers have shifted emphasis from low-cost, mass production toward high-quality, customer-tailored production. Spurred by heightened international competition and facilitated by new computer technologies and management theories, many manufacturers (and some services) now compete based on the quality and customer suitability of their product. They produce for niche markets rather than mass markets.

These shifts in competitive strategies have created, particularly in the context of globalization, a great deal more uncertainty and complexity in production and marketing. This is effectively a reverse of the "product cycle," and suggests a shift in some manufacturing toward more urban locations, where access to information, special services, and skilled workers is more available. Some analysts suggest that areas and regions will become more specialized as interrelated firms cluster to take advantage of "untraded interdependencies" (Storper 1997a) and compete in global markets (Porter 1998). These theories may be less relevant for rural areas than urban. As Falk and Lyson (1988) and Lyson (1989) have shown for the South, however, strong urban high tech clusters do not necessarily spread to the rural hinterland.

Again, however, Singelmann (1996) sounds a cautionary note. These new strategies have also reduced and perhaps in some industries even reversed advantages of scale. This, and more extensive subcontracting, may work in favor of manufacturers in smaller, more rural labor markets. Some have also felt that the development of the Internet and other information transmittal systems would permit a greater dispersion of industry, although the same technology that permits dispersion to rural areas also permits dispersion overseas.

There has been considerable debate about what post-Fordism would mean for labor. Harrison's (1994) research suggested that flexibility meant more temporary workers, outsourcing to nonunionized shops, and other corporate strategies to reduce labor costs in a time of uncertain demand. Others, however, have stressed the link between product quality and labor quality.

A 1996 survey of rural manufacturers supports the latter view. Users of advanced (post-Fordist) technologies and management practices reported substantial recent increases in skill needs (particularly in problem-solving, teamwork, and computer use) and much greater use of training (McGranahan 1999a). Independent of plant size and industry type, advanced technology manufacturers had more professional and technical workers and more highly schooled production workers than other manufacturers (McGranahan 2003). Not surprisingly, advanced technology manufacturers were relatively sensitive to local labor market skills. More often than others, they reported major problems in finding skilled labor and attracting managers and professionals to the area, particularly where education levels were low.

To some extent, the divergent findings with respect to labor quality may reflect when the studies were done. McGranahan (1999a) found that U.S. labor market areas ranked in the bottom quarter in high school completion were the only ones with a net gain in manufacturing jobs between 1979 and 1990, suggesting that, consistent with Harrison (1994), manufacturers were pursuing low-wage/low-skill strategies during the 1980s. In contrast, during the 1990–1997 period, when new technologies and management practices became more widespread, only labor markets ranked in the top quarter in education gained in manufacturing jobs. The same type of pattern showed up for the nonmetropolitan South.

Expansion of Services

Virtually all employment growth in both rural and urban areas in the 1980s was in services (Lahr 1993), and services continued to be the major source of new jobs in the 1990s. The economic boom of the late 1990s was driven by the expansion of high-end producer services—business and professional services, communications, and financial services—largely in urban areas, but with some rural spillover. Contributing to services growth has been the growing tendency for manufacturers and farmers to contract out for services that had previously been done internally. Consumer services are a major component of the rural economy—*the* major component according to some classification schemes—and it is their growth that has been perhaps most responsible for the predominance of service-sector jobs in the rural economy.

The expansion of services has been seen as, at best, a mixed blessing. Rural sociology has long been concerned about "good" versus "bad" jobs (see Bloomquist et al. 1993). Growth in the service sector is essentially seen as growth in bad jobs. The sector generally provides good jobs for the well-educated, but for others, the jobs may be part-time, temporary, low-pay, and without meaningful benefits—much worse than those found in the manufacturing sector. Gorham (1993) found that consumer and social services accounted for 44 percent of all nonmetropolitan jobs in 1987, but 56 percent of all low-pay jobs. However, while low-pay jobs had increased from 31 percent of all nonmetropolitan jobs in 1979 to 42 percent in 1987, little of the increase was associated with the expansion of services. Rather, the increase was pervasive across industries, suggesting that general economic conditions rather than a shift to low-end service-sector employment were responsible for the increases in economic hardship during the 1980s.

Employment Decline in Traditional Rural Industries

Jobs in farming, mining, and timber have all declined considerably over the past eighty years. This decline has not necessarily occurred evenly across time or space. Mining employment, for instance, grew briefly during the 1970s, and collapsed in the 1980s. In agriculture, recent declines in employment have been accompanied by "industrialization." This has meant not only large "mega-farms," but also an increase in contracting, where poultry, hog, and other farms raise animals for food processors according to standards set by, and sometimes with inputs from, meat processors. While Fordism characterizes much of new agriculture, there has also been a trend toward niche farming for farmers markets, restaurants, and other specialized customers. Most of this activity is confined to areas near major cities, however.

The decline in traditional rural industries has long meant that, unless rural areas succeed in attracting or developing other types of industries, they will have difficulty maintaining viable economies. While some have argued that many of these industries rise and fall over time, a strong case can be made that decline is inexorable (Freudenberg 1992).

The ecological analyses covered in the first section attempt to analyze and describe the broad constraints and opportunities that are associated with rurality, work force education, and natural resources and amenities. These analyses generally do not examine consequences for particular rural areas or residents. Industrial transformation in rural areas has been very uneven over space as well as time. While the globalization of production and markets has meant a substantial loss of rural apparel manufacturing jobs in parts of the South, for instance, other areas in the rural South have become suppliers for new foreign auto manufacturing. The decline in traditional rural industries has been offset by industrial agriculture in some areas and recreation industries in others, both of which bring new stresses.

Recognizing this unevenness, in the 1980s rural sociologists began to focus on particular areas or comparisons across areas and less on rurality per se. There were other reasons for this shift in focus as well. Some felt that rural and urban areas are under some of the same broad stresses (such as the expansion of services and manufacturing losses), so that to focus on rural/urban differences was to miss the commonalties. Also, and perhaps most significantly, rural sociologists were interested in issues such as local area inequality and poverty, which broad analyses address only indirectly.

Marginal Rural Economies

Globalization has brought home the fact that capital is geographically fluid, especially compared with labor forces (McMichael 1996a). This may particularly be true where ownership and control lie outside the community. While there are various versions of (and names for) what White (1998) calls the "internal colonial dependency" model, it basically posits that communities characterized by relative isolation, specialization in one or two industries with relatively well-paying, low-skill jobs for men, and outside ownership are extremely vulnerable to economic misfortune and decline. If the main industry becomes unprofitable in that location, capital moves on, leaving the community with few alternatives, as most investment has gone to support the given industry and profits have gone to the outside owners. Sometimes, the industry itself degrades the environment, reducing its usefulness for other purposes. The local workforce also has few alternatives, since the industry in question did not provide or require skills that are useful elsewhere. People may remain, hoping that the industry will return.

While Appalachia is probably the archetype for this kind of situation, this model may also apply to a number of rural areas now or previously dependent on extractive industries. Freudenburg (1992) provides an insightful view of the problems facing communities in the Western U.S. dependent on mining and timber. White (1998) has applied this model to southwestern Kansas, where meat packing and natural gas now dominate the economy. Lyson and Falk's (1993) edited volume covers many rural regions where industry declines or labor-saving technologies have created situations with few adequate jobs for the remaining population. Duncan (1999) contrasts the divisive legacies of Southern plantations and Appalachian coal mining with the more inclusive traditions of a New England mill town. Areas with significant American Indian populations, often comprising Federal reservations, tend to be marginal economies without a viable economic base (Snipp et al. 1993; see also Chapter 3 in this volume).

Comparative analyses across counties were also used in the 1990s to explore the issue of rural economic marginality. Rural sociology has historically been concerned with the effects that changes in the industrial structure in general, and the farm sector in particular, have on income inequality and poverty (Bloomquist et al. 1993; Lobao 1990; Lobao and Schulman 1991). As Brown and Hirschl (1995) note, these analyses have tended to treat the local economic environment and household characteristics (low schooling and single parenthood, for example) as separate factors contributing to poverty. Rural poverty research began in the 1990s to draw on Wilson's (1987) analysis of urban marginal economies, which posits that household characteristics (most notably single parenthood) may themselves be influenced by economic transformation. Briefly, Wilson argues that the decline of urban durable manufacturing left low-skill men used to union wages without comparable opportunities, and many dropped out of the formal labor market or left the area. At the same time, the growth in producer services provided opportunities for low-skilled women, but the new jobs were often in suburbs or other locations difficult to reach, and in any case paid poorly. This shift made men less attractive as spouses and contributed to a growth in female-headed families, thus amplifying the likelihood of inner-city poverty.

Rural economic transformation has been quite different from the urban situation described by Wilson (1987). The shift from manufacturing to services has been much less marked in rural areas (see Fig. 10.1). Many of the rural jobs lost have been in textiles and apparel, not durable goods. Apparel industries, especially, tend to employ women. Wilson's description is perhaps more analogous to areas that once had thriving mines or plantations than to manufacturing areas (Duncan 1999). Nonetheless, agriculture, mining, and manufacturing all did poorly in rural areas in the 1980s, the proportion of rural children in female-headed households rose markedly, and rural poverty rates climbed. If one can equate marginal rural areas with inner cities, the simultaneity of these trends suggested the possibility of similar dynamics (Lichter and McLaughlin 1995; McLaughlin, Gardner, and Lichter 1999; Albrecht et al. 2000).

In general, these studies have shown that single-female-headed families are more likely in rural areas to be characterized by economic hardship, particularly where opportunities for men are few (McLaughlin et al. 1999; Albrecht et al. 2000). This research has also reinforced the findings of other studies with respect to the deleterious effects of low levels of schooling on both the prevalence of two-parent families and income.

The roles of industrial structure and change have been considerably less clear. Results have varied from one study to the next, depending on the categorizations used. For instance, Albrecht et al. (2000) found service-sector employment highly associated with the prevalence of single-parent families and poverty. At the other extreme, Cook and Mizer (1994), using a very different categorization of services, show that "trade and services" counties had the lowest poverty rates of all their economic types. McLaughlin et al. (1999), in one of the few studies to look at change in family structure over time, found no straightforward association between change in county industry structure and change in family structure. Gains in industries typified by poor jobs for women were not associated with increases in female-headed families.

From the ecological perspective taken here, one source of the confusion may be that industry structure is related to poverty at two levels. First, different industries provide different types of jobs, so an industry mix that includes relatively well-paying jobs for low-skill workers is likely to have less poverty. Since poverty is rarer among householders who work in manufacturing than among those who work in services (Lichter, Johnston, and McLaughlin 1994), for instance, rural areas with more employment in manufacturing and less in services should tend to have lower poverty rates. A long-standing assumption of rural county-level analysis has been that the relationship of local industry structure to family structure, poverty, and income derives largely from the types of jobs provided within that structure.

At the same time, certain industry structures—namely, those with high proportions of employment in maintenance activities such as health, primary and secondary schools, social services, and personal services—may reflect economies lacking viability, i.e., economies that are largely dependent on transfers. At this level, the relationship of local industry structure to family structure and poverty results not from the poor quality of local jobs, but from the lack of jobs. Moreover, the lack of jobs would be especially high for men. In nonmetropolitan North Dakota, for example, 79 percent of the jobs in health, education, and social services were held by women, according to the 2000 Census of Population. Women held only 37 percent of jobs in the rest of the state's nonmetropolitan economy.

This contextual relationship may explain why several county-level studies have found the ratio of public sector to total employment to correlate with poverty (e.g., Lobao and Schulman 1991; Lichter and McLaughlin 1995), even though public sector employment is not associated with poverty at the householder level (Lichter et al. 1994). It may also explain why Albrecht et al. (2000), whose measure of service-sector employment is heavily weighted by community maintenance activities, found stronger relationships of county services employment to single parenthood and poverty than other studies. Cook and Mizer (1994) included all public-sector services (including public health and local schools) under government, and government counties had the largest proportion of single-female-headed households and the highest poverty of all their economic types. These patterns suggest that the viability of the local economy has been perhaps more central than the types of jobs generated by local industrial structures in determining where rural poverty rates are high.

Given the decline in manufacturing in many areas, the fall in farm incomes, and the continuing problems in forestry and mining, one of the issues for analysts of the 1980s was whether rural areas in general were developing marginal economies. As I discuss at the end of the chapter, the 1990s presented a different context, with renewed economic growth and declines, not increases, in poverty. This different context should allow rural sociologists to better separate out the different contributions of local industry structures, economic growth and decline, and household attributes for community and household economic viability. McLaughlin et al. (1999) studied change in the prevalence of female-headed households in rural counties, which incorporates local changes in both overall number and types of jobs, pointing us to the type of analysis that will be required.

Household Strategies

Rural sociology has a long history of looking at household economic strategies, much of it concerned with off-farm employment (e.g., Simpson, Wilson, and Young 1988). In the 1990s, concern about a persistent lack of jobs in some rural areas and industrial transformation in others prompted research on household strategies to increase income or reduce expenses outside of formal wage and salary jobs. Inspired by theorists such as Mingione (1991), who emphasized the importance of looking at all reciprocal relationships (not just market relationships), this chapter argues that one cannot understand how people in rural America make a living by focusing exclusively on formal employment.

Three types of economic strategies aside from regular jobs have been identified: subsistence activities or self-provisioning (e.g., hunting, fishing, gardening); household maintenance (e.g., money-saving activities such as doing ones own repairs, canning); and informal economy work (e.g., odd jobs, mowing lawns, haircutting) that involves pay or exchange. Although there are exceptions (e.g., Brown, Xiu, and Toth 1998), most research has focused on the informal economy.

The term "informal economy" was introduced to U.S. sociology by Portes and Sassen-Koob (1987), but originated in analyses of Third World urban labor markets in the 1970s. For many, including Portes and Sassen-Koob, the emphasis has been on the informal economy as a means for owners to avoid regulation and taxation, as in urban "sweatshops." For others, including most rural sociologists, the emphasis has been on the informal economy as a means for households to augment income or get by with less income.

Research in this vein has concentrated on the poor (e.g., Fitchen 1981; Duncan 1992) or on communities plagued by economic hardship (Campbell, Spencer, and Amonkra 1993; Nelson 1999), including American Indian communities (Pickering 2000). While the expectation has been that informal work, which may involve exchange as well as pay, is largely confined to people who otherwise have a hard time making ends meet, recent surveys in Pennsylvania (Jensen, Cornwall, and Findeis 1995), Kentucky (Tickamyer and Wood 1998), and Vermont (Nelson 1999) suggest that work outside one's main job is a much broader phenomenon (see also Parker 1997 on second jobs). In line with earlier work by British sociologists (e.g., Pahl 1985), Nelson (1999) found that, in fact, households that are better off gain the most from secondary activities. They can have the capital to establish side businesses. When households have poor regular jobs, then other work also tends to be low pay—often in personal services. This may reflect in part their lack of skills (Brown and Kulcsar 2001). The informal economy does not diminish inequalities, it increases them. At the same time, these activities appear to be economically more critical to those living on the margin (Jensen et al. 1995). The research has shown that, particularly for better off households, this type of activity is important for far more than economic gains (see especially Hinrichs 1998 on maple syrup production). Indeed, at times, economic gain is a minor motivation.

This new research area has proved difficult, and to date much of it has been exploratory. Survey responses have varied considerably depending on whether the survey was conducted by telephone or face-to-face (Nelson 1999), and on the wording and formatting of the questions (Tickamyer and Wood 1998). Respondents are reluctant to report some informal work, as the activities are unofficial and sometimes illegal. Other work may be unreported because respondents consider it as helping out neighbors, even though they receive compensation. The research has been largely confined to small, purposefully selected areas and often to particular types of households. Little attention has been given to who in the family does informal work or how much it contributes to household welfare. Finally, self-provisioning and household maintenance activities are relatively neglected in this body of work.

The interweaving of the social and economic aspects of informal work, however, may be a more sociologically interesting avenue to pursue than the exact amount of informal work that is carried out and by whom. In their study of Hungarian towns, Brown and Kulcsar (2001) found that households were less involved in exchange with other households when they were relatively poor and when they were socially isolated—feeling that they had no one to turn to in times of need. This sense of isolation is exactly what poorer families felt in Naples' (1994) case study of small, declining Iowa towns. Duncan's (1999) comparisons of three communities facing economic hardship show that social isolation is not endemic to low-income households, but in part a community outcome, dependent on the social rigidity of the local community. Naples' work suggests, however, that a loss of economic base may create social rigidity, even in areas that have taken pride in community inclusiveness.

This is an exciting new area of research. Even if it turns out that informal activities are a very small part of making a rural living, they may be a large part of producing and reproducing rural community life. The main hindrance is not a lack of interest or theory, but, as with much other rural sociology, a lack of appropriate information (Tickamyer 1996).

Looking Forward

Globalization and technological change have created considerable uncertainty for nations, regions, and communities over the past twenty years. For rural communities in the United States, the "Rural Renaissance" of the 1970s gave way in the 1980s to a loss of economic base, marginal local economies, and households struggling to survive on low-paying jobs and informal work. According to the Censuses of Population, over 60 percent of nonmetropolitan counties had higher poverty rates in 1989 than in 1979. Rural sociology spent much of the past decade trying to understand how communities and households, men and women, and different racial and ethnic groups were affected by and dealt with the troubled economic times. Central to this work was an understanding that change was having a very uneven impact. Some areas prospered even as others declined, and some households thrived as others lost their central livelihoods.

Recently released data from the 2000 Census of Population suggest that the 1990s were quite different for rural America—85 percent of nonmetropolitan counties had lower poverty in 1999 than a decade earlier. Reductions were both greater and more prevalent in counties with high poverty rates (over 20 percent) in 1990 than in areas with lower initial poverty. This turnaround occurred in metropolitan areas as well. As the number of people participating in welfare programs declined substantially in the late 1990s, it has become evident that these changes occurred largely because of changes in the job market. Slack and Jensen (2002) show significant reductions in rural underemployment in the late 1990s, particularly for African Americans.

What made the 1990s so different? Part of the difference lies simply in the number of jobs created. According to U.S. Bureau of Economic Analysis (2002) REIS data files, nonmetropolitan growth in jobs was nearly twice as high in the period 1989–99 (19 percent) than in the previous decade (10 percent), although the national rate of growth remained the same. While the growth in jobs may have drawn more people into the labor force and put pressure on wages, there was more to it than "trickle-down" growth (see Lyson et al. 1993). The federal minimum wage, seriously eroded by inflation in the 1980s, was raised substantially in the 1990s (Whitener and Parker 1999). Nonmetropolitan workers, especially, gained from these increases, as a relatively high proportion of them were working below the new minimum wage. Rises in the payments from the earned income tax credit program also played a potentially large role (Durst 1999). Both programs disproportionately affected service-sector workers and areas with high poverty. While these analyses are preliminary, it is possible that some of the most effective policy for rural development has not been policy targeted at rural areas but policy targeted at low-wage workers in a period of job growth.

The 1990s were not marked by a reversal in industrial transformation. Nonmetropolitan agricultural jobs continued to decline, if at a slower pace than in the 1980s. The number of manufacturing jobs increased overall, but at a much slower rate (4 percent) than jobs in general. The bulk of job growth continued to be in services. At least some of this growth stemmed from the development of new rural economic base services—prisons, casino resorts, and warehousing, for example. The decline in nonmetropolitan poverty in the 1990s suggests that it may be possible to build economically viable communities with viable households based around at least some service-sector industries.

These changes suggest a more nuanced industrial transformation paradigm; they do not necessarily make the paradigm less salient. Poverty rates remained over 20 percent in one out of five nonmetropolitan counties in 1999. Moreover, there are signs that the growth in jobs was not pandemic. While Jensen, Findeis, and Wang (2000) show that underemployment declined in the nonmetropolitan South between 1988 and 1998, they also show that labor force participation rates declined for white, Black, and Latino men in this region, and rose only for white and Latino women. While changes in survey methodology may have influenced these statistics, they suggest that more people, particularly more men, were opting out of formal work at the end of the decade (see also Fosset, Seibert, and Cready 1998).

Finally, the difference between the 1980s and 1990s is a challenge for ecological analysis. The pervasiveness of the change suggests that the broad forces tending to concentrate economic activity in urban areas in the 1980–90 period were much weaker from 1990–2000. While it should be possible to discern the nature of the growth in jobs, the real challenge is to develop an understanding of the unevenness of rural growth in jobs over time—why the 1970s and 1990s were a boon to rural areas and the 1980s were a period of decline. Only then will we be able to get a sense of what may lie ahead in the current decade.

11

Who Benefits from Economic Restructuring?

Lessons from the Past, Challenges for the Future

William W. Falk and Linda M. Lobao

The Process of Economic Restructuring and its Consequences for Rural America

The social science research on economic restructuring is large and diverse. Economic restructuring first received widespread attention in the post-1970s period, as analysts tried to explain the deindustrialization of northern manufacturing cities (Bluestone and Harrison 1982), but rural areas were not entirely overlooked (Summers et al. 1976; Singlemann 1978). Since then, "economic restructuring" has evolved into a shorthand expression for a variety of economic shifts, with the consequence that the term is often criticized for its overuse and vague meaning. To conceptualize economic restructuring, we build from research in sociology, rural sociology, and geography. Our discussion draws particularly from the critical political economy tradition, a conceptual perspective that spans each of the disciplines and offers a general framework from which to understand spatial and temporal changes in U.S. society (Aglietta 1979; Gordon et al. 1994; Lobao 1990; Peck 1996). In the social science literature, economic restructuring is generally seen to involve three sets of processes: first, changes in economic structure or industries, firms, and jobs in both the nonfarm and farm sectors; second, shifts in social relationships or long-standing patterns of institutionalized arrangements between employers, workers, government, and citizens; and finally, because economic restructuring has been spatially uneven, changes in the fortunes of people and places across regions and locales (Falk and Lyson 1988; Lobao 1990; Peck 1996). In addition, processes involving economic structure, social relationships, and space vary by historical period and by urban/rural location.

Economic restructuring is an important rural social issue for several reasons. First, restructuring has a major impact on American economic and social well-being. Changes in economic well-being, such as earnings, income, and employment, are among the most direct consequences of economic restructuring. In turn, changes in economic well-being are known to affect social well-being indicators, such as physical and mental health status; social disorganization (e.g., teenage fertility, substance abuse, and crime); quality and quantity of local public services, infrastructure, and housing; and environmental preservation. Second, economic restructuring imposes disproportionately harmful consequences for rural populations. Rural areas tend to be more vulnerable than urban areas to the detrimental effects of economic restructuring owing to their less diverse industrial structures, lower household incomes, and human capital attributes such as lower educational attainment. In the next two sections, we further describe the processes and consequences of economic restructuring. We focus primarily on rural/urban differences, and on consequences captured by economic well-being indicators, such as earnings, income, and employment. In general, social scientists expect that deterioration of a population's income and employment opportunities will jeopardize these extra-economic aspects of public well-being.

While we limit most discussion to generalizations about the rural and urban publics at large, such generalizations need to be tempered, where possible, by considering the extensive diversity within the rural category and within rural populations, not just as they compare with metropolitan populations. That is, there is variance within rural areas as well as between rural and urban areas. For example, nonmetropolitan people residing in counties adjacent to metropolitan counties tend to have better socioeconomic conditions than their more remote rural neighbors. Region of the country is another source of diversity, with the rural South still lagging behind other regions. Rural people are also differentiated by class, gender, race, and ethnicity; those higher in the stratification order generally have better employment opportunities and experience less deleterious effects of economic restructuring. Finally, rural people are not the only ones whose residential location jeopardizes their life chances. Comparisons of people living in remote rural areas with those at the urban core reveal striking similarities in terms of poorer economic conditions (Brown and Hirschl 1995).To understand the uneven consequences of economic restructuring, it is useful to examine three distinct stages of change since the post–World War II period. Scholars have produced a body of work on restructuring in each of these periods. The first stage, often termed the postwar "Fordist" period, extended from 1945 to the early 1970s, and is characterized by economic growth. The second stage, which lasted from the 1970s into the 1990s, is one of Fordist decline, or deindustrialization and restructuring. The third and present stage, which began in the 1990s, is a period of transformation that moves toward a new stage of capitalism. To contemporary observers, it may seem that each of these three decades had its own unique attributes; however, for us—and others casting a historical framework—these decades each constitute a coherent "era" during which widespread structural changes occurred in both rural and urban economies.

For each of these eras, one thing is certain—we know much more about urban populations than rural ones. Indeed, social scientists whose starting point is national-level restructuring usually fail to extend their inquiry to rural areas. Rural sociologists examine restructuring mainly by focusing on internal, rural-specific issues such as nonmetropolitan industrialization and farm structural change. Thus, to understand the fate of rural people and places in different periods of restructuring, one has to extrapolate downward from the national, urban-oriented literature and to generalize upward from rural-specific studies. We attempt to do this by drawing from the national and rural-specific literatures to piece together a portrayal of economic restructuring processes and consequences for rural well-being over time.

The Postwar Fordist Growth Period and Its Consequences for Rural Americans

Social scientists use the term "Fordism" to describe the historical pattern of U.S. development from about 1900 to the early 1970s. In this period, development was characterized by mass production industries, mass consumption markets, rapid national economic growth, and rising real earnings (Aglietta 1979; Gordon et al. 1982, 1994). Most research on Fordism focuses on its later stage, the period following World War II through the early 1970s, known as "postwar Fordism." We begin our discussion here as well.

Research on postwar Fordism denotes a distinct economic structure with accompanying social relationships and related spatial patterns. Researchers stress the importance of manufacturing employment in creating conditions for well-remunerated workers, relatively high family incomes, declining income inequality, and a strong middle class (Aglietta 1979; Gordon et al. 1982, 1994). Postwar manufacturing was based on consumer durables, and its wage levels helped create self-sustaining, effective national demand. Manufacturing facilitated unionization and helped drive up wages in other employment sectors as well. Since manufacturing is considered the leading sector of this period, some note the need to distinguish further within manufacturing. For example, Gordon et al. (1982, 1994) conceptualize a core sector of mainly durable manufacturing industries with large firms in concentrated markets, and a peripheral sector of nondurable manufacturing industries with small firms in competitive markets. Employees in core-sector manufacturing benefited from stronger union power and shared in oligopoly profits to a greater extent than those in peripheral manufacturing. Historically, core employment has been more predominant in urban areas, while peripheral employment has been more prevalent in rural areas (e.g., Falk and Lyson 1988).

Institutional factors worked in tandem with manufacturing to foster aggregate growth during this period. The structure of occupations, protected by unions and professional associations, served to reward seniority, educational attainment, and acquired skills. Strong workplace organizations not only benefited occupational incumbents, they also gave the U.S. workforce as a whole political leverage to demand sharing of economic surplus. The postwar period to the 1970s was also an era of Keynesian state policies. Capital accumulation expanded and economic benefits filtered down to workers and their families. This was made possible by a stable institutional environment facilitated by collective bargaining arrangements and relatively high levels of federal support for citizen welfare coupled with expenditures to stimulate demand.

Social scientists see the economic structure and institutional patterns of postwar Fordism as having a distinct spatial pattern, a quality most developed in the northern urban manufacturing belt (Lobao et al. 1999; Peck 1996). Here, high quality core employment—particularly in durable manufacturing—combined with greater unionization and government support for public welfare to raise earnings and total family incomes while reducing poverty and the deleterious consequences of labor market downturns. Portrayals of postwar Fordism often result in overly generalized accounts that neglect gender and region. Research focuses on formal (paid and documented) male employment structures, assuming a one-wage-earner model of the family. Nationally, rates of labor force participation by women began to grow in the 1960s, but poor and particularly minority women have always engaged in income-generating activities both in the formal and informal sectors. Women's informal-sector labor consists of undocumented paid work or unpaid work in family businesses in both farm and nonfarm sectors. Research on Fordism also has centered on the urban manufacturing belt, obscuring how Fordism played out in rural areas and outside the North. Regions such as the South, for instance, were less likely to share in the postwar prosperity brought by core industries and unionization.

Postwar Fordism and Rural Areas

What were the fates of rural places and people during this postwar era? Rural areas served as agriculture and energy reserves that fueled the Fordist economy (Page and Walker 1991). They were also the location of choice for employers seeking to move manufacturing branch plants, particularly in peripheral industries with routinized production. Some plants relocated within the United States, especially to the South, while others moved outside the United States, often just across the border to Mexico (Falk and Lyson 1988, 1993). The industrialization of nonmetropolitan communities had mixed effects (Summers et al. 1976). Rural communities gained employment and population growth; however, inequality among some population segments often increased. Poorer, less educated people were least likely to benefit from new incoming jobs, while the best positions were often reserved for individuals recruited by employers from outside the community. Population growth tied to industrial relocation drove up housing costs, leaving the poor and elderly worse off (Ziebarth and Tigges 2003).

While social science portrayals of Fordism centered on manufacturing, the farm sector underwent dramatic restructuring in the post–World War II period. Farms grew larger and became more capital intensive. From 1940 to 1970, the average acreage per farm more than doubled. Gross sales and real estate values per farm expanded fourfold in constant dollars over this period (Lobao 1990). As technology replaced labor, the farm population went into precipitous decline. Almost one-quarter of all Americans lived on farms in 1940, but by 1970, this figure had declined to 4.7 percent. The combination of larger and fewer farms spurred out-migration, contributing to rural population loss. Net out-migration from rural areas continued throughout the postwar period into the 1970s. As part-time farming and large-scale, industrialized farming increased, national farming patterns moved further away from the Jeffersonian family farm ideal.

Studies during this period found that industrialized farms had a number of detrimental effects on rural socioeconomic well-being, compared to family farms, a hypothesis first suggested by Walter Goldschmidt (1978). In brief, where industrial farms predominated, incomes tended to be lower, poverty rates and unemployment higher, and community services poorer (for an overview of related studies, see Lobao 1990). The mechanization of cotton production in the 1950s, combined with farm restructuring trends, adversely affected southern rural African Americans. Their historical trend of out-migration from the rural South continued, but small farm failures resulted in precipitous declines in Black land ownership. For those who remained in the South, this meant they lost the social, economic, and political power that land ownership confers in rural communities (Beauford 1986). Government institutions played a role in restructuring rural areas during the Fordist period in two significant ways. First, social programs expanded in line with the Keynesian-oriented, Great Society agenda. These programs targeted individuals and families affected by economic instability in both urban and rural areas. Second, farm income support programs continued, with little change. These served several interests, including large commercial farmers, the generally urban-based manufacturers that supplied inputs and consumer durables to these farmers, and urban employers in their desire for low-cost food (De Janvry, Runsten, and Sadoulet 1987). As this study and others have noted, farm programs were the nation's de facto rural development policy, as there was no coherent, formal policy aimed at improving the well-being of rural Americans. In practice, the growth of large farms and the loss of traditional family farms, in conjunction with the lack of a meaningful policy aimed at rural restructuring, functioned to "de-develop" many communities, eroding their population base and increasing socioeconomic inequality (De Janvry et al. 1987).

Economic Crisis and Its Consequences for Rural Americans: The 1970s and 1980s

Social scientists recognize the period beginning in and following the 1970s as ushering in national changes in industrial structure and institutional relationships that disrupted the Fordist system.[1] Broadly, manufacturing employment experienced steep declines while the lower-wage service sector expanded. The institutional structure of capital/labor and state/citizen relationships, which regulated the Fordist economy and assured rising earnings, began to break down. The bargaining power of workers vis-à-vis employers, manifest foremost in unionization, declined. The role of government also began to shift and concern with Keynesian demand management and support for citizen welfare diminished. Social scientists argue that these shifts in industrial employment and long-standing institutional

1. Social science frameworks see the causes of post-1970 restructuring in light of their distinct conceptual emphases. Some place emphasis on class struggle and political innovation, particularly the growing strength of unions and citizens' demand for increased social welfare, which severely stressed postwar social structure (see Gordon et al. 1994). Others tend to focus more on shifts in national and global production and consumption linkages that became disrupted particularly with the beginning of the 1973 oil crisis and the end of the Vietnam War (see Aglietta 1979).

relationships reduced labor's share of surplus and earnings, increased income inequality, and shrank the relative size of the middle class, although many continue to debate this topic (Harrison and Bluestone 1988; Lobao et al. 1999).[2] The restructuring of the Fordist system was manifest first in the urban manufacturing belt. In some sense, the urban misfortunes of the 1970s benefited rural areas, as industrial restructuring and social upheavals in northern cities were a source of urban-to-rural migration that partly fueled the nonmetropolitan population turnaround of the decade (Fuguitt et al. 1989; Brown and Wardwell 1980; Brown et al. 1993). Rural officials attracted urban-based and other new firms by touting their union-free and often tax-free locations, as well as their work forces' low bargaining power, "work ethic," and willingness to accept lower wages (see Rosenfeld 1988; Falk and Lyson 1988). Japanese automotive plants (e.g., Honda, Mitsubishi, and Nissan) found the rural Midwest particularly attractive for these reasons, while German manufacturers (e.g., BMW and Mercedes Benz) were more likely to locate in the South.[3] While the energy crisis adversely affected urban manufacturing in the 1970s, it stimulated the rural mining and oil industries (Johnson 1999). Finally, the 1970s brought increased global demand for U.S. farm products, rising real values for farmland, and widespread farm prosperity. Thus, while many urban areas stagnated, the rural economy boomed, and the earnings and income gap between metropolitan and nonmetropolitan areas began to close. In 1969 nonmetropolitan workers earned 76.4 cents for every dollar that metropolitan workers earned, which increased in real terms to 80.3 cents to the dollar in 1980 (Gale and McGranahan 2001). Correspondingly, the per capita income gap between metropolitan and nonmetropolitan people decreased, and the nonmetropolitan poverty rate declined from 20 percent in 1967 to 13 percent by the late 1970s (Rural Sociological Society Task Force on Persistent Rural Poverty 1993).

The 1980s brought a reversal of fortunes for rural people. As the energy crisis abated, the mining and oil industries declined. The migration of urban manufacturing firms to rural locations slowed. The farm economy went into a protracted crisis as farmers faced a worldwide recession that reduced demand for farm exports. Low farmland values eroded equity, which, coupled with lower farm incomes, made it difficult to service the large debt that many farmers accrued in the expansionist 1970s. Midwestern farmers were

2. Nationally, real earnings growth began to slow by the mid-1960s, then fell from 1973 until the 1990s. Real median family income growth has slowed similarly since 1973. Income inequality has increased gradually since the late 1960s and more dramatically since the early 1980s.

3. Toyota, a Japanese company, and Saturn, an American manufacturer, also located in the South.

particularly hard hit by these changes, and about 30 percent of them faced serious financial problems by 1989 (Lasley et al. 1995). By the time this crisis du jour arrived, past epochs of restructuring had already taken a toll on the nation's small farms. Starting with a smaller base, the relative farm decline in the 1980s (about 12 percent) was actually smaller than in the booming 1970s (about 17 percent) and previous postwar decades (Lobao and Meyer 2001).The impact of farm and nonfarm restructuring in the 1980s is clear when considering indicators of socioeconomic well-being. In contrast to the 1970s, there was net out-migration from rural areas during the 1980s (Johnson 1999:3). Rural workers' earnings slipped relative to their urban counterparts: by 1989, nonmetropolitan workers earned only 74 cents for every dollar earned by metropolitan workers, decreasing from 80.3 cents at the start of the decade (Gale and McGranahan 2001) and dipping below what they had earned in the 1970s. Rural unemployment rates tended to rise relative to urban areas during the 1980s, a significant factor contributing to the widening income gap between metropolitan and nonmetropolitan populations. As a corollary, the poverty rate for the nonmetropolitan population also rose relative to the past decade and relative to the metropolitan poverty rate (Rural Sociological Society Task Force on Persistent Rural Poverty 1993). As one would expect, these effects occurred unevenly across the country. The farm crisis hit midwestern farming-dependent communities and related agricultural industries particularly hard, and these areas experienced large population losses (Lasley et al. 1995).[4]

One latent consequence of economic restructuring is that it may benefit women insofar as it opens new employment opportunities, as happened during the 1980s. Rural economic sectors that traditionally employed men (e.g., mining, farming, and manufacturing) declined, while service sectors expanded relatively, creating opportunities for women at the same time that households needed additional wage earners to make ends meet. Over the decade, labor force participation by nonmetropolitan women increased relative to the past and relative to urban women. In 1980, 49.8 percent of metropolitan and 43.9 percent of nonmetropolitan women over the age of twenty-five were in the labor force. By 1994, these rates increased to 58.9 percent for metropolitan women and 54.8 percent for nonmetropolitan women (Rogers 1997). Indeed, the increasing number of women entering the labor force accounted for almost all of the nonmetropolitan labor force growth in the 1980s (Rogers 1997). The earnings gap between men and

---

4. Jane Smiley's (1992) book, *A Thousand Acres,* based in part on her students' diaries, produced a particularly gripping account of the disruptive and destructive affect on farm families and communities in the early 1980s.

women also narrowed over the decade, but this was partly a function of the decline in men's real earnings, which was more pronounced in urban areas. The restructuring of the 1980s had an especially significant impact on farm women. In contrast to the popular belief that women increased on-farm work activities to cope with the farm crisis of the 1980s, midwestern women appear to have responded mainly by increasing off-farm work relative to farm men and relative to the past (Lobao and Meyer 1995).

In the 1980s, federal government policy with regard to rural people continued much as in past decades. The "accumulation" and "concentration" aspects of large-scale capitalism—what some political economists have called "monopoly capital" (Braverman 1974)—came increasingly to characterize American agriculture. For example, small farms (defined by the USDA as those with gross sales less than $50,000) make up nearly 75 percent of the nation's farms but account for only 7 percent of farm sales, while the top 3.6 percent of farms (those with sales of over $500,000) account for more than 50 percent of all sales (Lobao and Meyer 2001; see also Sommer et al. 1998; Lyson 2002). Support for commercial agriculture was paramount, and there was a massive government bailout for farmers and agricultural lenders as a consequence of the crisis.

Farm policy continued as the de facto rural development policy (Marshall 2001). In contrast, as with the urban poor, the nonfarm rural poor were faced with a less generous social welfare system. Under the New Federalism of the 1980s, federal social programs were increasingly devolved to state and local governments. Indeed, some social scientists have argued that such devolution is, in effect, a dismantling effort under the guise of increasing local accountability (Kodras 1997). To adapt to the declining federal role in community development as well as the precarious conditions of 1980s, localities increasingly assumed economic development activities. Much of the social science discourse about rural development shifted to local-level strategies, rather than considering an expanded role for the federal government (see Barkley 1993). And the decades-old emphasis on "human capital" shifted dramatically to "social capital," especially as an empowerment strategy for rural communities (Flora and Flora 1996).

Post-1990 and Beyond: A New Stage of Development for Rural America?

From about 1994 onward, the nation and much of rural America began to recover from the downturns of the previous decades. Social scientists are somewhat divided as to whether or not the post-1990 period constitutes a fundamentally new stage of economic development. Some stress that the United States has entered a protracted restructuring phase in which the basic national industrial structure and institutional arrangements remain, but with diminishing social benefits (Gordon et al. 1994). Other social scientists see a new phase of capitalism, and debate extensively how this might be characterized—e.g., post-Fordism, flexible production, flexible accumulation (Peck 1996). While the popular media championed the vision of a "new economy," one driven by high technology and telecommunications, many are now rethinking this issue. As a recent *New York Times* article notes: "After the collapse of the dot-com bubble, a steady retreat in technology stocks this year and an old-fashioned recession surely under way, the new economy theory requires some revision, to put it mildly. Its biggest problem came first—the word new" (Lohr 2001, C3).

While analysts popularly proclaim a "new" stage of development, much of the old economy remains in place, nowhere more so than in rural America. For most Americans, the consequences of restructuring in the 1990s simply perpetuated many of the trends from the 1970s and 1980s discussed above. Nationally, income inequality continued to increase and even the incremental increases in median family income that occurred in the mid-1990s ceased by the end of the decade. The new century has ushered in some key shifts in industrial structure and institutional arrangements that have important implications for the well-being of rural people.

First, globalization and trade policy are affecting rural areas to a greater extent than in the past. Globalization particularly affects rural industrial structure, because rural areas are more likely to specialize in peripheral manufacturing sectors—such as routine manufacturing (e.g., textiles, apparel, furniture, metal working, rubber, plastics) and value-added manufacturing (e.g., food, wood, leather) that face global competition and whose production processes can more easily be moved partially or fully offshore. Many of these industries had negative earnings growth in the late 1990s (Gale and McGranahan 2001).

A second set of shifts involves industrial changes that have contributed to spatial polarization by benefiting urban areas to a greater extent than rural areas. Durable manufacturing was increasingly revitalized through the use of flexible production techniques and high technology. Large, core-sector firms and their heavily unionized work forces have remained primarily in urban areas. Although large firms have shed labor, they still offer higher wages and benefits than smaller peripheral firms (Harrison 1994). High technology manufacturing is more concentrated in urban areas, and had a particularly fast rate of earnings growth in the late 1990s (Gale and McGranahan 2001; Glasmeier and Howland 1995). Producer services (e.g., communications, finance, insurance, business and professional services) also contributed substantially to national growth in the 1990s. But this is another sector that is concentrated in urban areas, and its earnings grew much faster in metropolitan than nonmetropolitan areas in the 1990s.

Third, institutional changes that accompany the ongoing technological revolution and processes of globalization, particularly the continued decentralization of federal government functions, affect the ability of rural areas to respond to new economic changes. Under decentralization, state and local governments were to receive less aid from the federal government. Federal government income transfers, which rural people depend upon to a greater degree than urban people, slowed over the 1990s (Cook 2000). Important social programs, such as Aid to Families with Dependent Children (AFDC), were changed from open-ended, matching grants to block grants, often adding requirements that local governments engage in grant-writing to secure funds (see Chapter 19 in this volume). Temporary Assistance to Needy Families (TANF) replaced AFDC after 1996, and this program was devolved to the state level. By the end of the 1990s, sixteen states, including some of the nation's largest (e.g., California, Michigan, New York, Pennsylvania, and Texas), had further devolved welfare administration to counties. Sharp metropolitan/nonmetropolitan differences were evident, especially in the capacity of county officials to enact these programs (Kraybill and Lobao 2001). Nonmetropolitan counties exhibited less administrative capacity to secure needed resources from upper levels of government than their metropolitan counterparts. For example, nonmetropolitan counties employed fewer staff grant writers and had access to fewer resources to secure private-sector investment, such as economic development staff and funding. Employment programs developed by nonmetropolitan governments reported much less success finding jobs for former welfare recipients (White et al. 2003). There were also large gaps between nonmetropolitan counties, with those more remote from metropolitan areas having much less administrative capacity and fewer resources. With regard to farm programs, however, farmers' interests were generally preserved. The 1996 Farm Bill, designed to reduce government intervention, was pronounced a failure as massive government bailouts continued to prop up farm income shortfalls.

On balance, the period following the 1990s indicates a continued urban/rural gap in the quality of industrial structure and institutional arrangements. It is not surprising that many of the patterns of spatial inequality noted in previous decades persist. Rural areas continue to lag behind urban areas on many indicators (Gale and McGranahan 2001).

Between 1991 and 1998, earnings per nonfarm job increased by 0.6 percent in nonmetropolitan areas compared to 1.1 percent in metropolitan areas, and the earnings gap between nonmetropolitan and metropolitan Americans widened. Despite the 1990s expansion, more than a quarter of wage and salary workers aged twenty-five and older earned full-time equivalent wages below the poverty threshold for a family of four in 1999 (Cook and Gibbs 2000). In 1998, nonmetropolitan poverty rates remained higher (14.3 percent, compared to 12.3 percent in metropolitan areas), while median family income was lower (on average $11,000 less per family than for metropolitan residents), although over the course of the 1990s, the differences in these indicators began to narrow (Economic Research Service 2000a).

Among rural population subgroups, race and gender differences in poverty rates persisted. In 1998, nonmetropolitan African Americans, Latinos, Native Americans, and women living alone all manifested poverty rates at around 30 percent, and 36.5 percent of nonmetropolitan single-female-headed families remained in poverty (Economic Research Service 2000b). There were also net migration gains in nonmetropolitan America, but not at the level of the 1970s turnaround (Johnson 1999).[5] Regionally, many of the same historical patterns persist. The nonmetropolitan South continued to have the nation's highest poverty rates: in 1998, 53.5 percent of the nation's nonmetropolitan poor resided in the South (Economic Research Service 2000b). And in contrast to overall nonmetropolitan net migration gains, two regions had net migration losses, the Mississippi Delta—reflecting long-standing historical inequalities—and the farming dependent regions in the Great Plains—due to the more recent effects of the farm crisis (see Chapter 1 in this volume).

Conclusion

The post-1990s period suggests that rural America continues to be characterized by social and spatial inequalities, a legacy of the previous rounds of restructuring outlined in this chapter. On the one hand, this suggests a great deal of continuity with the past. On the other hand, given the broader national trend of increased inequality and the shifts accompanying industrial

5. Of potential significance is the marked increase in African American return migration to the South. While about 90 percent of this is to urban areas, the 10 percent going to rural areas reflects a population that is disproportionately older, female, and better educated than the local indigenous population, but like them, reflects historical ties to the area and land ownership (see Falk et al. 2002).

and institutional forces noted above, polarization not only between rural and urban people but within rural America is likely to intensify.

At least two changes are contributing to increased divergence among rural communities. The first is the expanded influence of urban economies and their integration with adjacent nonmetropolitan hinterlands, which is further expanding "metropolitan regions" as functional economic units. As we noted, nonmetropolitan adjacent communities historically have had better socioeconomic conditions than their more remote counterparts. This is even the case for historically African American counties, often the poorest of the poor in rural America (Rankin and Falk 1991). We believe this gap will only intensify as urban economic processes increasingly drive the restructuring of adjacent nonmetropolitan counties. Indeed, this likelihood is enhanced considerably in light of the massive development in some suburban counties that has led to the notion of "edge cities"—places with their own unique economic forces and spatial arrangements (Molotch et al. 2000). Second, while the fortunes of rural communities adjacent to metropolitan areas are increasingly driven by the development of their urban centers, more remote rural places are faced with the loss of their traditional industries and therefore their long-standing role in the national economy. More remote rural locales are adapting by carving out new niches in the national and, where possible, the global economy, although one consequence has been an even greater bifurcation in the fortunes of rural America. One set of strategies that many communities have employed involves capitalizing on consumption amenities, as opposed to production roles (Goe et al. 2003). Many rural places with natural amenities such as lakes and rivers, a pleasant climate, and mountains are the same places that have experienced net migration gains in the 1990s. Other rural communities have been successful in establishing "territorial consumption complexes" (Lobao et al. 2003), or what Ritzer (2001) has called "landscapes of consumption." Under this strategy the rural region itself serves as a marketing tool, legitimizing traditional products in the context of a presumed historical rural past. Many examples of these complexes are found around the country. New England employs the theme "Fall into New England" to highlight the region's foliage during the fall season. In the Midwest, areas that once specialized in pottery and glass draw a regional and sometimes national following, and are able to spin off related tourist industries. In the South, the beaches and the mountains are an adman's pitch for paying a visit. In the Southwest, working ranches become resorts and impoverished American Indian reservations become major sites for archaeological visits and shopping for crafts made (one presumes) by indigenous peoples. In the

West, it becomes axiomatic: the less densely populated, the more attractive for many tourists.

Communities that are least able to develop attractive consumption amenities are faced with a dilemma. Either they are left with no jobs or, alternatively, with jobs in businesses that provide minimal benefits and tend to stigmatize the community and hinder long-term development efforts (Kilborn 2001). Such industries include prisons, animal confinement operations, chicken, beef, or pork processing plants, and waste disposal facilities. Given such options, tourism may be the more favorable development strategy, but it obviously has social costs as well, as it changes the character of rural communities and typically fails to generate high quality employment. None of these options—neither tourism nor attracting less desirable industries—offers a solution for the loss of traditional employment sectors. To us, the situation is clear: the fortunes of remote rural communities are more at stake in the present period of development than ever before.

In this chapter, we have outlined the patterns of polarization between metropolitan and nonmetropolitan areas, between rural regions in different parts of the country, and within rural population subgroups. These patterns are the product of cumulative processes of restructuring that reshape economic conditions, institutional relationships, and the use of geographic space. We have also noted that the federal government has played a weak role in developing regional and spatially-based strategies to address the needs of rural Americans. Social scientists have increasingly recognized that divergence in socioeconomic well-being among populations results from the development path that Americans have chosen (Brown and Lee 1999). So who benefits from economic restructuring? Some do far more than others. Most predictably, the greatest benefits accrue to those who have benefited the most historically from other large economic transitions.

12

Commuting

A Good Job Nearby?

Leann M. Tigges and Glenn V. Fuguitt

With the increasing deconcentration of population and economic activities across the nation, rural and small-town America has become more and more interdependent with metropolitan areas. This process also has led to increased interdependence among nonmetropolitan counties, cities, and villages. Indeed, if it ever existed, the autonomous rural community is no longer with us. A major component of this interdependence is the separation between home and work.

Traveling a substantial distance to work appears to be increasing slightly over each census interval, as shown by the proportion of workers living in a county different from their place of work (from 19 percent in 1970 to 27 percent in 2000) and by the increased time spent traveling to work (the mean time in 2000 was twenty-four minutes, up from about twenty-two minutes in 1970 and 1980). Metropolitan/nonmetropolitan differences in these measures have not been large, though generally metropolitan residents appear to commute longer distances or spend more time commuting. Among nonmetropolitan and metropolitan residents alike, few people commute longer than an hour (So, Orazem, and Otto 2001).

The likelihood of travel from one's county of residence to work in another county is greater than expected in some parts of rural America. According to the U.S. Department of Agriculture (USDA 2002a), 381 nonmetropolitan counties had at least 40 percent of workers commuting to jobs in other counties in 1990. Nearly all of these "commuting counties" are in the South (65 percent) and Midwest (28 percent). The incidence of commuting can also be analyzed for cities, towns, or villages. According to analysis of 1990 census data, net out-commuting for nonmetropolitan incorporated places is the rule. Three-fourths of nonmetropolitan counties have at least 35 percent of working residents commute out of their towns or other places of residence (Aldrich, Beale, and Kassel 1997). Although there are some notable exceptions, in general, commuting rates are higher east of the Mississippi, where places are closer together and counties are smaller. Communities with high rates of out-commuting, serving mostly as residential centers or "bedroom communities," may face special challenges—an issue we take up in our concluding section.

In this chapter we look at commuting both as a community or macrolevel process and as an individual or microlevel process. We first consider the way commuting helps define community and labor market areas, and then discuss the role of commuting in the process of population deconcentration. Next we turn to social factors affecting individual commuting behaviors, with a discussion of three theoretical perspectives on commuting and employment opportunities for men, women, and minorities: spatial mismatch, spatial containment, and skills mismatch theories. Finally, we look at the consequences of commuting for the community and for the individual. Throughout the chapter, we point to areas where research is needed to address the special issues facing rural America.

Commuting Patterns and Flows: Helping to Define Spaces and Places

The entire area in and around a big city often has been viewed as an integrated social and economic system. In recognition of this, the U.S. government began to define and delineate metropolitan areas in 1950. Throughout most of the nation, whole counties have been one element of the definition. Counties with large urban cores are the basic components, but from the start there has been a question about including other counties nearby. Commuting patterns became an important criterion for including other counties beginning in 1960, when this information was first collected as part of the decennial census. Thus, some counties without a large city or a densely settled urban area have been designated as part of metropolitan areas because of their residents' commuting behavior.

Over time, more and more counties were designated "metropolitan," resulting in a continual loss of population and territory for nonmetropolitan America. As many as half of newly designated metropolitan counties since 1980 were not central counties, but instead shifted their designation as a result of the spread of commuting to and from nearby metropolitan areas. Although many nonmetropolitan counties are clearly in the metropolitan orbit, their levels of commuting or other forms of integration are not yet enough to trigger a change to metropolitan status.[1]

A political process created counties, but as the expansion of metropolitan areas shows, economic and labor market activities do not stop at county boundaries. This is true in rural America as well. In order to better capture the diversity of nonmetropolitan areas, the USDA Economic Research Service has grouped counties together into commuting zones. For 1990, 741 commuting zones were delineated. These commuting zones, developed without regard to population size, reflect the physical territory throughout which workers are matched to jobs. To generate a special 1990 Census Public Use Microdata Sample (PUMS-L) that identifies labor market areas in which individuals live and work, the commuting zones were aggregated into 394 labor market areas (LMAs) that met the Census Bureau's criterion of a 100,000 population minimum (Tolbert and Killian 1987; Tolbert and Sizer 1996). A similar file (PUMS-D) was created as part of the 1980 census. With the availability of commuting data for the smaller Census Block Groups from the 1990 and 2000 censuses, more precise delineations may soon be possible.

Deconcentration and Commuting

The importance of commuting extends well beyond its use for delineations of community, however conceived. Changes in commuting patterns should be associated with the shifts in the location of residences and employment that have received so much attention in recent years. The modulating patterns of nonmetropolitan population growth and decline have been labeled as the "population turnaround" of the 1970s, the 1980s "reversal," and the 1990s "rebound."[2]

The principal theoretical perspective used by sociologists to explain these trends has been termed "deconcentration" (Long 1981; Wardwell 1980). This perspective assumes that the movement and growth of the resident population in low-density settings is fueled by residential preferences for location amenities. These preferences are aided by transportation and communication improvements. The result is expanded community structures with more widespread commuting. An alternative perspective has

1. Recently, the Census Bureau has explored moving away from the use of county units, and commuting has formed a basis for delineating metropolitan areas with smaller geographic units (Census Block Groups) on an experimental basis (Morrill, Cromartie, and Hart 1999).
   2. For a discussion of these trends, see Fuguitt and Beale (1996) and Johnson (1999).

been termed "economic restructuring," which holds that the major force for population dispersal has been the shift in sources of employment to more remote locations. No doubt both processes are at work, but Frey (1987) and Renkow and Hoover (2000) have reported research contrasting the two perspectives and showing more support for the deconcentration explanation.

A careful look shows, however, that the empirical evidence for deconcentration is fraught with problems that need to be resolved. Although nonmetropolitan population trends varied widely between 1960 and 2000, parallel changes in residential preferences were not detectable (Brown et al. 1997), and commuting research has shown an unbroken increase in the importance of commuting over longer distances. Nor has there been a discernable deconcentration in commuting patterns over any period. Fuguitt (1991) examined the 1980 patterns (at the close of the turnaround) and concluded that commuting was predominantly toward larger places in the rural/urban hierarchy. Mohn (1997) confirmed these results through 1990. In further analysis for this chapter, we did find a slight increase between 1970 and 1990 in the proportion of nonmetropolitan-to-metropolitan commuters going to the smallest sized metropolitan areas (population less than 250,000), along with an increase in the proportion going to core counties of major metropolitan areas. The increase going to the smaller metropolitan areas in part reflects the spread of metropolitan areas, as larger nonmetropolitan cities expand and achieve metropolitan status. But the increased importance of movement into major metropolitan areas, which happened in both decades, is counter to any expectations regarding the deconcentration of employment.

The examination of nonmetropolitan commuting patterns must not be limited to a consideration of work in metropolitan areas. Between 1970 and 1990, only about half of the intercounty commuting by nonmetropolitan workers involved going to metropolitan areas. Consequently, a related question involves intercounty commuting to more urban counties, regardless of their metropolitan status. What is the likelihood that intercounty commuting will be to a county having a larger-sized place? Two-thirds of the nonmetropolitan-origin commutes were toward a more urban county, but this was true for only half of the metropolitan-origin commuting flows. Nonmetropolitan-origin commuting still appears to be rather different from metropolitan-origin commuting (Clemente and Summers 1975). Despite the 1970s rural turnaround and even the more recent rural rebound, the urban hierarchy is still alive and well, pulling nonmetropolitan resident commuters toward more urban settings.

Overall, this review of evidence supports a modification of the deconcentration perspective. Changes in commuting patterns are not associated with population trends over any decade. Instead, commuting is part of the infrastructure that makes population deconcentration possible, facilitating what may be rapid population shifts as a response to short-term changes in social and economic conditions.

With improved transportation and communications some nonmetropolitan residents who otherwise would have moved to more highly urbanized places for job opportunities may opt instead to stay put and commute to work. Similarly, metropolitan residents may decide that they can move to a nonmetropolitan setting for quality-of-life reasons while continuing to work in the city. Within dual-earner households these migration/commuting decisions may be complex as couples seek to maximize flexibility and security (Green 1997; Hoffmeister 2002). Although these are familiar phenomena, we could find little recent empirical research to document their importance or nature in nonmetropolitan America. It is particularly difficult, of course, to estimate the extent to which people choose to commute instead of moving. It is more feasible to examine the extent to which people migrate between metropolitan and nonmetropolitan locales, but continue to work in the residence category of their former residence. In 1980, at the end of the turnaround period, the number of migrants from metropolitan to nonmetropolitan areas almost equaled the number moving in the other direction. Of those moving from nonmetropolitan to metropolitan areas, only about 5 percent continued to work in nonmetropolitan areas. Most of these migrants must have been attracted by the jobs available in metropolitan areas. Of those moving from metropolitan to nonmetropolitan areas, on the other hand, about 20 percent worked in metropolitan areas. This percentage may be considered surprisingly low, but these data are for nonmetropolitan areas as a whole, and so include migrants to remote rural areas. Nevertheless, this percentage is low enough to suggest that local job availability is more important than sometimes assumed for these metropolitan-to-nonmetropolitan migrants. Postmigration employment is an important area for further research.

Commuting Behaviors: The Importance of Social Factors

In explaining individual decision-making concerning residence and work, economists often describe the logic of rural residence as trading lower housing costs for the lower wages of jobs in nonmetropolitan areas. Commuting to larger places, often to metropolitan counties, gives rural residents access to higher wages and a broader range of opportunities. But commuting costs money and time, and often creates stress.[3] The major factors explaining who commutes and how far they commute are often associated with the abilities to bear these costs given the benefits of commuting (So et al. 2001). Economists would expect workers, regardless of where they live, to evaluate potential economic benefits against costs; however, they generally acknowledge that people differentially value certain amenities or lifestyle considerations, such as small town safety or the pleasantness of a bucolic rural setting. These values influence commuting decisions, but are exogenous factors in an economic model.

In contrast to this model of economic rationality, sociologists and social geographers believe that noneconomic factors should be central to any model of commuting behaviors. Noneconomic factors generate local labor-market areas of different sizes for social groups defined by race, ethnicity, gender, and class (Hanson and Pratt 1992; Peck 1989). Thus, the metropolitan or commuting zones delineated by overall patterns of commuting may greatly overestimate the actual area accessible to certain social categories of workers. Their local labor markets may be constrained by their access to job information or reliable transportation and by employers' hiring practices. If the kinds of jobs appropriate for workers' skills or needs are not located within their local labor markets, they are unlikely to be adequately employed. The decentralization of manufacturing employment into some nonmetropolitan areas is but one part of the economic restructuring that centralized retail and service functions simultaneously. Thus, economic restructuring may have shrunk the local labor market for some occupational groups but expanded it for others (MacDonald and Peters 1994a).

These arguments about the socially constituted nature of local labor markets can help frame our understanding of the variations in rural commuting behaviors. For example, in his study of commuting from nonmetropolitan places, Fuguitt (1991) reports that women and individuals with higher income or more education are more likely to commute up the urban hierarchy than are men and those with lower income or less education. These gender differences may be related to spatial differences in the gender gap in wages and employment opportunities. Nonmetropolitan women could be expected to have a greater incentive than men to work in metropolitan areas because nonmetropolitan jobs provide lower returns to women's human capital (McLaughlin and Perman 1991), are more gender segregated (Cotter et al. 1996), are less likely to provide adequate hours or wages (Jensen et al. 1999), and often fail to provide health benefits (Peters

3. A study by White and Rotton (1998) found that commuters had less tolerance for frustration than noncommuters, and that commuting raised pulses and systolic blood pressure.

and MacDonald 1994). Despite these differences however, rural women, like their urban counterparts, on average work closer to home than do men.

Other research shows that commuting costs are not always offset by higher earnings—gender and residence are important factors. Howell and Bronson (1996) find that the wage benefit for commuting tends to "wash out" in models that control for human capital and regional location. Moreover, women living in nonmetropolitan counties with small urban places lose eighty-nine dollars in annual wages for each minute spent per day commuting, net of human capital and demographic characteristics, while the negative effect on men in this residential group is about half that amount. Men and women living in completely rural counties, however, receive a small but significant boost in earnings from commuting. The rurality of the area and the gender of the worker are important social factors shaping the economic consequences of commuting.

Our point here is that commuting is not merely a matter of traversing space to get to a job; instead, space mediates the labor market relationship, creating barriers for some but not others. Social scientists have emphasized the ways that social distinctions and relationships, especially those involving gender, race, and social class, affect the probabilities and patterns of commuting. These issues clearly emerge as we consider the relevance of theoretical perspectives for commuting by rural workers. In the following review, we discuss in turn the spatial mismatch, spatial entrapment or containment, and skills mismatch theories. These theories were developed to explain patterns of and barriers to commuting across large metropolitan areas, especially by minorities and women. Although these theories have seldom been applied to the study of rural commuting, we suggest some ways they could inform rural research on the ways spatial patterns of economic restructuring have affected different categories of workers.

Theoretical Perspectives on Commuting

The Spatial Mismatch Hypothesis

Originally, the spatial mismatch hypothesis was used to explain the employment disadvantage of inner-city African Americans (Kain 1968; 1992). According to this theory, the movement of lower-skilled jobs out of central cities spatially separated inner-city minority residents from the jobs appropriate to their skills. Unlike suburbanites, inner-city residents are unable to resolve this spatial mismatch because residential segregation limits their access to suburban housing markets and because they lack viable transportation options to the suburbs.

If the spatial mismatch applies to rural areas, the forces creating it would be quite different from the housing discrimination and employment deconcentration that generate this condition in urban America. Instead, we might look for persisting patterns of racial concentration and poverty and for patterns of economic restructuring that eliminate low-skill jobs. One rural region marked by these phenomena is the "Black Belt" of the deep South, where "runaway factories" from the "Rust Belt" avoided counties with high concentrations of African Americans (Colclough 1988). The spatial mismatch theory might help explain the fact that some counties in Mississippi and Alabama have lower than average rates of out-commuting from nonmetropolitan towns and places (Aldrich et al. 1997). These areas apparently lack jobs of sufficient quality to motivate commuting. Lack of public transportation and unreliable personal transportation reinforce the friction of distance in rural areas just as they do in the central city, but paternalistic employment relations and strict enforcement of racial and class privileges also may be important factors in creating a rural spatial mismatch in the Black Belt (Tomaskovic-Devey 1993).

One recent study used the spatial mismatch hypothesis to explain the labor market limitations faced by rural white women. MacDonald and Peters (1994b) argue that many rural white women hold low-wage jobs and thus, like lower-skilled inner-city residents, face limited payoffs for commuting. Although these women do not face racial discrimination in housing markets, higher priced housing in metropolitan areas may effectively restrict their ability to move closer to jobs. Further, although many rural women have access to private automobiles, the reliability of the vehicles may limit their commuting options. This study of commuting in four nonmetropolitan Iowa counties shows that differences in job rewards (specifically, receiving health insurance) and transportation resources are the most important determinants of these women's commuting decisions. Industrial sector employment is also related to the probability that rural women will commute to jobs in metropolitan locations, with the highest commuting rates associated with employment in manufacturing and related industries and in professional industries (MacDonald and Peters 1994b; Peters and MacDonald 1994).

The spatial mismatch theory has been criticized for neglecting gender differences in commuting (Thompson 1997) and for overemphasizing location, rather than skills, in labor market mismatches. The results of these criticisms are the spatial entrapment and skills mismatch theories, which we consider in turn.

The Spatial Entrapment Thesis

Developed to explain the shorter commutes of suburban women relative to suburban men, the spatial entrapment thesis holds that wives and mothers forgo the higher wages of the central business district in favor of local employment that allows them to more easily attend to their domestic responsibilities (Wyly 1998). Convenience comes at a price for women but not for men who have a larger job search area.[4]

Central to the spatial entrapment thesis is the idea that women's shorter work trips are a reflection of the segmented character of local labor markets (MacDonald 1999). The emphasis is not solely on gender differences in commute times but on the differences between women with various social and economic traits. Because of the gender division of domestic responsibilities, women with young children should be more spatially "contained" in their job search than other women. Employers who want to take advantage of this containment will locate their workplaces in the suburbs where many of these workers live. The data to support these ideas are equivocal in the urban literature (see MacDonald 1999) and generally absent in the rural literature. In their rural Iowa study, Peters and Mac-Donald (1994) find that, contrary to the containment thesis, younger women and those with children at home have longer work trips. However, if women's entrapment is seen as the result of their limited employment choices and the processes associated with occupational gender segregation, the Iowa study finds some support in that women in more feminized occupational sectors have shorter work trips. More research comparing the commuting behaviors of rural women with rural men and with urban or suburban women is needed to assess the applicability of the spatial containment theory beyond the suburbs. This research would require data on family and household responsibilities of workers, as well as on the gender segregation of their occupations.

The Skills Mismatch Theory

Debates over the validity of the spatial mismatch theory led some to argue that the main problem facing urban minorities is not inadequate transportation but inappropriate skills. The restructuring of the economy has not just shifted low-skill jobs out of the central city, it has changed the type of skills required to participate in the "new economy." Educational

4. Carlson and Persky (1999) show that wages paid to women in Chicago's suburbs are about 8 percent less than wages downtown, while male suburban/urban wages are nearly identical.

requirements have increased as information-handling jobs replace machine-tending jobs. In addition, "soft skills" (i.e., people skills) are required for even low-wage jobs in the service economy. The central problem facing urban African Americans and new immigrants, from this perspective, is the failure of educational systems to expand their skills at the same time that cities are becoming centers of information control and coordination. The result of this skills mismatch is continued high levels of African American unemployment (Kasarda 1990) and the unavailability of commuting as a solution to labor market mismatches.

The relatively low levels of education that plague many nonmetropolitan residents may create a skills mismatch for these workers as well, as manufacturing employment continues to decline. Many rural economic bases have been challenged by international competition for low-skill jobs. As a result, those workers who desire better jobs may increasingly need to look to metropolitan areas, where higher skills will be required. Thus, the skills mismatch may extend beyond the core of large cities into adjacent nonmetropolitan counties.

The Consequences of Commuting for Rural Communities

In this chapter we have shown that commuting represents a common and important way for nonmetropolitan workers to gain greater access to jobs. Workers generally commute to places more urban than those in which they live, though "back commuting" also occurs. Higher wages than those found locally may be a powerful motive for many commuters, but several studies we reviewed suggest that nonmetropolitan commuters do not always recoup their costs. Job quality, skill fit, work schedule, or fringe benefits may influence the decision to commute more than wages do. Future research should explore in greater depth the motives for commuting as well as the barriers to it, and how these motives and barriers differ across social groups and geographical spaces. In addition to the individual economic and social factors associated with commuting, the community-level consequences of commuting should be studied. By way of conclusion, we suggest a few of these consequences.

Although commuting can improve the match between workers and jobs, communities with large numbers of out-commuters can face serious challenges. One important challenge is financial. Local governments may find their tax base undermined if there are relatively few employers compared to residents. "Separation of work and residence could result in need for social services, housing, water and sewer facilities that do not decline when jobs do" (Aldrich et al. 1997, 26). In addition, local economies are affected by the spending behaviors of commuters (Shields and Deller 1998). According to a recent survey in a Wisconsin county, the average inter-county commuter spent seventy-five dollars per week on retail purchases outside the county while they were commuting (Green 2001). The cumulative effect of these changes in spending reduces local and county tax revenues and might be devastating to small local retailers.

Commuting also has important implications for community cohesion and structure. The journey to work may be combined with shopping, visiting, or other social activities that bind people into community relations (see Tolbert et al. 2002). A long commute adds greatly to the modern complaint about lack of time. What does this time drain do to local community participation and civic engagement? Putnam (2000) contends that every ten minutes of commuting time cuts involvement in community affairs by 10 percent. Whether or not this is precisely accurate, there is undoubtedly an association here that illustrates the significance of commuting for the community that extends beyond individual workers or their families. Commuting may be the result of better employment opportunities outside the community, and its economic costs for the commuter may be offset by higher wages, but the time it takes cannot be recovered. Commuters quite simply have less time for personal, family, and community activities than those who work closer to home.

13

Continuities and Disjunctures in the Transformation of the U.S. Agro-Food System

Frederick H. Buttel

Virtually every rural social scientist and rural policy-maker is conversant with the basic storyline of the twentieth-century development of U.S. agriculture. Much of this storyline is captured in Lobao and Meyer's (2001) overview of the "great agricultural transition" of the twentieth century. Lobao and Meyer note that the essence of this transition is "the abandonment of farming as a household livelihood strategy. This transition is evident in both the mass decline of the farm population and in the structural transformation of agriculture, whereby most remaining farm units are marginal units incapable of fully employing and sustaining families" (2001, 104). Over the course of the twentieth century, especially during the four or five decades after the Great Depression, there were successively fewer and larger farms, farm sales and assets became increasingly concentrated, farm enterprises and farming regions became more specialized, agribusiness concentration and control over farmers' management and technology choices progressively increased, and the federal agricultural policy apparatus provided enormous subsidies to the largest farms. At the same time, American government officials increasingly championed trade liberalization and were harsh in their condemnations of nations for protecting their agricultures with "market-distorting" subsidies and import restrictions. Most any social or policy analyst of U.S. agriculture at the beginning of the twenty-first century would identify these twentieth-century themes as the major ones that continue to characterize agro-food system change in our time.

As much as there is a good deal of continuity between the structural change processes that characterized the American agro-food system during the twentieth century and those that are predominant today, the basic argument of this paper is that for approximately one decade there have been some major and emergent discontinuities in the transformation of the American agro-food system. These discontinuities have not attenuated or reversed the master twentieth-century trends; indeed, the nature of these turn-of-the-century discontinuities is that they not only reinforce the familiar twentieth century trends, but also make them even more irreversible, more politicized, more global in scope, and more difficult to address from a public policy standpoint.

An American Agro-Food System with No Farmers?

One enlightening—though highly flawed—way to think about the emergent great transformation of American and world agricultures at the turn of the twenty-first century is from the perspective of the provocative "Blank hypothesis," proposed by Steven C. Blank, an agricultural economist and Assistant Vice Provost at the University of California-Davis. In Blank's hotly debated book, *The End of Agriculture in the American Portfolio* (Blank 1998), and in a series of related articles (e.g., Blank 1999), he makes the seemingly outrageous argument that in roughly two generations America agriculture will essentially disappear. Note that Blank's hypothesis is not that American agriculture will merely go through a "great transformation" (as Lobao and Meyer have depicted for the twentieth century) that will result in many fewer, larger, nonfamily farms cultivating about the same amount of land. Blank has in mind a far more radical disappearance of agriculture—not only the end of a way of life and a household livelihood strategy, but essentially the end of agriculture as a rural land use.

Blank argues that there are four major forces that will increasingly propel the disappearance of American agriculture. First, U.S. agriculture is already essentially uncompetitive with several powerhouse agro-food exporting nations (e.g., Brazil, Argentina, Australia, Canada, and New Zealand), and shortly will be uncompetitive with other major world regions (e.g., Ukraine, Russia, Mexico, Uruguay, Paraguay, and much of Eastern Europe) as they modernize and become low-cost agricultural producers. The lack of competitiveness of U.S. agriculture is revealed in the progressively worsening profitability squeeze in American farming—one that would have been truly devastating in its impacts if it were not for lavish federal subsidies (mostly "emergency" payments) that began in the late 1990s (Ray 2000) and that have continued under the 2002 Farm Bill. Second, global agribusiness, including firms with U.S. headquarters, is increasingly seeking out the least-cost suppliers of commodities on a global basis through multiple sourcing of agricultural inputs, strategic alliances, cross-border intersubsidiary movements of products, direct foreign investment, and other means of getting access to the cheapest sources of inputs into their processing and distribution industries.

Third, Blank argues that U.S. farmers are becoming decreasingly competitive in the domestic rural land market. Nonfarm owners and users of land (homeowners, real estate developers and speculators, governments, municipalities, tourist industries and vacationers, and so on) are increasingly outbidding farmers for rural land. Higher farmland values are contributing to high production costs and the profitability squeeze. Fourth, consumers and nonfarm people will continue to be well fed at cheap prices. In addition, they will value the rural land at their disposal for parks, vacationing, second homes, trout streams, water, subdivisions, tourist sites, and shopping centers more than they will value having farms in the hinterland. Consumers and citizens will thus be largely comfortable with the end of agriculture and the (mostly irreversible) conversion of rural land into nonfarm uses. Urban America, in Blank's view, is tired of subsidizing farmers. And now that there are well under one million full-time farmers in business, farmers will not have nearly enough clout to win any political battles against the over 260 million people who like cheap food that can be provided by the global market and who value nonfarm uses of rural land.

When Blank's book was originally published in the late 1990s, it did not generate much attention, and a good many people who read *The End of Agriculture in the American Portfolio* felt that it was an extreme perspective that ignored the persistence of noncorporate production forms in the agro-food system, especially in farm-level production (for a particularly insightful review by a well known agricultural economist, see Harl n.d.). Blank's ideas have been attacked even more vigorously by some members of the public (see, for example, the letters to the *UC Davis Magazine* [2000] in response to his article in a previous issue). Yet if the book has attracted a swarm of criticism, why has it become more widely read with each passing year since its publication date?

Blank deserves credit for putting his finger on the late twentieth century and early twenty-first century as being the confluence of several critical trends in agriculture: declining food agricultural commodity prices and the profit squeeze on American producers despite unprecedented federal subsidies, the shifting locus of control over the food system as multinational food firms increasingly make decisions on a global basis to ensure access to cheap commodity inputs, rising local (U.S.) costs of production due to competition on the rural land market, and technological changes that are facilitating very large production units and/or reduced labor demands. Indeed, below I will discuss the emerging, incipient great transformation of agriculture in the twenty-first century, my rendering of which has some superficial similarities to Blank's list of symptoms that currently affect U.S. agriculture. In addition, while agricultural policy has long been contested, and while there has been considerable similarity in the fault lines of agricultural policy conflict for more than two decades, there seems to be a growing, more widely shared sentiment that the current policy conjuncture will determine the course of development of American—even world—agriculture for decades to come. Thus, while Blank's book generated little disciplinary acclaim or policy attention when it was published—the flagship journal of the American Agricultural Economics Association did not even review it—the events and policy struggles of the ensuing years have given his ideas a certain cachet.

The Emergent Great Transformation of the Twenty-First Century

What are these turn-of-the-century discontinuous social forces that are reinforcing and rendering even more irreversible the "great agricultural transition" about which Lobao and Meyer have written so elegantly? In my view there are seven fundamental components of the new American agro-food milieu at the turn of the twenty-first century. Each of these fundamental components has implications for alternative policies and for the future agenda of rural sociological research.

The first major discontinuity is the elaboration of long-distance food supply chains—what economists typically refer to as "value chains" (Boehlje et al. 1999) and what sociologists more often refer to as "commodity chains" (which are buyer-driven, according to Gereffi 1994). Value or commodity chains are corporate agribusiness systems for managing and optimizing supply from farm inputs and farm-level production through processing, marketing, and consumption. Global value chains are a melding of socioeconomic relations and physical structures that are entered into by food processing, manufacturing, and retail firms in order to cheapen the cost of inputs, to obtain efficiencies through better flow scheduling, to improve food safety and reduce other risks, and to enable firms to respond as quickly as possible to changes in consumer demand. In sum, these strategies are undertaken because, for the dominant actors and with respect to most commodities, undertaking some combination of these strategies is obligatory to maximize profits, meet competition, and increase the chain's share of consumer food expenditures. The shift toward the predominance of value or commodity chains in the agro-food system is leading to increased interdependence across food chains, and to growth in mergers and acquisitions, strategic alliances, and networks among firms.

The chief manifestation of long-distance food supply systems or chains at the farm level is the growth of contractual relationships between farmers and processors and the disappearance of "open markets" (see Tweeten and Flora 2001; Heffernan 1999). At the extra-farm level, these long-distance food supply systems involve not only industrial consolidation and oligopoly, but also an increased prevalence of joint ventures, vertical integration, strategic alliances, and other types of interfirm networks (Heffernan 1999).

These value chains are increasingly global in nature (Bonanno et al. 1994; McMichael 1994; Heffernan 1999), and global vertical coordination is leading to a steady shift in the locus of decision-making power within the food system. During the great transformation of agro-food systems during the twentieth century, the master process was the quest for economies and rents that was undertaken mainly through horizontal integration (i.e., merger and consolidation), resulting in larger agribusiness firms with relatively centralized national decision-making. While many of these firms initiated multinational subsidiaries, each tended to operate mainly as a national-level firm. The beginning of the twenty-first century is an era in which new considerations are leading to global-scale vertical integration and other forms of cross-border coordination.[1] Some of these considerations are risk, food safety concerns, differentiated consumption, debates over new agricultural technologies (such as genetically modified foods), and the development of new technologies and techniques in agro-food chains (e.g., information, packing, transport, and other technologies in food manufacturing that enable "flow scheduling" in commodity chains, and an increased ability to control product attributes across the food chain). Accordingly, power in agro-food systems has increasingly shifted from the level of the nationally centered product sector to an increasingly global level of vertically coordinated interfirm relationships among transnational grain traders, food manufacturers, farm input suppliers, and retail chains.

The second major agro-food structural discontinuity is also revealed, albeit indirectly and imprecisely, in Blank's work. Blank writes tellingly in the closing paragraph of his contribution to the University of Georgia College of Agriculture and Environmental Science's 2001 Symposium on the Future of American Agriculture that "the difficulty American agriculture has in fighting these trends has this bottom line: everything that is happening in this development of a global market is good for U.S. agribusiness

---

1. It goes without saying, however, that the global integration of agro-food systems is by no means new. Indeed, in some sense it is the case that the turn-of-the-century version of global integration is less pronounced than that of the nineteenth century, when the world economy was characterized by British specialization in manufacturing and its importation of foodstuffs from its far-flung colonies.

firms and American consumers" (Blank 2001, 11). This second discontinuity is the global neoliberalization of agriculture. Note that while the neoliberalization of agriculture is closely related to the matter of (global) value chains, the former refers to a policy environment that makes certain structural changes such as value chains more logical and more imperative, while value chains themselves are a structural phenomenon that drives, as well as derives from, global neoliberalization.

Global neoliberalization is not simply "globalization" (the international integration of agricultural and food product markets and growth in the volume of world agricultural trade) or "trade liberalization" ("freer" trade or reduction of state subsidies of agriculture), though both globalization and trade liberalization play significant roles. Nominally, the global neoliberalization of agriculture involves major changes in national agricultural policies such as the reduction of national "market-distorting" subsidies of agriculture, the reduction of trade barriers on agricultural goods, the subordination of national food regulatory standard setting to globally "harmonized" standards, and especially the removal of import barriers and nontariff barriers to trade. Perhaps most fundamentally, though, neoliberalization is a set of procorporate policies that are aimed at creating profitable opportunities for private firms in agro-food and other sectors with the idea that stimulating private investment and encouraging mobility of investment capital will yield social benefits.

Since the ratification of the North American Free Trade Agreement (NAFTA) in 1994 and the World Trade Organization (WTO) in 1995, there has been a definite trend toward increasingly synchronized global markets in most agricultural commodities. The covariation of the implementation of these trade liberalization pacts with the downward trend in farm commodity prices suggests a causal relationship of some sort. An equally important consequence of these trade pacts is that they make it more difficult to advance alternative policies. Most fundamentally, global neoliberalization of agriculture involves the actual or self-imposed global veto over U.S. agricultural policy alternatives (and over alternatives available to other nation-states) that derives from the commitment to trade liberalization agreements such as those of the WTO (and NAFTA). The establishment of increasingly hypercompetitive conditions in world agriculture that have led to progressively lower price ceilings for most commodities also serves as an implicit veto over national policy alternatives. Nelson (2002), for example, points out how U.S. government obligations under the WTO—and perhaps even more fundamentally, the fact that government noncompliance with the WTO agricultural agreement would undermine U.S. leadership in seeking to deepen trade liberalization—might serve to rule out many alternatives for domestic support of and investment in agriculture.

It should be stressed, however, that as much as global neoliberalization of agriculture is a palpable trend, many of the components of global neoliberalization are proceeding in highly discontinuous and contentious ways. In practice, NAFTA, and especially the WTO, has been far less efficacious in "liberalizing" agriculture than many proponents and opponents of these policies accept. In the current unipolar world in which the United States dominates economically, militarily, and politically, American interests tend to dominate to a considerable degree. But while all of the U.S. administrations since the 1980s have favored trade liberalization, and the current administration does so with particular vigor, this administration has permitted—sometimes even encouraged—protectionism of various sorts (e.g., massive emergency payments to farmers in the late 1990s, import restrictions on sugar, and many of the provisions of the 2002 Farm Bill). Also, there is still sufficient support for farmers (not to mention steel and textile manufacturers) in Congress that it has continued to vote for huge farm subsidies, and seems scarcely more prepared than fifty years ago to let American farms be annihilated though unfettered global market forces. Most every world nation wants to be part of the World Trade Organization, but most would prefer to see its agricultural rules substantially changed. There is now very little active support for the U.S.-backed Uruguay Round Agreement on Agriculture (the WTO's current agriculture agreement) outside of the seventeen members of the U.S.-led "Cairns Group." Yet because most every nation reasons that it cannot survive economically without being in the world trading system, there does not seem to be a truly conceivable policy alternative or a viable coalition in opposition to current trade liberalization agreements and policies.

The third great turn-of-the-century discontinuity is that the structural differentiation of agriculture has now progressed so far—and so rapidly— that American farms now have very little in common with each other, despite the fact that they are among a handful of survivors of the great transformation about which Lobao and Meyer have written. For example, the Hoppe et al. (2001) Family Farm Report to Congress contains some revealing 1999 data on the current structure of agriculture, employing the U.S. Department of Agriculture Economic Research Service farm structure categories. For the vast bulk of American farms, and for all but about 10 percent of the largest operations, farm income is minimal and usually negative. Over 40 percent of farms are "residential or lifestyle" farms, and another 14.1 percent are "retirement farms." "Limited resource" farms have declined extremely rapidly over the past decade (from approximately

14 percent of farms in 1993 to 7.3 percent of farms in 1998). Another 20 percent of farms are "low-sales" family farms—farms whose annual sales volumes are under $100,000, and thus incapable of generating an adequate family income. These farms have essentially nothing in common with the roughly 18 percent of farms that fall in the "high-sales family farm," "large family farm," "very large family farm," and "nonfamily farm" categories that dominate U.S. agriculture in terms of sales and assets. The two larger-than-family-farm categories (large family farm, very large family farm) and the nonfamily farm category alone accounted for 68 percent of U.S. production in 1999.

The fourth great discontinuity is the extraordinary industrialization and concentration of livestock production. For the first few decades of the twentieth century, livestock production provided family farmers a means to intensify production without investing in more land, to utilize surplus family labor, and to capture "added value." Hogs, for example, were widely known as "mortgage burners" for family farm households. The last four decades of the twentieth century, however, have witnessed an extraordinary decline of commercially viable moderate-scale independent livestock production (McBride 1997). Similar independent production has largely disappeared in poultry. Moderate-scale independent production of fed cattle has also largely disappeared in its major production regions (the Great Plains and the Intermountain regions). Moderate-scale independent production is well on its way to disappearing in the pork sector, and is becoming increasingly threatened in dairy production, which is the only remaining family farming dominated livestock sector. The demise of commercially viable moderate-scale independent livestock production represents an enormous handicap to the survival of family-type farms, since one of the cornerstones of successful moderate-scale production of the basic crop commodities has traditionally been to supplement with animal and livestock enterprises in order to achieve the integration efficiencies of crop rotations and utilization of animal manures. This formula has also tended to be the foundation of sustainable agriculture practices.

The fifth major turn-of-the-century discontinuity is the role played by a new class of agricultural technologies, typified by genetically modified crop varieties such as Bt corn and cotton and herbicide-resistant (HR) soybeans. In contrast to the dominant forms of technological change during the heart of the twentieth century that generally required—and augmented—management skill, the nature of these new technologies is that they substitute for management, and substantially remove management barriers to enormous increases in the scale of field crop production. As these new technologies substitute for management, they reduce previous management limits on large-scale crop production. HR soybean varieties in the Midwest, for example, significantly reduce the need for managerial decision-making about weed control, and when combined with no-till technology, they enable one farmer to manage far larger acreages than was possible before the advent of HR soybeans.[2] These new technologies and the management simplification they facilitate would seem to make field crop agriculture more likely to become contractually integrated into the global value chains discussed earlier.

A sixth discontinuity in the structural configuration of agriculture is the culmination of the trend that began in the early 1970s—the relocation of agrarian protest outside of mainstream production agriculture. Agrarian protest no longer consists primarily of aggrieved rank-and-file farmers acting as leaders to contest established power relations in governments or in private agricultural organizations. Instead, the impetus to agricultural reform and protest—and even the provision of alternative policy ideas and research to support them—now comes largely from nonfarm groups (Benbrook 1996; Stumo 2000; Wallace Center 2001). A host of mostly nonfarm nongovernmental organizations (NGOs) and a few farm activists fight persistent battles—sometimes successful ones, others more future-oriented or rear-guard in nature—in Congress, as well as against agricultural-administrative agencies such as the USDA and against the agribusiness establishment. Even though these struggles seem to have low chances at success, the nature of agrarian movement mobilization—the availability of philanthropic foundation funds to support agrarian protest, the strength of the sentiments of prospective agrarian activists, and the political obstacles to elected politicians pulling the plug on the family farmers who remain—creates a milieu of endemic and indefinite politicization of agro-food issues. And while some farm people and groups (such as the National Farmers Union) remain involved in agricultural protest activities, aggrieved farm people are more prone to pessimism, disillusion, and cynicism from the many failed attempts at agricultural policy reform than they are to allegiance to agrarian policy reform movements.

The seventh great transformation of U.S. agriculture is its incipient "environmentalization," by which I mean agriculture is becoming increasingly subject to environmental criteria and regulations. To be sure, the environmentalization of agriculture has proceeded rather slowly. It is still the case, however, that among many farm groups, mention of the fact that

---

2. A further technological component of this fifth discontinuity is the growing importance played by information (explicit or formal, systematic information, as opposed to tacit knowledge and "mental models") and the ongoing privatization of important components of this information.

agriculture has for some time been the nation's biggest polluter or destroyer of water resources—or even that agriculture has much of an environmental impact at all—brings forth anger and denial. Many of the most powerful agricultural commodity groups and general farm organizations deny that the hypoxia zone (Boesch et al. 2001) in the Gulf of Mexico actually exists, has anything to do with agriculture, or is of any significance. Farm groups remain formidable in resisting state government regulations on agricultural sources of water pollution. But, slowly but surely, there is growing recognition that agriculture's environmental performance must be substantially improved. Some of the reasons why agriculture must deal with environmental constraints are obvious. There is general, though soft, public support for the environmental reform of agriculture. Increasingly, environmental groups of all sorts, ranging from national and international ones like the Sierra Club to regional ones such as Wisconsin's Environmental Decade and Wisconsin Citizens Action, are targeting agricultural sources of pollutants, nutrients, and toxics. Federal and state environmental regulatory agencies increasingly recognize that they are hamstrung in meeting legislated or administratively determined environmental quality goals unless they deal squarely and promptly with farmers and agribusinesses. Some farm groups, particularly organic farmers, local food systems groups, and sustainable agriculture groups, also stress the need for environmental reform of agriculture.[3]

As much as there is a certain momentum developing behind the environmental reform of agriculture, it remains unclear how this aspect of the twenty-first century transformation of agriculture will affect the other six components. There is some evidence that agricultural run-off and pollution could be substantially reversed if agriculture production units became smaller in scale and more agro-ecologically diverse, and if distribution chains became more local and regional in scale. To the degree that this is the case, one could imagine a trajectory of agricultural/environmental reform that would involve regulations or market incentives (strict taxes on agricultural chemicals, subsidies for crop rotations, and strict regulations on concentrated animal feeding operations [CAFOs]) that would make the

3. One additional impetus for environmental reform of agriculture comes from a number of world nations, especially the European Union nations and Japan, that see environmental protection not only as valuable in its own right, but also as a possible strategy to permit a certain level of support for family farmers (and also some measure of protectionism) within the rules of the WTO. The notion of multifunctionality—that agriculture performs a number of important nonmarket functions (such as rural development, tourism, biodiversity conservation, and so on) in addition to producing food commodities—has become a significant issue area in the Millennial (or Doha) Round of negotiations of the World Trade Organization's agriculture agreement.

cost structures of medium-sized farms advantageous. Import restrictions on food products produced under unsustainable conditions in other countries would dramatically reduce the vulnerability of American commodity producers to the global competitive forces about which scholars such as Blank (1998) have written. As logical as this policy option might seem, however, the overall thrust of the first six forces would seem to substantially militate against this scenario being the most likely one. Perhaps as likely or more likely is the marriage of the Cascadian Farms model of very large-scale, high-value, largely monocultural organic production, as depicted in a celebrated *New York Times Magazine* article by Michael Pollan (2001) on the "organic-industrial complex," with precision-farming techniques.

Alternative Policies and New Research Agendas

The 2002 Farm Bill involved subsidies to large commercial producers that are inconsistent with the spirit, if not the intent, of the Uruguay Round of the WTO. At this writing in 2003 the Doha Round agriculture agreement negotiations are just beginning. This is one of the most important social policy junctures for American and world agricultures, but a frank assessment of the course of these debates is that while rural sociologists potentially have much to offer, they have not been active players.[4] These policy discussions are dominated by agricultural economists as well as commodity and other agricultural groups, and the range of debate is limited to the range of views that exists within U.S. agricultural economics. To some degree the lack of involvement of rural sociologists in these debates is not surprising, since it is the nature of sociology to question institutional arrangements, power relations, and orienting assumptions such as the structures and policies of the contemporary agro-food system. But it is also worth mentioning that sociologists have not been as active as one would like in researching many of the key issues where their input is most needed.

Rural sociology's research agenda must include several new or expanded areas of work in order to make more definitive and effective responses to these policy issues in the future. There are, to be sure, some important areas of research among rural sociologists today (e.g., Heffernan 1999;

4. Rural sociologists do actively influence some areas of discussion within agriculture, such as the status of the structure of agriculture, the impacts of new technologies, and the relationships between agriculture and households. Rural sociologists have tended not to be active players in policy arenas such as the Farm Bill, WTO negotiations, and agricultural-environmental policy-making.

Bonanno et al. 1994; McMichael 1994) that are highly relevant; however, some of the needed areas of policy research have not been common among rural sociologists. In very rough terms, a model for some of the work that needs to be done is Lyle Schertz and Otto Doering's (1999) book *The Making of the 1996 Farm Act*. While this is a work of agricultural economics, it presents a detailed institutional and historical rendering of the coalitions, discourses, strategies, and unexpected turns of events that were involved in the passage of the 1996 Farm Bill. The same type of work is necessary to understand the nature of global neoliberalization and its institutional moorings. Another example of needed research is in the arena of the political economy of U.S. antitrust law and its relationships to agricultural laws and policies. Many groups contesting agricultural policy today lament the fact that agricultural transformation is characterized by concentration of agro-industrial sectors and anticompetitive practices. U.S. antitrust law was largely enacted in the early twentieth century and is increasingly outmoded in addressing the nature of power exercised by transnational agribusiness firms in global agro-food commodity chains in the early twenty-first century (Sexton 2000). There is a desperate need for rural sociological research on industrial structure in relation to antitrust laws of various sorts.

There has been some promising rural sociological research on agro-food commodity chains, the shifting sociopolitical relations of food regulation, and the role of consumption, but much of this work has been done outside of the United States. There is a need for this research to be policy relevant and to explore not only the benefits and costs of existing arrangements but also the possibilities for alternatives.

There is also a strong need for comprehensive rural sociological research (as well as multidisciplinary research) on the ecological implications and impacts of both the "great agricultural transition" discussed by Lobao and Meyer and the turn-of-the-century transformations that are now upon us. What are the ecological performance and risks associated with production systems of different types, including the impact of the socioeconomic characteristics of operators and of the ecological characteristics of farms? To what degree does thoroughgoing agro-ecological reform require structural changes in farming, and how would alternative agro-ecological reforms induce structural changes in agro-food systems?

There are two general types of alternative policies that have been discussed by various parties interested in the future of agricultural systems and rural sociologists who share these interests. One set of policy alternatives is that of localism, or what Kloppenburg et al. (1996) have referred to as "foodshed" analysis and policy, through efforts to build more direct local farmer/consumer relationships. The other set of policy alternatives is to seek either dramatic reforms in existing trade liberalization agreements (e.g., the pursuit of multifunctionality payment systems within the WTO agriculture agreement that would eliminate subsidies for overproduction and instead subsidize ecosystem service provision and social spin-offs from agriculture), or a significant roll-back of the provisions of the Uruguay Round Agreement on Agriculture. Rural sociological research is needed on these approaches to policy reform to understand their sociopolitical viability as well as their socioeconomic impacts and unintended consequences.

Imagine that well before the end of the twenty-first century one or more rural sociologists will write a review article much like that of Lobao and Meyer (2001), in which there is a qualitative and quantitative assessment of the great transformation of twenty-first-century agro-food systems. This article might well document a significant decline in the number of U.S. farms, but the outcome is unlikely to be the disappearance of production agriculture as a rural land use; indeed, two or three decades hence there could very well be citation to the Lobao and Meyer piece about the reasons why there tend to be substantial linkages between rural households and primary production of agro-food commodities. There will probably have been a profound elaboration of some of the new forces discussed in the present paper. Rural sociological research priorities will almost certainly have shifted, perhaps to some degree along the lines advocated above. It is quite likely that this future review article will chronicle the continued contestedness of the policies and practices regarding agro-food systems. One hopes that this article will also document how rural sociologists increasingly came to be major players in agro-food policy debates as the twenty-first century unfolded.

14

Tourism and Natural Amenity Development
Real Opportunities?

Richard S. Krannich and Peggy Petrzelka

The mountains, forests, rivers and lakes, open spaces, and scenic vistas that characterize portions of America's rural landscape have for many years attracted population growth, tourism and recreational visitation, and associated economic development to certain locales where natural amenity values are high. As McGranahan (1999b) notes, natural amenities involving mild climate conditions, topographic variation, and the presence of water areas are closely linked to population growth. From 1970 through 1996 nonmetropolitan counties in the United States that rated high on six natural amenity factors[1] grew by an average of 125 percent, compared to an average growth of just 1 percent among counties that rated low on those same measures (McGranahan 1999b; see also Beale and Johnson 1998; Johnson and Beale 1994; Rudzitis 1999; Rudzitis and Johansen 1989; Shumway and Davis 1996).

Natural-amenity-based growth and development are by no means new phenomena in rural America. A number of tourism-based communities became well established during the first half of the twentieth century, most notably in areas adjoining the entrances to major recreation destinations such as Rocky Mountain and Great Smoky Mountains National Parks (Rothman 2000). Growth and development in "gateway" locations adjoining such natural areas has become increasingly widespread in recent decades (Howe, McMahon, and Probst 1997). Elsewhere, the development of major winter and summer resorts at places like Park City in Utah, Apostle Islands in Wisconsin, Mississippi river towns in Iowa and Illinois, and

---

1. These six factors include warm winters, winter sun, temperate summer, low summer humidity, topographic variation, and water areas.

Hilton Head and surrounding areas in South Carolina has driven both seasonal tourism and extensive land and housing development. Other rural locales such as Idaho's Teton Valley and Georgia's Putnam County have experienced substantial growth from a surging in-migration of retirees, telecommuting professionals, and urban refugees attracted to high-amenity sites as year-round residential locations.

The economic changes and population growth that appear to characterize these kinds of high-amenity locales often occur as a result of factors beyond the scope of local initiatives or development efforts. Examples include decisions by federal or state agencies to designate new parks and monuments or to build reservoirs or other resource-based recreation attractions, or decisions by nonlocal development interests to build large-scale resort facilities. However, in other instances the changes associated with amenity-based growth are the result of purposive local actions. As Humphrey (2001) recently observed, tourism-based growth promotion is a key facet of community-level development initiatives in many locales.

Increasingly, the potential for amenity-based development has been held out as a key economic development strategy for rural communities, particularly those wishing to counter the erosion of traditional rural economies; however, it is important to raise several cautionary points regarding the prospects for such development. First, amenity-based development is simply not a realistic option for many rural areas. In many locales the kinds of natural features needed to attract tourism or other amenity-based activities are not present. Also, many rural areas that do exhibit certain amenity characteristics still find it very difficult to capitalize on those features due to locational disadvantages (e.g., being in very remote and hard-to-access settings) or an inability to compete effectively with other areas that have even greater amenity resource endowments.

In short, not every community can expect to successfully recruit an influx of tourists or new residents on the basis of surrounding natural amenities, and amenity-based development cannot reasonably be expected to serve as the salvation of all communities confronted by an erosion of traditional rural economic enterprises. Moreover, it is important to recognize that, as is true for virtually any form of economic development activity, both "opportunities" and "threats" (Freudenburg and Gramling 1992) are associated with amenity-based development. Communities that are confronted by, or hope to pursue, such development need to be aware of both positive and negative consequences experienced in other amenity-rich settings where growth and development outcomes have already occurred. The remainder of this chapter addresses this need by reviewing some of the major consequences of tourism and amenity-based development that have been reported.

Opportunities and Threats from Amenity-Based Development

Economic Benefits and Costs

The available literature suggests that a mixture of both economic benefits and costs needs to be considered when assessing the consequences of amenity-based development efforts. A review of studies focusing on the effects of tourism activity indicates that "parks and park-related tourism generate millions of dollars of income, sizeable multiplier effects, and new jobs in neighboring regions" (Achana and O'Leary 2000, 72). English, Marcouiller, and Cordell (2000) found significantly higher per capita income levels, faster rates of population growth, and higher housing prices in counties that are economically dependent on tourism. In addition, Johnson and Fuguitt (2000) observed a strong tendency for older adults to represent a major component of the migration stream to high-amenity recreation counties, an outcome that prior research has shown to create new income and employment opportunities in destination communities (Glasgow and Reeder 1990).

While some areas may be able to capitalize on tourism as a means of developing a more diversified local economy (Power 1996; Rasker 1995), other places become so heavily "tourism-dependent" that they can be as vulnerable to downturns as places dependent on more traditional resource extraction economies. Furthermore, employment opportunities associated with amenity-based growth tend to be in lower-wage service-sector industries, often on a part-time basis, with lack of opportunity for advancement and few benefits, if any. While such jobs can represent important employment options for some residents, they may not generate incomes sufficient to fully support a family. Also, these types of jobs often are highly volatile, due to the inherent seasonality of tourism-based activity and second-home residency in many settings. Indeed, the magnitude of seasonal fluctuations can rival that of traditional extractive industries, but with a far greater frequency of upswings and downturns (Keith, Fawson, and Chang 1996). In addition, a substantial leakage of income out of the local area often occurs, particularly when income and profits are siphoned away by nonlocal corporations that often control much of the development in such settings (Miles 2000).

Studies of residents' perceptions of tourism-based economic activity seem to confirm the notion that the effects are mixed, with several noting a tendency for residents to express skepticism if not outright dissatisfaction with the consequences of tourism in their communities (Lankford 1994; Smith and Krannich 1998). Even where other employment opportunities have withered, many individuals are likely to spurn the prospects of working in tourism-related industries due to low wages and seasonal employment. In addition, some rural residents balk at working in amenity-based occupations because they consider them inconsistent with the cultural traditions and lifeways associated with more traditional rural occupations such as logging, mining, or agriculture (Carroll 1995).

An additional economic consequence of amenity-based development is the change in cost of living that may occur (English et al. 2000). Property value inflation can lead to windfall profits for those who choose to sell or develop their land and other properties; however, such inflation can also contribute to residential displacement of persons who have limited or fixed incomes. For example, with the building of upscale resorts and elite gated communities on the rural Sea Islands of South Carolina (primarily populated by upper-class whites), land values and taxes have increased, forcing some longtime residents to sell their land and move (Ritzer 1999). Similar effects have been observed in North Carolina counties experiencing high levels of amenity-based retirement in-migration (Bennett 1992).

Throughout the rural West, service-sector workers at major winter resorts such as Aspen and summer destinations such as Jackson Hole find it necessary to commute from more affordable locations, often at a substantial distance. Property value inflation can also cause dissension within families when some heirs want to sell their lands at high prices while others want to maintain it for agricultural or other established uses (Tibbetts 2001).

Another important consideration involves the fiscal effects on local governments. Some analyses suggest that fiscal impacts of amenity-based development can in certain situations generate revenues that offset increased government costs (e.g., Deller, Marcouiller, and Green 1997). However, most studies suggest that revenues generated by new businesses and populations are often exceeded by the additional costs associated with the need to expand public infrastructure and services. While tourists spend money that circulates in the local economy and adds to sales tax revenues, they do not pay the state or local income and property taxes that are the primary revenue sources for local governments. In addition, seasonal spikes in visitation can require an expansion of public services to levels far in excess of what would be needed to serve the needs of permanent populations. Similarly, large numbers of seasonal homes can generate substantial increases in public-sector expenditures and the local tax burden for infrastructure, while seasonal occupancy may limit revenues derived from property, sales, and local income taxes (Bennett 1996; Burchell et al. 1998; English et al. 2000; Fritz 1982).

Population Growth: Effects on Social Organization and Community Capacity

The population growth that often occurs in high-amenity rural areas has multiple consequences for the social contexts of affected communities. The arrival of new residents can substantially enhance the human capital of many rural areas, as in-migrants bring occupational, organizational, and leadership experiences, skills, and talents to their new communities. Population growth also has the potential to generate the critical mass of residents needed to reinvigorate or even create churches, civic organizations, and interest groups that are often moribund if not entirely absent in many rural areas. Thus, amenity-driven population growth has the potential to enhance community capacity to respond to change and address the needs of local residents (Doak and Kusel 1996; Flora and Flora 1993; Kretzmann and McKnight 1993a).

This potential for enhanced community capacity may be compromised if growth occurs at levels exceeding either local preference or the ability of established social structures and institutions to respond. Where growth rates are excessive, informal social structures as well as public institutions and formal organizations can experience substantial strain. Increased population, along with the presence of larger numbers of both recently arrived residents and seasonal visitors, can reduce the "density of acquaintance-ship," which tends to be high in more stable rural places and can contribute in important ways to social solidarity and informal social support processes (Freudenburg 1986).

Population growth has also been associated with a so-called culture clash, when traditional and newcomer values collide (Smith and Krannich 2000). Prior research suggests that divergent views about growth and environmental protection can become a focal point for tensions between established and in-migrant populations (Beyers and Nelson 2000; Blahna 1990; Cockerham and Blevins 1977; Graber 1974; Jobes 1999; Ploch 1978; Price and Clay 1980; Rudzitis 1999; Spain 1993). It is important to note some evidence suggesting that newcomers' and long-term residents' perspectives on such issues may be more similar than is often assumed (Fortmann and Kusel 1990; Smith and Krannich 2000). Where such divisions are present, however, the potential for broad-based civic engagement and collective actions in pursuit of community interests and needs is likely reduced (Wilkinson 1991).

Effects on Cultural Traditions and Identities

There is also a potential for affecting cultural traditions and identities in communities experiencing amenity-based growth. As noted by Hester, tourism development can lead to a situation where "a small dying town takes an economic U-turn by capitalizing on its smallness, intimacy, natural beauty, village character, and rural past. Unfortunately, for many communities, this turnaround spells the demise of community traditions, destruction of valued places, and their replacement by a phony folk culture" (1990, 5).

There are innumerable examples where this scenario has played out. Tennessee's Gatlinburg and Pigeon Forge area adjoining the Great Smoky Mountains National Park has been described as a place that "grew seemingly without plan or limit, offering park visitors ... every conceivable choice of tacky gift shop, recreation pastime (hillbilly golf), amusement park (Dollywood), fast food, and roadside motel" (Jarvis 2000, 222), in effect becoming a "cathedral of consumption" where individuals go to "practice our consumer religion" (Ritzer 1999, x).

This process contributes to the near elimination of long-established local lifeways and cultural traditions. Concerns that large-scale tourism and amenity-based growth will overwhelm and obliterate the customs and cultures of rural and indigenous communities have become a focal point of local opposition and efforts to resist or limit such growth in a variety of settings (Canan and Hennessy 1989; Milman and Pizan 1988).

Furthermore, amenity-based development affects "place," by which we mean the spaces within which "social relationships transpire" (Lobao 1996, 78) and that serve as "centers of meaning to individuals and groups" (Tuan 1977, 198). Strong symbolic and emotional attachments to place(s) are found among both residents and visitors (Mitchell et al. 1993; Brandenburg and Carroll 1995), and may be at times unconscious, with the importance of place noticed only once it has been destroyed or is threatened (Hester 1985; Hiss 1990).

Natural settings valued because of their ability to provide opportunities for privacy, reflection, solitude, communion with nature, and a spiritual linkage with the natural world (Brandenburg and Carroll 1995) become less conducive to such outcomes when they are visited by growing numbers of tourists, used by a increasing numbers of new residents, or transformed by altered land use patterns associated with growth (Mitchell et al. 1993; Hiss 1990). In such cases, established residents often feel that their opportunities to pursue recreation in and preserve the character and symbolic meanings of such places are threatened (Martin and McCool 1992).

At the same time, under certain conditions amenity-based development can enhance the meanings associated with place. The presence of "newcomers" moving into the community or of tourists finding it attractive enough to visit can alter local residents' awareness and recognition of their place. For example, in the Loess Hills of western Iowa, tourism promotion brought attention to the scenic beauty of the landform, resulting in long-term residents viewing both the landform and themselves differently. While many locals had a tendency to minimize their place due to the stigma of being "from the hills" and therefore a "hillbilly," many note they now take pride in the fact they are from the hills and indicate that external attention focused on the landform has given them some dignity (Petrzelka 1999).

Environmental Consequences

Finally, it is important to address some of the implications of amenity-based development for the natural environment. Paradoxically, while environmental qualities are the magnets that often attract development, the growth pressures and land use changes that occur can frequently result in significant environmental damage (American Society of Planning Officials 1976).

In some locations, increased numbers of people create traffic volumes that exceed the capacity of small-town streets and rural highways, creating both congestion and safety problems. Sprawling residential development can contribute to a transformation of agricultural land uses, loss of open space, and increased public safety problems where housing developments extend into forested landscapes and exacerbate the risks associated with wildfire. Emissions from vehicles and wood-burning stoves can contribute to deteriorating air quality. Increased volumes of wastewater and disturbance of vegetative cover can affect water quality, often to the point that federal water-quality requirements for total maximum daily load are violated even in seemingly pristine locations. Finally, the effects on wildlife are among the most significant environmental consequences associated with amenity-based development. Land fragmentation resulting from residential development disturbs wildlife habitat and can lead to declines in wildlife numbers and species diversity (Buehler et al. 1991; Croonquist and Brooks 1993; Heimberger, Euler, and Barr 1983; Jules et al. 1999; Morrison, Marcot, and Mannan 1992; Schindler, Geib, and Williams 2000; Voigt and Broadfoot 1995).

Implications and Policy Recommendations

Do tourism and natural amenity development represent real opportunities for rural communities? Based on the range of evidence reviewed here, the answer to that question appears to be quite uncertain, and definitely in need of qualification. For some rural communities such development may be the only available option, particularly where traditional rural economies have withered and there are few prospects for alternative industrial or business development. Certainly there are cases where amenity-based development has helped to create economically and socially vibrant communities, often in settings once characterized by stagnation and decline; however, such cases appear to be atypical. Clearly, the types of development that are associated with natural amenity values do not represent a panacea for the economic and community development needs that confront much of rural America. Overall, research findings suggest that the consequences of such development are at best mixed, and often negative. Indeed, Rothman concludes that tourism-based development is "a devil's bargain" that "typically fails to meet the expectations of communities and regions that embrace it as an economic strategy" (1998, 10).

For tourism and amenity-based development to contribute positively to rural communities, several key issues require additional attention on the part of both local community leaders and planners and those responsible for devising and implementing rural development policies. First, communities and development professionals need to address the risks associated with substituting one form of resource dependency for another. Overreliance on tourism or other amenity-based activities can contribute to problems of economic instability and rural poverty. This is due both to the seasonal nature and service-sector wage rates that characterize many such activities and their susceptibility to periodic downturns due to regional, national, and international conditions and events. Little snowfall can lead to major economic downturns in winter resource communities; hurricanes, floods, and similar natural disasters can reduce or eliminate visitation to other types of tourist destinations. Extended periods of national or international economic stagnation can dramatically alter the patterns of vacationing and second home development. During the fall and winter of 2001 many major resort and entertainment destinations experienced a virtual collapse of visitation in the wake of the September 11th terrorist attacks on America. In short, communities that rely heavily on tourism or any other single industry are more vulnerable to disruption than those with diversified economies.

Attention should also be directed to efforts designed to encourage local business development and investment, so that profits from tourism and growth are not largely siphoned away from the local economy by outside investment interests. Implementation of user fees, lodging and other visitor taxes, land development taxes, and other revenue-generating mechanisms beyond the more traditional property and sales tax mechanisms can help to better balance the fiscal consequences for local units of government.

Where substantial amenity-based growth does occur or is anticipated, attention needs to be focused on both the social and environmental disturbances that can occur. Growth that exceeds the carrying capacity of the natural landscape, that overwhelms valued traditions, cultures, and interests of established populations, or that displaces residents as a result of cost of living increases certainly does not contribute positively to the well-being of rural people and communities. Efforts to involve new residents in community organizations and activities, and to seek out areas of common interest to bridge potential gaps in the interests and values of newcomer and established populations, can help to reduce the tensions that often arise when such growth occurs. Careful consideration of zoning and other land use ordinances, establishment of open space protection programs, and enforcement of standards for things like wastewater management are also important to minimize the adverse effects of increased human activity, land use change, and habitat fragmentation.

Communities that choose to pursue amenity-based development need to learn from the lessons of places that have been overwhelmed and irrevocably altered by excessive growth and implement planning practices that can contain growth at levels that are socially, economically, and ecologically sustainable. As an example, the Sea Island residents mentioned earlier established a "cultural-protection overlay district" as part of their county's zoning ordinance. Included in the ordinance are prohibitions against "gated communities, golf courses, and resorts" (Tibbetts 2001, 31), all developments the residents felt threatened their culture and way of life.

Unfortunately, many rural communities are ill equipped to engage in the kinds of planning activities needed to maximize the opportunities of amenity-based development while minimizing the threats that can accompany it. Rural planning departments are often inadequately funded and staffed, and in some areas nonexistent. Also, a strong adherence to a private property rights orientation in many rural locales can make efforts to engage in comprehensive planning politically difficult at best.

Studies that examine ways to accomplish "success" with amenity-based development suggest the importance of adopting a participatory research approach and including *all* voices from the beginning of the planning process. For example, in his article "Subconscious Landscapes of the Heart," Randy Hester (1985) details his community and tourism planning work in Manteo, North Carolina. Through the use of surveys, behavior mapping, and in-depth interviews, Hester and his colleagues identified places perceived as important by residents of Manteo, and developed a list of the community's "sacred structures" (public yet sacred places). The community intentionally sacrificed an estimated half-million dollars in retail sales per year by not commodifying these sacred structures for tourism.

Hester (1985) argues that identification and protection of these sacred structures helped preserve the local culture while simultaneously providing a foundation for new development. These thoughts are echoed by Mitchell et al. (1993) in arguing for the importance of recognizing the "uniqueness and spirit of place in the planning process." Such participatory planning efforts consume resources, both in time and money. When resources are so lacking that evaluative studies of the impact of amenity-based development cannot be conducted, however, real problems can arise (Luloff et al. 1994). However, in the long run, the participatory approach appears to be the most successful one available for accomplishing equitable community outcomes.

PART III

The Rural Community: Is It Local? Is It a Community?

Perspectives on Community

15

Community Agency and Local Development

A. E. Luloff and Jeffrey C. Bridger

Post–World War II economic, social, cultural, and technological changes radically reshaped life at the local level. The growth of the interstate highway system coupled with loan programs that provided more than eleven million mortgages for returning servicemen set the stage for the building boom now recognized as the beginning of suburban sprawl (Duany et al. 2000). Although jobs remained in cities for several years after the war, by the 1960s and 1970s many corporations had moved to the suburbs where most of their workforces lived. At the same time, the development of new communication and transportation technologies brought previously isolated rural areas into the economic and cultural mainstream.

Given the scale and pace of these transformations, it is not surprising that community change became an important topic of inquiry. At first, attention was focused on explaining why and how local communities persisted in an increasingly mobile and footloose society. Later, many scholars began to question whether the community was any longer a fundamental unit of social organization. By the 1970s, the local community had become largely incidental to the study of other phenomena, often serving as the physical setting for what were presumably more important topics. Sociologists were studying things that happened in communities, but the community itself was rarely a central focus of inquiry.

In our view, this trend has not been sociologically productive. Although the great transformations of the twentieth century reshaped the structural and cultural dimensions of the community, events at the local level continue to affect material, social, and mental well-being in fundamental ways. In fact, over the last decade many scholars have rediscovered the community as a concept, and now argue that the local ecological context is central to understanding the factors that affect such diverse processes as socialization, workforce participation, persistent poverty, intellectual development, successful aging, and physical and mental health (Berkman 1995; Berkman and Syme 1979; Claude et al. 2000; Flora and Luther 2000; Furstenberg 1993; Hylton 1995; Tigges et al. 1998; Wacquant and Wilson 1993; Wilkinson 1991; Wilson 1987, 1995, 1996). From a practical standpoint then, it is important to create policies and programs that can provide direction for local actions aimed at building stronger, healthier communities.

We hope to contribute to this debate by articulating an interactional approach to community and community action. To lay the groundwork for our argument, we begin with a discussion of the most prominent theories of community decline, especially Robert Putnam's thesis that the collapse of community can be traced to a widespread loss of social capital. We argue that this line of reasoning is flawed, and suggest that an interactional theory (Wilkinson 1991) of community provides a better understanding of the relationship between community agency and community development. The chapter concludes with a discussion of the policy implications that proceed from the interactional approach.

"The Eclipse of Community"

In his book *The Eclipse of Community,* Maurice Stein (1960) argued that as modern societies became larger, more dense, and more complex, communal relationships were necessarily attenuated. This reasoning can be traced to analyses of urbanism by Simmel (1950) early in the twentieth century, and later by Wirth (1938), which suggested that modernization and urbanization destroyed the personal, long-lasting, and interconnected relationships characteristic of smaller and rural communities, replacing them with fragmented, transitory, and impersonal ties. In the course of this process, anomie and alienation increased, especially as the values, attitudes, and behaviors of the dominant culture filtered into the nation's hinterland.

The Great Change

Roland Warren (1963, 1971, 1978) took a slightly different approach to the transformation of community life in his "Great Change" theory. He argued that as communities became increasingly reliant on extra-local institutions and sources of income, they were overwhelmed by forces they could not control. The community, from his perspective, became little more than a stage where extra-local groups, organizations, and businesses pursued their interests with little concern for how their actions affected local residents. The logic of Warren's assertion was intuitively appealing and straightforward. As communities became more internally differentiated and increasingly linked to larger systems beyond their borders, the local ties that once connected all parts of a community into a system began to break down. With the solidification of this trend in the decades following World War II, local decisions, policies, and programs increasingly were formulated outside the community and "guided more by their relations to extra-community systems than by their relations to other parts of the local community" (Warren 1963, 53). Over time, this process diminished the importance of the community and local relationships in people's daily lives, and individuals and organizations became more and more oriented to happenings beyond the local community.

Mass Society

The Great Change coincided with the emergence of the theory of the mass society (Shils 1972), which, in contrast to Warren's argument that increased connections to larger systems undermined community and threatened individual and social well-being, suggested that integration into a central value system and set of institutions would improve community life. Wilkinson summarized this perspective succinctly: "The mass society is a welfare society promoting egalitarian ideals. It is a form of community to be achieved as a societal goal, and not something to be resisted as a sign of the decay of community" (1991, 21). The mass society thesis provided a strong argument for abandoning the territorial element common to most definitions of community, while its emphasis on the integration of local populations into the value system of the larger society meant the community was no longer coterminous with the local society.

"Bowling Alone"

Over the past decade, the community decline thesis has been reembraced, most notably by Robert Putnam in a series of influential articles (1993a, 1995, 1996) and in his recent book, *Bowling Alone: The Collapse and Revival of Community* (2000). Drawing on many sources of data (e.g., declining participation in bridge clubs, the percent of people attending public meetings, and changes in charitable giving), Putnam argues that we have become increasingly disconnected from family, friends, and important social institutions. He describes this growing disconnectedness as the direct result of a breakdown in the nation's stock of social capital, which he defines as "connections among individuals, social networks and the norms of reciprocity and trustworthiness that arise from them" (Putnam 2000, 19). In communities characterized by high levels of trust, strong norms of reciprocity, and dense networks of civic engagement, people feel an obligation toward one another and are better able to work together for the common good. Social capital develops as trust, reciprocity, and engagement reinforce one another. The argument can be briefly summarized as follows: "Networks involve mutual obligations. . . . Networks of community engagement foster strong norms of reciprocity. . . . A society characterized by generalized reciprocity is more efficient than a distrustful society. . . . Trustworthiness lubricates social life. Frequent interaction among a diverse set of people tends to produce a norm of generalized reciprocity. Civic engagement and social capital entail mutual obligation and responsibility for action" (20–21).

Putnam's analysis suggests that trends in virtually all types of civic engagement indicate that social capital has declined sharply in communities throughout the nation. The prescription for correcting this situation lies in rebuilding the locality-based relationships that have been lost. We must, in Putnam's view, "resolve to become reconnected with our friends and neighbors" (414).

This argument has resonated with both academics and policy-makers because it offers a rather simple approach to complex social and economic problems that have not been solved by market mechanisms, government programs, or legislative action. Many scholars (Flora 1998; Flora and Flora 1993; Flora et al. 1997; Potapchuk 1996; Ritchey-Vance 1996) have embraced it as part of their call for new community development activities and agendas. And some of our highest elected officials have invoked the term "social capital" as a key component of strategies to address such disparate policy issues as neighborhood revitalization and nation-building in the former Soviet block (Portes 1998). President Clinton was so impressed with Putnam's thesis that he invited the author to meet with him at the White House (Portes 1998).

Despite its appeal, social capital is freighted with confusing conceptual baggage. For this reason, the term deserves more scrutiny before it is embraced as an element of sound public policy. First, and perhaps most important, it is critical to understand that the concept of social capital, especially as used by Putnam, is rooted in James Coleman's version of rational choice theory (1988, 1990b). In Coleman's (1988) framework, people are viewed as purposive agents who make rational, deliberate choices to maximize their utility. In contrast to traditional economic approaches that tend to view the actor in isolation, however, Coleman explicitly incorporates the social context. As he puts it, "persons' actions are shaped, redirected, constrained by the social context; norms, interpersonal trust, social networks, and social organization are important in the functioning not only of society but also of the economy" (1988, S96). Although the inclusion of social organization imposes limits on action, the underlying conception of the individual still resembles *homo economis:* people maximize their utility by conducting a cost-benefit analysis of alternative courses of action. In the end, as Alexander argues, Coleman retains "the picture of discrete, separated, and independent individuals" (1992, 209).

Although there are numerous theoretical and practical difficulties with such a conceptualization of action, perhaps the most serious shortcoming is its inability to account for social structure and collective action (Bridger and Luloff 2001). In order to reconcile structure and order with autonomous individuals in this framework, people must relinquish control over activities and resources for conscious and calculated reasons that are in their best interests. This conceptualization requires a mechanism that reconciles differences among short-term self-interest, long-term self-interest, and long-term collective interest. Putnam (2000), following Coleman, argues that the norm of reciprocity resolves this problem. According to this line of reasoning, if I can expect that if I do you a favor now, you (or someone else) will repay me in the future, then the distinction between short-term self-interest, long-term self-interest, and long-term collective interest melts away. Practically, however, the norm of generalized reciprocity would only seem to hold when an actor can expect that a favor will be repaid within the foreseeable future. In many instances, this is an untenable assumption.

Ultimately, rational choice theory tries to solve this dilemma by relying on the concept of trust. As actors come to trust one another, they are less tempted to take actions that serve only their own short-term (or long-term) self-interest. Trust results in a shared commitment to the long-term collective interest. But it is important to realize that according to rational choice theory trust itself is a product of calculated decision-making. The decision to place trust in an individual, organization, or decision-making process when one is not sure of the future payoff is analogous to the reasoning involved in placing a bet: the individual calculates the odds (Coleman 1990b). If the odds favor her, then she would be rational to place trust in the other party and she would be rational to cooperate. If the odds are against her, it is not rational to cooperate.

When it comes to the kinds of situations that typically confront those involved in community action and community development, there is no simple way for a rational actor to calculate accurately the odds of loss or gain. Consider two activities that figure prominently in many community development efforts: planning and zoning. Decisions made in these institutional realms often include acceptance of limits on property rights and cooperative agreements aimed at reducing externalities associated with production and processing activities. Such decisions involve major concessions, and it is difficult to envision how a rational individual could calculate the odds that long-term benefits will somehow make up for losses incurred in the short run.

A more basic problem with this line of reasoning is that it fails to capture the motivations of donors in the exchanges that are essential to the creation and maintenance of social capital. It is easy to understand why recipients participate, since they receive tangible benefits in the form of favors, gifts, and/or loans. For donors, however, the motives that lead them to participate are less clear. As Portes (1998) notes, the fact that donors are expected to provide assets with no expectation of immediate reciprocity raises a host of questions that neither Coleman nor Putnam addresses. There are arguably a wide range of motivations behind the donations that are critical to the creation and maintenance of social capital, and these deserve considerably more attention insofar as "they are the core processes that the concept . . . seeks to capture" (Portes 1998, 5).

When discussing the applicability of social capital to community development, it is also important to address the extent to which social capital is transferable across different domains of local action. Coleman is well aware of this problem: "Social capital is not completely fungible. . . . A given form of social capital that is valuable in facilitating certain actions may be useless or even harmful in others" (1990b, 302). Social capital, therefore, is not always transferable across networks and domains of action. To the extent that social capital remains locked within specific networks, it makes little sense to talk about a community's stock of social capital. Whether or not social capital can be aggregated across individuals or networks to the community level remains an empirical question.

This issue is particularly salient given the patterns of stratification that divide most communities. To take a simple example, every community contains voluntary groups and organizations. Often, these are formed along class and/or racial and ethnic lines. Each organization may be characterized by dense networks of civic engagement, a high level of generalized reciprocity, and strong norms regarding the behavioral expectations of members. Further, there may be much interaction between organizations drawing members from the same class, racial, or ethnic groups. In most communities, however, there are few linkages among organizations composed of people from different backgrounds and societal positions. This hampers the development of the trust necessary for effective collaboration and successful community action. Instead, most communities are best characterized by pockets of social capital that are isolated from one another.

Putnam attempts to solve this problem by distinguishing between bonding and bridging social capital. Bonding social capital is what he calls a "sociological superglue" (Putnam 2000, 23). It is found in dense networks such as those characteristic of some ethnic groups. Bridging social capital is similar to Granovetter's (1973) concept of weak ties and encompasses "people across diverse social cleavages" (Putnam 2000, 22). Communities that strike a healthy balance between these types of social capital should be most likely to undertake successful collective actions. Unfortunately, Putnam finds no examples of communities containing both bonding and bridging social capital, which leads him to issue the following caveat: "In our empirical account . . . this distinction will be less prominent than I would prefer" (24).

Even if it were possible to identify ways to build bonding and bridging social capital, high levels of trust would not necessarily emerge because, as Coleman points out, the development of trust depends upon "the actual needs that persons have for help, the existence of other sources of aid . . . and the degree of affluence" (Coleman 1990b, 307). Stratification powerfully affects each of these factors regardless of the extent of interaction among groups and individuals.

The Interactional Approach to Community Development

Our approach to community action and local development is driven by interactional theory (Wilkinson 1991), and requires a different conceptualization of social interaction and individual calculus. While acknowledging the massive changes that have affected communities over the last century, this approach focuses on persistent features of local life. Despite the fact that local society is not the integrated, holistic unit it might once have been, people sharing a common territory tend to interact with one another on place-relevant matters, even as they participate in more far-flung networks and extra-local systems. Locality-based social interaction has not disappeared, and is still the essential element of community: "Social interaction delineates a territory as the community locale; it provides the associations that comprise the local society; it gives direction to processes of collective action; and it is the source of community identity" (Wilkinson 1991, 13).

Interaction affects social behavior in important ways. We behave and act purposively in response to the concept we have of our connections with others. This is a point Tönnies (1957) made long ago in his distinction between the natural will and the rational will. The natural will is impulsive; it is nondeliberative and noncalculative. In contrast, the rational will is deliberative; means and ends are considered and recognition is given to the necessity of suppressing impulses in order to attain goals. In all relationships, the type of will varies. At times it is natural, while at others it is quite rational. *Gemeinschaft* refers to those associations in which the natural will predominates, and *Gesellschaft* refers to those characterized primarily by the rational will. However, *Gemeinschaft* and *Gesellschaft* are not polar opposites—elements of both are present in all relationships.

Schmalenbach (1961) begins with Tönnies' concepts of *Gemeinschaft* and *Gesellschaft,* but argues that the typology is incomplete as formulated. He suggests that a third category is needed to avoid the confusing uses to which Tönnies' concepts have been put, especially *Gemeinschaft* (Wilkinson 1991). In Schmalenbach's scheme, community is a natural state of being in relation to others. The formative conditions of this state are not consciously experienced. Instead, they are experienced in an unreflective manner; the mere fact of human existence leads people into multiple and natural relationships with others. Community "simply refers to the fact that one naturally is connected to other people" (Wilkinson 1991, 16).

When community is consciously recognized and responded to emotionally, and the emotion is shared in social interaction, a new state emerges. This state is different from community, *Gemeinschaft,* or *Gesellschaft.* Schmalenbach calls it *Bund,* a term that, loosely translated, means communion. Communion is a celebration of community. It is important to note that although communion cannot exist in the absence of community, the opposite relation does not hold. Community exists whether it is emotionally responded to or not.

Wilkinson draws on this conception of community to argue that it is a natural and ubiquitous phenomenon: "It is natural because people . . . engage in social relationships with others on a continuing basis and . . . derive their social being and identities from social interaction . . . all people engage in it almost all of the time, whether or not they recognize that fact. . . . Community, therefore, is a natural disposition among people who interact with one another on matters that comprise a common life" (16–7).

The locality orientation that characterizes much of this interaction contains a special form of *Gemeinschaft* that creates a generalized bond: people who inhabit the same territory inevitably interact over common issues, and this interaction gives structure to local life. Locality-oriented interaction also provides an explanation for the convergence of self and collective interest because "each actor has a real interest in the *local* aspects of local social life. This interest . . . is pursued in social interaction and thus is shared" (39).

Local life is further structured as people organize to accomplish various tasks and pursue their interests. From the interactional perspective, this organization is viewed in dynamic, process-oriented terms. Organized groupings are conceptualized as unbounded fields of interaction. The community, in turn, is composed of several more or less distinct social fields through which people act on various interests and accomplish different goals. For instance, in most communities it is possible to identify social fields composed of people and organizations dedicated to social services, environmental issues, and economic development. The actions that occur in the community field connect these more limited spheres of activity. Although this field is similar to other social fields, it does not pursue specific interests. Instead, the community field pursues the larger community interest: "The community field cuts across organized groups and . . . other interaction fields. . . . It abstracts and combines the locality-relevant aspects of specialized interest fields, and integrates the[m] . . . into a generalized whole. It does this by creating and maintaining linkages among fields that otherwise are directed toward more limited interests. As the community field arises . . . it in turn influences those special interest fields and asserts the common community interest in the various spheres of local social activity" (36). The actions that occur in the community field coordinate the more narrowly focused actions that occur in other social fields and, in the process, bind them into a larger, more inclusive, whole.

Community Development from an Interactional Perspective

A local capacity to address important issues and improve local well-being depends upon the strength of the community field. Thus, community development involves purposive efforts to create and strengthen the community field. The most distinctive feature of these efforts is their focus on developing relationships and lines of communication across interest groups. This involves the conscious attempt to create linkages among actions and actors in different social fields. From this perspective, then, community development is the process of building relationships that increase the adaptive capacity of people who share a common territory; it requires that residents work purposively to increase the number or reinforce the strength of the relationships among "the various fields of locality-oriented action" (Wilkinson 1991, 92).

Adaptive capacity is reflected in the ability of people to manage, utilize, and enhance the resources available to them to address local issues and problems. From an interactional perspective, then, every community has the potential for collective action.[1] It is this capability that differentiates a community from an aggregation of individuals who simply share a common territory. We call this ability "community agency," and define it as the capacity for collective action. Fostering community agency is central to community development efforts.

Here it is useful to draw the distinction between development *in* community and development *of* community (Claude et al. 2000; Summers 1986; Wilkinson 1991). Development in community refers to such instrumental activities as job creation, infrastructure improvements , and business retention, expansion, and recruitment. In contrast, development of community focuses on the social aspects of local life, and emphasizes the enhancement of local problem-solving capacities. The development of the community field is synonymous with the development of community.

In many rural communities and small towns there are obvious needs for jobs, income, and social services; however, narrowly focusing on such sustenance needs misses the essential contribution that development of community makes to local well-being. Community development is a broad, multi-faceted process requiring the simultaneous advancement and mutual reinforcement of development of community and development in community.

When specific projects are pursued with an emphasis on building the relationships and lines of communication that make up the community field, community development has occurred regardless of whether or not a project met specific outcomes (Claude et al. 2000; Wilkinson 1991). Trying is enough. In fact, from the perspective articulated here, objective success is not the most important measure of community development. Communities develop and well-being is enhanced when residents work together to address common issues and problems—that is, when they exhibit community agency (Bridger and Luloff 1999, 2001; Luloff 1998; Luloff and Swanson 1995; Wilkinson 1991).

Evidence of the relationship between community development, well-being, and action have been documented in a series of recent studies. For instance, Claude et al. (2000) studied four rural communities in Pennsylvania and found that in those communities characterized by high levels of activeness, residents rated community well-being higher than in communities

1. We are not suggesting that the community "acts" in a literal sense. People act; community development occurs as "[members'] actions connect with the acts of others to form action fields" (Wilkinson 1991, 92).

characterized by low levels of activeness. Moreover, in those places characterized by low levels of success and high levels of activeness, residents were more likely to rank social well-being higher than their counterparts in communities characterized by high levels of success and low levels of activeness (Claude 1995; Luloff 1998).

There is also evidence that community activeness is associated with well-being at the individual level. For instance, Jacob, Luloff , and Bridger (2001) found that communities characterized by macrolevel factors including community solidarity (an aspect of local life that can be seen as emerging from collective action) contributed to mental well-being. Those respondents who lived in communities with higher levels of community solidarity were less depressed than residents who lived in places with low solidarity.

Implications

Community development strategies based on the concept of social capital direct attention to rebuilding connections that have been lost in the course of modernization. Their aim, to borrow from Coleman's 1992 American Sociological Association presidential address, is a rational reconstruction of society—one in which new institutions would replace the traditional ties that once held our communities together. In contrast, the interactional approach focuses on features of local social life that persist, and suggests that community development efforts can build from existing fields of interaction among a local population. From this perspective, community can emerge whenever people share a common territory. By beginning with this premise, the interactional approach directs attention to community development policies that nurture this potential. Of course, effective policies must recognize and address the fact that many of the problems facing local communities have extra-local origins. Community is not likely to emerge when residents struggle to meet basic needs. At the same time, however, the persistent linkage between community action and well-being suggests that efforts to foster the development of community at a local level must be a key component of rural development policy.

16

Social Capital

Cornelia Butler Flora and Jan L. Flora

Human interaction is the foundation of all communities. People may inhabit the same place for extended periods of time and never interact; conversely, people are increasingly interacting with others who live outside of their geographic community. Interactions in human communities are not based solely on proximity, but also on history. Understanding the configuration of interactions, along with the inequalities and power differentials that structure interactions, requires an understanding of the historical context as well as of current processes.

Human interactions can build or diminish social capital. Social capital is a community attribute, and is one of the resources that organizations and communities can invest in. Social capital can positively or negatively affect wider social goals of equity, ecosystem health, and vital economies. Understanding both the structure and content of social capital and its relationship to other types of capital can contribute to community analysis and community building.

Social Capital Defined

Social capital is often characterized by norms of reciprocity and mutual trust (Coleman 1988). Norms can be reinforced through a variety of processes: forming groups, collaborating within and among groups, developing a united view of a shared future, or engaging in collective action. Robert Putnam describes social capital as referring to "features of social organization, such as networks, norms, and trust, that facilitate coordination and cooperation for mutual benefit. Social capital enhances the benefits of investment in physical and human capital" (Putnam 1993a, 35–36).

A number of scholars regard social capital as an individual attribute, focusing on the importance of networks as a personal resource (Coleman 1988; Bourdieu 1986). Employing an approach rooted in rational action theory—a variation of public choice theory—they conclude that investments in social capital are declining because individuals retain few of the benefits derived from their investment. From this we can deduce that social capital has characteristics associated with public goods. We propose that structural factors, rather than individual motivation, increase bias against the formation of social capital. For example, the way that built capital is designed or used can either aid or impair social capital development: for example, when housing improvements are delivered in a top-down fashion, and decisions and resources are produced entirely outside the community, social capital often decreases and dependency increases, as verified by many urban renewal projects of the 1960s and 1970s.

Communities can build sustainable social capital by strengthening relationships and communication on a community-wide basis and encouraging community initiative, responsibility, and adaptability (Flora et al. 1999). Clearly, however, it takes time for these processes to unfold and for social capital to develop. Strengthened relationships and communications can result from fostering increased interactions among unlikely groups inside and outside of the community and increased availability of information and knowledge among community members. Community initiative, responsibility, and adaptability are enhanced by developing a shared vision, building on internal resources, looking for alternative ways to respond to constant changes, and discarding a victim mentality, which only causes the community to focus on past wrongs rather than future possibilities.

Interactions of Different Forms of Capital

Favoring only one form of capital can deplete all capital within a community in the future; however, each form of capital has the potential to enhance the productivity of the others. For instance, increasing social capital greatly reduces transaction costs, making other resource uses more efficient. Granovetter (1997) proposed that social capital (or embeddedness) has an independent effect on the functioning of economic systems, and increasingly, scholars have built on this insight (see also Landolt 2001;

Triglia 2001; Talmud and Mesch 1997; Portes and Zhou 1992). Transaction cost economics suggests the importance of social capital in increasing competitiveness, from firms to nations (Möllering 2002; Dasgupta and Serageldin 2000; Pamuk 2000; Wilson 2000; Lorenz 1999; Knack and Keefer 1997; Siles, Hanson, and Robison 1994).

Often, social capital is not seriously considered in the state and market sectors. For example, schools in communities with high levels of social capital, measured by such indicators as high attendance at varsity sports events, a perceived safe and drug-free school and community environment, and low student-teacher ratio, have fewer dropouts than comparable schools with low levels of social capital (Buckley 1997). The challenge is to maintain and strengthen social capital in order to enhance other forms of capital.

Additionally, overemphasis on generating financial and built capital without regard to the pollutants emitted can reduce the value of human capital through negative impacts on health. Destroying soil and water quality can negatively affect natural capital, and if local networks are bypassed and replaced with impersonal bureaucratic structures with top-down mandates, social capital can be undermined. Attention solely to natural capital can lead to a wasting of human capital and a decline in financial and built capital, as natural capital preservation is pursued.

Sources of Social Capital

The impetus for building social capital often comes from civil society groups. However, the state plays a key role in redirecting resources and changing rules in order for nongovernmental entities, with appropriate accountability, to receive state funds. The state also provides a safe space where civic interaction can occur, which is crucial because when space or safety is denied, social capital declines. Governmental inflexibility, particularly when it defends bureaucratic turf, tends to destroy social capital. Additionally, social capital does not substitute for government services, especially those that assist excluded people to participate in society with a degree of dignity.

Decisions by governments regarding the use of physical space—whether to individualize it or to provide a place for people to meet informally—can destroy or create social capital. When police protection is denied or the police are viewed as the enemy, when fire protection is withdrawn from an area, and when landlords allow property to deteriorate, personal and collective safety decreases. Terrorism is another threat to safety, making it legally and psychologically difficult for diverse groups to converge.

Types of Social Capital

Social capital can be divided into two elements similar to the classical for-mulations by Tönnies (*Gemeinschaft/Gesellschaft*), Durkheim (organic and mechanical solidarity), and more recent dichotomies, including Gra-novetter's (1973) strong and weak ties. Bonding social capital consists of connections among homogeneous individuals and groups, which may be based principally on class, ethnicity, gender, or another social characteris-tic. Specifically, it means that members of a group with high bonding capi-tal know one another in multiple settings or roles (see also Freudenburg 1986 for the concept of "density of acquaintanceship" and Coleman 1988 for the concept of "closure"). Bridging social capital, in contrast, connects diverse groups within the community to each other and to groups outside the community.[1]

Bridging social capital can enable change, but when this is the only type of social capital, outsiders or local elites establish agendas. Narayan (1999) uses the term "cross-cutting ties" to explain bridging social capital and to contrast it with bonding social capital. She explains it this way: "Primary social group solidarity [bonding social capital] is the foundation on which societies are built. The impact of primary social groups depends on their resources and power. But when power between groups is asymmetrically distributed, it is cross-cutting ties, the linkages between social groups, that are critical to both economic opportunity and social cohesion" (Narayan 1999, 13).

Consequently, not only are boundary maintenance and in-group/out-group notions incorporated into this dichotomy,[2] but the concept of power is introduced: "While primary groups and networks undoubtedly provide opportunities to those who belong, they also reinforce pre-existing social stratification, prevent mobility of excluded groups, minorities or poor people, and become the bases of corruption and co-optation of power by the dominant social groups. Cross-cutting ties which are dense and voluntary,

---

1. Narayan (1999) distinguishes between bridging and linking social capital. Both are cross-cutting ties among groups that hold different values; the former are horizontal and the latter are vertical ties. We have included vertical ties within the concept of bridging social cap-ital in order to emphasize the distinction between intimate, multipurpose (bonding) ties and instrumental, single-purpose, and non-redundant (bridging) ties.

2. Young (1970), using a Durkheimean approach, emphasized the exclusionary aspects of social solidarity, but his notion of boundary maintenance exercised by solidarity groups did not explicitly include notions of differential power. In fact, he saw solidarity movements as a strategy for excluded groups to gain symbolic recognition of their particular *Weltanschauung* as a way of bringing about social change. The perspective that we take in this chapter is that the access to information and resources that bridging social capital can bring to excluded groups can also be an important source of social change from below.

though not necessarily strong . . . help connect people with access to different information, resources and opportunities" (13).

Thus, Narayan suggests that the development of "weak ties"[3] (Granovetter 1973) is important for breaking down inequalities of power and
access. Both Granovetter (1973) and Loury (1977) conclude that a contributing factor to racial inequality is the lack of information available to
African American youth about where they can find "good" jobs. Furthermore, a lack of parental connections to smooth the way for African American children to gain access to those jobs contributes to inequality. These
notions of exclusion are complementary to those presented by Bourdieu
(1986), who proposes that elite families and upwardly mobile middle-class
families in France use family economic and cultural capital to gain strategic
class-based ties (social capital) for their children, thereby excluding children of those parents who lack resources and the necessary strategic
impulses for moving their children up the social ladder.

Narayan (1999) focuses on relating state governance to the overall character of civil society, specifically whether cross-cutting ties are high or low
at the national level. We are interested in how bridging and bonding social
capital interact at the (geographic) community level in order to determine
the extent of collective action that takes place in those communities. We
have employed a simple four-fold table in an effort to predict levels of collective action (see Fig. 16.1).

It is arguable that bridging and bonding social capital can reinforce one
another: when both are high we get effective community action, or entrepreneurial social infrastructure (ESI).[4] When both bridging and bonding
capital are low and ESI does not prevail extreme individualism dominates,
reflected at the community level in social disorganization. Community
action is low when apathy is the predominant way in which residents relate
to their community. When bridging social capital is high but bonding social
capital is low, there is clientelism, and relationships formed within and outside the community are predominantly vertical. When bonding social capital is high but bridging social capital is low, there is conflict. The
community may be organized against an outside entity or against itself. In
the latter case, bonding social capital occurs within homogeneous groups
within the community that are then in conflict with one another.

3. Weak ties, because they are cross-cutting, are generally used for a single purpose, and
hence more likely to be instrumental than strong ties, which indicate bonding social capital.

4. Entrepreneurial social infrastructure is a form of structural community action that
involves legitimation of alternatives, inclusive and diverse networks, and resource mobilization. This concept is discussed in detail later in this chapter.

		Bridging Social Capital	
		High	Low
Bonding social capital	High	Inclusion: horizontal ties within community, diverse horizontal and vertical ties to outside	Conflict with outside, internal factionalism
	Low	Clientelism: internal and external ties are mainly vertical	Apathy, extreme individualism

Fig. 16.1 Community social capital typology

Four characteristics of networks strengthen ESI and build bridging social capital. First, networks include a horizontal dimension. Lateral learning is critical in networks—communities learn best from each other. Social capital is built in the course of lateral learning, both between communities and within communities. Second, networks include a vertical dimension. It is critical that communities are linked to regional, state, and national resources and organizations; however, it is also critical that there is not just one gatekeeper who makes that linkage. Elected officials and members of organizations need to attend regional, state, and national meetings so that one person is not saying "Well, the rules won't let us." Other points of view that are still within the rules can uncover alternatives. Third, networks are flexible—being part of a network should not be a lifetime commitment. Participation increases and burnout decreases when people are asked to participate in a network that has a finite life span. People are willing to participate where they can make a difference, and they are asked to participate primarily in projects in which they have a real interest, although care must be taken that the larger vision is shared. Flexibility means that more people have the opportunity to become leaders. Fourth, networks have permeable boundaries—the community of interest is expanded and the community of place grows larger as new partnerships and collaborations are formed. Yet when very local action is required, the boundaries can become temporarily narrowed. Permeable and flexible networks are critical for community sustainability.

Dimensions of Social Capital

Exploring how the two dimensions of social capital relate to community change is a vital component in this discussion (see Fig. 16.2).

		Bridging Social Capital	
		High	Low
Bonding social capital	High	Locally initiated change driven by community-defined goals, with links to external resources	Community resists externally initiated change or in-fighting negates community change efforts
	Low	Community change dominated by local/extralocal "bosses" or "power elite"	Wealthy residents solve problems with financial capital; the poor have few options

Fig. 16.2 Social capital typology and community change

Absence of Social Capital: Low Bridging and Bonding

Communities lacking bonding or bridging social capital also lack the capacity for change. Individuals in these types of communities view themselves as self-reliant—or as totally adrift. In the absence of social capital, some people can succeed by substituting financial capital for social capital. For communities without financial capital, the absence of social capital can be fatal, as health studies are increasingly showing (Galea et al. 2002; Hendryx et al. 2002; Hyyppä and Mäki 2001; Rose 2000; Weitzman and Kawachi 2000; Kawachi et al. 1999; Kennedy et al. 1998; Runyan et al.1998; Kawachi et al. 1997).

Crime rates are high where there is an absence of social capital; personal security is a major problem. Skogan (1990) sees this disorder and incivility resulting in individual residents barricading themselves against the outside and against each other. The wealthy can protect themselves with expensive security systems (Blakely and Snyder 1997). They install alarms and even hire their own police, whereas no similar protection is available to poorer communities.

Conflict with the Outside/Internal Factionalism: High Bonding and Low Bridging

When bonding is high and bridging is low, communities resist change. This may occur in two ways. The community may organize in opposition to the outside in a kind of reactive solidarity (Young 1970): newcomers are viewed with suspicion in such communities. Alternatively, homogeneous groups or factions within the community may have varied perspectives on the kinds of change that might benefit their community. The groups do not trust each other and therefore are unwilling to cooperate with one another. Conflict, rather than being focused outside the community, is turned inward, and becomes the dominant community-level attribute. Although collective action may occur within groups in the geographic community, it is difficult to organize and carry out at the community level if internal conflict dominates.

External Influence via Local Elites: High Bridging and Low Bonding

Where bridging social capital is high but bonding capital is low, some degree of control from outside the community is expected and exercised through community elites or, in the most extreme form, local "bosses." This arrangement does not preclude collective action on the part of community residents, but is more apt to benefit outsiders and/or their local surrogates. While this pattern of social capital is also built on norms of reciprocity and mutual trust (or at least mutual obligation), those relationships are vertical rather than horizontal. Power is clearly concentrated. Traditional patron/client relationships, typical of urban gangs (Portes and Sensenbrenner 1993) or boss-run political machines, are created. Those at the bottom of the hierarchy—who are obviously beholden to the few at the top—are the majority of the population in such communities. As a result, recipients of favors owe substantial loyalty to their patron when it is time to vote for public office, to collect from a loser in the numbers racket, or to settle a score with a rival gang. As a result, horizontal networks are actively discouraged, particularly outside the sphere of influence of the patron, godfather, or elite clique. Such systems create dependency.

This type of social capital is prevalent in some persistently impoverished communities. For instance, an Appalachian coal-mining community studied by Duncan (1992) involved absentee ownership of most of the resources, businesses, and services by the coal companies. When coal employment declined, jobs were in short supply. An elite group of families controlled many public- and private-sector jobs through their control of local government. Gaining employment depended on whether one came from a "good" or a "bad" family. A more "modern" version of this hierarchical social capital is the "power elite" community model, in which social and economic inequalities are generally substantial. There is clearly a ruling clique that maintains its social distance from the rest of the community, but preserves political influence either directly or through pliable middle- or working-class officeholders (see Lynd and Lynd 1937 for an example of this approach to political power).

Participatory Community Action: High Bridging and Bonding

Horizontal social capital implies egalitarian forms of reciprocity, without necessarily implying a flat structure or equal wealth, education, or talents. Community resources or capital are broadly defined. Not only is each member of the community expected to give, thereby earning status and pleasure from doing so, but each is expected to receive as well. Each person in the community is deemed capable of sharing something valuable with all members, including contributions to a collective project, from parades to the volunteer fire department to Girl Scouts. Norms of reciprocity are reinforced, but payback to the donor is not required or even expected.

Such communities also have diverse contacts with the outside, which provide needed information to the community that can often be used to generate outside resources without exercising control over the community. One such example is Solidale, a small community of less than five thousand people located in the rich farming country of the northern Great Plains a few miles from a transcontinental Interstate highway (Sharp 2001). Over the past few decades, this community has had impressive economic growth (small manufacturing and value-added agricultural plants), resulting in substantial population growth. The leadership has followed a few simple rules. First, they are not afraid to use local funds if a potential economic enterprise or amenity looks like a good risk; local funds beget outside investments and industries in part because local investments send the message that the community is willing to partner with others. Second, there is a conscious effort to recruit young males (community leaders have failed to equitably recruit males and females) into community leadership, particularly through the private development corporation. Third, it is an attractive place to live, with amenities such as an excellent library, a community center, agricultural landscapes, and a science museum. All were financed largely through trusts and a community foundation, endowed (at least initially) by bankers without progeny. Thus, good fortune for the community, not necessarily for the bankers, also played a role. Now estate planners routinely ask their clients if they would like to will part of their estate to one of the multiple local trusts or foundations in addition to providing for their children. This is a community that encourages bonding capital, but also ensures that bridging or crosscutting ties are strengthened within the community and beyond. Clearly, Solidale has high bonding and bridging social capital.

Entrepreneurial Social Infrastructure

Communities that are high on both bridging and bonding social capital are poised for action, what Wilkinson (1991) would call engaging the "community field." We use the term "entrepreneurial social infrastructure" (ESI), which is a related term because it must be conceptualized and measured at the community or collective level. ESI is a measurable form of community action. It is conceptually distinct from social capital, and is hypothesized to be a consequence of high bridging and high bonding social capital.

Three characteristics distinguish ESI from social capital. First, indicators of ESI do not involve aggregation of individual characteristics, but are measured at an institutional level. Second, ESI can be changed through an explicit collective effort; it links social capital to agency. A community with a well-developed social infrastructure tends to engage in collective action for community betterment, which is why we call this phenomenon entrepreneurial social infrastructure (Flora and Flora 1993).[5] ESI is less abstract than the elements of social capital. For example, it is difficult to directly change levels of community trust, but it may be possible to encourage previously combative groups to cooperate through conflict management or by redefining issues.

Third, while diversity and inclusion are central to bridging social capital, ESI focuses on the outcomes of diversity—the willingness to consider and accept alternatives. In a community planning process, diverse types of information are sought from individuals and groups with different values and in diverse socioeconomic locations inside and outside of the community. When the flow of information is not channeled exclusively to or from a particular group but is dispersed widely throughout the community, decisions are more generally accepted. Furthermore, the inclusion of all citizens, not only in communications networks but also in the decision-making process itself, ensures greater commitment to carrying out those decisions (Flora 1998).

Flora and Flora (1993) identified some basic social structures within communities indicating that high levels of ESI are present, including legitimation of alternatives, inclusiveness and diversity of networks, and widespread resource mobilization.

Legitimation of Alternatives

Some communities seek simplistic solutions, while in others various perspectives are both accepted and valued. In communities that explore alternative options, there is an understanding that there are multiple ways of meeting shared goals. As with continuous improvement in industry, definitive solutions

---

5. The term "social infrastructure" was chosen because the name suggests that it operates in a parallel way to physical infrastructure (which we include under the term "built capital") in community development.

are not sought. Instead, countermeasures are implemented as progress is monitored and alternative ways of achieving goals are examined.

This leads to the acceptance of controversy, as opposed to conflict. Acceptance of controversy means that people can disagree and still maintain mutual respect. Where there is conflict, lines are drawn and labels are assigned according to one's stance on a particular issue. Conflict-prone communities may tacitly agree to avoid conflict, thereby suppressing controversy. New issues are not brought forward, visions of the future are not shared, and alternative ways of achieving goals are not developed. In this situation, conflict often lies right beneath the surface.

In communities that accept controversy, politics are depersonalized. Ordinary citizens are likely to run for public office, and feel able to implement countermeasures to resolve community issues without being castigated. There is awareness that the public sector is vital to provoking change at the local level; consequently, participation increases in both civic and governmental organizations. Furthermore, it has been shown that social capital is effectively produced when market actors are involved. Their involvement is based on determining how building social capital can aid the market's efficiency. Thus market actors may be involved last, but are still critical for social capital creation to successfully achieve equity and ecosystem health (See Flora et al. 2000 for a discussion of how the addition of market and state actors to a diversity group allowed it to succeed where it previously had failed).

In such communities, great attention is given to community process. There are celebrations of collective identities and individual and collective successes within the community. In contrast, in some communities where it is not legitimate to look at alternatives, the notion of a "limited good" is strong (Nash 1958). One person's success is considered to have occurred at the expense of another. These are communities where controversy does not occur, because people are unwilling to risk expressing contrasting viewpoints. Focusing on process allows for the assessment of progress toward goals. When progress does not meet expectations, a discussion of countermeasures for advancement occurs. There is less concern about notions like "Whose crummy idea was that?" or "Why didn't you listen to me? I had a better idea," and more consideration of questions like "What did we learn from this last effort?" and "What will we try now?"

Inclusive and Diverse Networks

Networks in communities with high social capital are diverse and inclusive. While there is room for subgroups with high levels of social capital, namely interest groups within communities, communities of place also require diversity. The best approach to diversity is not to ask "Are we being politically correct?" A more appropriate question is "Whose viewpoint is necessary as we move forward toward our goals?" For example, if a community development project's goal is to create more jobs, local people who might take those jobs need to be part of the process so there can be a better link between human capital and the built capital that offers employment opportunities.

Diversity involves directly asking nonparticipants why they are not involved in decision-making measures: Is it the time of day? Day of the week? Is the meeting place too expensive for lunch? Is it the location? Organizers need to take into account the concerns and availability of various participants. For example, meeting at lunch on work days is impossible for people who work in factories or in hourly wage employment. In addition, people who are poor or have little access to transportation may find meeting places difficult to access because of the lack of transportation.

Blanket invitations do not promote inclusiveness. Personal invitations are preferred over advertisements in newspapers. People who do not receive personal invitations and who are not part of the planning team generally only attend meetings if they are really incensed and want to protest. Personal invitations that include a chance to share and explain how that person or institution is critical to the effort and vice versa are vital to building inclusive networks.

Inclusiveness and diversity must go together. Being inclusive does not simply mean having a range of people at the table. This has been discovered in some youth programs that are supposed to teach leadership skills that young participants can then share with their community; however, the actual response to their presence is often something like: "Wonderful, here is someone to sell the donuts and do the cleanup." The youths may be willing to do these tasks, but they are also prepared to participate in planning the development activities. But when they try to participate in the planning, response of the established leaders is likely to be "Well, we don't do it that way here" or "We tried that twenty years ago and it didn't work." The mere presence of young people does not satisfy the criteria for inclusiveness; only a real effort to incorporate all participants meaningfully does this.

Resource Mobilization

Resource mobilization is the last critical piece of structured community action or ESI. First, resources in the community must be fully accessible. This applies to private resources, such as access to credit, as well as public resources, such as quality schooling, recreation, and other opportunities. This does not mean there cannot be criteria for access, but the criteria should be publicized, and opportunities for people to increase their chances for access need to be provided.

When mobilizing private resources, financial institutions need to decide how to disperse appropriate loan amounts with the appropriate terms to all levels of entrepreneurs and citizens. In such a community, private citizens of all levels contribute financial aid when there is a need, and opportunities are available for individuals to contribute their time and goods to worthwhile causes. The ability to mobilize private resources is an important element of community action, and gives everyone a chance to contribute.

Social capital building for development, or ESI, includes communities of interest and place. We also find that ESI is enhanced by forming advocacy and action coalitions among institutional actors of different sectors (e.g., market, state, and civil society) and at different levels (e.g., international, national, regional, provincial, and local). Civil society is key to adding sustainability to the policy mix, while the state is uniquely able to provide rewards for market actors who conserve and protect natural and human resources, and punishments for those who do not. Although market firms may initially resist regulation regarding treatment of employees or pollution, in the longer term many firms discover that pollution and undervaluing workers are forms of waste; profits can be enhanced through environmental cost accounting and building employee commitment.

Conclusion

As Putnam's (1993b) research in Italy and other studies suggest (e.g., Knack and Keefer 1997; World Bank 2001, chapter 7), development is enhanced when social capital exists. But when bonding social capital is not tempered by bridging social capital, it creates barriers to change. When existing social capital is "right," development happens—local resources are innovatively combined and augmented by outside resources.

Our research on environmental protection projects in the United States suggests that collective monetary incentives work when there is effective monitoring by the funder to ensure widespread participation and sharing (Gasteyer et al. 2002). Incentives with accountability can strengthen social capital, but simply urging participation does not. Mary Emery's (1994) research in Idaho demonstrates that focusing on network inclusiveness is a positive starting point for increasing bridging capital. Other research shows that simply inviting new people to the discussion does not automatically result in enhanced social capital. Situations must be established so that all actors have a chance to contribute to the collective endeavor—and have their contributions appreciated. For example, in her study of Head Start mothers in a medium-sized community in the United States, Barbara Peters (1998) found that bridging social capital was built by carefully recording volunteer hours that matched a number of grants. That practice, with the intention of integrating Head Start mothers into the staff, greatly increased social capital and human development. However, an increasing professionalization of the staff since the study has decreased that option.

Some factions of the market sector have recognized the importance of both bonding and bridging social capital for market effectiveness. In such firms, employees are carefully selected for their relational as well as their technical skills. Government organizations are less likely to seek relational skills in their bureaucrats; however, voluntary organizations often seek members who have strong interpersonal skills. Cultivating interpersonal skills in an institution that encourages the development of social capital helps to create effective organizations. The following questions must be considered in order to improve the market effectiveness of social capital: To what degree can communities of place learn from the organizational models for building social capital? Or is the applicability of the business models that use social capital for market ends limited because of firms' power to select their workforce and measure their success according to net worth and quarterly profits? These are qualities that may not readily translate into community practices. Forms and degrees of social capital are part of communities and they change slowly; however, interventions to enhance bridging social capital can be critical, particularly in areas of high distrust among different groups.

While a balance of bridging and bonding social capital is needed at all levels of society, building the bridging social capital of excluded groups is crucial. Unless excluded groups have a certain a mount of social capital, it is difficult to develop community-wide social capital. And unless there is a certain degree of community bridging social capital—an inclusive orientation by the dominant community groups—increased social capital on the part of excluded groups may lead to reactive solidarity on the part of the dominant group within the community, further distancing a now well-organized excluded group. This will diminish community, and reduce the prospects for accomplishing communal goals and enhancing social well-being.

17

Civil Society, Civic Communities, and Rural Development

Thomas A. Lyson and Charles M. Tolbert

Rural communities and local economies in the United States today are being woven into global circuits of mass production and consumption, as large national and multinational corporations have come to set the development agenda. In a scenario of corporate-led economic development, communities become places where production and consumption are concentrated. Left with few choices but to play the global development game, rural communities are forced to amass arsenals of business incentives in the hope of attracting jobs. Global capital flows to places that offer the highest return on investment. Rural communities and small towns, because they have less to offer prospective employers, are clearly placed in a structurally disadvantaged position vis-à-vis larger urban places.

Yet despite disruptions in local economies, resilient rural communities that bind people to place do exist (Irwin, Tolbert, and Lyson 1997, 1999). In these communities, small firms with local ownership, regional trade associations, and local entrepreneurs are firmly integrated with local government, local churches, and social associations, forming potentially important though often neglected structures for community development. A growing body of theory and research shows that these civic communities can be safe islands in the sea change of rural global economic transformation (Mills and Ulmer 1946; Tolbert, Lyson, and Irwin 1998; Tolbert et al. 2002). These communities have civic foundations that perpetuate community-oriented institutions amenable to community problem-solving efforts and that create cultural attachment to locality.

For most of the twentieth century, economic development in rural America was guided by the precepts of free-market capitalism. In agriculture, farmers were told to think of themselves as "managers" and not laborers. The Land

Grant Universities and the USDA developed agricultural technologies that were designed to make food production both more productive and more efficient. At the same time, farmers who adopted these technologies were supposed to earn a modicum of profit. The technologies were disseminated across the countryside by extension services, and the "good manager" was exhorted to quickly adopt them. Those farmers who failed to adopt the technologies and went out of business were deemed "bad managers." Millions of "bad managers" have left the land over the past hundred years.

For localities in which agriculture was not economically viable, rural development strategies centered on putting in place the modern transportation and communication infrastructures that businesses needed to compete in an increasingly competitive marketplace. Enhancing human capital through vocational education programs and job training was another key ingredient in the industrial development mix. Communities that did not invest in their infrastructure or in their residents, as well as those that did all of the right things but were unable to attract business, were simply "forgotten" (Lyson and Falk 1993).

The precepts of neoclassical economics provided workers and communities alike with a blueprint to follow on the path to development. In many respects, the free-market capitalist way was the only way. The fact that rural America was plagued by pockets of persistent poverty (Economic Research Service 1995), income inequality (Tolbert and Lyson 1992), and uneven development (Lyson and Falk 1993) throughout the last century was not part of the free-market plan. And indeed, when confronted with the inability to find a market-based solution to the rural problem, academics and government leaders began to look elsewhere for help.

By the beginning of the twenty-first century, rural America had become part of the global economy. Larger family farms were subsumed under the control of large national and multinational agribusiness firms (Heffernan 1999). Family farm incomes had fallen to the point that the federal government was pumping tens of billions of dollars into rural areas to keep people on the land. And American farmers found themselves in competition with producers from around world.

The situation for communities not dependent on farming was not much better. Many rural communities, especially in the South, have been forced to compete with third world countries for low-wage jobs. Large multinational corporations moved their facilities from one low-wage area to another, always looking for places where labor was cheap and unorganized and environmental regulations were weak. Not surprisingly, for the past forty years the gap between urban America and rural America has been growing (Lyson 1989).

The current restructuring of the rural economy toward increased global integration is premised on the assumption that large national and multinational corporations will be the primary engines of change and development (Barber 1995; Drabenstott 1999; Harrison 1994; McMichael 1996b). According to this perspective, rising productivity in the long run should translate into higher wages and presumably more prosperous rural communities (Thurow 1996). In the short run, though, some workers and rural areas may fare less well than others.

In a system tending toward global accumulation and regulation, the nation-state's role in directing economic development and in protecting the welfare of rural workers and communities has been weakened (McMichael 1996a; see also Chapter 19 in this volume). In the United States, for example, the deindustrialization of large segments of the rural economy in the 1970s and 1980s showed that the state did little to prevent large multinational corporations from succumbing to competition from lower-cost competitors in other parts of the world (Bluestone and Harrison 1982).

The lessons for local communities were clear. As Tolbert et al. note, "history suggests that large corporations rarely, if ever, make good neighbors. From the coal mining communities of Appalachia (Caudill 1963) . . . to the automobile and steel cities of the Midwest (Bluestone and Harrison 1982), and even to the so-called 'high-tech' enclaves in the Northeast (U.S. Congress 1995), the story has been the same. The social and economic fate of the community is integrally tied to the competitive position of the corporation in the global economy. Over the long term, the vitality of all globally oriented industries and the communities that are dependent on them will be challenged" (1998, 402–3).

Consider farmers in the United States and elsewhere, for example: the globalization of the food system means that a much smaller number of producers will articulate with a small number of multinational processors in a highly integrated business alliance. Drabenstott (1999) estimates that "forty or fewer chains will control nearly all U.S. pork production in a matter of a few years, and that these chains will engage a *mere fraction* [italics added] of the 100,000 hog farms now scattered across the nation." In a similar vein, Gary Hanman, the CEO of Dairy Farms of America, the U.S.'s largest dairy cooperative, recently noted that "we would need only 7,468 farms (out of over 100,000 today) with 1,000 cows if they produced 20,857 pounds of milk which is the average on the top four milk producing states" (Northeast Dairy Business 1999, 11). The consequences are clear, in that "supply chains will locate in relatively few rural communities. And with fewer farmers and fewer suppliers where they do locate, the economic impact will be different from the commodity agriculture of the past" (Drabenstott 1999).

Since at least the 1980s, the task of sheltering workers and communities from the disruptions of the marketplace has increasingly devolved from the nation-state to local communities (Grant 1995; Mander and Goldsmith 1996). This devolution has sparked a reexamination of the "bigger is better" model as the favored blueprint for economic development. A small but growing body of theory and research has focused attention on small firms, regional trade associations, industrial districts, and local entrepreneurs as potentially important, though often neglected, agents of development. Piore and Sabel (1984) articulated a set of precepts by which advanced industrial societies that are organized around smaller scale, flexibly specialized production enterprises can contribute to both economic growth and individual and community welfare. Perrow (1993), Bagnasco and Sabel (1995), Fukuyama (1995), Pyke and Sengenberger (1992), and others have further illuminated the conceptual foundation for an economy in which smaller scale, flexibly organized, municipally supported units of economic production can serve as a significant source of goods and services in advanced industrial societies. And over the last fifteen years, a small body of empirical research has demonstrated that economies organized around smaller scale, locally controlled economic enterprises are associated with a more balanced economic life and high levels of social welfare (Lyson and Tolbert 1996. See also Tolbert et al. 1998; Tolbert et al. 2002; Piore and Sabel 1984).

Civic Community and Balanced Socioeconomic Development

The emerging perspective on the benefits of smaller, locally-based enterprises as engines of rural economic development (Perrow 1993; Piore and Sabel 1984; Tolbert et al. 1998) was foreshadowed over fifty years ago by Walter Goldschmidt (1978) and C. Wright Mills and Melville Ulmer (1946). They showed that localities in which the economic base consisted of many small, locally-owned firms manifested higher levels of social, economic, and political welfare than places where the economic base was dominated by a few large absentee-owned firms.

Goldschmidt studied agricultural communities in the Central Valley of California. One community, Dinuba, was supported by relatively small, family-operated farms. The other community, Arvin, was surrounded by large, corporate-run enterprises. According to Goldschmidt, these communities were "selected for their divergence in scale of farm operations." However, they were also very similar in "most fundamental economic and geographic factors, particularly richness of potential resources, agricultural production, relationship to other communities, and the more general techniques and institutional patterns of production." Using a broad array of data collection and analysis techniques, Goldschmidt concluded that "the community surrounded by large-scale farm operations offered the poorer social environment according to every test made" (1978, 420).

The study by Mills and Ulmer (1946) was similar in design to the Goldschmidt study; however, Mills and Ulmer focused on manufacturing communities. They studied three matched pairs of small to medium-sized American cities. Two pairs provided big/small business contrasts, while the third provided an intermediate case. Their findings were consonant with those of Goldschmidt. According to Mills and Ulmer: "(1) Small business cities provided their residents a considerably more balanced economic life than did big business cities; (2) The general level of civic welfare was appreciably higher in the small business cities; (3) These differences between life in big and small business cities were due largely to differences in industrial organization—that is, specifically to the dominance of big business on the one hand and the prevalence of small business on the other" (1946, 1–2).

The perspective set forth by Goldschmidt and by Mills and Ulmer in the 1940s fits within a current renewed interest in civil society, civic community, and civic engagement that is challenging the assumption that a more globally integrated and corporately managed economy is the "best" and perhaps "only" development path that will lead to enhanced social and economic welfare for rural workers and communities (Barber 1995; Putnam 1993b; Tolbert et al. 1998). The civil society perspective posits that small to medium-sized economic enterprises can serve as the foundation of modern industrial economies. At the local level, the civic community is one in which residents are bound to place by a range of local institutions and organizations (Irwin et al. 1997). Business enterprises are embedded in institutional and organizational networks (Bagnasco and Sabel 1995; Piore and Sabel 1984). And the community, not the corporation, is the source of personal identity, the topic of social discourse, and the foundation for social cohesion (Barber 1995).

Recent research suggests that there may be many positive benefits to localities that embrace a community capitalism model of economic development (Lyson and Tolbert 1996; Tolbert et al. 1998; Tolbert et al. 2002). Places that nurture local systems of production as one part of a broader plan of diversified economic development can gain greater control over their economic destinies. They can also enhance the level of social capital among their residents, contribute to rising levels of civic welfare and socioeconomic well-being, revitalize rural landscapes, improve environmental quality, and ultimately, promote long-term sustainability (Berry 1996).

A Turn Toward Civil Society and Civic Communities

A theory of civil society and civic community as it relates to rural development is now being constructed. The contours of such a theory show that there are several fundamental differences between the dominant market-based approach to development and one based on civic community.

Modernization versus Sustainable Development

Neoclassical economics and civic community studies both reference bodies of social science theory. When they are applied to issues of social and economic development, however, they do so under the rubric of modernization and sustainability. Modernization efforts, whether at the community, regional, or societal levels, are frequently grounded on the precepts of neoliberalism. Under the modernization approach, the motor of development is the market economy. Modernization processes take root and are most successful in those societies that put the fewest constraints on the market. According to this scenario, economic globalization is the ultimate and preferred outcome of development.

In contrast to modernization, advocates of sustainability and sustainable development look for an explanation of development that is driven by social processes other than economics. Alexis de Tocqueville (1836) provided starting points for inquiries into civic community. Tocqueville showed that the norms and values of civic community are embedded in distinctive social structures and practices. In particular, Tocqueville pointed to civic associations as cornerstones of the civic community. Writing from this perspective, Robert Putnam notes that "a dense network of secondary associations both embodies and contributes to effective social collaboration" (1993b, 90). Esman and Uphoff also relate civic community to development when they report "a vigorous network of membership organizations is essential to any serious effort to overcome mass poverty under conditions that are likely to prevail in most developing countries" (1984, 40).

In many ways, civic community provides a counterpoint to free-market, neoclassical economics. Rather than pursue "rational" self-interest and assume that everyone else will do the same, "citizens in a civic community, though not selfless saints, regard the public domain as more than a battleground for pursuing personal interest" (Putnam 1993b, 88).

Production versus Development

The neoclassical model is at heart a "production" model, with the emphasis on economic efficiency and productivity. Low-cost production is the guiding principle. The civic community perspective can best be described as a "development" model, where economic efficiency is but one yardstick by which to measure success or failure. Equity issues within the community are given equal weight. Decisions are not made solely on economic grounds, but on social grounds as well.

Corporations versus Communities

The civic community approach is oriented toward local social and economic systems, while the conventional or neoclassical approach is directed toward economic globalization. The desired outcome for neoclassical economics is a global (mass) market articulating with standardized, low-cost, mass production. Sustainable development rests on production and consumption maintaining at least some linkages to the local community.

In the neoclassical model, the ideal form of production is the large firm. These are able to capture "economies of scale" and hence produce goods more cheaply than smaller and presumably less efficient firms. From the neoclassical perspective, large producers link with large wholesalers, large wholesalers connect with large retailers, and large retailers serve the mass market. Large multinational corporations are the driving engines in the development scenario.

The civic community perspective advocates smaller, well-integrated firms cooperating with each other to meet the needs of consumers in local (and global) markets. The ideal form is the "industrial district" (Piore and Sabel 1984). Firms share information and combine forces to market their products. The state supports this economic venture by ensuring that all firms have access to the same resources (e.g., information, labor, infrastructure).

Corporate Middle Class versus Independent Middle Class

From the modernization perspective, a worker's social class position is part and parcel of the corporate hierarchy. As the corporation goes, so goes the employment prospects of the individual. Not surprisingly, in an economy dominated by large corporations an individual's engagement with the civic affairs of the local community is tempered by his or her allegiance to the corporation. Like William Whyte's *Organization Man* (1956), the corporate employee moves from one homogeneous urban, suburban, or rural locale to the next, primarily at the behest of one corporation or another.

The economically independent middle class is rooted in the local community. As Mills and Ulmer showed, the independent middle class is more likely to participate in civic affairs and to concern itself with finding solutions to local social problems. What is "good" for the socioeconomic health and well-being of the local community is integrally tied to the welfare of the small business community. City-dwelling members of the independent middle class are the heroes of the New Urbanism (Hall and Porterfield 2001). They recreate community in close, planned residential areas that sport small shops, cafes, and services. The savvy urban professional or proprietor can choose between walking to work or commuting from the sprawling edge. Similarly, in some rural communities, the offices and storefronts of the independent middle class line a thriving Main Street. Still other communities have boarded up the downtown facades and reoriented business life along a bypass highway anchored by a "big box" retailer.

Human and Social Capitals versus Civic Community

In the neoclassical tradition, individuals with relatively high human capital (e.g., abilities, training, skills) and social capital (social network resources) naturally fare better. As the term "capital" implies, human and social capital are the property of individuals. Even within the same community, individual actors have variable amounts of human and social capital. These variations lead to uneven socioeconomic outcomes even in the best of communities.

The properties of civic communities are available to virtually all residents and are not reducible to tangible individual properties. Civic structure is not a commodity that can be produced, marketed, and accumulated by individuals. The vitality of the civic community rests on institutions that mediate individual variations in social and human capital.

Political Processes

Civic communities are fundamentally democratic. Community problem-solving around social, economic, and environmental issues requires that all citizens have a say in community life. Indeed, citizen participation in voluntary organizations and associations is a cornerstone of a civic community.

The free-market system of corporate community development, on the other hand, does not necessarily benefit from democracy. Benjamin Barber recently noted that "capitalism requires consumers with access to markets; such conditions may or may not be fostered by democracy" (1995, 15). The neoliberal paradigm is compatible with a wide range of political regimes and, in fact, may be challenged in places where widespread democratic participation prevails.

Motors for Development

From the corporate community, modernization perspective, a person's human and social capital are translated into better labor force outcomes in a free market. Human capital can take many forms, but it is typically manifested in investments in education, vocational training, and work experience. It is assumed that the "market" is the institution that is best able to efficiently allocate human resources. Social capital enhances the effectiveness of human capital by building bridges between actors who can mutually enhance each others' attainments and achievements.

The motors for development from the civic community perspective are civic engagement and social movements. Civic communities are best seen as problem-solving places in which residents come together in formal and informal associations to address common social problems. Communities that have rich associational and organizational structures nurture civic engagement and are best able to meet the social and economic needs of all of their residents (see Chapter 16 in this volume). Instead of individual rational actors being the foundation of the community, groups of individuals organized into social movements are fundamental to the civic community approach.

Regrettable Imperfections versus Surmountable Inequities

While markets may efficiently allocate resources, they are less than perfect. Market discrimination is an enduring feature of all capitalist economies. The result is uneven development. Some communities prosper, while others decline. In declining communities, sources for community income generation dry up. Poverty and unemployment increasingly prevail, and those people with viable options migrate elsewhere. Some communities may hold up better than others due to diversity in their economic bases. Even in resilient communities, however, racial, ethnic, and gender discrimination can lead to socioeconomic disadvantage for some groups. Discrimination-based inequalities manifest themselves in a variety of ways, ranging from income inequality to residential segregation. Remedies for these problems are frequently sought in the market's tendency to equilibrium.

Though more efficient markets can help to ameliorate labor market discrimination, a more perfect (efficient) market will still leave many inefficient communities behind. Implicit in the market model is the notion that a human settlement system that consists in part of many small communities is inefficient. Remote, isolated small towns are an anomaly in the global market regime. It follows that the demise of small towns is the result of natural market forces.

In the civic community tradition, market imperfections are community problems that need to be resolved. The interconnectedness of local civic institutions gives a structural impetus to problem solving. At the community level, research has shown that relatively more associations, churches, and locally oriented businesses are associated with higher income levels, lower poverty levels, less unemployment, less out-migration, and lower crime levels (Irwin et al. 1999; Lee and Ousey 2001; Lyson and Tolbert 1996; Tolbert et al. 1998; Tolbert et al. 2002). Within communities, evidence shows the same civic institutions associated with lower levels of Black/white residential segregation (Irwin et al. 2002). In sharp contrast to their place in a global free market, small towns occupy a prominent place in the civic community traditions.

Conclusion

The implications of the civic community, problem-solving perspective for social and economic welfare programs and community and rural development policy are clear. Communities dominated by large national or multinational firms are more vulnerable to greater inequality, lower levels of welfare, and increased rates of social disruption than localities where the economy is more diversified. In the current era of economic globalization and political devolution, an effective rural economic development strategy should be geared toward fostering an economically independent middle class everywhere. Policies to promote and strengthen regional trade associations, local industrial districts, producer cooperatives, and other forms of locally-based entrepreneurship should be part and parcel of a comprehensive community-based, rural economic development strategy. These groups and organizations are at the heart of the problem-solving capacity of local communities.

The core assumptions that underlie our understanding of both socioeconomic attainment processes and approaches to rural, regional, and community development need to be revisited. In traditional economic development paradigms, the economy is distinct from community and firms, and workers are cast as independent, competitive units. The civic community requires a fusion of cooperation and competition. As communities turn more civic, structure shades into infrastructure, competition into cooperation, and economy into society (Piore and Sabel 1984). The reemergence of an economy organized around locally coordinated, smaller-scale, technologically sophisticated, and globally competitive enterprises is both theoretically and practically possible.

The Social Institutions That Maintain
and Reproduce Community

18

The Global/Local Interface

Alessandro Bonanno and Douglas H. Constance

Although global social relations[1] between peoples and countries have existed for many centuries, recent trends toward increased political, economic, and cultural globalization have created a new context for understanding the interface between the local and the global. A crucial result of these trends is that the quality of life of many rural peoples and their respective communities depends less and less on nation-based policies and to an increasing degree on socioeconomic events taking place at the global level. The decisions and practices of global actors such as transnational corporations (TNCs), multi-national trade agreements such as the North American Free Trade Agreement (NAFTA), and global economic regulatory organizations such as the International Monetary Fund (IMF) and World Trade Organization (WTO) have serious implications for rural peoples. Local, regional, and national public policy-makers must take into consideration this new context in order to optimize the chances of creating and implementing effective initiatives designed to better the lives of rural peoples.

What is new and different today is the recognition that contemporary global social relations cannot be adequately understood through the continued use of the nation-state as the central unit of study. As local markets expanded into national and international forms, scholars who analyzed the growth of society employed the concepts of "local" and "international" in relation to the nation or the nation-state. Through the existence of the nation-state it was possible to identify and define the existence of "the less than national," i.e., the local and regional, and "the more than national," i.e., the international. From this perspective, the "inter-national" realm

1. The concept of "social relations" refers to the ways in which individuals and groups interact with each other and the outcomes of these interactions.

was cast in terms of social relations among sovereign nation-states. The decreasing utility of the nation-state[2] as the appropriate unit of analysis for studies of socioeconomic development opened the door for new conceptualizations of the local, the international, and the global as sites of study.

This scholarly debate on the features and nature of the relationship between locally-based social relations and globally-based social relations is the subject of this chapter. The first section covers early to contemporary views of the "local." The second section discusses the manner in which aspects other than the local, i.e., first "society" and later "world," were used and opposed to the local. The following section on the emergence of the global reveals that current understandings of the local/global relationship often conceives of them as two sides of the same coin. The next section covers perspectives that simultaneously address the local and global levels. While some views stress the importance of the global over the local, and others take alternative positions, all conclude that it is impossible to correctly understand the local/global interface without considering each of these aspects as mutually interdependent. The final section illustrates some research gaps, future developments, and possible policy implications.

Early Understandings of the "Local" and Its Relationship with "Society"

Early American sociology employed a dualistic approach that cast the "local" in opposition to "society." Localness was conceptualized in terms of community, tradition, and precapitalism, in opposition to society, modernity, and capitalism. This dualistic view is grounded in the works of Ferdinand Tönnies (1963) and Emile Durkheim (1984). For Tönnies, the local was synonymous with community, and the growth of modern society meant the loss of community. Durkheim was also concerned about the negative societal effects of the growth of capitalism and modern social relations, but he considered the growth of society as ultimately positive, as traditional, locally-based social relations lacked the necessary characteristics to sustain balanced socioeconomic progress. For both Tönnies and Durkheim, the alteration of locally-based social relations was a component of the natural evolution of society as a whole.

In the early 1900s, a group of scholars at the University of Chicago—known as the "Chicago School"—developed human ecology theory (e.g.,

2. It is important not to confuse our statement about the end of the centrality of the nation-state with the often-argued concept of the irrelevance of the nation-state as a political, economic, and social entity. Despite the growth of globalized social relations, the nation-state continues to maintain important powers and roles.

Park 1952). This approach employed a biological perspective that viewed the local community as an organism made up of particular social groups in competition with other social groups. As these groups competed, they had to adapt to existing conditions and changes brought on by endogenous and exogenous forces. This characterization of the local—as communities trying to adapt and survive in an increasingly industrial world—became a primary area of investigation for the nascent discipline of rural sociology. By the mid-twentieth century, Talcott Parsons (1971) presented a novel view of the local that departed from the dualistic notion. His theory of social action suggested that the local is one extreme on a continuum, with the broader society at the other pole. For most of the three decades following World War II, the view of the local as a part of a local/society continuum remained popular in rural sociological analyses.

From "Society" to the "World"

By the 1960s the dominant view of the relationship between society and the local was largely framed in terms of evolution and penetration. Evolution referred to the process through which localities developed and were absorbed by the modernized external society. Penetration referred to the processes through which these external social forces brought change to localities. Research remained centered on the consequences that contact between society and locality brought to local communities. Two versions of this approach became particularly influential within academic and policy-making circles. The first acknowledged that the penetration of extra-local forces through "vertical linkages" decreased the autonomy of local actors, but stressed that the positive effects of modern industrial growth outweighed their negative consequences on local communities (e.g., Warren 1963). The second position stressed the negative impacts—such as increased social and economic inequalities and decreased quality of local life—associated with the industrialization of local social relations (e.g., Goldschmidt 1947). The scientific debate shifted in the late 1960s as domestic and international events changed the organization of society. The disrupting effects of the Civil Rights movement, the anti–Vietnam War protests, the student movement, and national liberation and anti-Western movements in developing countries called into question previous evolutionary perspectives that highlighted the increased levels of social stability, consensus, and shared values associated with modernization and industrialization (Parsons 1971; Warren 1963). Alternative approaches emerged that provided strong critiques of established views of the positive relationship between the local and society.

In the 1970s, dependency theory (Frank 1979), world system theory (Wallerstein 1974), and critical theory (Lefebvre 1991) recast localness as part of a historically determined world order. These approaches place the relationship between the local and society in complementary terms. More specifically, they posit that the local cannot exist unless there is a society that defines and gives it meaning, and that an entity larger than the local (society) cannot exist without a local to represent its counterpart. In these views, society and locality referred to historically determined dimensions of space that were the outcome of established social relations. Because many theorists and policy-makers of the time believed that the primary objective of modern society was the creation of markets for the enhancement of socioeconomic development, these approaches viewed spatial relations in terms of the creation, maintenance, and expansion of markets. Despite their emphasis on world relations, the most fundamental market was created and reproduced within the space of the nation-state. National societies constituted the venue through which world social relations took shape. The elaboration of rural policies was generally framed in a nation-centered context in which the local was a regional variation of national social, economic, and political trends and processes.

The Global

In response to significant socioeconomic changes in the late twentieth century, a new perspective on the local/society relationship developed. This view argued that the study of local social relations had to take into account the actions of individuals and groups whose spheres of influence reached far beyond individual nations. Moreover, the view of the world as a system of nations (the "inter-national") was also seen as increasingly questionable. In essence, it became clear to many that if events could not be explained by using the nation as a spatial unit of analysis, then the study of the world as a system of nations was also flawed.

The crisis of nation-centered analyses was one outcome of changes that took place at the social, political, and economic levels. At the social level, the introduction of new means of communication—primarily computers and the Internet—created modes of interaction that were unthinkable only a few decades earlier. These new developments fostered the growth of a global culture—a way of acting that transcends locally- and/or nationally-based cultural norms. In essence, many people around the world who have the means find themselves thinking and acting in ways that are remarkably similar (Barber 1995). For instance, they eat at McDonald's, watch MTV,

Baywatch, and Michael Jordan on cable and satellite TV, use e-mail to communicate with people around the world, drink Coca Cola, wear Nike and Gap brand clothing, and so forth. At the political level, the new global culture was accompanied by a growing consensus opposed to trade barriers and in support of the free circulation of people and commodities among countries, resulting in initiatives such as NAFTA and the WTO. This neoliberal understanding of the new world order informed not only geopolitical but also regional policy decisions worldwide. At the economic level, the new cultural and political climates translated into companies having the ability to move about the globe with greater freedom. This situation allowed such companies to enhance their competitiveness and profits and, for some of them, to sever traditional linkages to their countries of origin and became global corporations (e.g., TNCs).The concepts "global" and "globalization" captured these changes and their consequences. Global refers to the tendency for local events to be, to a great extent, affected by economic, political, and cultural forces that operate at a level greater than the national and the inter-national. Globalization refers to the processes through which global social relations are established and reproduce themselves. The idea of the global and its implications are illustrated by the British sociologist Anthony Giddens' (1990) discussion of the distinction between place and space. Giddens maintains that the distinction between the concepts of place and space becomes visible only with the advent of modernity and capitalism. In premodern societies local events generally unfolded within a single location (the place). Because they were contained within the local community where they originated, it was possible to maintain independence from external forces. With the emergence of capitalism and modernity, local events became increasingly affected by, and linked to, other events that occurred outside the local and that were distant in space from it. For Giddens, the distinction between place (local) and space (global) emerged out of the transformation of social relations through space and time. While these transformations separated the local from the global, the interconnection between these two settings became much more evident. In other words, social change at the local level was most often linked to social relations established at the global level.

Giddens further contends that the distancing of place from space evolved through the various phases of the expansion of capitalism. In the global era, however, the relationship between the local and the global has reached a new and qualitatively different level that can be illustrated through the concept of the "hyper-mobility of capital" (Harvey 1989). This refers to the ability of economic actors to operate in ways that avoid specific local (as well as regional and/or national) laws and regulations and that allow them to significantly erode identification with, and loyalty to, countries of origin (Antonio and Bonanno 2000). It also refers to the ability that TNCs have to move their operations and assets beyond regional and national borders relatively quickly and easily, despite resistance from local actors (e.g., Dicken 1998; Gray 1998). This has been viewed as one of the prominent features defining globalization. Among globalization scholars, there is very little disagreement regarding why TNCs engage in this new behavior.[3] TNCs relocate their plants and assets worldwide in order to obtain more desirable conditions of production[4] and avoid limitations and restrictions demanded by other social actors (e.g., governments, workers, private organizations, social movements). Hypermobility is global because it is based on the establishment of social relations that go beyond the national and multinational levels. More specifically, the economy has gone global while the nation-state is still restricted to acting within its territorial borders.

Although the hypermobility of capital, as well as other aspects of globalization, is not homogeneously experienced in every location of the world, it does require the local dimension to exist. This means that the potential for mobility is global, and that a variety of locations and their social relations (e.g., labor markets, work forces, social institutions) are now linked together through processes of capital accumulation and spatial reorganization. Linking various locations around the world redefines the meaning of the local. Hypermobility mandates the existence of localities where global strategies materialize. For instance, in the event of plant relocation, the local is relevant in at least two ways, as conditions change both at the location that loses the plant and at the location that receives the relocated factory. These two localities, although experiencing different consequences of hypermobility, represent concrete aspects of global socioeconomic processes.

3. To be sure, some interpretations of the globalization of the economy and society and the role of TNCs depart from those indicated above. In particular, some accounts identify the concept of globalization exclusively in terms of the end and/or reduction of barriers to the circulation of commodities and labor (e.g., Friedman 2000). They argue that this is chiefly the result of advancements in technology and the implementation of neoliberal policies. While the importance of these factors is also shared by other interpretations, this segment of the literature takes for granted the use of new technologies and the implementation of neoliberal policies. More importantly, they do not problematize the actions of TNCs whose economic and social behaviors they largely support.

4. This phenomenon often has been described in terms of global sourcing (Heffernan and Constance 1994). Global sourcing refers to the ability of TNCs to search for desirable conditions and factors of production around the globe. This is a prerogative that was not available in other phases of the development of capitalism. As indicated by a variety of studies (e.g., Antonio and Bonanno 2000; Carnoy et al. 1993; Harvey 1989) the restructuring of the economy and society and advancements in technology have allowed the development of production structures and social conditions that permit enhanced mobility of financial capital, productive structures, and labor.

Continuing with this example, it is evident that the local is not simply the end stage of a process that began at the global level. This process finds a part of its roots at the local level, making the local and the global two sides of a unified process. As illustrated in many documented instances, plant and asset relocations from one place to another often respond to these locations' different labor markets, industrial legislations, environmental regulations, market access, and other local conditions that make one more (or less) attractive than the other in terms of capital accumulation strategies. The conditions that mandated global mobility cannot transcend the local. Additionally, this process creates the existence of locations that are "left out," that is, they are not included in global processes. Global relations will not necessarily eventually penetrate these locations. Again, globalization is not a homogenous set of processes that links localities and global actors in uniform manners across time and space. The heterogeneity of the process of the hypermobility of capital is evident in two ways. First, mobility assumes a variety of forms. Empirical studies (e.g., Storper 1997) indicate that along with plant relocations, mobility refers to events such as the reorganization of commodity-chain production (units of the production chain are replaced with others located in different areas or regions), decentralization of production (delegation of production processes to smaller production units), and even the strategy of threatening to move production facilities. Indeed, these last three phenomena have been interpreted in terms of the ideology of mobility. In this case, the possibility of relocating is employed by companies to extract concessions from labor, local and regional administrations, and nation-states. In other words, TNCs employ global sourcing strategies and play one locality off another to get the best deal. To be sure, mobility should not be understood in absolute terms, as localities can mobilize power to carry out successful dialogues with TNCs (e.g., Swyngedouw 1997). In particular, groups within localities endowed with natural, social, and human resources can be powerful counterparts to corporate strategies.

While most contributions to the understanding of the local/global interface have been published outside of rural sociology, a number of rural sociologists have probed this topic and generated valuable research. The works of Heffernan (2000), Friedland (1994), and McMichael (2000) represent fundamental contributions to the definition of the connection between global processes and local outcomes. While they all clearly stress the mutual interdependence between the global and the local, a common characteristic of these works is their attention to the dominant power of the global over the local. In his seminal work on corporate concentration in the agro-food industries, Heffernan documents the ability of global food

TNCs to shape markets and defeat resistance at the local level. Similarly, Friedland points out that while appearing to be locally-based operations, the proliferation of specialized commodities designed to cater to "localized" markets (market nichification) are in fact controlled by a few TNCs. Finally, McMichael stresses the power that financial forces such as the IMF and the WTO have at the global level and how these dominant institutions of the "globalization project" shape local situations. In particular, he highlights the crisis of the powers of the nation-state and argues its transformation into an "agent" of TNCs.

Other Interpretations of the Local/Global Interface

The idea that the local/global interface is dominated by the global sphere has also been questioned by rural sociologists (e.g., Arce 1997; Arce and Fisher 1997; Marsden 1997a; 1997b; Marsden et al. 1996; Marsden and Arce 1995). Employing an actor network approach, these scholars disagree with positions that view results of globalization as phenomena that can be almost exclusively explained through macro-socioeconomic analyses. Arce and Marsden contend that global processes are fragmented and reinterpreted at the local level. Global phenomena, in other words, are mediated and reconfigured by local actors. Therefore, it is important to underscore the differences and peculiarities of these aspects through a "close-up analysis." Documenting the life histories of individuals involved in agricultural production, Arce points out how knowledge of far and near events has been reinterpreted and embedded in the everyday lives of actors to create conditions for their expansion and success. For these authors, economics is not the primary factor for understanding globalization; rather, cultural and aesthetic dimensions such as fashion and taste are as crucial as economic factors to explain the emergence of global relations. The taken for granted ordering of the world, therefore, needs to be deconstructed in order to understand these basic processes of interpretation and action. They argue that macroanalyses neglect these aspects and therefore provide only limited interpretations of global processes. Macroanalyses have very little to say in terms of how actors "interpret and translate" global phenomena (Arce 1997, 82). While defending the value of the local (micro), Arce and Marsden do not disregard the importance of the global (macro) sphere in their view of contemporary society. Both are careful in underscoring the importance of macroanalyses as they call for a rural sociology that simultaneously takes into account both macro- and microperspectives. The two dimensions must be read as intrinsically interrelated sides of the same process.

Saskia Sassen's (1998, 2000) network theory provides another alternative interpretation to the dominance of the global sphere. She argues that globalization has fundamentally altered local social relations through the denationalization of socioeconomic processes. Denationalization is the practice of "offshoring" economic activities, placing them outside the regulatory umbrella of nation-states. This process, however, is not simply a strategy of TNCs, but it has been fostered by local entities such as nation-states and regional states (e.g., NAFTA), which through the introduction of neoliberal policies and deregulation have promoted processes that opened local economies and societies. Similarly, the control of global processes does not simply take place at the global level. Because flexible global actions materialize at the local level, the local centers where these materializations occur (e.g., the global cities) represent new important components of the global system. Through bypassing national and supranational organizations, global cities constitute networks of local entities that are central in the development and maintenance of global flows of capital and natural and human resources. Due to the fact that these networks are needed for the continuous growth of the global economy, they represent new forms of local empowerment. In essence, some authors (e.g., Friedland, Heffernan, and McMichael) identify the global as the locus of power, while others (e.g., Arce and Marsden) remind us of the local as a source of power, and Sassen transcends the separation of the local from the global. In her interpretation, the local/global relationship is presented in terms of the creation of networks in which the two dimensions are reconfigured and reshape each other.

Our research conducted over the past few years on the community impacts of industrialized animal production in the United States provides further insights into the local/global interface (Bonanno and Constance 2000; Constance and Bonanno 1999; Constance et al. 2003a; Constance et al. 2003b). Through case studies of corporate penetration and expansion of confined animal feeding operations (CAFOs) in the swine and poultry industries in Missouri and Texas, we discovered that TNCs do employ global sourcing strategies to identify and select the locations with the most lucrative factors of production. Dominant agro-food TNCs sourced low-cost labor, cheap land, abundant water, lax regulatory environments, and vulnerable depressed rural economies to set up their "export platforms" to service global markets. Similar to Sassen's perspective, we also found that in both examples the states of Texas and Missouri changed their corporate farming laws to make them more attractive to corporate investments. In both cases we found that these CAFO-based business development strategies supported in cooperation with the states and TNCs soon met with increased criticisms as local social movement groups organized and declared the CAFO forms of industrial animal production illegitimate socioeconomic development projects. The social movements organizations argued that the negative impacts of CAFOs, including environmental degradation, human health hazards, and property value depreciations, outweighed the positive contributions, such as jobs and tax base increases. In the Missouri case, the social movement coalition was successful in halting the expansion of CAFO forms of development through the enactment of stricter corporate farming laws. In the Texas case, in contrast, legislation was passed to decrease the barriers to corporate farming, resulting in a steady increase in both swine and poultry CAFOs. In fact, one of the TNCs that was restricted in Missouri is now expanding in Texas.

We conclude that the globalization project is a contested terrain whereby the attempts of TNCs to globally source rural localities as production sites are countered at the local level through the emergence of locality-based social movements. Although these social movement organizations are often successful in restricting corporate activities in their localities, our research indicates that more often than not the TNCs simply relocate to another state (e.g., from Missouri to Texas) or another country (e.g., from Missouri and Texas to Mexico) where the factors of production are more supportive for their particular type of business development.

Research Gaps, Future Directions, and Policy Implications

Despite the fact that some rural sociologists actively examine the issue of the local/global interface, most of the debate, research, and theorizing on this topic have taken place outside the venues where rurality and rural problems have been traditionally studied. To rectify this situation, steps should be taken to qualitatively enhance the discussion on the local/global interface within the community of scholars, practitioners, and policy-makers who are concerned with rural issues. In this regard, we recommend that American intellectuals interested in rural issues become more receptive to new approaches and paradigms and follow the example of their European (e.g., Marsden and Arce 1995), South American (e.g., Gras 1997), and Oceanic (e.g., Curtis 2001; Lockie and Lyons 2001) counterparts, who have adopted alternative approaches in their study of rural issues. North Americans should amend perspectives that view the local as a self-contained entity composed of a set of social relations whose evolution is shaped by the mobilization of local resources. Too often, this view has resulted in the development of narrowly focused policies that underestimated the constraints imposed on local actors by global forces. Similarly, efforts should be made to analyze the global in terms that transcend the view that sees it only as a background force against which local actors ultimately operate. In essence, North American scholars, practitioners, and policy-makers should engage more actively in, and learn from, pertinent debates stemming from geographical areas and academic communities beyond North America.

The most significant effort, however, should be to avoid the common error of focusing attention exclusively on either local or global contexts. Given the current conditions of the evolution of social relations, it is almost impossible to study any setting without making specific references to both its local and global connections. This is a situation to which policy-makers should pay particular attention. The effort to study the local/global interface in new ways should be accompanied by the adoption of fresh views about the policy implications of living in a more open global society. While local characteristics still play a fundamental role, the opening of social and economic spaces and the much enhanced global flow of human and nonhuman resources create conditions that make it very difficult to act locally without careful consideration of global factors. Motivated by the increasing inability of local political actors to respond to global forces, a number of scholars have argued the demise of local and national state powers. In their view, local political forces are ultimately incapable of developing and implementing policies that do not conform to global trends and objectives. More accurate analyses, however, have recognized the ability of local, regional, and national authorities to respond effectively to global initiatives and flows. Regardless of these differences, the consensus is that the basic conditions for policy interventions have changed, in at least two ways. First, despite expanding confidence in the free market to generate solutions to current issues, existing social problems require some form of public and/or private intervention and action. Second, the scope of action of global flows transcends the spheres of jurisdiction of local and national agencies and representatives. Therefore, policy interventions designed to improve the lives of rural peoples should be conceptualized in different terms than in the past and in ways that take into account the porous and flexible boundaries of action in the global era. Because of these changes, successful socioeconomic development initiatives need to seek broader coordination across localities and rest on a dialogue between locally-based constituencies and global forces. In other words, actions at the local level should be coordinated in ways that contemplate the effects of global flows and interests of global forces while maintaining the objectives and fostering the aspirations of local groups. While this new dimension of policy intervention presents obvious difficulties, it must be recognized and contended with in a world in which the local and the global are increasingly interconnected, yet remain two equally important constitutive components of the new society.

19

Competition, Cooperation, and Local Governance

Mildred E. Warner

Privatization, decentralization, and civic participation are common themes characterizing the changing structure and organization of local governments. At national, state, and local levels, governments have sought to decentralize programs so that decisions about service delivery and policy design would be made closest to the beneficiary to enhance efficiency and civic participation. Governments also are exploring the possibility of market forms of service delivery. Traditionally, public services have been defined as services the private market cannot provide due to the collective nature of their consumption and the inability to exclude free riders; however, many local governments provide public services via contracts with private providers, and user fees are becoming more common. Privatization and decentralization are based on the positive power of competition to ensure governmental efficiency and responsiveness to citizen voice.

These trends represent important innovations, but they also bring new challenges. Successful decentralization requires administrative and financial capacity, as well as effective citizen participation, but many rural governments lack the necessary revenue base or sufficient professional management capacity to decentralize. Although civic capacity is strong in some rural communities, in others it is challenged by uneven or hierarchical social capital that undermines representation and voice. Rural residents have relied more on private markets than government for many services; however, rural areas have also suffered from underdevelopment due in part to uneven markets. Privatization, in the face of uneven markets, may result in greater inequality in governmental service levels.

As we move into the twenty-first century, government innovation based on competition may give way to innovations based on cooperation. Cooperation between levels of government and with private sector and civil society actors may offer greater potential for efficiency and equity than competitive markets; however, cooperation will also bring challenges. The governance of cooperative networks will require new mechanisms for accountability and voice. Ensuring equity and participation in these new governance structures will be especially important for rural communities.

Theoretical Foundations: Competition and Democracy

What drives these governance trends? Competitive markets and democracy are linked in both the popular and theoretical imaginations. In the last third of the twentieth century we have shifted from the notion of a voter with political voice to the notion of a consumer-voter—one who votes more regularly through consumer choices than at the ballot box. This argument was first promoted by Charles Tiebout in 1956. In response to complaints that local governments would always produce more goods and services than the public really wants, Tiebout (1956) argued that in fact there is a public market among local governments that encourages them to be efficient and responsive to citizen needs. The consumer-citizen chooses a community based on the mix of services and taxes desired, and local governments compete for mobile citizens by offering differentiated mixes of public services and taxes.

Competition does not have to be just between governments, but also can occur between governments and private markets. Private providers are assumed to be more efficient and innovative than government because they operate in competitive markets (Savas 2000). The book *Reinventing Government*, by David Osborne and Ted Gaebler (1992), recognized the potential of private-sector management and promoted a revolution in thinking about local government. Widely popular and read by many local government officials across the nation, this book encouraged governments to shift from the old provider, regulator, and enforcer roles to new roles of facilitator, networker, and enabler. Although this weakens government's traditional forms of control and representation, it enhances the involvement of a wider array of partners in a network system of governance.

The twin processes of devolution and privatization reflect decentralization from state to local levels of government and from government to market forms of provision. At the close of the twentieth century, markets, democracy, and decentralized decision-making are viewed as the paths to effective governance. Competition, consumer choice, and greater public engagement, it is argued, should result in more efficient and responsive government. But there are important cracks in this story that point to alternative possibilities for the future.

Critical Challenges: Inequality and the Fiscal Constraints Facing Rural Communities

Public choice theory gives limited attention to equity and redistribution. Citizens are assumed to have mobility and real choice in their selection of communities, and local governments are assumed to have the capacity to compete. Under these theoretical assumptions, inequality in the level of local government services is justified as "what people want." Historically, U.S. rural development policy has attempted to redress uneven development processes by investing in technical infrastructure and human capital. Poverty in the rural South and Appalachia was not viewed as a "choice" by local residents, but rather as the historical legacy of extractive economies (plantation agriculture and mining) built upon highly unequal social structures of slavery and company-owned towns (Brown and Warner 1991). Nationally sponsored regional development programs such as the Appalachian Regional Commission recognized the need for redistributional investment to promote economic development.

National policy is shifting from a focus on redistribution to a focus on devolution and development. Redistributive programs are assumed to create dependence, whereas policies that promote competition are assumed to stimulate local development. Widespread support for infrastructure development in lagging rural regions is *not* under discussion. Instead, the federal government is playing a new facilitator role, encouraging poor communities to compete for funding, as in the Empowerment Zone–Enterprise Community program. Communities that win the competition receive increased federal aid, but most poor rural communities are left behind. Similarly, the New Markets Initiative is focused on providing subsidies to private business to invest in depressed rural communities. Such policies are common at the state level as well, where states provide tax breaks to firms that invest in lower-income economic development zones.

Federal funds are increasingly disbursed in the form of block grants to the states, which can then decide whether they will invest in lagging rural communities or in more economically vibrant communities that can serve as engines of economic growth. Evidence from the 1990s suggests that some states are playing a redistributive role toward their lagging rural communities (Warner 2001). But the 1990s was a decade of overall economic growth. Simulations of state expenditure patterns show that caps on federal block grants may prevent states from redistributive expenditures in times of economic recession (Powers 1999).

Devolution permits greater variety in the implementation of federally funded programs. Increasing the use of block grants in the social welfare arena results in considerable variation in eligibility, program design, and funding levels across states. This is seen dramatically in areas such as child health insurance, day care subsidies, job training, and welfare assistance. Some states have designed programs to provide important transitional support to low-income workers, while others have been aggressive in removing people from welfare dependency through more punitive means. Often states with the highest poverty rates (which have traditionally offered the most limited benefits) have implemented the most restrictive programs (Weinstein 1998). Even before welfare reform in 1996, eighteen states had decentralized part of the administrative costs and eleven states had decentralized part of the fiscal responsibility for welfare benefits to localities (Urban Institute n.d.).

The process of devolution also masks an overall reduction in the welfare state. Worldwide, national welfare states are under pressure to reduce costs and benefits to ensure national competitiveness in a global economy. Beginning in the 1980s with the Reagan administration, the federal government has devolved responsibility without increasing funds, thereby creating a crisis of fiscal stress for many localities. Devolution has also fostered competition between state and local governments. The process of decentralizing expenditure responsibility to localities is occurring without an increase in local revenue-raising authority. In fact the trend is in the opposite direction—to further restrict local revenue-raising authority. Since the passage of Proposition 13 in California in the 1970s, half of the states have preempted local revenue-raising authority by placing state restrictions on local property tax rates or revenue earnings (ACIR 1995). Not surprisingly, local revenue from property taxes has been flat in real terms since the 1980s. In response, local governments have increased reliance on sales taxes and user fees; however, the increased use of Internet commerce (which still enjoys a tax moratorium) undercuts sales tax revenue. Fiscal stress undermines the potential of decentralization. Close articulation of financial capacity and local government expenditure ensures that local governments will invest in activities that promote economic development and build the tax base, creating a local "developmental state." Local governments that lack the fiscal capacity to respond to development challenges will be caught in a vicious circle. Poor economic development leads to limited government revenues, which in turn limit government investment, in turn reducing future economic development. For communities with strong fiscal capacity, the cycle is virtuous: increased economic development yields more government revenue, which is invested in better services, promoting still more development. A USDA study of government finance in 1990 showed that the poorest rural communities have the poorest governments (Reeder and

Jansen 1995). With declining access to a redistributive state, even more rural local governments may be left behind.

Inequality in government services as a result of decentralized fiscal responsibility is now being recognized in the public education arena. Beginning with the Serrano suit in California in the late 1970s, seventeen states with public education based on the local property tax have had their systems of financing education declared unconstitutional because the level of service for children from poor districts was found inequitable. Twelve more states have similar litigation pending (Long 1999). In California, however, research shows that under centralization, overall levels of education funding have not kept pace with rising enrollments since the 1970s. Taxpayers with higher incomes may not support increased overall levels of funding for education if they cannot ensure the taxes they pay benefit their own communities (Silva and Sonstelie 1995). Decentralization promotes competition and inequality, but it appears that centralization may reduce political support for redistributive programs. To ensure equity, some level of cooperation needs to be present in the fiscal system.

The Local Capacity for Response: Privatization, Cooperation, and Civic Engagement

Decentralization requires both fiscal and administrative capacity. The previous section outlined the fiscal structures of constraint. In this section I will discuss the structural limits to markets and civic engagement. Rural communities have always depended more on private service provision due to the limited size and scope of rural local government; however, private providers of public services may not offer a viable alternative to many of the poorest rural communities where profit potential is low. We can expect a similar unevenness in the capacity of civic engagement to promote development across rural communities. Civil society varies according to the social capital of the rural community, from the highly engaged town meetings of New England to the patron/client relations typical of communities in Appalachia and the deep South (Duncan 1999). Communities with more egalitarian social capital structures are better able to create networks of governance that support cooperative competition and promote development, while those with hierarchical structures of social capital will continue to see patronage-style politics that stifle development prospects.

Clearly there is a role for local agency in promoting rural development, but the capacity for local action is uneven. Under decentralization and privatization, the results of this uneven capacity should become even more pronounced.

Privatization

Privatization advocates claim that governmental production stifles the development of private markets for service delivery (Savas 2000). Given that local governments depend on local taxes, developing private markets could increase the local tax base. Contracting public services to private businesses could meet public needs and stimulate economic development. Privatization has appeal to rural governments with limited resources and lacking the technical or managerial capacity to administer complex public services. As technical requirements for water and waste system management have increased, some rural governments have found it convenient to turn to private environmental firms for assistance. Private providers offer economies of scale and scope, and in many cases can reduce the cost and improve the quality of service delivery beyond what a small rural government could provide on its own.

My research on the contracting behavior of local governments since the early 1980s, however, has shown that privatization has increased only slightly. National survey data on 1,500 local governments (of which roughly four hundred are nonmetropolitan) show that rural governments rely less heavily on privatization than either their metropolitan or suburban counterparts (Warner and Hefetz 2003). Detailed statistical analysis shows that privatization is favored by richer, medium-sized suburbs. From the perspective of private providers, suburbs—with their medium densities, homogeneous populations, and higher incomes—are more attractive and more profitable markets. Relying on markets may leave poorer rural communities behind.

One way that rural governments are providing services more efficiently is through cooperation with other local governments to achieve economies of scale. This is especially true for more isolated rural communities. For services that are capital intensive, such as public works, equipment sharing across municipalities can save money. Economies of scale are also present in many back office services such as dispatching and payroll. While local governments may maintain their own small police force, dispatching is best handled at a more centralized level, such as the county. With respect to human services, urban communities can rely on nonprofit providers, but such groups are less common in rural areas. Intermunicipal cooperation allows local governments to gain scale while maintaining a strong community orientation in service delivery.

The trend is for rural governments to contract to an intergovernmental system—an approach that is based on cooperation—rather than to a private system, an approach based on competition. Public choice theory argues that competition is the key to efficiency, but rural local government behavior suggests an alternative. Frustrated by limited private and nonprofit market alternatives in their areas, rural local governments are creating a public market of cooperating governments to gain scale and efficiency.

Cooperation and Civic Engagement

While the theories guiding local government reform in the later half of the twentieth century focused on the benefits of competition to promote efficiency and democracy, theories guiding governmental reform in the twenty-first century may focus more on the positive value of cooperation. Competition through decentralization and privatization has left rural governments at a disadvantage. Rural governments that lack the fiscal capacity to meet local needs face decreased development prospects as a result of decentralization. Rural areas are less attractive to private suppliers, so local governments must create public markets based on intergovernmental cooperation to achieve efficiency.

Both privatization and decentralization have shown that innovation and efficiency can be encouraged when citizens are more engaged in the governing process and private actors are brought into partnership with government to deliver public services; however, both trends may exacerbate inequalities (Warner and Hefetz 2002). Rural development practitioners know that such inequality reflects the lack of opportunity that promotes uneven development. Thus, competitive theories of government may fail the development test and leave too many communities behind. Cooperative theories of governance provide an alternative.

What do I mean by cooperation? Over the last few decades, rural local governments have learned to cooperate with private businesses, nonprofit organizations, local citizen groups, and other local governments to meet local needs. The relationship with state and federal government is shifting from one of dependency to one of partnership, although too often this is an unequal partnership that excessively burdens local governments. All levels of government have moved from hierarchically organized, authoritative bureaucracies to multi-agency, collaborative networks. At the local level, we have witnessed a shift from formal, elected representation to informal networks of civic participation and business/government partnership (Rhodes 1996).

Earlier I described the Empowerment Zone–Enterprise Community (EZ-EC) initiative as an example of decentralized policy based on competition between communities. But it is also a policy designed to promote collaboration within communities. Successful applicants incorporated local government, private business, and community groups in proposal design. One of the challenges of the program has been to sustain these collaborative networks when the interests of different members diverge. Recognizing that rural poverty springs in part from unequal social relations, the EZ-EC initiative has given attention to strengthening civic engagement among the most disadvantaged groups in rural communities. These initiatives seek to build new partnerships between government, business, religious, and nonprofit interests to improve the quality of life in the poorest neighborhoods.

Collaborative approaches such as these reflect the asset-building strategy of community development (Kretzmann and McKnight 1993b). Rather than looking at what is wrong in a community and how government can fix it, the asset-building approach capitalizes on and supports a community's strengths. Government becomes an enabler, facilitator, and networker rather than a provider and enforcer. In rural areas, public schools often play the same roles that neighborhood nonprofits might play in more urban areas. Public schools are connected to families and to community power structures and thus may offer a broader vision than government alone (see Chapter 21 in this volume). One challenge for rural communities, however, is to find ways to enhance the voices of disadvantaged groups (Warner 1999).

Although this networked system of governance is based on cooperation, competition is still present among the partners for funding, recognition, and authority. For example, there is hierarchical competition between state and local governments for political credit and taxes. State governments can offer tax breaks at the expense of local government services, either through unfunded mandates or reductions in state aid. New Jersey largely paid for its tax breaks in the 1990s through reductions in local education aid. Wisconsin recently considered cutting local revenue aid. Even among local governments—where cooperation is voluntary—it is still primarily based on self-interest. Communities with greater needs, and higher costs, may be excluded from cooperative agreements. Increasingly, intergovernmental cooperation has resulted in the formation of special districts that are highly technocratic and have limited accountability to citizens. Cooperation among government, private, and nonprofit partners requires trust and long-term relationships, but these can be undermined by competition. Concessions may be granted to important partners to keep them in the coalition. Weaker partners may lose voice as power and influence trump formal voting to determine representation in these networks, raising new and important challenges for governance. How do we ensure representation? How can we prevent capture of program benefits by elites? How do we distinguish collaboration from collusion, civic participation from cronyism, and development from corruption?

New Challenges: Governing Cooperative Networks

As we stand at the beginning of a new century, rural local governments face many opportunities—and many challenges. Decentralized decision-making gives rural communities the opportunity to design policies that better fit their needs. Partnerships between government, business, and civic organizations offer the potential for synergy and asset-based development strategies. That is the promise of decentralized, cooperative, networked systems of governance.

While many contemporary challenges are similar to the challenges of the past, the stakes are greater. Uneven markets led to uneven rural economic development in the past, but today uneven markets may also contribute to uneven governmental services as rural governments find they cannot compete with suburbs for the most advantageous private-sector contracts. Whereas federal aid helped redress uneven governmental financial and managerial capacity in the past, under decentralization greater fiscal inequality will result and there will be less emphasis on redistributive aid. Finally, persistent rural poverty has been a reflection, in part, of hierarchical social capital arrangements. With increased emphasis on civic engagement in governmental programs, communities lacking more egalitarian social relations will fall even further behind.

The logic behind privatization and decentralization rests on the positive value of competition, but to be successful, these new forms of governance must include greater attention to cooperation. Three forms of cooperation stand out. First, state and local governments must cooperate to ensure that redistributive goals are maintained. Second, local governments and private providers must cooperate to ensure that market efficiencies are present, even in higher cost rural markets. And finally, local government, the private sector, and civil society must cooperate to ensure that representation is broadened.

The principal challenge of the new century will be to structure the governance of these networks to ensure that diverse interests are represented, and to balance the tension between cooperation and competition, so that the broader well-being of the rural community is addressed. Past definitions of governmental accountability rested on the necessary separation of government, civil society, and private sector action. Now, however, the lines between state, market, and civil society are blurred (Rhodes 1996). Cooperation across networks is critical to success, yet accountability, representation, and equity must still be addressed or cooperation may create its own forms of uneven development. The great challenge to rural local governments in the twenty-first century is to ensure participation, representation, accountability, and equity under systems of both cooperation and competition.

20

Religion

Leland Glenna

Christian fundamentalism in the United States, Islamic fundamentalism in Iran, and the rise of Islamic militants in Egypt are examples of religion-oriented issues that are dramatically affecting world politics as we enter the twenty-first century. Moreover, these issues are experienced locally and are connected to rural people's efforts to make meaning of an urbanizing and industrializing world (Riesebrodt 1993; Araghi 1989; Ibrahim 1985). A host of scholars have examined how rural people construct meaning at the intersection of politics, economics, and religion (Araghi 1989; Gilbert 2000; Flora 1976; Bradley 2000; Rikoon 1995; Young 1967; Tolbert, Lyson, and Irwin 1998). But for the most part, anyone interested in twentieth-century rural religion would be better served by reading anthropology, history, or even fiction than rural sociology.

One obstacle to the study of religion is that rural sociologists, and sociologists in general, assume secularization. They take for granted that religion permeated all other institutions in premodern society. But in modern society, religion has become just one of many institutions, and of secondary or tertiary importance to economic institutions (Sorokin et al. 1931). Moreover, sociologists tend to be "fixated on the church as a historically relative institutionalization of religion" and ignore the social process through which people construct a sacred cosmos (Berger 1969, 177). Thus, sociologists expect religion to decline in significance as time passes and gauge that expectation by the rise and fall in church membership and doctrinal adherence.

Durkheim's frequently cited definition—"A religion is a unified system of beliefs and practices relative to sacred things, that is to say, things set apart and forbidden—beliefs and practices which unite into one single moral community called a Church, all those who adhere to them" (1965,

62)—is used to justify fixating on the church. But there are at least two reasons why Durkheim's definition should not limit sociological investigation of religion to measuring church members and doctrinal commitment. First, Durkheim's own research on religion was not limited to studying churches. For example, he analyzed the "elementary forms of religious life" that existed before the Christian church (Durkheim 1965). Second, the word "church" itself has roots in a broader meaning than it connotes today: the French word for church, "eglise," is derived from the Greek "ekkalesia," an assembly of citizens. The Greeks used the concept to refer to any moral community, as did Durkheim.[1] Even science could be considered a religion according to this functionalist definition because it provides universalizing beliefs and rituals; however, Durkheim adds a substantive component to the definition of religion. Science directs itself at describing men and the world—the social and the natural—while religion is more interested in the meaning of the world—the metaphysical and the supernatural (Durkheim 1965, 478).

Berger (1969) extends Durkheim's insight by defining religion as a moral community that assigns supernatural significance to the beliefs and rituals that connect members of the community with the natural and social world. That may happen in a church (or synagogue, mosque, temple, or other such cultural site) or in other settings. This definition of religion is important if we are to understand the ways people assign meaning to their lives in this time of global interaction and reintegration. Whether examining overtly religious organizations, such as a rural Catholic church, or seemingly secular ones, such as the World Bank, analyzing the social process of constructing a sacred cosmos offers the opportunity for a deeper understanding of rural society.

Rural America's Religious History

Since the family and the church were often the first institutions that European settlers established as they claimed territory in North America, attempts to understand contemporary rural America, and the United States in general, would benefit from considering their religious foundations (Burkart 1997). Spanish settlers in the 1500s conquered the native people with the intent of perpetuating the Catholic religion (Diamond 1999). And

---

1. Since Durkheim's understanding of religion was greatly influenced by his teacher Numa Denis Fustel de Coulanges, who wrote a prominent book in 1864 on the religion, laws, and institutions of ancient Greece, it seems clear that Durkheim was thinking more broadly than the contemporary manifestation of church when he wrote his definition (Lemert 1999).

wars among these early settlers were more religious than nationalistic. An admiral sent by Spain's King Philip II in 1565 to eliminate French Lutherans who had settled in Spanish territory claimed that "We slew them not as Frenchman, but as Lutherans" (Wolf 1965, 1).

Many of the Northern Europeans who moved to the New World in the seventeenth and eighteenth centuries were members of Protestant sects fleeing religious persecution. Some scholars credit that flight from persecution and the subsequent struggles between the various Protestant denominations with inspiring the Constitutional framers to seek "to avoid the domination of past tyrannies" through the establishment of religious tolerance in the form of the separation of church and state (Forcinelli 1990, 45–46).

Although American Jews are most often identified with cities, they too have a history of viewing the American countryside as a sanctuary from persecution. The eight thousand Jews who settled on farms in the Midwest between 1880 and 1940 fled prohibitions against land ownership and pogroms in Russia and Eastern Europe, as well as anti-Semitism and anti-Sephardic sentiments in American cities (Rikoon 1995).

America was not a place of religious freedom for Africans. Slaveholders wanted to "wipe out African religious beliefs," but resisted converting slaves to Christianity at first. They feared that the Africans would be emboldened to ask for better treatment and that white Christians would want Christian slaves to be liberated (Hudson and Corrigan 1999, 121). However, to enable proselytizing, the British declared in 1727 that Christianization would not affect a person's status as property, and slaves were asked to pledge "in the presence of God and before this Congregation that you do not ask for holy baptism out of any design to free yourself from the Duty and Obedience that you owe to your Master while you live" (Hudson and Corrigan 1999, 122).

Although Catholics and Jews from Europe and Latin America and African American Protestants have contributed to rural life over the past five hundred years, rural America is more homogenous than urban America. Little has changed since Sorokin et al. asserted that "contemporary rural America is predominantly Protestant, while urban America has a considerably higher proportion of the followers of other religions" (1931, 373). My analysis of a 1998 survey from the American Religion Data Archive reveals that almost 72 percent of those who live in rural counties (counties having no towns of ten thousand or more) identify themselves as Protestant, 16 percent as Catholic, and 12 percent as other or none. Only 46 percent of those in central cities identify as Protestant, 25 percent as Catholic, 4 percent as Jewish, and 25 percent as other or none (American Religious Data Archives 1998). These findings lend evidence to the assertion by Sorokin et al. that the "history of diffusion of new religions in the societies of the past shows that they spread much more successfully in the cities and among the nonagricultural classes than in the rural parts and among agricultural classes" (1931, 373).

The Decaying Church and the Decline of Religion

The figures cited above support the rural sociological assumption that as societies modernize and urbanize, people convert to other religions, become more tolerant of diverse religions, abandon organized religion, or become atheists. Rural societies modernize too, and experience a weakening of commitment to traditional doctrines. The process is simply slower in rural areas than in cities. Taylor argued that the church must accept and adapt to secularization: in relation to the "five great social institutions" of education, government, family, business, and the church, "the church must find its place in team work and cooperation with the other four" (1926, 212). But Sorokin et al. portray such a strategy as a mere attempt to "revitalize churches by means of salesmanship and business enterprise" while failing to "interrelate and fuse religion and daily activities, to give religious sanctity to life, [and] . . . only introduce[s] into the churches and temples, the last shelters of religion, secular and profane things" (1931, 357). The implication is that religion is quaint but doomed. If one wants to understand the norms and forms that actually affect modern life, one needs to examine the other "great social institutions."

Religion becomes interesting within this framework only to the extent that it tends to linger longer in rural than urban areas. Larson (1978) documented that 69 percent of rural people in 1974 believed that "religion can answer 'all or most of today's problems,'" compared to only 44 percent of those in large cities. He also found that rural people are more likely than people in small, medium, and large cities to attend church services, to read the Bible, and to hold more conservative beliefs and values regarding gender roles, sex, and the work ethic. Politically, they are more likely to want lower taxes and a smaller federal government. Larson (1978) concludes that government agencies should be aware of these differences in beliefs and values when they seek to implement rural policies.

Recent surveys reveal that rural people are still more conservative. According to my analysis of the American Religion Data Archive survey (1998), 33 percent of those in rural counties call themselves "conservative," compared to 26 percent of urban residents (in the 112 largest metropolitan areas). Larson (1978) found that 61 percent of rural people surveyed in

1973 said that premarital sex is wrong, compared to 34 percent of those in large cities. Those figures dropped in 1998, but the rural/urban gap remained: 42 percent of rural people said that premarital sex is always or almost always wrong, while 28 percent of urban residents did. And a recent survey of rural and nonrural churches by the Evangelical Lutheran Church in America (2001) found that rural churches are less likely to welcome change. Nearly 93 percent of rural Lutheran churches seldom consider social change to be a "challenge rather than a problem," whereas only 16 percent of nonrural Lutheran churches do not welcome the challenge of social change.

Rural churches are also resistant to consolidation in the face of declining membership. A Midwestern county that had eighty-seven schools and eighty-five churches in 1900 had only three schools in 1960, but seventy-three churches. Rogers et al. cite this as evidence that the "rural church is often the local institution most resistant to social change in society" (1988, 166). But the consolidation of rural churches in the latter half of the twentieth century reveals that resistance to change has been futile (Rogers et al. 1988).

By analyzing church membership, church consolidation, and adherence to "old-fashioned" values, one could find support for the theory that religion wanes as people become modernized, even in the conservative rural communities; however, this perspective may fail to capture the complexity of religion in modern society. As Lester argues, because "religion mutates with Darwinian restlessness," talking of "'established' or 'traditional' faith becomes oxymoronic" (2002, 37).

The Dynamics of Rural Religion

The secularization thesis ignores how religious movements have emerged at various stages of history to challenge or legitimize social change. The Great Awakening of the 1830s in the United States, which was characterized by evangelical revivals throughout the countryside, began as a movement of commercial farmers and urban businessmen to proclaim God's support for middle-class values. This movement "was critical to the social and ideological transformations that accompanied the market revolution" (Wilentz 1997, 73). The Progressive movement of the early 1900s, which sought to help displaced farmers and unemployed workers during a time of industrialization-induced economic upheaval, also had religious undertones (Lash and Urry 1987). For example, organizations like the Young Men's Christian Organization (YMCA) sought to improve the lives of the disaffected by substituting prayer and Bible study for life on the streets. John Dewey's *A Common Faith* (1934) served as a theological appeal to set aside bickering over religious differences and to work instead in a utilitarian spirit to achieve public good. Its argument was that all people share core beliefs about making the world better, which would happen if everyone simply trusted in the scientific method, as opposed to religion, to solve social problems.

Many rural churches resisted the Progressive movement at the outset. When the Country Life movement sought to use churches to industrialize rural areas, the pastor at one rural church argued that it would be wrong if the Church's "chief concern is to make roads as 'a way of salvation,' 'to raise fat pigs for the glory of God.'" And aware of the economic implications of efforts to increase farm production, a Kansas minister warned in 1916, "To feed the flaming passion for big crops is not the task of the country church, and if it stoops to this it will ultimately become the farmer's worst enemy" (Quoted in Danbom 1979, 82). But when Progressivism became an effort to address the problems associated with industrialization through the New Deal, which was this movement's ultimate expression according to Lash and Urry (1987, 76), the churches assisted. In an article on agrarian intellectuals who helped construct Roosevelt's New Deal, Gilbert explains how "crusading Christianity contributed to progressive reform" by describing how many of these agrarians had a Protestant upbringing in the Social Gospel movement (2000, 166–7).

The American Christian fundamentalist movement of the 1910s reflects the church's paradoxical relationship with modernity. Although fundamentalists define themselves as antimodern, particularly opposing scientific theories of evolution, they also welcome high-tech innovations for propagating their message. And a fundamentalist may "lash out against alcoholism, and yet feel comfortable taking sleeping pills, drinking coffee, or working for a multinational corporation that rapes the environment" (Wuthnow 1993, 122). Some argue that fundamentalism emerges as "persons with low incomes and meager cultural resources ... tend to form small, insulated groups marked by distinctive and unconventional religious beliefs," which suggests that they are merely reacting to modern economic conditions (Young 1967, 137). Furthermore, the contention that the Bible is infallible and should be interpreted literally, the primary tenet of fundamentalism, did not exist prior to 1900. Thus, a religious organization may alter itself to be persistently nonconformist to modernity, even as this makes it beholden to modernity (Riesebrodt 1993).

Nor is the portrayal of religion as reifying traditional gender roles is as straightforward as some may assume. For example, Pentecostalism, which was a nineteenth-century American sectarian "Holiness" movement with roots in Methodism, is a growing movement in the United States and South and Central America. It promotes a church hierarchy of man above woman and a family hierarchy of husband above wife. Lawless (1988) has discovered, however, that women in Pentecostal churches often have unique characteristics that propel them to leadership roles in the church. Once they are in those roles, their sermons and their interactions transform gender relations. And Nason-Clark (1995) has discovered that women within conservative churches are able to draw upon family values rhetoric to defend each other when they are in abusive households. Even more counterintuitive, Neitz (1995) has found that female-privileged Witchcraft organizations lack the structure necessary to enforce punishment for sexual abuse, which amounts to a sanctioning of it.

As noted earlier, religion has played a paradoxical role for African Americans. Since many African slaves were converted to Christianity during the time of the Great Awakening, which was characterized by more spirited worship, they found in Christianity a medium for preserving components of their African religious heritage of drumming, singing, dancing, and shouting. Although slaves pledged not to rebel against their masters during their baptisms, and many Southern clergy appealed to the Bible to justify slavery, Christians in the North drew from the Bible to justify the abolitionist movement (Hudson and Corrigan 1999). And although religion remains one of the most racially segregated institutions in the United States, Black churches helped to integrate African Americans into urban life during the Black migration into the cities during and after World War I. Moreover, many Black and some white churches promoted political, social, and economic desegregation and civil rights during the 1950s and 1960s (Hudson and Corrigan 1999). The Civil Rights movement actually spanned Christian and Jewish denominations (Gaustad 1990).

Latin Americans have also experienced both religious oppression and liberation in America. Immigrants from Latin America tended to be excluded from positions of leadership in the Catholic Church (only one of 225 American bishops was Hispanic in 1973), even though they made up about one-quarter of Catholics. Yet Caesar Chavez drew upon his Catholic faith to organize "the migrant Mexican-American laboring force in California with sufficient effectiveness as to win wide attention and support" (Gaustad 1990, 334). Although most Latin American immigrants locate in urban areas, the migrant laborers who work on farms and in food processing factories draw attention beyond what their numbers would justify. For example, I worked in a small town church in Southwestern Minnesota where people talked about the "Mexican problem," even though Latin

Americans made up only 3 percent of the town's population. Rural sociologists could learn much about religion and race in rural areas by examining this issue.

The rural church retains an important role in socially integrating people in rural settings as the society's socioeconomic institutions are extending beyond local and even national boundaries. Tolbert et al. (1998) demonstrate that rural areas with small manufacturing operations, family-run farms, and civically engaged churches are more likely to gain socioeconomic benefits in the globalizing economy than rural areas with large manufacturing and farm operations and less civically engaged churches (see Chapter 17 in this volume). And Bradley (2000) describes how churches in Warrensburg, Missouri, have taken on the goal of promoting social integration as their population has become more transient.

Religion Surfaces in Multiple Social Arenas

The theme of the previous section was to challenge the portrayal of churches as a premodern relic, a conception that ignores the dynamic function that they may play in society. In this section, I will examine an even broader application of the definition of religion.

One underexplored facet of rural religion is the myth of the family farm ("myth" here refers to a traditional story that explicates a world-view, not a counterfactual statement). Jeffersonian agrarianism, the basis for claims that the farmer is the "backbone of society," conjures the image of God working through small, family-run farms to uphold society morally and materially, just as the spine upholds the primate. William Jennings Bryan and the Grangers used this religion-charged ideology to rally support in the village and rural churches of the South and Midwest in the late nineteenth century as they fought the railroads, banks, and industrialists who were exploiting the farmers. However, this connection between God and farmer was ignored at the time because the urban-based religious presses showed little interest in agrarian issues (Hudson and Corrigan 1999, 308). Today, politicians and agribusinesses draw upon this family farm myth to rally support for policies that hurt small family farmers.

The environmental movement has connections to the American Transcendentalists, who merged European Romanticism and Native American religions to construct the myth of the Native Americans as prototypical environmentalists, or "the noble savage." This perspective is incomplete, however, because Jewish and Christian religions also have traditions promoting harmonious society/nature relationships (Hiebert 1996). And

Native Americans did not always have relationships with nature that are worthy of emulation. For example, some Native Americans exploited buffalo herds in unsustainable ways, in part at least because of their religious belief that buffalo existed in infinite supplies underground (Flores 1991). This myth of the noble savage becomes intriguing in contemporary social settings when environmental groups who claim a connection to Native American spirituality are surprised to find themselves in opposition to Native Americans such as the Makah Tribe of Western Washington, which wants to revive its whaling tradition (see Chapter 25 in this volume).

Another overlooked area of inquiry is the religious origin of economic rationality. The notion that less government and more markets are panaceas to social ills has become dominant in the United States and other parts of the world. Often labeled the "Washington Consensus," this argument is used by the IMF and World Bank to suggest that any environmental or social problem can be alleviated with deregulated markets and free trade (Krugman 1999). This belief system is rooted in a theological presupposition that greedy competition yields more social benefits than altruistic cooperation. Adam Smith first articulated this presupposition when he drew upon Christian and Stoic religious doctrines to contend that the market's God-ordained natural laws transubstantiate selfish and greedy actions into social benefits (Glenna 2002).

The religious origins of economic rationality may help us to explain other phenomena. For example, Kintz (1997) documents how liberal economics, patriotism, and fundamentalist Christianity have become fused into a right-wing political movement that has considerable political influence in the United States. And Dudley (1996) has demonstrated that religious, economic, and patriotic values of sanctimony, competitive efficiency, and American superiority were behind a conservative ideology that blamed individual farmers when farm numbers declined in the 1980s, instead of blaming the economic conditions that promoted their demise.

Rural sociologists have examined the role religion has played in efforts to export economic rationality to developing countries. For example, Flora (1976) found that in Columbia the Pentecostal movement was more effective than the Catholic Church in facilitating worker solidarity movements because Pentecostalism emphasized "boundary maintenance and cooperation, rather than desires of individual members to prove their individual election to the Kingdom of God" (228). In stark contrast, psychologist Martin-Baro (1990) explains how the American-supported military government in El Salvador used the Pentecostal movement to promote the acceptance of capitalism. He states that Pentecostalism's emphasis on submission to the social order and individual salvation was considered more conducive to United States economic interests that Catholicism's criticism of the oppressive government and its emphasis on social justice. The varying ways that religious belief systems serve as the means to resist or promote economic interests could be especially important areas of investigation as globalization brings economic changes to the developing world and to the rural United States.

Durkheim's notion of religion as an individual's sense of connection to the larger society becomes especially useful when attempting to understand extreme religious movements like fundamentalist strains of Christianity, Islam, Judaism, Hinduism, and Buddhism. In contrast to Young (1967), some argue that fundamentalism emerges out of newly formed middle classes, not the impoverished masses. For example, Araghi (1989) has argued that the rise of fundamentalist Islam in Iran was connected to rural people in the 1960s and 1970s moving into Tehran under an oppressive government. Ibrahim (1985) makes a similar observation by pointing to the prominence of "rural urbanites" in Egyptian Islamic militant circles. Riesebrodt (1993) concurs that fundamentalist movements emerge as a religious revitalization during a crisis of consciousness in response to a dramatic social change, rather than poverty. Based on this theoretical insight, as globalization continues to generate social change and migrations, we may expect to see a rise in crises of consciousness and religious revitalization in rural America.

Conclusion

Observing that there are many jokes about lawyers, economists, and psychologists, but few about sociologists, Berger (1963) concludes that sociology is comparatively irrelevant. He argues that until we accept our responsibility to become a humanistic science and examine questions of meaning, instead of specialized empirical studies that merely confirm what everyone already knows, we will remain irrelevant. Understanding the place of religion in society presents sociologists with an opportunity to produce more relevant work. According to Wood, "Religious culture matters because it is taken seriously by large numbers of people—and thus orients their lives either toward or away from political engagement and the habits of the heart that can sustain it" (1999, 329). In an article describing how religion has exploded in diversity in the twentieth century, Lester argues that new religions emerge and flourish "because they provide community and foster relationships that help people deal with challenging new social and political realities" (2002, 44).

With a history of being in the forefront of examining rural social change as the result of the industrialization of agriculture and natural resource use, and economic and political restructuring, rural sociologists are well positioned to study the worldviews and social relationships of rural Americans that emerge alongside the new economic and political realities. Attending to the work of rural sociologists who have demonstrated that religion is something more than a stagnant organization that perpetuates premodern superstitions will help us to understand these developments.

21

Promoting Educational Achievement

A Partnership of Families, Schools, and Communities

Lionel J. Beaulieu, Glenn D. Israel, and Ronald C. Wimberley

There remains a state of unease in this country regarding the quality of our nation's kindergarten through twelfth grade (K–12) educational system.[1] Despite ongoing federal and state policy efforts to bring about measurable improvements in the educational advancement of our nation's public school students, many young people continue to be labeled "low achievers." According to the National Education Association (2001), significant numbers of these low-performing youth are enrolled in public schools located in our nation's rural areas.

Inferior achievement levels in rural places are said to be linked to a number of factors, including inadequate school facilities, a large pool of educators teaching outside their fields of expertise, the limited availability of specialized and advanced courses for students, a high proportion of minority students, a sizable number of students from low-income and low-education families, a limited number of local residents with college degrees, and the lack of quality local jobs requiring well-educated workers (Ballou and Podgursky 1998; Greenberg and Teixeira 1998; Jensen and McLaughlin 1995; National Education Association 2001; Stallmann et al. 1995; Swaim 1998). Despite the myriad forces affecting student performance, it is disquieting that strategies commonly devised by state and federal policy-

1. The apparent concern with the educational progress of our nation's youth is linked, in part, to the changed economic environment in which youth will find themselves as they move into the labor force. Due to the increased integration of computer and information technologies into the workplace, and the expanded need for workers with analytical, mathematical, and verbal skills, the demand for better-educated workers is accelerating (Swaim 1998). As a result, individuals with solid educational credentials, problem-solving capabilities, and technological expertise are in demand (Beaulieu et al. 2001; Gibbs, Swaim, and Teixeira 1998). Those who lack these skills are likely to face a future of unsteady employment and declining real wages (Judy and D'Amico 1997; Reich 1992).

makers to improve the academic performance of rural students remain largely confined to school-based solutions.

This chapter is intended to inspire parents, educators, and civic leaders to engage in policy discussions that look beyond schools as the principal agent for improving the academic achievement of students. We contend that educational success is not a singular product of what happens within the school. Rather, families and communities are important conduits for promoting the educational progress of youth (Lerner 1995; Schorr 1988), a fact that must become an integral part of the policy designs of federal, state, and local education leaders.

As such, we outline a set of factors within the family, school, and community that can pay big dividends in advancing the academic performance of rural students. We suggest that select structural and process-oriented features of families, schools, and communities play key roles in facilitating the emergence of social capital. We assert that children embedded in families, schools, and communities with high levels of social capital generally perform better in school. As a result, we argue that the long-standing disparities in the educational success of metropolitan versus nonmetropolitan youth may be less a matter of geographical location and more a factor of variations in the strength of family, school, and community social capital available to youth living in these geographic settings.

We begin this chapter by examining the current state of education in rural America. We do so to gain some insight into the nature and extent of educational advances among nonmetropolitan and metropolitan adults during the 1990s. This information serves as an important contextual anchor for assessing the local educational environment in which rural youth live. Next, we highlight important features of social capital, giving special attention to the set of family, school, and community components seen as important in promoting the academic success of youth. We then synthesize a number of empirical studies, showcasing attributes of family, school, and community that have emerged again and again as critical elements in helping or hindering the educational achievement of nonmetropolitan students. Finally, we propose options for the policy community as it searches for ways to improve the educational achievement of rural youth.

The State of Education in Rural America

The challenges of progressing through an area's K–12 educational system are greater for children living in communities with poorly educated adults (Carter 1999). When students find themselves surrounded by adults with low achievement and aspirations, their own educational progress tends to suffer (Stockard and Mayberry 1992). Thus, it is important to take stock of the current state of educational attainment in rural America since it may have an important bearing on the academic climate of local schools (Beaulieu and Israel 1997).

Historically, rural areas have consistently lagged behind metropolitan areas with regard to the educational attainment of their adults (Killian and Beaulieu 1995; Pollard and O'Hare 1990). But do educational disparities persist today? The information presented in Table 21.1 reveals that the educational standing of nonmetropolitan adults has improved somewhat over the 1990–2000 period. In particular:

- The proportion of adults at the lowest rung of the educational ladder has declined in nonmetropolitan America. As a result, the percentage of nonmetropolitan adults with less than a high school education is virtually identical to that found in metropolitan areas of the country.
- The largest percentage of nonmetropolitan adults has completed high school, a figure that is higher than that found in metropolitan areas.
- The completion of some college education through community or technical colleges or other postsecondary education outlets has accelerated at a faster pace among nonmetropolitan than metropolitan adults during the 1990s (50 percent versus 39 percent, respectively).

Despite these important advances, nonmetropolitan areas have made no appreciable gains in closing the metropolitan/nonmetropolitan gap on the proportion of residents with baccalaureate degrees or higher.

When the issue of educational attainment is examined by race and ethnicity (Table 21.2), disparities between metropolitan/nonmetropolitan areas become quite pronounced. For example:

- The proportion of nonmetropolitan African Americans with terminal high school degrees, or who have taken part in some type of college experience beyond high school, has steadily increased. But the proportion completing a college degree has not progressed at all in ten years.
- The metropolitan/nonmetropolitan gap in college-educated residents has widened over the course of the last decade for both whites and African Americans, suggesting that metropolitan areas are experiencing greater success in retaining and capturing the most highly educated adults from these two racial groups.
- Nonmetropolitan Latinos remain entrenched in the lowest tier of the education ladder. In fact, the percentage of Latinos with less than a high

Table 21.1 Educational attainment of persons 25 years old and over, by metropolitan/nonmetropolitan residence, 1990–2000

Level of education	Metropolitan			Nonmetropolitan		
	1990	1994	2000	1990	1994	2000
Less than high school	17.2	14.7	13.9	20.3	16.8	13.8
High school only	37.7	32.5	30.7	45.6	40.5	39.0
Some college or Associate's degree	19.9	26.2	26.6	18.4	26.2	27.7
Bachelor's degree or more	25.2	26.6	28.8	15.7	16.5	19.5
	(n=44,250)	(n=56,915)	(n=54,042)	(n=13,825)	(n=18,278)	(n=15,070)

Source: Current Population Survey, various years.

Table 21.2 Educational attainment of persons 25 years old and over, by race/ethnicity and metropolitan/nonmetropolitan residence, 1990–2000

Level of education	Metropolitan			Nonmetropolitan		
	1990	1994	2000	1990	1994	2000
White						
Less than high school	11.2	8.7	6.7	17.8	14.4	10.0
High school only	39.0	33.1	30.9	46.6	41.4	39.8
Some college or Associate's degree	21.0	27.5	28.4	18.9	26.8	28.7
Bachelor's degree or more	28.7	30.7	34.0	16.7	17.3	21.4
	(n=32,134)	(n=40,138)	(n=35,816)	(n=12,033)	(n=15,855)	(n=12,602)
African American						
Less than high school	24.5	19.2	15.0	38.1	29.8	25.4
High school only	40.4	37.7	35.5	38.4	41.0	42.3
Some college or Associate's degree	21.2	27.7	30.0	15.1	20.3	24.2
Bachelor's degree or more	13.9	15.4	19.5	8.4	8.9	8.1
	(n=4,439)	(n=5,786)	(n=5,500)	(n=817)	(n=1,000)	(n=743)
Latino						
Less than high school	44.8	41.5	39.4	44.6	45.6	45.1
High school only	31.4	28.1	29.1	39.1	28.4	30.4
Some college or Associate's degree	13.7	20.1	19.8	11.1	18.0	17.4
Bachelor's degree or more	10.1	10.3	11.8	5.2	8.0	7.1
	(n=5,906)	(n=8,298)	(n=10,093)	(n=542)	(n=783)	(n=1,125)

Source: Current Population Survey, various years.

school education is virtually identical today to that in 1990. Moreover, only one in fifteen Latinos now holds a bachelor's degree or more.

So, there are some encouraging signs regarding the improved state of educational attainment among nonmetropolitan adults, but a baccalaureate degree continues to elude better than nine of every ten nonmetropolitan African Americans. And for Latinos, finishing high school and pursuing a postsecondary education remains as much a dream as a reality.

With the educational status of rural America as a backdrop, an important question remains: "What can be done in rural areas to ensure that local youth of all backgrounds are provided a real opportunity for educational success?" We argue that helping rural youth to succeed academically is the collective responsibility of families, schools, and communities. In the next section, we highlight the important social capital features of the family, school, and community that social science researchers have identified as being of value in promoting educational achievement.

Understanding Family Social Capital

Family social capital refers to the norms, social networks, and relationships between adults and children that are of value for the child while growing up (Coleman 1990a). When parents create a home environment in which social capital is strong, it often translates into dramatic improvements in the educational success of their kids. According to Smith, Beaulieu, and Seraphine (1995), the creation of family social capital is spurred by key structural and process features of the family. Structure refers to factors that give shape to the opportunity, frequency, and duration of interpersonal interactions between children and parents. Process symbolizes the quality of involvement that parents have in the lives of their children.

Parental education and family income are two important structural components of family social capital that give shape to the educational achievement and aspirations of children (Choy 2001). For students with college-educated parents, for example, better than 80 percent enter college upon graduation from high school. Among students with high-school-educated parents, the figure is one in three (Choy 2001). Furthermore, children whose families are poor have a higher risk of failing in school since low income severely constrains the opportunities these children have to learn (Huang 1999).

Two additional family structural characteristics that can help influence the emergence of social capital are the presence of one or both parents in the home and the number of siblings. Children in two-parent families have a greater opportunity than those of single parents to interact with, secure emotional support from, and be under the watchful eye of their parents (Astone and McLanahan 1991). And when more siblings are present in the home, the amount of time and energy that parents can devote to any single child is effectively diminished (Downey 1995; Fields and Smith 1998).

The process elements of family social capital include parents' nurturing activities such as interacting with their children on important school matters and voicing high aspirations for their children's educational progress. Monitoring children's activities, such as limiting the time children spend watching television and ensuring that an adult is present in the home when children return from school, is also a relevant component of family social capital. Together, these activities help advance the personal growth and academic success of children (Epstein 1995; Maynard and Howley 1997).

Rural places have serious barriers that might limit the creation of family social capital. For example, rural families tend to be larger, and the education and income levels of parents are generally lower (Dagata 2000; Ghelfi 2000). These structural traits tend to diminish the chances that frequent parent-child interactions will take place, interactions that can play a key role in stimulating academic advancement. Furthermore, parental aspirations and expectations tend to be lower in rural areas, conditions that often lead to lower educational attainment and aspirations on the part of their children (Hansen and McIntire 1989; Paasch and Swaim 1998). On the other hand, nonmetropolitan students are more likely to live in married-couple families (Fields and Casper 2001), thus increasing the chances that parents are present to nurture and monitor their children's activities.

Social Capital Features of the School

Achievement among school-aged children can be influenced by a variety of school-related factors (Neisser 1986). Among the structural features of a school that can give shape to educational achievement are the socioeconomic background of the student population, the learning climate evident in the school or classroom, and school size and organization (Stockard and Mayberry 1992).

Schools whose students come from high socioeconomic status (SES) families, who interact with high-status peers, are more likely to realize higher achievement (Blau 1960; Coleman et al. 1966). One reason for this phenomenon is that students attending higher SES schools are more likely to establish friendships with individuals having solid academic habits and high educational aspirations (Stockard and Mayberry 1992). Second, higher status schools are likely to have well established norms and values that place a premium on good academic performance (Alexander and Eckland 1975), and high teacher expectations generally translate into better academic outcomes for students (Hoffer, Greeley, and Coleman 1987; Rutter et al. 1979). Third, orderly environments in the school and classroom help students excel since norms of behavior tend to be well-articulated and problem behaviors on the part of students are limited (Lightfoot 1978; Rutter et al. 1979). And fourth, higher SES schools are typically located in communities that place a priority on quality education and play an active part in supporting these schools (Friedkin and Necochea 1988).

Closely related to the socioeconomic context of the school are the race and ethnic profiles of schools. Schools consisting of largely white students are more likely to be drawn from middle-class backgrounds, while those composed of more racial and ethnic minorities have a greater tendency to come from lower status communities (Stockard and Mayberry 1992). Financial resources represent another structural element of the school than can affect student achievement (Mortimore et al. 1988). With greater funding, schools are able to expand the breadth of courses and programs available to support the education of their students.

The structural feature of the school that has commanded considerable attention is school size. Some researchers have asserted that larger schools are more effective since they offer students a richer and more varied set of course offerings (McDill and Rigsby 1973). Others contend that smaller schools have many positive features, such as lower student-teacher ratios and greater awareness by teachers of their students' needs (Howley 1995; Gregory and Smith 1987; Walberg 1992). In fact, studies have found little evidence that small schools inhibit academic performance, particularly when controls for family factors and regional location of the schools are considered (Greenberg and Teixeira 1998; Hobbs 1995).

With regard to the process aspects of school social capital, certain features of a school can enable students to be successful. Students who build caring relationships with teachers, and who see such teachers as role models, are more likely to succeed in school (Noddings 1988; Werner and Smith 1989). Similarly, students that have opportunities to participate in school activities and who serve in positions of leadership in school-related organizations tend to thrive academically (Israel, Beaulieu, and Hartless 2001). In a nutshell, these various activities facilitate the building of social relationships with adults and peers that are useful in promoting achievement (Lerner 1995).

Parental investment in school activities is another important process component of school social capital. Strong partnerships between parents and schools result in better academic outcomes for students (Eccles and Harold 1993; Hickman, Greenwood, and Miller 1995; Maynard and Howley 1997). In fact, students whose parents are involved in their schools, irrespective of family SES, perform better in their academic courses and are less inclined to drop out of high school (Epstein 1995; Stevenson and Baker 1987; Walberg 1984).

One important advantage of most rural schools is their smaller enrollment size. Smaller school size increases the odds that students will be able to engage in frequent interactions with teachers, and become an active part of school-related organizations. Furthermore, rural schools are less likely to experience a host of school problems,[2] thus providing a favorable environment for learning (Ballou and Podgursky 1998). On the other hand, rural schools are more likely to experience greater constraints in funding than urban schools, translating into lower per student expenditures (Hobbs 1995). With their small size and more limited resources, rural schools are typically unable to offer students a wide array of specialized courses (Ballou and Podgursky 1998). Moreover, rural schools are more likely to be composed of students from lower SES homes, a factor that can hamper the academic performance of these students (Hobbs 1995; Paasch and Swaim 1998). At the same time, smaller school enrollments and class sizes allow rural teachers to interact with, and seek the support from, students' parents (Ballou and Podgursky 1998).

The Relevance of Community Social Capital

Schools are embedded in communities, and just as classmates, teachers, and other school-related resources affect the academic performance of students, so too can the communities in which they live (Stockard and Mayberry 1992, 59). Community social capital—that which is available outside the home or school—can influence student achievement.

The notion of community field theory, conceptualized by Wilkinson (1991), provides an important framework for understanding the link between community social capital and educational achievement. Localities with high community social capital are marked by extensive civic engagement and

2. For example, rural schools are less likely to experience student tardiness and absenteeism, students cutting classes, physical conflicts among students, school vandalism, or verbal abuse of teachers (Ballou and Podgursky 1998).

patterns of mutual support (Putnam 2000). Community activeness builds social capital since the network of relationships that develop from past local activities can be tapped whenever new efforts to address educational or other community needs are initiated.

There are certain structural features of a community that can boost the creation and accumulation of social capital. These factors include socioeconomic capacity, proximity, stability, and equality (Israel et al. 2001; Wilkinson 1991). With regard to socioeconomic capacity, certain localities are large enough to support a variety of institutions and organizations that help meet most of the daily needs of its residents. Such places have a cadre of people with extensive experience, knowledge, and expertise that can be used to guide local activities or to attract quality jobs. Furthermore, some communities have greater access to outside resources that can be tapped to deal with an array of challenging community issues (Luloff and Wilkinson 1979). The sum of these human, organizational, and institutional resources serves as the foundation of a community's socioeconomic capacity.

In most instances, the socioeconomic capacity of rural areas has lagged behind those of suburban and urban areas. Lower-skilled, low-paying production jobs have been concentrated in rural areas, while more highly skilled managerial and technical positions have clustered in urban places (Hobbs 1995; Jensen and McLaughlin 1995). Low-capacity rural towns, where educational attainment, income levels, job skills, and community engagement are more limited, can create a milieu where education is not given high priority. This may reduce rural students' educational achievement and aspirations relative to those of metropolitan students (Cobb, McIntire, and Pratt 1989; Smith et al. 1995).

Proximity increases opportunities for interaction among local residents. Such interactions are necessary for building community bonds among a locality's residents (Wilkinson 1991). Residents living in the sparsely populated rural countryside incur the added cost of distance in maintaining social networks, especially the "weak ties" made up of more transitory interactions that underpin much of community interaction (Granovetter 1973). Likewise, residents who work in the locality are better able to remain connected because they have more time available for establishing and/or maintaining local ties.

Residential stability also contributes to the emergence of strong links between local people. Communities that experience limited residential turnover, or that are home to many long-term residents, have ample opportunities to develop relationships that can be used to coordinate activities to improve the community and build community social capital (Putnam 2000). Residential instability, on the other hand, can disrupt local relationships, thereby reducing the social capital available to community members.

Finally, equality can reduce social divisions that affect the quality of interaction (Blau 1994). Insofar as certain racial or ethnic minorities may have less access to a locality's resources, such disparities can become the basis for durable cleavages between powerful local elites and disadvantaged local populations, particularly when community priorities are being determined. When residents feel alienated, participation in local affairs declines and collective action is fragmented. One outcome of high inequality is that less social capital is available to improve local education. Increasingly, rural America is becoming an area of great racial and ethnic diversity as witnessed by the rapid expansion of Latino and African American populations in nonmetropolitan areas over the 1990–2000 period (U.S. Bureau of the Census 2001c). This increasing complexity poses challenges for rural areas as they seek to reduce social and economic cleavages.

The process components of community social capital can be demonstrated by the level of interest and caring that adult members of the community have for the welfare of another person's child, and by the efforts of individuals and organizations to engage children in community programs and activities that make effective use of their time and energy (Beaulieu and Mulkey 1995; Coleman and Hoffer 1987; Smith et al. 1995). These include campaigns for voters to support initiatives that improve facilities, such as schools, sports arenas, and community centers. Moreover, it encompasses programs that involve students in adult/youth relationships through church-based and community-based organizations (Beaulieu and Israel 1997). When these activities involve adults with higher levels of educational attainment, youth are immersed in an environment in which educational achievement is encouraged.

Where the Rubber Meets the Road: Social Capital Features That Matter the Most

Having outlined social capital features of families, schools, and communities that are theoretically important in shaping the educational achievement of rural students, we showcase the subset of social capital features that have consistently emerged through empirical research as having the most important affect on student achievement levels. Drawing mainly from studies that we and others have undertaken over the course of the past fifteen years,[3] we outline the factors that have served to contribute to or limit

3. We draw upon a number of social capital related studies that we and others have conducted during the 1990s. These include Beaulieu and Israel (1997); Beaulieu et al. (2001); Israel et al. (2001); Israel and Beaulieu (2002); Lee (1993); Muller and Kerbow (1993); Smith, Beaulieu, and Israel (1992); Smith et al. (1995); and Sun (1999).

or inhibit the educational progress of youth. The intent is to sharpen our focus on the social capital forces that matter most to the educational achievement of rural youth.

Table 21.3 outlines the variables that play a statistically significant role in promoting academic performance. These are classified into four major groups: (1) individual background characteristics; (2) social capital features of the family; (3) social capital characteristics of the school; and (4) social capital traits of the community. While not inclusive of all the factors that influence student achievement, the table details the key elements of the family, school, and community having substantive impacts on achievement. For purposes of this chapter, math and reading composite test scores of a national representative group of eighth graders are used to measure achievement (see Ingels et al. 1998 for a detailed description of the study's methodology). As a general rule, these factors prove important for metropolitan and nonmetropolitan students alike, although the magnitude of their impacts tends to vary slightly among students attending schools in different locational settings.

Two key social capital factors reported in Table 21.3 have sizable positive effects on achievement. The first is parents who discuss school matters with their child, and the second is parents who have high aspirations with regard to their child attending college. Four features have large negative impacts on achievement. These include two background characteristics of students—being African American or Latino; one family social capital variable—parents who frequently monitor their child's homework; and one school social capital variable—parents who have contact with the school on a frequent basis.

A host of social capital variables offers modest contributions to student educational performance. Within the family arena, these include having a college-educated parent, higher family income, two parents or a single parent in the home, parents who limit their child's television time, and the presence of adult supervision in the home after school. As for school social capital features, the positive features include schools with higher per student expenditures, an emphasis on academics, and a positive school climate. Moreover, students who get involved in school organizations, who have teachers that nurture them, and who have parents that are involved in parent-teacher or other school-related groups, tend to have better test scores.

Within the context of the community, residential stability actually lowers the performance of rural students. Such areas may offer limited attraction to people living elsewhere, and without the infusion of people with new ideas, educational expectations on the part of the community may

Table 21.3 Impact of background characteristics and social capital attributes on educational achievement

Variable	Level of Impact on Achievement
Individual background characteristics	
African American	− − −
Hispanic	− −
Male	+
School social capital	
Structural features	
Per student expenditures	+
School size	NS
Percent of students from low income families	−
School emphasizes academics	+
Positive school climate	+
Process features	
Student involved in school clubs	+
Teachers nurture students	+
Teachers/students talk outside of class	−
Parents contact the school	− − −
Parents involved in PTO or PTA	+
Parents involved in other school-related organizations	+
Family social capital	
Structural features	
At least one parent with a college degree	+
Income level of family	+
Number of siblings	−
Number of siblings who are high school dropouts	−
Two parents in the home	+
Single parent in the home	+
Process features	
Parent/child discuss school matters	+ + +
High aspirations for child attending college	+ +
Parents monitor homework	− −
Parents limit TV time	+
Adult supervision after school	+
Community social capital	
Structural features	
Socioeconomic capacity	+
Proximity	+
Residential stability	−
Community equality (civic involvement)	+
Process features	
No moves since 1ˢᵗ grade	+
Student involved in religious organization	+
Student involved in non-religious organization	+

Key: +/− = Improves/reduces test score by up to 2.99 points; + +/− − = Improves/reduces test score from 3–5.99 points; + + +/− − − = Improves/reduces score by 6 or more points. NS = not significant.
Note: Test scores have a mean of 50 and a standard deviation of 10.

remain low. If a community shows signs of extensive civic involvement (as measured by voting in major national elections), has resources in place that contribute to its socioeconomic capacity, and has people living in reasonable proximity to one another, student achievement improves. Also, if students' community ties have not been disrupted through frequent moves to other schools since they started first grade, their parents know their friends' parents personally, and these young people get involved in religious and nonreligious community organizations, their achievement levels tend to increase.[4]

On the other side of the coin, a small number of social capital elements have modest negative influences on achievement. Having siblings, including siblings who have dropped out of high school, inhibits the emergence of family social capital. Detrimental school factors include the presence of a high percentage of students from low-income families, and teachers and students who talk outside of class on a frequent basis. This latter item may reflect the fact that these types of teacher/student interactions are occurring mainly to address difficulties that students may be experiencing inside the classroom.

There is one feature related to social capital that has no significant bearing on student achievement, namely, size of the school (in terms of student enrollment). When other key factors of the family, school, and community are considered, school size does not emerge as important in shaping the academic achievement of students.

Fitting the Pieces Together

Table 21.3 summarizes the specific set of individual, family, school, and community variables having positive and negative influences on the academic achievement of young people. The impact of any variable may seem limited when viewed in isolation, but when considered collectively, each one plays an important part in shaping the academic performance of students. The combined effects of the four sets of variables (background, family social capital, school social capital, and community social capital) on achievement levels (i.e., standardized math and reading tests scores) are represented in Figure 21.1.[5] Results are reported by the four geographic locations (metropolitan core, metropolitan other, nonmetropolitan adjacent, nonmetropolitan nonadjacent) of the schools that students attend. This

4. Student involvement in nonreligious groups is good up to a point. If students are involved in too many local organizations, their composite test scores suffer a negative impact.

5. The statistical data employed to generate the information presented in this table are available upon request from the senior author.

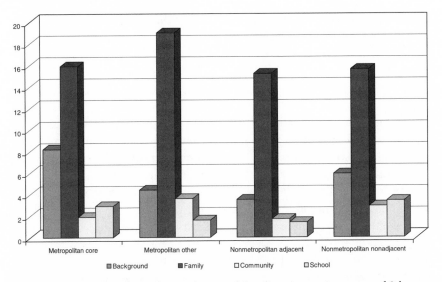

Fig. 21.1 Influences of social capital on math/reading composite scores of 8th graders, by place of residence

allows one to study how the impact of the social capital features might vary across metropolitan/nonmetropolitan areas.

Despite the continued attention given within policy circles to schools as the prime engine for improving educational performance of students, schools have only modest impacts on test scores. In fact, school social capital features captured in Figure 21.1 account for only 1.6 to 3.4 percent of the variance in student test scores (depending upon the geographic location of their schools).

Family social capital variables prove to be the vital in shaping test score outcomes for students—ranging from 15.2 to 19 percent of the variability in achievement scores across the four geographic settings. At the same time, background characteristics account for 3.5 to 8.2 percent of the variance in test scores. The combined set of community social capital variables help explain 1.4 to 3.4 percent of the difference in tests scores of students attending schools in the four metropolitan/nonmetropolitan areas of the United States.

For students attending schools in nonmetropolitan areas (be they located in adjacent or nonadjacent nonmetropolitan areas), family social capital features prove to be principally responsible for student test score outcomes. Community features appear to have their most sizable impacts in nonadjacent nonmetropolitan and in other metropolitan localities. School social capital forces play their most important role in shaping achievement levels for students attending schools in nonadjacent non-metropolitan areas.

Conclusion

Rural America has made important strides in improving the quality of its human capital resources. More nonmetropolitan residents are completing their high school education and enrolling in community colleges and technical institutions than ever before. Nevertheless, in an ever-changing world in which the need for well-educated workers is accelerating (Swaim 1998), the modest educational improvements registered by rural Americans may not be enough. Creating, retaining, and attracting well-educated individuals, especially those with a Bachelor's degree or higher, will be vital to the long-term social and economic health of rural areas.

Attending to the educational progress of youth is an important part of the constellation of strategies that rural areas must consider if they want to improve their chances of expanding their pool of college-educated residents. If history is any guide, the policies they enact (or implement as a result of state and federal mandates) will place the burden of strengthening student success squarely on the shoulders of local schools. This chapter has shown that the social capital attributes of schools, regardless of their spatial location, have only modest effects on student performance improvements (although their impacts tend to be greatest for students enrolled in schools located in nonmetropolitan nonadjacent areas). For nonmetropolitan students, the family is the most important conduit for realizing educational success, while the broader community in which they are embedded plays a secondary role. The set of family social capital attributes captured in Figure 21.1 had five to ten times more impact on standardized test scores for nonmetropolitan eighth graders than did the structural and process features of schools. While our chapter does not consider all the items that could affect educational achievement, those considered did prove to be critical in explaining test score results of rural students.

Given these findings, we offer four recommendations that would place rural students on a path of educational success. First, expanded investments are needed to help rural parents understand the vital role they play in shaping the academic progress of their children. While the message that parents are their child's first teacher is a commonly accepted fact, a concrete set of programs is necessary to help parents become an active part of their child's life through the school years. This includes equipping them with the skills to engage in positive discussions with their kids about school matters, alerting them to the importance of parental monitoring of their child's activities, and helping them realize the key role that parental aspirations play in shaping their child's long-term educational plans.

Second, schools must create additional mechanisms to involve parents in their child's school life. For too many parents, contact with schools only occurs as a result of their child's misbehavior or academic problems. Finding positive channels for meaningful parental involvement in the school is important to a child's educational progress. At the same time, teachers must seek to nurture and guide students inside and outside the classroom setting in a positive and sustained manner.

Third, children who have been uprooted from their school and community each time that they move are at risk of doing poorly in school. In many communities, new residents are not actively welcomed. Communities and neighborhoods must find ways to effectively integrate new families and children into the life of their schools and communities in a timely fashion.

Fourth, rural communities can play meaningful roles in promoting the educational success of youth by ensuring that kids have access to adult mentors as well as programs and activities that can guide them through life's challenges. For children living in homes where parents are indifferent or apathetic, contact with caring adults and mentors in the community can set these young people on a path to educational excellence.

While not designed to be comprehensive, these four strategies will expand the spotlight on factors outside of the classroom that can affect the educational achievement of rural youth. Certainly, policy-makers should not abandon their focus on school-based strategies. But this chapter gives notice that success inside the school depends greatly on investments made outside the building—in the families and communities that are essential partners with America's rural schools.

22

Rural Health Policy

Lois Wright Morton

Rural health policy in the United States is an unintentional byproduct of national health policy. As a result it suffers from the assumption that a market-driven medical/industrial complex can solve rural health problems. The goals of current national health policies are cost containment and economic efficiencies, rather than the goals set forth by Healthy People 2010, which advocates a U.S. health promotion agenda emphasizing reduced health disparities and increased longevity and quality of life (U.S. Department of Health and Human Services 2000). Current policies reinforce the biomedical production of goods and services, and have led to an increasingly fragmented health care system that is most responsive to consumers who can afford to purchase health commodities. In this chapter, I examine the disconnection between current health policy and health goals for rural America. First, two major crises in rural health are discussed—health disparities both between urban and rural places and within rural areas, and inadequate rural health infrastructure. Then, health policies and their impacts on rural places are analyzed. Next, two underlying assumptions about health policies are challenged—that the main health issues are competitive markets and improved rural health care infrastructure, and that these will solve rural health problems. Lastly, basic assumptions about which future rural health policies should be developed are offered, and future solutions are framed to meet health status goals and socioeconomic concerns.

Crises in Rural Health

Healthy People 2010, a national health promotion and disease prevention initiative developed by the U.S. Department of Health and Human Services, set out two overarching goals for the U.S. population in 1998. The first is to increase health quality and the number of years of healthy life. The second is to eliminate health disparities among populations regardless of race, ethnicity, disability, socioeconomic status, gender, age, or geography. These two goals frame the rural health crisis. Health disparities between urban and rural regions and among rural populations have existed historically, and in some cases inequality seems to be increasing. Inadequate medical infrastructure limits access to and quality of the health care that rural populations are able to obtain. Further, underlying rural economic and social conditions—such as employment and occupational opportunities, income, education, civic structure, and transportation—influence the capacities of rural places to solve their population health problems.

Health Status Disparities

The U.S. National Center for Health Statistics reported a number of health differences between metropolitan and nonmetropolitan counties for the period 1996–1998 (Eberhardt et al. 2001). Death rates for children and young adults (ages one to twenty-four years) in the most rural counties in all regions except the Northeast were over 50 percent higher than the lowest rates reported in fringe counties of large metropolitan areas. In the South, death rates for working-age adults (ages twenty-five to sixty-four) during this period were highest in nonmetropolitan counties. Ischemic heart disease death rates in the South were over 20 percent higher in the most rural counties than in fringe counties of large metropolitan areas. Using a gradient of counties from more to less urban, the death rates from unintentional injuries increased nationally and within each region as counties become less urban. Most rural counties experienced death rates from motor vehicle traffic–related injuries that were twice as high as central counties of large metropolitan areas. Suicide rates for males fifteen years and over increased steadily from urban to nonmetropolitan counties. Male suicide was steepest in the West—almost 80 percent higher than large metropolitan county rates.

Using longitudinal mortality data from the U.S. Centers for Disease Control for the period 1968 to 1997, distinct patterns of mortality emerge as these data are disaggregated by urban influence (Fig. 22.1) (U.S. Centers for Disease Control 2001). Nonmetropolitan counties that are not adjacent to metropolitan areas and have places with populations less than 10,000 (codes 8 and 9 in Fig. 22.1) consistently experienced higher rates of age-adjusted mortality than counties with more populated places. A lag in health over time for the most rural counties (code 9 in Fig. 22.1) was also

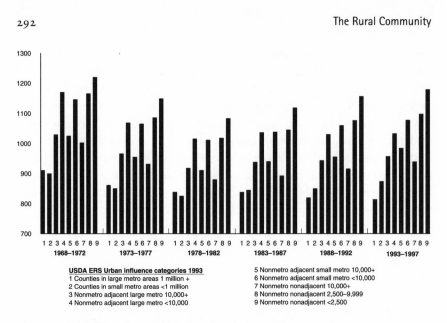

Fig 22.1 Age-adjusted mortality rates, by county, 1968–1997 (per 100,000 population)*Notes:* Alaska not included. Funded by the Iowa State University Agriculture Experiment Station under research project AES NC1001.

Source: Centers for Disease Control (2001), CDC Compressed Mortality Files 1968–97; age-adjusted to 2000 standard U.S. population.

evident in age-adjusted death rates for a number of diseases, including diseases of the heart, cerebrovascular disease (stroke), diabetes, nutritional deficiencies, and digestive organ cancers (data not shown). Although heart disease and stroke—the first and third leading causes of death in the United States, respectively—have declined over time nationally and in rural areas, geographic disparities have not been eliminated. Diabetes mortality rates for the most rural counties during the 1993–1997 period were 43 percent higher than in large metropolitan counties with populations over one million (data not shown).

Crises in Rural Health Care Infrastructure

Health care infrastructure—anchored by rural hospitals, public health departments, and emergency medical services—has played an important role in decreasing mortality rates and increasing well-being and health. However, this aging infrastructure and system of care is unraveling as chronic diseases have become more prevalent than acute illnesses, as medical technologies and innovations have proliferated, as health care delivery and health insurance institutions have restructured, and as declining rural economic conditions have undermined the ability of local communities to finance health care services. Most rural hospitals were built in the 1950s with federal matching funds obtained through the Hill Burton Act. Financing and administration crises plague rural hospitals as they struggle to modernize and respond to changing market conditions. County-level public health departments, the traditional provider of last resort, are responsible for collecting data on population health, assuring environmental quality and disease prevention, and carrying out health care planning. These institutions are experiencing budget stress due to declining local revenues, expectations for cost efficiencies and accountability, and new competition from the private sector. Emergency medical services (EMS) provide essential transportation and first response care. Composed primarily of local volunteers, rural EMS units across the United States report critical shortages of volunteers and resources for training, and underfunding to upgrade and replace equipment.

The traditional role of the hospital as the foundation of rural health care is undergoing reevaluation as health care costs burden rural citizens. Almost 10 percent of the nation's rural hospitals closed between 1980 and the late 1990s (Reif, DesHarnais, and Bernard 1999). Many of these hospitals had comparatively less technologically sophisticated equipment and strained budgets, which made it difficult for them to compete with urban hospitals or to be able to purchase the ever-expanding array of technical and biomedical innovations (Reardon 1996). Overall admission rates in rural hospitals declined as residents bypassed their local hospitals for the more sophisticated services provided by urban facilities (Morrisey et al. 1995). Rural hospitals are caught between providing basic medical care to an aging and increasingly chronically ill population, and a burgeoning medical infrastructure that focuses on specialization and technology. Bad debts, a higher percentage of Medicare patients than urban hospitals (Reardon 1996), and changes in Medicaid reimbursement have undermined the financial stability of many rural hospitals.

Rural hospital restructuring in the past two decades took one of several possible pathways—closure, merger with neighboring rural hospitals or urban health systems, development of rural health care networks or alliances with multiple health institutions, and/or downsizing to a critical access hospital. Hospital closures resulted in resident distress over the loss of local emergency rooms, greater travel distances for hospital services, difficulty in recruiting physicians for routine care, and health services access issues for vulnerable populations such as the elderly and those with low incomes (Reif et al. 1999). Rural physicians who are expected to deliver a comprehensive set of health care services to their patients depend upon the rural hospital (Phelps 1992; Krein, Christianson, and Chen 1997). Patient volume and the profitability of physician practices and pharmacy services are linked to the location of the nearest hospital and hospitals that provide specialty services. Thus, loss or changes in the rural hospital affect rural physician practices, as well as a number of auxiliary medical services. Expansion of managed care under Medicaid waivers increased urban competition for primary care physicians (Rural Policy Research Institute 1996) and undermined an already short supply of rural medical providers. The U.S. Office of Rural Health Policy (1997) estimates that people who live in nonmetropolitan areas are almost four times more likely to live in an area with a shortage of health professionals, compared to residents of metropolitan areas.

Health departments, the second major health institution in rural areas, are experiencing new competition from the private sector, loss of their ability to cross-subsidize services to the needy and medically underserved, and new opportunities to partner with the medical community. Various factors shift many Medicaid services away from public health departments, including competition from private providers, the Child Health Insurance Program, and Medicaid managed care requirements that a primary care provider refer patients prior to the delivery of health services. In several states with fully capacitated Medicaid managed care programs, rural health departments eliminated or decreased services such as rural well-child clinics (Slifkin, Goldsmith, and Ricketts 2000). A number of health department directors reported substantial loss of Medicaid reimbursements for these services and reduced health department financial stability.

What do reduced or eliminated public health clinical services mean to rural populations? Loda et al. (1997) report that in the rural Southeast, health departments are the primary source of services that prevent pregnancy and poor birth outcomes for adolescents, in contrast to urban areas that have a variety of family planning providers. In eleven states east of the Mississippi River, rural children who were immunized by public health clinics had higher immunization completion rates than urban children in 1995 (Slifkin et al. 1997). Slifkin et al. (1997) suggest that rural families are more dependent on public health clinics, and that rural health department professionals know their clientele more personally, allowing them to better target families with children. These examples offer evidence that continued financial instability for rural public health departments could result in poorer health outcomes for low-income rural populations.

The third major component of rural medical infrastructure, emergency medical services, is experiencing labor and equipment crises. In 2000, a survey of rural EMS units identified a variety of needs—73 percent required communication equipment, 68 percent needed medical equipment, and 54 percent needed ambulances (Heinrich et al. 2001). As the rural economy shifts from many small farmers to a few large farmers, and as more of the rural nonfarm workforce commutes to neighboring urban centers, emergency medical services are finding it increasingly difficult to recruit volunteers for daytime shifts. Lack of advanced-care equipment and training and low volumes of some types of services prevent the transport team from maintaining adequate patient care skills (Morrisey et al. 1995). According to the U.S. General Accounting Office, one rural state reported that medical direction to EMS staff could be from a physician as far as one hundred miles away (Heinrich et al. 2001). The loss or downsizing of rural hospitals increases the distances that EMS personnel have to travel, and can double the time spent transporting patients. This makes it even more difficult to attain the Healthy People 2010 objective of a greater proportion of rural people reached by EMS within ten minutes. Without investments in rural EMS infrastructure, the current differences between rural and urban (whose goal is EMS service in five minutes) are likely to increase rather than decrease. For an aging rural population that is increasingly less able to drive and more likely to need emergency assistance, the availability and expertise of emergency medical services is an essential resource for extending longevity and quality of life.

The high fixed costs of rural hospitals, public health departments, and twenty-four-hour emergency service are major financing challenges for rural places. In 1992, rural local governments spent $10.8 billion to support local health infrastructure (Wellever and Radcliff 1998). Zimmerman and McAdams (1999) reported that although an average of 12.1 percent of Kansas' 1996 county-level public budgets were spent on health care, ten of the 105 counties spent one-fourth to one-third of their budgets on health care. Morton's (1997) study of upstate New York counties from 1984 to 1995 found an upward trend over time with rural periphery and rural-suburban counties' total health spending (including local Medicaid share) in 1995 close to 30 percent of all county expenditures.

The ability to pay taxes to support a health care infrastructure and personally purchase medical services is dependent upon rural residents' employment, income, and health insurance. Although rural people have similar insurance coverage rates as urban populations, they are more likely to be underinsured (Comer and Mueller 1992). More rural than urban residents rely on individual health insurance plans or coverage purchased through small employers (Pol 2000). Uninsured rural residents are more likely to have low or modest incomes, and be self-employed—15 percent rural versus 9.5 percent urban—or employed in agriculture, mining, forestry, or fishing.

Fragile Social and Economic Conditions

Although rural health care institutions offer intervention strategies for disease and illness, they do not adequately address prevention issues and cannot address the root causes of disease and mortality (Morton 2001a). Albrecht, Clarke, and Miller noted the "large and consistent net effects on health status" (1998, 249) of rural community structural characteristics, such as percent with less than a ninth grade education, percent of Latino residents, and percent of people who do not speak English. Young and Lyson (2001) found that the social organization of communities (number of voluntary organizations, membership organizations, small businesses, and percentage who voted in national elections) explained 49 percent of the variance in mortality across U.S. counties.

There is a great deal of science that links poor health to lower education, lower income, lower social standing, and increasing age (Evans, Barer, and Marmor 1994). Some health outcomes are the result of limited access to health care services, but Evans et al. conclude that "there are underlying factors that influence susceptibility to a whole range of diseases" (1994, 46). This suggests that general, nonspecific risk factors are sources of poor health. Rural social and economic conditions such as schools, employment opportunities, economic conditions, transportation systems, and civic structure are general factors that are only beginning to be understood in relationship to attaining health and well-being. These conditions are elaborated in other chapters of this book and are important underlying factors that must be considered in order for health intervention policies to be effective.

Health Care Policies

Transformations in rural health care in the past decades were precipitated in most places by the devolution of Medicaid regulatory practices to state and local health departments and revisions to the federal Medicare reimbursement rate structure. Corporate America embraced managed care practices as "their favorite techniques for controlling health care costs for their own employees" (Leyerle 1994, 109). By the mid-1990s, government dollars financed more than 44 percent of all U.S. health care expenditures (U.S. Department of Health and Human Services 1996), and efforts intensified to control public medical costs. Business pressures to embrace managed care and more competitive health care markets inevitably led the government to enact policies and practices that supported freer and more competitive health care markets (Morton 2001a). Competitive markets respond to individual demands for health services, but are not able to redistribute resources across populations.

A shift in 1982 to the prospective payment system for Medicare, and state-by-state adoption of Medicaid-managed care changed the rules for reimbursal and the amount of reimbursement dollars available to insurance companies, rural health care providers, and rural county health departments. Managed care combines the insurance and the delivery of health care, and redirects profits from hospitals and doctors to insurance companies. Managed care organizations compete primarily on the basis of price; incentives in the marketplace for quality and access are weak or nonexistent (American Public Health Association 1997). The federal Balanced Budget Act of 1997 allowed provider-sponsored networks to receive Medicare-managed care contracts, and supported the transition from fee-for-service payments for health care services to managed care payments. Despite rhetoric about preventative care, the real goals of these new policies were to achieve cost efficiencies and reduce the public economic burden of financing the health care system.

The critical access hospital (CAH) created by the Balanced Budget Act of 1997 offered rural hospitals flexibility in staffing and the potential to offset financial losses. The average number of rural hospital beds ranges from forty-eight to 132 beds per hospital (Reardon 1996). Conversion to a CAH means that rural hospitals must downsize to no more than fifteen acute beds (and ten swing beds), limit hospital stays to ninety-six hours, provide twenty-four-hour emergency services, and form a network with at least one other acute care hospital. This model defines rural medical services as basic health care only, with little or no specialty care. If this model is replicated across rural America, the extreme difference in availability of specialty care will produce an even more distinctly different set of services between rural and urban places than is true today. The impact on population health is yet unknown. If accompanied by investments in medical services that respond to chronic illness and increases in primary care providers, this could be an effective policy to reduce acute care costs without loss of longevity or quality of health. Without investments, disparities in access to health care between rural and urban places will increase with negative effects on rural health status.

The Disparity Between Health Status and Health Policies

U.S. health policy primarily focuses on the health care system and its ability to respond to sick individuals' demands for health care (Henly et al. 1998;

Morton 2001a). As long as health issues are framed as individual rather than population concerns, competitive market strategies will continue to be applied in hopes of controlling costs. However, the health care system lacks many of the critical components necessary for markets to efficiently operate—disease and illness are not voluntary, so patients are captive to market offerings and cannot voluntarily exit the market; patients often lack the technical knowledge to rationally purchase health services; and health care providers (the real demanders of services) are accountable to health insurers, not patients.

The source of the disconnection between health policies that attempt to control medical costs and the ability to reach Healthy People 2010 goals of eliminating health disparities and increasing longevity and quality of life lies in the conflict between individual and population health. Pooling resources that target population health averages out what each person has to pay for health care, and allocates care efficiently across patients (Eddy 1991). This is in contrast to individual patients choosing resources that optimize their own personal care. Competitive markets and managed care curtail cost shifting in order to squeeze out excess payments, yet small hospitals (Ginzberg 1996) and public health depend on cross-subsidization to cover patient-care losses. Mechanisms that spread the high financial costs of medical care among populations are dismantled by policies that reward competitive markets that operate based on individual demand.

Rural areas lack the population characteristics, geographic density, and economic conditions that are necessary to make competitive health care markets efficient and effective. Competitive markets merely accentuate the differences between consumers who can afford and those who cannot afford the growing array of medical services. Wysong et al. (1999) reported that managed care firms found rural markets less attractive than urban ones because rural areas had lower incomes and higher poverty rates. Policies whose main foci are competitive markets cannot eliminate health disparities among rural and urban populations unless economic disparities are also eliminated. Moreover, these policies reinforce medical solutions, when improvements to health may actually be gained through a host of different actions and policies that have nothing directly to do with health care. For example, smoking and obesity, two risk factors associated with major chronic health conditions, have population-level interventions that target disease prevention rather than medical responses.

The 1960 U.S. Surgeon General report on smoking and cancer bore fruit in the 1990s with successful private and public lawsuits against tobacco firms. Higher tobacco taxes and indoor smoking bans that local and state governments have enacted are examples of socially constructed political interventions designed to reduce smoking and cancer rates (Sturm 2002). However, adults and adolescents living in the most rural counties were found to smoke more than those in central counties of large metropolitan areas. The South—where tobacco is a major agricultural cash crop in some areas—experienced large increases in smoking in 1999 (Eberhardt et al. 2001). Are Southern counties less likely than others to have indoor smoking bans or incentives that deter smoking due to economic and cultural biases? Are incomes and occupations the real sources of poor health? Research is necessary to answer these questions.

The effects of obesity on chronic health are now recognized as larger than excessive drinking or current or past smoking (Sturm 2002). Declared a national epidemic in 2001, obesity is considered one of the nation's most important health problems because of associations with heart disease, stroke, cancer, and diabetes, and health care costs for overweightness and obesity are estimated at $117 billion annually (Squires 2001). Iowa, a highly rural state, reported a substantial increase (from 25.3 percent to 32.7 percent) in the incidence of obesity from 1989 to 1997 (USDHHS 2000c). Diet and the structure of our food systems are implicated as sources of obesity. The International Obesity Task Force causal web depicts the interrelationships of health to global food marketing, media, national and state policies related to food and agriculture, urban design, education, and transportation systems (Kumanyika 2001). Smoking and obesity are only two examples of proximate causes of poor health that will not be alleviated by competitive health care markets. Underlying smoking and obesity behaviors are poverty and low education levels—both disproportionate problems in rural areas.

Putting the "Rural" into Health Policy

Why do rural regions need special attention in health policy? Healthy People 2010 lists six categories where health disparities exist: race and ethnicity, socioeconomic status, gender, age, disability, and geographic location. As noted in other chapters of this book, rural areas have age, socioeconomic status, and race and ethnicity disparities that are critical factors in explaining geographic differences in population health. A large proportion of American resources is invested in a medical/industrial complex in the hopes that we can achieve longer and higher quality lives and reduce disparities among populations. While policies that target the medical infrastructure may reward cost efficiencies and encourage medical science to continue to innovate, they will not reduce health disparities until rural populations have an equal ability to purchase these products and services. Further, an increasingly elderly rural population, the high costs of medical care, and the fact that almost 30 percent of all hospitalized Medicare patients die within twelve months (Ginzberg 1996) suggest that investments in the rural medical infrastructure may increase quality of life (comfort and reduced pain) but will not reduce mortality.

If better health for rural populations is the goal, I suggest that policymakers start with five assumptions. First, nationwide and rural policies must be evaluated on their ability to achieve improved population health as reflected in Healthy People 2010 goals rather than individual health gains. Second, generalized risk factors such as social and economic infrastructures affect population health. Rural regions differ among themselves and in comparison to urban regions on a number of characteristics: geography, population density, racial and ethnic mix, age, occupations, and social and economic conditions. These differences influence inequities in health status and the adequacy of rural medical infrastructures. Third, connections among rural and urban insurance risk pools and medical infrastructures are necessary to share costs and risks. Rural primary care services must be networked into a larger system that incorporates interventions for primary, secondary, and tertiary care. Fourth, health decisions are political. Local civic structures, including human and social capitals, affect capacities for local problem solving, including the integration of rural health, social, and economic goals. Fifth, rural population characteristics prevent competitive market solutions from solving basic rural health problems. Place-based interventions will be necessary if health and well-being are to be shared across U.S. populations.

Solutions to rural health issues lie in policies and incentives that encourage partnerships among public and private rural institutions and connections with urban resources (Morton 2001b). One of the most critical needs is to increase access to affordable health insurance. This means that public policies should be structured to spread the risk-of-disease cost burden among populations, rather than providing incentives to form niche, profitable markets for insuring healthy populations. The Child Health Insurance Program (CHIP) is a beginning, but it targets a generally already healthy population. The greatest risk-sharing need is for our aging, chronically ill population. Young and old, healthy and sick populations must share the risk and cost burdens for disparities to be reduced. The transformation of rural health care infrastructure to serve chronic health needs, while responding to continuing critical acute care needs, means the rural hospital must reevaluate the kinds of services it offers and work with local, state, and national public and private groups to link specialty care and to share the costs of uninsured and charity cases. Further, rural models of health care require more functional overlap among health professions than urban models (Henly et al. 1998) because of limited specialty professionals. The job descriptions and expectations of rural health professionals and their supporting infrastructures look very different from their highly specialized urban counterparts.

Investments in public health, an institution whose goals are population health, are necessary for continued monitoring and assessment of rural health, as benchmarked by Healthy People 2010 nationally and at state levels. Further, public health must work with voluntary organizations, local leaders, and private health care firms to address population health prevention and coordinate services to under- and uninsured populations. Telemedicine infrastructure links specialized knowledge available in urban centers to many rural medical sites; however, its full potential is not currently being utilized.

Lastly, integrated approaches to rural health research and interventions need to examine the associations among generalized socioeconomic factors and health. This acknowledges the complex interrelatedness of rural economies, civic structure, occupations, incomes, poverty, agricultural structure, and environmental health to rural population health. Examples of public policies that would benefit from this understanding are national farm bills, Health Care Financing Administration rules and regulations that distinguish between place-based population characteristics, Environmental Protection Agency policies and practice recommendations on land use and water quality, nutritional policies that affect food systems and food safety, and a new structure for emergency medical services that designates a lead agency instead of four federal agencies offering fragmented guidance and direction.

Conclusion

Healthy People 2010 goals were not lightly chosen on the whim of one sector or interest group. They were developed through the broad input of public institutions and private citizens, organizations and firms, employers, health departments, and health care providers. As such they represent the aspirations of an America that tries to practice democracy (representation of diverse interests and populations) and strives toward fairness. To effectively achieve these goals, public leaders must incorporate three important areas: the sciences of diseases and their relationships to rural people and their environments, evaluations of policies and interventions based on their

impacts on rural health, and mobilization of the political will to enact policies in the rural interest. The test of any rural health policy should be this:
Does it reduce health disparities within rural populations and between
rural and urban places and increase the quality of life that they experience?
This does not mean that strategies that encourage market efficiencies are
avoided. It does mean, however, that rural health policies go beyond incentives to the medical infrastructure, and address social and economic
inequalities that are the root cause of poor health.

PART IV

People and the Environment: Tough Tradeoffs in
an Era with Vanishing Buffers

23

Transforming Rural America

The Challenges of Land Use Change in the Twenty-First Century

Douglas B. Jackson-Smith

The last decade has witnessed a significant amount of social and political debate regarding patterns of urban growth in the United States. Under the banner of movements like "Smart Growth," "Sustainable Communities," and "Comprehensive Planning," an impressive number of citizens, activists, and political leaders have sought to reevaluate the traditional, land-extensive suburban growth model that has defined residential housing development since the 1950s. Most proposed solutions call for planning, land use regulations, and incentives to encourage higher housing densities, reinvestment in existing urbanized areas, and protection of open spaces and parks as green-space buffers (Duany, Plater-Zyberk, and Speck 2000).

Although the modern land use planning movement has a decidedly urban character, many rural communities have also begun to reevaluate their own patterns of growth and development. The resurgence of urban-to-rural migration in the early 1990s (see Chapter 1 in this volume), combined with heightened economic stress in traditional rural economic sectors, has generated increased conflict between those who seek to preserve the rural character of these areas and those who want to take advantage of the economic opportunities that new types of rural growth provide.

Not surprisingly, much of the research and applied policy literature on rural land use change approaches the subject from a decidedly urbanist perspective. Scholars and policy-makers have tended to emphasize the rural land use changes that are taking place right at the urban fringe—the fuzzy geographic zones at the margins where metropolitan counties and urbanized places shade into less densely populated rural areas (Burchell and Shad 1999; Nickerson 2001). While urban deconcentration (often called "urban sprawl") is indeed a key to understanding the process of rural land use change in America, the dominant emphasis on urban fringe issues has contributed to a relative lack of research and analysis of the forces of change in the extended rural landscape. For example, we have a vastly greater understanding of agricultural land preservation programs in relatively urbanized communities than we do in the places that produce the bulk of our nation's food and fiber.

In addition, there is considerable disagreement among rural citizens, policy-makers, and academics concerning the role of agriculture in twenty-first century land use planning. On the one hand, there is a pervasive tendency toward agricultural essentialism—the view that agriculture and other traditional rural economic sectors are still the critical engines of economic activity and the basis of rural community life. In this view, the proper focus of rural land use research and policy is to find ways to protect and preserve agriculture from the threats posed by unregulated rural development. In response to concerns about agricultural essentialism, however, many have reacted with a form of agricultural minimalism. They argue that because agriculture is economically and socially unimportant, any focus on farmers or agricultural lands in the land use discussion diverts attention from the real story of economic and social life in modern rural America.

This chapter summarizes what we do (and do not) know about the nature, causes, and impacts of recent land use changes in rural America. I then discuss the challenge of developing effective policies to manage rural land use change. The influence of the urbanist perspective and the tension between the extreme agricultural essentialists and minimalists become quite apparent as we examine the gaps in our knowledge base and the failure of most land use policies to make a marked impact on the overall trajectory of rural land use and development. Many of the examples presented here are drawn from the Midwest and the western United States; however, the discussion is generally applicable to most of the advanced industrialized world.

Changes in the Use of Private Rural Lands

Given the extensive governmental resources devoted to measuring changes in population, economic conditions, and environmental quality, it is perhaps surprising that we have only indirect and imperfect measures of changes in rural land use in the United States. To some degree this reflects the sheer size of the rural landscape and problems with relying on structured census questionnaires and remotely sensed data for evaluating subtle changes in land use.

The results of the 1997 USDA National Resource Inventory (NRI) confirm that America remains a predominantly rural country with respect to land use (U.S. Department of Agriculture 2000). In addition to roughly four hundred million acres of federal land, the almost 1.5 billion acres of private land in the lower forty-eight states mainly consists of cropland[1] and pasture (36 percent), rangeland (27 percent), and forestland (27 percent). By contrast, developed land represents only 6.6 percent of the private land base.

Comparisons of NRI data over time suggest that there has been considerable stability in the use of rural land. Over 91 percent of private land acres remained in the same category between 1982 and 1997, and this increases to over 95 percent if shifts among the cropland, conservation reserve program (CRP), and pasture categories are ignored. However, while the overall pattern of land use change is one of stability, patterns of rural land use change during the 1980s and 1990s do reflect two important trends. One trend entails the conversion of all types of rural lands into urbanized or other developed uses. Between 1982 and 1997, developed land uses increased by twenty-five million acres (or 1.4 million acres per year). Newly developed lands were drawn in roughly equal fashion from former agricultural lands (45 percent) and forested lands (40 percent). Between 1992 and 1997 most newly developed rural land was located in metropolitan counties, and the vast majority was located in the eastern third of the country.

The other major trend reflects the deintensification of rural lands, particularly the conversion of agricultural lands into forest cover. NRI data suggest that the total acres of cropland, pasture, and CRP declined by more than twenty-three million acres between 1982 and 1997. Most of these "lost" acres were converted into forestland (thirteen million acres) or developed uses (eleven million acres). During the same period forestland acres increased by a net 3.6 million acres, reflecting both the addition of over thirteen million forest acres (shifting from cropland and pasture use) and the loss of over ten million acres of forestland to development.

Socioeconomic Dimensions of Rural Land Use Change

Demographic Forces

The NRI data allow us to measure changes in land cover and land use that are easily visible from aerial photographs. However, from a sociological

---

1. Cropland here refers both to cultivated cropland as well as acres of cropland that have been idled under the federal Conservation Reserve Program for ten-year periods.

perspective, some of the most important trends in rural land use reflect changes in land tenure, landowner characteristics, and more subtle shifts in land management approaches that remote sensing technologies may be unable to detect.

Heimlich and Anderson (2001) have identified two major types of residential patterns that affect rural lands. The first—urban fringe development—reflects a classic form of "urban sprawl" (Williams 2000). It is driven by growth in suburban residential developments close to the edge of existing urban and metropolitan areas, with a concomitant increase in average lot size and the development of extensive transportation, employment, and retail networks to provide services for the increasingly dispersed population (Benfield, Raimi, and Chen 1999; Lewis 1995; Rome 2001).

The second residential development pattern—beyond urban fringe development—consists of large lot, residential, or recreational land developments located farther away from existing urban areas. This "rural sprawl" is less well understood and documented (Daniels 2000), and usually involves far fewer numbers of people but significantly increased amounts of land per person. It can consist of the construction of houses on relatively large parcels of rural land, the purchase of existing housing by inmigrants, and the purchase of large acreages for use as recreational, vacation, or hunting properties, often without any building construction.

Rural sprawl is difficult to detect using conventional data sources; however, using data from the Population Census and the American Housing Survey, Vesterby and Krupa (2001) found that two-thirds of the 110 million acres used for residential purposes in America were located in rural areas. Between 1980 and 1997, 70 percent of the new residential acreage was located in places that remained rural, with an average of 1.4 million acres being converted to new residential uses each year. New rural housing lots tend to be much larger than their urban counterparts. Over 60 percent of new rural housing acreage consisted of lots over ten acres.

Demographic forces are clearly a driver of rural land use change. In the 1970s and again in the early 1990s, there was a notable "population turnaround" associated with net migration from urban into rural areas in many parts of the country (Johnson and Beale 1998). At the same time, the declining average size of U.S. households has caused new housing construction to exceed the rate of population growth. Urban and rural forms of sprawl also reflect residential preferences for rural and suburban homes (Brown et al. 1997; Drabenstott and Smith 1995), significant growth in retirement, seasonal or recreational housing (Summers and Hirschl 1985), the decreased real cost of transportation, the growth of the digital and service economies, and the rise of telecommuting (Johnson 2001; Margherio et al. 1998).

The Economics of Commodity Production

Any discussion of rural land use change must also recognize changing rural economic conditions. The twentieth century was characterized by the steady deterioration of agricultural and other natural resource commodity markets relative to the manufacturing and service sectors (Mills 1995). This makes traditional land uses less viable and increases the appeal of developing rural lands for new residential, recreational, or conservation purposes (see Chapters 13 and 14 in this volume).

A closer examination of American agriculture helps illustrate the historical macroeconomic conditions in most basic commodity sectors. On the one hand, we have moved from a nation of rural people living on farms to one in which most Americans rarely set foot on a commercial farming operation. Between 1920 and 1997, the number of farms declined by over 70 percent, and employment in agriculture declined by over 80 percent (U.S. Department of Agriculture 1999). On the other hand, the total land area devoted to agricultural production decreased by only 3 percent during that same period.

Agriculture has become decidedly less important to rural areas socially and culturally; however, its economic importance depends on how one frames the issue. Figure 23.1 provides an overview of the inflation-adjusted aggregate value of farm receipts, expenses, and net farm income between 1924 and 1999. While productivity and output have continued to grow throughout the century, the rising cost of doing business has outstripped increases in farm output and gross receipts. The result has been stagnating

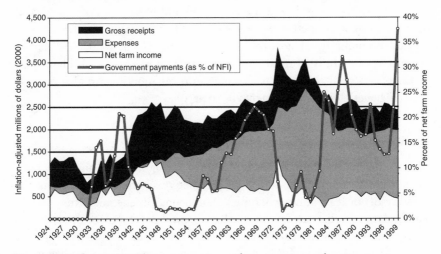

Fig. 23.1 Gross receipts, farm expenses, net farm income, and government payments, 1924–1999

and declining net farm income. Not coincidentally, government farm program payments have become an increasingly significant component of net farm income since the early 1980s.

A similar story can be told for most of the other traditionally rural, natural resource based economic sectors. Increased automation and technological change has allowed total output to increase, while local employment and producer net income levels decline (Cochrane 1979; Cook 1995; Freudenburg 1992). Moreover, in both farming and forestry, there has been a rapid increase in the number of smaller, noncommercial landowner/operators. These people may well market products from their farm and forest lands, but rarely depend on these assets for their household income and often manage them less intensively than larger commercial operators.

In sum, traditional natural resource industries may generate significant amounts of gross sales but relatively low amounts of net income. Even accounting for the secondary businesses that provide inputs and services or process the output of these traditional industries, it is rare that they will generate more than 20 percent of total employment or personal income in even the most remote rural communities (Power 1996). On the other hand, from a landscape perspective (in terms of land cover and visual impacts), farms, forests, and other natural resource industries usually dominate rural land use and define the aesthetic character of a rural community.

The Impacts of Urban and Rural Sprawl on Rural Places

Recent patterns of rural land use change would hardly be controversial if they were not associated with a wide range of potentially negative impacts on rural communities, landscapes, and the environment. While this chapter approaches the study of rural land conversion from a social problems perspective, it is clear that land use change in rural America can also provide positive benefits to some segments of society.

Farmland Loss

Perhaps the most oft-cited concern about rural land use change has been the perceived threat to the supply of productive agricultural lands and the viability of local farming economies (Sorenson, Greene, and Russ 1997). The growth of urban areas and rural residential development often occurs on productive agricultural lands. Overall, estimates of annual "loss" of farmland in the 1980s and 1990s range from 3.7 million acres from the

Census of Agriculture (U.S. Department of Agriculture 1999), to 4.4 million acres from the NRI figures for changes in cropland, pasture, and rangeland (U.S. Department of Agriculture 2000), to 4.8 million acres from the National Agricultural Statistics Service (NASS) statistics for land in farms (U.S. Department of Agriculture 2002b). In addition, over 157 million acres of farmland were purchased by nonoperator landlords and rented back out to farmers between 1988 and 1999 (U.S. Department of Agriculture 2001).

Is this rate of loss a threat to our nation's food supply? In the short run, the answer seems to be no. This is both because the total cropland base is relatively large (roughly four hundred million acres) and because the rate of productivity increase on the remaining acreage appears to be keeping pace with the rate of farmland loss (Heimlich and Anderson 2001). However, longer-term projections suggest that domestic population growth, declining rates of productivity increase, increased global demand for food, and continued farmland losses may produce a situation where this could change (Olson and Olson 1999).

Urban development affects farming in many ways other than merely "consuming" the land for other uses. For example, there is growing evidence that rural nonfarm housing development can increase complaints and conflicts over the dust, noise, and smells associated with modern agricultural activities. Farm supply dealers also need a "critical mass" of farm operations to remain viable within an area. As land gets split into smaller parcels, remaining farmers are forced to deal with more landlords and travel longer distances to access rented fields.

Perhaps most critical, people seeking to use farmland for nonagricultural purposes are usually willing to pay higher prices than the commercial farm economy would warrant (Brown, Phillips, and Roberts 1981; Healy and Short 1979; Stewart and Libby 1998). From a farmer's perspective, the inflated land value associated with development pressure is both a blessing and a curse (Daniels and Bowers 1997). Appreciating land values enable exiting farmers to realize significant financial gains when they sell their farmland assets. Proceeds from selling farmland are often the only source of retirement funds for older farm families. However, rising farmland values attract nonfarm land speculators (Lins 1994) and can make it difficult for new farmers to buy or even rent a farm of their own (Daniels 1999).

Overall, empirical studies of farmer exits have shown that development pressure alone is not usually the most important determinant of whether a farm stays in business or closes its doors. Rather, normal lifecycle events (e.g., retirement), the availability of a successor, and economic conditions within the farm sector are likely to be the most crucial (Hirschl and Long 1993; Saupe and Bentley 1990); however, areas experiencing intense nonfarm growth pressure do tend to have lower rates of new entry and investment in the agricultural sector (Jackson-Smith 1995).

Community Changes

Changes in rural land use can also affect the economic and social dynamics of rural households and communities (Lobao and Meyer 2001). Economically, while few nonmetropolitan counties now depend exclusively on the farming, forestry, or mining sectors, natural resource industries and the processing of raw commodities can still be a significant source of income and employment in specific communities (Beckley 1998; Stokes, Watson, and Mastran 1997). Traditional rural activities also serve as a source of rural cultural identity and social networks (Salamon 1995). In an increasingly urban society, many Americans still idealize the work ethic, independence, and closeness to nature that they associate with farming, logging, and other rural occupations.

From a fiscal standpoint, agricultural and forested lands generally provide significant property tax revenues to local governments and demand relatively few services in return—particularly in contrast to residential land uses that often cost municipalities more to service than they return in local property taxes (American Farmland Trust 2001; Burchell et al. 1998; Edwards and Jackson-Smith 2001). Though difficult to quantify, the rural and open character of agricultural landscapes also provides the community with attractive views and a high quality of life (Olson 1999). All of this makes rural communities a desirable place for people and businesses to visit, move to, and live in.

The empirical evidence is decidedly mixed on the impact of new rural residents on the culture, politics, and dynamics of rural communities. Many have reported the loss of traditional rural community values like informal labor exchange, neighborliness, and trust (Diamond and Noonan 1996; Fitchen 1991); however, differences in the values, attitudes, and community involvement of long-standing residents and newcomers may be overstated. Systematic surveys of rural residents have found that aggregate levels of community attachment, satisfaction, involvement, and perceived well-being are not significantly lower in places that have experienced rapid population growth, nonfarm development, or amenity in-migration when compared to places that have remained relatively static or "traditionally rural" (Greider, Krannich, and Berry 1991; Smith and Krannich 2000; Smith, Krannich, and Hunter 2001; Theodori and Luloff 2000).

Environmental Impacts

Natural resource based economic activities have certainly been a mixed blessing from the point of view of environmental and ecosystem health. Agriculture has been implicated as a major nonpoint source of water pollution both to surface and ground waters in the United States (U.S. Environmental Protection Agency 2000a), and there is growing concern about the impact of livestock farming on odors, greenhouse gases, and air quality (U.S. Environmental Protection Agency 2000b). Similarly, mining and commercial forestry operations are often cited as potential sources of environmental degradation (Kesler 1994; Langston 1995).

Agriculture and forestry are not always seen as environmentally negative, however. A growing number of scientists have identified certain "ecosystem" services provided by agriculture and forests (Olson 1999). These include the maintenance of wildlife habitat, enhanced water recharge capacity of local watersheds, and the ability to sequester or tie up atmospheric carbon in growing crops and plants.

Ultimately, environmental assessments of changes in rural land use depend on the particular landscape, the types of land uses being compared, the intensity of management, and the regional patterns and intermingling of land uses. If a subdivision is developed on former agricultural fields, the net overall impact on water quality and quantity, nutrient pollution, and wildlife habitat may be quite negative (Kahn 2000); however, if a former farm field reverts to grasslands or forest it may actually produce net gains in some environmental indicators.

The Challenges of Developing Rural Land Use Policies

Most rural areas have little experience with land use planning and typically have few growth management ordinances in place. The absence of guidelines and rules tends to generate haphazard patterns of development that can be aesthetically displeasing, aggravate land use conflicts, and create inefficiencies for public service provision. Moreover, where growth pressures are strong, local politics tend to be dominated by a "growth machine"—a loose coalition of pro-growth real estate, business, and civic interests (Logan, Whaley, and Crowder 1997; Molotch 1976). Where rural land use policies have been adopted, the most common approaches have involved community visioning or planning processes, zoning regulations that prevent or discourage rural housing development, and/or financial incentives to induce the desired patterns of land development.

Visioning and planning can help communities determine what they want their community to look like. Many rural communities have engaged in planning processes—often with extensive citizen involvement—and produced impressive vision statements and plan documents. However, producing a solid plan does not always lead to dramatic changes in local land use policies or practices. One reason is because most planning professionals and many of the local citizens active in rural planning efforts are not native to their communities and have a rather naive understanding of rural politics and governance, traditional rural land uses, and rural culture. Ironically, those most supportive of preserving traditional ways of life—the agricultural essentialists—are often nonfarmers, while opponents of such efforts—the agricultural minimalists—are disproportionately drawn from the ranks of older or retired farmers or other groups with close ties to the development community invested in showing that the importance of agriculture is overblown.

Regulatory approaches to rural land use typically involve the adoption of zoning ordinances that identify parts of the landscape where residential or commercial development is restricted. Conventional rural zoning ordinances designate most of the rural countryside as "agricultural" or "rural" zones and require large minimum lot sizes for future development (Daniels and Bowers 1997). However, experience has shown that these large lot sizes (usually twenty to sixty acres in size) do not serve as an effective disincentive for residential development, and are not big enough to create viable agricultural operations in most instances. In fact, because they consume much more land per unit of housing, they can accelerate the conversion of working lands (Roth 2000). Increasingly fragmented land ownership patterns also provide challenges to natural resource management agencies (Egan and Luloff 2000).

If zoning ordinances were rigorously enforced they could be powerful tools to shape development patterns; however, many local preservation plans and zoning ordinances are written without full consideration of the complexity of enforcement or implementation. Land use plans are often not treated as binding documents for making land use decisions, and local zoning boards routinely approve waivers, variances, or rezonings. Local government officials often find it difficult to turn down development proposals that would infringe upon an individual's private property rights (Daniels and Bowers 1997; Bukovac 1999). This is particularly true in rural areas when the landowner is a former farmer or rancher with few retirement savings, and a longtime resident of the area with close ties to local officials.

Recognizing the political difficulties (and economic hardships) associated with implementing strict regulatory controls on rural land use, a growing number of local leaders, landowners, and policy experts have advocated the use of financial incentives—preferential tax policies, economic development programs, and conservation easement purchases—to protect open rural landscapes.

Tax relief programs for rural lands are designed to reward landowners who choose not to develop their rural lands, and can increase the income-earning potential of farm and forest lands in the short run. However, as land parcels change hands, much of the financial windfall received by the original owners is capitalized into the underlying value of the land (Anderson and Bunch 1989; Henneberry and Barrows 1990). Economic development programs seek to make traditional rural industries more economically viable by attracting new capital investment, promoting enterprise diversification, and encouraging local processing of value-added products. The agricultural essentialists see this as a way to restore the centrality of agriculture to the rural economy, though they probably overestimate how important agriculture will ever be as an engine of economic success. By contrast, the agricultural minimalists resent the channeling of scarce economic development resources toward these traditional natural resource industries, and argue for more efforts to encourage new forms of rural economic activity (e.g., tourism, recreation, and high-tech industry), not all of which may be compatible with protecting farming and forestry.

An increasingly popular approach to rural land preservation involves the purchase of agricultural conservation easements (PACE) to protect open rural landscapes (American Farmland Trust 1997). Under a PACE program, a landowner voluntarily sells the rights to develop a parcel to a public or nonprofit entity. In return, they receive cash compensation, tax benefits, or other financial incentives. The value of the "development right" is usually determined by comparing the market value of the parcel with and without the easement restriction. While popular and effective, PACE programs are limited by the tremendous expense that would be required to purchase easements on any significant portion of the rural landscape, particularly where development pressures are high. Moreover, without a framework of planning and zoning, PACE programs run the risk of producing a checkerboard of protected lands surrounded by unprotected (and often highly developed) parcels (Daniels and Bowers 1997).

From an academic standpoint, we have very little solid empirical research about the impacts of rural land use policies and programs. Virtually all of the published literature reflects descriptive case studies of a particular program (see American Farmland Trust 1997; Daniels and Bowers 1997; Olson and Lyson 1999; Stokes et al. 1997) with little follow-up information about whether the program had a measurable impact on land development patterns. The absence of systematic data collection on land use and development in rural America prevents a careful assessment of policy impacts across localities or regions (Barrows and Trout 1989; Hiemstra and Bushwick 1989). Meanwhile, the few existing studies that evaluate the effectiveness of rural land use policies have found tenuous or nonexistent support for the idea that land use policies have materially affected the trajectories of rural land use change (Daniels and Nelson 1986; Jackson-Smith and Bukovac 2000; Kline and Alig 1999; Klein and Reganold 1997).

Future Research and Policy Directions

As we enter the twenty-first century, it is likely that the pace and direction of rural land use transformations will continue and even accelerate. Rural sociologists are well poised to interpret the social dimensions of these trends and develop programs and policies that help rural communities anticipate and adapt to the forces of change. To be effective, they will have to confront the three major conceptual blinders—urbanism, agricultural essentialism, and agricultural minimalism—that have limited our ability to understand and meet the challenges of rural land use policy development.

There are several critical areas of research that also need to advance at a more methodical and rapid pace. First, we need systematically collected data on the socioeconomic character of rural land use changes, including digitized land records and information on the characteristics of land buyers and sellers, and land tenure changes. Second, we must refocus on rural sprawl—the widespread and often "invisible" rural land use changes that take place beyond the immediate urban fringe, including low-density rural housing or recreational development. We also need to know more about the different land management practices and decision-making processes of the "new" types of landowners that increasingly populate rural America. Third, we need to improve our understanding of the impacts of rural land use shifts, including changes in the structure of rural economies, the influence of population in-migration on rural community character and function, and the ecological consequences of land management practices. Fourth, we need empirical evaluations of the performance of various rural land use policy tools, including a critical analysis of the social, cultural, and political factors that drive policy adoption and implementation.

Finally, there is a growing need to develop a "sociology of planning," whereby rural sociologists contribute to our understanding of the social dimensions of the land use planning process itself. How do the urban background and training of professional planners influence the character of rural land use planning efforts? What kinds of people participate, whose interests get represented, and how is rural land use policy shaped by these interests?

24

Community and Resource Extraction in Rural America

Lynn England and Ralph B. Brown

The Issues

Rural life is often characterized by two contrasting landscape types—agricultural and extractive. For many Americans, the social landscapes of agriculture are represented by a serene, calmly individualistic, and structured life. It is the way individual, family, and community life is "supposed to be." Life has a rhythm based on the seasons, and responds to weather patterns and cycles. The lifestyle is not intrusive, but harmonious with the rhythms of nature. Crises such as drought and downturns in macroeconomic trends are considered natural to this landscape, and they are outside of human control. This rural landscape is managed through stewardship combining peaceful coexistence with nature and being one's own boss. In short, "Family farming is rural America. The image of rural America as the storehouse of the traditional values that built the nation—self-reliance, resourcefulness, civic pride, family strength, concern for neighbors and community, honesty, and friendliness—persists, as many recent surveys show" (Garkovich et al. 1995, 9).

The other landscape of American rural life is the disorderly, wildly individualistic, and nonconforming world of extraction—minerals, oil, and timber. The mining town, the logging camp, the oil town, the company town, and the boomtown—all characterized by ethnic complexities, labor disputes, liquor, prostitutes, riotous living, and booms and busts—stand in juxtaposition to the placid midwestern farm town or the rustic New England village. While exogenous factors (e.g., the depletion of resources or swings in economic cycles) are prone to produce crises in these places, we tend to emphasize the endogenous factors, such as inherent company and labor conflict, dangerous work settings, and a lifestyle characterized by

violence and volatility as the causes of crises. In the rural landscape of
extraction, people live in conflict with nature; the companies rape the land
and seek to dominate the people and their communities. Neither nature nor
the individual is the boss.

Extraction: Rural America's Other Social Landscape

The extraction landscape has never been considered central to the national
character or a paragon of values. It is a symbol of moral disorder, and is
metaphorically associated with the rough economic growing pains of the
country; its redeeming society-wide feature is its importance as a supplier
of resources to fuel the national economy. We tolerate its problems and
crises because of its economic importance. At the dawn of this new century,
a more penetrating examination of this other rural landscape is past due. In
our discussion of rural landscapes characterized by extraction, we will provide a view of extractive communities and their values that argues they are
as central to our rural fabric as agriculture.

Extractive Communities

"Extractive industries, as the name implies, involve removal of raw materials from nature; this category thus excludes agriculture, but it includes a
significant fraction of the other forms of employment that have traditionally been seen as rural" (Freudenburg 1992, 307). An important feature of
extractive enterprises is that they are always in a position of dependence,
because raw materials acquire value through processing. They must be
mined, pumped, cut, milled, or refined, and made into something else—fin-
ished products whose sale and potential profit justifies the ongoing investment in their extraction. Raw materials undergo major transformations to
make them consumable, as opposed to agriculture, where the transformation is comparatively minor—harvesting, rounding up, butchering, or
packaging. The decision to extract raw materials is typically made by people whose interests are outside of the location where the materials are
found, and as a result they also lack interest in the local social world. Most
of the value found in a raw material accrues at the output end of the trans-
formative process, and is dependent on the state of technology. For example, coal, oil, and timber became significant raw materials with the growth
of steam engines, gas powered transportation, and the paper and housing
industries. Uranium became a valuable raw material when governments
and manufacturers found it important to weapons and commercial energy.

Raw materials must be extracted where they occur, and they are not necessarily found in convenient locations. Remote rural locations are thus a major part of the extraction landscape.

As we move into a new century, what are some of the primary issues confronting rural America as far as extractive industries, communities, and their associated social conditions are concerned? We are experiencing heated controversies over proposals to drill for oil in remote and pristine areas, to explore and develop coal-bed methane, and to extract other valued raw materials. We have started the new century the same way we ended the last one—trying to come to grips with the conflicts and problems associated with this other rural landscape. In the three sections that follow, we begin by examining some of the characteristics that are common to this extractive rural landscape; next, we examine the diversity of extractive sectors and responses to depletion; and finally, we present some conclusions and recommendations.

Universal Features of Extraction

Five features commonly accompany extraction. First, modern extractive activities are embedded in national and global systems. The nature of the embeddedness of extractive activities differs from other types of activities. Second, the people, communities, and regions where extraction takes place are characterized by exploitation. Third, extractive activities are accompanied by a set of historical phases that include founding, normal operation, and depletion. Fourth, the individuals, communities, and regions directly affected by resource extraction often undergo rapid and extreme fluctuations in their economic conditions and social well-being due to the volatile nature of the economy of extractive enterprises. And fifth, in spite of the other four conditions, the residents of extractive communities and regions develop emotional and cultural attachments to the locale and experience a sense of cohesiveness—the community becomes "home."

Embeddedness

The history of extraction and exploitation can only be understood in the context of its extensive embeddedness in a national or global system. Extraction involves linkages to national and world markets. Extractive enterprises are owned by entities whose management, manufacture, and markets are far removed from the location of the raw materials. This is especially evident in the history of the western United States. While some prospecting and exploration was done by people seeking personal fortune, development of the resources required large amounts of capital not readily available in the West—capital from the East and later the Pacific Coast was necessary. Robbins points out that even at present "it is big money–outside capital that is the most prominent feature in the remaking of that rural New West" (1994, 191). The railroads, oil companies, mining enterprises, and timber operations are all funded by outside capital, which exercises local control.

Extractive enterprises are also distant from the bureaucratic centers that exercise regulatory control. The federal government has a long history of involvement in extractive industries west of the Mississippi. This began with ownership, management, and in many cases, disposal of large tracts of "public domain" lands (see Robbins 1994). Government not only influenced the nature of extractive activities through land grants and sales, but continues to do so today through leasing and land use policies. This situation is further complicated by the fact that an array of federal bureaucracies with diverse goals and missions continue to administer federal lands, among them the Forest Service, the Bureau of Land Management, the Bureau of Reclamation, the Fish and Wildlife Service, the Bureau of Indian Affairs, and the National Park Service. The federal government is involved in policies dealing with safety, air and water quality, water supply, wilderness, and energy. State governments have their own controlling agencies and departments as well.

One example of the ways in which government can dramatically change the region and communities involved in extraction can be seen in the consequences of federal silver policies during the 1890s. As the federal government withdrew its price supports and purchasing policies related to silver, mines throughout much of the West closed, mining operations went bankrupt, and once growing and vibrant communities suddenly became places of severe poverty, suffering, and unemployment. Large numbers of victims lived on the streets of Denver—hungry, destitute, and despairing due to the sudden changes brought about by the stroke of a pen in Washington, D.C.

Terms like "colony," "empire," and "dependency" are often used to describe the relationship between local extractive communities and national and international entities because economic and political embeddedness undermine local control. The theoretical argument is supported empirically (see Humphrey et al. 1993): extractive communities, because they are often dependent on a single raw material owned by interests distant from the location of the resource, have little control over their own destinies and remain relatively poor and powerless. At the same time, other regions become enriched, expanding their power and influence.

Exploitation

Extraction leads to exploitation. The basic theory of exploitation originated with Marx's (1964, 1973) analysis of conditions under capitalism. Exploitation occurs when workers use tools to transform raw materials into commodities that can be sold for substantially more than the combined cost of the tools, labor, and raw materials used in their creation. The workers are paid only enough to ensure basic survival and are treated as commodities themselves, with the owners of the tools pocketing the majority of the profits.

The exploitative nature of extractive industries is based on the way in which the embeddedness discussed above is structured. Raw materials, the tools to extract them, and the tools to process them into commodities are owned by entities located at a geographical and cultural distance from where the raw material is extracted. For example, the ownership of many of the coal-fields of Utah and western Colorado continually shifts from one distant place to another due to acquisitions and mergers. The owners often have little commitment to the area where the raw materials are located, and the profits flow to these shifting, remote centers. The corporate entities answer to stockholders and interests that typically have little to do with the locale where extraction occurs.

Workers, however, usually live near the raw materials. While their wages and benefits far exceed anything envisioned by Marx, they remain meager when compared to those of the managers, owners, and stockholders. The exploitation includes not only workers but communities and regions as well, as profits are expatriated, leaving them with low incomes, high unemployment, and polluted environments.

Historical Phases

Raw materials are either nonrenewable or renewable only in the long term. Oil, coalfields, minerals, and metal deposits become depleted or are replaced by more profitable sources in other locations, often severely altering and scarring the environment. This raises the issue of "life after extraction" for the workers and their families, communities, and regions that have specialized in the rural landscape of extraction. Many communities often overspecialize—relying on only one resource—so that the slightest fluctuation in its supply or value becomes amplified throughout the community, as so many of its institutions depend on this one resource. Freudenburg (1992) describes these as "addictive economies." At times, the downturn experienced by extractive communities may be so severe that they do not survive. Occasionally, all that remains are the physical scars on the landscape, and these produce scars on the social landscape as well. Other extractive communities simply refuse to disappear, even after their raw materials have all been extracted or they have lost their markets. The survival of extractive communities—themselves the product of the characteristics of extractive industries—make sustainability a central concern. Sustainability refers to the community's capacity to continue in the long term—do physical and social communities survive beyond the life of their extractive raw materials? Sustainability, consequently, is not only an issue of preservation of the raw materials, but of the community, region, and the physical environment where the raw materials are located.

Extraction is a process, and its social organization follows a specific developmental sequence consisting of three phases. The first is the foundational phase, during which the resource is prepared for extraction. In some cases, this phase may involve the construction of a refining or processing facility—for example, coal may be developed along with an adjacent coal-fired power plant. Communities entering the foundational phase of resource extraction attract large numbers of construction workers, who typically will only remain for the duration of this phase and then move on. Schools, stores, and other services are needed to accommodate the influx of workers to the site, and as a result a secondary construction industry emerges. This is especially the case for many remote western locales where distances between communities are vast. Early researchers assumed that the construction workers, and those who would follow them, were very different from local residents, and they characterized the construction phase as highly disruptive to the social fabric of the community and region. In-migration of workers was presumed to be the primary cause of social disruptions in extraction communities; however, more recent work suggests that most of the disruption occurs among the long-term residents themselves before new residents move in. The long-term residents take sides and reorient themselves to the new reality shaping their community (see Brown et al. 1989). Though the foundational phase does place heavy demands on small-town infrastructure, which must be expanded in a very short period of time, the magnitude of the problem is often matched by local efforts and preconstruction community aid from the government or the corporations undertaking the development.

Once the foundation is completed, the project enters an operational phase, in which miners, oil riggers, lumber jacks, and other extractive workers come to be central figures in the region. New technology has reduced the degree to which most extractive enterprises are dependent on such labor, but skilled workers are still needed. These workers often have their own unique lifestyles and worldviews, which include beliefs and styles for dealing with danger, economic ups and downs, and gender roles. These become part of the organic nature of the evolving community. During this period, the embeddedness and exploitative nature of extraction affects the communities through the influence of remote power centers, leading to struggles by the residents to preserve local control and promote community.

At some point in the operation, the raw materials are either depleted or they no longer occur in a quantity and quality that can support the extractive effort. At this point, the community and region face the effects of shutdown and closure—a downturn phase. When the industry leaves, some communities simply close; however, these are the exceptions. Most others endure an out-migration of younger workers, while the older ones remain and either retire, live on unemployment, or rely on the informal economy. The community itself continues, though its composition has changed. When closures occur, they often leave problems at the extraction site— decaying facilities, polluted water and soil, and waste left over from the extraction that is often simply dumped nearby are some of the environmental problems that these communities face. Often, clean-up or removal of these remnants is an expensive proposition for the federal or local government, and the communities must wait in a toxic limbo for a solution. Thus, even when the extractive era of a community comes to a close, the community may still find itself at the mercy of outside entities. Lack of local control remains part of the organic nature of these communities. Today, many such communities search for ways to establish local control through coalitions with outside entities and the courts. Many of these efforts have met with considerable success.

Rapid and Extreme Fluctuation

Extractive communities are characterized by economic and population booms and busts. Because they occupy the bottom of the economic food chain, fluctuations in the economy are amplified for extractive industries. As a result, extractive activities are sensitive to fluctuations in raw material prices. In addition, economic booms are often accompanied by population booms. The boom phase has been studied extensively by rural sociologists, well summarized by Hunter et al. (2002). Early research claimed that the boom phase was highly disruptive to the social fabric of the communities and the region in question. Subsequent research, however, has "generally revealed that rapid growth is not associated uniformly with extreme disruption, disorganization, and social malaise" (Hunter et al. 2002, 73). Some aspects of the community improve, others are unaffected, and still others decline. It has also been noted that the communities adapt and reestablish themselves following the boom. Due to inherent fluctuations, the boom condition is often not a one-time event, but something that occurs several times during the operational phase. Communities and their residents develop mechanisms to cope with and find ways to anticipate the boom period.

Periods of economic busts are accompanied by declines in the local population and rising unemployment and poverty. The bust phase in extractive communities has not been as widely studied as the boom phase. Population loss usually involves the young. Many people, however, remain due to an attachment to the physical landscape or social linkages, and they find ways to survive through these economic fluctuations. Repeated bust events lead to the adoption of a lifestyle centered around the recognition that busts will occur and that they are survivable. Pick-up trucks, double-wide mobile homes, and do-it-yourself mentalities become part of a valued way of life (see Harvey 1993). Periods of unemployment or reduced employment are opportunities to find temporary employment, send the spouse to work, hunt, fish, hang out, or drink more than usual.

Attachment to Place

Despite the volatility of extractive communities, residents demonstrate a clear pattern of attachment to these places. Even company towns can, and do, become home. When workers view the area as home they develop a localized sense of community. In many mining towns, even if they were company towns, workers built their own churches, lodges, and civic centers for use alongside the company store, company taverns, and company houses of ill repute. They established baseball teams and boxing clubs to compete with other towns. The houses they lived in were often personalized and improved. When, in the 1970s, many company towns were put up for sale, miners bought the homes they had been living in. In Castle Gate, Utah, when the company town was to be destroyed to make room for expanded coal mining, the residents negotiated with the company to buy their company-owned homes and move them to a nearby town. There, they set up a subdivision called Castle Gate as well, and attempted to reproduce their former community. Even so-called ghost towns often hold reunion days when former residents return and recall their home.

In summary, extractive enterprises lead to some clear commonalities. While they continue to pose the threat of serious environmental damage, exploitation, and rapid change, they also foster efforts by residents to preserve their distinctive home.

Diversity in Exploitation and Depletion

In addition to common features, significant local diversity has developed out of several of the features of extraction. First, the technologies and structure that characterize extractive activities have important consequences for the environment, community, and region. The nature of coal mining has led to a way of life and regional structure that is unique to the effort, and very different from those practices attached to oil extraction or timber. Second, the region in which the extraction takes place is significant (Nord and Luloff 1993). Appalachia, for example, has regional features of extraction that differ from those of the Intermountain West. Third, though much extraction is characterized by long distance ownership, certain types of extractive activities—such as timber and coal mining—also feature small-scale, locally owned operations.

Another major form of diversity occurs at the end of the operational phase of extraction: depletion. Depletion hangs as a dark specter over almost all extractive endeavors. A common response has been to change technologies or develop new ones to allow for the extraction of less accessible or less pure raw materials. Hence oil fields are mined using technologies that free more of the resource. In areas where pine forests are no longer available for logging, the timber industry has turned to the harvest of less valuable aspen to use for chipping and gluing. Additionally, efforts are made to develop faster growing varieties of pine, and alternative forest industries are created.

Even if technologies fail to avoid depletion, regions and communities often make adjustments to survive, using depletion and past history as a local resource for adaptation. We suggest four successful types of such adjustments. First, places such as Park City, Utah and Aspen, Colorado, went from centers of mineral extraction—with the lifestyle that accompanied such places—to resort towns and upscale developments. They used the mine remnants and architectural themes of the mining days as a way of creating a commodified atmosphere to attract a specific high-end clientele. Dwellings in these locales are often second or third homes, typically beyond the means of locals—one recent development near Park City indicated they would not market their land and dwellings in Utah because Utah natives simply would not be able to afford them. They were for the "Eastern market." Local residents typically remain outside the loop of control—just as in the days of productive extraction—because these developments are often funded and operated in the same way that the mines and mills that preceded them were: capital and management is located far from the communities.

A second adaptation strategy occurs when residents of an area attempt to exert local control through zoning and land use planning in the face of outside efforts to create high-end developments. They resist becoming a Park City or Aspen, while fighting to survive. These communities present themselves as old-time mining towns by preserving some aspects of the traditional lifestyle, but they also market skiing, mountain biking, and carefully restricted second-home developments. They fight external control and seek to preserve the community for the "locals." Crested Butte, Colorado, is famous for its successful fights to avoid large-scale ski resorts and future mineral extraction that would dramatically alter the town's current environment.

A third approach is to strive to preserve the local flavor in a genuine way, while also promoting tourism and recreation without new developments of any sort. Leadville, Colorado, is one of Colorado's most famous mining towns. When the silver mines went bankrupt in the 1890s, they were replaced by alternative mining operations, especially those mining molybdenum. Now even this mineral is no longer mined, yet locals have started to promote tourist activities that capture the danger and adventure of the old silver days as a mechanism to keep the town and its mining flavor. Alternative funding sources preserve the old lifestyle. Leadville is the home of one-hundred-mile ultra marathons, the world's most demanding one-hundred-mile mountain bike race, and "boom days" that feature teams of people and burros racing forty to one hundred miles and contests requiring the skills used by the old silver miners.

Finally, there are the communities and areas that persist without attracting any such schemes. Clear Creek, Utah, was once a mining town of over one thousand people. When the mines closed, some people stayed. Their attachment to their community is now such that some currently commute over one hundred miles each way to work. Others who did move away have kept their homes for retirement—when they retire, they return "home." The community bills itself as "America's Front Porch." Resistance to outside developments or outsiders in this rural landscape is palpable. The land is theirs, no matter who owns it, and they defend it with a mine-town vigor, including violence if necessary.

Conclusion

The landscapes of agriculture and extraction have long been treated as two distinct and diverse sectors of rural America. In the past century, both have presented dynamic traits that promise to continue well into the new century with some interesting changes, ironic twists, and convergences.

Agriculture, once the American cultural symbol of individualism, self-reliance, and independence, has largely been removed from its historical base, the family farm (see Chapter 13 in this volume). In the past century, agriculture has become more intensive, less organic, larger in size, increasingly industrialized, and corporate in nature. It has developed in ways that are remote from the rural owner-operator, who continues to characterize our idealistic image of rurality. Ironically, at the turn of the twenty-first century, ownership and management of agricultural enterprises have more in common with the characteristics typically associated with extractive industries—loss of local control, outside ownership, and large-scale intensive exploitation of the land. The factory-like processing of hogs and chickens now resembles the processing of coal and oil more than the classical image of agriculture. In an unsettling fulfillment of Goldschmidt's (1947) thesis, many farming communities now are experiencing increased external control and exploitation in ways that also characterize extractive communities.

Extractive communities have experienced continued importance and dramatic shifts. Extraction of energy-related raw materials retains an important role in rural America. Metals such as iron, copper, and others show no signs of declining in significance. The timber industry has adopted new technologies and produced new types of wood products. Extraction now requires fewer workers with greater technical skills.

Extractive industries continue to exercise considerable control over the communities where they are located. It is unlikely that the locus of ownership and the intensive involvement of federal and state governments will change; however, there are clear indications that a movement is underway in extractive communities and regions to gain greater local control. These communities have discovered how to use the courts to fight state and federal governmental regulations and multinational extractive corporations. For example, Gunnison County, Colorado, has filed suit to dispute a multinational corporation's proposal to develop a major molybdenum deposit, and to keep water resources in the county instead of allowing them to go to the major metropolitan areas of the state. These same communities have formed coalitions with other groups that, in the past, have been their bitter enemies. The Gunnison County court cases have included not only coalitions of local groups such as local ranchers and environmental groups, the local Chamber of Commerce, and local governments, but also entities like the Sierra Club, the U.S. Forest Service, and the National Park Service.

Another dimension of increased local control is in the application of federal regulations and land use planning, elements that locals have long seen as the enemy. These are now being used as tools to support local interests and power. Extraction-dependent communities develop land use plans and zoning laws to stop undesired actions by the federal government and corporations. Increasingly, they use agency planning and hearing requirements to assure that their voice is heard. Federal requirements for consideration of cultural and social impacts are sources of local control and power. The irony is that the very tools—such as the formal legal structure—that once led to and supported external control are now being tapped by extractive communities to enhance local control. Perhaps years of interacting with these entities have provided local entities with a "formal education," equipping them to use the formal structures of the political system to argue their case and gain a measure of local power.

At the beginning of a new century and millennium, a hundred or so years of analyzing rural life has given us a unique opportunity to assess where we have been and where we are going. It allows us to adjust our biases and the myths they may be based on. Rural landscapes—both agricultural and extractive—are now shaped by a complex and dialectical set of forces. The numbers of people involved in agriculture and extraction continue to decline. Both industrial sectors face challenges of economic dependency and external control; however, extractive communities also shows clear signs of a growing ability to exercise local control and fight to maintain their unique flavor. As we study and become involved in these dynamic dialectics, it is important to recall Markoff's (1996) comment that we often take a snapshot, when what is needed is a movie with multiple cameras and sensors. Our myths of rural life continue to be still-life snapshots of the autonomous rural family farm, even as these become further effaced by modern corporate structure. All the while, continued exposure to the corporate, legal, and other formal structures of society has provided the extractive community a unique command of the tools of modern society to be wielded in defense of local control. Only the advantage of a time-exposed photographic technique has allowed us to see the ironies of our rural myths at the turn of the century as they concern these two rural landscapes.

25

Fur, Fins, and Feathers

Whose Home Is It Anyway?

Steven E. Daniels and Joan M. Brehm

The broad area of human/wildlife interaction[1] raises a number of intriguing sociological and policy questions. This chapter focuses on how major social forces of the recent decades have created largely positive views of wildlife, living in peaceful coexistence with humans, and how various events are simultaneously challenging those attitudes. We then assess the major piece of federal wildlife policy—the Endangered Species Act—and surmise that it may gradually lose its base of public support if mechanisms to address the localized impacts of species conservation cannot be developed. Finally, these ideas are blended into a set of future challenges for U.S. society, as we attempt to craft a more sophisticated set of principles defining our relationships with wildlife.

Blending Demographics, Environmental Sociology, and Cognitive Hierarchy Theories

Many demographers have recognized that the classic rural/urban dichotomy is an increasingly bad metaphor for American society. The dominant condition in which most people lived in the late twentieth century was in fact suburban, which is distinctly different from conventional notions of either urban or rural. The great population movement from rural to urban areas that began in the late nineteenth century was

---

1. "Wildlife" is being used as an all-encompassing term that includes terrestrial animals, fish, and birds. While our colleagues whose interests are primarily in fish and birds may feel that this terminology is somehow dismissive toward their interest, we ask their forbearance for the sake of brevity and style.

supplanted by the 1950s with a movement out of cities and into suburban areas, producing what demographers have termed the "doughnut effect."

Research into the emergence of the environmental movement clearly shows it to be firmly rooted in metropolitan areas, and therefore it is more likely to reflect urban or suburban values. It is not surprising that our society's dominant views about wildlife have been affected by these demographic shifts. Theories of cognitive hierarchy contend that attitudes about specific issues (e.g., abortion or gun control) tend to be derived from, and compatible with, more fundamental beliefs and value systems (e.g., religion). This integration of concepts would lead us to suspect that there are attitudes toward wildlife that are characteristic of distinct rural, urban, and suburban experiences, and that these are derived from larger attitudes about the appropriate relationship between humans and nature. These attitudes are socially constructed on the basis of direct experience, and they are both reinforced and mediated by a person's immediate social milieu and broader cultural context. The potential differentiation in viewpoint as a result of differing life experiences lies at the intellectual foundation of much of the discussion that follows.

This approach very much echoes Fred Buttel's presidential address to the Rural Sociological Society in 1991. His contention was that even though environmentalism is a socially constructed and "especially indeterminate, malleable" ideology (Buttel 1992, 14), it was at the core of a set of new social movements—largely attracting urban professionals—that were filling a void left by the decline of more traditional social-democratic institutions. In short, he represented environmentalism as a specific manifestation of a broader ideational conflict between social-democratic and neoconservative worldviews, which was likely to have significant impacts on rural areas and peoples. In much the same way, attitudes toward wildlife can be understood as a specific manifestation of environmental attitudes and beliefs about the appropriate relationship between nature and humanity.

At the risk of presenting a perspective that is overly glib and simplistic, it is necessary to draw some broad distinctions between a rural, an urban, and a suburban view of wildlife. A rural view sees wildlife as "varmints, vermin, and venison." Thus undomesticated animals are varmints when they eat your crops, vermin when they carry disease or infest your home, and venison when you can eat them. In a rural setting, wildlife is an everyday part of existence, and is more likely to be assigned a utilitarian value than a symbolic one. This is in stark contrast to a classic urban experience in which daily interaction with wildlife has been largely eliminated. Apart from incidental interaction (e.g., pigeons in a park), wildlife becomes an "out of sight, out of mind" aspect of the urban experience: it simply becomes unimportant and distant. The suburban perspective is more complicated than merely a blending of the rural and urban viewpoints. If migration out of urban areas is motivated at least in part by a desire to be closer to nature, having wildlife around is tangible proof of having achieved that good life. The desire to move to suburbia is a desire to inhabit an idyllic, park-like setting that is clean, safe, and natural. As such, wildlife is viewed as a co-inhabitant of this Eden that serves to validate its authenticity. Wildlife is an attraction and a selling point. People are pleased to see wildlife, and engage in various activities to attract it (landscaping, bird feeders, and so forth). The more wildlife there is—both in terms of numbers and diversity—the better.

In short, we assert that the dominant view of wildlife in the late twentieth century was this suburban perspective. It assigns a highly positive affect to wildlife and involves a moderate amount of daily interaction, but it is also highly mediated. A ready supply of cultural evidence can be called upon to buttress this assertion: the rate of participation in hunting has steadily fallen, while fishing participation has remained strong (perhaps due to the simultaneous emergence of a strong catch-and-release ethic). Bird-watching and feeding is practiced by millions and has spawned its own industry and periodicals. An initiative on the ballot in Oregon in 1992 restricted bear hunting; roughly 80 percent of the voters in the three-county metropolitan area of Portland supported it, and roughly 80 percent of a very rural county in eastern Oregon opposed it. The emergence of animated Disney features ranging from "Bambi" to "The Lion King," the millions of children who receive "Ranger Rick" (the youth publication of the National Wildlife Federation), and the proliferation of nature-related programming on cable television are indicative of the highly positive yet mediated nature of the human/wildlife relationship.

Cracks in the Suburban View of Wildlife

As we enter the twenty-first century, the idealized suburban view of wildlife has begun to fray notably around the edges. There are some increasingly clear signals that our unabashedly positive view of wildlife is being confounded by generalizable evidence and anecdotal events. Perhaps the most important of these is when the reality of living in close proximity to wildlife begins to depart from the ideal experience. There may be no more striking example that the emergence of Lyme disease in recent decades.

Lyme disease (*Lyme borreliosis*) is widespread in the eastern United States. It is caused by a spirochete that is vectored by a tick, commonly named the deer tick. The tick is hosted primarily by white-tailed deer, and to a lesser extent by birds and small mammals. The disease owes its name to a localized outbreak near Lyme, Connecticut, in the late 1970s. As Figure 25.1 indicates, the number of reported Lyme disease cases has risen significantly over the past two decades. Some portion of the increase is no doubt due to increased awareness among both health professionals and the lay public, but it is also due to increased deer and deer tick populations. There is evidence that deforestation and the virtual elimination of white-tailed deer in the nineteenth century destroyed the population densities of deer ticks. Only after 1926 were habitat conditions suitable for the proliferation of deer—and therefore deer ticks—reestablished (Randolph 2001). It is the combination of high human and deer populations coexisting in the same areas that has created this public health problem. Suburban residents who might have initially been attracted by deer now must regard them as a potential hazard, and may make landscaping choices to discourage deer. They may also have heightened concern about allowing their children to play in wooded or brushy areas for fear of deer ticks. That fear is not unfounded, as in some areas the proportion of ticks infected with the spirochete approaches 25 percent (Randolph 2001).

Nor is Lyme disease the only animal-vectored disease of note. Rocky Mountain spotted fever is another tick-vectored disease; rabies has long been a concern; the West Nile virus, which is vectored by mosquitoes and birds, has spread rapidly in recent years, with fatalities in new states every summer; chronic wasting disease (a variant of mad cow disease) and foot and mouth disease are concerns in cervid populations; and hantavirus (vectored by

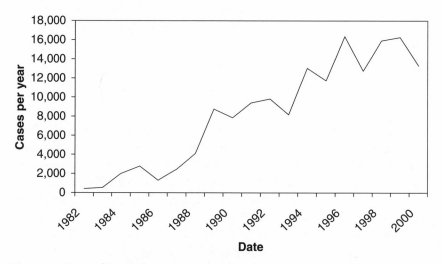

Fig. 25.1 Cases of Lyme disease, 1982–2000

rodents) has proven fatal to humans in the Southwest. Collectively these diseases indicate that close proximity to wildlife, particularly at the high population densities that allow disease to be readily transmitted, is not without risks.

Disease is not the only concern that arises from wildlife. The high populations of white-tailed deer in the mid-Atlantic states have produced a large number of vehicle accidents in recent years and may be altering the species composition of forests to an alarming extent. High elk populations are a notable problem in parts of Colorado; even though 92 percent of survey respondents from Evergreen, Colorado, were interested in seeing elk near their homes, a substantial portion of the community either have reservations about the problems elk cause (33 percent) or even want the elk population to decrease (29 percent) (Chase and Decker 1998). Canada geese have invaded suburbs in Minnesota, Virginia, and Maryland, tormenting golfers as they protect their territory, nests, or goslings. Black bears in Colorado, Idaho, and New Mexico have broken into homes. In one widely publicized case, a jogger in California was killed by a lactating cougar.[2] Coyotes have attacked both people and domesticated animals across the country. As alligator populations have rebounded in the southeast, human contact has increased as well. In many regions of the country, private animal control firms have their hands full removing a broad assortment of raccoons, bats, snakes, and alligators that set up housekeeping in habitats we prefer to keep to ourselves—such as our chimneys, basements, and swimming pools.

This description of the emergence of Lyme disease and of other cases of wildlife/human conflict is not intended to present a frightful or sinister picture. Rather, it serves to illustrate that nature neither conforms to our will nor adheres to culturally constructed and mediated scripts. The notion of "Bambi as bummer" is not one that many of us prefer to embrace, nor is it one that our nursery rhymes and picture books have prepared us for. It is, however, one that we must come to terms with. It is also not appropriate to attribute the cause of these conflicts to nature. In many cases, residential sprawl has exacerbated these situations as people have encroached upon important habitats. In recent years, for example, grizzly bear/human conflict has increased in the foothills of the Mission Mountain range in western Montana. This has occurred on slopes where the bears forage in the spring as they emerge from their dens. The number of interactions is not increasing because the bears are venturing farther down the mountains; rather, it is because the homes extend farther up.

---

2. This case received notoriety because donations provided for the orphaned cougar kittens initially surpassed those given to the children of the jogger.

The Endangered Species Act

The second major source of social turmoil and mobilization over wildlife relates to the Endangered Species Act of 1973 (ESA). While most wildlife policy is controlled by states, the ESA is federal law, and is by far the most significant legal structure for managing sensitive species in the country. It is so dominant in both our thinking and management that its terminology— threatened and endangered species—has become the shorthand phrase for any kind of species of special concern even in those cases where the ESA in not specifically at issue. The ESA is intended to preserve species at risk of extinction. It initially attempted to prevent extinctions by focusing on the "taking" (i.e., hunting, killing, trapping, harassing) of threatened or endangered species and their commercial utilization—the sale and transport of endangered organisms or their parts. An amendment enacted in 1978 provided an important conceptual modification: in addition to conserving individual members of wildlife populations, their critical habitat must also be identified, protected, and potentially expanded. This amendment codified the decades-earlier recognition among wildlife scientists that we are fundamentally unable to manage wildlife populations if we cannot simultaneously manage critical features of their habitat. Without a doubt, the ESA's habitat requirements have proven to be much more controversial than the prohibition against taking individual organisms. In recent years, many of the high-profile conflicts over fish and wildlife issues have involved the ESA.

There are a number of thorough explanations of the ESA (e.g., Czech and Krausman 2001; Stanford Environmental Law Society 2001); here, we simply wish to mention several aspects of it that are relevant to this discussion. The ESA was originally enacted in 1973. Amendments passed in 1978 added critical habitat conservation and an exemption process (the so-called God Squad), while a 1982 amendment added the incidental take permit/ habitat conservation plan process. The potential impact on people is not a factor in a decision to list a species as threatened or endangered, but it can be motivation for an exemption. The Secretary of the Interior has the authority to constrain private land management practices, and other public agencies must consult with the U.S. Fish and Wildlife Service (USFWS) or the National Marine Fisheries Service (NMFS) prior to undertaking any land management activities to ensure that they will not jeopardize the viability of listed species.

The ESA has been referred to as the "bulldog" of federal environmental law; once it gets its teeth locked (i.e., a species is listed), it is almost impossible to call it off. This is because the ESA is a regulatory process of last resort. It is invoked when the best scientific information on species viability indicates there is a probability of extinction, and because of its last-resort character, it tends to be unyielding. While other environmental laws may include language such as "to the degree practicable," or "may," the ESA and the case law pursuant to it is replete with "shall." It leaves managers with far less discretion than do other pieces of federal environmental law, which are often more procedural than substantive.

The ESA has been the legal mechanism behind some huge swings in the economic fortunes of industries in particular regions, as well as significant disruptions for particular locations and landowners. Federal timber harvest in the Pacific Northwest dropped by 80 percent between 1989 and 1994 (Raettig and Christensen 1999), driven by the need to respond to a series of legal decisions related to the listing of the northern spotted owl, as well as concern for the viability of a host of other terrestrial and aquatic species that are dependent on mature forests.

While relatively few people will debate the value of the ESA's intent, their sentiments become far more divided over the restrictions on land use that are often necessary to achieve recovery. In the early 1990s, *Reader's Digest* published an article on the ESA entitled "When a Law Goes Haywire" (Fitzgerald 1993). This article was not based on systematic research and used a series of carefully selected cases of seeming regulatory excess to make its point. *Readers' Digest* is not a premier publisher of cutting-edge conservation biology or environmental law, but it is a good barometer of the mental state of the American body politic—it is in too many waiting rooms to be ignored. Its editors carefully choose articles that mirror the attitudes of its huge readership, and it in turn has a notable influence on the attitudes of its readership. For many, this may be the only article on the ESA they ever read.

There is a substantial concern among rural residents and people employed in various productive and extractive industries (e.g., farming, ranching, logging, mining) that the ESA is used by interest groups to drive them out of business. While this may sound unduly escalatory and extremist, Fred Buttel would contend that many of the activities that these industries engage in are in fact inconsistent with a symbolic view of rural areas that would be associated with environmentalism: "What, then, will be the future of rural America if it becomes defined in strong symbolic terms as forest sites or prospective forest acreage needed to curb the greenhouse effect, as pristine ecosystems to ensure clean water for urban use, and as more desirable to the degree that fewer people are there to pollute, disrupt natural habitats, and the like?" (Buttel 1992, 23).

As an unsurprising extension of that logic, it bothers some people—particularly rural people who hold a utilitarian perspective on wildlife—that the ESA puts the welfare of animals, oftentimes obscure ones, above the needs of people. And indeed the law does just that, as the U.S. Supreme Court concluded in the well-known Tellico Dam controversy of the 1970s: "It may seem curious to some that the survival of a relatively small number of three-inch fish among the countless millions of species extant would require the permanent halting of a virtually completed dam for which Congress has expended more than $100 million.... We conclude, however, that the explicit provision of the Endangered Species Act requires precisely that result. Congress intended endangered species to be afforded the highest of priorities.... The plain intent of Congress in enacting this statute was to halt and reverse the trend toward species extinction, whatever the cost" (*Tennessee Valley Authority v. Hill*, 437 US 153, 174, 184 [1978]).

Future Challenges

Values toward wildlife are a human construct shaped through complex social processes. In that sense, we are fully in agreement with the social constructivist tradition (Berger and Luckmann 1966). Meaning is continually being negotiated as events occur, as groups vie for political and economic advantage, and as science provides new information. "Overpopulation," "pest," and "problem" are not objective terms but value-laden interpretations subject to continual revision. As the idealized suburban view of wildlife continues to be challenged, it may well be that a new perspective will supplant it. Sociologists can contribute to a renegotiation of the meaning of wildlife through research and participation in the process.

Wildlife populations tend to increase unchecked in residential and protected areas because of abundant food and the absence of predation or hunting. Managing wildlife in such areas can be profoundly vexing. Public controversy and political maneuvering seem to eliminate every option for reducing populations. Attitudes about management techniques have been extensively studied, with a fairly consistent set of results. Lethal means are universally controversial, with opposition centering on the safety, ethics, and risks to nontarget species. Nonlethal means (e.g., aversive conditioning, trapping and relocation, contraceptives) are generally preferable, although typically they are far more expensive and arguably less effective. Support for lethal means tends to increase if the respondent has had a negative interaction with the species or lives in close proximity to it.[3]

3. A special issue of the *Wildlife Society Bulletin* (1997, 25 [2]) was devoted to the challenge of deer overabundance in the twenty-first century. It offers an excellent overview of the biological, attitudinal, and public participation issues related to deer management.

A robust postsuburban wildlife perspective will likely incorporate a number of attributes. First, this perspective must incorporate an understanding of wildlife population dynamics and the carrying capacity of habitats. Second, it must recognize the extent to which wildlife enhances our daily lives. Third, it must include a tolerance toward a diversity of ways to value wildlife, moving beyond an oversimplified view of "Bambi lovers" and "magnum maulers." Fourth, it must acknowledge that science and technology cannot make all negative aspects of cohabitation disappear, and it must generate realistic expectations regarding the ability to respond to the hazards presented by close proximity to wildlife. Finally, this perspective must accept that many wildlife conflicts arise because we have moved into their habitat, not vice versa.

For reasons that the authors do not entirely comprehend, the ESA has become the cornerstone of wildlife conservation in the United States, even though there is no evidence that the Congressional intent was for it to become so. While it is clear that the ESA is intended to be the nation's ultimate conservation safety net, there is no indication that the Congressional intent was to leave conservation issues unaddressed until the ESA becomes applicable. But a strange convergence of agency budget constraints, interest group litigation, and political conflict avoidance has concentrated a disproportionate share of our conservation efforts on the listed species. As a result, other species receive relatively little attention, even though our options for their conservation are far more plentiful than they will be if their populations dwindle.

In effect, we collectively watch the viability of a species decline until it crosses the threshold for being listed as threatened, and then the floodgates of regulatory control are opened. Both the legal obligation and administrative means to preempt the need for an ESA listing are relatively weak. Recent innovations in candidate conservation assurance agreements are a possible exception, but they are both too rare and too new to evaluate. The rationale for a species protection policy that swings so dramatically from passivity to zealotry lacks a basis in conservation biology and is likely to increase the social disruptions associated with conservation.

We should assume that we can improve the law through amendments, particularly as our experience reveals its shortcomings. As a number of authors have noted (e.g., Rohlf 1991), the ESA still has some shortcomings in its integration of conservation biology and law. Certainly the original 1973 Act was deeply flawed because it recognized no linkage between conserving the individual members of a species and the adequacy of habitat upon which they depend. The ESA has evolved significantly as the result of amendments: the critical habitat provisions were added in 1978, and the capacity for habitat conservation planning was added in 1982. Both

amendments added to our ability to target the law's power on those ecological factors most critical to species conservation, while minimizing
impacts elsewhere.

In its present state, the ESA clearly falls short as an equitable mechanism
for conservation planning. Examples such as the recent economic plight of
farmers in the Klamath Basin, Oregon, due to irrigation water being with-
held for the endangered sucker fish, and the reams of case law revolving
around the issue of inequitable "takings" due to critical habitat preservation, provide ample evidence of a select few bearing the costs and burdens
of conservation intended to benefit the larger society (Jehl 2001; Coggins,
Wilkinson, and Leshy 1993). From a sociological perspective, a potential
link appears to be emerging between the ESA and the concept of environmental justice. This possible link admittedly goes beyond the historical
conceptualization of environmental justice as pertaining more narrowly to
the correlation of race, class, facility siting decisions, and toxic exposure
(Anderton et al. 1994; Oakes, Anderton, and Anderson 1996; Pollock and
Vittes 1995; Szasz and Meuser 2000); however, the authors argue it is one
worthy of further consideration and examination.

It is easy to see the forces that create the ESA's mal-distribution of the
costs and benefits of species preservation. The benefits of conservation are
very diffuse: they accrue to all of humanity in this and future generations.
The costs of conservation are inevitably more concentrated, and in cases
where critical habitat designations greatly constrain economic activity, the
costs can be both significant and highly concentrated. If, for example, you
were expecting to fund your retirement with the proceeds from a stand of
long leaf pine from the Coastal Plain of Georgia, only to have harvesting
prohibited for the sake of a red-cockaded woodpecker colony, the financial
cost and personal impact could be devastating. Quite understandably, your
enthusiasm for this specific woodpecker and for the ESA more generally
might pale considerably.

According to Pellow (2000), environmental inequalities can be viewed
as relationships constituted through a process of continuous change involving negotiation and often conflict among multiple stakeholders. The listing
of endangered species and related habitat is an ongoing process that is sure
to expand, and has the potential for incalculable impacts to a mélange of
stakeholders across time and place. There is clearly a need to develop a policy that retains its protection of endangered species, yet does so in a manner that distributes the burden and cost of that protection in a more
equitable manner.

It is difficult to imagine how a conservation movement that disregards
the social impacts of its agenda can maintain its political base. Like

environmentalism more broadly, wildlife conservation has few direct bene-
ficiaries: "unlike most old or even new social movements, such as the
women's movement, the civil rights movement, ethnic separatist movements and labor movements, [environmentalism] has no natural constituency or bearers. Opposition to environmentalism, on grounds of
threatened material interests or aversion to state intervention, is actually
easier to explain than environmental advocacy itself. For many environmental issues, those who act to protect the environment can expect to
receive no personal material benefits" (Buttel 1992, 14).

There is also reason to surmise that endangered species controversies
may become more rancorous rather than less so. Much of the political controversy around endangered species protection has been in the West, with
its high percentage of federal land. But the majority of endangered species
occur in the East, which is predominantly in private ownership. To date we
have lacked the political will to demand the same high level of land use
modification on private land that we have been willing to accept on public
land. But to ensure conservation of predominantly eastern species, significant regulation of private land will be required, most likely through use
restrictions. If regulations fail to address the distributive impacts of the
ESA, the result may be a political conflict that surpasses the spotted owl
episode in the Pacific Northwest in rancor and duration. In addition, if
landowners do not support land use restrictions, the level of policing necessary to coerce their compliance could be extremely costly. One option is
to build a collaborative decision-making framework that would involve
landowners and other affected stakeholders in a process of mutual planning and decision-making before a species or its habitat actually became
threatened. A proactive strategy that is more inclusive of the various stakeholders might prove to be more effective than the current reactive and coer-
cive regulatory approach.

In short, addressing the equity dimensions of wildlife conservation will
be critical to building and maintaining meaningful support, particularly
among the landowners whose compliance is essential. Such a process of
civic discourse would allow us to socially construct a new set of values and
relationships between people and wildlife, simultaneously permitting us to
transcend twentieth century suburban attitudes toward wildlife as well as
the perpetrator/victim mindset with regard to the ESA that seems so common in rural areas.

PART V

Changing National and International Policies:
New Uncertainties and New Challenges

26

What Role Can Community Play in Local Economic Development?

Gary Paul Green

Why do rural localities promote growth, and how effective have these efforts been? Historically, economic development has been the responsibility of federal and state governments. In the past, the federal government has influenced local economies through investment in the physical infrastructure, such as the interstate highway system and the projects of the Tennessee Valley Authority. During the 1970s and 1980s, however, local governments began to actively promote growth. The economic recession of the early 1980s pushed many local governments, especially in the Midwest and Northeast, to become more entrepreneurial and to seek new sources of revenue because of lost jobs and income during this period (Eisinger 1988). The rise of local economic development policies also represents a growing recognition by policy-makers that it is essential to engage local residents in decisions affecting their community and that local involvement improves the effectiveness of these policies (Green and Haines 2002).

Changes in the location of economic development activities have given rise to the field of community economic development. This domain not only involves actions to promote local economic development, but also is based on a process of public participation in decision-making (Boothroyd and Davis 1993). Most research on local economic development has emphasized the important role of market forces on the decisions of local officials, yet social forces are critically important in the effectiveness of their growth efforts. Social factors can influence local economic development in several ways, such as providing access to resources and information, overcoming collective action problems of individual firms, and improving the functioning of local markets (e.g., financial, labor, and land).

Following a review of the social science research on local efforts to promote growth, I examine how community-based approaches to economic development help address the weaknesses of markets and government programs in addressing local needs. I also consider how community-based development approaches the trade-off between efficiency and equity.

Research on Local Economic Development

Research on local economic development has taken a significant turn in recent years. Much of the previous empirical work on this topic focused on two broad issues—first, the adoption of economic development policies and business incentives by local governments, and second, the determinants of local and regional growth. However, there has been a growing interest in how social factors influence local economic development. In the following section, I discuss the major theoretical debates and empirical findings pertaining to these issues and questions.

What Factors Influence Growth Promotion?

Localities have adopted a wide range of policies and incentives to promote growth. Research on this topic has primarily focused on population and employment growth. There is considerable debate in the literature regarding how much flexibility local economic development officials have in their policy decisions. Can they pursue progressive policies in the context of globalization and increasing capital mobility? Or do external pressures dictate that local governments must provide more and larger incentives to business rather than increase expenditures on things like local social services?

Two broad theories address these questions. A structuralist approach posits that local development is shaped primarily by economic forces beyond the control of local policy-makers. According to this perspective, local officials must compete with other localities to attract new firms and residents by keeping taxes low and maintaining service levels. Peterson (1981) argues that the federal system of governance pushes localities to focus on development rather than redistributive policies that shift resources from high-income to low-income residents, as redistributive policies may have a negative effect on efforts to attract businesses and new residents. Thus, the market and structural forces determine the policies and strategies of local governments. A key assumption of structuralist theory is that development policies will benefit the entire community, not just corporations or developers (see Bartik 1991). In other words, localities must focus on efficiency, which only indirectly affects equity considerations.

An alternative view, often referred to as regime theory, suggests that local policy-makers do have some autonomy, and, moreover, that their decisions seldom benefit the entire community but instead tend to favor one set of interests over another (Logan and Molotch 1987; Stone 1989). This theory suggests that although localities face several structural constraints (e.g., fiscal and economic stress), there is wide variation in what localities do to promote growth and development. In most localities, however, realtors and developers have a disproportionate influence on local policy. It is possible for other groups such as homeowners and neighborhood organizations to shape policy as well, but it is unlikely that local officials can ignore efficiency concerns.

The empirical evidence on these issues shows that most localities are actively promoting growth. Those most likely to promote growth are large municipalities experiencing fiscal stress, high rates of unemployment, and competition from other municipalities in their region for jobs (Wolman and Spitzley 1996). Although there is considerable attention in the literature on localities that have a stated policy of "no-growth," they are clearly exceptions. The evidence also suggests that business recruitment activities and many other forms of growth promotion have little impact on opportunities for the poor and unemployed (Logan and Molotch 1987). There is only anecdotal evidence on the long-term impact of local progressive policies on the poor and unemployed.

Do Incentives Work?

The media have focused on several instances where large corporations received large subsidies to locate in a particular state or municipality. Two of the most publicized cases have been South Carolina's deal to attract a BMW plant—subsidized at $71,000 per job—and Alabama's successful effort to attract a Mercedes plant—with subsidies totaling $169,000 per job. These cases have raised questions about how necessary these subsidies are. Research on this topic has principally been concerned with the relative role of public policies (e.g., tax levels, business incentives, or government spending) and area characteristics (e.g., labor market conditions, education, access to markets, demographic characteristics, and industrial composition) on economic growth or activity (usually measured by employment, earnings, and per capita income). A related empirical issue is whether the subsidies actually influence corporate decision-making.

There continues to be debate over the effects of public policy, especially incentives to attract businesses, on economic growth. Timothy Bartik (1991)—one of the strongest advocates of business incentives—finds that municipalities that reduce taxes by 10 percent increase their business activity by 2.5 percent. He also argues that in the long run these policies will lower unemployment rates, especially for minorities.

Other research has suggested that the adoption of economic development incentives has little or no effect on employment growth, when controlling for other market or locality factors (Feiock 1991; Green et al. 1996). Blair and Premus (1987) have argued that the decision by a firm to locate in a community may be a two-step process. First, firms decide on a region in which to locate, based on factors such as labor costs, taxes, and proximity to markets. After they decide on the region, firms then narrow their choices using a different set of criteria, such as education, infrastructure, and quality of life.

Overall, most studies suggest that market factors are more important than government actions in influencing the performance of local economies. Innovative policies may have more of an effect, but may lose their "punch" over time (Goetz 1994). The effects of policies may vary across the business sector or economic sector (manufacturing versus service firms) as well. The benefit/cost ratio also may decrease over time as the cost of the subsidies increases faster than the benefits. Finally, there continue to be concerns that recruiting new industries may have a minimal impact on the poor and unemployed workers in the community.

Do Social Factors Matter?

One way that researchers have addressed the role of social factors has been to examine how citizen involvement influences local economic development strategies. Sharp (1991), for example, found that citizen involvement—measured by the existence of an appointed advisory committee, public hearings, citizen surveys, and elected neighborhood commissions—increased local officials' efforts to promote growth. Citizen and neighborhood groups, however, tend to be more interested in policies that lead to more equal distribution of development outcomes, but there is little evidence that citizen involvement influences policy outcomes.

Fleischmann and Green (1991) take a different approach, by examining how the organization of economic development within the local bureaucracy affects growth efforts. They found that centralizing these activities in a single agency or in the mayor's office tends to increase the growth effort, but does not have much influence on job growth.

A third approach is to examine how the level of social capital influences local and regional growth. Putnam's (1993b) work on the role that civic traditions play in economic development in Italy has been especially influential in this area. In his pivotal book, Putnam found that differences in the economic performance of northern and southern Italy can be attributed to the different histories of civic organizations and public participation. Northern Italy has a history of active civic organizations, while southern Italy does not. Active civic organizations provide the social basis for the networks necessary for the flexible production of northern Italy.

Woolcock's (1998) comprehensive review of the literature on social capital and economic development focuses on two broad types of social capital: microlinkages that are based on intra- and intercommunity networks, and macrolinkages that are based on institutional access to public officials and the level of organizational integrity in the government. Contacts within the community and with outside actors are important because these ties provide information and resources facilitating economic development. Macrofactors are important because they bolster the level of public trust and organizational capacity of the government to stimulate economic development.

Overall, there is a growing body of research that shows that social factors do influence local growth efforts, and they do have an effect on job, income, and population growth (Reese and Rosenfeld 2002). This literature is limited in its usefulness, however, because of the variety of ways in which social influences are measured and the lack of data on social influences in most communities. Research on public participation in local economic development suggests that the existence of strong community and neighborhood organizations has a much larger impact than simply increasing citizen input.

Implications for Rural America

Increased competition among communities for economic development has been referred to as the new "arms race." Communities have increased the level of incentives and/or subsidies they offer to businesses in response to the growing competition between communities for economic development. Nonmetropolitan communities tend to lag behind in their growth efforts, either because they possess fewer resources, they lack specific expertise, or they exhibit lower levels of political entrepreneurship (Green and Fleischmann 1991). Their efforts also may be less effective due to structural forces, such as distance to markets and a shortage of human and physical capital. In addition, nonmetropolitan communities may lack the social ties and networks that facilitate local economic development. Many small communities may have a sufficient supply of strong ties, but lack weak

ties—relationships based on relatively low levels of social contact that
facilitate contact with a broad range of individuals—across various groups
(Granovetter 1973) (see also Chapter 16 in this volume). Local officials in
small towns also may have fewer ties and contacts with state officials and
utility companies than do officials in large cities.

Although research on the effects of social capital on economic development continues to be debated, there is a growing consensus that social factors do matter. For example, research suggests that the size of networks
and the level of interaction have an independent effect on job growth.
Rural communities face some additional challenges. The literature on
social capital emphasizes the importance of extracommunity linkages and
weak ties within the community as a means of promoting information and
accessing resources. Yet, the social structure of many rural communities is
characterized by strong social ties within the community and a lack of connections to external organizations and resources.

In the next section, I briefly consider some alternative directions for
rural communities. Most of these alternatives have been adapted in urban
settings, and could be modified to work in rural areas as well.

Alternative Policy Directions

Rural communities face a variety of obstacles in promoting growth and
development. Those that are heavily dependent on resource-extractive
industries—such as agriculture, forestry, fishing, and mining—are vulnerable to fluctuating prices, which produces periods of boom and bust (see
Chapter 25 in this volume). During the 1960s and 1970s, a large number
of rural communities successfully attracted new manufacturing firms, but
they tended to provide low-wage, low-skilled work, because higher-wage
firms are more dependent on urban amenities (Summers et al. 1976). Rural
communities also tend to be dependent on a small number of employers,
resulting in a lower level of diversification. Typically, rural communities
also are disadvantaged because of their small size and distance from urban
centers. Because of the low population densities in many rural communities, the cost of providing education, health care, transportation systems,
and other services is higher than in more densely populated communities.
The low level of service provision may discourage businesses and people
from moving to these areas.

Many rural communities also suffer because their employers tend to
take the "low road" competitive strategy of cutting production costs, primarily by keeping labor costs as low as possible. This usually means rural

workers likely receive low wages, few benefits, and few opportunities for upward mobility. Levels of productivity gains tend to be low, and employees receive little training. Conversely, employers that take a "high road" competitive strategy offer high wages, benefits, and opportunities for mobility, high levels of technological adoption, investments in worker training, and continuous improvements in productivity.

Why do most rural employers continue down the "low road?" What obstacles do they face if they attempt to pursue a "high road" strategy? Although credit and infrastructure may be factors, the central issue tends to be a collective action problem—it is in the interests of all the employers to increase productivity, but it is illogical for individual employers to bear the costs. Fearing that they will lose their investment in job training if workers leave for other jobs, rural employers tend to limit training to specific skills that are not easily transferred to other work sites—or they do no training at all (McGranahan 1998). As a result, employers are reluctant to invest in new technologies that will require more skilled workers, and are thus unable to improve wages, benefits, or opportunities for advancement in the firm.

One strategy is to use social mechanisms to address these problems. In particular, it may be possible to promote cooperative strategies among employers to overcome some of the limits on the capabilities of individual employers. Similarly, social mechanisms can address some of the obstacles in rural capital markets. Not all communities are likely to be successful in taking this "high road" approach. Although there is little research on which to base predictions, there are reasons to believe that communities with producer services or a larger manufacturing base may be more likely to make this transition.

In the following section, I discuss two broad approaches—workforce development strategies and community development credit institutions—that integrate "community" into local economic development strategies. These strategies attempt to link equity and efficiency concerns directly at the local level.

Workforce Development

Localities face several obstacles in developing their workforce. If the community attracts new employers demanding skills that are not available locally, employers will face a skills shortage or be forced to hire workers outside the region. If employers provide training to workers for jobs that are not available locally, workers may move to where the jobs are or they may obtain higher paying jobs outside the area. Information is frequently a problem in labor markets as well. Employers lack sufficient information about the productivity of applicants, and job searchers lack adequate information about the availability and demands of jobs in the area. Community-based organizations (CBOs) can address these problems by helping to improve the flow of information between employers, workers, and training institutions, and reducing some of the costs and risks of training workers by spreading the costs across several organizations. For example, it may be too costly for independent firms to provide training in basic skills, but it may be possible for groups of employers to offer it by sharing the costs of the program.

A growing number of communities have established networks of organizations to improve job training and information in the labor market. Harrison and Weiss (1998) identify three distinct ways of organizing workforce development networks. First are hub-spoke employment networks, which have a CBO at the center of a network that links employers, trainers, and public officials. Second, peer-to-peer networks consist of several CBOs at the core of the network. Third, intermediary training networks have a regional training institution at the center of the network. These networks provide stronger coordination between trainers and employers, improve the information flow in the local labor market, and involve a wider variety of activities than just training—including job search assistance, mentoring, and retention. Below, I discuss two community-based strategies for building human capital.

The first of these is to build career ladders that link opportunities for mobility across the labor market rather than within firms. Career ladders tend to replace the internal labor markets that generally exist in large, unionized firms. Career ladders link employers that hire unskilled or semi-skilled workers with employers hiring primarily skilled workers. The system is based on the premise that unskilled workers will remain with their employers if they are participating in the career ladder program because it provides opportunities for upward mobility—employers in the high-skill sector hire directly from employers in the low-skill sector. Employers in the low-skill sector benefit because they can reduce their turnover rate, which also means they are more willing to invest in job training. Similarly, employers demanding more skilled workers will benefit from a steady stream of trained workers who have demonstrated their work ethic. This approach may be most effective for communities on the rural/urban fringe, where linkages with higher paying employers would be more accessible.

A second community-based strategy for addressing the problems of labor markets in rural areas is to apply a sectoral or cluster approach—working with a group of employers in a single industry to develop training programs that promote skills that are common across the industry. By developing training programs across industry lines, employers can reduce some of their risk in investing in training, and workers benefit by obtaining additional skills and possibly greater upward mobility. This strategy also reduces some of the cost of providing training to individual employers as well. Large firms that have some capacity for on-site formal training may be willing to develop partnerships with public/private agencies to provide this training to small firms that have less capacity.

A variation on the sectoral or cluster approach is for large firms to assist their suppliers with job training programs. The large firms have an incentive to maintain a stable supply of inputs and to improve the productivity of these firms. Many of these suppliers are likely to be located in lower-cost areas, such as in rural communities.

Community Development Banks

There continues to be some debate over whether financial markets in rural areas are seriously affecting economic development (Economic Research Service 1997). Some policy-makers and community activists argue that rural communities, especially those with large minority populations and/or high rates of poverty, do not have enough access to credit. Discriminatory lending practices by financial institutions also may contribute to the credit gap. Others argue that the credit gap is due to the risk of investing in these areas. Rural communities also may have been disadvantaged by the mergers and acquisitions that occurred in the banking industry over the past few decades. Finally, some analysts suggest that the problems are not due to the financial system, discrimination, or information, but the creditworthiness of applicants.

In response to these problems, a variety of community development credit institutions have been created. Examples of these types of institutions are community development credit unions, revolving loan funds, community development loan funds, and microenterprise loan funds. These institutions may allocate credit differently than private lenders for several reasons. First, because these institutions are more actively tied to community-based organizations they may be able to provide more complete information on the risk of loan applicants, which may increase the level of lending in these areas. Second, although these institutions are interested in profit making, they also have a set of social objectives they are trying to achieve. So, most of these institutions only make loans to applicants in a geographic area or to individuals who may have less access to credit, such as low-income women in the case of some microenterprise loans or small businesses in the case of revolving loan funds. Although market and regulatory approaches to addressing the credit needs of poor and minority communities may have some impact on the flow of capital, community-based credit institutions offer the most promise because they consider "community" at the heart of the investment decision.

Although some of these models of community development banking are promising, they are having only a limited impact in most poor and minority communities today. Many of these credit institutions have received most of their support from foundations and the federal government, but few have become self-sustaining. To promote these community-based lending institutions, some outside support for seed capital will be necessary.

Conclusion

Purely market or bureaucratic strategies to promote rural economic development fail to consider the important role of social forces. Several emerging models for addressing problems in labor and capital markets are built around community-based organizations and rely heavily on social ties and networks for them to work properly. These models, however, are still dependent on resources from external organizations, such as federal and state governments. At the same time, they rely heavily on "local knowledge" and networks to make them work. Community-based approaches to economic development are especially important for rural areas.

This brief review of research on local economic development reveals that all communities are not participating in the "race to the bottom" by offering higher levels of subsidies to attract low-paying jobs. A growing number of communities are developing models that address the weaknesses of pure market or bureaucratic solutions to local development. A key element of these strategies is the allocation of decisions to the local level, where relationships between development, the environment, and social needs are most transparent. These models also are based on a logic that broadens the profit-maximization goals of the market and embeds economic decisions in social and environmental objectives as well. Many federal and state policies tend to minimize the importance of community for the functioning of market or bureaucratic solutions. Emerging models will require recognition and support from federal and state policies for the importance of community economic development.

27

Devolution

Who Is Responsible for Rural America?

Jeffrey S. Sharp and Domenico M. Parisi

Devolution became a public policy buzzword during the last decades of the twentieth century to describe ongoing shifts in the balance of responsibilities among national, state, and local levels of government. Devolution refers to a process whereby the federal government transfers some degree of responsibility for the control, development, and support of public policy to states and local jurisdictions (Kodras 1997; Watson and Gold 1997). This shift is viewed as a means to accomplish several objectives, such as increasing the efficiency and flexibility of public policy to better serve local populations. An underlying justification for such a shift is that states and local communities are better able to manage and cope with local problems and needs (Harrigan 1998; Stein 1999). Devolution, however, has not gone unchallenged. Critics point out that the limited fiscal, technical, and civic capacity of many communities can pose a serious problem for meeting local needs (Warner 1998; Peterson 1995), exacerbating spatial inequality between communities with and without adequate local resources. Though the full implications of the current pattern of devolution are not yet fully known, it is clear this trend will continue to have a substantial impact on rural America and its social, economic, and environmental well-being.

In this chapter we briefly describe the historical division of responsibilities among federal, state, and local governments in the United States. We then consider some of the challenges wrought by devolution and the commensurate increased responsibility of localities for meeting the economic, social, and environmental needs of local populations. Devolution in three policy arenas—welfare, rural economic development, and natural resource management—provides illustrative examples of some of these challenges. We conclude by identifying research, policy, and community development issues that may require attention to enable communities to more effectively manage the responsibilities and expectations of the twenty-first century.

A Brief History of Federalism and Devolution

In the United States, the governance system is dynamic, based on the allocation of responsibilities across national (or federal), state, and local governments. While the U.S. Constitution outlines the structure and responsibilities of the national government, the Tenth Amendment affirms that powers not directly allocated to the national government reside with the states (referred to as the Reserved Powers clause). Throughout the nation's history, the actual distribution of responsibility across the various levels of government in question has not been static, but has evolved to meet the challenges of the day and the public's needs. One of the nation's earliest presidential transitions (Jefferson succeeding Adams) reflected, in part, a philosophical concern that the national government had exceeded the responsibilities that had been granted to it by the Constitution. Tension and change in the balance of responsibilities has continued, with three distinctive eras of intergovernmental responsibilities identifiable in the twentieth century (Conlan 1998). During the first period, national and state government had limited responsibility for social and economic well-being in comparison to local government. In the second period, the national government's responsibility for social and economic welfare increased dramatically. The third period, which continues today, is marked by a return or devolution of responsibility back to state and local government.

Limited Government

Prior to the 1930s, the role of the federal government was limited to a few activities such as the operation of a postal system and the maintenance of an army and navy. The role of state and local governments was also relatively limited, focusing primarily on development of public infrastructure and provision of basic services. In this period, each level of government had its own authority over well-specified areas of responsibility. Each level in this system operated relatively independently of any other level.

Expanded Federal Control

In the 1930s and 1940s, as a result of the Great Depression, the New Deal, and World War II, roles began to change as the national government took on greater responsibility for the economic and social welfare of the nation (Conlan 1998). Social security, unemployment assistance, and greater involvement in economic planning and regulation were roles taken on by the national government as part of the New Deal, and there was also an expansion of federal fiscal and bureaucratic capacity. During the 1950s and 1960s, the role of the national government further increased with the development of additional social programs such as those directed at eradicating poverty, and an increased role in setting national standards such as those related to health and environmental quality. During this period, national, state, and local government increasingly worked together on domestic issues. In this newly "cooperative system," however, the national government was the dominant partner among the three levels.

The expanded role of the national government resulted in a variety of positive outcomes, including reductions in poverty and improved civil rights protections. But there were problems associated with the national government's increased programmatic responsibilities, including growing conflicts between national and state or local governments, perceptions by some of an intrusive national government, and ideological concerns about an activist national government and a preference for greater local authority (Conlan 1998). As a result of these administrative and philosophical concerns, a tendency toward devolution of governmental functions and responsibilities began to emerge.

Devolution

During the Nixon administration, there was a selective devolution of administrative responsibilities of formerly national programs as well as a redirection of resources to states, in the form of block grants, which allowed greater discretion by lower levels of government in meeting local needs and securing the resources to do so (Conlan 1998; Liner 1989). During the Reagan administration, there was a further shift in responsibilities among national, state, and local governments. Most significant were budget and tax changes at the national level that resulted in substantial reductions in resources available for state and local governments to provide for the programs and needs previously devolved (Peterson 1995). In the 1990s, the balance of responsibilities was further influenced by moves to consolidate federal programs and to provide state and local governments with greater discretion in how limited resources were expended to meet local needs (Peterson 1995; Conlan 1998; Kodras 1997). This new orientation required collaborative efforts both within and across local communities that share similar interests, along with an increased emphasis on participatory democracy at the local level. The trend of devolution has continued into the twenty-first century, with state and local governments still grappling with the opportunities and challenges of developing, administering, and funding local policies to meet social, economic, and environmental goals (see Chapter 19 in this volume).

The paradigmatic shift toward more local responsibility has created a variety of policy and development challenges for many localities. This is especially true for those places situated in rural settings. In the next section we identify three topics of rural social research that illuminate some of the challenges and/or opportunities created by the trend toward increased local responsibility. These three research topics include spatial inequality, resource mobilization and community civic capacity, and collaborative decision-making. Three policy areas, welfare reform, community economic development, and natural resource management, are the contexts that highlight this particular body of research.

Challenges of and Possibilities for Increased Local Responsibility

Spatial Inequality

Generally, U.S. welfare policies were conceived in order to alleviate poverty. Over the years, these policies became expensive and had limited success in removing low-income people from the public assistance rolls. Some began to believe that public assistance was a more significant cause of persistent poverty than lack of opportunity. As a result, in 1996 President Clinton signed into law the Personal Responsibility and Work Reconciliation Act. This act ended welfare's sixty-year status as a nationally funded entitlement, and more importantly, it altered the roles and responsibilities of the state and local community. The primary role of developing the welfare policy agenda now resides with state government, while the local community is urged to assume certain administrative responsibilities and to compensate, to some degree, for cuts in federal funding. Specifically, under the new welfare system, local communities are asked to take more local responsibility for job promotion and workforce development (Parisi et al. 2002).

However, it may be difficult for some rural places to fully meet the expectations of the new welfare system (see Chapters 8 and 27 in this volume). One basic problem is limited job opportunities in more remote, underdeveloped rural regions, particularly jobs that provide sufficient income to lift a family out of poverty (Zimmerman and Garkovich 1998;

Garkovich 1998). This can be a particularly serious concern due to the limits the new welfare policy imposes on the assistance an individual can receive, with no more than twenty-four months of continuous aid and a total of five years assistance in a lifetime. Even where jobs may exist within a rural region, public services enabling potential workers to become employed may be lacking. For example, the absence of regional public transportation services can limit the accessibility of some employment opportunities, and the limited availability of child care services can further diminish the ability of some would-be workers to meet the employers' expectations. In more urban locations, where the population and tax base is sufficient to support these types of services, barriers such as transportation and child care may not be as great.

An underlying problem for some rural places to support the local population in need of assistance is limited local resources and a local economy characterized by decline and stagnation (as is the case in some regions dependent on natural resource extraction and some types of heavy manufacturing). While economic decline and stagnation is not solely a "rural" phenomenon, nor is it a characteristic of all rural places, the uneven distribution of opportunities and resources across the United States can create limits for how well some rural regions can manage their own destinies (Lyson and Falk 1993). A general disparity between metropolitan and non-metropolitan communities in terms of their capacity to raise revenue has been reported (Warner 1998), with lower per capita income in more remote nonmetropolitan areas and a steady decline of per capita incomes over time relative to metropolitan areas. As a result, some rural local governments have fewer resources to fund effective poverty alleviation programs such as workforce development. Moreover, they are less able to provide other services necessary to facilitate the movement of the rural poor into the workforce compared with better off rural and urban locales.

Resource Mobilization and Community Civic Capacity

While spatial inequality can limit the effectiveness of welfare reform efforts in some rural areas, research identifying possible methods for overcoming some of the constraints associated with rurality and remoteness exists. Much of this research emerged from policy shifts arising during the mid-1980s related to economic development. During the 1970s and the early 1980s, federal resources in the form of community development block grants and other national programs provided local governments with substantial resources that they could use for economic development purposes (Clarke and Gaile 1999). Federal resources for these purposes began to diminish during the mid- and late 1980s, resulting in local communities either relying more on state level resources or attempting to identify new local resources, or both. At about the same time, a shift occurred in the type of state and local economic development strategies pursued by some communities. Enthusiasm began to wane for industrial recruitment strategies that pitted localities against each other in a zero-sum competition to attract large employers. The realization that the benefits of industrial recruitment did not necessarily justify the costs of recruitment gave rise to more entrepreneurial strategies that focused on market development and firm creation to fill local market needs (Eisinger 1999, 1988).

During the 1990s, a team of rural researchers disseminated a series of reports identifying self-development as an alternative to industrial recruitment in rural places (Flora et al. 1991; Flora et al. 1993; Green et al. 1990). From this analysis the concept of social infrastructure was identified as a key local resource that could enhance capacity for development despite limited fiscal or technical capacity. Social infrastructure has several dimensions, but a key element is the extent to which resources are mobilized within the community (see Chapter 25 in this volume). This research identified a relationship between successful self-development and a willingness by local citizens, organizations, and institutions to invest in the community. Another important element of social infrastructure is whether community network structures tend to operate internally among organizations and individuals (Sharp 2001), or externally between the community and higher levels of government or other similarly situated communities (Flora et al. 1997). Community networks are viewed as an important mechanism through which financial resources and technical information can be pooled and accessed for the collective good.

Research related to social infrastructure is consistent with other work in the social sciences identifying social capital (Putnam 2000, 1993a, 1993b) or civic engagement (Tolbert, Lyson, and Irwin 1998; Kemmis 1990) as valuable resources for local social well-being. Putnam concludes that "voluntary cooperation is easier in a community that has inherited a substantial stock of social capital, in the form of norms of reciprocity and networks of civic engagement" (1993b, 167). Thus for rural places shouldering greater responsibility for local economic development and other functions related to local social welfare, the research suggests that there is utility in developing a community's social structure to increase the social, financial, and technical resources available to manage additional responsibilities. Community development practice has long recognized the importance of social development to the community (Christenson and Robinson 1989; Wilkinson 1991), and rural places may need to give increased attention to this type of development in an era of devolution.

Collaborative Decision-Making

Popular perceptions of rurality might suggest that building social capital and social infrastructure in rural places may be an easy task due to notions of small town cohesiveness and traditions of town meetings where collective problems are easily resolved. Unfortunately, the community and institutional arrangements enabling effective administration of new responsibilities at the local level can be quite challenging to develop. Rural America is increasingly diverse (Castle 1995), and it is important that institutions and organizations recognize this diversity when policies are formulated and implemented. For example, the ongoing decline in the number of farmers in combination with the influx of nonfarm residents into the countryside can lead to disagreements over how the rural environment should be managed, in areas such as water quality or livestock manure management. Guidance for working through complex issues with diverse local stakeholders is emerging in the field of natural resource management, where collaborative decision-making processes have been developed for solving local environmental problems.

Initially, environmental policies were designed in response to environmental threats created by economic development during the postwar period. During the 1970s, economic development was viewed as a serious threat to the quality of the environment, and at the beginning of the 1980s, public concern for the environment had grown (Dunlap 1991). The initial response to many environmental concerns originated with the national government, which set standards and regulations for what was and was not permissible (John 1994). During the 1980s, there was a decline in environmental protection and enforcement resources at the national level, and some devolution of responsibility to states and localities occurred. At the same time it was found that national, one-size-fits-all types of policies did not always work, especially in situations where many actors affected environmental quality, as opposed to one or a few large industrial polluters (John 1994). Environmental policies were criticized for failing to reflect the opportunities and constraints inherent in a particular community (Bridger and Luloff 1999).

One response to changes in natural resource management policy has been the emergence of "civic environmentalism," in which localities focus on local environmental problems and develop local solutions to these problems that attempt to overcome fragmentation of interests among stakeholders (John 1994). Research in this area is ongoing, but several factors have been identified as enhancing local decision-making processes and their effectiveness in overcoming differences and finding solutions. Findings about what is important to the success of local environmental policy include the existence of open and inclusive decision-making processes, the development of a common language among participants in the process, and the participation of extra-local organizations and stakeholders who can provide technical and/or financial support to local efforts (Swanson 2001; Kellert et al. 2000; Parisi et al. 2002; Weber 2000; John 1994).

The devolution of some environmental policy-making and the move to more collaborative processes may require rethinking institutional roles. For example, because greater responsibility for finding solutions to problems in some policy domains is increasingly centered in the locality, the state and national role may need to shift from rule-making, monitoring, and enforcement to include the provision of technical information necessary for informed decision-making at the local level (see Chapter 19 in this volume). This means that in policy arenas such as the environment and rural development, federal agencies such as the Environmental Protection Agency (EPA) and the U.S. Department of Agriculture (USDA) need to continue and enhance their capacity to generate knowledge relevant to problems and opportunities of diverse rural places. Of course, to be effective generators and clearinghouses of information, the national and state institutions involved in the gathering and delivery of technical information will have to become familiar with the diversity of interests and concerns that exist within and between rural communities so that the information they provide is credible and relevant. In the case of rural economic development and welfare reform issues, this may create an opportunity as well as a need for an institution such as the USDA to further expand its purview beyond agriculture to a more general goal of improving rural life quality.

Defining the basic roles and relationships among various local and extra-local actors is just a single facet of one of the biggest challenges of successful collaborative decision-making: the ability to sustain the process over an extended period of time. For example, legislative efforts in Iowa to reduce agricultural chemical use took many years of sustained educational and legislative work to come to fruition (John 1994). Ostrom (1990), in another context, identifies successful collective resource management arrangements in several case studies that evolved over generations. These examples reveal a need for local civic culture or social infrastructure that enables sustained and inclusive public deliberation (Swanson 2001; Wilkinson 1991). In communities where civic culture or a community-oriented field of interaction does not exist, it first may be necessary to facilitate increased awareness among rural residents and various local and extra-local institutions of their shared interests before contentious resource management issues can be successfully tackled.

Meeting the Challenge of Devolution

The current era of federal devolution seeks to improve citizen and community well-being by shifting some policy responsibility to the state and local levels, but as the research outlined in the previous section illustrates, it is important to recognize the possible limitations of certain divisions of responsibilities among national, state, and local governments. While the current policy bias may be to shift greater responsibility to lower levels of government, in practice it may be that different levels of government are best suited for different roles associated with the delivery, administration, and funding of particular policies (Liner 1989; Hovey 1989). For example, although local government may be quite responsive in program delivery or administration, there may be a need for funding responsibilities at higher levels of government to smooth out spatial inequality. An important issue that policy-makers as well as rural social scientists must continue to explore is the optimal division of responsibilities to meet the needs of rural people and communities. An important development question for local leaders, researchers, and development practitioners is how to build the capacity to fulfill their policy responsibilities, and also capitalize on local strengths and abilities to successfully shoulder some policy responsibilities.

There may be some barriers, though, for rural social scientists to generate research-based knowledge that can contribute to crafting policy or assist in its implementation. Research questions relevant to policy audiences and local decision-makers may not align with topics currently in vogue within the academic or disciplinary outlets that set the standards for evaluating scholarly contributions and merit. This may require some adjustment of norms by professional societies in order to enhance the extent to which scholars are rewarded for conducting policy-relevant research. There may also be a need for researchers to explore alternative approaches to research to better understand the diversity within and between rural places as well as the context within which problems must be solved. A substantial amount of rural research relies on county-level secondary data, which easily masks the diversity of actual jurisdictions within a county (such as villages, small cities, and townships) as well as the differences among these jurisdictions. More refined spatial analysis utilizing geographic information systems (GIS), case study research (e.g., Duncan 1999), and comparative community studies (e.g., Ryan, Terry, and Woebke 1995; Sharp 2001) may be examples of research methodologies that can illuminate important contextual factors that influence local capacity and decision-making associated with new responsibilities. Research that is more closely linked to particular places as well as the aggregation of data at levels of analysis relevant to the particular problem (such as watershed management) through the use of GIS can lead to better information for policy decision-making (Parisi et al. 2002).

Devolution is ultimately a multifaceted issue that affects rural America in many different ways. For some communities, such as those blessed with abundant local resources and a history of local civic engagement, devolution may result in enhanced community and resident well-being. But in those communities with limited resources and limited local civic capacity, the shift of responsibilities to the local level may not achieve the intended goals. It is this latter scenario that necessitates ongoing interest in the subject of devolution by researchers, policy-makers, and citizens in a quest to find the optimal division of responsibilities among national, state, and local governments across a variety of policy arenas.

28

Welfare Reform in Rural Areas

A Voyage through Uncharted Waters

Julie N. Zimmerman and Thomas A. Hirschl

Just as the face and circumstances of poverty in rural areas differ from those in urban centers, rural families needing cash assistance face different constraints than urban families (Rural Policy Research Institute [RUPRI] 1999). However, the 1996 welfare reform legislation and regulations did not contain specific rural provisions (U.S. Department of Health and Human Services [USDHHS] 2002). Instead, the legislation gave greater flexibility to the states with the intention that they would be in the best position to design programs better tailored to "respond more effectively to the needs of families within their own unique environments" (USDHHS 1997, preamble).

Despite the unprecedented amount of welfare reform research that has emerged since this legislation was enacted, research focused on rural areas has been much more limited (Weber et al. 2002). Even less common are investigations that examine differences across the diversity of rural areas. We examine several studies, though limited in number and ranging broadly in their research focus, that did attempt to assess rural/urban outcomes. Overall, these studies indicate that while some trends may be similar, important rural/urban differences remain. Less clear are the implications of these differences.

Especially during times of economic growth, welfare recipients are often the object of negative political rhetoric, even though many Americans are at risk of needing to use welfare at some time during their life course (Rank and Hirschl 2002). Public opinion polls in the early and mid-1990s revealed a widespread perception that the welfare system was persistently failing, and a willingness to accept fundamental programmatic change.

Weaver puts it this way: "Welfare, in short, was perceived as being at odds with the widely shared American belief in individualism and the work ethic" (2000, 174). This was a particularly potent belief as the unprecedented economic boom of the 1990s took shape.

Policy shifts in cash assistance that first saw limited expression in the 1980s, such as expanding state-level decision-making and attaching work requirements, were subject to a different political environment a decade later. Among other factors, increasing use and flexibility of waivers to Aid to Families with Dependent Children (AFDC), Democratic political repositioning, and Republican gains in Congress opened new political space for the passage of the 1996 welfare reform (Weaver 2000). The nature of changes directed at recipients burgeoned out of two dominant explanations for poverty—lack of labor market participation and irresponsible personal behavior.

Comparative analyses have generally demonstrated that no other advanced country relies so heavily upon markets and spends so little upon income maintenance as the United States (Esping-Andersen 1990; Moller et al. 2001). Welfare reform represents yet another escalation of market reliance, demonstrating an unparalleled experiment in self-reliance to provide for the needy. With its emphasis on labor market attachment and lifetime limited access, the future human consequences of these policy changes are unclear. This is because so much depends upon the economic climate, the ability of labor markets to provide adequate employment, and the ability of the remaining programs to supplement low-wage jobs.

What Is Welfare Reform?

The 1996 Personal Responsibility and Work Opportunities Reconciliation Act (PRWORA) ended cash assistance "as we have known it." Among the changes that came with this legislation, AFDC, Job Opportunities and Basic Skills (JOBS) training programs, and Emergency Assistance (EA) were eliminated, and the Temporary Assistance to Needy Families (TANF) Block Grant was created. The legislation also introduced changes to other programs including food stamps and the Social Services Block Grant (SSBG), and introduced the Child Care Development Block Grant (CCDBG). The most sweeping changes, however, were associated with the new TANF cash assistance program.

Following a period of state experimentation through federally granted waivers to AFDC, the 1996 PRWORA legislation changed the cash assistance system from being an entitlement to one that is limited and contingent. Among the changes for recipients, TANF introduced time limits, required participation in "work or work related activities," and contained financial sanctions for noncompliance. New attention was also brought to unwed childbearing and family formation (Lichter and Jayakody 2002). As a result, welfare reform is characterized as having the twin strategies of "requiring work and responsibility and rewarding families" (USDHHS 2000a, 1).

Along with changes directed at recipients, the legislation also affected the organization of the cash assistance provision system, moving to a block grant program. This change increased decision-making and latitude for the states within federal requirements, fixed federal funding based on states' funding under AFDC, and froze funding differences across states. Together, these changes represented the confluence of two philosophies: devolution of federal governmental responsibilities to the states, and a philosophy of "work" in place of long-term dependency. In general, the goals of welfare reform are to increase states' flexibility in operating a program designed to do the following:

1. provide assistance to needy families so that children may be cared for in their own homes or in the homes of relatives;
2. end the dependence of needy parents on government benefits by promoting job preparation, work, and marriage;
3. prevent and reduce the incidence of out-of-wedlock pregnancies and establish annual numerical goals for preventing and reducing the incidence of these pregnancies;
4. encourage the formation and maintenance of two-parent families.

These goals shall not be interpreted to entitle any individual or family to assistance under any state program funded under AFDC.

With the new federal TANF block grants, states organized their own TANF programs, variously named and within federal parameters. Each state made a series of decisions regarding the exact nature of their programs. These decisions included aspects such as the possibility of time limits less than the federal sixty months; the form, timing, and severity of sanctions; the option to have a family cap or exempting a vehicle from the asset limitations; devolving decision-making to the county level; and establishing diversion programs or specialized assistance for victims of domestic violence, among many others (Zedlewski 1998; Gallagher et al. 1998; USDHHS 2000a). As a result, while most state programs are uniform within their states, across the states TANF programs can differ markedly from one another.

Funding and the role of governments also changed as a result of the new block grant approach to cash assistance. Under the block grants, states are required to meet certain standards in order to maintain their federal funding levels such as reaching caseload work participation rates and maintenance of effort (MOE) requirements. There are also high performance bonuses and illegitimacy bonuses. For states with lower than average funding levels or high population growth, separate supplemental funds were provided. States could also choose to have their own separate state-funded program, which would not be subject to the federal requirements.

Tribal governments have the option to administer separate programs or to be included in their state TANF program. There are twenty-two tribal TANF plans covering ninety-four tribes and Alaska Native villages; nineteen of these are administered by individual tribes, while three are administered by "multi-tribal consortia" (USDHHS 2000a). In contrast to the state plans, tribal TANF plans can include traditional and culturally relevant activities in their definitions of "work or work related activities."

Finally, as a federal policy approach to alleviating poverty, cash assistance does not stand alone. In addition to establishing TANF, the PRWORA legislation restricted access to food stamps for able-bodied single adults without children. It also brought increased attention to collecting child support, and increased funding for child care, both through the ability to transfer TANF funds for child care and an overall increase in funding. When eligible, families remain able to receive other forms of assistance such as food stamps, housing, and medical assistance, all of which remain federal categorical assistance programs.

Are There Rural/Urban Differences in Welfare Reform Outcomes?

While welfare recipients face many similar issues across rural and urban areas—meeting work requirements, gaining economic independence, and maintaining family and child well-being—rural areas experience economic, political, and service landscapes different from their urban counterparts (USDHHS 2002). These differences include fewer economic opportunities, lower earnings, and variation in occupational skill levels, as well as issues associated with less access to formal child care, lack of transportation options, limitations in housing, and the availability of health care (RUPRI 1999). Before the 1996 welfare reform, the face of cash assistance looked different in rural areas. The same may be the case after welfare reform.

Even before the 1996 legislation, cash assistance caseloads had begun to decline from their 1994 historic high. Many states had obtained an AFDC waiver, and the economy was expanding. Between 1994 and 2000, the number of families receiving cash assistance (either AFDC or TANF) declined by 56 percent, with 2,845,000 fewer families receiving cash assistance nationwide (USDHHS 2000b). Heralded by many as a harbinger of success, caseload decline was seen as evidence of declining dependency on cash assistance.

However, cash assistance caseload declines were not evenly shared across the nation. State declines ranged considerably, from a 16 percent decrease in Hawaii to a 91 percent decline in Wyoming (USDHHS 2000b). Regionally, the South shifted from having the highest number of recipients to being the region with the second lowest (Zimmerman 1999).

Just as caseload declines have not been shared evenly across states and regions, this is also the case across rural and urban areas, though the pattern varies. For example, researchers found that rural areas in Tennessee and Wisconsin experienced a higher rate of caseload decline than their urban counterparts (Fox et al. 1998; Cancian et al. 1999). On the other hand, results of studies in Texas, Kentucky, and Virginia report slower rates of caseload decline for rural areas (Swensen et al. 2002; Bosley and Mills 1999; Dyk and Zimmerman 2000). Even more variation emerged when rural areas were disaggregated (see RUPRI 1999).

While recipients leave cash assistance for myriad reasons, employment has become one of the overriding policy concerns. Some results suggest that rural recipients exhibit higher rates of employment while on welfare, but have lower rates of employment after leaving assistance. For example, Bosley and Mills (1999) found that the rural southwestern region of Virginia had lower rates of moving from welfare to employment. In Oregon, Acker et al. (2001) found lower rates of employment for TANF leavers in the predominantly rural central and eastern regions of the state. Among closed and denied cases in Oklahoma, Kickham et al. (2000) found that rural areas had a statistically significant lower proportion of full-time employment and a higher proportion of part-time employment.

There also appear to be differences for those remaining on assistance. Among those cases in Kentucky that either are or were work eligible (excluding child-only cases and those exempt from work requirement), Dyk and Zimmerman (2000) found a higher share of adult recipients in nonmetropolitan areas being employed and remaining on assistance. In an analysis of Iowa's AFDC waiver from 1993–1995, Jensen et al. (2000) found that a higher share of recipients in nonmetropolitan areas received wage income compared to metropolitan areas. In Tennessee, a larger proportion of rural recipient families were employed, with even larger rural/urban differences for two-adult cases (Fox et al. 1998). Even for those employed while receiving assistance, there is also evidence of lower incomes for rural recipients (Kickham et al. 2000; Fox et al. 1998; Schexnayder et al. 2001; Bosley and Mills 1999).

McKernan et al. (2001) cite a familiar list of barriers to employment for recipients living in rural communities, including a lack of affordable housing; limited availability of services such as mental health services, substance abuse treatment, and domestic violence services; and more limited availability of emergency food and shelter. The types of employment found by recipients were predominantly minimum wage with little advancement opportunities, and many were part-time or intermittent.

Employment is not the only reason recipients leave welfare. The new TANF program also brought the possibility of financial sanctions for noncompliance in the form of benefit reduction or termination for recipients. Westra and Routley (2000) found that Arizona's rural counties had a lower share of cases closed due to sanctions. By contrast, Swensen et al. (2002) found evidence in Texas that while overall sanctions were applied fairly evenly across rural and urban areas in the state, since access to job services varied for rural and urban areas, sanctions associated with access to these services were not evenly distributed. Swensen et al. (2002) also found that while recipients with less education were more likely to be sanctioned in both rural and urban areas of the state, this effect was greater in rural areas.

While outcomes such as caseload declines and employment have produced some variation in results, other issues provide more consistent evidence of a rural/urban difference. For example, transportation is often found to be a key difference between rural and urban areas (Acker et al. 2001; Fox et al. 1998; Schexnayder et al. 2001; Fletcher and Jensen 2000). In Oregon, Acker et al. (2001) found that those rural recipients who had the use of a vehicle were more likely to be employed. In Iowa, Fletcher and Jensen (2000) found that the lack of reliable transportation posed a barrier not only to employment, but also to accessing child care and other daily needs. Those who owned a car often described them as old and unreliable, and as a result, many recipients relied on a "patchwork of friends and family," which often included reciprocating rides. Except for the school bus, public transportation was rarely mentioned. Recipients in a rural Texas county reported driving up to fifty miles round-trip not only to jobs, but also to welfare offices and health services, resulting in "more frequent and severe examples of difficulties in acquiring medical treatment" (Schexnayder et al. 2001, 4).

There were also rural/urban differences in overall service provision and availability. For example, in one rural county in Iowa, while emergency food assistance was available, the service was only open for two hours at a time, two days a week (Fletcher et al. 2000). Swensen et al. (2002) report that the job service program in Texas was first implemented in all of the state's urban areas and a selection of rural areas, with service more sparsely distributed in rural areas. This resulted in a larger share of the urban case-load receiving job services compared to rural areas. Kraybill and Lobao (2001) found that rural county governments were much less likely to have implemented an employment program in response to welfare reform. More-over, even when they did have a program, they were less successful at plac-ing former TANF recipients in jobs than programs in metropolitan areas.

Child care and child support provision also received increased attention under welfare reform. Jensen et al. (2000) found that during Iowa's waiver, a higher proportion of households in nonmetropolitan areas received child support. Similar results were found in Tennessee (Fox et al. 1998). By con-trast, in Kentucky the proportion of work-eligible cases with child support collection was lower in nonmetropolitan parts of the state (Dyk and Zim-merman 2000). Rural/urban differences are also evident in relation to child care, with recipients in rural areas relying less on formal child care and more on a family member or friend to meet their child care needs (Fox et al. 1998; Schexnayder et al. 2001).

Rural Diversity: One Size Doesn't Fit All

While it is common to contrast rural and urban areas, rural areas also dif-fer considerably from one another. And, while this diversity of rural areas could hold different implications for welfare reform, research that exam-ines these differences is even more limited. For example, in an analysis of AFDC/TANF and food stamp caseloads in Mississippi and South Carolina, Henry et al. (2000) found that all else being equal, rural areas in these states would have a more difficult time reducing dependence on both cash assistance and food stamps. This was especially the case for rural areas such as those located in the Mississippi Delta region.

RUPRI (1999) examined trends in caseload levels for metropolitan, non-metropolitan adjacent, and nonmetropolitan nonadjacent counties in Mis-sissippi, Missouri, Oregon, South Carolina, and Kentucky. Their results revealed considerable variation not only between rural and urban areas, but across rural areas as well; however, the pattern was not the same in all of the states. In Oregon and Mississippi, the greatest declines were in met-ropolitan areas, with lower declines in rural areas. On the other hand, in Missouri and South Carolina, metropolitan areas had the lowest rates of caseload decline, with greater rates of decline in rural areas. For Kentucky, declines were greatest in nonmetropolitan areas adjacent to metropolitan areas, but were the least in nonmetropolitan areas not adjacent to a metro-politan area.

Brady et al. (2000) also examined cash assistance participation across rural areas in California from 1985 to 1997. They found that the patterns differed for rural and agricultural counties compared to urban counties. For example, a larger share of the local population in rural and agricultural counties relied on assistance. There were shorter spells and more cycling on and off of assistance in rural areas. They further identified seasonal changes in rural and agricultural counties with an increased likelihood that these recipients would exit assistance during the summer. This seasonality was "correlated with agricultural employment in the agricultural and mixed counties and with retail and other forms of nonagricultural employment in rural counties" (Brady et al. 2000, 2).

In Mississippi, Howell (2000) estimated the prospects for local labor markets to meet the employment needs of recipients by spatially comparing the educational characteristics of those receiving assistance with the projected job growth at those educational levels. Access to transportation (vehicle and major road access) and child care were also examined. The results suggested wide variability across the state. Those areas most challenged by the mismatch between jobs and recipients included rural areas of the Mississippi Delta region.

An analysis in Kentucky revealed even more caseload variation across rural areas and regions in the state (Haleman et al. 2000; Zimmerman and Renfro-Sargent 2000). Econometric analyses in Kentucky by Goetz et al. (1999) indicated the importance of place-based characteristics, caseload characteristics, and rurality in accounting for declining caseloads across the state. Examining only those cases that either are or were work eligible, Dyk and Zimmerman (2000) found differences in the caseload composition not only across the different rural areas of Kentucky but across its regions as well. Results also indicated the impact of different rural areas in the state on the likelihood of recipients' cycling on and off of assistance, the likelihood of being a recent recipient, and the likelihood of long-term receipt of cash assistance.

Parisi et al. (2002) took a different approach. Their research examines the role of place and space in accounting for caseload declines across Mississippi. In addition to identifying the importance of local economic conditions, the results suggest the importance of community structure rather than rurality in accounting for variations in caseload declines across the state.

Issues and Implications

While many questions about welfare reform are similar across rural and urban areas, some are unique to rural areas. As stated in a RUPRI report, "rural areas and communities are not just smaller, poor substitutes for urban areas. Rather, they are qualitatively different, and those differences are consequential" (RUPRI 2001, 3). Particularly in rural areas, issues facing recipients interplay with broader issues facing rural communities. For instance, changes such as recent declines in Medicaid hold particular implications for rural communities, as Medicaid is a critical income stream for the economic viability of rural hospitals (RUPRI 1999). Fewer economic and job advancement opportunities, child care alternatives, and transportation options are issues faced by all community members, not just current and former TANF recipients.

It is also unclear whether or not all communities are equally situated to be able to respond to these newly devolved responsibilities. For many rural communities, local elected officials are part-time employees, attending to their other job duties while also serving their communities. Rural leadership networks tend to be smaller in size, sometimes overlapping or centered on a few families. There are also fewer nonprofit organizations to fill potentially receding services gaps and smaller faith-based institutions with limited capacity to provide services (cf. Bartkowski and Regis 2003; Ferguson et al. 2002). Fewer social service resources and sparse population densities can also stretch already limited resources by increasing cost-per-client ratios, even when services are available (RUPRI 1999; Duffy et al. 2002).

On the other hand, rural communities do offer examples of sectors and organizations working together (see Pindus 2001). Small leadership structures that may hinder one community can help another work together across traditional lines. For example, McConnell and Ohls (2000) found that while rural participants felt that they would be likely to meet someone they know while shopping at the grocery store; they also found that service delivery in rural areas was perceived as being more courteous.

But cash assistance does not stand alone. Rather, it is one piece of a larger system of programs directed at those with low or no income. And, in addition to TANF, these other programs have also begun to be redefined and devolved. The Workforce Investment Act brought a new focus to what used to be the Job Training Partnership Act program. The Children's Health Insurance Program now seeks to provide health care to children of the working poor. There is also new funding for child care and transportation programs, and greater flexibility in how TANF surpluses can be spent. Other federal policies such as the minimum wage and the federal Earned Income Tax Credit are also critical for the future prospects of welfare recipients, particularly those in rural areas where incomes are lower and a higher share of workers rely on the minimum wage (Parker and Whitener 1997).

Indeed, with the devolution of cash assistance, the structure of federal funding streams themselves can have hidden implications for rural areas

(Weber et al. 2001; Weber and Duncan 2001). Separate from the TANF state grant, Supplemental Fund grants for TANF were provided to states with lower than average funding levels or high population growth. Of those states receiving Supplemental Fund grants for low spending, all are in the South with large rural populations. However, these funds are not in the TANF "baseline" block grant funds; consequently, their continuance requires separate Congressional reauthorization and funding, making this important funding stream especially vulnerable. Since a large share of the nation's rural population lives in the South, and states in the South receive a disproportionate share of these funds, any discontinuance would disproportionately affect these rural states (Weber and Duncan 2001).

It is also unclear whether block grants actually empower the decision-makers closest to the issues at hand. State administrators face political landscapes within their own states that can pose barriers to responding to rural needs. For instance, in a state where politics are dominated by urban interests, rural areas may be neglected in a block grant environment (Reeder 1996).

Finally, welfare reform was implemented in a time of national economic growth. Macroanalyses have indicated that this strong economic climate was a critical component of declining caseloads (Blank 1997; Council of Economic Advisers 1999; Danziger 1999; Martini and Wiseman 1997; Schott, Greenstein, and Primus 1999; Rector and Youssef 1999). With a higher proportion of recipients in rural areas working and still remaining eligible for assistance, the impact of time limits—particularly in a recessionary period—may hit rural areas particularly hard. Moreover, in meeting the federal work participation requirements, many states have relied on a "caseload reduction credit" wherein the federally required work participation rates for their caseloads could be reduced. Still unknown is how these work participation rates will be met as both the economy declines and caseloads increase.

Conclusion

While research on welfare reform has grown exponentially, the knowledge base for rural areas constitutes only a very small piece in this body of work. While it is suggestive of rural/urban differences in some areas, we know very little about others. For example, does welfare reform affect rural child well-being differently than in urban settings (see Chapter 7 in this volume)? Are there implications for rural minorities (cf. Moreland-Young et al.

2002)? And what are the long term outcomes for families residing in persistent poverty areas (cf. Braun et al. 2002)?

One reason for the relative scarcity of rural research lies in the methodologies themselves and the challenges of easy access to suitable data. A common approach for assessing the impacts of welfare reform has been to conduct a statewide assessment such as a survey of those leaving TANF (cf. Isaacs and Lyon 2000; Zedlewski and Alderson 2001). However, while researchers may include rural families in order to ensure a statewide representative sample, they rarely separate the rural voices from the sample, and even more rarely do they examine difference across the diversity of rural areas.

Even when rural areas are examined, the lack of any uniform definition of place confounds the ability to provide a clear interpretation of findings. For instance, in some cases urban areas are defined by the major urban counties, with all remaining counties combined into a single rural category (e.g., Westra and Routley 2000; Kickham et al. 2000). Others forego a rural/urban distinction and use a regional approach within the state (e.g., Acker et al. 2001; Bosley and Mills 1999). In one instance, rural and urban areas in one part of the state are combined into a single region, while rural and urban places are disaggregated for the remainder of the state (Cummings and Nelson 1999). Klemmack et al. (2002) compare major metropolitan and other metropolitan counties with persistent-poverty rural and other rural counties. Less common are analyses that use standardized county classifications such as that provided by the Office of Management and Budget or the USDA Economic Research Service (Dyk and Zimmerman 2000; Jensen et al. 2000; McKernan et al. 2001; RUPRI 1999).

While analyses using national surveys such as the Current Population Survey are often used to assess federal policy changes, these data sources are restricted in their ability to portray the diversity of rural areas. Indeed, this approach may be least relevant as devolution to state and local decision making increases. The National Research Council (Moffitt and Ver Ploeg 2001) has argued that because decisions for TANF vary by state and local areas, sampling frames and sample sizes from national surveys are not appropriate. While the new American Community Survey will allow for better analyses of small areas, its implementation has only recently begun (Moffitt and Ver Ploeg 2001). Without a national county-level database or other adequate means to easily and systematically examine outcomes across the diversity of rural areas in the nation, knowledge about the impacts and outcomes of welfare reform for rural America will remain scattered and limited.

While devolution and block grants opened the possibility for policies to be more responsive to rural needs (see Chapters 19 and 27 in this volume), and employment of all TANF recipients has increased, it is less clear whether these changes have increased the well-being of those in rural areas or increased their vulnerability, especially in the long term (cf. Singelmann, Davidson, and Reynolds 2002). Because rural poverty is already disproportionately found among those who are working, it is unclear whether an employment-focused cash assistance program with time limits will be an effective policy for many rural areas. Moreover, what happens when families who are poor live in places that are poor (Brown and Warner 1991)? Rural areas encompass some of the highest persistent-poverty regions of the nation (e.g., the Mississippi Delta, Appalachia, the Southern Black Belt, Native American reservations, Rio Grande), which are characterized by disproportionate dependence on cash assistance (Nord and Beaulieu 1997). How effective is a block grant environment when these regions cross state lines (Wimberley and Morris 2002)? How can families in persistent poverty areas make the transition from welfare to work when there are few employment opportunities to begin with?

Welfare reform represents yet another stage in America's social experiment of using markets to provide for the needy. Whether this experiment will succeed or fail remains to be seen. There are indications that market mechanisms are not working as well in rural America, but the evidence for this is not strongly compelling. With policies varying by state—each facing its own political and economic changes—and with the diversity of places found in rural America, the prospects for welfare reform in rural areas are variable as well. In the end, "perhaps the ultimate test of welfare reform lies in how it is faring for families and recipients in the most distressed communities in the most remote areas" (RUPRI 2001, 3).

29

The Impact of Global Economic Practices on American Farming

Philip McMichael

The implications of agricultural trade policies for U.S. farmers are profound and double-edged. More than one-third of U.S. agricultural production depends on export markets for sales. The quid pro quo for opening markets overseas is to open the U.S. market to imports of agricultural products. Not only do these imports, many of which are low-cost, compete with the products of American farmers, but they are increasingly farm products produced offshore by U.S. corporations. Policies of economic liberalization sponsor this situation, whereby firms are encouraged to seek lower-cost production opportunities overseas, and trade rules encourage the transnational movement of agricultural commodities. These policies threaten the American family farmer (see Chapter 13 in this volume). In this chapter, I address the source, character, and impact of global economic policies, and identify trends, and resistances to these trends, in the American farming economy.

Global Economic Policy Themes

Over the past two decades, free trade has become a mantra of policy-makers in both major U.S. political parties. The key tenet of free trade is the neoliberal belief in the ability of the market to allocate resources more efficiently than government. Hence the social protections and tariff policies associated with the welfare state have been targeted as legacies of government intervention bridling entrepreneurship and economic growth. Despite U.S. policies to the contrary, such as George W. Bush's protection of the steel industry and the 2002 Farm Bill's expanded set of subsidies to agricultural producers, free trade remains the rhetorical principle for global economic policies. Free trade has assumed the status of a self-fulfilling prophecy, insofar as it is associated with globalization, which is generally understood as inevitable. This perspective is, in some sense, a function of the perceived rationality (and nonterritoriality) of market forces. Neoliberal economics replaced Keynesian economics (the champion of national protectionism), when the latter lost legitimacy during the 1970s crisis of welfare capitalism. Accordingly, contemporary economic theory champions free market policies, with trade rules that destabilize farming across the world, including in the United States.

Agricultural liberalization policies begin from the proposition that in a global market, the most efficient farmers will survive. In this scenario, food security is no longer a local or national responsibility; rather it is provided through the marketplace by globally efficient agriculture (global "breadbasket regions"). Analogously, local or national entrepreneurs in any industry will prosper or decline depending on their "comparative advantage" (the ability to exploit local natural or technological resources) in an increasingly global marketplace (see Chapter 18 in this volume).

In contrast to the neoliberal view of markets promoting cross-border efficiencies, John Ikerd (2001, 3) argues that none of the assumptions about the market and its invisible hand apply today. He offers the provocation that "as agriculture has moved from competitive capitalism to corporatism, it has changed from a market economy to a 'central planned' economy," and that under a corporate global food system "Americans would be at least as dependent on the rest of the world for food as we are today for oil. Perhaps we could keep the food imports flowing, as we maintain the inflow of oil today. But how large a military force would it take? ... Would 'cheap food' be worth the cost we might ultimately be forced to pay?"

The issues here are complex, but one thing is certain: while agribusiness may have come to dominate the structure and terms of food production, agriculture is not solely a market phenomenon. Unlike commercial business, farming is handicapped by vagaries of climate, differential land fertility, dependence on biological rhythms and processes, and other constraints. Farmers are not mobile, unlike firms. Herein lies the quandary for farmers in a global market: as integration proceeds, under the influence of global economic policies and through the activity of global agribusiness, farmers are brought increasingly into competitive relation with one another, *as if* they are simply business units surviving in a deterritorialized market system. In this context, global prices (following a downward trend as lower-cost producers come on line) confront rising local costs. This is the reality facing (relatively high-cost) American farmers.

What is at issue here, perhaps, is the discrepancy between economic theory and reality. Theory tells us market competition leads to efficiency, while the reality is that farmers are neither equal nor equally served by global markets that privilege large-scale agribusiness. This discrepancy suggests that neoliberal economic theory is deployed to legitimize the liberalization of farm policy and agricultural trade across the world, as if it were a global marketplace. The question that concerns farmers and citizens is whether the global economy operates as a market, as asserted by policymakers, or whether the rules governing agricultural trade promote exchanges within and among corporations that systematically disadvantage the majority of farmers. In other words, how does economic rationality threaten rural culture, food sovereignty, and sustainable farming?

Corporate Agriculture

In the United States, 2 percent of farms grow 50 percent of agricultural produce, with the average family farm earning only 14 percent of its income from farming. Ninety-five percent of American food is manufactured and sold by corporations (Lehman and Krebs 1996). To dramatize the corporatization of food, whereas in 1956 the cost of a box of Wheaties was $.28 to the consumer, and the farmer received two cents, in 2001 a box of Wheaties costs $3.51, and the farmer receives four cents. Further, while the American farmer produces grain to feed 180 people per year, the farmer's income from that is not sufficient to feed a family of four during that same year (Catholic Conference of Illinois 2001).

Corporate influence, however, does not simply concern subsuming family farming under the corrosive effect of contract arrangements (Mooney 1988), and removing profitability to the processing and marketing of food. It also concerns the organization of world agriculture, encouraging a shift from national farm sectors to global farm regions as firms use global sourcing to maximize profitability in an uneven world market.

Current trends in the global restructuring of agriculture intensify a global division of labor, where trade in low-value temperate cereals and oilseeds has been historically dominated by countries such as the United States, Canada, and Australia, and trade in high-value products has been controlled increasingly by corporate agro-exporters (or their contract farmers) producing in the developing nations (the global "South"). These southern exports of high-value products are dramatized in two recent developments: since the North American Free Trade Agreement (NAFTA) began in 1994, roughly one-third of winter vegetable producers in Florida have gone out of business; and China, where the farm labor cost differential is one-sixth of the cost of U.S. harvest labor, is producing seven times the amount of vegetables and twice as much fruit as the United States, threatening Asian markets valuable to West coast producers (Iritani 2001).

We are seeing a new process at work: the widespread subordination of producing regions to global production and consumption relations organized by transnational food companies. Such global sourcing increasingly underwrites a system of profiteering in food products, in which food travels from farm gate to dinner plate over thousands of kilometers, and often food from the same source travels in opposite directions. Transnational corporations are most likely to gain from a free trade regime, which enhances and rewards capital mobility and facilitates it by reducing transactional costs. Not surprisingly, agribusinesses were instrumental in the 1980s in the General Agreement on Tariffs and Trade (GATT) Uruguay Round's multilateral push to liberalize agriculture and the trade in agricultural commodities. Indeed, Cargill's former senior vice president (and former officer of the U.S. Department of Agriculture) drafted the original U.S. proposal. Cargill and Continental share roughly 50 percent of U.S. grain exports. Across the board, food companies, grain traders, and the chemical industry favor using the WTO to phase out farm programs, eliminating supply management and driving down prices by exposing producers to worldwide differential labor costs. Price support reduction helps corporations to structure comparative advantages in the world market, and to source their inputs from the variety of producing regions incorporated into the "free" world market.

Global Economic Policy-Making

The United States, as the dominant agro-exporter and home base of half of the world's largest food processors (accounting for one-third of U.S. agro-exports), has sought to organize the world food economy to its advantage—levying what the French referred to as "green power" (Revel and Riboud 1986). Beginning with the Uruguay Round, the United States has advocated a steady liberalization of farming and agricultural trade, directed at the Common Agricultural Policy (CAP) as much as markets.

The neoliberal economics underlying this advocacy reached perhaps its most direct formulation in the notion of food security as a global arrangement. This formulation laid the groundwork for the 1994 WTO Agreement on Agriculture (AoA), and was articulated by the U.S. representative as such: "The United States has always maintained that self-sufficiency and food security are not one and the same. Food security—the ability to acquire the food you need when you need it—is best provided through a smooth-functioning world market" (quoted in Ritchie 1993, 14 n. 25). The AoA was designed to open agricultural markets across the world by adopting minimum import requirements and tariff and producer subsidy reductions.

AoA reforms included reductions in trade protection, farm subsidies, and government intervention. Southern nations signed on in the hopes of improving their foreign currency income from expanded agro-exports (under the imperative of servicing foreign debt). The effect has been to open markets for Northern ("developed" countries) products, supported by export subsidies. Critics, especially in these "less developed" countries, argue that these rules favor the globally dominant states and corporations (whose internal transactions account for 70 percent of the international food trade).

Meanwhile, northern nations continued farm support, with effective subsidies of 49 and 30 percent for farmers from the United States and Europe, respectively, according to one estimate (Malhotra 1996). In the absence of public capacity in less developed countries, unprotected farmers are exposed to a structure of unfair trade. Oxfam asks, "how can a farmer earning U.S. $230 a year (average per capita income in LDCs) compete with a farmer who enjoys a subsidy of U.S. $20,000 a year (average subsidy in OECD [Organization for Economic Cooperation and Development] countries)?" (quoted in Bailey 2000, 7). Conservative estimates are that between twenty and thirty million people lost their land as a result of trade liberalization (Madeley 2000). In northern nations, by the mid-1990s, 80 percent of farm subsidies in the OECD countries concentrated on the largest 20 percent of (corporate) farms, rendering small farmers increasingly vulnerable to the vicissitudes of a deregulated (and increasingly privately managed) global market for agricultural products. As a result most American farmers and ranchers, for example, obtain almost 90 percent of their total income from off-farm earnings (Lilliston and Ritchie 2000).

The pressures on farming across the world have intensified since the 1996 Farm Bill, dubbed "Freedom to Farm" by its bipartisan proponents. This neoliberal bill removed the New Deal system of production controls, and proposed the total elimination of federal price supports by 2002 (Lilliston and Ritchie 2000). The effects were revealing. For traders, as a Cargill spokesman told the Ontario Financial Post in 1996, "Freedom to Farm has really positioned the United States very well to take advantage of the opportunities in the world market" (quoted in Lilliston and Ritchie

2000, 10). But many farmers have been devastated. Not only did all grain exports drop by nearly 10 percent, but farm prices for the major commodities in world trade have fallen 30 percent or more since the WTO agreement was signed in December 1994 (Ritchie 1999). *The Economist* (1999) reported that commodity prices were at an all-time low for the last century and a half. Many countries could not meet their commitments to the AoA because of this price collapse. In particular, the United States abandoned its commitments by increasing farm subsidies (as proposed in the 2002 Farm Bill) and intensifying export dumping—in part to use supply management to restore crop prices (Ritchie 1999), and in part to capture overseas markets.

Case Study: The End of Farming As We Know It?

A recent report on NAFTA from the Public Citizen's Global Trade Watch documents a common process of elimination of small farmers across the whole North American region as the legacy of NAFTA. While millions of Mexican *campesinos* have lost their maize farms, U.S. farmers are faced with an intensification of competitive imports from Mexico and Canada, replacing crops grown in the United States. Since 1994 33,000 U.S. farms with under $100,000 in annual income have disappeared (six times the decline for 1988–1993). Meanwhile, during the 1990s a massive demographic shift occurred in Mexico, where overall population growth was 20 percent; however, urban population grew 44 percent and rural only 6 percent (Public Citizen 2001).

As representative of a world region, NAFTA is a telling case study of the impact of liberalization. This shows up in two ways. First, there has been a general decline in U.S. agricultural trade surpluses as agriculture has shifted offshore (a noticeable trend since 1985). Second, during the period the WTO and NAFTA have been in effect, while the U.S. world trade surplus has declined 29.6 percent, the U.S. NAFTA trade surplus has declined more than twice that, by 71 percent (Public Citizen 2001). This particular decline fuels a global "substitution effect," whereby competitive imports (fruit, vegetables, and other labor-intensive foodstuffs) represented 80 percent of all U.S. agricultural imports during the decade of the 1990s (Public Citizen 2001).

Policy changes such as these express and enhance agribusiness power. The ethos of liberalization is that the generalization of an export model would render agricultural protections unnecessary because of expanding global food flows. As a Public Citizen report observes with respect to

U.S. policy, "Proponents of the legislation contended it would make farming more efficient and responsive to market forces; in reality it essentially handed the production of food to agribusiness. . . . Ironically, to counteract the predictable failure of NAFTA and the similar farm deregulation policies embodied in the Freedom to Farm Act, Congress has had to appropriate emergency farm supports—in massive farm bailout bills—every year since the legislation went into effect" (Public Citizen 2001, 16).

As in Europe, 56 percent of U.S. emergency taxpayer assistance went to the largest 10 percent of farms. As states that could afford farm support ran up huge relief bills, agribusiness corporations took the opportunity to restructure, with input industries and output industries consolidating "within and across their narrow sectors and (creating) alliances with other food industries to encircle farmers and consumers in a web . . . from selling seeds and bioengineering animal varieties to producing the pesticides, fertilizers, veterinary pharmaceuticals and feed to grow them to transporting, slaughtering, processing and packaging the final 'product'" (Public Citizen 2001, 19).

Such "food chain clustering" (Heffernan et al. 1999) exemplifies general trends in the global restructuring of capital, where, for example, 60 percent of foreign direct investment in 1998 involved cross-border mergers and acquisitions (Public Citizen 2001). The Canadian National Farmers Union testified in 2000 that "almost every link in the chain, nearly every sector, is dominated by between two and ten multibillion-dollar multinational corporations" (quoted in Public Citizen 2001, 20). And in Mexico, once NAFTA opened the door to 100 percent foreign investor rights in Mexican agriculture, Pillsbury's Green Giant subsidiary relocated its frozen food processing from California to Mexico to take advantage of cheap wages, minimal food safety standards, and zero tariffs on re-export to the United States. Cargill purchased a beef and chicken plant in Saltillo, and Cargill de Mexico invested nearly $200 million in facilities such as vegetable oil refining and soybean processing in Tula. Meanwhile, anticipating the Free Trade Area of the Americas (FTAA), or "NAFTA on steroids," Tyson Foods developed cross-border operations in Mexico, Brazil, Argentina, and Venezuela; ConAgra processes oilseed in Argentina; Archer Daniels Midland crushes and refines oilseed and mills corn and flour, and bioengineers feeds in Mexico and Central and South America; and Wal-Mart operates in Argentina and Brazil (Public Citizen 2001).

Through the device of cross-border operations, global firms exploit food market asymmetries between "more" and "less developed" countries, undercutting northern nations' entitlement structures and their institutional supports by optimizing the strategy of global sourcing. In relation to the neoliberal regime institutionalized via NAFTA, Public Citizen observes: "Multinational agribusinesses were positioned uniquely to take advantage of trade rules that force countries to accept agricultural imports regardless of their domestic supplies. The companies utilized their foreign holdings as export platforms to sell imported agriculture goods in the United States, and by thus increasing supply, put negative pressures on U.S. agriculture prices" (2001, 13).

Conclusion

The story unfolding in American agriculture appears to confirm the thesis of the disappearing family farmer in a globalizing market incorporating lower-cost producers. But there are issues regarding this scenario as simply driven by a multitude of rational decisions by market minded individuals.

First, the "lower-cost producers" are often constituted by the very policies stemming from the consolidation of corporate power in the agro-food system. The effect of dumping farm goods on the world market routinely undercuts southern producers, driving them into contract relations with agribusinesses, or to work as casual and migrant labor on agro-*maquilas* springing up across "less developed" nations (see, e.g., Barndt 1999). These low-cost producers are not there by virtue of some inevitable developmental trend within individual nations involving the commercialization of farming for export. While the modernization thesis assumes a linear development from low-tech agriculture to the informational economy, the politics of global agriculture suggest that this continuum is relational rather than sequential. That is, the expansion of agro-exporting is neither a natural process in southern countries, nor a simple shedding of a superfluous economic sector. Rather, neoliberal policies and related agribusiness practices suggest that low-cost producers emerge as both an unintended consequence of, and a competitive condition for, a corporate strategy of global market success.

Second, the question of costs is far more complex. Farm prices for American farmers are artificially low because they face oligopolistic corporate processors on the one hand, and, on the other, they compete with farmers under corporate processors overseas. The real costs of "developed" nations' government subsidies to corporate farmers in deficiency payments, in natural resource depletion, and in oil and transport infrastructure far outweigh the minimal supports to producers. But this cost differential is not accounted for in national accounting statistics, which do not include "external" costs.

Third, economists view the world as if it is a natural market. Here life imitates art in very real sense, since global economic policies are premised on the assumption of the superiority of markets in making efficient and profitable allocation of resources. As noted above, the market is essentially a political construct, expressing a balance of forces favoring corporate actors. But to recognize this is to posit and legitimize alternatives. The debates over the American farm bill increasingly reveal the contradictory interests of different stakeholders in the farm system, in particular those of family farmers versus corporate farmers and processors. There is a mounting opposition to the neoliberal policy of privileging corporate agriculture. In March of 2000, over three thousand farmers rallied in Washington, D.C., for rural America, drawing their strength from a coalition of family farm, church, labor, and consumer and environmental groups, who called for a new farm bill that would restore a competitive market, support farmers with cost of production loans, enact conservation measures to reduce overproduction, create a farmer-owned grain reserve to ensure food security in times of scarcity and price stability in times of plenty, negotiate fair trade agreements with assurances that countries retain the right to develop farm programs responsive to the needs of their producers and consumers first, eliminate export dumping, and so forth (Lilliston and Ritchie 2000). In the spring of 2001, a group of Catholic bishops called for the reversal of corporate farming, "which creates concern about market control and leaves little room for independent producers. These forces threaten to change the face of food production in our state and nation. They are already taking an enormous human toll on those involved in family farming. . . . Low prices and rising uncertainty about the future place a toll on personal relationships, marriages and the fabric of family life. Meanwhile the precarious situation of family farming threatens the welfare of businesses, schools, churches and community services" (Catholic Conference of Illinois 2001).

Fourth, the social consequences of U.S. farm policy are sufficiently severe that the U.S. Congress' emergency support of farmers clearly violates its public position on "free trade" as promoted through WTO policy. The issue of subsidies was a central sticking point in the failed WTO Seattle Ministerial Round in 1999. Southern nations view the AoA as protecting the farm systems of the more developed countries of the North, and in fact the United States has made it clear in negotiations for the Free Trade of the Americas (FTAA) that it will not negotiate the issue of farm subsidies. Commentators from Brazil, which is ambivalent about the FTAA, observe that the financial power of the North sustains its inefficient agriculture (Osava 2001). Within Washington, the difference between the WTO-

oriented agricultural bureaucracy and the Congressional attempt to preserve farm supports feeds growing foreign criticism of the U.S. position,
even to the extent of the WTO finding that "while the United States
demanded subsidy reductions internationally, it had tripled payouts to its
domestic agricultural and food producers between 1997 and 2000" (Keene
2001). These divisions currently define the WTO as a giant with feet of
clay, since the extant policies regarding agricultural trade have become
contentious. They continually confirm that liberalization acts as a "protection racket," ostensibly for American farming, but in reality for agribusiness, which gains most from the use of subsidies to depress commodity
prices at home and abroad.

For American agriculture, the growing recognition of the contradictory
policy of supporting a corporate food system via mechanisms in violation
of WTO commitments is a condition for generating real alternatives. Real
reforms and/or alternative forms of agriculture will surely emerge to fill the
gap left by corporate agriculture. There is already a healthy movement for
Community Supported Agriculture across the United States, implementing
the desire for localization (based potentially in new spaces like bioregions
rather than nations per se) and sustaining communities and farming simultaneously. Niche farming, for example, with organics and other local
cuisines, is evolving in the wake of failed conventional farming. As
U.S. farmers pull back from genetically modified crops and face the dis-
pleasure of the processors, they find their way toward alternative agricultures. Meanwhile, global economic policy controversies spotlight the
subsidy system and its subversion of WTO protocols, and transnational
movements like *Via Campesina* highlight the growing movement for food
sovereignty based in democratic politics rather than food security based in
euphemistic policies of "free trade."

There is no question that global policies are stalled precisely because
while all nations are presumed equal, some are "more" equal than others.
The different stances and groupings of nations in the WTO negotiations
regarding agricultural trade policies appear to be insurmountable, especially as governments experience growing pressure from destabilized farming populations. This provides an opening for a new envisioning of
agricultural organization and food systems.

30

Catalytic Community Development

A Theory of Practice for Changing Rural Society

Kenneth E. Pigg and Ted K. Bradshaw

How is rural community development practice changing in our increasingly complex society? Previous models of rural community development saw the community developer as a specialist providing technical assistance, an organizer forming grassroots organizations to work for community agendas, a leader who promoted community self-help efforts, and a mediator of community conflicts (Christenson and Robinson 1989; Voth and Brewster 1990). Community developers knew how to build infrastructure and use Robert's Rules of Order, help attract firms into the community to provide jobs, or write grants to fund community services. The old model of locality-centered development focused on the mobilization of local resources to address community problems. In this model each community was the locus of an independent development project that required specific technical skills for success, and the community developer was the specialist responsible for bringing these skills.

What is new in rural community development is the emergence of a loose collection of approaches we call catalytic development, that are likely to lead to more effective community development practice in rural places. In catalytic development the emphasis is on leveraging local resources and networks to find local solutions in regional and global exchanges that expand capacity and investments. The community developer as catalyst does not entirely abandon locality-centered development practices, but is no longer the technician. Instead, the developer's goal is to mobilize the capacity of local groups and organizations to achieve expanded objectives. Presciently, Bradshaw and Blakely (1979) argued that rural community development practice passed through three phases, and the third stage was that of "resource coordinator and network facilitator," whose tasks involve region-ally-based, collaborative approaches to problem-solving. Today, community developers recognize that no community can have—nor should try to have—all the specialists increasingly necessary for development, but that collaborative arrangements are more effective. Of course, these catalytic processes are not themselves new. What is new is that it is time to make them central and essential. In a complex society, communities lacking cat-alytic development processes and the organizations that support them are unlikely to be as successful as those that do adopt or develop them.

One example of how catalytic community development operates is the Redwood Community Action Agency, one of the original Community Development Corporations (CDCs). This organization's success is closely tied to the strategy of spinning off dozens of nonprofit organizations and for-profit businesses that are more effective than if they were still organiza-tionally tied to the parent CDC. A community developer from Kansas who claims that he does not really do anything other than just getting people together provides another example. For instance, to create a marker for the entrance to their town—a brick planter with two flags—he did not suggest that the city build it. Instead, he persuaded the garden club (interested in flowers) and the Boy Scouts and Veterans of Foreign Wars (interested in symbols of patriotism) to adopt the idea and build it.

Locality-centered development is inadequate today because rural com-munities are increasingly complex. Rural communities are linked in increas-ingly specialized networks, the economy is in flux, the community of place is being complemented by communities of interest, uncertainty replaces blind confidence in rational choice, and globalization reduces isolation (Schuh 2001). Rural community policy is in a state of disarray: programs are fragmented and do not turn out as intended, and poor communities and their populations get poorer rather than better off. Some observers, such as Kretzmann and McKnight (1993b), believe that institutions create narrowly focused programs that produce results that are the opposite of those antici-pated—prison systems teach crime, schools reduce children's natural instinct for learning, hospitals and medical systems thrive on unhealthy individuals, and welfare systems create dependency. Faced with these fail-ures, local problem-solving capacity must overcome significant barriers.

Complexity theory provides many insights to the process by which rela-tively autonomous participants self-organize to create large system net-works (Johnson 2001). Ecosystems have feedback apparatus and communications to the group that provide efficient functioning without explicit controls. Many of the processes involved in community change are similar from place to place. As Innes and Booher (1999) point out, the old equilibrium-seeking model of community has been replaced by one that sees communities at the edge of chaos, where the system is too complex and too random for mechanistic policy models, but not so disorganized that learning and action cannot take place (see also Bradshaw 2000; Cilliers 1998; Rupasingha, Wojan, and Freshwater 1999; Waldorp 1992).

In complex society the catalytic community developer is no longer the individual who does development; the community developer is the agent who helps many individuals work together in a loosely coupled way. The role of the community developer is not to try to control the system but to help all participants take a role in the process. Like a chemical catalyst that stimulates reactions in industrial processes without itself being consumed, the community developer, as catalyst, is more important for organizing the reactions of community members, and less so as the person responsible for getting things done. However, like the chemical catalyst, the community developer is an actor required to facilitate the change that takes place. Our analysis presents a somewhat different conclusion than others that acknowledge the transition in approaches to practice in the community development literature. The dynamics indicate a transition is underway from program-focused, top-down, direct-assistance models to community-centered, capacity-building, coordinated approaches (Campfens 1997; Flora et al. 1997; Pigg 1999; Rupasingha et al. 1999). Further, community development has made a transition through a limited capacity-building phase to emphasize leadership, organizational development, and increasing the social capital of rural communities (Dhesi 2000). Some of the approaches characteristic of this phase include the collaborative, interagency-interorganizational approach, the social learning or educational approach, the social integration approach, and the community-building approach.

Characteristics of Catalytic Community Development Practice

We believe that the growing complexity facing rural communities gives rise to six characteristics of catalytic community development practice that will help improve the effectiveness of rural community development activities. These are interrelated and not intended to be an exhaustive list but, like complex systems themselves, are evolving and self-organizing.

From Technical Expert to Capacity Builder

According to Flora and Luther (2000) and Chaskin et al. (2001), the "community capacity-building" approach is the most recent community development approach to emerge. The purpose of "capacity building" is to engender an "entrepreneurial social infrastructure" that establishes a direction to guide development activity and enhances the community's ability to successfully implement these plans (Flora et al. 1997, 623). To Chaskin et al. (2001) this approach, derived mostly from urban neighborhood development experience, consists of four elements: leadership development, organization development, organizing, and networking. Flora et al. (1997) have presented a set of elements more suited to rural areas that include diverse, inclusive citizen participation; expanding leadership base; strengthened individual skills; widely-shared vision; strategic community agenda; tangible progress toward goals; effective community organizations and institutions; and enhanced resource utilization (see Chapter 16 in this volume).

The focus on capacity building resolves historical tensions in rural development over the role of government, markets, and civil society. Beginning with the New Deal period, we placed our confidence in politics to resolve rural development issues. Galston and Baehler (1995) argue this was an attempt to resolve development tensions through top-down programs that essentially ignored the role of the market and the civic sector. The post–World War II period saw a shift away from the big government that we had grown to distrust because of its ineffectiveness. Top-down policies were replaced with others that emphasized the role of markets, at the expense of politics and the civic sector. These, too, have largely failed, Galston and Baehler argue, because they concentrated on industries rather than communities (at least pertaining to rural areas). As a result, Galston and Baehler argue that what is now necessary is a different approach that balances the three-way relationship by placing greater emphasis on the civic sector, and less on markets and politics. While they associate the civic sector with nongovernmental and volunteer organizations, we argue that this is, in effect, community capacity-building—although the focus on the "civic sector" obscures the need to build community as the foundation for civic engagement (Graham 2001).

Capacity-building in rural communities is not new: training leaders and honing organizational skills have long been central to rural community development. What is new is the extent to which the notion of "capacity" has expanded. For example, the Rural Development Leadership Network, a national nonprofit organization, sponsors a one-month university-based seminar, where community leaders learn basic facts about rural communities, communication skills, program development, and research methodologies. Participants develop solidarity with each other and with the network of individuals who were previously in the program. The skills developed in these programs help individuals function under the guidance of local, established leaders, giving them the ability and confidence to take initiative themselves when necessary.

From Involvement to Empowerment

One challenge that rural community developers increasingly face is to balance effective community participation with the technical expertise of outsiders commissioned to find effective solutions to the complex problems rural communities face. On the one hand, community participation is a sacred premise of community development—people must be involved since the goal of community development is to achieve the wishes of a community (Botes and van Rensburg 2000). On the other hand, participation is a process, and it is often slow, costly, complicated, and uncertain. When participation becomes an end in itself, housing does not get built and training programs are not implemented. Alternatively, professionals working in communities without local participation create programs that do not effectively meet local needs or, at worst, fail with significant negative consequences.

A growing literature on community participation in development projects highlights three topics: first, concerns over the type of participation (White 1996); second, barriers to participation (Botes and van Rensburg 2000); and third, strategies to increase participation. The classic formulation of different types of participation is Sherry Arnstein's (1969) "ladder of citizen participation." While this continuum applies to all rural communities, capacity-building not only requires participation in community development projects by a more diverse set of community residents, but full empowerment of the participants as well (Richardson 2000). A number of barriers must be overcome to achieve this level of community participation. Funders, including government, see community improvement tasks as technical, as opposed to empowering to community residents. This creates what Botes and Van Rensberg call the "hard issue bias" (2000, 46).

Real participation from a diverse population is hard to achieve (Aigner et al. 1999). For example, many rural communities hold dozens of public meetings while creating new general plans. However, these meetings are often held during the day, and the only participants are ones who are paid to attend, such as developers, reporters, governmental officials, and affected business owners. Representative participation often substitutes for broad-based public input. Some experts suggest that authentic participation is not important, as long as citizens are informed, while others, like Putnam (2000), are concerned that the lack of civic engagement represents a failure to build social capital. Organizational proliferation and specialization gives representatives of organizations more apparent legitimacy, but many community members are not really involved. Finally, as more people become more involved, conflict—or at least the potential for conflict—increases. As a result, more effort must be dedicated to resolving conflicts.

Increasingly, the issue for participation is empowerment, because mere attendance at meetings fails to achieve the benefits of broad participation (Peterman 2000). Empowerment is the product of a long process, however, since full participation restructures the system and equips individuals to assume greater control of development on behalf of local interests. Participation must be focused on "empowerment" (Stoecker 1998; Mesch 1998) in order to create a political infrastructure for participation that empowers citizens and gives them an authentic voice in decision-making about community direction and the means to achieve their goals. Especially important is the rural middle class, which Stauber (2001) argues must be the target to retain in rural areas. Empowerment should also be part of the agenda for the multitude of community leadership education programs being implemented by states; effective tools exist to empower individuals and groups for community betterment and action (Pigg 2002).

Forms of political infrastructure that illustrate this point include the neighborhood associations of Columbus, Ohio, which are granted direct access to government decision-making in arenas such as land use planning committees, and the local economic development corporations that provide leadership in small Wisconsin communities (Sullivan 1998). Without an authentic voice in governance structures, citizens cannot be empowered and community capacity is restricted (Mesch 1998).

From Independent Action to Collaboration

Collaboration is an increasingly common term in rural community development, and refers to the facilitation and operation of multi-organizational problem solving not easily achievable by one organization alone (McGuire 2000). However, there is still a lack of specificity about how collaborations differ from coalitions, partnerships, or networks. As with participation, there are degrees of collaboration, based on intensity of multi-organizational sharing and the extent to which goals are interwoven (Winer and Ray 1994). Collaboration encompasses forms of interaction like communication, coalitions, coordination, and cooperation.

Collaboration is most important when problems exceed the capacity of one community development organization. These situations exist when the problem is ill-defined or beset by conflict. Also, when there is a lack of trust among participants, the historical failures to solve the problem become a barrier to future efforts. Typically, collaboration is most successful when no stakeholder has power over the others, but each knows that they are essential to a solution and that they have something to contribute to reaching a commonly held goal (Gray 1989).

One example of collaboration is the Quincy Library Group, respected in environmental circles for working together to resolve conflicts between environmentalists and logging interests in the northern Sierra Nevada of California (Kiester 1999). Revisions of U.S. Forest Service policies on logging, awareness of serious environmental problems with logging practices, and stern opposition by environmental groups reduced logging activity and resulted in substantial unemployment and economic distress in local communities. Local leaders proposed a collaborative effort by environmental, logging, Forest Service, and local government interests to find a solution benefiting all parties. Meeting at the Quincy library, the group worked out a proactive strategy—not a compromise—to meet collective goals of economic vitality in the community and higher levels of environmental protection through restoration of previous damage.

The challenge for catalytic community development is that there are significant benefits from moving up the scale of multi-organizational activities from simply communicating about activities and interests with other organizations working in the same domain, to forming networks and cooperative relations. Collaboration requires new ways of making decisions, planning, and project management (see Foster-Fishman et al. 2001). The benefit of collaboration is that, as situations change and as more is learned about the complex dimensions of a problem, the collaborative goal is modified so that the capacity for action represented by partnerships can be maintained (Gray 1989; Korsching et al. 1992).

Collaboration produces formal structures that allow organizations to recognize and manage their interdependence (Alexander 1995). Intermediaries, planning frameworks, programs and projects, markets, and governing commissions and boards are all formal structures that facilitate collaboration among interdependent organizations. Higher levels of government often play the role of structuring collaboration, as do foundations and other funding sources that wish to share risk by bringing together multiple participants in complex projects.

Collaboration is costly, however, especially for rural communities. Distance makes joint work more difficult than sequential or parallel efforts, and rural community development organizations often lack the flexibility and resources to subordinate their goals to those of the collaborators.

Moreover, organizational collaboration and citizen participation are frequently disconnected (Aigner et al. 1999). To manage the challenges of rural community development, collaborative activity must also be directed beyond the jurisdictional boundaries of the locality to include regional activities, public and private organizations, communities of interest, and nongovernmental organizations (Galston and Baehler 1995).

Community Is Local and Relational

The locus of the activity circumscribed by community development activity may be communities of place (e.g., neighborhood, city, town, or village) or communities of interest, including virtual communities. Historically, nearly all discussions of rural community development have focused on communities of place, specifically small, well-bounded, largely agrarian collectivities (Reiss 1959; Batten and Batten 1967; Cary 1970). We argue that, in the global society, this limited perspective constrains practice in ways that fail to acknowledge existing fragmentation and complexity (Richardson 2000). Further, the creation of extra-local and virtual communities, especially those involving Internet technologies, demands a redefinition of the theory from which practice is derived, to focus on "relationships" as well as the development of solidarity and agency in local places (Bhattacharya 1995). As earlier chapters have already dealt with topics related to solidarity and agency (see Chapters 15, 16, and 17 in this volume), we focus on the effect of adding relationships such as those found in regional efforts to the working definition of community development.

Regional efforts may be the most significant response to change in rural areas. While the Tennessee Valley Authority, Appalachian Regional Commission, and other regional efforts have long helped shape rural community development, the growth of mid-level and smaller-scale regional efforts around entities such as industrial clusters or transportation networks is impressive as well. Rural communities join together based on political jurisdictions, economic "laborsheds" or market areas, industrial clusters, watersheds and bioregions, and transportation networks. The regional framework is valuable in terms of interdependency of communities that together constitute different parts of a larger whole. In some areas the small communities constitute what has been described as a "ruralplex," or an integrated network of small communities with specializations and divisions of labor. For example, in Wisconsin, one community has a university, another is the county seat with abundant government programs, a third is the retail center, and another has heavy industry. And very small towns around Gackle, North Dakota, pay attention to how their economic development efforts "complement those of others on the Great Plains" (Richardson 2000, 233). In each community there are different assets and capacities, but they work together like neighborhoods in an urban area.

Wells (1990) described a multi-community cluster program to develop rural leadership where regional identity is developed and intercommunity competition is replaced by cooperation. Regional planning organizations have been established under federal and state mandates. In some places common economic interests have led to the formation of regional organizations that work to expand business opportunities including marketing, identify formation, and especially research to assist business expansion. Regionalism must become manifest in other ways, such as in the "learning regions" described by Florida (1995). Learning regions provide a manufacturing infrastructure of interconnected vendors and suppliers; a human infrastructure that produces knowledgeable workers organized around life-long learning; a physical and communication infrastructure that supports information sharing, just-in-time delivery of goods and services, and integration into the global economy; and capital allocation and industrial governance systems that serve the needs of knowledge-intensive organizations (Florida 1995, 534). Where rural communities are adjacent to urban areas, greater linkages and the organization of economic infrastructure must take place with those urban counterparts (Galston and Baehler 1995). Where they are not nearby, rural areas' efforts to create new forms of connections with urban areas' markets and sources of innovation must take place using communication technology and publicly supported diffusion processes. Where isolation prevents location-specific strategies from being employed, multijurisdictional collaborations must be organized—and supported in policy—to mobilize and create comparative advantages in tourism, amenity settlements, regional manufacturing clusters, and so forth (Ndubisi and Dyer 1992; Parks and Oakerson 2000; Savitch and Vogel 2001).

From Dissemination to Open Access to Information

Rupasingha et al. (1999) discuss the importance of information as a critical resource in dealing with complex situations. Without open access to information of various types, community capacity to self-organize is limited. In order to be empowered and enact the capacity they possess in leadership and organization resources, communities need access to technical and innovational information about external resources available to assist development activities, examples of lessons from successful and unsuccessful change efforts, national and international trends and changes that might provide opportunities for niche strategies to be established, and other forms of information such as the activities of nearby jurisdictions that can support and/or leverage community development action between or among communities.

Access to information provided by state and federal governments, higher education institutions, and national nonprofit organizations must be increased. Perhaps an expanded National Rural Development Partnership or other coordinated alliance could more easily organize information about resources available and structures created so that community capacity-building can benefit from the information. Community networks, if supported by a targeted rural development policy, could be created and linked to bring access directly to individuals in their homes (Schuler 1996). This access can be structured using current software tools created in the "knowledge networking" field (Milner 2000; Skyrme 1999). There are two important features of these tools. One is the integration of the formal knowledge of experts with the tacit knowledge of practitioners and citizens so that both are accessible. The second is the necessity of converting descriptive information to prescriptive; that is, from an understanding of "what" to a presentation of "how" in the form of examples and illustrations from experience and practice.

From Categorical to Comprehensive

Finally, catalytic development encourages development activities that are comprehensive, not categorical (Coffey 1990). Comprehensive or integrated activities have been adopted in rural and urban communities due to growing awareness of interconnections among programs and how progress in one area (e.g., housing) is undermined if there is no progress in other areas (such as employment and crime prevention). Comprehensive community development activities may involve coalitions assembling flexible categorical programs within one collaborative structure so that the service provided is seamless (Wolff 2001).

Comprehensive activities can save time and expense in dealing with clients, but the more comprehensive a program is, the greater the chance that the specialists needed by the client will not be available or included. Rural community development programs have dealt with this problem in a number of ways. Richardson (2000) documents the holistic, integrated, community-based approach used by the participants in Vermont's Environmental Programs/Partnerships in Communities (EPIC) program. This program employed tools like small seed grants; leadership development; the empowerment of women, youth, and the elderly; a systems approach that addressed all segments of the community identified by local people as valuable; and collaboration with government agencies and neighboring communities.

Conclusion

Rural development in an increasingly complex community setting must become more catalytic to deal with a greater number of needs, participants, and opportunities. For the most part, rural programs remain stuck with locality-based approaches that either do not work or are much less effective than what is needed to stimulate the development. Community development practitioners are too often wedded to approaches that emphasize locality and technical assistance without the capacity to serve in a catalytic role and focus on new ways of serving their communities.

Effective rural policy needs to stimulate catalytic development at three levels. At the assistance level, categorical funding programs remain counterproductive (McDowell 1995). Program funding has gained flexibility by incorporating changes like increasing block grants and workforce investment act consolidated service centers, but much remains to be done. Disconnected activities now in place to improve transportation, health, education, and agricultural policies mean that funds going to rural areas get diluted rather than effectively leveraging other assets to produce the desired results.

Second, policy needs to stimulate catalytic development at the organizational level. Ongoing evaluation has shown the comprehensive organizational development of the War on Poverty era, via CDCs and Community Action Agencies, was more successful than believed at the time. In fact, programs of this type are quite suited to today's complex environment. Moreover, the most successful new nonprofit organizations in rural areas are more like CDCs than single-focus service delivery providers. Federal policy should be focused on supporting comprehensive, self-organized efforts demonstrating broad collaboration and planning activities that recognize the impact of global change on their future, rather than creating new initiatives from the top down.

Third, rural policy needs to promote and encourage catalytic development processes. Whereas rural development agents have become increasingly specialized and isolated from local community involvement, what is needed are people who understand the interrelations of disciplines and programs. In conjunction, existing federal programs that emphasize short-term grants for specific projects, such as infrastructure, should focus instead on supporting the efforts made to create and sustain "learning regions" (Florida 1995). Sustainability is an important element of development strategy in this approach, and sustainability is best attained when it is community-based and community-driven, based on community knowledge and skills, and a realistic, collaborative process of assessment and planning (Green and Haines 2002).

Rural community development practice should be framed in the context posed by Sears and Reid (1995), who differentiate between a policy that is "program-based" and one that is "community-based." This provides a rationale to shift federal policy from emphasizing programs to one that supports diverse efforts and approaches formulated community by community. Coupled with a catalytic approach to community development, a community-based approach could make substantial differences in rural areas. It is a safe generalization to say that it is the community that is important to rural people. The programs are merely tools to be used to meet local goals. However, it is the capacity of local leaders and citizens to employ these programs and other community assets that is instrumental for achieving this success. Catalytic community development practice, framed in complexity theory and capacity-building, emphasizing collaborative comprehensive programs, and focused on regional dimensions of cooperative activity, is more likely than other approaches to be a successful intervention to meet rural needs and secure a brighter future for rural people.

Conclusion

Challenges Become Opportunities:
Trends and Policies Shaping the Future

Louis E. Swanson and David L. Brown

Daryl Hobbs, coeditor of the first volume in this series on rural America, is attributed one of the better aphorisms describing rural society: "when you've seen *one* rural community, you have seen *one* rural community." As with any useful framing statement, this one encompasses multiple meanings. Most obviously, it underscores the great ethnic, cultural, regional, economic, and social diversity of rural people and places. The statement also limits simplistic, often deterministic and partisan assumptions concerning rural societies, for instance that "rural" is synonymous with "agriculture"—which it obviously is not. Less obvious are the ways in which this statement sets up theoretical and methodological concerns that occur with inquiry on exceedingly diverse social phenomena. If rural society is as diverse as Hobbs' pithy dictum implores, then for sociologists who systematically look for patterns and trends, identifying and documenting common conceptual themes among this great diversity becomes a keen intellectual challenge. The chapters in this book provide a broad spectrum of themes shaping rural sociological understanding of the well-being, social interaction, social structural characteristics, and potential future paths of the United States' rural areas. In turn, these themes are connected to the use of public policies that address or ignore persisting social problems or emerging opportunities. These chapters point to significant barriers to the improved well-being of rural America, but they also provide challenges for a better future. In the introduction we presented demographic criteria and data that describe essential population realities of rural America. Additionally, we provided a thematic map of the chapters to come. Here we the editors share with you some of our general musings on the chapters and their collective wisdom. We will not summarize each section and the chapters within: our emphasis is on the policy implications. We, and implicitly most of the authors, believe that not only are the people and the environment of rural America important in and of themselves, but they are important for those who live in the tall buildings of metropolitan areas and the vast web of suburbs that characterize early twenty-first-century America.

Institutional Neglect of Nonfarm Rural Issues: The Question of Rural Policy

Nonagricultural national rural policies have been characterized as suffering from a historic condition of "institutional neglect" (Browne 2001).[1] Rural people are penalized by nonagricultural institutions, by a metropolitan policy myopia, and by their "friends" in agriculturally-oriented institutions who find it convenient to assume that farming interests are the same as rural. Such neglect does not indicate an inherent fatalism for national rural policies, but the political inertia of this neglect is difficult to overcome. The great diversity within rural America and a historic inability for rural interests to organize a national political constituency beyond well-heeled agricultural interests suggests a need for at least a critical review of, and possibly even serious reform for, rural policies at all levels of society. Among the more salient themes emerging from these chapters are calls for policies that appropriately address both the breadth of diverse conditions and local realities. Among nonagricultural institutions (for example, education and health and social welfare), a salient theme is the need to fashion policies that are sensitive to the peculiar conditions found in rural America, rather than influenced by assumptions reflecting metropolitan and suburban conditions and constituencies.

Plainly, some rural interests enjoy the benefits of national attention or cultural mythification.[2] Among these, agricultural and environmental issues capture significant attention and resources from Congress and federal

1. Among policy researchers on rural issues, the observation that there is a systematic institutional neglect of nonfarm rural issues is common (Browne 2001). A shortcoming of this volume is the absence of a chapter on institutional neglect in general, but especially by the Land Grant Universities that have a unique institutional obligation to rural people. Our omission does not lessen the seriousness of addressing an engagement of the Department of Agriculture and the 1862 Land Grant Universities on nonfarm rural development.

2. Here the term myth refers to foundational cultural framing assumptions and not to a false statement, though it is a false statement that at a national level rural and farming interests are one and the same.

agencies. Unfortunately for most rural people and places, agricultural and environmental interests have demonstrated little concern for rural development. Agricultural interests have given neither much attention nor many resources to the needs of farmers' nonagricultural neighbors, even though their plights are exceedingly important in determining local social services and economic vitality. For example, institutions such as the Department of Agriculture and the 1862 Land Grand Universities have never directed significant resources to nonfarm rural America, even though both have Congressional mandates to do so (Browne 2001; Swanson and Freshwater 1999). Furthermore, there is little evidence that either set of public institutions will willingly reform their programmatic assumptions and reallocate scarce—even dwindling—resources to nonfarm rural development. To make matters worse, other public institutions responsible for providing services to rural people and places are unfamiliar—or unconcerned—with finding ways to make their programs fit the diversity of rural America. National environmental groups exhibit a great interest in rural environments and landscapes but are "disconnected" from on-the-ground rural social and economic issues, since the great majority of their stakeholders live in suburbs and metropolitan areas. Rural development may even be antithetical to goals of "preserving" the environment. Institutional influence primarily resides in national and state environmental protection agencies that tend to rely on regulatory programs to achieve their goals; however, particularly in the West, regulatory programs have tended to pit environmental groups against local private property interests, or against the interests of extractive and recreational users of public lands. Rural land use policies must be crafted to address and resolve these inherent political tensions. Also essential is the inclusion of local interests in program development and implementation; however, similar to many agriculturally-oriented public institutions, environmental institutions tend to be nationally focused agencies with bureaucratic silos that do not welcome substantive local partnerships, especially with people who tend not to be programmatic stakeholders. To make matters worse, agricultural and environmental agencies and their stakeholders often see one another as the "enemy."

So where do we look for policy reform? Where are the untried ideas that can provide a more optimistic future for rural America? One answer proposed in this volume is to formulate policies that enhance the capacity of rural people and communities to help themselves. This is much easier to suggest than it is to achieve, but it certainly makes sense in the context of current institutional neglect. The assumption underlying this approach is not that people will make a positive difference in their local communities if given the tools; rather, the assumption is that they should be given real opportunities to do so. It calls upon cultural values for civil engagement and democracy to be used as tools for development and programmatic administration. Current tendencies to decentralize federal and state programs to counties and municipalities create some political traction for localities, but significant shifts in institutional support and programmatic paradigms will also be required.

Community, Civility, and Devolution

Three loosely associated themes converge among our authors' recommendations. These are: (1) the recognition among government managers and academicians that experiences in local societies, in communities, is important; (2) the renewed emphasis on the rights and responsibilities of citizenship and civility in proactively addressing social problems and enhancing quality of life; and (3) the decentralization, or devolution, of authority for federal social and economic development programs to the states and their localities. While these three trends seem to be related, they have emerged virtually independently of one another. If our authors are representative of broader social science perspectives, and we think they are, these three themes are coalescing as broad sets of remedies for current challenges before rural societies. Unlike earlier policy remedies, these trends do not carry with them exuberant promises of success. Rather, they represent throwbacks to traditional policy principles, even last ditch efforts, to address seemingly intractable development quandaries by institutionalizing framing principles of the America political economy: democracy, local initiative, civility and tolerance for our neighbors, recognition of the importance and obligations of private property, and the value of community. Institutionalizing foundation values will be more difficult if the current government and educational institutions serving rural America do not actively participate; however, it is difficult to imagine a better starting point for creating and realizing new policy opportunities for rural America.

The Importance of Community, for Better or Worse

For better or worse we live our lives in local societies. The basic physical, social, and economic infrastructures that we depend upon are primarily local. Much of the material and cultural quality of our lives is dependent upon the provision of these necessities in our local societies, whether a suburb, a metropolitan central city, a rural village, or a rural open country neighborhood. Considering the tendency of sociologists for the last half of the twentieth century to dismiss the relevance of local society as having been eclipsed by the social forces of mass society, the academic revival of interest in and inquiry about both local society and civility is welcomed. Among rural sociologists, local society has been an important focus of inquiry since the inception of the Rural Sociological Society in the late 1930s. Given rural communities' small scale and involuntary intimacy— which have proven to be both an advantage and a bane—ignoring communities and open country neighborhoods simply was not possible. What is new, or at least renewed, is the vigor with which past assumptions are being tested and reconceptualized in sociological research.

Community, as an ecological unit of analysis, is traditionally conceived of in isolation or in a subregional context. But today's communities, especially American rural communities, are influenced by global markets, global migration, and the currents of global culture. The commercial resource extraction upon which much of rural America was founded has been located within a global economy in competition with other areas of the world since colonial times. But the acceleration of interaction with national and global markets and cultures during the twentieth century has profoundly reshaped the capacities of rural people and places to sustain themselves. A theme among many of the chapters is the degree to which localities can maintain effective self-determination—culturally and economically—in the context of their global connections. While the environmental moniker is to "think globally—act locally," the converse has become a reality for much of rural America—think locally but understand global connections. A conceptual tension brought forward in this volume is the degree to which communities can carve out a local identity that contributes to self-determination given the economic and social forces of globalization. This tension concerning the degree of local self-determination is an unresolved debate. Some of our authors, working from the position that rural people are at a great disadvantage in a global economy, may be correct. Others propose that citizens can adopt strategies associated with civic community, a development scenario that champions local small-scale entrepreneurship. But for local societies to seize these opportunities, these authors state in various ways the need to enhance inclusiveness and democracy, address social inequities correlated with persistent poverty, and overcome historic cultural legacies associated with ethnic diversity.

Locality-Based Policy and Beyond

If one assumes that there is a continuing importance for local society even when confronted with the forces of globalization, then it seems reasonable that federal and state policies should be founded on varying degrees of partnership with localities. Therefore, the decentralization or devolution of federal social and economic development programs should be viewed as a positive trend. But the decentralization of federal and state programs is not without its challenges, particularly for rural communities with a small core of civil servants, a limited tax base, and limited capacities to achieve economies of scale in the provision of essential services. The public administration challenges for this new policy environment have forced rural governments to address a wide variety of policy options that range from exclusive public provision of services to privatization of public services.

Several of the chapters examine the consequences of devolution. They note that politically, such decentralization addresses fiscal and legitimacy crises at the federal and state government levels by transferring the immediate political liabilities of program administration to local and municipal authorities. They also observe that while decentralization has been championed by most political observers, including advocates for greater local autonomy, as a political and programmatic response to make public policies locally appropriate, the general experience has been for fewer resources and greater political liability to be devolved to rural places. Greater program responsibility with fewer resources has overstretched local governments' ability to effectively administer these programs. Given past criticism by local leaders of federal and state authorities, this political turn of the tables may seem deserved. Unfortunately, rural people, their communities, and often the local environment are left wanting. Moreover, since some states and localities have more capacity than others, devolution has the potential to create increased geographic inequality among rural places and regions.

A challenge and opportunity for rural governments will be to find innovative ways of managing their scarce resources. Cooperation offers one the more promising means for doing so. Sharing program responsibilities with neighboring communities increases the likelihood of achieving the benefits of economies of scale and utilizes the limited time of public servants more efficiently. This is perhaps ironic, as it implies some erosion of community autonomy without firm knowledge of how such spatially horizontal partnerships might allocate available resources. Greater coordination, cooperation, and sharing of resources between local governmental bodies are more easily proffered than realized.

The provision of public services may be more effectively administered by private venders. Privatization may ease the administrative personnel binds experienced by local governments with a thin civil service base. Several of our authors point to the need to consolidate the provision of health care, education, and welfare without losing local identities and the positive factors associated with more intimate knowledge of those who are served. Others propose the sensible option of local governments acting as facilitators and networkers of services instead of incurring the costs of directly providing essential services.

What is evident is that the dividends of devolution have not been the windfall that county and rural municipal leaders expected. Nor is devolution simply another cruel example of institutional neglect, though for many rural communities this may be the final consequence. In this case, the benefits from gains in programmatic authority may be well worth innovative efforts by local officials to capture their enhanced jurisdiction over key federal and state programs.

Belief in the Power of Individual and Collective Agency

A pervasive theme among our authors is the belief that civic engagement, civility, inclusiveness, and democracy are necessary framing principles for effective rural development. This theme is in contrast to more elitist perspectives that place emphasis on the belief that private entrepreneurship will automatically provide for the public good. While civility, inclusiveness, and democracy can guide private entrepreneurial decision-making, they are by no means assured to do so. An equally important ancillary theme is enhancing local decision-making capacity by improving local social capital; that is, the enrichment of the quality of social interactions meant to achieve public goals. In concert, these themes underscore a general call for social development as a necessary condition for economic development. The chapters in this volume indicate that investments in people and the quality of social interactions within and outside of their communities are key dimensions for rural development strategies. They also indicate that such emphases on people and social relationships are presently underutilized and unappreciated in rural development policies. It may be that this is simply wishful thinking on the part of a broad range of rural sociologists. Conceivably, rural sociologists suffer from self selection biases that include a fundamental belief in the potential for conscientious and informed people acting in a civil manner to work out their individual differences and thereby achieve a common good. This bias is no different than that of economists who accept a belief that if left alone markets generally will achieve a common good. The emphasis given to the benefits of informed collective action and civility is apparent through much of this volume. So too are pervasive concerns that structural and cultural conditions may present significant challenges to the efficacy of sustained collective action.

Structural Constraints

This volume presents myriad social structural and spatial conditions that pose significant challenges for improving the quality of rural life. Perhaps the single most important demographic transformation is increased ethnic diversity. It is not possible to frame the social and economic opportunities for rural people without including the plight of rural minorities. This volume has devoted several chapters to race and ethnicity. Without exception, the authors have pointed to the richness of human experiences and capacity that diversity brings to rural communities. Yet a prevailing theme is that rural nonwhite populations often confront higher rates of poverty, occupy the most economically and politically vulnerable sectors of rural labor markets, and, in the case of Native Americans, African Americans, and Latino Americans, must deal with legacies of discrimination and weak public investments in their education, job training, and health care. For rural America to prosper, the economic and social conditions that impede full access to economic and social opportunities for all citizens must be overcome. Among places experiencing economic stagnation and population decline, investments only in strengthening social relationships and civic participation are unlikely to induce development without other forms of investments. In the rural South, the persistence of poverty accompanied by inadequate educational, health, and welfare programs create enormous challenges. In the 1960s this area was declared a region "left behind." It still has a long ways to go to catch up. The Great Plains present a different set of challenges. There the economic and cultural dependency on farming has ebbed almost as fast as the decline of its farm population. Yet in the Great Plains there have been greater investments in people. Democratic processes occurring in communities with relatively homogenous social structures is common. Again, investing in people may not be enough.

Other areas of rural America, such as the intermountain West, the Northeast, and areas of the South close to prosperous metropolitan areas or recreational and retirement amenities, are growing. In the past, population growth was considered to be a "good" indicator of quality of life. But the positive character of this growth is seriously questioned in this volume. Rapid growth, particularly associated with urban sprawl, has triggered intense political conflicts over land use and the continuing prosperity of agriculture. This type of social change can intensify the spatial polarization of class structure. Metropolitan sprawl and the growth of rural trade centers in recreational and public land areas are likely to continue to energize intense political conflict over land use conversion and environmental degradation.

Perhaps the most important structural transformations noted in these chapters are associated with shifting patterns of employment. Today, services are the primary engine of economic growth in both urban and rural America, yet compared with urban economies, growth in the rural service sector is much more likely to be in the consumer or personal categories rather than in high-wage producer services. This trend of differential development will exacerbate already significant economic disparities between urban and rural America.

The continuing social changes in the structure of American farming are also particularly important. The globalization of agricultural markets and the accompanying market hegemony of transnational corporations are not just limiting local options, they are potentially threatening to traditional commercial farming operations. Farming may confront the greatest social changes in the coming years of any economic sector. And yet farming at a smaller, community-oriented level may provide innovative opportunities that fully engage the nonfarm rural residents. This is an old idea that perhaps is becoming more possible, in part due to globalization.

Final Observations

Emery Castle observes that "[e]conomic distress does not characterize all of nonmetropolitan America, but social adjustment does" (1995, 495). We agree with Castle. Like Hobb's comment, Castle's has multiple meanings. It, too, gives emphasis to diversity of social, economic, and demographic experiences. But his highlight on the importance of social adjustment and social change is the focus and value of our volume's tour of issues confronting rural America. Public and private policies cannot simply focus on economic issues and well-worn assumptions of the efficiency of markets. To be holistic, to be relevant at the local level, and to tap the development capacities of rural residents, future rural policies need to be as attentive to social issues as they are to economic and environmental concerns. Social change is to a great extent steered both by local circumstances and by relationships with regional and global markets and institutions. The immediate sites of these "adjustments" are the lives of rural people. The great transformations of rural societies are expressed through the myriad social interactions of rural people among themselves and in their relationships with the larger society. Rural people and places are worthy of our interest and public investment. Hopefully, this volume has not just helped you frame your understanding of challenges and opportunities, but also has provided conceptual frameworks and evidence for greater investment in rural people themselves.

REFERENCES

Achana, Francis T. and Joseph T. O'Leary. 2000. "The Transboundary Relationship between National Parks and Adjacent Communities." In *National Parks and Rural Development: Practice and Policy in the United States,* ed. G. E. Machlis and D. R. Field, 67–87. Washington, D.C.: Island Press.

Acker, Joan, Sandra Morgen, Terri Heath, Kate Barry, Lisa Gonzales, and Jill Weigt. 2001. "Oregon Families Who Left Temporary Assistance to Needy Families (TANF) or Food Stamps: A Study of Economic and Family Well-Being from 1998 to 2000." Eugene: Center for the Study of Women in Society, University of Oregon. Available at: http://wnw.uoregon.edu/welfvol1.shtml.

Advisory Commission on Intergovernmental Relations (ACIR). 1995. "Tax and Expenditure Limits and Local Governments." Information Report M-194, March, U.S. Advisory Commission on Intergovernmental Relations. Washington, D.C.

Aglietta, Michel. 1979. *A Theory of Capitalist Regulation: The U.S. Experience.* Trans. D. Fernbach. London: Verso.

Aigner, Stephen M., Cornelia B. Flora, Syed N. Tirmizi, and Carrie Wilcox. 1999. "Dynamics to Sustain Community Development in Persistently Poor Rural Areas." *Community Development Journal* 34 (1): 13–27.

Ainsworth-Darnell, James W., and Vincent J. Roscigno. 2001. "Stratification, School-Work Linkages, and Vocational Education." Presented at the Annual Meeting of the American Sociological Association, August 18–21. Anaheim, Ca.

Albrecht, Don E., Carol M. Albrecht, and Stan L. Albrecht. 2000. "Poverty in Nonmetropolitan America: Impacts of Industrial, Employment, and Family Structure Variables." *Rural Sociology* 65 (1): 87–103.

Albrecht, Stan L., Leslie L. Clarke, and Michael K. Miller. 1998. "Community, Family, and Race/Ethnic Differences in Health Status in Rural Areas." *Rural Sociology* 63 (2): 235–52.

Aldrich, Lorna, Calvin Beale, and Kathleen Kassel. 1997. "Commuting and the Economic Function of Small Towns and Places." *Rural Development Perspectives* 12 (3): 26–31.

Alesch, Daniel J. 1997. "The Impact of Indian Casino Gambling on Metropolitan Green Bay." *Wisconsin Policy Research Institute Report* 10 (6): 1–35.

Alexander, Ernest R. 1995. *How Organizations Act Together: Interorganizational Coordination in Theory and Practice.* Luxembourg: Gorden and Breach Publishers.

Alexander, Jeffrey C. 1992. "Shaky Foundations: The Presuppositions and Internal Contradictions of James Coleman's Foundations of Social Theory." *Theory and Society* 21 (2): 203–17.

Alexander, Karl, and Bruce K. Eckland. 1975. "Contextual Effects in the High School Attainment Process." *American Sociological Review* 40 (3): 402–16.

Allan Guttmacher Institute. 1999. *Contraception Counts: New Jersey [Mississippi] Information.* New York: Alan Guttmacher Institute.

American Farmland Trust. 1997. *Saving American Farmland: What Works.* Northampton, Mass.: AFT Publications.

———. 2001. "Cost of Community Service Studies, Fact Sheet." Northampton, Mass.: Farmland Information Center, American Farmland Trust. Available at: http://www.farmlandinfo.org/fic/tas/COCS9-2001.pdf.

American Indian Policy Review Commission. 1977. *Final Report.* Washington, D.C.: U.S. Government Printing Office.

American Public Health Association (APHA). 1997. "Supporting National Standards of Accountability for Access and Quality in Managed Health Care." Policy 9615(PP), January 1, 1995. Washington, D.C.: American Public Health Association.

American Religious Data Archive. 1998. Available at: http://www.thearda.com/.

American Society of Planning Officials. 1976. *Subdividing Rural America: Impacts of Recreational Lot and Second Home Development.* Washington, D.C.: Council on Environmental Quality, Office of Policy Development and Research, U.S. Department of Housing and Urban Development.

Anders, Gary C. 1998. "Indian Gaming: Financial and Regulatory Issues." *Annals of the American Academy of Political and Social Science* 556 (March): 98–108.

Anderson, Cynthia D., and Michael D. Schulman. 1999. "Women, Restructuring, and Textiles: The Increasing Complexity of Subordination and Struggle in a Southern Community." In *Neither Separate nor Equal: Women, Race, and Class in the South,* ed. B. E. Smith, 91–108. Philadelphia: Temple University Press.

Anderson, John E., and Howard C. Bunch. 1989. "Agricultural Property Tax Relief: Tax Credits, Tax Rates, and Land Values." *Land Economics* 65 (1): 13–22.

Anderton, Douglas L., Andy B. Anderson, John M. Oakes, and Michael R. Fraser. 1994. "Environmental Equity: The Demographics of Dumping." *Demography* 31 (2): 229–48.

Antonio, Robert J., and Alessandro Bonanno. 2000. "A New Global Capitalism? From 'Americanism and Fordism' to 'Americanization-Globalization.'" *American Studies* 41 (2/3): 33–77.

Araghi, Farshad A. 1989. "Land Reform Policies in Iran: Comment." *American Journal of Agricultural Economics* 71 (4): 1046–49.

Arce, Alberto. 1997. "Globalization and Food Objects." *International Journal of Sociology of Agriculture and Food* 6: 77–107.

Arce, Alberto, and Elizabeth Fisher. 1997. "Global Configurations and Food Objects and Commodities—Apples, Honey & Coca." Presented at the International Conference on Agricultural Commodity Systems in Comparative Perspective. Toronto, Ontario.

Arnstein, Sherry R. 1969. "A Ladder of Citizen Participation." *Journal of the American Institute of Planners* 35 (4): 216–24.

Astone, Nan Marie, and Sara S. McLanahan. 1991. "Family Structure, Parental Practices, and High School Completion." *American Sociological Review* 56 (3): 309–20.

Bagnasco, Arnaldo, and Charles F. Sabel. 1995. *Small and Medium-Size Enterprises*. London: Pinter Publishers.

Bailey, Michael. 2000. "Agricultural Trade and the Livelihoods of Small Farmers." Oxfam GB Discussion Paper 3/00, March, Oxfam GB Policy Department, Oxford, UK. Available at: http://www.oxfam.org.uk/policy/papers/agricultural_trade/agric.htm.

Ballou, Dale, and Michael Podgursky. 1998. "Rural Teachers and Schools." In *Rural Education and Training in the New Economy: The Myth of the Rural Skills Gap*, ed. R. M. Gibbs, P. L. Swaim, and R. Teixeira, 3–21. Ames: Iowa State University Press.

Barber, Benjamin R. 1995. *Jihad vs. McWorld*. New York: Times Books.

Barker, Kathleen, and Kathleen Christensen. 1998. *Contingent Work: American Employment Relations in Transition*. Ithaca: ILR Press.

Barkley, David L. 1993. *Economic Adaptation: Alternatives for Nonmetropolitan America*. Boulder, Co.: Westview Press.

Barndt, Deborah. 1999. *Women Working the NAFTA Food Chain: Women, Food, and Globalization*. Toronto: Second Story Press.

Barrows, Richard, and Elizabeth Troutt. 1989. "A National Perspective on Data Needs for Agricultural Land Use in Urbanizing Areas." In *Land Use Transition in Urbanizing Areas: Research and Information Needs. Proceedings of a Workshop Sponsored by the Economic Research Service, USDA and the Farm Foundation, Washington, DC, June 6–7, 1988*, ed. R. E. Heimlich, 1–13. Washington, D.C.: The Farm Foundation.

Bartfeld, Judi, and Daniel R. Meyer. 2001. "The Changing Role of Child Support Among Never-Married Mothers." In *Out of Wedlock: Causes and Consequences of Nonmarital Fertility*, ed. L. L. Wu and B. Wolfe, 229–55. New York: Russell Sage Foundation.

Bartik, Timothy J. 1991. *Who Benefits From State and Local Economic Development Policies?* Kalamazoo, Mich.: W. E. Upjohn Institute for Employment Research.

Bartkowski, John P., and Helen A. Regis. 2003. *Charitable Choices: Religion, Race, and Poverty in the Post-Welfare Era*. New York: New York University Press.

Batten, Thomas R., and Madge Batten. 1967. *The Non-Directive Approach in Group and Community Work*. London: Oxford University Press.

Beach, Betty A. 1995. "What Do We Know About Rural Child Care? An Overview of Issues." *Journal of Research in Rural Education* 11 (2): 114–20.

Beale, Calvin L. 1966. "The Negro in American Agriculture." In *The American Negro Reference Book*, ed. J. P. Davis, 163–204. Washington, D.C.: U.S. Department of Agriculture.

Beale, Calvin L. 1996. "The Ethnic Dimension of Persistent Poverty in Rural and Small-Town Areas." In *Racial/Ethnic Minorities in Rural Areas: Progress and Stagnation, 1980–90*, ed. L. L. Swanson, 26–32. Agricultural Economic Report 731, August, Rural Economy Division, Economic Research Service, U.S. Department of Agriculture. Washington, D.C.

Beale, Calvin L. 2000. "Nonmetro Population Growth Recedes in a Time of Unprecedented National Prosperity." *Rural Conditions and Trends* 11 (2): 27–31.

Beale, Calvin L., and Kenneth M. Johnson. 1998. "The Identification of Recreational Counties in Nonmetropolitan Areas of the USA." *Population Research and Policy Review* 17 (1): 37–53.

Beauford, E. Yvonne. 1986. "Dilemmas Facing Minority Farm Operators in Agricultural Crisis." In *Agricultural Change: Consequences for Southern Farms and Rural Communities,* ed. J. J. Molnar, 25–37. Boulder, Co.: Westview Press.

Beaulieu, Lionel J., and Glenn D. Israel. 1997. "Strengthening Social Capital: The Challenge for Rural Community Sustainability." n *Rural Sustainable Development in America,* ed. I. Audirac, 191–233. New York: John Wiley & Sons.

Beaulieu, Lionel J., Glenn D. Israel, Glen Hartless, and Patricia Dyk. 2001. "For Whom Does the School Bell Toll? Multi-Contextual Presence of Social Capital and Student Educational Achievement." *Journal of Socio-Economics* 30 (2): 121–27.

Beaulieu, Lionel J., and David Mulkey. 1995. *Investing in People: The Human Capital Needs of Rural America.* Boulder, Co.: Westview Press.

Beckley, Thomas M. 1998. "The Nestedness of Forest Dependence: A Conceptual Framework and Empirical Exploration." *Society and Natural Resources* 11 (2): 101–20.

Benbrook, Charles M. 1996. *Pest Management at the Crossroads.* Yonkers, N.Y.: Consumers Union.

Benfield, F. Kaid, Matthew D. Raimi, and Donald D. T. Chen. 1999. *Once There Were Greenfields: How Urban Sprawl is Undermining America's Environment, Economy, and Social Fabric.* New York: Natural Resources Defense Council.

Bengtson, Vern, Carolyn Rosenthal, and Linda Burton. 1996. "Paradoxes of Families and Aging." In *Handbook of Aging and the Social Sciences,* Fourth Edition, ed. R. H. Binstock and L. K. George, 253–83. San Diego: Academic Press.

Bennett, D. Gordon. 1992. "The Impact of Retirement Migration on Carteret and Brunswick Counties, N.C." *The North Carolina Geographer* 1: 25–38.

———. 1996. "Implications of Retirement Development in High-Amenity Nonmetropolitan Coastal Areas." *Journal of Applied Gerontology* 15 (3): 345–60.

Berger, Peter L. 1963. *Invitation to Sociology: A Humanistic Perspective.* New York: Anchor Books.

———. 1969. *The Sacred Canopy: Elements of a Sociological Theory of Religion.* Garden City, N.Y.: Doubleday/Anchor Books.

Berger, Peter L., and Thomas Luckmann. 1966. *The Social Construction of Reality: A Treatise in the Sociology of Knowledge.* New York: Irvington Publishers.

Berkman, Lisa F. 1995. "The Role of Social Relations in Health Promotion." *Psychosomatic Medicine* 57 (3): 245–54.

Berkman, Lisa F., and S. Leonard Syme. 1979. "Social Networks, Host Resistance, and Mortality: A Nine-Year Follow-Up Study of Alameda County Residents." *American Journal of Epidemiology* 109 (2): 186–204.

Bernstein, Alison R. 1991. *American Indians and World War II: Toward a New Era in Indian Affairs.* Norman: University of Oklahoma Press.

Berry, Brian J. L. 1973. *Growth Centers in the American Urban System. Vol. 1: Community Development and Regional Growth in the Sixties and Seventies.* Cambridge, Mass.: Ballinger Publishing.

Berry, Brian J. L., and John D. Kasarda. 1977. *Contemporary Urban Ecology.* New York: Macmillan Publishers.

Berry, Wendell. 1977. *The Unsettling of America: Culture and Agriculture.* San Francisco: Sierra Club Books.

———. 1996. "Conserving Communities." In *The Case Against the Global Economy and For a Turn Toward the Local,* ed. J. Mander and E. Goldsmith, 407–18. San Francisco: Sierra Club Books.

Beyers, William B., and Peter B. Nelson. 2000. "Contemporary Development Forces in the Nonmetropolitan West: New Insights from Rapidly Growing Communities." *Journal of Rural Studies* 16 (4): 459–74.

Bhattacharyya, Jnanabrata. 1995. "Solidarity and Agency: Rethinking Community Development." *Human Organization* 54 (1): 60–69.

Billings, Dwight B., and Kathleen M. Blee. 2000. *The Road to Poverty: The Making of Wealth and Hardship in Appalachia.* Cambridge: Cambridge University Press.

Blahna, Dale J. 1990. "Social Bases for Resource Conflicts in Areas of Reverse Migration." In *Community and Forestry: Continuities in the Sociology of Natural Resources,* ed. R. G. Lee, D. R. Field, and W. R. Burch Jr., 139–78. Boulder, Co.: Westview Press.

Blair, John P., and Robert Premus. 1987. "Major Factors in Industrial Location: A Review." *Economic Development Quarterly* 1 (1): 72–85.

Blakely, Edward J., and Mary G. Snyder. 1997. *Fortress America: Gated Communities in the United States.* Washington, D.C.: Brookings Institution Press.

Blank, Rebecca M. 1997. "What Causes Public Assistance Caseloads to Grow?" Working Paper 6243, December, National Bureau of Economic Research, Cambridge, Mass. Available at: http://papers.nber.org/papers/W6343.

Blank, Steven C. 1998. *The End of Agriculture in the American Portfolio.* Westport, Conn.: Quorum Books.

———. 1999. "The End of the American Farm?" *The Futurist* 33 (4): 22–27.

———. 2001. "Threats to American Agriculture." Presented at the Third Annual Symposium on the Future of American Agriculture, August 16–17. Athens, Ga. Available at: http://www.uga.edu/caes/symposium01/sblank.html.

Blau, Peter M. 1960. "Structural Effects." *American Sociological Review* 25 (2): 178–93.

———. 1994. *Structural Contexts of Opportunities.* Chicago: University of Chicago Press.

Bloomquist, Leonard E. 1988. "Performance of the Rural Manufacturing Sector." In *Rural Economic Development in the 1980's: Prospects for the Future,* ed. D. L. Brown, J. N. Reid, H. Bluestone, D. A. McGranahan, and S. M. Mazie, 49–75. Rural Development Research Report 69, September, Agriculture and Rural Economy Division, Economic Research Service, U.S. Department of Agriculture. Washington, D.C.

Bloomquist, Leonard E., Christina Gringeri, Donald Tomaskovic-Devey, and Cynthia Truelove. 1993. "Work Structures and Rural Poverty." In *Persistent*

Poverty in Rural America, ed. Rural Sociological Society Task Force on Persistent Rural Poverty, 68–105. Boulder, Co.: Westview Press.

Bluestone, Barry, and Bennett Harrison. 1982. *The Deindustrialization of America: Plant Closings, Community Abandonment, and the Dismantling of Basic Industry.* New York: Basic Books.

Boehlje, Michael D., Steven L. Hofing, and R. Christopher Schroeder. 1999. "Value Chains in Agricultural Industries." Staff Paper 99-10, Department of Agricultural Economics, Purdue University, West Lafayette, Ind.

Boesch, Donald F., Richard H. Burroughs, Joel E. Baker, Robert P. Mason, Christopher L. Rowe, and Ronald L. Siefert. 2001. *Marine Pollution in the United States.* Arlington, Va.: Pew Oceans Commission.

Bonanno, Alessandro, Lawrence Busch, William H. Friedland, Lourdes Gouveia, and Enzo Mingione. 1994. *From Columbus to ConAgra: The Globalization of Agriculture and Food.* Lawrence: University Press of Kansas.

Bonanno, Alessandro, and Douglas H. Constance. 2000. "Mega Hog Farms in the Texas Panhandle Region: Corporate Actions and Local Resistance." *Research in Social Movements, Conflicts, and Change* 22: 83–110.

Boothroyd, Peter, and H. Craig Davis. 1993. "Community Economic Development: Three Approaches." *Journal of Planning Education and Research* 12 (3): 230–40.

Bosley, Sarah, and Bradford Mills. 1999. "How Welfare Reform Impacts Non-Metropolitan and Metropolitan Counties in Virginia." Virginia Cooperative Extension Publication 448-244/REAP R046, September, Rural Economic Analysis Program, Virginia Polytechnic Institute and State University, Blacksburg, Va. Available at: http://www.reap.vt.edu/publications/reports/r46.pdf.

Botes, Lucius, and Dingie van Rensburg. 2000. "Community Participation in Development: Nine Plagues and Twelve Commandments." *Community Development Journal* 35 (1): 41–58.

Bourdieu, Pierre. 1986. "The Forms of Capital." In *Handbook of Theory and Research for the Sociology of Education,* ed. J. G. Richardson, 241–58. New York: Greenwood Press.

Bradley, Karen. 2000. "Making Space for Church Life at the Rural-Urban Crossroads." Presented at the Annual Meeting of the Association for the Sociology of Religion, "Religion and Global Civil Society," August. Washington, D.C.

Bradshaw, Ted K. 2000. "Complex Community Development Projects: Collaboration, Comprehensive Programs, and Community Coalitions in Complex Society." *Community Development Journal* 35 (2): 133–45.

Bradshaw, Ted K., and Edward J. Blakely. 1979. *Rural Communities in Advanced Industrial Society: Development and Developers.* New York: Praeger Publishers.

Brady, Henry E., Mary H. Sprague, Fredric C. Gey, and Michael Wiseman. 2000. "The Interaction of Welfare-Use and Employment Dynamics in Rural and Agricultural California Counties." Presented at Rural Dimensions of Welfare Reform: A Research Conference on Poverty, Welfare, and Food Assistance, May 4–5. Washington, D.C. JCPR Working Paper 201, July 31, Joint Center for Poverty Research, Northwestern University and University of

Chicago, Evanston, Ill. Available at: http://www.jcpr.org/wp/wpdownload.
cfm?pdflink=wpfiles/brady_gey_sprague.pdf.

Bramlett, Matthew D., and William D. Mosher. 2001. "First Marriage Dissolution, Divorce, and Remarriage: United States." Advance Data from Vital
and Health Statistics 323, May 31, National Center for Health Statistics,
Hyattsville, Md. Available at: http://www.cdc.gov/nchs/data/ad/ad323/pdf.

Brandenburg, Andrea M., and Matthew S. Carroll. 1995. "Your Place or Mine?:
The Effect of Place Creation on Environmental Values and Landscape
Meanings." Society and Natural Resources 8 (5): 381–98.

Braun, Bonnie, Frances C. Lawrence, Patricia H. Dyk, and Maria Vandergriff-
Avery. 2002. "Southern Rural Family Economic Well-Being in the Context
of Public Assistance." Southern Rural Sociology 18 (1): 259–93.

Braverman, Harry. 1974. Labor and Monopoly Capital: The Degradation of
Work in the Twentieth Century. New York: Monthly Review Press.

Bridger, Jeffrey C., and A. E. Luloff. 1999. "Toward an Interactional Approach to
Sustainable Community Development." Journal of Rural Studies 15 (4):
377–87.

———. 2001. "Building the Sustainable Community: Is Social Capital the
Answer?" Sociological Inquiry 71 (4): 458–72.

Bronfenbrenner, Urie. 1992. "Principles for the Healthy Growth and Development
of Children." In Marriage and Family in a Changing Society, 4th ed., ed.
J. M. Henslin, 243–49. New York: The Free Press.

Brown, Adell, Ralph D. Christy, and Tesfa G. Gebremedhin. 1995. "Structural
Changes in U.S. Agriculture: Implications for African-American Farmers."
In Blacks in Rural America, ed. J. B. Stewart and J. E. Allen-Smith, 45–65.
New Brunswick, N.J.: Transaction Publishers.

Brown, Anita C., Gene H. Brody, and Zolinga Stoneman. 2000. "Rural Black
Women and Depression." Journal of Marriage and the Family 62 (1): 187–98.

Brown, David L. 2002. "Migration and Community: Social Networks in a Multi-
level World." Rural Sociology 67(1): 1–23.

Brown, David L., and John B. Cromartie. 2003. "The Nature of Rurality in Postin-
dustrial Society." In New Forms of Urbanization: Beyond the Urban-Rural
Dichotomy, ed. Tony Champion and Graeme Hugo. Aldershot: Ashgate.

Brown, David L., Donald R. Field, and James J. Zuiches. 1993. The Demography
of Rural Life. University Park, Pa.: Northeast Regional Center for Rural
Development.

Brown, David L., Glenn V. Fuguitt, Tim B. Heaton, and Saba Waseem. 1997.
"Continuities in Size of Place Preferences in the United States, 1972–1992."
Rural Sociology 62 (4): 408–28.

Brown, David L., and Thomas A. Hirschl. 1995. "Household Poverty in Rural and
Metropolitan-Core Areas of the United States." Rural Sociology 60 (1): 44–66.

Brown, David L., and Marlene A. Lee. 1999. "Persisting Inequality Between Metropolitan and Nonmetropolitan America: Implications for Theory and Policy." In A Nation Divided: Diversity, Inequality, and Community in
American Society, ed. Phyllis Moen, Donna Demster-McClain, and Henry
Walker, 151–67. Ithaca: Cornell University Press.

Brown, David L., and Laszlo Kulcsar. 2001. "Household Economic Behavior in
Post-Socialist Rural Hungary." Rural Sociology 66 (2): 157–80.

Brown, David L., and John M. Wardwell. 1980. *New Directions in Urban-Rural Migration: The Population Turnaround in Rural America.* New York: Academic Press.

Brown, David L., and Mildred E. Warner. 1991. "Persistent Low-Income Nonmetropolitan Areas in the United States: Some Conceptual Challenges for Development Policy." *Policy Studies Journal* 19 (2): 22–41.

Brown, H. James, Robyn S. Phillips, and Neal A. Roberts. 1981. "Land Markets at the Urban Fringe: New Insights for Policy Makers." *Journal of the American Planning Association* 47 (2): 131–44.

Brown, Ralph B., H. Reed Geertsen, and Richard S. Krannich. 1989. "Community Satisfaction and Social Integration in a Boomtown: A Longitudinal Analysis." *Rural Sociology* 54 (4): 568–86.

Brown, Ralph B., Xia Xu, and John F. Toth Jr. 1998. "Lifestyle Options and Economic Strategies: Subsistence Activities in the Mississippi Delta." *Rural Sociology* 63 (4): 599–623.

Browne, William P. 2001. *The Failure of National Rural Policy: Institutions and Interests.* Washington, D.C.: Georgetown University Press.

Bryson, Ken. 1997. "America's Children at Risk." Census Brief 97-2, U.S. Bureau of the Census. Washington, D.C.

Buckley, Barbara A. 1997. "High School Dropout Rates and Social Capital Influences in Missouri's School Districts." M.S. Thesis, Department of Sociology, Iowa State University.

Buehler, David A., Timothy J. Mersmann, James D. Fraser, and Janis K. D. Seegar. 1991. "Effects of Human Activity on Bald Eagle Distribution on the Northern Chesapeake Bay." *Journal of Wildlife Management* 55 (2): 282–90.

Bukovac, Jill K. 1999. "Town Government's Role in Explaining the Spatial Variation of the Rate of Farmland Loss: Dane County, Wisconsin." M.S. Thesis, Institute for Environmental Studies, University of Wisconsin.

Bultena, Gordon L. 1969. "Rural-Urban Differences in the Familial Interaction of the Aged." *Rural Sociology* 34 (1): 5–15.

Bumpass, Larry, and Hsien-Hen Lu. 2000. "Trends in Cohabitation and Implications for Children's Family Contexts in the U.S." *Population Studies* 54 (1): 29–41.

Burchell, Robert W., and Naveed A. Shad. 1999. "A National Perspective on Land Use Policy Alternatives and Consequences at the Rural-Urban Fringe." In *Increasing Understanding of Public Problems and Policies: Proceedings of the 1998 National Public Policy Education Conference,* September 20–23, 1998, Clackamas, Or., ed. D. P. Ernstes and D. M. Hicks, 13–33. Oak Brook, Ill.: Farm Foundation.

Burchell, Robert W., Naveed A. Shad, David Listokin, Hilary Phillips, Anthony Downs, Samuel Seskin, Judy S. Davis, Terry Moore, David Helton, and Michelle Gall. 1998. "The Costs of Sprawl—Revisited." Transportation Cooperative Research Program Report 39, Transportation Research Board, National Research Council. National Academy Press. Washington, D.C.

Burkart, Gary. 1997. "Religion." In *Encyclopedia of Rural America: The Land and People,* vol. 2, ed. G. A. Goreham, 605–10. Santa Barbara: ABC-CLIO.

Buttel, Frederick H. 1992. "Environmentalization: Origins, Processes, and Implications for Rural Social Change." *Rural Sociology* 57 (1): 1–27.

Buttel, Frederick H., and Jessica R. Goldberger. 2002. "Gender and Agricultural Science: Evidence from Two Surveys of Land-Grant Scientists." *Rural Sociology* 67 (1): 24–45.

Campbell, Rex R., John C. Spencer, and Ravindra G. Amonkra. 1993. "The Reported and Unreported Missouri Ozarks: Adaptive Strategies of the People Left Behind." In *Forgotten Places: Uneven Development in Rural America*, ed. T. A. Lyson and W. W. Falk, 30–52. Lawrence: University Press of Kansas.

Campfens, Hubert. 1997. *Community Development Around the World: Practice, Theory, Research, and Training*. Toronto: University of Toronto Press.

Canan, Penelope, and Michael Hennessy. 1989. "The Growth Machine, Tourism, and the Selling of Culture." *Sociological Perspectives* 32 (2): 227–43.

Canby, William C. 1988. *American Indian Law in a Nutshell*. St. Paul: West Publishing.

Cancian, Maria, Robert Haveman, Thomas Kaplan, and Barbara Wolfe. 1999. "Post-Exit Earnings and Benefit Receipt among Those Who Left AFDC in Wisconsin." Special Report 75, January, Institute for Research on Poverty, University of Wisconsin, Madison. Available at: http://www.ssc.wisc.edu/irp/sr/sr75.pdf.

Carlson, Virginia L., and Joseph J. Persky. 1999. "Gender and Suburban Wages." *Economic Geography* 75 (3): 237–53.

Carnoy, Martin, Maneul Castells, Stephen S. Cohen, and Fernando H. Cardoso. 1993. *The New Global Economy in the Information Age: Reflections on Our Changing World*. University Park: Pennsylvania State University Press.

Carroll, Matthew S. 1995. *Community and the Northwestern Logger: Continuities and Changes in the Era of the Spotted Owl*. Boulder, Co.: Westview Press.

Carstensen, Fred, William Lott, Stan McMillen, Bobur Alimov, Na Li Dawson, and Tapas Ray. 2000. *The Economic Impact of the Mashantucket Pequot Tribal Nation Operations on Connecticut*. Storrs: Connecticut Center for Economic Analysis, University of Connecticut.

Carter, Carolyn S. 1999. "Education and Development in Poor Rural Communities: An Interdisciplinary Research Agenda." ERIC Clearinghouse on Rural Education and Small Schools, EDO-RC-99-9, December. Available at: http://www.ael.org/eric/digests/edorc999.htm.

Cary, Lee J. 1970. *Community Development as a Process*. Columbia: University of Missouri Press.

Castle, Emery N. 1995. *The Changing American Countryside: Rural People and Places*. Lawrence: University Press of Kansas.

Catholic Conference of Illinois. 2001. "A Catholic Perspective on Rural Life in Illinois." Bishop Statements, Spring, National Catholic Rural Life Conference, Des Moines, Iowa.

Caudill, Harry M. 1963. *Night Comes to the Cumberlands: A Biography of a Depressed Area*. Boston: Little, Brown and Co.

Chase, Lisa C., and Daniel J. Decker. 1998. "Citizen Attitudes Toward Elk and Participation in Elk Management: A Case Study in Evergreen, Colorado." *Human Dimensions of Wildlife* 3 (4): 55–56.

Chaskin, Robert J., Prudence Brown, Sudhir Venkatesh, and Avis Vidal. 2001. *Building Community Capacity*. New York: Aldine de Gruyter.

Chevan, Albert, and J. Henry Korson. 1972. "The Widowed Who Live Alone: An Examination of Social and Demographic Factors." *Social Forces* 51 (1): 45–53.

Choy, Susan P. 2001. "Students Whose Parents Did Not Go to College: Postsecondary Access, Persistence, and Attainment." In *The Condition of Education, 2001,* NCES 2001-072, ed. the National Center for Education Statistics, U.S. Department of Education, xviii–xliii. Washington, D.C.: U.S. Government Printing Office.

Christaller, Walter. 1966. *Central Places in Southern Germany.* Trans. C. W. Baskin. Englewood Cliffs, N.J.: Prentice-Hall.

Christenson, James A., and Jerry W. Robinson Jr. 1989. *Community Development in Perspective.* Ames: Iowa State University Press.

Cilliers, Paul. 1998. *Complexity and Postmodernism: Understanding Complex Systems.* New York: Routledge.

Citro, Constance F., and Robert T. Michael. 1995. *Measuring Poverty: A New Approach.* Washington, D.C.: National Academy Press.

Clarke, Susan E., and Gary L. Gaile. 1999. "The Next Wave: Postfederal Local Economic Development Strategies." In *Approaches to Economic Development: Readings from Economic Development Quarterly,* ed. J. P. Blair and L. A. Reese, 165–77. Thousand Oaks, Ca.: Sage Publications.

Claude, Lumane P. 1995. "Community Activeness, Success, and Well-Being: A Comparative Case Study of Four Pennsylvania Rural Communities." Ph.D. dissertation, Department of Agricultural Economics and Rural Sociology, Pennsylvania State University.

Claude, Lumane P., Jeffrey C. Bridger, and A. E. Luloff. 2000. "Community Well-Being and Local Activeness." In *Small Town and Rural Economic Development: A Case Studies Approach,* ed. P. V. Schaeffer and S. Loveridge, 39–45. Westport, Conn.: Praeger Publishers.

Clemente, Frank, and Gene F. Summers. 1975. "The Journey to Work of Rural Industrial Employees." *Social Forces* 54 (1): 212–19.

Climo, Jacob. 1992. *Distant Parents.* New Brunswick: Rutgers University Press.

Cobb, Robert A., Walter G. McIntire, and Phillip A. Pratt. 1989. "Vocational and Educational Aspirations of High School Students: A Problem for Rural America." *Research in Rural Education* 6 (2): 11–16.

Cochrane, Willard W. 1979. *The Development of American Agriculture: A Historical Analysis.* Minneapolis: University of Minnesota Press.

Cockerham, William C., and Audie L. Blevins Jr. 1977. "Attitudes Toward Land-Use Planning and Controlled Population Growth in Jackson Hole." *Journal of the Community Development Society* 8 (1): 62–73.

Coffey, W. J. 1990. "Comprehensive Bases for Locally Induced Development." In *Alternative Perspectives on Development: Prospectives for Rural Areas, AAEA Meetings,* ed. D. Otto and S. C. Deller, 51–78. Vancouver, British Columbia.

Coggins, George C., Charles F. Wilkinson, and John D. Leshy. 1993. *Federal Public Land and Resources Law.* Third Edition. Westbury, N.Y.: Foundation Press.

Cohen, Felix S. 1942. *Handbook of Federal Indian Law.* Washington, D.C.: U.S. Government Printing Office.

Colclough, Glenna. 1988. "Uneven Development and Racial Composition in the Deep South: 1970–1980." *Rural Sociology* 53 (1): 73–86.

Coleman, James S. 1988. "Social Capital in the Creation of Human Capital." *American Journal of Sociology* 94 (Supplement): S95–S120.

———. 1990a. *Equality and Achievement in Education.* Boulder, Co.: Westview Press.

———. 1990b. *Foundations of Social Theory.* Cambridge, Mass.: Belknap Press.

Coleman, James S., Ernest Q. Campbell, Carol J. Hobson, James McPartland, Alexander M. Mood, Frederic D. Weinfeld, and Robert L. York. 1966. *Equality of Educational Opportunity.* Washington, D.C.: U.S. Government Printing Office.

Coleman, James S., and Thomas Hoffer. 1987. *Public and Private High Schools: The Impact of Communities.* New York: Basic Books.

Comer, John, and Keith Mueller. 1992. "Correlates of Health Insurance Coverage: Evidence from the Midwest." *Journal of Health Care for the Poor and Underserved* 3 (2): 305–20.

Conlan, Timothy J. 1998. *From New Federalism to Devolution: Twenty-Five Years of Intergovernmental Reform.* Washington, D.C.: Brookings Institution Press.

Constance, Douglas H., and Alessandro Bonanno. 1999. "CAFO Controversy in the Texas Panhandle Region: The Environmental Crisis of Hog Production." *Culture and Agriculture* 21 (1): 14–26.

Constance, Douglas H., Alessandro Bonanno, Caron Cates, Daniel L. Argo, and Mirenda Harris. 2003a. "Resisting Integration in the Global Agro-Food System: Corporate Chickens and Community Controversy in Texas." In *Globalisation, Localisation and Sustainable Livelihoods,* ed. R. Almås and G. Lawrence. London: Ashgate Publishing.

Constance, Douglas H., Anna M. Kleiner, and J. Sanford Rikoon. 2003b. "The Contested Terrain of Swine Production: Deregulation and Reregulation of Corporate Farming Laws in Missouri." In *Fighting for the Farm: Rural America Transformed,* ed. J. Adams, 76–95. Philadelphia: University of Pennsylvania Press.

Cook, Annabel K. 1995. "Increasing Poverty in Timber-Dependent Areas in Western Washington." *Society and Natural Resources* 8 (2): 97–109.

Cook, Peggy J. 2000. "Food Stamp and Family Assistance Benefits Sharply Decline in the Post-Welfare-Reform Era." *Rural Conditions and Trends* 11 (2): 68–74.

Cook, Peggy J., and Robert M. Gibbs. 2000. "Favorable Rural Socioeconomic Conditions Persist, but Not in All Areas." *Rural Conditions and Trends* 11 (2): 4–8.

Cook, Peggy J., and Karen L. Mizer. 1994. "The Revised ERS County Typology: An Overview." Rural Development Research Report 89, December 1, Economic Research Service, U.S. Department of Agriculture. Washington, D.C.

Corcoran, Mary. 1995. "Rags to Rags: Poverty and Mobility in the United States." *Annual Review of Sociology* 21: 237–67.

Cornell, Stephen, Joseph P. Kalt, Matthew Krepps, and Jonathan Taylor. 1998. *American Indian Gaming Policy and Its Socio-Economic Effects: A Report to the National Gambling Impact Study Commission.* Cambridge, Mass.: The Economics Resource Group.

Cotter, David A., JoAnn DeFiore, Joan M. Hermsen, Brenda M. Kowalewski, and Reeve Vanneman. 1996. "Gender Inequality in Nonmetropolitan and Metropolitan Areas." *Rural Sociology* 61 (2): 272–88.

Council of Economic Advisers. 1999. "The Effects of Welfare Policy and the Economic Expansion on Welfare Caseloads: An Update." Technical Report, August 3, White House Council of Economic Advisers. Washington, D.C.

Couto, Richard A., and Catherine S. Guthrie. 1999. *Making Democracy Work Better: Mediating Structures, Social Capital, and the Democratic Prospect.* Chapel Hill: University of North Carolina Press.

Coward, Raymond T., Gary R. Lee, and Jeffrey W. Dwyer. 1993. "The Family Relations of Rural Elders." In *Aging in Rural America,* ed. C. N. Bull, 216–31. Newbury Park, Ca.: Sage Publications.

Cready, Cynthia M., Mark A. Fossett, and K. Jill Kiecolt. 1997. "Mate Availability and African American Family Structure in the U.S. Nonmetropolitan South, 1960–1990." *Journal of Marriage and the Family* 59 (1): 192–203.

Cromartie, John B. 2001. "Nonmetro Outmigration Exceeds Inmigration for the First Time in a Decade." *Rural America* 16 (2): 35–37.

Croonquist, Mary Jo, and Robert P. Brooks. 1993. "Effects of Habitat Disturbance on Bird Communities in Riparian Corridors." *Journal of Soil and Water Conservation* 48 (1): 65–70.

Cummings, Scott ,and John P. Nelson. 1999. "Kentucky Transitional Assistance Program: A Statewide and Regional Evaluation, Administrative Data Analysis." June, Center for Policy Research and Evaluation, Urban Studies Institute, University of Louisville, Louisville, Ky.

Curtis, Bruce M. 2001. "Reforming New Zealand Agriculture: The WTO Way or Farmer Control?" *International Journal of Sociology of Agriculture and Food* 9 (1): 29–42.

Dagata, Elizabeth M. 2000. "Rural Poverty Rate Declines, While Family Income Grows." *Rural Conditions and Trends* 11 (2): 62–67.

Danbom, David B. 1979. *The Resisted Revolution: Urban America and the Industrialization of Agriculture, 1900–1930.* Ames: Iowa State University Press.

Daniels, Thomas L. 1999. *When City and Country Collide: Managing Growth in the Metropolitan Fringe.* Washington, D.C.: Island Press.

———. 2000. "What To Do About Rural Sprawl." *Small Town and Rural (STaR) Newsletter,* Small Town and Rural Planning, American Planning Association, January.

Daniels, Thomas L., and Deborah Bowers. 1997. *Holding Our Ground: Protecting America's Farms and Farmland.* Washington, D.C.: Island Press.

Daniels, Thomas L., and Arthur C. Nelson. 1986. "Is Oregon's Farmland Preservation Program Working?" *Journal of the American Planning Association* 52 (1): 22–32.

Danziger, Sheldon H. 1999. *Economic Conditions and Welfare Reform.* Kalamazoo, Mich.: W. E. Upjohn Institute for Employment Research.

Dasgupta, Partha, and Ismail Serageldin. 2000. *Social Capital: A Multifaceted Perspective.* Washington, D.C.: World Bank.

DeHaan, Laura, and James E. Deal. 2001. "Effects of Economic Hardship on Rural Children and Adolescents." In *The Hidden America: Social Problems in Rural America for the Twenty-First Century,* ed. R. M. Moore III, 42–56. Selinsgrove: Susquehanna University Press.

De Janvry, Alain, David Runsten, and Elisabeth Sadoulet. 1987. "Toward a Rural Development Program for the United States: A Proposal." In *Agriculture and Beyond: Rural Economic Development,* ed. G. F. Summers, J. Bryden, K. Deavers, H. Newby, and S. Sechler, 55–93. Madison: College of Agriculture and Life Sciences, University of Wisconsin.

Deller, Steven C., David W. Marcouiller, and Gary P. Green. 1997. "Recreational Housing and Local Government Finance." *Annals of Tourism Research* 24 (3): 687–705.

Deloria, Vine, Jr. 1984. *The Nations Within: The Past and Future of American Indian Sovereignty.* New York: Pantheon Books.

———. 1985. "The Evolution of Federal Indian Policy Making." In *American Indian Policy in the Twentieth Century,* ed. V. Deloria Jr., 239–56. Norman: University of Oklahoma Press.

Dewey, John. 1934. *A Common Faith.* New Haven: Yale University Press.

Dewit, David J., Andrew V. Wister, and Thomas K. Burch. 1988. "Physical Distance and Social Contact Between Elders and their Adult Children." *Research on Aging* 10 (1): 56–80.

Dhesi, Autar S. 2000. "Social Capital and Community Development." *Community Development Journal* 35 (3): 199–214.

Diamond, Henry L., and Patrick F. Noonan. 1996. *Land Use in America.* Washington, D.C.: Island Press.

Diamond, Jared M. 1999. *Guns, Germs, and Steel: The Fates of Human Societies.* New York: W. W. Norton.

Dicken, Peter. 1998. *Global Shift: Transforming the World Economy.* New York: Guilford Press.

Dickens, William T., and Kevin Lang. 1985. "A Test of Dual Labor Market Theory." *American Economic Review* 75 (4): 792–805.

Dill, Bonnie Thornton, and Bruce B. Williams. 1992. "Race, Gender, and Poverty in the Rural South: African American Single Mothers." In *Rural Poverty in America,* ed. C. M. Duncan, 97–109. New York: Auburn House.

Dillman, Don A., and Daryl J. Hobbs. 1982. *Rural Society in the U.S.: Issues for the 1980s.* Boulder, Co.: Westview Press.

Doak, Sam C., and Jonathan Kusel. 1996. "Well-Being in Forest Dependent Communities, Part II: A Social Assessment Focus." Report 37, Sierra Nevada Ecosystem Project, Final Report to Congress, Status of the Sierra Nevada. Vol. II: *Assessments and Scientific Basis for Management Options.* Centers for Water and Wildland Resources, Davis, Ca.

Doeringer, Peter B. 1984. "Internal Labor Markets and Paternalism in Rural Areas." In *Internal Labor Markets,* ed. P. Osterman, 271–89. Cambridge: MIT Press.

Doeringer, Peter B., and Michael J. Piore. 1971. *Internal Labor Markets and Manpower Analysis.* Lexington, Mass.: Heath Lexington Books.

Doherty, William J. 1997. *The Intentional Family: Simple Rituals to Strengthen Family Ties.* New York: Avon Books.

Donnermeyer, Joseph F. 1993. "Rural Youth Usage of Alcohol, Marijuana, and Hard Drugs." *International Journal of the Addictions* 28 (3): 249–55.

Downey, Douglas B. 1995. "When Bigger Is Not Better: Family Size, Parental Resources, and Children's Educational Performance." *American Sociological Review* 60 (5): 746–61.

Drabenstott, Mark. 1999. "New Futures for Rural America: The Role for Land-Grant Universities." William Henry Latch Memorial Lecture, presented at the Annual Meeting of the National Association of State Universities and Land-Grant Colleges, November 8. San Francisco, Ca.

Drabenstott, Mark, and Tim R. Smith. 1995. "Finding Rural Success: The New Rural Economic Landscape and Its Implications." In *The Changing American Countryside: Rural People and Places,* ed. E. N. Castle, 180–96. Lawrence: University Press of Kansas.

Duany, Andres, Elizabeth Plater-Zyberk, and Jeff Speck. 2000. *Suburban Nation: The Rise of Sprawl and the Decline of the American Dream.* New York: North Point Press.

DuBois, W. E. B. 1967. *Black Reconstruction in America: An Essay Toward a History of the Part Which Black Folk Played in the Attempt to Reconstruct Democracy in America, 1860–1880.* New York: Meridian Books.

Dudley, Kathryn M. 1996. "The Problem of Community in Rural America." *Culture and Agriculture* 18 (2): 47–57.

Duffy, Patricia A., Ginger Grayson Hallmark, Joseph J. Molnar, LaToya Claxton, Conner Bailey, and Steve Mikloucich. 2002. "Food Security of Low-Income Single Parents in East Alabama: Use of Private and Public Programs in the Age of Welfare Reform." *Southern Rural Sociology* 18 (1): 48–81.

Duncan, Cynthia M. 1992. *Rural Poverty in America.* New York: Auburn House.

———. 1999. *Worlds Apart: Why Poverty Persists in Rural America.* New Haven: Yale University Press.

Duncan, Greg J., and Jeanne Brooks-Gunn. 1997. "Income Effects Across the Life Span: Integration and Interpretation." In *Consequences of Growing Up Poor,* ed. J. Brooks-Gunn and G. J. Duncan, 596–610. New York: Russell Sage Foundation.

Dunlap, Riley E. 1991. "Trends in Public Opinion Toward Environmental Issues, 1965–1990." *Society and Natural Resources* 4 (3): 285–312.

Dupree, Allen, and Wendell Primus. 2001. "Declining Share of Children Lived with Single Mothers in the Late 1990s: Substantial Differences by Race and Income." June 15, Center on Budget and Policy Priorities. Washington, D.C.

Durkheim, Émile. 1984 [1893]. *The Division of Labor in Society.* Trans. W. D. Halls. New York: The Free Press.

———. 1965 [1915]. *The Elementary Forms of the Religious Life.* Trans. J. W. Swain. New York: The Free Press.

Durst, Ron L. 1999. "Additional Farm Tax Relief Among the New Tax Measures." *Rural Conditions and Trends* 10 (1): 46–48.

Dyk, Patricia H., and Julie N. Zimmerman. 2000. "The Impacts and Outcomes of Welfare Reform across Rural and Urban Places in Kentucky." Final Report, Policy Outcome Grant, Administration for Families and Children, U.S. Department of Health and Human Services, College of Agriculture, University of Kentucky, Lexington. Available at: http://www.ca.uky.edu/SNARL/Reportfiles/ReportFrontPage.htm.

Easterlin, Richard A. 1996. "Economic and Social Implications of Demographic Patterns." In *Handbook of Aging and the Social Sciences,* 4th ed., ed. R. H. Binstock and L. K. George, 73–93. San Diego: Academic Press.

Eberhardt, Mark S., Deborah D. Ingram, Diane M. Makuc, Elsie R. Pamuk, Virginia M. Freid, Sam B. Harper, Charlotte A. Schoenborn, and Henry

Xia. 2001. *Urban and Rural Health Chartbook. Health, United States, 2001.* Hyattsville, Md.: National Center for Health Statistics.

Eccles, Jacquelynne S., and Rena D. Harold. 1993. "Parent-School Involvement During the Early Adolescent Years." *Teachers College Record* 94 (3): 568–87.

Economic Research Service (ERS). 1995. "Understanding Rural America." Agricultural Information Bulletin 710, February, Economic Research Service, U.S. Department of Agriculture. Washington, D.C.

———. 1997. "Credit in Rural America." Agricultural Economics Report 749, Rural Economy Division, Economic Research Service, U.S. Department of Agriculture. Washington, D.C.

———. 2000a. "Appendix Table 10—Poverty Rates and Family Income by Residence, 1990–98." *Rural Conditions and Trends* 11 (2): 103.

———. 2000b. "Appendix Table 9—Poverty Rates by Residence, Region, and Selected Characteristics, 1998." *Rural Conditions and Trends* 11 (2): 102.

Economist. 1999. "A Raw Deal for Commodities." *Economist* 351 (8115): 75–76.

Eddy, David M. 1991. "Clinical Decision Making: From Theory to Practice: The Individual vs. Society: Resolving the Conflict." *Journal of the American Medical Association* 265 (18): 2399–2401, 2405–6.

Edwards, Mary E., and Douglas B. Jackson-Smith. 2001. "An Innovative Approach to Cost of Community Service Studies in Wisconsin." *Journal of the Community Development Society* 32 (2): 271–89.

Edwards, Ruth W. 1992. *Drug Use in Rural American Communities.* Binghamton, N.Y.: Haworth Press.

Egan, Andrew F., and A. E. Luloff. 2000. "The Exurbanization of America's Forests: Research in Rural Social Science." *Journal of Forestry* 98 (3): 26–30.

Eisinger, Peter K. 1988. *The Rise of the Entrepreneurial State: State and Local Economic Development Policy in the United States.* Madison: University of Wisconsin Press.

———. 1999. "State Economic Development in the 1990s: Politics and Policy Learning." In *Approaches to Economic Development: Readings from Economic Development Quarterly,* ed. J. P. Blair and L. A. Reese, 178–90. Thousand Oaks, Ca.: Sage Publications.

Elder, Glen H., Jr., and Rand D. Conger. 2000. *Children of the Land: Adversity and Success at Century's End.* Chicago: University of Chicago Press.

Elder, Glen H., Jr., Rand D. Conger, E. Michael Foster, and Monika Ardelt. 1992. "Families Under Economic Pressure." *Journal of Family Issues* 13 (1): 5–37.

Elder, Glen H., Jr., Elizabeth B. Robertson, and E. Michael Foster. 1994. "Survival, Loss, and Adaptation: A Perspective on Farm Families." In *Families in Troubled Times: Adapting to Change in Rural America,* ed. R. D. Conger and G. H. Elder Jr., 105–26. New York: Aldine de Gruyter.

Elkind, David. 1994. "Young Children in the Postmodern World." In *Resources for Early Childhood: A Handbook,* ed. H. Nuba, M. Searson, and D. L. Sheiman, 449–54. New York: Garland Publishing.

Elo, Irma T., and Calvin L. Beale. 1984. *Rural Development, Poverty, and Natural Resources: An Overview.* Washington, D.C.: Resources for the Future.

Emery, Mary E. 1994. "Leadership Needs in Idaho: Competing Paradigms or Confronting Community Hierarchies: A Report from the Idaho Rural Development Council's Leadership Project." Presented at the Annual Meeting of the Community Development Society, July. Lincoln, Nebraska.

English, Donald B. K., David W. Marcouiller, and H. Ken Cordell. 2000. "Tourism Dependence in Rural America: Estimates and Effects." *Society and Natural Resources* 13 (3): 185–202.

Epstein, Joyce L. 1995. "School/Family/Community Partnerships: Caring for the Children We Share." *Phi Delta Kappan* 76 (9): 701–12.

Erickson, Rodney A. 1981. "Corporations, Branch Plants, and Employment Stability in Nonmetropolitan America." In *Industrial Location and Regional Systems: Spatial Organization in the Economic Sector,* ed. J. Rees, G. J. D. Hewings, and H. A. Stafford, 135–53. Brooklyn: J.F. Bergin Publishers.

Eschbach, Karl. 1993. "Changing Identification Among American Indians and Alaska Natives." *Demography* 30 (4): 635–52.

———. "The Enduring and Vanishing American Indian: American Indian Population Growth and Intermarriage in 1990." *Ethnic and Racial Studies* 18 (1): 89–108.

Esman, Milton J., and Norman T. Uphoff. 1984. *Local Organizations: Intermediaries in Rural Development.* Ithaca: Cornell University Press.

Esping-Andersen, Gøsta. 1990. *The Three Worlds of Welfare Capitalism.* Princeton: Princeton University Press.

Evangelical Lutheran Church in America. 2001. "Rural Congregations." ELCA Education and Evangelism Team, Chicago. Available at: http://www.elca.org/eteam/resources/RuralCngrsLocations.htm.

Evans, Robert G., Morris L. Barer, and Theodore R. Marmor. 1994. *Why Are Some People Healthy and Others Not? The Determinants of Health of Populations.* New York: Aldine de Gruyter.

Evans, William P., Carla Fitzgerald, Dan Weigel, and Sarah Chvilicek. 1999. "Are Rural Gang Members Similar To Their Urban Peers? Implications for Rural Communities." *Youth & Society* 30 (3): 267–82.

Fahs, Pamela S. Stewart, Blenda E. Smith, A. Serdar Atav, Mary X. Britten, Mary S. Collins, Lindsay C. Lake Morgan, and Gale A. Spencer. 1999. "Integrative Research Review of Risk Behaviors Among Adolescents in Rural, Suburban, and Urban Areas." *Journal of Adolescent Health* 24 (4): 230–43.

Falk, William W., Larry R. Hunt, and Matthew O. Hunt. 2002. "Coming 'Home'?: The Return Migration of African-Americans to the 'New South.'" Unpublished manuscript. Department of Sociology, University of Maryland, College Park.

Falk, William W., and Thomas A. Lyson. 1988. *High Tech, Low Tech, No Tech: Recent Industrial and Occupational Change in the South.* Albany: SUNY Press.

———. 1993. "Forgotten Places Redux." In *Forgotten Places: Uneven Development in Rural America,* ed. Thomas A. Lyson and William A. Falk, 257–69. Lawrence: University Press of Kansas.

Falk, William W., Michael D. Schulman, and Ann R. Tickamyer. 2003. *Communities of Work: Rural Restructuring in Local and Global Perspective.* Athens: Ohio University Press.

Feiock, Richard C. 1991. "The Effects of Economic Development Policy on Local Economic Growth." *American Journal of Political Science* 35 (3): 643–55.

Feldman, Shelley, and Rick Welsh. 1995. "Feminist Knowledge Claims, Local Knowledge, and Gender Divisions of Agricultural Labor: Constructing a Successor Science." *Rural Sociology* 60 (1): 23–43.

Felton, Gwen M., Mary Ann Parsons, Russell R. Pate, Dianne Ward, Ruth Saunders, Robert Valois, Marsha Dowda, and Stewart Trost. 1996. "Predictors of Alcohol Use Among Rural Adolescents." *Journal of Rural Health* 12 (5): 378–85.

Ferguson, Miguel, Dennis Poole, Diana DiNitto, and A. James Schwab. 2002. "Raising a Flag of Caution in the Race for Community-Based Approaches to Rural Welfare Reform: Early Findings from Texas." *Southern Rural Sociology* 18 (1): 204–11.

Fields, Jason M., and Kristen E. Smith. 1998. "Poverty, Family Structure, and Child Well-Being: Indicators from the SIPP." Population Division Working Paper 23, April, Population Division, U.S. Bureau of the Census. Washington, D.C.

Fields, Jason, and Lynne M. Casper. 2001. "America's Families and Living Arrangements: March 2000." Current Population Reports, P20-537, June, U.S. Census Bureau. Washington, D.C.

Findeis, Jill L., Leif Jensen, and Qiuyan Wang. 2000. "Underemployment Prevalence and Transitions in the U.S. Nonmetropolitan South." *Southern Rural Sociology* 16: 122–44.

Fink, Deborah. 1986. *Open Country, Iowa: Rural Women, Tradition, and Change.* Albany: SUNY Press.

Fitchen, Janet M. 1981. *Poverty in Rural America: A Case Study.* Boulder, Co.: Westview Press.

———. 1991. *Endangered Spaces, Enduring Places: Change, Identity, and Survival in Rural America.* Boulder, Co.: Westview Press.

———. 1992. "On the Edge of Homelessness: Rural Poverty and Housing Insecurity." *Rural Sociology* 57 (2): 173–93.

———. 1995. "Spatial Redistribution of Poverty through Migration of Poor People to Depressed Rural Communities." *Rural Sociology* 60 (1): 181–201.

Fitzgerald, Randall. 1993. "When a Law Goes Haywire." *Reader's Digest* 143 (September): 49–53.

Fixico, Donald L. 1986. *Termination and Relocation: Federal Indian Policy, 1945–1960.* Albuquerque: University of New Mexico Press.

Fleischmann, Arnold, and Gary P. Green. 1991. "Organizing Local Agencies to Promote Economic Development." *American Review of Public Administration* 21 (1): 1–15.

Fletcher, Cynthia N., Jan L. Flora, Barbara J. Gaddis, Mary Winter, and Jacquelyn S. Litt. 2000. "Small Towns and Welfare Reform: Iowa Case Studies of Families and Communities." Presented at Rural Dimensions of Welfare Reform: A Research Conference on Poverty, Welfare, and Food Assistance, May 4–5. Washington, D.C. JCPR Working Paper 190, June 26, Joint Center for Poverty Research, Northwestern University and University of Chicago, Evanston, Ill. Available at: http://www.jcpr.org/wp/wpdownload.cfm?pdflink=wpfiles/Fletcher.pdf.

Fletcher, Cynthia N., and Helen H. Jensen. 2000. "Transportation Needs and Welfare Reform in Rural Iowa: A Case Study." *Consumer Interests Annual* 46: 30–36.

Flora, Cornelia B. 1976. *Pentecostalism in Colombia: Baptism by Fire and Spirit.* Cranbury, N.J.: Associated University Presses.

Flora, Cornelia B., and James A. Christenson. 1991. *Rural Policies for the 1990s.* Boulder, Co.: Westview Press.

Flora, Cornelia B., and Jan L. Flora. 1993. "Entrepreneurial Social Infrastructure: A Necessary Ingredient." *Annals of the American Academy of Political and Social Science* 529 (September): 48–58.

———. 1996. "Creating Social Capital." In *Rooted in the Land: Essays on Community and Place,* ed. V. W. Vitek and W. Jackson, 217–25. New Haven: Yale University Press.

Flora, Cornelia B., Jan L. Flora, Gary P. Green, and Frederick E. Schmidt. 1991. "Rural Economic Development Through Local Self-Development Strategies." *Agriculture and Human Values* 8 (3): 19–24.

Flora, Cornelia B., Michael Kinsley, Vicki Luther, Milan Wall, Susan Odell, Shanna Ratner, and Janet Topolsky. 1999. "Measuring Community Success and Sustainability: An Interactive Workbook." RRD 180, North Central Regional Center for Rural Development, Ames, Iowa. Available at: http://www.ncrcrd.iastate.edu/Community_Success/about.html.

Flora, Cornelia B., and Vicki Luther. 2000. "An Introduction to Building Community Capacity." In *Small Town and Rural Economic Development: A Case Studies Approach,* ed. P. V. Schaeffer and S. Loveridge, 1–3. Westport, Conn.: Praeger Publishers.

Flora, Jan L. 1998. "Social Capital and Communities of Place." *Rural Sociology* 63 (4): 481–506.

Flora, Jan L., Edward Gale, Frederick E. Schmidt, Gary P. Green, and Cornelia B. Flora. 1993. "From the Grassroots: Case Studies of Eight Rural Self-Development Efforts." Staff Report AGES 9313, Agriculture and Rural Economy Division, Economic Research Service, U.S. Department of Agriculture. Washington, D.C.

Flora, Jan L., Jeff Sharp, Cornelia B. Flora, and Bonnie Newlon. 1997. "Entrepreneurial Social Infrastructure and Locally-Initiated Economic Development in the Nonmetropolitan United States." *Sociological Quarterly* 38 (4): 623–45.

Flores, Dan. 1991. "Bison Ecology and Bison Diplomacy: The Southern Plains from 1800 to 1850." *Journal of American History* 78 (2): 465–85.

Florida, Richard. 1995. "Toward the Learning Region." *Futures* 27 (5): 527–36.

Forbes, Douglas, W. Parker Frisbie, Robert A. Hummer, Starling G. Pullum, and Samuel Echevarria. 2000. "A Comparison of Hispanic and Anglo Compromised Birth Outcomes and Cause-Specific Infant Mortality in the United States, 1989–1991." *Social Science Quarterly* 81 (1): 439–58.

Forcinelli, Joseph. 1990. *The Democratization of Religion in America: A Commonwealth of Religious Freedom by Design.* Lewiston, N.Y.: E. Mellen Press.

Fortmann, Louise, and Jonathan Kusel. 1990. "New Voices, Old Beliefs: Forest Environmentalism Among New and Long-Standing Rural Residents." *Rural Sociology* 55 (2): 214–32.

Fosset, Mark A., M. Therese Seibert, and Cynthia M. Cready. 1998. "Ecological and Structural Determinants of Declining Labor Force Participation of African-American Men: Evidence from Southern Nonmetropolitan Labor Markets, 1940–1980." In *Continuities in Sociological Human Ecology,* ed. M. Micklin and D. L. Poston Jr., 317–44. New York: Plenum Press.

Foster-Fishman, Pennie G., Shelby L. Berkowitz, David W. Lounsbury, Stephanie Jacobson, and Nicole A. Allen. 2001. "Building Collaborative Capacity in

Community Coalitions: A Review and Integrative Framework." *American Journal of Community Psychology* 29 (2): 241–61.

Fox, William F., Mark Boyer, Vickie C. Cunningham, and Betty B. Vickers. 1998. "Families First 1997 Case Characteristics Study." June, Center for Business and Economic Research, College of Business Administration, University of Tennessee-Knoxville. Available at: http://cber.bus.utk.edu/tdhs/ccs1997/ccs1997.htm.

Frank, Andre G. 1979. *Dependent Accumulation and Underdevelopment.* New York: Monthly Review Press.

Frenzen, Paul D. 1997. "Births to Unmarried Mothers Are Rising Faster in Rural Areas." *Rural Conditions and Trends* 8 (2): 66–69.

Freudenburg, William R. 1986. "The Density of Acquaintanceship: An Overlooked Variable in Community Research?" *American Journal of Sociology* 92 (1): 27–63.

———. 1992. "Addictive Economies: Extractive Industries and Vulnerable Localities in a Changing World Economy." *Rural Sociology* 57 (3): 305–32.

Freudenburg, William R., and Robert Gramling. 1992. "Community Impacts of Technological Change: Toward a Longitudinal Perspective." *Social Forces* 70 (4): 937–55.

Frey, William H. 1987. "Migration and Depopulation of the Metropolis: Regional Restructuring or Rural Renaissance?" *American Sociological Review* 52 (2): 240–57.

———. 1996. "Immigration, Domestic Migration, and Demographic Balkanization in America: New Evidence for the 1990s." *Population and Development Review* 22 (4): 741–63.

Frey, William H., and Kenneth M. Johnson. 1998. "Concentrated Immigration, Restructuring, and the 'Selective' Deconcentration of the U.S. Population." In *Migration into Rural Areas: Theories and Issues,* ed. P. J. Boyle and K. H. Halfacree, 79–106. Chichester, UK: John Wiley and Sons, Ltd.

Friedkin, Noah E., and Juan Necochea. 1988. "School System Size and Performance: A Contingency Perspective." *Educational Evaluation and Policy Analysis* 10 (3): 237–49.

Friedland, William H. 1994. "The New Globalization: The Case of Fresh Produce." In *From Columbus to ConAgra: The Globalization of Agriculture and Food,* ed. A. Bonanno, L. Busch, W. H. Friedland, L. Gouveia, and E. Mingione, 210–31. Lawrence: University Press of Kansas.

Friedman, Samantha, and Daniel T. Lichter. 1998. "Spatial Inequality and Poverty Among American Children." *Population Research and Policy Review* 17 (2): 91–109.

Friedman, Thomas L. 2000. *The Lexus and the Olive Tree.* New York: Anchor Books.

Fritz, Richard G. 1982. "Tourism, Vacation Home Development, and Residential Tax Burden: A Case Study of the Local Finances of 240 Vermont Towns." *American Journal of Economics and Sociology* 41 (4): 375–85.

Fuguitt, Glenn V. 1985. "The Nonmetropolitan Population Turnaround." *Annual Review of Sociology* 11: 259–80.

———. 1991. "Commuting and the Rural-Urban Hierarchy." *Journal of Rural Studies* 7 (4): 459–66.

Fuguitt, Glenn V., and Calvin L. Beale. 1996. "Recent Trends in Nonmetropolitan Migration: Toward a New Turnaround?" *Growth and Change* 27 (2): 156–74.

Fuguitt, Glenn V., David L. Brown, and Calvin L. Beale. 1989. *Rural and Small Town America: The Population of the United States in the 1980s.* New York: Russell Sage Foundation.

Fuguitt, Glenn V., Richard M. Gibson, Calvin L. Beale, and Stephen J. Tordella. 1998. "Elderly Population Change in Nonmetropolitan Areas: From the Turnaround to the Rebound." Presented at the 37th Annual Meeting of the Western Regional Science Association, February 18–22. Monterey, Ca.

Fuguitt, Glenn V., and Timothy B. Heaton. 1995. "The Impact of Migration on the Nonmetropolitan Population Age Structure, 1960–1990." *Population Research and Policy Review* 14 (2): 215–32.

Fukuyama, Francis. 1995. *Trust: The Social Virtues and the Creation of Prosperity.* New York: The Free Press.

Furstenberg, Frank F., Jr. 1993. "How Families Manage Risk and Opportunity in Dangerous Neighborhoods." In *Sociology and the Public Agenda,* ed. W. J. Wilson, 231–58. Newbury Park, Ca.: Sage Publications.

Gale, Fred, and David McGranahan. 2001. "Latest Trends in Nonmetro Jobs and Earnings: Nonmetro Areas Fall Behind in the 'New Economy.'" *Rural America* 16 (1): 44–52.

Galea, Sandro, Adam Karpati, and Bruce Kennedy. 2002. "Social Capital and Violence in the United States, 1974–1993." *Social Science and Medicine* 55 (8): 1373–83.

Gallagher, L. Jerome, Megan Gallagher, Kevin Perese, Susan Schreiber, and Keith Watson. 1998. "One Year After Federal Welfare Reform: A Description of State Temporary Assistance for Needy Families (TANF) Decisions as of October 1997." May, The Urban Institute. Washington, D.C. Available at: http://newfederalism.urban.org/pdf/tanf2.pdf.

Galston, William A., and Karen J. Baehler. 1995. *Rural Development in the United States: Connecting Theory, Practice, and Possibilities.* Washington, D.C.: Island Press.

Garkovich, Lorraine, Janet L. Bokemeier, and Barbara Foote. 1995. *Harvest of Hope: Family Farming/Farming Families.* Lexington: University Press of Kentucky.

Garkovich, Lori. 1998. "The New Federalism: Confounding Effects of Devolution." Welfare Reform Information Brief 4, August, Southern Rural Development Center, Mississippi State University.

Gasteyer, Stephen P., Cornelia B. Flora, E. Fernandez-Baca, Damayanti Banerji, S. Bastian, S. Aleman, M. Kroma, and A. Mears. 2002. "Community Participation for Conservation and Development of Natural Resources: A Summary of Literature and Report of Research Findings." *Delta Development Journal* 1 (2): 57–75.

Gaustad, Edwin S. 1990. *A Religious History of America.* San Francisco: Harper and Row.

Gereffi, Gary. 1994. "The Organization of Buyer-Driven Global Commodity Chains: How U.S. Retailers Shape Overseas Production Networks." In

Commodity Chains and Global Capitalism, ed. G. Gereffi and M. Korze-niewicz, 95–122. Westport, Conn.: Praeger Publishers.

Ghelfi, Linda M. 2000. "Rural Nonfarm Earnings Increase in 1997, But Lag Urban Earnings Growth." *Rural Conditions and Trends* 11 (2): 51–55.

Gibbs, Robert M., and Timothy S. Parker. 2001. "Nonmetro Earnings Continue Upward Trend." *Rural America* 16 (2): 38–40.

Gibbs, Robert M., Paul L. Swaim, and Ruy Teixeira. 1998. *Rural Education and Training in the New Economy: The Myth of Rural Skills Gap.* Ames: Iowa State University Press.

Giddens, Anthony. 1990. *The Consequences of Modernity.* Stanford: Stanford University Press.

Gilbert, Jess. 2000. "Eastern Urban Liberals and Midwestern Agrarian Intellectu-als: Two Group Portraits of Progressives in the New Deal Department of Agriculture." *Agricultural History* 74 (2): 162–80.

Ginzberg, Eli. 1996. *Tomorrow's Hospital: A Look to the Twenty-First Century.* New Haven: Yale University Press.

Gittell, Ross J., and Avis Vidal. 1998. *Community Organizing: Building Social Capital as a Development Strategy.* Thousand Oaks, Ca.: Sage Publications.

Glasgow, Nina. 1980. "The Older Metropolitan Migrant as a Factor in Rural Population Growth." In *Rebirth of Rural America: Rural Migration in the Midwest,* ed. A. J. Sofranko and J. D. Williams, 153–70. Ames: North Central Regional Center for Rural Development, Iowa State University.

———. 1988. "The Nonmetro Elderly: Economic and Demographic Status." Rural Development Research Report 70, Economic Research Service, U.S. Department of Agriculture. Washington, D.C.

———. 2000. "Rural/Urban Patterns of Aging and Caregiving in the United States." *Journal of Family Issues* 21 (5): 611–31.

Glasgow, Nina, and Calvin L. Beale. 1985. "Rural Elderly in Demographic Per-spective." *Rural Development Perspectives* 2 (1): 22–26.

Glasgow, Nina, and David L. Brown. 1998. "Older, Rural, and Poor." In *Aging in Rural Settings: Life Circumstances and Distinctive Features,* ed. R. T. Cow-ard and J. A. Krout, 187–207. New York: Springer Publishing.

Glasgow, Nina, Karen Holden, Diane McLaughlin, and Graham Rowles. 1993. "The Rural Elderly and Poverty." In *Persistent Poverty in Rural America,* ed. Rural Sociological Society Task Force on Persistent Rural Poverty, 259–91. Boulder, Co.: Westview Press.

Glasgow, Nina, and Richard J. Reeder. 1990. "Economic and Fiscal Implications of Nonmetropolitan Retirement Migration." *Journal of Applied Gerontol-ogy* 9 (4): 433–51.

Glasmeier, Amy K. 1991. *The High-Tech Potential: Economic Development in Rural America.* New Brunswick, N.J.: Center for Urban Policy Research.

Glasmeier, Amy K., and Marie Howland. 1995. *From Combines to Computers: Rural Services and Development in the Age of Information Technology.* Albany: SUNY Press.

Glenna, Leland L. 2002. "Liberal Economics and the Institutionalization of Sin: Christian and Stoic Vestiges in Economic Rationalism." *Worldviews: Envi-ronment, Culture, Religion* 6 (1): 31–57.

Goe, W. Richard, Sean Noonan, and Sherry Laman. 2003. "Economic Restructur-
ing and the Growth of Missoula, MT: From Timber to the Consumption of
Services." In *Communities of Work: Economic Restructuring in Local and
Global Context,* ed. W. W. Falk, M. Schulman, and A. Tickamyer. Athens:
Ohio University Press.

Goetz, Edward G. 1994. "Expanding Possibilities in Local Development Policy:
An Examination of U.S. Cities." *Political Research Quarterly* 47 (1):
85–109.

Goetz, Stephan J., Fisseha Tegegne, Julie N. Zimmerman, David L. Debertin,
Surendra P. Singh, Safdar Muhammed, and Enefiok Ekanem. 1999. "Eco-
nomic Downturns and Welfare Reform: An Exploratory County-Level
Analysis." November 8, Southern Rural Development Center, Mississippi
State University. Available at: http://ext.msstate.edu/srdc/activities/
grantrecipt98.htm.

Goldschmidt, Walter R. 1947. *As You Sow.* Glencoe, Ill.: The Free Press.

———. 1978. *As You Sow: Three Studies in the Social Consequences of Agribusiness.* Montclair, N.J.: Allanheld, Osmun and Co.

Gonzales, Angela A. 1998. "The (Re)Articulation of American Indian Identity:
Maintaining Boundaries and Regulating Access to Ethnically Tied
Resources." *American Indian Culture and Research Journal* 22 (4): 199–225.

———. 2003. "Gaming and Displacement: Winners and Losers in American
Indian Casino Development." *International Social Science Journal* 55 (175).

Gordon, David M., Richard Edwards, and Michael Reich. 1982. *Segmented
Work, Divided Workers: The Historical Transformation of Labor in the
United States.* Cambridge: Cambridge University Press.

———. 1994. "Long Swings and Stages of Capitalism." In *Social Structures of
Accumulation: The Political Economy of Growth and Crisis,* ed.
D. M. Kotz, T. McDonough, and M. Reich, 11–28. Cambridge: Cambridge
University Press.

Gorham, Lucy S. 1993. "The Slowdown in Nonmetropolitan Development: The
Impact of Economic Forces and the Effect on the Distribution of Wages." In
*Population Change and the Future of Rural America: A Conference Pro-
ceedings,* ed. L. L. Swanson and D. L. Brown, 60–78. Staff Report AGES
9324, November, Agriculture and Rural Economy Division, Economic
Research Service, U.S. Department of Agriculture. Washington, D.C.

Graber, Edith A. 1974. "Newcomers and Oldtimers: Growth and Change in a
Mountain Town." *Rural Sociology* 39 (4): 502–13.

Graefe, Deborah Roempke, and Daniel T. Lichter. 1999. "Life Course Transitions
of American Children: Parental Cohabitation, Marriage, and Single Mother-
hood." *Demography* 36 (2): 205–17.

Graham, Garth. 2001. "Community: The Link across Digital Divides." Presented
at the Second World Conference of Citizens Networks: Renewing Communities in the Digital Era, December 5–7. Buenos Aires, Argentina.

Granovetter, Mark S. 1973. "The Strength of Weak Ties." *American Journal of
Sociology* 78 (6): 1360–80.

———. 1997. "Economic Action and Social Structure: The Problem of Embeddedness." In *Social Structures: A Network Approach,* ed. B. Wellman and
S. D. Berkowitz, 430–51. Greenwich, Conn.: JAI Press.

Grant, Don S, II. 1995. "The Political Economy of Business Failures Across the American States, 1970–1985: The Impact of Reagan's New Federalism." *American Sociological Review* 60 (6): 851–73.

Gras, Carla. 1997. "Complejos Agroindustriales y Globalización: Cambios en la Articulación del Sector Agrario." *International Journal of Sociology of Agriculture and Food* 6: 55–75.

Gray, Barbara. 1989. *Collaborating: Finding Common Ground for Multiparty Problems.* San Francisco: Jossey-Bass.

Gray, John. 1998. *False Dawn: The Delusions of Global Capitalism.* New York: New Press.

Green, Anne E. 1997. "A Question of Compromise? Case Study Evidence on the Location and Mobility Strategies of Dual Career Households." *Regional Studies* 31 (7): 641–57.

Green, Gary P. 2001. "Kenosha County Commuter Study." Report, Kenosha County Economic Development Corporation, University of Wisconsin, Madison.

Green, Gary P., and Arnold Fleischmann. 1991. "Promoting Economic Development: A Comparison of Central Cities, Suburbs, and Nonmetropolitan Communities." *Urban Affairs Quarterly* 27 (1): 145–54.

Green, Gary P., Arnold Fleischmann, and Tsz Man Kwong. 1996. "The Effectiveness of Local Economic Development Policies in the 1980s." *Social Science Quarterly* 77 (3): 609–25.

Green, Gary P., Jan L. Flora, Cornelia B. Flora, and Frederick E. Schmidt. 1990. "Local Self-Development Strategies: National Survey Results." *Journal of the Community Development Society* 21 (2): 55–73.

Green, Gary P., and Anna Haines. 2002. *Asset Building and Community Development.* Thousand Oaks, Ca.: Sage Publications.

Greenberg, Elizabeth J., and Ruy Teixeira. 1998. "Educational Achievement in Rural Schools." In *Rural Education and Training in the New Economy: The Myth of the Rural Skills Gap,* ed. R. M. Gibbs, P. L. Swaim, and R. Teixeira, 23–39. Ames: Iowa State University Press.

Gregory, Thomas B., and Gerald R. Smith. 1987. *High Schools as Communities: The Small School Reconsidered.* Bloomington, Ind.: Phi Delta Kappa Educational Foundation.

Greider, Thomas, Richard S. Krannich, and E. Helen Berry. 1991. "Local Identity, Solidarity, and Trust in Changing Rural Communities." *Sociological Focus* 24 (4): 263–82.

Gringeri, Christina E. 1994. *Getting By: Women Workers and Rural Economic Development.* Lawrence: University Press of Kansas.

Guo, Guang. 1998. "The Timing of the Influences of Cumulative Poverty on Children's Cognitive Ability and Achievement." *Social Forces* 77 (1): 257–88.

Guo, Guang, and Kathleen Mullan Harris. 2000. "The Mechanisms Mediating the Effects of Poverty on Children's Intellectual Development." *Demography* 37 (4): 431–47.

Haleman, Diana L., Matthew Sargent, Julie N. Zimmerman, and Dwight Billings. 2000. "The Impact of Welfare Reform on Kentucky's Appalachian Counties." May, Appalachian Center, University of Kentucky, Lexington. Available at: http://www.uky.edu/RGS/AppalCenter/welformreport.doc.

Hall, Kenneth B., Jr., and Gerald A. Porterfield. 2001. *Community By Design: New Urbanism for Suburbs and Small Communities.* New York: McGraw-Hill.

Hansen, Thomas D., and Walter G. McIntire. 1989. "Family Structure Variables as Predictors of Educational and Vocational Aspirations of High School Seniors." *Research in Rural Education* 6 (2): 39–49.

Hanson, Sandra M., and William J. Sauer. 1985. "Children and Their Elderly Parents." In *Social Support Networks and the Care of the Elderly: Theory, Research, and Practice,* ed. W. J. Sauer and R. T. Coward, 41–66. New York: Springer Publishing.

Hanson, Susan, and Geraldine Pratt. 1992. "Dynamic Dependencies: A Geographic Investigation of Local Labor Markets." *Economic Geography* 68 (4): 373–405.

Hareven, Tamara K. 1996. *Aging and Generational Relations Over the Life Course: A Historical and Cross-Cultural Perspective.* New York: Aldine de Gruyter.

Harl, Neil E. n.d. "Review of The End of Agriculture in the American Portfolio, by Steven C. Blank." Available at: http://www.econ.iastate.edu/faculty/harl/Book_Review.html.

Harper, Sarah. 1987. "The Kinship Network of the Rural Aged: A Comparison of the Indigenous Elderly and the Retired Inmigrant." *Aging and Society* 7 (3): 303–27.

Harrigan, John J. 1998. *Politics and Policy in States and Communities.* New York: Addison-Wesley Longman Educational Publishers.

Harris, David R. 1994. "The 1990 Census Count of American Indians: What Do the Numbers Really Mean?" *Social Science Quarterly* 75 (3): 580–93.

Harrison, Bennett. 1994. *Lean and Mean: The Changing Landscape of Corporate Power in the Age of Flexibility.* New York: Basic Books.

Harrison, Bennett, and Barry Bluestone. 1988. *The Great U-Turn: Corporate Restructuring and the Polarizing of America.* New York: Basic Books.

Harrison, Bennett, and Marcus Weiss. 1998. *Workforce Development Networks: Community-Based Organizations and Regional Alliances.* Thousand Oaks, Ca.: Sage Publications.

Harvey, David. 1989. *The Condition of Postmodernity: An Enquiry into the Origins of Cultural Change.* Oxford: Basil Blackwell.

Harvey, David L. 1993. *Potter Addition: Poverty, Family, and Kinship in a Heartland Community.* New York: Aldine de Gruyter.

Healy, Robert G., and James L. Short. 1979. "Rural Land: Market Trends and Planning Implications." *Journal of the American Planning Association* 45 (3): 305–17.

Heffernan, William D. 2000. "Concentration of Ownership and Control in Agriculture." In *Hungry for Profit: The Agribusiness Threat to Farmers, Food, and the Environment,* ed. F. Magdoff, J. B. Foster, and F. H. Buttel, 61–75. New York: Monthly Review Press.

———. 1999. "Consolidation in the Food and Agriculture System." Report to the National Farmers Union, February 5. Available at: http://nfu.org/.

Heffernan, William D., and Douglas H. Constance. 1994. "Transnational Corporations and the Globalization of the Food System." In *From Columbus to*

ConAgra: The Globalization of Agriculture and Food, ed. A. Bonanno, L. Busch, W. H. Friedland, L. Gouveia, and E. Mingione, 29–51. Lawrence: University Press of Kansas.

Heffernan, William, Mary Hendrickson, and Robert Gronski. 1999. "Consolidation in the Food and Agricultural System." Report to the National Farmer's Union, February 5, Department of Rural Sociology, University of Missouri, Columbia. Available at: http://nfu.org/images/heffernan_1999.pdf.

Heimberger, Marianne, David Euler, and Jack Barr. 1983. "The Impact of Cottage Development on Common Loon Reproductive Success in Central Ontario." *Wilson Bulletin* 95 (3): 431–39.

Heimlich, Ralph E., and William D. Anderson. 2001. "Development at the Urban Fringe and Beyond: Impacts on Agriculture and Rural Land." ERS Agricultural Economic Report 803, June, Economic Research Service, U.S. Department of Agriculture. Washington, D.C.

Heinrich, Janet, Katherine Iritani, Tim Bushfield, Leslie Spangler, and Stan Stenersen. 2001. "Emergency Medical Services: Reported Needs Are Wide-Ranging, With a Growing Focus on Lack of Data." GAO-02-28, October, U.S. General Accounting Office. Washington, D.C.

Hendryx, Michael S., Melissa M. Ahern, Nicholas P. Lovrich, and Arthur H. McCurdy. 2002. "Access to Health Care and Community Social Capital." *Health Services Research* 37 (1): 87–103.

Henly, Susan J., Elizabeth A. Tyree, Deborah L. Lindsey, Sharon O. Lambeth, and Christine M. Burd. 1998. "Innovative Perspectives on Health Services for Vulnerable Rural Populations." *Family and Community Health* 21 (1): 22–31.

Henneberry, David M., and Richard L. Barrows. 1990. "Capitalization of Exclusive Agricultural Zoning into Farmland Prices." *Land Economics* 66 (3): 249–58.

Henry, Mark S., and Willis Lewis. 2001. "Welfare Reform: Remedy for Persistent Poverty in the South?" *Rural America* 15 (1): 59–67.

Henry, Mark S., Willis Lewis, Lynn Reinschmiedt, and Darren Hudson. 2000. "Reducing Food Stamp and Welfare Caseloads in the South: Are Rural Areas Less Likely to Succeed than Urban Centers?" Presented at Rural Dimensions of Welfare Reform: A Research Conference on Poverty, Welfare, and Food Assistance, May 4–5. Washington, D.C. JCPR Working Paper 188, June 19, Joint Center for Poverty Research, Northwestern University and University of Chicago, Evanston, Ill. Available at: http://www.jcpr.org/wp/wpdownload.cfm?pdfling=wpfiles/Henry-Lewis.pdf.

Hernandez-Leon, Ruben, and Victor Zuniga. 2002. "Mexican Immigrant Communities in the South and Social Capital: The Case of Dalton, Georgia." Presented at the Latinos in the South Symposium, Sponsored by the Farm Foundation and the Southern Rural Development Center. Atlanta, Ga.

Hess, Beth B., and Beth J. Soldo. 1985. "Husband and Wife Networks." In *Social Support Networks and the Care of the Elderly: Theory, Research, and Practice,* ed. W. J. Sauer and R. T. Coward, 67–92. New York: Springer Publishing.

Hester, Randy. 1985. "Subconscious Landscapes of the Heart." *Places* 2 (3): 10–22.

Hester, Randolph T., Jr. 1990. "The Sacred Structure of Small Towns: A Return to Manteo, North Carolina." *Small Town* 20 (4): 4–21.

Hickman, Catherine W., Gordon Greenwood, and M. David Miller. 1995. "High School Parent Involvement: Relationships with Achievement, Grade Level, SES, and Gender." *Journal of Research and Development in Education* 28 (3): 125–34.

Hiebert, Theodore. 1996. *The Yahwist's Landscape: Nature and Religion in Early Israel.* New York: Oxford University Press.

Hiemstra, Hal, and Nancy Bushwick. 1989. "Plowing the Urban Fringe: An Assessment of Alternative Approaches to Farmland Preservation." Joint Center for Environmental and Urban Problems, Florida Atlantic University, Fort Lauderdale.

Hill, Michael. 2002. "Census Finds More Grandparents Assuming Primary Parental Role." *Ithaca Journal,* May 25, p. 3A.

Hines, Fred K., David L. Brown, and John M. Zimmer. 1975. "Social and Economic Characteristics of the Population in Metropolitan and Nonmetropolitan Counties, 1970." Agricultural Economic Report 272, Economic Research Service, U.S. Department of Agriculture. Washington, D.C.

Hinrichs, C. Clare. 1998. "Sideline and Lifeline: The Cultural Economy of Maple Syrup Production." *Rural Sociology* 63 (4): 507–32.

Hirschl, Thomas A., and Christine R. Long. 1993. "Dairy Farm Survival in a Metropolitan Area: Dutchess County, New York, 1984–1990." *Rural Sociology* 58 (3): 461–74.

Hiss, Tony. 1990. *The Experience of Place: A New Way of Looking at and Dealing with Our Radically Changing Cities and Countryside.* New York: Vintage Books.

Hobbs, Daryl J. 1991. "Rural Education." In *Rural Policies for the 1990s,* ed. C. B. Flora and J. A. Christenson, 151–65. Boulder, Co.: Westview Press.

Hobbs, Daryl. 1995. "Capacity Building: Reexamining the Role of the Rural School." In *Investing in People: The Human Capital Needs of Rural America,* ed. L. J. Beaulieu and D. Mulkey, 259–84. Boulder, Co.: Westview Press.

Hodson, Randy. 1983. *Worker's Earnings and Corporate Economic Structure.* New York: Academic Press.

———. 1984. "Companies, Industries, and the Measurement of Economic Segmentation." *American Sociological Review* 49 (3): 335–48.

Hoffer, Thomas, Andrew M. Greeley, and James S. Coleman. 1987. "Catholic High School Effects on Achievement Growth." In *Comparing Public and Private Schools: School Achievement,* vol. 2, ed. E. H. Haertel, T. James, and H. M. Levin, 67–88. New York: Falmer Press.

Hofferth, Sandra L., and John Iceland. 1998. "Social Capital in Rural and Urban Communities." *Rural Sociology* 63 (4): 574–98.

Hoffmeister, Heather A. 2002. "Couples' Commutes to Work Considering Workplace, Household, and Neighborhood Contexts." Ph.D. dissertation, Cornell University.

Hoppe, Robert A., James Johnson, Janet E. Perry, Penni Korb, Judith E. Sommer, James T. Ryan, Robert C. Green, Ron Durst, and James Monke. 2001. "Structural and Financial Characteristics of U.S. Farms: 2001 Family Farm

Report." ERS Agriculture Information Bulletin 768, Economic Research Service, U.S. Department of Agriculture. Washington, D.C.

Hovey, Harold A. 1989. "Analytic Approaches to State-Local Relations." In *A Decade of Devolution: Perspectives on State-Local Relations,* ed. E. B. Liner, 163–82. Washington, D.C.: Urban Institute Press.

Howe, Jim, Ed McMahon, and Luther Probst. 1997. *Balancing Nature and Commerce in Gateway Communities.* Washington, D.C.: Island Press.

Howell, Frank M. 2000. "Prospects for 'Job Matching' in the Welfare-to-Work Transition: Labor Market Capacity for Sustaining the Absorption of Mississippi's TANF Recipients." Presented at the Rural Dimensions of Welfare Reform: A Research Conference on Poverty, Welfare, and Food Assistance, May 4–5. Washington, D.C. JCPR Working Paper 202, August 14, Joint Center for Poverty Research, Northwestern University and University of Chicago. Evanston, Ill. Available at: http://www.jcpr.org/wp/wpdownload.cfm?pdflink=wpfiles/Howell_rural.pdf.

Howell, Frank M., and Deborah R. Bronson. 1996. "The Journey to Work and Gender Inequality in Earnings: A Cross-Validation Study for the United States." *Sociological Quarterly* 37 (4): 429–47.

Howley, Craig. 1995. "The Matthew Principle: A West Virginia Replication?" *Education Policy Analysis Archives* 3 (18): 1–25.

———. 2001. "The Rural School Bus Ride in Five States." The Rural School and Community Trust. Washington, D.C. Available at: http://www.rsct.org/bus.html.

Huang, Gary G. 1999. "Sociodemographic Changes: Promises and Problems for Rural Education." ERIC Digest EDO-RC-98-7, January, ERIC Clearinghouse on Rural Education and Small Schools, AEL. Charleston, W.V.

Hudson, Winthrop S., and John Corrigan. 1999. *Religion in America: An Historical Account of the Development of American Religious Life.* Upper Saddle River, N.J: Prentice Hall.

Hummon, David M. 1990. *Commonplaces: Community Ideology and Identity in American Culture.* Albany: SUNY Press.

Humphrey, Craig R. 2001. "Disarming the War of the Growth Machines: A Panel Study." *Sociological Forum* 16 (1): 99–121.

Humphrey, Craig R., Gigi Berardi, Mathew S. Carroll, Sally Fairfax, Louise Fortmann, Charles C. Geisler, Thomas G. Johnson, Jonathan Kusel, Robert G. Lee, Seth Macinko, Michael D. Schulman, and Patrick C. West. 1993. "Theories in the Study of Natural Resource-Dependent Communities and Persistent Rural Poverty in the United States." In *Persistent Poverty in Rural America,* ed. Rural Sociological Society Task Force on Persistent Rural Poverty, 136–72. Boulder, Co.: Westview Press.

Hunter, Lori M., Richard S. Krannich, and Michael D. Smith. 2002. "Rural Migration, Rapid Growth, and Fear of Crime." *Rural Sociology* 67 (1): 71–89.

Hylton, Thomas. 1995. *Save Our Land, Save Our Towns: A Plan for Pennsylvania.* Harrisburg, Pa.: RB Books.

Hyyppä, Markku T., and Juhani Mäki. 2001. "Individual-Level Relationships Between Social Capital and Self-Rated Health in a Bilingual Community." *Preventive Medicine* 32 (2): 148–55.

Ibrahim, Saad E. 1985. "Egypt's Islamic Militants." In *Arab Society: Social Science Perspectives,* ed. S. E. Ibrahim and N. S. Hopkins, 494–507. Cairo, Egypt: American University in Cairo Press.

Ikerd, John. 2001. "Twenty-First Century Agriculture: The End of the American Farm or the New American Farm?" Presented at the Conference on Partnerships for Sustaining California Agriculture: Profit, Environment, and Community, March 27–28. Woodland, Ca.

Indian Health Service. 2001. *Trends in Indian Health, 1998–1999.* Washington, D.C.: U.S. Department of Health and Human Services.

Ingels, Steven J., Leslie A. Scott, John R. Taylor, Jeffrey Owings, and Peggy Quinn. 1998. "National Education Longitudinal Study of 1998 (NELS:88) Base Year Through Second Follow-Up: Final Methodology Report." Working Paper 98-06, May, National Center for Education Statistics, U.S. Department of Education. Washington, D.C.

Innes, Judith E., and David E. Booher. 1999. "Consensus Building and Complex Adaptive Systems: A Framework for Evaluating Collaborative Planning." *Journal of the American Planning Association* 65 (4): 412–23.

Inter-University Program for Latino Research. 2001. "Population Change for the Hispanic Population from 1990 to 2000 by County, Sorted by State, Table 3.2." Notre Dame, Ind.: Inter-University Program for Latino Research. Available at: http://www.nd.edu/~iuplr/cic/4St_county.html.

Iritani, Evelyn. 2001. "U.S. Farmers' Fears Growing: Groups Are Seeking Protections Amid Concerns About a Glut of Cheap Fruits and Vegetables." *Los Angeles Times,* August 8, p. A1.

Irwin, Michael D., Troy Blanchard, Charles M. Tolbert, and Thomas A. Lyson. 2002. "Dwelling Together: Civic Community and Residential Segregation in U.S. Counties." Presented at the Annual Meeting of the Southwestern Sociological Association, March. New Orleans, La.

Irwin, Michael D., Charles M. Tolbert, and Thomas A. Lyson. 1997. "How to Build Strong Home Towns." *American Demographics* 19 (2): 42–47.

———. 1999. "There's No Place Like Home: Non-Migration and Civic Engagement." *Environment and Planning A* 31 (12): 2223–38.

Isaacs, Julia B., and Matthew R. Lyon. 2000. "A Cross-State Examination of Families Leaving Welfare: Findings from the ASPE-Funded Leavers Studies." Presented at the 40th Annual Workshop of the National Association for Welfare Research and Statistics, August 1. Scottsdale, Arizona. Available at: http://aspe.hhs.gov/hsp/leavers99/cross-state00/.

Israel, Glenn D., and Lionel J. Beaulieu. 2002. "The Influence of Social Capital on Test Scores: How Much Do Families, Schools, and Communities Matter?" Presented at the 2002 Annual Meeting of the Southern Rural Sociological Society, February 3–5. Orlando, Fla.

Israel, Glenn D., Lionel J. Beaulieu, and Glen Hartless. 2001. "The Influence of Family and Community Social Capital on Educational Achievement." *Rural Sociology* 66 (1): 43–68.

Jackson, Wes. 1980. *New Roots for Agriculture.* San Francisco: Friends of the Earth.

Jackson-Smith, Douglas B. 1995. "Understanding the Microdynamics of Farm Structural Change: Entry, Exit and Restructuring Among Wisconsin Family

Farmers in the 1980s." Ph.D. dissertation, Department of Sociology, University of Wisconsin.

Jackson-Smith, Douglas B., and Jill Bukovac. 2000. "Explaining Spatial Variation in Farmland Loss: Evidence from Wisconsin Towns Between 1990–1997." PATS Staff Paper 3, Program on Agricultural Technology Studies, University of Wisconsin.

Jacob, Steve, A. E. Luloff, and Jeffrey C. Bridger. 2001. "Rural Communities and Individual Mental Health." Unpublished manuscript.

Jarvis, T. Destry. 2000. "The Responsibility of National Parks in Rural Development." In *National Parks and Rural Development: Practice and Policy in the United States,* ed. G. E. Machlis and D. R. Field, 219–30. Washington, D.C.: Island Press.

Jehl, Douglas. 2001. "Cries of 'Save the Suckerfish' Rile Farmers' Political Allies." *New York Times,* June 20, pp. A1, A20.

Jensen, Helen H., Shao-Hsun Keng, and Steven Garasky. 2000. "Location and the Low Income Experience: Analyses of Program Dynamics in the Iowa Family Investment Program." Presented at the Rural Dimensions of Welfare Reform: A Research Conference on Poverty, Welfare, and Food Assistance, May 4–5. Washington, D.C. JCPR Working Paper 194, June 26, Joint Center for Poverty Research, Northwestern University and University of Chicago. Available at: http://www.jcpr.org/wp/wpdownload.cfm?pdflink= wpfiles/Jensen.pdf.

Jensen, Leif. 1995. "Employment Hardship and Rural Minorities: Theory, Research, and Policy." In *Blacks in Rural America,* ed. J. B. Stewart and J. E. Allen-Smith, 119–38. New Brunswick, N.J.: Transaction Publishers.

Jensen, Leif, Gretchen T. Cornwell, and Jill L. Findeis. 1995. "Informal Work in Nonmetropolitan Pennsylvania." *Rural Sociology* 60 (1): 91–107.

Jensen, Leif, and David J. Eggebeen. 1994. "Nonmetropolitan Poor Children and Reliance on Public Assistance." *Rural Sociology* 59 (1): 45–65.

Jensen, Leif, Jill L. Findeis, Wan-Ling Hsu, and Jason P. Schachter. 1999. "Slipping Into and Out of Underemployment: Another Disadvantage for Nonmetropolitan Workers?" *Rural Sociology* 64 (3): 417–38.

Jensen, Leif, Jill L. Findeis, and Qiuyan Wang. 2000. "Labor Supply and Underemployment in the Southern United States." *Southern Rural Sociology* 16: 96–124.

Jensen, Leif, and Diane K. McLaughlin. 1995. "Human Capital and Nonmetropolitan Poverty." In *Investing in People: The Human Capital Needs of Rural America,* ed. L. J. Beaulieu and D. Mulkey, 111–38. Boulder, Co.: Westview Press.

———. 1997. "The Escape from Poverty Among Rural and Urban Elders." *The Gerontologist* 37 (4): 462–68.

Jensen, Leif, and Marta Tienda. 1989. "Nonmetropolitan Minority Families in the United States: Trends in Racial and Ethnic Economic Stratification, 1959–1986." *Rural Sociology* 54 (4): 509–32.

Jobes, Patrick C. 1999. "Residential Stability and Crime in Small Rural Agricultural and Recreational Towns." *Sociological Perspectives* 42 (3): 499–524.

John, DeWitt. 1994. *Civic Environmentalism: Alternatives to Regulation in States and Communities.* Washington, D.C.: Congressional Quarterly Press.

Johnson, Kenneth M. 1993. "When Deaths Exceed Births: Natural Decrease in the United States." *International Regional Science Review* 15 (2): 179–98.

———. 1999. "The Rural Rebound." *PRB Reports on America* 1 (3): 1–20. Population Reference Bureau. Washington, D.C.

———. 2000. "Migration to Rural America: Historical Trends and Future Prospects." Presented at the NASA Land Use Land Cover Change Program Conference on Changing Landscapes of Rural America, September 22–24. Yellowstone National Park, Wyo.

Johnson, Kenneth M., and Calvin L. Beale. 1992. "Natural Population Decrease in the United States." *Rural Development Perspectives* 8 (1): 8–15.

———. 1994. "The Recent Revival of Widespread Population Growth in Nonmetropolitan Areas of the United States." *Rural Sociology* 59 (4): 655–67.

———. 1998. "The Continuing Population Rebound in Nonmetro America." *Rural Development Perspectives* 13 (3): 2–10.

Johnson, Kenneth M., and Glenn V. Fuguitt. 2000. "Continuity and Change in Rural Migration Patterns, 1950–1995." *Rural Sociology* 65 (1): 27–49.

Johnson, Kenneth M., John P. Pelissero, David B. Holian, and Michael T. Maly. 1995. "Local Government Fiscal Burden in Nonmetropolitan America." *Rural Sociology* 60 (3): 381–98.

Johnson, Steven. 2001. *Emergence: The Connected Lives of Ants, Brains, Cities, and Software.* New York: Scribner.

Johnson, Thomas G. 2001. "The Rural Economy in a New Century." *International Regional Science Review* 24 (1): 21–37.

Jones, Jacqueline. 1985. *Labor of Love, Labor of Sorrow: Black Women, Work, and the Family From Slavery to the Present.* New York: Vintage Books.

Judy, Richard W., and Carol D'Amico. 1997. *Workforce 2020: Work and Workers in the 21st Century.* Indianapolis: Hudson Institute.

Jules, Erik S., Evan J. Frost, L. Scott Mills, and David A. Tallmon. 1999. "Ecological Consequences of Forest Fragmentation in the Klamath Region." *Natural Areas Journal* 19 (4): 368–78.

Kahn, Matthew E. 2000. "The Environmental Impact of Suburbanization." *Journal of Policy Analysis and Management* 19 (4): 569–86.

Kain, John F. 1968. "Housing Segregation, Negro Employment, and Metropolitan Decentralization." *Quarterly Journal of Economics* 82 (2): 175–97.

———. 1992. "The Spatial Mismatch Hypothesis: Three Decades Later." *Housing Policy Debate* 3 (2): 371–460.

Kalt, Joseph P., and Stephen Cornell. 1994. "The Redefinition of Property Rights in American Indian Reservations: A Comparative Analysis of Native American Economic Development." In *American Indian Policy: Self-Governance and Economic Development,* ed. L. H. Legters and F. J. Lyden, 121–50. Westport, Conn.: Greenwood Press.

Kasarda, John D. 1990. "The Jobs-Skills Mismatch." *NPQ: New Perspectives Quarterly* 7 (4): 34–38.

Kawachi, Ichiro, Bruce P. Kennedy, and Roberta Glass. 1999. "Social Capital and Self-Rated Health: A Contextual Analysis." *American Journal of Public Health* 89 (8): 1187–93.

Kawachi, Ichiro, Bruce P. Kennedy, Kimberly Lochner, and Deborah Prothrow-Stith. 1997. "Social Capital, Income Inequality, and Mortality." *American Journal of Public Health* 87 (9): 1491–98.

Keene, Chris 2001. "WTO Criticises U.S. Trade Policies." *Anti-Globalization Network Newsletter,* September 17.

Keith, John, Christopher Fawson, and Tsangyao Chang. 1996. "Recreation as an Economic Development Strategy: Some Evidence from Utah." *Journal of Leisure Research* 28 (2): 96–107.

Kellert, Stephen R., Jai N. Mehta, Syma A. Ebbin, and Laly L. Lichtenfeld. 2000. "Community Natural Resource Management: Promise, Rhetoric, and Reality." *Society and Natural Resources* 13 (8): 705–15.

Kemmis, Daniel. 1990. *Community and the Politics of Place.* Norman: University of Oklahoma Press.

Kennedy, Bruce P., Ichiro Kawachi, Deborah Prothrow-Stith, Kimberly Lochner, and Vanita Gupta. 1998. "Social Capital, Income Inequality, and Firearm Violent Crime." *Social Science and Medicine* 47 (1): 7–17.

Kesler, Stephen E. 1994. *Mineral Resources, Economics, and the Environment.* New York: Macmillan College Publishing.

Kickham, Kenneth, Robert Bentley, Nury Effendi, and Angela Harnden. 2000. "Health and Well-Being in Oklahoma: A Long Term Analysis of Welfare Reform." May, Office of Planning, Policy and Research, Oklahoma Department of Human Services, Oklahoma City. Available at: http://www.okdhs.org/ioppr/Research_Studies/TANF_May2000.htm.

Kiester, Edwin, Jr. 1999. "A Town Buries the Axe." *Smithsonian* 30 (4): 70–79.

Kilborn, Peter T. 2001. "Rural Towns Turn to Prisons to Reignite Their Economies." *New York Times,* August 1, pp. A1, A11.

Killian, Molly S., and Lionel J. Beaulieu. 1995. "Current Status of Human Capital in the Rural U.S." In *Investing in People: The Human Capital Needs of Rural America,* ed. L. J. Beaulieu and D. Mulkey, 23–46. Boulder, Co.: Westview Press.

Kintz, Linda. 1997. *Between Jesus and the Market: The Emotions That Matter in Right-Wing America.* Durham: Duke University Press.

Klein, Linda R., and John P. Reganold. 1997. "Agricultural Changes and Farmland Protection in Western Washington." *Journal of Soil and Water Conservation* 52 (1): 6–12.

Klemmack, David L., Lucinda L. Roff, Debra Moehle McCallum, and John T. Stem. 2002. "The Impact of Welfare Reform on Rural Alabamians." *Southern Rural Sociology* 18 (1): 186–203.

Kline, Jeffrey D., and Ralph J. Alig. 1999. "Does Land Use Planning Slow the Conversion of Forest and Farm Lands?" *Growth and Change* 30 (1): 3–22.

Kloppenburg, Jack, Jr., John Hendrickson, and G. W. Stevenson. 1996. "Coming Into the Foodshed." *Agriculture and Human Values* 13 (3): 33–42.

Knack, Stephen, and Philip Keefer. 1997. "Does Social Capital Have an Economic Payoff? A Cross-Country Investigation." *Quarterly Journal of Economics* 112 (4): 1251–88.

Kodras, Janet E. 1997. "Restructuring the State: Devolution, Privatization, and the Geographic Redistribution of Power and Capacity in Governance." In *State Devolution in America: Implications for a Diverse Society,* ed. L. A. Staeheli, J. E. Kodras, and C. Flint, 79–96. Thousand Oaks, Ca.: Sage Publications.

Komro, Kelli A., Carolyn L. Williams, Jean L. Foster, Cheryl L. Perry, Kian Farbakhsh, and Melissa H. Stigler. 1999. "The Relationship Between

Adolescent Alcohol Use and Delinquent and Violent Behavior." *Journal of Child and Adolescent Substance Abuse* 9 (2): 13–28.

Korsching, Peter F., Timothy O. Borich, and Julie Stewart. 1992. *Multicommunity Collaboration: An Evolving Rural Revitalization Strategy, Conference Proceedings.* RRD 161, July, North Central Regional Center for Rural Development. Ames, Iowa.

Krause, Louis E., and Susan Stoddard. 1989. *Chartbook on Disability in the United States.* Washington, D.C.: National Institute on Disability and Rehabilitation Research.

Kraybill, David, and Linda Lobao. 2001. "County Government Survey: Changes and Challenges in the New Millenium." Rural County Governance Center Research Report 1, July, National Association of Counties. Washington, D.C. Available at: http://www.naco.org/programs/comm_dev/rcgsurvey.pdf.

Krein, Sarah L., Jon B. Christianson, and Mei-Mei Chen. 1997. "The Composition of Rural Hospital Medical Staffs: The Influence of Hospital Neighbors." *Journal of Rural Health* 13 (4): 306–19.

Kretzmann, John P., and John L. McKnight. 1993a. "Asset-Based Community Development: Mobilizing an Entire Community." In *Building Communities from the Inside Out: A Path Toward Finding and Mobilizing a Community's Assets,* ed. J. P. Kretzmann and J. L. McKnight, 345–54. Chicago: ACTA Publications.

———. 1993b. *Building Communities from the Inside Out: A Path Toward Finding and Mobilizing a Community's Assets.* Evanston, Ill.: Institute for Policy Research, Northwestern University.

Kritz, Mary M., and Douglas T. Gurak. 2001. "The Impact of Immigration on the Internal Migration of Natives and Immigrants." *Demography* 38 (1): 133–45.

Krout, John A. 1984. "The Utilization of Formal and Informal Support of the Aged: Rural Versus Urban Differences." Final Report to the Andrus Foundation, American Association of Retired Persons, Fredonia State College. Fredonia, N.Y.

———. 1988. "Rural versus Urban Differences in Elderly Parents' Contact with Their Children." *The Gerontologist* 28 (2): 198–203.

Krugman, Paul. 1999. *The Return of Depression Economics.* New York: W. W. Norton.

Kumanyika, Shiriki K. 2001. "Minisymposium on Obesity: Overview and Some Strategic Considerations." *Annual Review of Public Health* 22: 293–308.

Kusel, Jonathan. 1996. "Well-Being in Forest Dependent Communities, Part I: A New Approach." In *Sierra Nevada Ecosystem Project Final Report to Congress: Volume II, Assessments and Scientific Basis for Management Options,* ed. Sierra Nevada Ecosystem Project Science Team, 361–74. Wildland Resources Center Report 39, June, Centers for Water and Wildlands Resources, University of California. Davis, Ca.

Lahr, Michael L. 1993. "Service Industries Dominate Nonmetro Employment Growth." *Rural Conditions and Trends* 4 (3): 40–43.

Landolt, Patricia. 2001. "Salvadoran Economic Transnationalism: Embedded Strategies for Household Maintenance, Immigrant Incorporation, and Entrepreneurial Expansion." *Global Networks* 1 (3): 217–41.

Langston, Nancy. 1995. *Forest Dreams, Forest Nightmares: The Paradox of Old Growth in the Inland West.* Seattle: University of Washington Press.

Lankford, Samuel V. 1994. "Attitudes and Perceptions Toward Tourism and Rural Regional Development." *Journal of Travel Research* 32 (3): 35–43.

Larson, Alice C. 2000a. "Migrant and Seasonal Farmworker Enumeration Profiles Study: California." September, Bureau of Primary Health Care, U.S. Department of Health and Human Services. Bethesda, Md. Available at: http://www.bphc.hrsa.gov/migrant/enumeration/enumerationstudy.htm.

———. 2000b. "Migrant and Seasonal Farmworker Enumeration Profiles Study: Texas." September, Bureau of Primary Health Care, U.S. Department of Health and Human Services. Bethesda, Md. Available at: http://www.bphc.hrsa.gov/migrant/enumeration/enumerationstudy.htm.

Larson, Olaf F. 1978. "Values and Beliefs of Rural People." In *Rural U.S.A.: Persistence and Change,* ed. T. R. Ford, 91–114. Ames: Iowa State University Press.

Lash, Scott, and John Urry. 1987. *The End of Organized Capitalism.* Madison: University of Wisconsin Press.

Lasley, Paul. 1994. "Rural Economic and Social Trends." In *Families in Troubled Times: Adapting to Change in Rural America,* ed. R. D. Conger and G. H. Elder Jr., 57–78. New York: Aldine de Gruyter.

———. 1997. "Farms." 258–62 in *Encyclopedia of Rural America: The Land and People,* ed. G. A. Goreham, 57–78. Denver: ABC-CLIO.

Lasley, Paul, F. Larry Leistritz, Linda M. Lobao, and Katherine Meyer. 1995. *Beyond the Amber Waves of Grain: An Examination of Social and Economic Restructuring in the Heartland.* Boulder, Co.: Westview Press.

Lawless, Elaine J. 1988. *Handmaidens of the Lord: Pentecostal Women Preachers and Traditional Religion.* Philadelphia: University of Pennsylvania Press.

Lee, Gary R., Raymond T. Coward, and Julie K. Netzer. 1994. "Residential Differences in Filial Responsibility Expectations Among Older Persons." *Rural Sociology* 59 (1): 100–109.

Lee, Gary R., Jeffrey W. Dwyer, and Raymond T. Coward. 1990. "Residential Location and Proximity to Children Among Impaired Elderly Parents." *Rural Sociology* 55 (4): 579–89.

Lee, Matthew R., and Graham C. Ousey. 2001. "Size Matters: Examining the Link Between Small Manufacturing, Socioeconomic Deprivation, and Crime Rates in Nonmetropolitan Communities." *Sociological Quarterly* 42 (4): 581–602.

Lee, She-Ahn. 1993. "Family Structure Effects on Student Outcomes." In *Parents, Their Children, and Schools,* ed. B. Schneider and J. S. Coleman, 43–75. Boulder, Co.: Westview Press.

Lefebvre, Henri. 1991. *The Production of Space.* Trans. D. Nicholson-Smith. Cambridge, Mass.: Blackwell Publishers.

Lehman, Karen, and Albert Krebs. 1996. "Control of the World's Food Supply." In *The Case Against the Global Economy and For a Turn Toward the Local,* ed. J. Mander and E. Goldsmith, 122–30. San Francisco: Sierra Club Books.

Lemert, Charles. 1999. "The Might Have Been and Could Be of Religion in Social Theory." *Sociological Theory* 17 (3): 240–63.

Lerner, Richard M. 1995. *America's Youth in Crisis: Challenges and Options for Programs and Policies.* Thousand Oaks, Ca.: Sage Publications.

Lester, Toby. 2002. "Oh, Gods!" *Atlantic Monthly* 289 (2): 37–45.

"Letters: End of Agriculture?" 2000. *U.C. Davis Magazine* 17 (3). Available at: http://www-ucdmag.ucdavis.edu/spoo/Letter_Ag.html.

Lewis, Oscar. 1966. "The Culture of Poverty." *Scientific American* 215 (4): 19–25.

Lewis, Peirce. 1995. "The Urban Invasion of Rural America: The Emergence of the Galactic City." In *The Changing American Countryside: Rural People and Places,* ed. E. N. Castle, 39–62. Lawrence: University Press of Kansas.

Leyerle, Betty. 1994. *The Private Regulation of American Health Care.* Armonk, N.Y.: M. E. Sharpe.

Lichter, Daniel T. 1997. "Poverty and Inequality Among Children." *Annual Review of Sociology* 23: 121–45.

Lichter, Daniel T., Gretchen T. Cornwell, and David J. Eggebeen. 1993. "Harvesting Human Capital: Family Structure and Education Among Rural Youth." *Rural Sociology* 58 (1): 53–75.

Lichter, Daniel T., and Martha L. Crowley. 2002. "Poverty in America: Beyond Welfare Reform." *Population Bulletin* 57 (2): 3–35.

Lichter, Daniel T., and David J. Eggebeen. 1992. "Child Poverty and the Changing Rural Family." *Rural Sociology* 57 (2): 151–72.

Lichter, Daniel T., and Rukmalie Jayakody. 2002. "Welfare Reform: How Do We Measure Success?" *Annual Review of Sociology* 28: 117–41.

Lichter, Daniel T., and Leif Jensen. 2002. "Rural America in Transition: Poverty and Welfare at the Turn of the Twenty-First Century." In *Rural Dimensions of Welfare Reform,* ed. B. A. Weber, G. J. Duncan, and L. Whitener, 77–110. Kalamazoo, Mo.: W. E. Upjohn Institute for Employment Research.

Lichter, Daniel T., Gail M. Johnston, and Diane K. McLaughlin. 1994. "Changing Linkages Between Work and Poverty in Rural America." *Rural Sociology* 59 (3): 395–415.

Lichter, Daniel T., and Diane K. McLaughlin. 1995. "Changing Economic Opportunities, Family Structure, and Poverty in Rural Areas." *Rural Sociology* 60 (4): 688–706.

Lichter, Daniel T., Michael J. Shanahan, and Erica L. Gardner. 2002. "Helping Others? The Effects of Childhood Poverty and Family Instability on Prosocial Behavior." *Youth & Society* 34 (1): 89–119.

Lightfoot, Sara L. 1978. *Worlds Apart: Relationships Between Families and Schools.* New York: Basic Books.

Lilliston, Ben, and Niel Ritchie. 2000. "Freedom to Fail: How U.S. Farming Policies Have Helped Agribusiness and Pushed Family Farmers Toward Extinction." *Multinational Monitor* 21 (7/8): 9–12.

Lin, Nan. 2001. *Social Capital: A Theory of Social Structure and Action.* Cambridge: Cambridge University Press.

Liner, E. Blaine. 1989. "Sorting Out State-Local Relations." In *A Decade of Devolution: Perspectives on State-Local Relations,* ed. E. B. Liner, 3–25. Washington, D.C.: Urban Institute Press.

Lins, David A. 1994. "Anatomy of the Land Market: Evolving Through the Winds of Change." *Agri Finance* 36 (4): 20–22.

Lobao, Linda M. 1990. *Locality and Inequality: Farm and Industry Structure and Socioeconomic Conditions.* Albany: SUNY Press.

———. 1996. "A Sociology of the Periphery Versus a Peripheral Sociology: Rural Sociology and the Dimension of Space." *Rural Sociology* 61 (1): 77–102.

Lobao, Linda M., Lawrence A. Brown, and Jon Moore. 2003. "Old Industrial Regions and the Political Economy of Development: The Ohio River Valley." In *Communities of Work: Economic Restructuring in Local and Global Context,* ed. W. W. Falk, M. Schulman, and A. Tickamyer. Athens: Ohio University Press.

Lobao, Linda M., and Katherine Meyer. 1995. "Economic Decline, Gender, and Labor Flexibility in Family-Based Enterprises: Midwestern Farming in the 1980s." *Social Forces* 74 (2): 575–608.

———. 2001. "The Great Agricultural Transition: Crisis, Change, and Social Consequences of Twentieth Century U.S. Farming." *Annual Review of Sociology* 27: 103–24.

Lobao, Linda M., Jamie Rulli, and Lawrence A. Brown. 1999. "Macrolevel Theory and Local-Level Inequality: Industrial Structure, Institutional Arrangements, and the Political Economy of Redistribution, 1970 and 1990." *Annals of the Association of American Geographers* 89 (4): 571–601.

Lobao, Linda M., and Michael D. Schulman. 1991. "Farming Patterns, Rural Restructuring, and Poverty: A Comparative Regional Analysis." *Rural Sociology* 56 (4): 565–602.

Lockie, Stewart, and Kristen Lyons. 2001. "Renegotiating Gender and the Symbolic Transformation of Australian Rural Environments." *International Journal of Sociology of Agriculture and Food* 9: 43–58.

Loda, Frank A., Ilene S. Speizer, Kerry L. Martin, Julia DeClerque Skatrud, and Trude A. Bennett. 1997. "Programs and Services to Prevent Pregnancy, Childbearing, and Poor Birth Outcomes Among Adolescents in Rural Areas of the Southeastern United States." *Journal of Adolescent Health* 21 (3): 157–66.

Logan, John R. 1996. "Rural America as a Symbol of American Values." *Rural Development Perspectives* 12 (1): 19–21.

Logan, John R., and Harvey L. Molotch. 1987. *Urban Fortunes: The Political Economy of Place.* Berkeley and Los Angeles: University of California Press.

Logan, John R., Rachel B. Whaley, and Kyle Crowder. 1997. "The Character and Consequences of Growth Regimes: An Assessment of 20 Years of Research." *Urban Affairs Review* 32 (5): 603–30.

Lohr, Steve. 2001. "New Economy: Despite its Epochal Name, the Clicks-and-Mortar Age May Be Quietly Assimilated." *New York Times,* October 8, p. C3.

Long, David. 1999. "School Finance Litigation." August, Education Finance Statistics Center, National Center for Education Statistics. Washington, D.C. Available at: http://nces.ed.gov/edfn/litigation.

Long, John F. 1981. "Population Deconcentration in the United States." Special Demographic Analysis CDS-81-5, Bureau of the Census, U.S. Department of Commerce. Washington, D.C.

Long, Larry, and Alfred Nucci. 1997. "The 'Clean Break' Revisited: Is U.S. Population Again Deconcentrating?" *Environment and Planning A* 29 (8): 1355–66.

Longino, Charles F., Jr. 1990. "Geographical Distribution and Migration." In *Handbook of Aging and the Social Sciences,* 3d ed., ed. R. H. Binstock and L. K. George, 45–63. San Diego: Academic Press.

Lonsdale, Richard E., and H. L. Seyler. 1979. *Nonmetropolitan Industrialization.* Washington, D.C.: V. H. Winston.

Lorenz, Edward. 1999. "Trust, Contract, and Economic Cooperation." *Cambridge Journal of Economics* 23 (3): 301–15.

Loury, Glenn C. 1977. "A Dynamic Theory of Racial Income Differences." In *Women, Minorities, and Employment Discrimination,* ed. P. A. Wallace and A. M. LaMond, 153–86. Lexington, Mass.: D. C. Heath.

Luloff, A. E. 1998. "What Makes a Place a Community?" The Fifth Sir John Quick Bendigo Lecture, October 1. Bendigo, Australia: La Trobe University Press.

Luloff, A. E., Jeffrey C. Bridger, Alan R. Graefe, Mary Saylor, Kenneth Martin, and Richard Gitelson. 1994. "Assessing Rural Tourism Efforts in the United States." *Annals of Tourism Research* 21 (1): 46–64.

Luloff, A. E., and Louis E. Swanson. 1995. "Community Agency and Disaffection: Enhancing Collective Resources." In *Investing in People: The Human Capital Needs of Rural America,* ed. L. J. Beaulieu and D. Mulkey, 351–72. Boulder, Co.: Westview Press.

Luloff, A. E., and Kenneth P. Wilkinson. 1979. "Participation in the National Flood Insurance Program: A Study of Community Activeness." *Rural Sociology* 44 (1): 137–52.

Lynd, Robert S., and Helen M. Lynd. 1937. *Middletown in Transition: A Study in Cultural Conflicts.* New York: Harcourt Brace.

Lyson, Thomas A. 1989. *Two Sides to the Sunbelt: The Growing Divergence Between the Rural and Urban South.* New York: Praeger Publishers.

———. 2002. "Agricultural Biotechnologies, the Structure of Agriculture, and the Future of the Food System." In *Perspectives on Agricultural Biotechnology: Proceedings from "Biotechnology: Progress or Problem?" A Conference for Developing Community Leaders,* 83–89. January 17–19, Binghamton, N.Y. NRAES Publication 144, Natural Resource, Agricultural, and Engineering Service, Ithaca, N.Y.

Lyson, Thomas A., and William W. Falk. 1993. *Forgotten Places: Uneven Development in Rural America.* Lawrence: University Press of Kansas.

Lyson, Thomas A., William W. Falk, Mark Henry, JoAnn Hickey, and Mildred Warner. 1993. "Spatial Location of Economic Activities, Uneven Development, and Rural Poverty." In *Persistent Poverty in Rural America,* ed. Rural Sociological Society Task Force on Persistent Rural Poverty, 106–35. Boulder, Co.: Westview Press.

Lyson, Thomas A., and Charles M. Tolbert. 1996. "Small Manufacturing and Nonmetropolitan Socioeconomic Well-Being." *Environment and Planning A* 28 (10): 1779–94.

MacDonald, Heather I. 1999. "Women's Employment and Commuting: Explaining the Links." *Journal of Planning Literature* 13 (3): 267–83.

MacDonald, Heather I., and Alan Peters. 1994a. "Spatial Constraints on Rural Women Workers." *Urban Geography* 15 (8): 720–40.

———. 1994b. "Rural Women in a Restructuring Economy: Work and Commuting in Eastern Iowa." *Economic Development Quarterly* 8 (2): 171–85.

MacLeod, Jay. 1987. *Ain't No Makin' It: Leveled Aspirations in a Low-Income Neighborhood.* Boulder, Co.: Westview Press.

MacTavish, Katherine. 2001. "Going Mobile in Rural America: Community Effects of Trailer Parks on Children and Youth." Ph.D. dissertation, Department of Human and Community Development, University of Illinois.

MacTavish, Katherine, and Sonya Salamon. 2001. "Mobile Home Park on the Prairie: A New Rural Community Form." *Rural Sociology* 66 (4): 487–506.

Madeley, John. 2000. *Hungry for Trade: How the Poor Pay for Free Trade.* New York: Zed Books.

Maggard, Sally W. 1998. "'We're Fighting Millionaires!': The Clash of Gender and Class in Appalachian Women's Union Organizing." In *No Middle Ground: Women and Radical Protest,* ed. K. M. Blee, 289–306. New York: New York University Press.

———. 1999. "Gender, Race, and Place: Confounding Labor Activism in Central Appalachia." In *Neither Separate nor Equal: Women, Race, and Class in the South,* ed. B. E. Smith, 185–206. Philadelphia: Temple University Press.

Malecki, Edward J. 1997. *Technology and Economic Development: The Dynamics of Local, Regional, and National Competitiveness.* Essex, UK: Addison Wesley Longman.

Malhotra, Kamal. 1996. "The Uruguay Round of GATT, the World Trade Organization, and Small Farmers." Presented at the Regional Conference on MonoCultural Cropping in Southeast Asia: Social/Environmental Impacts and Sustainable Alternatives, June 3–6. Songkhla, Thailand. Available at: www.focusweb.org/focus/library/Alternatives_to_Trade_and_Finance/uruguay_round_of_gatt.htm.

Mander, Jerry, and Edward Goldsmith. 1996. *The Case Against the Global Economy and For a Turn Toward the Local.* San Francisco: Sierra Club Books.

Mandle, Jay R. 1992. *Not Slave, Not Free: The African-American Economic Experience Since the Civil War.* Durham: Duke University Press.

Margherio, Lynn, Dave Henry, Sandra Cooke, and Sabrina Montes. 1998. "The Emerging Digital Economy." April, Economics and Statistics Administration, U.S. Department of Commerce. Washington, D.C. Available at: http://www.ecommerce.gov/emerging.htm.

"Market Gorilla." 1999. *Northeast Dairy Business* 1 (6): 11.

Markoff, John. 1996. *The Abolition of Feudalism: Peasants, Lords, and Legislators in the French Revolution.* University Park: Pennsylvania State University Press.

Markusen, Ann R. 1985. *Profit Cycles, Oligopoly, and Regional Development.* Cambridge: MIT Press.

———. 1987. *Regions: The Economics and Politics of Territory.* Totowa, N.J.: Rowman and Littlefield.

Marsden, Terry K. 1997a. "Creating Space for Food: The Distinctiveness of Recent Agrarian Developments." In *Globalising Food: Agrarian Questions and Global Restructuring,* ed. D. Goodman and M. J. Watts, 169–91. London: Routledge.

———. 1997b. "Reshaping Environments: Agriculture and Water Interactions and the Creation of Vulnerability." *Transactions of the Institute of the British Geographers* 22 (3): 321–37.

Marsden, Terry K., and Alberto Arce. 1995. "Constructing Quality: Emerging Food Networks in the Rural Transition." *Environment and Planning A* 27 (8): 1261–79.

Marsden, Terry K., Josefa S. B. Cavalcanti, and José F. Irmão. 1996. "Globalisation, Regionalisation, and Quality: The Socio-Economic Reconstruction of Food in the San Francisco Valley, Brazil." *International Journal of Sociology of Agriculture and Food* 5: 85–114.

Marsden, Terry, Philip Lowe, and Sarah Whatmore. 1990. *Rural Restructuring: Global Processes and Their Responses*. London: David Fulton Publishers.

Marshall, Ray. 2001. "Rural Policy in the New Century." *International Regional Science Review* 24 (1): 59–83.

Martin, Philip, and Elizabeth Midgley. 1999. "Immigration to the United States." *Population Bulletin* 54 (2): 3–44.

Martin, Steven R., and Stephen F. McCool. 1992. "Attitudes of Montana Residents Toward Tourism Development." Research Report 23, Institute for Tourism and Recreation Research, School of Forestry, University of Montana.

Martin-Baro, Ignacio. 1990. "Religion as an Instrument of Psychological Warfare." *Journal of Social Issues* 46 (3): 93–107.

Martini, Alberto, and Michael Wiseman. 1997. "Explaining the Recent Decline in Welfare Caseloads: Is the Council of Economic Advisors Right?" July, Income and Benefits Policy Center, The Urban Institute. Washington, D.C. Available at: http://www.urban.org/welfare/cea.htm.

Marx, Karl. 1964. *Economic and Philosophic Manuscripts of 1844*. New York: International Publishers.

———. 1973. *Grundrisse: Foundations of the Critique of Political Economy*. New York: Vintage Books.

Mather, Mark. 2002. "Patterns of Poverty in America." June, Population Reference Bureau. Washington, D.C. Available at: http://www.prb.org/Template.cfm?Section=PRB&template=/ContentManagement/ContentDisplay.cfm&ContentID=5985.

Mayer, Susan E. 1997. *What Money Can't Buy: Family Income and Children's Life Chances*. Cambridge, Mass.: Harvard University Press.

Maynard, Stan, and Aimee Howley. 1997. "Parent and Community Involvement in Rural Schools." ERIC Clearinghouse on Rural Education and Small Schools, EDO-RC-97-3, June. Available at: http://www.ael.org/eric/digests/edorc973.htm.

McBride, William D. 1997. "Change in U.S. Livestock Production, 1969–92." Agricultural Economics Report 754, Economic Research Service, U.S. Department of Agriculture. Washington, D.C.

McConnell, Sheena M., and James C. Ohls. 2000. "Food Stamps in Rural America: Special Issues and Common Themes." Presented at the Rural Dimensions of Welfare Reform: A Research Conference on Poverty, Welfare, and Food Assistance, May 4–5. Washington, D.C. JCPR Working Paper 182, June 5, Joint Center for Poverty Research, Northwestern University and University of Chicago, Evanston, Ill. Available at: http://www.jcpr.org/wp/wpdownload.cfm?pdflink=wpfiles/Ohls.pdf.

McDill, Edward L., and Leo C. Rigsby. 1973. *Structure and Process in Secondary Schools: The Academic Impact of Educational Climates*. Baltimore: Johns Hopkins University Press.

McDonnell, Janet A. 1991. *The Dispossession of the American Indian: 1887–1934.* Bloomington: Indiana University Press.

McDowell, George R. 1995. "Some Communities Are Successful, Others Are Not: Toward an Institutional Framework for Understanding the Reasons Why." In *Rural Development Strategies,* ed. D. W. Sears and J. N. Reid, 269–81. Chicago: Nelson-Hall Publishers.

McGranahan, David A. 1988. "Rural Workers in the National Economy." In *Rural Economic Development in the 1980's: Prospects for the Future,* ed. D. L. Brown, J. N. Reid, H. Bluestone, D. A. McGranahan, and S. M. Mazie, 29–47. Rural Development Research Report 69, September, Agriculture and Rural Economy Division, Economic Research Service, U.S. Department of Agriculture. Washington, D.C.

———. 1998. "Local Problems Facing Manufacturers: Results of the ERS Manufacturing Survey." Agricultural Information Bulletin 736-03, March, Economic Research Service, U.S. Department of Agriculture. Washington, D.C.

———. 1999a. "The Geography of New Manufacturing Technology: Implications for the Rural South." *Southern Rural Sociology* 15: 84–103.

———. 1999b. "Natural Amenities Drive Rural Population Change." Agricultural Economic Report 781, October, Food and Rural Economics Division, Economic Research Service, U.S. Department of Agriculture. Washington, D.C.

———. 2002. "Local Context and Advanced Technology Use by Small, Independent Manufacturers in Rural Areas." *American Journal of Agricultural Economics* 84 (5): 1237–45.

McGranahan, David A., and Linda M. Ghelfi. 1998. "Current Trends in the Supply and Demand for Education in Rural and Urban Areas." In *Rural Education and Training in the New Economy: The Myth of the Rural Skills Gap,* ed. R. M. Gibbs, P. L. Swaim, and R. Teixeira, 131–71. Ames: Iowa State University Press.

McGranahan, David A., and Kathleen Kassel. 1996. "Education and Rural Minority Job Opportunities." In *Racial/Ethnic Minorities in Rural Areas: Progress and Stagnation, 1980–90,* ed. L. L. Swanson, 5–25. Agricultural Economic Report 731, August, Rural Economy Division, Economic Research Service, U.S. Department of Agriculture. Washington, D.C.

McGrath, Daniel J., Raymond R. Swisher, Glen H. Elder Jr., and Rand D. Conger. 2001. "Breaking New Ground: Diverse Routes to College in Rural America." *Rural Sociology* 66 (2): 244–67.

McGuire, Michael. 2000. "Collaborative Policy Making and Administration: The Operational Demands of Local Economic Development." *Economic Development Quarterly* 14 (3): 276–91.

McKernan, Signe-Mary, Robert Lerman, Nancy Pindus, and Jesse Valente. 2001. "The Relationship Between Metropolitan and Non-Metropolitan Locations, Changing Welfare Policies, and the Employment of Single Mothers." February, The Urban Institute. Washington, D.C. Available at: http://www.urban.org/pdfs/welfarepolicies.pdf.

McLaughlin, Diane K. 1995. "Becoming Poor: The Experience of Elders." *Rural Sociology* 60 (2): 202–23.

McLaughlin, Diane K., Erica L. Gardner, and Daniel T. Lichter. 1999. "Economic Restructuring and Changing Prevalence of Female-Headed Families in America." *Rural Sociology* 64 (3): 394–416.

McLaughlin, Diane K., and Leif I. Jensen. 1993. "Poverty Among Older Americans: The Plight of Nonmetropolitan Elders." *Journal of Gerontology: Social Sciences* 48 (2): S44–S54.

———. 1998. "The Rural Elderly: A Demographic Portrait." In *Aging in Rural Settings: Life Circumstances and Distinctive Features,* ed. R. T. Coward and J. A. Krout, 15–46. New York: Springer Publishing.

———. 2000. "Work History and U.S. Elders' Transitions into Poverty." *The Gerontologist* 40 (4): 469–79.

McLaughlin, Diane K., and Lauri Perman. 1991. "Returns vs. Endowments in the Earnings Attainment Process for Metropolitan and Nonmetropolitan Men and Women." *Rural Sociology* 56 (3): 339–65.

McLaughlin, Diane K., and Carolyn Sachs. 1988. "Poverty in Female-Headed Households: Residential Differences." *Rural Sociology* 53 (3): 287–306.

McLeod, Jane D., and Michael J. Shanahan. 1996. "Trajectories of Poverty and Children's Mental Health." *Journal of Health and Social Behavior* 37 (3): 207–20.

McMichael, Phillip. 1994. *The Global Restructuring of Agro-Food Systems.* Ithaca: Cornell University Press.

———. 1996a. "Globalization: Myths and Realities." *Rural Sociology* 61 (1): 25–55.

———. 1996b. *Development and Social Change: A Global Perspective.* Thousand Oaks, Ca.: Pine Forge Press.

———. 2000. "The Power of Food." *Agriculture and Human Values* 17 (1): 21–33.

MDC Research Committee. 2000. *The State of the South: A Report to the Region and Its Leadership.* Chapel Hill, N.C: MDC.

Mele, Christopher. 2000. "Asserting the Political Self: Community Activism Among Black Women Who Relocate to the Rural South." *Sociological Quarterly* 41 (1): 63–84.

Mesch, Gustavo S. 1998. "Community Empowerment and Collective Action." In *Research in Community Sociology: American Community Issues and Patterns of Development,* vol. 8, ed. D. A. Chekki, V. Stamford: JAI Press.

Metropolitan Life. 1996. *The Metropolitan Life Survey of the American Teacher, 1984–1995.* New York: Metropolitan Life Insurance and Louis Harris and Associates.

Meyer, Katherine, and Linda M. Lobao. 1994. "Engendering the Farm Crisis: Women's Political Response in the USA." In *Gender and Rurality,* ed. S. Whatmore, T. Marsden, and P. Lowe, 69–86. London: David Fulton Publishers.

Mezey, Naomi. 1996. "The Distribution of Wealth, Sovereignty, and Culture through Indian Gaming." *Stanford Law Review* 48: 711–37.

Mika, Karin. 1995. "Private Dollars on the Reservation: Will Recent Native American Economic Development Amount to Cultural Assimilation?" *New Mexico Law Review* 25 (1): 23–34.

Miles, John C. 2000. "Three National Parks of the Pacific Northwest." In *National Parks and Rural Development: Practice and Policy in the United States,* ed. G. E. Machlis and D. R. Field, 91–109. Washington, D.C.: Island Press.

Mills, Edwin S. 1995. "The Location of Economic Activity in Rural and Non-metropolitan United States." In *The Changing American Countryside: Rural People and Places*, ed. E. N. Castle, 103–33. Lawrence: University Press of Kansas.

Milman, Ady, and Abraham Pizam. 1988. "Social Impacts of Tourism on Central Florida." *Annals of Tourism Research* 15 (2): 191–204.

Milner, Eileen M. 2000. *Managing Information and Knowledge in the Public Sector.* New York: Routledge.

Mingione, Enzo. 1991. *Fragmented Societies: A Sociology of Economic Life Beyond the Market Paradigm.* Trans. P. Goodrich. Cambridge, Mass.: Basil Blackwell.

Mills, C. Wright, and Melville J. Ulmer. 1946. "Small Business and Civic Welfare." Report of the Smaller War Plants Corporation to the Special Committee to Study Problems of American Small Business, 79th Congress, 2nd Session, U.S. Senate Document 135, February 13, U.S. Government Printing Office. Washington, D.C.

Mitchell, M. Y., J. E. Force, M. S. Carroll, and W. J. McLaughlin. 1993. "Forest Places of the Heart: Incorporating Special Places into Public Management." *Journal of Forestry* 91 (4): 32–37.

Moffitt, Robert A., and Michele Ver Ploeg. 2001. "Evaluating Welfare Reform in an Era of Transition." Committee on National Statistics, National Research Council, National Academies Press. Washington, D.C. Available at: http://books.nap.edu/books/0309072743/html/.

Mohn, David J. 1997. "Commuting Flows in Nonmetropolitan America, 1970–1990." M.S. thesis, Department of Sociology, University of Wisconsin.

Moller, Stephanie, David Bradley, Evelyne Huber, Francois Nielsen, and John D. Stephens. 2001. "The State and Poverty Alleviation in Advanced Capitalist Democracies." Luxembourg Income Study Working Paper 278, August, Center for the Study of Population, Poverty, and Public Policy. International Networks for Studies in Technology, Environment, Alternatives, Development. Differdange, Luxembourg.

Möllering, Guido. 2002. "Perceived Trustworthiness and Inter-Firm Governance: Empirical Evidence from the UK Printing Industry." *Cambridge Journal of Economics* 26 (2): 139–60.

Molotch, Harvey. 1976. "The City as Growth Machine: Toward a Political Economy of Place." *American Journal of Sociology* 82 (2): 309–32.

Molotch, Harvey, William Freudenburg, and Krista E. Paulsen. 2000. "History Repeats Itself, but How? City Character, Urban Tradition, and the Accomplishment of Place." *American Sociological Review* 65 (6): 791–823.

Mooney, Patrick H. 1988. *My Own Boss?: Class, Rationality, and the Family Farm.* Boulder, Co.: Westview Press.

Moore, Kristin A., and Dana Glei. 1995. "Taking the Plunge: An Examination of Positive Youth Development." *Journal of Adolescent Research* 10 (1): 15–40.

Moreland-Young, Curtina, Kristie Roberts, Jody Fields, and Royal Walker Jr. 2002. "Racial Disparities and Welfare Reform in Mississippi." *Southern Rural Sociology* 18 (1): 111–53.

Morissey, Michael A., Robert L. Ohsfeldt, Victoria Johnson, and Richard Treat. 1995. "Rural Emergency Medical Services: Patients, Destinations, Times, and Services." *Journal of Rural Health* 11 (4): 286–94.

Morrill, Richard, John Cromartie, and Gary Hart. 1999. "Metropolitan, Urban, and Rural Commuting Areas: Toward a Better Depiction of the United States Settlement System." *Urban Geography* 20 (8): 727–48.

Morrison, Michael L., Bruce G. Marcot, and R. William Mannan. 1992. *Wildlife-Habitat Relationships: Concepts and Applications.* Madison: University of Wisconsin Press.

Mortimore, Peter, Pamela Sammons, Louise Stoll, David Lewis, and Russell Ecob. 1988. *School Matters: The Junior Years.* Berkeley and Los Angeles: University of California Press.

Morton, Lois W. 1997. "Medicaid Managed Care and Community Economic Development." Community-Based Health Planning, New York State College of Human Ecology Policy Perspectives Series, November, Cornell University.

———. 2001a. *Health Care Restructuring: Market Theory vs. Civil Society.* Westport, Conn.: Auburn House.

———. 2001b. "The Contributions of Business and Civil Society Sectors to Rural Capacity to Solve Local Health Issues." *Journal of Rural Health* 17 (3): 41–73.

Muller, Chandra, and David Kerbow. 1993. "Parent Involvement in the Home, School, and Community." In *Parents, Their Children, and Schools,* ed. B. Schneider and J. S. Coleman, 13–42. Boulder, Co.: Westview Press.

Murdock, Steve H., and Kenneth M. Johnson. 2001. "Migration and Demographic Change by Race and Hispanic Origin for Central City, Suburban, and Nonmetropolitan Counites of the United States, 1990–2000." Presented at the 64th Annual Meeting of the Rural Sociological Society, August 15–19. Albuquerque, N.M.

Murray, James M. 1993. *The Economic Benefits of American Indian Gambling Facilities in Wisconsin.* Green Bay: University of Wisconsin-Cooperative Extension

Nagel, Joane. 1996. *American Indian Ethnic Renewal: Red Power and the Resurgence of Identity and Culture.* New York: Oxford University Press.

Naples, Nancy A. 1994. "Contradictions in Agrarian Ideology: Restructuring Gender, Race-Ethnicity, and Class." *Rural Sociology* 59 (1): 110–35.

Naples, Nancy A., and Carolyn Sachs. 2000. "Standpoint Epistemology and the Uses of Self-Reflection in Feminist Ethnography: Lessons for Rural Sociology." *Rural Sociology* 65 (2): 194–214.

Narayan, Deepa. 1999. "Bonds and Bridges: Social Capital and Poverty." Policy Research Working Paper 2167, Poverty Division, Poverty Reduction and Economic Management Network, The World Bank, August. Available at: http://www.worldbank.org/poverty/scapital/library/narayan.pdf.

Nash, Manning. 1958. *Machine-Age Maya: The Industrialization of a Guatemalan Community.* Chicago: University of Chicago Press.

Nason-Clark, Nancy. 1995. "Conservative Protestants and Violence Against Women: Exploring the Rhetoric and the Response." In *Sex, Lies, and Sanctity: Religion and Deviance in Contemporary North America,* ed. M. J. Neitz and M. S. Goldman, 109–30. *Religion and the Social Order* Series, vol. 5, ed. D. G. Bromley. Greenwich, Conn.: JAI Press.

National Advisory Commission on Rural Poverty. 1967. *The People Left Behind: A Report.* Washington, D.C.: U.S. Government Printing Office.

National Center for Farmworker Health. 2001. "Migrant Health Issues: Monograph Series." October, National Center for Farmworker Health, Buda, Tx. Available at: http://www.ncfh.org/docs/monograph.pdf.

National Education Association. 2001. "Making Low-Performing Schools a Priority: An Association Resource Guide." National Education Association. Washington, D.C.

National Indian Gaming Association. 2002. "National Indian Gaming Association (NIGA): A Legislative and Public Policy Resource on Indian Gaming Issues and Tribal Community Development." National Indian Gaming Association (NIGA). Washington, D.C. Available at: http://www.indiangaming.org.

Navarro, Vicente. 2000. "Neoliberalism, 'Globalization,' Unemployment, Inequalities, and the Welfare State." In *The Political Economy of Social Inequalities: Consequences for Health and Quality of Life,* ed. V. Navarro, 33–107. Amityville, N.Y.: Baywood Publishing.

Ndubisi, Forster, and Mary Dyer. 1992. "The Role of Regional Entities in Formulating and Implementing Statewide Growth Policies." *State and Local Government Review* 24 (3): 117–27.

Neisser, Ulric. 1986. *The School Achievement of Minority Children: New Perspectives.* Hillsdale, N.J.: Lawrence Erlbaum Associates.

Neitz, Mary Jo. 1995. "Defining and Sanctioning Sexual Deviance in Contemporary Witchcraft." In *Sex, Lies, and Sanctity: Religion and Deviance in Contemporary North America,* ed. M. J. Neitz and M. S. Goldman, 223–35. *Religion and the Social Order* Series, vol. 5, ed. D. G. Bromley. Greenwich, Conn.: JAI Press.

Nelson, Frederick J. 2002. "Aligning U.S. Farm Policy with World Trade Commitments." *Agricultural Outlook* AGO-288 (January/February): 12–16.

Nelson, Margaret K. 1999. "Economic Restructuring, Gender, and Informal Work: A Case Study of a Rural County." *Rural Sociology* 64 (1): 18–43.

Nelson, Margaret K., and Joan Smith. 1999. *Working Hard and Making Do: Surviving in Small Town America.* Berkeley and Los Angeles: University of California Press.

Nickerson, Cynthia. 2001. "Smart Growth: Implications for Agriculture in Urban Fringe Areas." *Agricultural Outlook* AGO-280 (April): 24–27.

Noddings, Nel. 1988. "Schools Face 'Crisis in Caring.'" *Education Week* 8 (14): 32.

Nord, Mark. 1994. "Natural Resources and Persistent Poverty: In Search of the Nexus." *Society and Natural Resources* 7 (3): 205–20.

———. 1997. "Overcoming Persistent Poverty—And Sinking Into It: Income Trends in Persistent-Poverty and Other High-Poverty Rural Counties, 1989–94." *Rural Development Perspectives* 12 (3): 2–10.

———. 2000. "Does it Cost Less to Live in Rural Areas? Evidence from New Data on Food Security and Hunger." *Rural Sociology* 65 (1): 104–25.

Nord, Mark, and Bo Beaulieu. 1997. "Spatial Mismatch: The Challenge of Welfare-to-Work in the Rural South." *Southern Perspectives* 1 (1): 4–5. Available at: http://ext.msstate.edu/srdc/publications/decsp97.pdf.

Nord, Mark, and A. E. Luloff. 1993. "Socioeconomic Heterogeneity of Mining-Dependent Counties." *Rural Sociology* 58 (3): 492–500.

Northeast Dairy Business. 1999. "Market Gorilla." *Northeast Dairy Business* 1 (6): 11.

Oakes, John M., Douglas L. Anderton, and Andy B. Anderson. 1996. "A Longitudinal Analysis of Environmental Equity in Communities with Hazardous
Waste Facilities." *Social Science Research* 25 (2): 125–48.

Oberhauser, Ann M., and Anne-Marie Turnage. 1999. "A Coalfield Tapestry:
Weaving the Socioeconomic Fabric of Women's Lives." In *Neither Separate
nor Equal: Women, Race and Class in the South,* ed. B. E. Smith, 109–22.
Philadelphia: Temple University Press.

O'Connor, Alice. 2001. *Poverty Knowledge: Social Science, Social Policy, and the
Poor in Twentieth-Century U.S. History.* Princeton: Princeton University
Press.

Ogunwole, Stella U. 2002. "The American Indian and Alaska Native Population:
2000." Census 2000 Brief C2KBR/01-15, February, U.S. Census Bureau,
U.S. Department of Commerce. Washington, D.C.

Olson, Richard K. 1999. "A Landscape Perspective on Farmland Conversion." In
Under the Blade: The Conversion of Agricultural Landscapes, ed.
R. K. Olson and T. A. Lyson, 53–95. Boulder, Co.: Westview Press.

Olson, Richard K., and Thomas A. Lyson. 1999. *Under the Blade: The Conversion of Agricultural Landscapes.* Boulder, Co.: Westview Press.

Olson, Richard K., and Allen H. Olson. 1999. "Farmland Loss in America." In
Under the Blade: The Conversion of Agricultural Landscapes, ed.
R. K. Olson and T. A. Lyson, 15–51. Boulder, Co.: Westview Press.

Osava, Mario. 2001. "Trade: Agricultural Limits Unmask Free Market Illusions."
Inter Press Service, August 22, Rio de Janeiro, Brazil.

Osborne, David, and Ted Gaebler. 1992. *Reinventing Government: How the
Entrepreneurial Spirit is Transforming the Public Sector.* Reading, Mass.:
Addison-Wesley.

Osgood, D. Wayne, and Jeff M. Chambers. 2000. "Social Disorganization Outside
the Metropolis: An Analysis of Rural Youth Violence." *Criminology* 38 (1):
81–115.

Ostrom, Elinor. 1990. *Governing the Commons: The Evolution of Institutions for
Collective Action.* New York: Cambridge University Press.

Paasch, Kathleen M., and Paul L. Swaim. 1998. "Rural High School Completion." In *Rural Education and Training in the New Economy: The Myth of
the Rural Skills Gap,* ed. R. M. Gibbs, P. L. Swaim, and R. Teixeira, 41–59.
Ames: Iowa State University Press.

Page, Brian, and Richard Walker. 1991. "From Settlement to Fordism: The Agro-
Industrial Revolution in the American Midwest." *Economic Geography* 67
(4): 281–315.

Pahl, R. E. 1985. "The Restructuring of Capital, the Local Political Economy, and
Household Work Strategies." In *Social Relations and Spatial Structures,* ed.
D. Gregory and J. Urry, 242–64. New York: St. Martin's Press.

Pamuk, Ayse. 2000. "Informal Institutional Arrangements in Credit, Land Markets, and Infrastructure Delivery in Trinidad." *International Journal of
Urban and Regional Research* 24 (2): 379–96.

Parisi, Domenico, Diane K. McLaughlin, Michael C. Taquino, Steven M. Grice,
and Neil R. White. 2002. "TANF/Welfare Client Decline and Community
Context in the Rural South, 1997–2000." *Southern Rural Sociology* 18 (1):
154–86.

Parisi, Domenico, Michael C. Taquino, Steven M. Grice, and Duane A. Gill. 2003. "Promoting Environmental Democracy Using GIS as a Means to Integrate Community into the EPA-BASINS Approach." *Society and Natural Resources* 16 (2): 205–19.

Park, Robert E. 1952 [1925]. *Human Communities: The City and Human Ecology.* Glencoe, Ill.: The Free Press.

Parker, Timothy S. 1997. "Nonmetro Multiple Jobholding Rate Higher than Metro." *Rural Conditions and Trends* 8 (2): 18–21.

Parker, Timothy S., and Leslie A. Whitener. 1997. "Minimum Wage Legislation: Rural Workers Will Benefit More than Urban Workers from Increase in Minimum Wage." *Rural Conditions and Trends* 8 (1): 48–52.

Parks, Roger B., and Ronald J. Oakerson. 2000. "Regionalism, Localism, and Metropolitan Governance: Suggestions from the Research Program on Local Public Economies." *State and Local Government Review* 32 (3): 169–79.

Parsons, Talcott. 1971. *The System of Modern Societies.* Englewood Cliffs, N.J.: Prentice-Hall.

Passel, Jeffrey S. 1976. "Provisional Evaluation of the 1970 Census Count of American Indians." *Demography* 13 (3): 397–409.

———. 1996. "The Growing American Indian Population, 1960–1990: Beyond Demography." In *Changing Numbers, Changing Needs: American Indian Demography and Public Health,* ed. G. D. Sandefur, R. R. Rindfuss, and B. Cohen, 79–102. Washington, D.C.: National Academy Press.

Passel, Jeffrey S., and Patricia A. Berman. 1986. "Quality of 1980 Census Data for American Indians." *Social Biology* 33 (3/4): 163–82.

Peck, Jamie A. 1989. "Reconceptualizing the Local Labour Market: Space, Segmentation, and the State." *Progress in Human Geography* 13 (1): 42–61.

Peck, Jamie. 1996. *Work-Place: The Social Regulation of Labor Markets.* New York: Guilford Press.

Pellow, David N. 2000. "Environmental Inequality Formation." *American Behavioral Scientist* 43 (4): 581–601.

Perrow, Charles. 1993. "Small Firm Networks." In *Explorations in Economic Sociology,* ed. R. Swedberg, 377–402. New York: Russell Sage Foundation.

Perry-Jenkins, Maureen, and Sonya Salamon. 2002. "Blue-Collar Kin and Community in the Small-Town Midwest." *Journal of Family Issues* 23 (8): 927–49.

Peterman, William. 2000. *Neighborhood Planning and Community-Based Development: The Potential and Limits of Grassroots Action.* Thousand Oaks, Ca.: Sage Publications.

Peters, Alan, and Heather I. MacDonald. 1994. "The Worktrips of Rural Nonmetropolitan Women in Iowa." *Growth and Change* 25 (3): 335–51.

Peters, Barbara J. 1998. *The Head Start Mother: Low-Income Mothers' Empowerment through Participation.* New York: Garland Publishing.

Peterson, Paul E. 1981. *City Limits.* Chicago: University of Chicago Press.

———. 1995. *The Price of Federalism.* Washington, D.C.: Brookings Institution.

Petrzelka, Peggy. 1999. "The (Loess) Hills: Power and Democracy in a 'New' Landform." Ph.D. dissertation, Department of Sociology, Iowa State University.

Pezzin, Liliana E., and Barbara S. Schone. 1999. "Parental Marital Disruption and Intergenerational Transfers: An Analysis of Lone Elderly Parents and Their Children." *Demography* 36 (3): 287–97.

Phelps, Charles E. 1992. *Health Economics.* New York: Harper Collins.

Pickering, Kathleen. 2000. "Alternative Economic Strategies in Low-Income Rural Communities: TANF, Labor Migration, and the Case of the Pine Ridge Indian Reservation." *Rural Sociology* 65 (1): 148–67.

Pigg, Kenneth E. 1999. "Community Development in the New Millennium." Presented at the Annual Meeting of the Community Development Society, July 25–28. Spokane, Wa.

Pigg, Kenneth E. 2002. "The Three Faces of Empowerment in Community Development." *Jounal of the Community Development Society* 33 (1): 107–23.

Pillemer, Karl, and Nina Glasgow. 2000. "Social Integration and Aging: Background and Trends." In *Social Integration in the Second Half of Life,* ed. K. Pillemer, P. Moen, E. Wethington, and N. Glasgow, 19–47. Baltimore: Johns Hopkins University Press.

Pindus, Nancy M. 2001. "Implementing Welfare Reform in Rural Communities." February, The Urban Institute. Washington, D.C. Available at: http://www.urban.org/pdfs/rural-welfarereform.pdf.

Piore, Michael J., and Charles F. Sabel. 1984. *The Second Industrial Divide: Possibilities for Prosperity.* New York: Basic Books.

Ploch, Louis A. 1978. "The Reversal in Migration Patterns—Some Rural Development Consequences." *Rural Sociology* 43 (2): 293–303.

Pol, Louis. 2000. "Health Insurance in Rural America." Rural Policy Brief PB2000-11, August, vol. 5 (11), RUPRI Center for Rural Health Policy Analysis. Omaha, Neb.

Pollan, Michael. 2001. "Naturally: How Organic Became a Marketing Niche and a Multibillion-Dollar Industry." *New York Times Magazine,* May 13, pp. 30–37, 57–58, 63–64.

Pollard, Kelvin M., and William P. O'Hare. 1990. *Beyond High School: The Experience of Rural and Urban Youth in the 1980s.* Washington, D.C.: Population Reference Bureau.

Pollock, Philip H., and M. Elliot Vittes. 1995. "Who Bears the Burdens of Environmental Pollution? Race, Ethnicity, and Environmental Equity in Florida." *Social Science Quarterly* 76 (2): 294–310.

Population Reference Bureau. 2000. "1999 World Population Data Sheet." Washington, D.C.: Population Reference Bureau.

Porter, Michael E. 1998. "Clusters and the New Economics of Competition." *Harvard Business Review* 76 (6): 77–90.

Portes, Alejandro. 1998. "Social Capital: Its Origins and Applications in Modern Sociology." *Annual Review of Sociology* 24: 1–24.

Portes, Alejandro, and Saskia Sassen-Koob. 1987. "Making It Underground: Comparative Material on the Informal Sector in Western Market Economies." *American Journal of Sociology* 93 (1): 30–61.

Portes, Alejandro, and Julia Sensenbrenner. 1993. "Embeddedness and Immigration: Notes on the Social Determinants of Economic Action." *American Journal of Sociology* 98 (6): 1320–50.

Portes, Alejandro, and Min Zhou. 1992. "Gaining the Upper Hand: Economic Mobility among Immigrant and Domestic Minorities." *Ethnic and Racial Studies* 15 (4): 491–522.

Potapchuk, William R. 1996. "Building Sustainable Community Politics: Synergizing Participatory, Institutional, and Representative Democracy." *National Civic Review* 85 (3): 54–59.

Power, Thomas M. 1996. *Lost Landscapes and Failed Economies: The Search for a Value of Place*. Washington, D.C.: Island Press.

Powers, Edward A., and Vira R. Kivett. 1992. "Kin Expectations and Kin Support Among Rural Older Adults." *Rural Sociology* 57 (2): 194–215.

Powers, Elizabeth. 1999. "Block Granting Welfare: Fiscal Impact on the States." Occasional Paper 23, May, The Urban Institute. Washington, D.C.

Preston, Samuel H. 1984. "Children and the Elderly: Divergent Paths for America's Dependents." *Demography* 21 (4): 435–57.

Price, Michael L., and Daniel C. Clay. 1980. "Structural Disturbances in Rural Communities: Some Repercussions of the Migration Turnaround in Michigan." *Rural Sociology* 45 (4): 591–607.

Prucha, Francis P. 1984. *The Great Father: The United States Government and the American Indians*. Lincoln: University of Nebraska Press.

Public Citizen. 2001. "Down on the Farm: NAFTA's Seven-Year War on Farmers and Ranchers in the U.S., Canada and Mexico." June 26, Public Citizen. Washington, D.C. Available at: www.citizen.org/documents/ACFF2.pdf.

Putnam, Robert D. 1993a. "The Prosperous Community: Social Capital and Public Life." *American Prospect* 4 (13): 35–42.

———. 1993b. *Making Democracy Work: Civic Traditions in Modern Italy*. Princeton: Princeton University Press.

———. 1995. "Bowling Alone: America's Declining Social Capital." *Journal of Democracy* 6 (1): 65–78.

———. 1996. "The Strange Disappearance of Civic America." *American Prospect* 7 (24): 34–48.

———. 2000. *Bowling Alone: The Collapse and Revival of American Community*. New York: Simon and Schuster.

Puzzanchera, Charles M. 2000. "Self-Reported Delinquency by 12-Year-Olds, 1997." OJJDP Fact Sheet 3, February, Office of Juvenile Justice and Delinquency Prevention, U.S. Department of Justice. Washington, D.C.

Pyke, Frank, and Werner Sengenberger. 1992. *Industrial Districts and Local Economic Regeneration*. Geneva: International Institute for Labour Studies.

Radeloff, Volker C., Roger B. Hammer, Paul R. Voss, Alice E. Hagen, Donald R. Field, and David J. Mladenoff. 2001. "Human Demographic Trends and Landscape Level Forest Management in the Northwest Wisconsin Pine Barrens." *Forest Science* 47 (2): 229–41.

Raettig, Terry L., and Harriet H. Christensen. 1999. "Timber Harvesting, Processing, and Employment in the Northwest Economic Adjustment Initiative Region: Changes and Economic Assistance." General Technical Report PNW-GTR-465, U.S. Department of Agriculture, Forest Service, Pacific Northwest Research Station. Portland, Or.

Randolph, Sarah E. 2001. "The Shifting Landscape of Tick-Borne Zoonoses: Tick-Borne Encephalitis and Lyme Borreliosis in Europe." *Philosophical Transactions: Biological Sciences* 356 (1411): 1045–56.

Rank, Mark R., and Thomas A. Hirschl. 2002. "Welfare Use as a Life Course Event: Toward a New Understanding of the U.S. Safety Net." *Social Work* 47 (3): 237–48.

Rankin, Bruce H. and William W. Falk. 1991. "Race, Region, and Earnings: Blacks and Whites in the South." *Rural Sociology* 56 (2): 224–37.

Rasker, Ray. 1995. *A New Home on the Range: Economic Realities in the Columbia River Basin*. Washington, D.C.: The Wilderness Society.

"A Raw Deal for Commodities." 1999. *Economist* 351 (8115): 75–76.

Ray, Daryll E. 2000. "The Failure of the 1996 Farm Bill: Explaining the Nature of Grain Markets." In *A Food and Agriculture Policy for the 21st Century*, ed. M. C. Stumo, 66–75. Lincoln, Neb.: Organization for Competitive Markets.

Reardon, Jack. 1996. "The Presence of Hospital Systems in Rural Areas." *Journal of Economic Issues* 30 (3): 859–76.

Rector, Robert E., and Sarah E. Youssef. 1999. "The Determinants of Welfare Caseload Decline." Center for Data Analysis Report 99-04, May 11, Heritage Center for Data Analysis, Heritage Foundation. Washington, D.C. Available at: http://www.heritage.org/library/cda/cda99-04.html.

Reeder, Richard J. 1996. "Issues in Agriculture and Rural Finance: How Would Rural Areas Fare Under Block Grants?" Agricultural Information Bulletin 724-03, April, Economic Research Service, U.S. Department of Agriculture. Washington, D.C.

Reeder, Richard J., and Anicca C. Jansen. 1995. "Rural Government—Poor Counties, 1962–87." Rural Development Research Report 88, February 1, Agriculture and Rural Economy Division, Economic Research Service, U.S. Department of Agriculture. Washington, D.C.

Reese, Laura A., and Raymond A. Rosenfeld. 2002. *The Civic Culture of Local Economic Development*. Thousand Oaks, Ca.: Sage Publications.

Reich, Robert B. 1991. *The Work of Nations: Preparing Ourselves for 21st-Century Capitalism*. New York: A. A. Knopf Publishing.

———. 1992. "Prepared Statement of Robert B. Reich: High-Wage Jobs in a Competitive Global Economy." Hearing Before the Joint Economic Committee, Congress of the United States, September 16. Washington, D.C.

Reif, Susan S., Susan DesHarnais, and Shulamit Bernard. 1999. "Community Perceptions of the Effects of Rural Hospital Closure on Access to Care." *Journal of Rural Health* 15 (2): 202–9.

Reiss, Albert J., Jr. 1959. "The Sociological Study of Communities." *Rural Sociology* 24 (2): 118–30.

Renkow, Mitch, and Dale Hoover. 2000. "Commuting, Migration, and Rural-Urban Population Dynamics." *Journal of Regional Science* 40 (2): 261–87.

Revel, Alain, and Christophe Riboud. 1986. *American Green Power*. Trans. E. W. Tanner. Baltimore: Johns Hopkins University Press.

Rhoades, Everett R. 2000. *American Indian Health: Innovations in Health Care, Promotion, and Policy*. Baltimore: Johns Hopkins University Press.

Rhodes, R. A. W. 1996. "The New Governance: Governing Without Government." *Political Studies* 44 (4): 652–67.

Richardson, Jean. 2000. *Partnerships in Communities: Reweaving the Fabric of Rural America*. Washington, D.C.: Island Press.

Riesebrodt, Martin. 1993. *Pious Passion: The Emergence of Modern Fundamentalism in the United States and Iran*. Trans. D. Reneau. Berkeley and Los Angeles: University of California Press.

Rikoon, J. Sanford. 1995. *Rachel Calof's Story: Jewish Homesteader on the Northern Plains*. Bloomington: Indiana University Press.

Riley, Linda Ann, Bahram Nassersharif, and John Mullen. 1999. "Assessment of Technology Infrastructure in Native Communities." Report prepared for the Economic Development Administration, U.S. Department of Commerce. Available at: http://alpha.nmsu.edu/~tech.

Ritchey-Vance, Marion. 1996. "Social Capital, Sustainability, and Working Democracy: New Yardsticks for Grassroots Development." *Grassroots Development Journal* 20 (1): 3–9.

Ritchie, Mark. 1993. *Breaking the Deadlock: The United States and Agricultural Policy in the Uruguay Round.* Minneapolis: Institute for Agriculture and Trade Policy.

———. 1999. "The World Trade Organization and the Human Right to Food Security." Presented at the International Cooperative Agriculture Organization General Assembly, August 29. Quebec City, Canada. Available online at http://www.agricoop.org/activities/mark_ritche.pdf.

Ritzer, George. 1999. *Enchanting a Disenchanted World: Revolutionizing the Means of Consumption.* Thousand Oaks, Ca.: Pine Forge Press.

———. 2001. "Landscapes of Consumption (Plenary Address)." Presented at the 64th Annual Meeting of the Rural Sociological Society, August 15–19. Albuquerque, N.M.

Robbins, William G. 1994. *Colony and Empire: The Capitalist Transformation of the American West.* Lawrence: University Press of Kansas.

Rogers, Carolyn C. 1996. "Age and Family Structure, by Race/Ethnicity and Place of Residence." In *Racial/Ethnic Minorities in Rural Areas: Progress and Stagnation, 1980–90,* ed. L. L. Swanson, 42–53. Agricultural Economic Report 731, August, Rural Economy Division, Economic Research Service, United States Department of Agriculture. Washington, D.C.

———. 1997. "Changes in the Social and Economic Status of Women by Metro-Nonmetro Residence." Agricultural Information Bulletin 732, February, Economic Research Service, United States Department of Agriculture. Washington, D.C.

———. 2001. "Factors Affecting High Child Poverty in the Rural South." *Rural America* 15 (4): 50–58.

Rogers, Everett M., Rabel J. Burdge, Peter F. Korsching, and Joseph F. Donnermeyer. 1988. *Social Change in Rural Societies: An Introduction to Rural Sociology.* 3d ed. Englewood Cliffs, N.J.: Prentice Hall.

Rohlf, Daniel J. 1991. "Six Biological Reasons Why the Endangered Species Act Doesn't Work—And What to Do About It." *Conservation Biology* 5 (3): 273–82.

Rome, Adam W. 2001. *The Bulldozer in the Countryside: Suburban Sprawl and the Rise of American Environmentalism.* Cambridge: Cambridge University Press.

Roscigno, Vincent J., and James W. Ainsworth-Darnell. 1999. "Race, Cultural Capital, and Educational Resources: Persistent Inequalities and Achievement Returns." *Sociology of Education* 72 (3): 158–78.

Roscigno, Vincent J., and Martha L. Crowley. 2001. "Rurality, Institutional Disadvantage, and Achievement/Attainment." *Rural Sociology* 66 (2): 268–93.

Rose, Richard. 2000. "How Much Does Social Capital Add to Individual Health? A Survey Study of Russians." *Social Science and Medicine* 51 (9): 1421–35.

Rosenfeld, Stuart A. 1988. "The Tale of Two Souths." In *The Rural South in Crisis: Challenges for the Future,* ed. Lionel J. Beaulieu, 51–71. Boulder, Co.: Westview Press.

Rossi, Alice S., and Peter H. Rossi. 1990. *Of Human Bonding: Parent-Child Relations Across the Life Course.* New York: Aldine de Gruyter.

Roth, Philip D. 2000. "Large-Lot Zoning and Agricultural Preservation: Poison or Cure." *Small Town and Rural Planning, American Planning Association Small Town and Rural (STaR) Newsletter,* January.

Rothman, Hal K. 1998. *Devil's Bargains: Tourism in the Twentieth-Century American West.* Lawrence: University Press of Kansas.

———. 2000. "A History of U.S. National Parks and Economic Development." In *National Parks and Rural Development: Practice and Policy in the United States,* ed. G. E. Machlis and D. R. Field, 51–65. Washington, D.C.: Island Press.

Rowley, Thomas D. 1996. "The Value of Rural." *Rural Development Perspectives* 12 (1): 2–4.

Rudzitis, Gundars. 1999. "Amenities Increasingly Draw People to the Rural West." *Rural Development Perspectives* 14 (2): 9–13.

Rudzitis, Gundars, and Harley E. Johansen. 1989. "Migration into Western Wilderness Counties: Causes and Consequences." *Western Wildlands* 15 (1): 19–23.

Ruggles, Patricia. 1990. *Drawing the Line: Alternative Poverty Measures and their Implications for Public Policy.* Washington, D.C.: Urban Institute Press.

Ruggles, Steven. 1996. "Living Arrangements of the Elderly in America: 1880–1980." In *Aging and Generational Relations over the Life Course: A Historical and Cross-Cultural Perspective,* ed. T. K. Hareven, 254–71. New York: Walter de Gruyter.

Runyan, Desmond K., Wanda M. Hunter, Rebecca R. S. Socolar, Lisa Amaya-Jackson, Diana English, John Landsverk, Howard Dubowitz, Dorothy H. Browne, Shrikant I. Bangdiwala, and Ravi M. Mathew. 1998. "Children Who Prosper in Unfavorable Environments: The Relationship to Social Capital." *Pediatrics* 101 (1): 12–18.

Rupasingha, Anil, Timothy R. Wojan, and David Freshwater. 1999. "Self-Organization and Community-Based Development Initiatives." *Journal of the Community Development Society* 30 (1): 66–82.

Rural Policy Research Institute (RUPRI)—Rural Health Delivery Expert Panel. 1996. "Changes in the Health Care Marketplace: What is the Future for Rural Health Care Delivery?" Policy Paper P96-2, January 11, Rural Policy Research Institute, Columbia, Mo. Available at: http://www.rupri.org/pubs/archive/old/health/P96-2.html.

Rural Policy Research Institute (RUPRI). 1999. "Rural America and Welfare Reform: An Overview Assessment." Policy Paper P99-3, February 10, Rural Welfare Reform Initiative, Rural Policy Research Institute, University of Missouri. Available at: http://www.rupri.org.

———. 2001. "Welfare Reform in Rural America: A Review of Current Research." Policy Paper P2001-5, February 2, Rural Welfare Reform Initiative, Rural Policy Research Institute, University of Missouri. Available at: http://www.rupri.org.

Rural Sociological Society Task Force on Persistent Rural Poverty. 1993. *Persistent Poverty in Rural America.* Boulder, Co.: Westview Press.

Rutter, Michael, Barbara Maughan, Peter Mortimore, and Janet Ouston. 1979. *Fifteen Thousand Hours: Secondary Schools and Their Effects on Children.* Cambridge, Mass.: Harvard University Press.

Ryan, Vernon D., Andy L. Terry, and Danyal Woebke. 1995. "Sigma: A Profile of Iowa's Communities." RDI-0101, College of Agriculture, Iowa State University.

Sachs, Carolyn E. 1994. "Rural Women's Environmental Activism in the USA." In *Gender and Rurality,* ed. S. Whatmore, T. Marsden, and P. Lowe, 117–35. London: David Fulton Publishers.

———. 1996. *Gendered Fields: Rural Women, Agriculture, and Environment.* Boulder, Co.: Westview Press.

Salamon, Sonya. 1992. *Prairie Patrimony: Family, Farming, and Community in the Midwest.* Chapel Hill: University of North Carolina Press.

———. 1995. "The Rural People of the Midwest." In *The Changing American Countryside: Rural People and Places,* ed. E. N. Castle, 352–65. Lawrence: University Press of Kansas.

———. 2003. *Newcomers to Old Towns: Suburbanization of the Heartland.* Chicago: University of Chicago Press.

Sassen, Saskia. 1998. *Globalization and its Discontents.* New York: New Press.

———. 2000. "Territory and Territoriality in the Global Economy." *International Sociology* 15 (2): 372–93.

Sauer, William J., and Raymond T. Coward. 1985. "The Role of Social Support Networks in the Care of the Elderly." In *Social Support Networks and the Care of the Elderly: Theory, Research, and Practice,* ed. W. J. Sauer and R. T. Coward, 3–20. New York: Springer Publishing.

Saupe, William E., and Susan E. Bentley. 1990. "Adjusting to Farm Financial Stress in the 1980s." In *Status of Wisconsin Farming, 1990,* ed. E. V. Jesse, 35–50. Department of Agricultural Economics and Cooperative Extension, University of Wisconsin.

Savas, Emanuel S. 2000. *Privatization and Public-Private Partnerships.* Chatham, N.Y.: Chatham House.

Save the Children. 2002. "America's Forgotten Children: Child Poverty in Rural America." June, Save the Children. Westport, Conn.

Savitch, H. V., and Ronald K. Vogel. 2001. "Paths to New Regionalism." *State and Local Government Review* 32 (3): 158–68.

Schertz, Lyle P., and Otto C. Doering III. 1999. *The Making of the 1996 Farm Act.* Ames: Iowa State University Press.

Schexnayder, Deanna, Daniel Schroeder, Laura Lein, David Dominguez, Karen Douglas, and Freddie Richards. 2001. "Texas Families in Transition/Surviving Without TANF: A Preliminary Analysis of Families Diverted from or Leaving TANF." Preliminary Report, March, Ray Marshall Center for the Study of Human Resources, and Center for Social Work Research, University of Texas, and Center for Innovative Projects for Economic Development, Prairie View A&M University. Available at: http://www.utexas.edu/research/cshr/pubs/TFITfullreport.pdf.

Schindler, Daniel E., Sean I. Geib, and Monica R. Williams. 2000. "Patterns of Fish Growth Along a Residential Development Gradient in North Temperate Lakes." *Ecosystems* 3 (3): 229–37.

Schmalenbach, Herman. 1961. "The Sociological Category of Communion." In *Theories of Society: Foundations of Modern Sociological Theory,* vol. 1, ed. T. Parsons, E. Shils, K. D. Naegele, and J. R. Pitts, 331–47. New York: Free Press of Glencoe.

Schorr, Lisbeth B. 1988. *Within Our Reach: Breaking the Cycle of Disadvantage.*
Garden City, N.Y.: Anchor Press/Doubleday.
———. 1997. *Common Purpose: Strengthening Families and Neighborhoods to
Rebuild America.* New York: Anchor Books.
Schott, Liz, Robert Greenstein, and Wendell Primus. 1999. "The Determinants of
Welfare Caseload Decline: A Brief Rejoinder." June 22, Center on Budget
and Policy Priorities. Washington, D.C. Available at: http://www.cbpp.org/
6-22-99wel.htm.
Schuh, Edward J. 2001. "The Impact of Globalization on Rural America:
Prospects for Development." Presented at the Annual Meeting of the Com-
munity Development Society, July 23–25. Duluth, Minn.
Schuler, Douglas. 1996. *New Community Networks: Wired for Change.* Reading,
Mass.: Addison-Wesley Publishing.
Schulman, Michael D., and Cynthia Anderson. 1999. "The Dark Side of the
Force: A Case Study of Restructuring and Social Capital." *Rural Sociology*
64 (3): 351–72.
Schwartz, Gary. 1987. *Beyond Conformity or Rebellion: Youth and Authority in
America.* Chicago: University of Chicago Press.
Sears, David W., and J. Norman Reid. 1995. *Rural Development Strategies.*
Chicago: Nelson-Hall.
Seebach, Michelle. 1992. "Small Towns Have a Rosy Image." *American Demo-
graphics* 14 (10): 19.
Sexton, Richard J. 2000. "Industrialization and Consolidation in the U.S. Food
Sector: Implications for Competition and Welfare." *American Journal of
Agricultural Economics* 82 (5): 1087–104.
Sharp, Elaine B. 1991. "Institutional Manifestations of Accessibility and Urban
Economic Development Polity." *Western Political Quarterly* 44 (1): 129–47.
Sharp, Jeff S. 2001. "Locating the Community Field: A Study of Interorganiza-
tional Network Structure and Capacity for Community Action." *Rural Soci-
ology* 66 (3): 403–24.
Shields, Martin, and Steven C. Deller. 1998. "Commuting's Effect on Local Retail
Market Performance." *Review of Regional Studies* 28 (2): 71–89.
Shils, Edward. 1972. *The Intellectuals and the Powers, and Other Essays.*
Chicago: University of Chicago Press.
Shumway, J. Matthew, and James A. Davis. 1996. "Nonmetropolitan Population
Change in the Mountain West: 1970–1995." *Rural Sociology* 61 (3): 513–29.
Siegel, Jacob S. 1993. *A Generation of Change: A Profile of America's Older Pop-
ulation.* New York: Russell Sage Foundation.
Siles, Marcelo, Steven D. Hanson, and Lindon J. Robison. 1994. "Socio-Econom-
ics and the Probability of Loan Approval." *Review of Agricultural Econom-
ics* 16 (3): 363–72.
Silva, Fabio, and Jon Sonstelie. 1995. "Did *Serrano* Cause a Decline in School
Spending?" *National Tax Journal* 48 (2): 199–215.
Simmel, Georg. 1950. "The Metropolis and Mental Life." In *The Sociology of
Georg Simmel,* ed. K. H. Wolff, 404–24. New York: The Free Press.
Simpson, Ida H., John Wilson, and Kristina Young. 1988. "The Sexual Division of
Farm Household Labor: A Replication and Extension." *Rural Sociology* 53
(2): 145–65.

Singelmann, Joachim. 1978. *From Agriculture to Services: The Transformation of Industrial Employment.* Beverly Hills, Ca.: Sage.

———. 1996. "Will Rural Areas Still Matter in the 21st Century? (or) Can Rural Sociology Remain Relevant?" *Rural Sociology* 61 (1): 143–58.

Singelmann, Joachim, Theresa Davidson, and Rachel Reynolds. 2002. "Welfare, Work, and Well-Being in Metro and Nonmetro Louisiana." *Southern Rural Sociology* 18 (1): 21–47.

Skatrud, Julia D., Trude A. Bennett, and Frank A. Loda. 1998. "An Overview of Adolescent Pregnancy in Rural Areas." *Journal of Rural Health* 14 (1): 17–27.

Skocpol, Theda. 1991. "Targeting Within Universalism: Politically Viable Policies to Combat Poverty in the United States." In *The Urban Underclass,* ed. C. Jencks and P. E. Peterson, 411–36. Washington, D.C.: Brookings Institution.

Skogan, Wesley G. 1990. *Disorder and Decline: Crime and the Spiral of Decay in American Neighborhoods.* New York: Free Press.

Skyrme, David J. 1999. *Knowledge Networking: Creating the Collaborative Enterprise.* Woburn, Mass.: Butterworth-Heinemann.

Slack, Tim, and Leif Jensen. 2002. "Race, Ethnicity, and Underemployment in Nonmetropolitan America: A 30-Year Profile." *Rural Sociology* 67 (2): 208–33.

Slifkin, Rebecca T., Sarah J. Clark, Suzanne E. Strandhoy, and Thomas R. Konrad. 1997. "Public-Sector Immunization Coverage in 11 States: The Status of Rural Areas." *Journal of Rural Health* 13 (4): 334–41.

Slifkin, Rebecca T., Laurie J. Goldsmith, and Thomas C. Ricketts. 2000. "Race and Place: Urban-Rural Differences in Health for Racial and Ethnic Minorities." NC RHRP Working Paper Series 66, January, N.C. Rural Health Research and Policy Analysis Program, University of North Carolina. Chapel Hill, N.C.

Smiley, Jane. 1992. *A Thousand Acres.* New York: Ballantine Books.

Smith, Mark H., Lionel J. Beaulieu, and Glenn D. Israel. 1992. "Effects of Human Capital and Social Capital on Dropping Out of High School in the South." *Journal of Research in Rural Education* 8 (1): 75–87.

Smith, Mark H., Lionel J. Beaulieu, and Ann Seraphine. 1995. "Social Capital, Place of Residence, and College Attendance." *Rural Sociology* 60 (3): 363–80.

Smith, Michael D., and Richard S. Krannich. 1998. "Tourism Dependence and Resident Attitudes." *Annals of Tourism Research* 25 (4): 783–802.

———. 2000. "'Culture Clash' Revisited: Newcomer and Longer-Term Residents' Attitudes Toward Land Use, Development, and Environmental Issues in Rural Communities in the Rocky Mountain West." *Rural Sociology* 65 (3): 396–421.

Smith, Michael D., Richard S. Krannich, and Lori M. Hunter. 2001. "Growth, Decline, Stability, and Disruption: A Longitudinal Analysis of Social Well-Being in Four Western Communities." *Rural Sociology* 66 (3): 425–50.

Smith, Stephen M. 1993. "Service Industries in the Rural Economy: The Role and Potential Contributions." In *Economic Adaptation: Alternatives for Nonmetropolitan Areas,* ed. D. L. Barkley, 105–26. Boulder, Co.: Westview Press.

Snipp, C. Matthew. 1986. "American Indians and Natural Resource Develop-
    ment: Indigenous Peoples' Land, Now Sought After, Has Produced New
    Indian-White Problems." *American Journal of Economics and Sociology* 45
    (4): 457–74.
———. 1989. *American Indians: The First of This Land*. New York: Russell Sage
    Foundation.
Snipp, C. Matthew, Hayward D. Horton, Leif Jenson, Joane Nagal, and Refugio
    Rochin. 1993. "Persistent Rural Poverty and Racial and Ethnic Minorities." In
    Persistent Poverty in Rural America, ed. the Rural Sociological Society Task
    Force on Persistent Rural Poverty, 173–99. Boulder, Co.: Westview Press.
So, Kim S., Peter F. Orazem, and Daniel M. Otto. 2001. "The Effects of Housing
    Prices, Wages, and Commuting Time on Joint Residential and Job Location
    Choices." *American Journal of Agricultural Economics* 83 (4): 1036–48.
Sommer, Judith E., Robert A. Hoppe, Robert C. Green, and Penelope
    J. Korb. 1998. "Structural and Financial Characteristics of U.S. Farms,
    1995: 20th Annual Family Farm Report to Congress." Agricultural Infor-
    mation Bulletin 746, December, Resource Economics Division, Economic
    Research Service, U.S. Department of Agriculture. Washington , D.C.
Sorensen, A. Ann, Richard P. Greene, and Karen Russ. 1997. *Farming on the
    Edge.* Washington, D.C.: American Farmland Trust.
Sorkin, Alan L. 1978. *The Urban American Indian.* Lexington, Mass.:
    D. C. Heath.
Sorokin, Pitirim A., Carle C. Zimmerman, and Charles J. Galpin. 1931. *A System-
    atic Source Book in Rural Sociology,* vol. 2. Minneapolis: University of
    Minnesota Press.
Spain, Daphne. 1993. "Been-Heres Versus Come-Heres: Negotiating Conflicting
    Community Identities." *Journal of the American Planning Association* 59
    (2): 156–71.
Spitze, Glenna, and John R. Logan. 1991. "Sibling Structure and Intergenerational
    Relations." *Journal of Marriage and the Family* 53 (4): 871–84.
Squires, Sally. 2001. "Report in Hand: Surgeon General Calls for Action Against
    Obesity." *Des Moines Register,* December 14, p. 6A.
Stack, Carol B. 1996. *Call to Home: African-Americans Reclaim the Rural South.*
    New York: Basic Books.
Stallmann, Judith I., Ari Mwachofi, Jan L. Flora, and Thomas G. Johnson. 1995.
    "The Labor Market and Human Capital Investment." In *Investing in Peo-
    ple: The Human Capital Needs of Rural America,* ed. L. J. Beaulieu and
    D. Mulkey, 333–49. Boulder, Co.: Westview Press.
Stauber, Karl N. 2001. "Why Invest in Rural America?" In *Exploring Policy
    Options for a New Rural America,* ed. the Center for the Study of Rural
    America, 9–29. Center for the Study of Rural America, Federal Reserve
    Bank of Kansas City. Kansas City, Mo.
Stein, Maurice R. 1960. *The Eclipse of Community: An Interpretation of Ameri-
    can Studies.* New York: Harper and Row.
Stein, Robert M. 1999. "Devolution and Challenge for State and Local Gover-
    nance." In *American State and Local Politics: Directions for the 21st Cen-
    tury,* ed. R. E. Weber and P. Brace, 21–37. New York: Chatham House
    Publishers, Seven Bridges Press, LLC.

Stevenson, David L., and David P. Baker. 1987. "The Family-School Relation and the Child's School Performance." *Child Development* 58 (5): 1348–57.

Stewart, Patrick A., and Lawrence W. Libby. 1998. "Determinants of Farmland Values: The Case of DeKalb County, Illinois." *Review of Agricultural Economics* 20 (1): 80–95.

Stockard, Jean, and Maralee Mayberry. 1992. *Effective Educational Environments.* Newbury Park, Ca.: Corwin Press.

Stoecker, Randy. 1998. "Capital Against Community." In *Research in Community Sociology: American Community Issues and Patterns of Development,* vol. 8, ed. D. A. Chekki, 15–43. Greenwich, Conn.: JAI Press.

Stokes, Samuel N., A. Elizabeth Watson, and Shelley S. Mastran. 1997. *Saving America's Countryside: A Guide to Rural Conservation.* Baltimore: Johns Hopkins University Press.

Stoller, Eleanor P. 1998. "Families of Elderly Rural Americans." In *Aging in Rural Settings: Life Circumstances and Distinctive Features,* ed. R. T. Coward and J. A. Krout, 127–46. New York: Springer Publishing.

Stone, Clarence N. 1989. *Regime Politics: Governing Atlanta, 1946–1988.* Lawrence: University Press of Kansas.

Storper, Michael. 1997a. *The Regional World: Territorial Development in a Global Economy.* New York: Guilford Press.

———. 1997b. "Territories, Flows, and Hierarchies in the Global Economy." In *Spaces of Globalization: Reasserting the Power of the Local,* ed. K. R. Cox, 19–44. New York: Guilford Press.

Storper, Michael, and Richard Walker. 1989. *The Capitalist Imperative: Territory, Technology and Industrial Growth.* New York: Basil Blackwell.

Stull, Donald D., Michael J. Broadway, and David Griffith. 1995. *Any Way You Cut It: Meat Processing and Small-Town America.* Lawrence: University Press of Kansas.

Stumo, Michael C. 2000. *A Food and Agriculture Policy for the 21st Century.* Lincoln, Neb.: Organization for Competitive Markets.

Sturm, Roland. 2002. "The Effects of Obesity, Smoking, and Drinking on Medical Problems and Costs." *Health Affairs* 21 (2): 245–53.

Sullivan, David. 1998. "Local Economic Development Organizations in Small- and Middle-Sized Communities: The Case of Wisconsin." In *Research in Community Sociology: American Community Issues and Patterns of Development,* vol. 8, ed. D. A. Chekki, 143–57. Stamford, Conn.: JAI Press.

Summers, Gene F. 1986. "Rural Community Development." *Annual Review of Sociology* 12: 341–71.

———. 1991. "Minorities in Rural Society." *Rural Sociology* 56 (2): 177–88.

———. 1995. "Persistent Rural Poverty." In *The Changing American Countryside: Rural People and Places,* ed. E. N. Castle, 213–28. Lawrence: University Press of Kansas.

———. 2000. "Rural Sociology." In *Encyclopedia of Sociology,* 2d ed., ed. E. F. Borgatta and R. J. V. Montgomery, 2425–36. New York: Macmillan Reference USA.

Summers, Gene F., Sharon D. Evans, Frank Clemente, E. M. Beck, and Jon Minkoff. 1976. *Industrial Invasion of Nonmetropolitan America: A Quarter Century of Experience.* New York: Praeger Publishers.

Summers, Gene F., and Thomas A. Hirschl. 1985. "Retirees as a Growth Industry." *Rural Development Perspectives* 1 (2): 13–16.

Sun, Yongmin. 1999. "The Contextual Effects of Community Social Capital on
Academic Performance." *Social Science Research* 28 (4): 403–26.

Swaim, Paul L. 1998. "Job Training for Rural Workers." In *Rural Education and
Training in the New Economy: The Myth of the Rural Skills Gap*, ed.
R. M. Gibbs, P. L. Swaim, and R. Teixeira, 97–113. Ames: Iowa State Uni-
versity Press.

Swanson, Linda L. 1996. "Racial/Ethnic Minorities in Rural Areas: Progress and
Stagnation, 1980–90." Agricultural Economics Report 731, August, Rural
Economy Division, Economic Research Service, U.S. Department of Agricul-
ture. Washington, D.C.

Swanson, Linda L., and Laarni T. Dacquel. 1996. "Rural Child Poverty and the
Role of Family Structure." In *Racial/Ethnic Minorities in Rural Areas:
Progress and Stagnation, 1980–90,* ed. L. L. Swanson, 33–41. Agricultural
Economics Report 731, August, Rural Economy Division, Economic
Research Service, U.S. Department of Agriculture. Washington, D.C.

Swanson, Louis E. 2001. "Rural Policy and Direct Local Participation: Democracy, Inclusiveness, Collective Agency, and Locality-Based Policy." *Rural
Sociology* 66 (1): 1–21.

Swanson, Louis E., and David Freshwater. 1999. "From New Deal to No Deal."
Forum for Applied Research and Public Policy 14 (1): 84–89.

Swanson, Louis E., Rosalind Harris, Jerry Skees, and Lionel Williamson. 1995.
"African-Americans in Southern Rural Regions: The Importance of
Legacy." In *Blacks in Rural America,* ed. J. B. Stewart and J. E. Allen-Smith,
103–18. New Brunswick, N.J.: Transaction Publishers.

Swensen, Tami, Steve White, and Steve Murdock. 2002."Time Limit and Sanction
Effects of the Texas TANF Waiver." *Southern Rural Sociology* 18 (1):
82–110.

Swyngedouw, Erik. 1997. "Neither Global nor Local: 'Glocalization' and the Politics of Scale." In *Spaces of Globalization: Reasserting the Power of the
Local,* ed. K. R. Cox, 137–66. New York: Guilford Press.

Szasz, Andrew, and Michael Meuser. 2000. "Unintended, Inexorable: The Production of Environmental Inequalities in Santa Clara County, California."
American Behavioral Scientist 43 (4): 602–32.

Tallichet, Suzanne E. 2000. "Barriers to Women's Advancement in Underground
Coal Mining." *Rural Sociology* 65 (2): 234–52.

Talmud, Ilan, and Gustavo S. Mesch. 1997. "Market Embeddedness and Corporate Instability: The Ecology of Inter-Industrial Networks." *Social Science
Research* 26(4):419–41.

Taylor, Carl C. 1926. *Rural Sociology: A Study of Rural Problems.* New York:
Harper and Brothers.

Teachman, Jay D., Lucky M. Tedrow, and Kyle D. Crowder. 2000. "The Changing Demography of America's Families." *Journal of Marriage and the Family* 62 (4): 1234–46.

Texas Water Development Board. 1997. "Texas Water Development Board's
Water and Wastewater Survey of Economically Distressed Areas." December, 1996, Texas Water Development Board. Austin, Tx. Available at:
http://www.twdb.state.tx.us/colonias/1996%20colonias.pdf.

Theodori, Gene L., and A. E. Luloff. 2000. "Urbanization and Community Attachment in Rural Areas." *Society and Natural Resources* 13 (5): 399–420.

Thompson, Alton. 1995. "Determinants of Poverty Among Workers in Metro and Nonmetro Areas of the South." In *Blacks in Rural America,* ed. J. B. Stewart and J. E. Allen-Smith, 153–71. New Brunswick, N.J.: Transaction Publishers.

Thompson, Mark A. 1997. "The Impact of Spatial Mismatch on Female Labor Force Participation." *Economic Development Quarterly* 11 (2): 138–45.

Thompson, Wilbur R. 1965. *A Preface to Urban Economics.* Baltimore: Johns Hopkins University Press.

Thompson, William, Ricardo Gazel, and Dan Rickman. 1995. "The Economic Impact of Native American Gaming in Wisconsin." *Wisconsin Policy Research Institute Report* 8 (3): 1–48.

Thurow, Lester C. 1996. *The Future of Capitalism: How Today's Economic Forces Will Shape Tomorrow's Future.* New York: W. Morrow.

Tibbetts, John. 2001. "Africa-on-the-South-Carolina-Coast." *Utne Reader* 107 (September/October): 30–31.

Tickamyer, Ann R. 1996. "Sex, Lies, and Statistics: Can Rural Sociology Survive Restructuring? (or) What Is Right with Rural Sociology and How Can We Fix It." *Rural Sociology* 61 (1): 5–24.

Tickamyer, Ann R., Janet Bokemeier, Shelley Feldman, Rosalind Harris, John P. Jones, and DeeAnn Wenk. 1993. "Women and Persistent Rural Poverty." In *Persistent Poverty in Rural America,* ed. Rural Sociological Society Task Force on Persistent Rural Poverty, 200–29. Boulder, Co.: Westview Press.

Tickamyer, Ann R., Debra A. Henderson, Julie A. White, and Barry L. Tadlock. 2000. "Voices of Welfare Reform: Bureaucratic Rationality Versus the Perceptions of Welfare Participants." *Affilia* 15 (2): 173–92.

Tickamyer, Ann R., and Teresa A. Wood. 1998. "Identifying Participation in the Informal Economy Using Survey Research Methods." *Rural Sociology* 63 (2): 323–39.

Tiebout, Charles M. 1956. "A Pure Theory of Local Expenditures." *Journal of Political Economy* 64 (5): 416–24.

Tigges, Leanne M., Irene Browne, and Gary P. Green. 1998. "Social Isolation of the Urban Poor: Race, Class and Neighborhood Effects on Social Resources." *Sociological Quarterly* 39 (1): 53–77.

Tocqueville, Alexis de. 1836. *Democracy in America.* London: Saunders and Otley.

Tolbert, Charles M., Patrick M. Horan, and E. M. Beck. 1980. "The Structure of Economic Segmentation: A Dual Economy Approach." *American Journal of Sociology* 85 (5): 1095–1116.

Tolbert, Charles M., Michael D. Irwin, Thomas A. Lyson, and Alfred R. Nucci. 2002. "Civic Community in Small-Town America: How Civic Welfare is Influenced by Local Capitalism and Civic Engagement." *Rural Sociology* 67 (1): 90–113.

Tolbert, Charles M., and Molly S. Killian. 1987. "Labor Market Areas for the United States." Staff Report AGES870721, August, Agriculture and Rural Economy Division, Economic Research Service, U.S. Department of Agriculture. Washington, D.C.

Tolbert, Charles M., and Thomas A. Lyson. 1992. "Earnings Inequality in the Nonmetropolitan United States: 1967–1990." *Rural Sociology* 57 (4): 494–511.

Tolbert, Charles M., Thomas A. Lyson, and Michael D. Irwin. 1998. "Local Capitalism, Civic Engagement, and Socioeconomic Well-Being." *Social Forces* 77
(2): 401–27.

Tolbert, Charles M., and Molly Sizer. 1996. "U.S. Commuting Zones and Labor
Market Areas: A 1990 Update." Staff Paper AGES-9614, Rural Economy
Division, Economic Research Service, U.S. Department of Agriculture.
Washington, D.C.

Tolnay, Stewart E. 1999. *The Bottom Rung: African American Family Life on
Southern Farms.* Urbana: University of Illinois Press.

Tomaskovic-Devey, Donald. 1988. "Industrial Structure, Relative Labor Power,
and Poverty Rates." In *Poverty and Social Welfare in the United States,* ed.
D. Tomaskovic-Devey, 104–29. Boulder, Co.: Westview Press.

———. 1993. *Gender and Racial Inequality at Work: The Sources and Consequences of Job Segregation.* Ithaca, N.Y.: ILR Press.

Tönnies, Ferdinand. 1957. *Community and Society (Gemeinschaft und
Gesellschaft).* Trans. C. P. Loomis. East Lansing: Michigan State University
Press.

———. 1963 [1887]. *Community and Society (Gemeinschaft und Gesellschaft).*
New York: Harper and Row.

Torres, Cruz C. 2000. "Emerging Latino Communities: A New Challenge for the
Rural South. The Rural South: Preparing for the Challenges of the 21st Century." Policy Brief 12, August, Southern Rural Development Center, Mississippi State University.

Triglia, Carlo. 2001. "Social Capital and Local Development." *European Journal
of Social Theory* 4 (4): 427–42.

Tuan, Yi-Fu. 1977. *Space and Place: The Perspective of Experience.* Minneapolis:
University of Minnesota Press.

Tweeten, Luther G., and Cornelia B. Flora. 2001. "Vertical Coordination of Agriculture in Farming-Dependent Areas." Task Force Report 137, Council for
Agricultural Science and Technology. Ames, Iowa.

Uhlenberg, Peter. 1993. "Demographic Change and Kin Relationships in Later
Life." In *Annual Review of Gerontology and Geriatrics: Kinship, Aging,
and Social Change,* vol. 13, ed. G. L. Maddox and M. P. Lawton, 219–38.
New York: Springer Publishing.

Uhlenberg, Peter, and Sonia Miner. 1996. "Life Course and Aging: A Cohort Perspective." In *Handbook of Aging and the Social Sciences,* 4th ed., ed.
R. H. Binstock and L. K. George, 208–28. San Diego: Academic Press.

Urban Institute. n.d. "Assessing the New Federalism: State Database." The Urban
Institute. Washington, D.C. Available at: http://www.urban.org/content/
Research/NewFederalism/Data/StateDatabase/StateDatabase.htm.

U.S. Bureau of the Census. 1980. *Census of Population and Housing.* Washington,
D.C.: U.S. Bureau of the Census.

———. 1990. *Census of Population and Housing.* Washington, D.C.: U.S. Bureau
of the Census.

———. 2000. *Census of Population and Housing.* Washington, D.C.: U.S. Bureau
of the Census.

———. 2001a. *Agricultural Statistics.* Washington, D.C.: Department of Commerce.

———. 2001b. "Current Population Survey." March, 2000, Ethnic and Hispanic Statistics Branch, U.S. Census Bureau. Washington, D.C. Available at: http://www.census.gov/population/socdemo/hispanic/p20-535/tab09-1.txt.

———. 2001c. "Population by Race and Hispanic or Latino Origin for the United States: 1990 and 2000." Census PHC-T-1, April, U.S. Bureau of the Census. Washington, D.C.

———. 2001d. "Small Area Income and Poverty Estimates: Intercensal Estimates for States, Counties, and School Districts." Small Area Estimates Branch, Housing and Household Economic Statistics Division, U.S. Bureau of the Census. Available at: http://www.census.gov/hhes/www/saipe.html.

———. 2002. "Annual Demographic Survey (March Current Population Survey Supplement)." U.S. Bureau of the Census and Bureau of Labor Statistics. Washington, D.C. Available at: http://www.bls.census.gov/cps/ads/ads-main.htm.

U.S. Bureau of Economic Analysis. 2002. "Regional Economic Information System (REIS) CD-ROM, 1969–2000." RCN-0295, June 3, Bureau of Economic Analysis, U.S. Department of Commerce. Washington, D.C.

U.S. Bureau of Indian Affairs. 1997. "Annual Report of Indian Lands." Office of Trust Responsibilities, Bureau of Indian Affairs, U.S. Department of the Interior. Washington, D.C. Available at: www.doi.gov/bia/realty/consol/97.html.

U.S. Centers for Disease Control. 2001. "Compressed Mortality Files 1968–1997, All U.S. Counties." Centers for Disease Control and Prevention, U.S. Department of Health and Human Services. Washington, D.C.

U.S. Congress. 1995. "Corporate Restructuring and Downsizing: Hearings Before the Committee on the Budget." House of Representatives, 104th Congress, First Session, March 23, U.S. Government Printing Office. Washington, D.C.

———. 1996. "Personal Responsibility and Work Opportunity Reconciliation Act of 1996 (P.L. 104-193)" H.R. 3734, 104th Congress, August 22. Washington, D.C.

U.S. Department of Agriculture (USDA). 1999. 1997 Census of Agriculture. Washington, D.C.: National Agricultural Statistics Service, U.S. Department of Agriculture. Available at: http://www.nass.usda.gov/census/.

———. 2000. "Summary Report: 1997 National Resources Inventory." December, 1999, Natural Resources Conservation Service, U.S. Department of Agriculture. Washington, D.C. Available at: http://www.nrcs.usda.gov/technical/NRI/1997/summary_report/.

———. 2001. "1997 Census of Agriculture: Agricultural Economics and Land Ownership Survey (1999)." National Agricultural Statistics Service, U.S. Department of Agriculture. Washington, D.C. Available at: http://www.nass.usda.gov/census/census97/aelos/aelos.htm.

———. 2002a. "Measuring Rurality: County Typology Codes." Economic Research Service, U.S. Department of Agriculture. Washington, D.C. Available at: http://www.ers.usda.gov/Briefing/Rurality/Typology/index.htm.

———. 2002b. "Farms and Land in Farms." February, National Agricultural Statistics Service, U.S. Department of Agriculture. Washington, D.C. Available at: http://www.usda.gov/nass/aggraphs/landinfarms.htm.

U.S. Department of Education. 1992. *Second Follow-Up of the National Education Longitudinal Survey.* Washington, D.C.: National Center for Education
Statistics.

————. 1996. *Schools and Staffing Survey, 1993–94: Electronic Codebook
and Public Use Data.* Washington, D.C.: National Center for Education
Statistics.

————. 1997. *High School and Beyond (Sophomore Cohort).* Washington, D.C.:
National Center for Education Statistics.

————. 1999. *Fast Response Survey System, Survey on the Condition of Public
School Facilities.* Washington, D.C.: National Center for Education Statistics.
Available at: http://nces.ed.gov/surveys/ruraled/data/Condition_Rating.asp.

U.S. Department of Health and Human Services (USDHHS). 1996. "Health Care
Financing Review: Medicare and Medicaid Statistical Supplement, 1996."
Publication 03386, October, Office of Research and Demonstrations,
Health Care Financing Administration, U.S. Department of Health and
Human Services. Baltimore, Md.

————. 1997. "Notice of Proposed Rule Making: Temporary Assistance for
Needy Families." Administration for Children and Families, U.S. Department of Health and Human Services. Washington, D.C. Available at:
http://www.acf.dhhs.gov/hypernews/topics2.htm.

————. 2000a. "Temporary Assistance for Needy Families (TANF) Program:
Third Annual Report to Congress." August, Administration for Children
and Families, U.S. Department of Health and Human Services. Washington,
D.C. Available at: http://www.acf.dhhs.gov/programs/opre/annual3.pdf.

————. 2000b. "Change in TANF Caseloads: Total TANF Families and Recipients."
Administration for Children and Families, U.S. Department of Health and
Human Services. Washington, D.C. Available at: http://www.acf.dhhs.gov/
news/stats/case-fam.htm.

————. 2002c. "Healthy People 2010." Office of Disease Prevention and Health
Promotion of the Office of Public Health and Science. Available at:
http://www.healthypeople.gov/.

————. 2002. "One Department Serving Rural America." HHS Rural Task Force,
Report to the Secretary, July, U.S. Department of Health and Human Services. Washington, D.C. Available at: ftp://ftp.hrsa.gov/ruralhealth/Publi-
cReportJune2002.pdf.

U.S. Department of Justice. 1996. "School Crime Supplement to the National
Crime Victimization Survey, 1989 and 1995." Bureau of Justice Statistics,
U.S. Department of Justice. Washington, D.C.

U.S. Environmental Protection Agency. 2000a. "Profile of the Agricultural Crop
Production Industry." EPA Report 310-R-00-001, September, EPA Office of
Compliance Sector Notebook Project. U.S. Government Printing Office.
Washington, D.C.

————. 2000b. "Profile of the Agricultural Livestock Production Industry." EPA
Report 310-R-00-002, September, EPA Office of Compliance Sector Notebook Project. U.S. Government Printing Office. Washington, D.C.

U.S. Office of Management and Budget. 2000. "Standards for Defining Metropolitan and Micropolitan Statistical Areas." *Federal Register* 65 (249), December 27: 82228–38.

U.S. Office of Rural Health Policy. 1997. *Facts About . . . Rural Physicians.* Washington, D.C.: Health Resources and Services Administration, U.S. Department of Health and Human Services.

Valenzuela, Angela. 1999. *Subtractive Schooling: U.S.-Mexican Youth and the Politics of Caring.* Albany: SUNY Press.

Valle, Isabel. 1994. *Fields of Toil: A Migrant Family's Journey.* Pullman: Washington State University Press.

Ventura, Stephanie J., Joyce A. Martin, Sally C. Curtin, Fay Menacker, and Brady E. Hamilton. 2001. "Births: Final Data for 1999." *National Vital Statistics Reports* 1 (1), April 17, National Center for Health Statistics, U.S. Department of Health and Human Services. Hyattsville, Md.

Vesterby, Marlow, and Kenneth S. Krupa. 2001. "Major Uses of Land in the United States, 1997." ERS Statistical Bulletin 973, Resource Economics Division, Economic Research Service, U.S. Department of Agriculture. Washington, D.C.

Vining, D. R., Jr. and A. Strauss. 1977. "A Demonstration that the Current Deconcentration of Population in the United States Is a Clean Break with the Past." *Environment and Planning A* 9 (7): 751–58.

Voigt, Dennis R., and Jim D. Broadfoot. 1995. "Effects of Cottage Development on White-Tailed Deer, *Odocoileus Virginianus,* Winter Habitat on Lake Muskoka, Ontario." *Canadian Field-Naturalist* 109 (2): 201–4.

Voss, Paul R. 2001. "Growth of Minority Populations in the Nonmetro Midwest." Presented at the 64th Annual Meeting of the Rural Sociological Society, August 15–19. Albuquerque, N.M.

Voth, Donald E., and Marcie L. Brewster. 1990. "Community Development." In *American Rural Communities,* ed. A. E. Luloff and L. E. Swanson, 169–80. Boulder, Co.: Westview Press.

Wacquant, Loïc J. D. and William J. Wilson. 1993. "The Cost of Racial and Class Exclusion in the Inner City." In *The Ghetto Underclass: Social Science Perspectives,* ed. W. J. Wilson, 25–42. Newbury Park, Ca.: Sage Publications.

Walberg, Herbert J. 1984. "Improving the Productivity of America's Schools." *Educational Leadership: Journal of the Association of Supervision and Curriculum Development* 41 (8): 19–26.

———. 1992. "On Local Control: Is Bigger Better?" In *Source Book on School and District Size, Cost, and Quality,* 118–34. Oak Brook, Ill.: North Central Regional Educational Laboratory.

Waldrop, M. Mitchell. 1992. *Complexity: The Emerging Science at the Edge of Order and Chaos.* New York: Simon and Schuster.

Walker, Richard A. 1978. "Two Sources of Uneven Development Under Advanced Capitalism: Spatial Differentiation and Capital Mobility." *Review of Radical Political Economics* 10 (3): 28–37.

Wallace Center. 2001. "Making Changes: Turning Local Visions into National Solutions." Henry A. Wallace Center for Agricultural and Environmental Policy at Winrock International. Arlington, Va.

Wallace, Rachel E., and Robert B. Wallace. 1998. "Rural-Urban Contrasts in Elder Health Status: Methodological Issues and Findings." In *Aging in Rural Settings: Life Circumstances and Distinctive Features,* ed. R. T. Coward and J. A. Krout, 67–83. New York: Springer Publishing.

Wallerstein, Immanuel. 1974. *The Modern World System.* New York: Academic Press.

Wardwell, John M. 1980. "Toward a Theory of Urban-Rural Migration in the Developed World." In *New Directions in Urban-Rural Migration: The Population Turnaround in Rural America,* ed. D. L. Brown and J. M. Wardwell, 71–118. New York: Academic Press.

———. 1982. "The Reversal of Nonmetropolitan Migration Loss." In *Rural Society in the U.S.: Issues for the 1980s,* ed. D. A. Dillman and D. J. Hobbs, 23–33. Boulder, Co.: Westview Press.

Warner, Mildred E. 1998. "Local Government Financial Capacity and the Growing Importance of State Aid." *Rural Development Perspectives* 13 (3): 27–36.

———. 1999. "Social Capital Construction and the Role of the Local State." *Rural Sociology* 64 (3): 373–93.

———. 2001. "State Policy Under Devolution: Redistribution and Centralization." *National Tax Journal* 54 (3): 541–56.

Warner, Mildred E., and Amir Hefetz. 2002. "Applying Market Solutions to Public Services: An Assessment of Efficiency, Equity, and Voice." *Urban Affairs Review* 38 (1): 70–89.

———. 2003. "Rural-Urban Differences in Privatization: Limits to the Competitive State," *Environment and Planning C: Government and Policy* 12 (5).

Warren, Roland L. 1963. *The Community in America.* Chicago: Rand McNally.

———. 1971. *The Community in America.* 2d ed. Chicago: Rand McNally.

———. 1978. *The Community in America.* 3d ed. Chicago: Rand McNally

Watson, Keith, and Steven D. Gold. 1997. "The Other Side of Devolution: Shifting Relationships Between State and Local Governments." Occasional Paper 2, August, The Urban Institute. Washington, D.C.

Wear, David N., and Paul Bolstad. 1998. "Land-Use Changes in Southern Appalachian Landscapes: Spatial Analysis and Forecast Evaluation." *Ecosystems* 1 (6): 575–94.

Wear, David N., Monica G. Turner, and Robert J. Naiman. 1998. "Land Cover along an Urban-Rural Gradient: Implications for Water Quality." *Ecological Applications* 8 (3): 619–30.

Weaver, R. Kent. 2000. *Ending Welfare as We Know It.* Washington, D.C.: Brookings Institution.

Weber, Bruce A., Emery N. Castle, and Ann L. Shriver. 1988. "Performance of Natural Resource Industries." In *Rural Economic Development in the 1980's: Prospects for the Future,* ed. D. L. Brown, J. N. Reid, H. Bluestone, D. A. McGranahan, and S. M. Mazie, 103–33. Rural Development Research Report 69, September, Agriculture and Rural Economy Division, Economic Research Service, U.S. Department of Agriculture. Washington, D.C.

Weber, Bruce A., and Greg J. Duncan. 2001. "Welfare Reform Reauthorization and Rural America: Implications of Recent Research." June, Joint Center for Poverty Research, Northwestern University and University of Chicago. Available at: http://www.jcpr.org/RuralPovertyReport.pdf.

Weber, Bruce A., Greg J. Duncan, and Leslie A. Whitener. 2002. *Rural Dimensions of Welfare Reform.* Kalamazoo, Mi.: W. E. Upjohn Institute for Employment Research.

Weber, Edward P. 2000. "A New Vanguard for the Environment: Grass-Roots Ecosystem Management as a New Environmental Movement." *Society and Natural Resources* 13 (3): 237–59.

Weinstein, Deborah. 1998. *Race to the Bottom: Plummeting Welfare Caseloads in the South and the Nation.* Washington, D.C.: Children's Defense Fund.

Weitzman, Elissa R., and Ichiro Kawachi. 2000. "Giving Means Receiving: The Protective Effect of Social Capital on Binge Drinking on College Campuses." *American Journal of Public Health* 90 (12): 1936–39.

Wellever, Anthony, and Tiffany A. Radcliff. 1998. "The Contributions of Local Government Financing to Rural Hospitals and Health Systems: Marginal Benefit or Safety Net?" Working Paper 25, November, Rural Health Research Center, School of Public Health, University of Minnesota.

Wells, Betty L. 1990. "Building Intercommunity Cooperation." *Journal of the Community Development Society* 21 (2): 1–17.

Werner, Emmy E., and Ruth S. Smith. 1989. *Vulnerable but Invincible: A Longitudinal Study of Resilient Children and Youth.* New York: Adams, Bannister, and Cox.

Westra, Karen L., and John Routley. 2000. "Arizona Cash Assistance Exit Study." First Quarter 1998 Cohort, Final Report, January, Office of Evaluation, Arizona Department of Economic Security. Phoenix, Az. Available at: http://www.de.state.az.us/links/reports/exitstudy.html.

Whatmore, Sarah. 1991. *Farming Women: Gender, Work and Family Enterprise.* London: Macmillan Publishers.

Whatmore, Sarah, Terry Marsden, and Philip Lowe. 1994. *Gender and Rurality.* London: David Fulton Publishers.

White, Julie, Ann Tickamyer, Debra Henderson, and Barry Tadlock. 2003. "Does Welfare-to-Work Work? Rural Employers Comment." In *Communities of Work: Rural Restructuring in Local and Global Perspective,* ed. William W. Falk, Michael Schulman and Ann R. Tickamyer. Athens: Ohio University Press.

White, Robert H. 1990. *Tribal Assets: The Rebirth of Native America.* New York: Henry Holt and Co.

White, Sarah C. 1996. "Depoliticising Development: The Uses and Abuses of Participation." *Development in Practice* 6 (1): 6–15.

White, Stephen E. 1998. "Migration Trends in the Kansas Ogallala Region and the Internal Colonial Dependency Model." *Rural Sociology* 63 (2): 253–71.

White, Steven M. and James Rotton. 1998. "Type of Commute, Behavioral Aftereffects, and Cardiovascular Activity: A Field Experiment." *Environment and Behavior* 30 (6): 763–80.

Whitener, Leslie A., and Timothy S. Parker. 1999. "Increasing the Minimum Wage: Implications for Rural Poverty and Employment." *Rural Development Perspectives* 14 (1): 2–8.

Whitener, Leslie, Bruce Weber, and Greg Duncan. 2002. "Reforming Welfare: What Does It Mean for Rural Areas?" Food Assistance and Nutrition Report 26-4, June, Economic Research Service, U.S. Department of Agriculture. Washington, D.C.

White Riley, Matilda, and Peter Uhlenberg. 2000. "Essays on Age Integration." *The Gerontologist* 42 (3): 261–308.

Whyte, William H. 1956. *The Organization Man.* New York: Simon and Schuster.

Wilentz, Sean. 1997. "Society, Politics, and the Market Revolution, 1815–1848." In *The New American History,* ed. E. Foner, 61–84. Philadelphia: Temple University Press.

Wilkins, David E. 1997. *American Indian Sovereignty and the U.S. Supreme Court: The Masking of Justice.* Austin: University of Texas Press.

Wilkinson, Charles F. 1987. *American Indians, Time, and the Law: Native Societies in a Modern Constitutional Democracy.* New Haven: Yale University Press.

Wilkinson, Kenneth P. 1991. *The Community in Rural America.* New York: Greenwood Press.

Williams, Donald C. 2000. *Urban Sprawl: A Reference Handbook.* Santa Barbara, Ca.: ABC-CLIO.

Wilson, Paul N. 2000. "Social Capital, Trust, and the Agribusiness of Economics." *Journal of Agricultural and Resource Economics* 25 (1): 1–13.

Wilson, William J. 1987. *The Truly Disadvantaged: The Inner City, the Underclass, and Public Policy.* Chicago: University of Chicago Press.

———. 1995. "Jobless Ghettos and the Social Outcome of Youngsters." In *Examining Lives in Context: Perspectives on the Ecology of Human Development,* ed. P. Moen, G. H. Elder Jr., and K. Lüscher, 527–43. Washington, D.C.: American Psychological Association.

———. 1996. *When Work Disappears: The World of the New Urban Poor.* New York: Alfred A. Knopf.

Wimberley, Ronald C., and Libby V. Morris. 1997. *The Southern Black Belt: A National Perspective.* Lexington: TVA Rural Studies, University of Kentucky.

———. 2002. "The Regionalization of Poverty: Assistance for the Black Belt South?" *Southern Rural Sociology* 18 (1): 294–306.

Winer, Michael B., and Karen Ray. 1994. *Collaboration Handbook: Creating, Sustaining, and Enjoying the Journey.* St. Paul: Amherst H. Wilder Foundation.

Wirth, Louis. 1938. "Urbanism as a Way of Life." *American Journal of Sociology* 44 (1): 1–24.

Wolf, Richard C. 1965. *Lutherans in North America.* Philadelphia: Lutheran Church Press.

Wolf, Steven A. 1998. *Privatization of Information and Agricultural Industrialization.* Boca Raton, Fl.: CRC Press.

Wolf, Steven A., and David Zilberman. 2001. *Knowledge Generation and Technical Change.* Boston: Kluwer Academic Publishers.

Wolff, Thomas. 2001. "Community Coalition Building—Contemporary Practice and Research: Introduction." *American Journal of Community Psychology* 29 (2): 165–72.

Wolman, Harold, and David Spitzley. 1996. "The Politics of Local Economic Development." *Economic Development Quarterly* 10 (2): 115–50.

Wood, Richard L. 1999. "Religious Culture and Political Action." *Sociological Theory* 17 (3): 307–32.

Woolcock, Michael. 1998. "Social Capital and Economic Development: Toward a Theoretical Synthesis and Policy Framework." *Theory and Society* 27 (2): 151–208.

World Bank. 2001. "World Development Report, 2000–2001: Attacking Poverty." New York: Oxford University Press. Available at: http://www.worldbank.org/poverty/wdrpoverty/.

Wright, Arthur W., John M. Clapp, Dennis R. Heffley, Subhash C. Ray, and Jon Vilasuso. 1993. *The Economic Impacts of the Foxwoods High-Stakes Bingo and Casino on New London County and Surrounding Areas.* Hartford, Conn.: Arthur W. Wright and Associates.

Wu, Lawrence L., and Barbara Wolfe. 2001. *Out of Wedlock: Causes and Consequences of Nonmarital Fertility.* New York: Russell Sage Foundation.

Wuthnow, Robert. 1993. *Christianity in the Twenty-First Century: Reflections on the Challenges Ahead.* New York: Oxford University Press.

Wyly, Elvin K. 1998. "Containment and Mismatch: Gender Differences in Commuting in Metropolitan Labor Markets." *Urban Geography* 19 (5): 395–430.

Wysong, Jere A., Mary K. Bliss, Jason W. Osborne, Robin P. Graham, and Denise A. Pikuzinski. 1999. "Managed Care in Rural Markets: Availability and Enrollment." *Journal of Health Care for the Poor and Underserved* 10 (1): 72–84.

Young, Frank W. 1967. "Adaptation and Pattern Integration of a California Sect." In *The Sociology of Religion: An Anthology,* ed. R. D. Knudten, 136–46. New York: Appleton-Century-Crofts.

———. 1970. "Reactive Subsystems." *American Sociological Review* 35 (2): 297–307.

Young, Frank W., and Thomas A. Lyson. 1993. "Branch Plants and Poverty in the American South." *Sociological Forum* 8 (3): 433–50.

———. 2001. "Structural Pluralism and All-Cause Mortality." *American Journal of Public Health* 91 (1): 136–38.

Zedlewski, Sheila R. 1998. "'States' New TANF Policies: Is the Emphasis on Carrots or Sticks?" *Policy and Practice of Public Human Services* 56 (2): 56–64.

Zedlewski, Sheila R., and Donald W. Alderson. 2001. "Before and After Reform: How Have Families on Welfare Changed?" Series B, No. B-32, April, The Urban Institute. Washington, D.C. Available at: http://newfederalism.urban.org/pdf/anf_b32.pdf.

Ziebarth, Ann, Kathleen Prochaska-Cue, and Bonnie Shrewsbury. 1997. "Growth and Locational Impacts for Housing in Small Communities." *Rural Sociology* 62 (1): 111–25.

Ziebarth, Ann, and Leann M. Tigges. 2003. "Earning a Living and Building a Life: Income-Generating and Income-Saving Strategies of Rural Wisconsin Families." In *Communities of Work: Rural Restructuring in Local and Global Perspective,* ed. William W. Falk, M. Schulman and Ann R. Tickamyer. Athens: Ohio University Press.

Zimmerman, Julie N. 1999. "Counting Cases: Changes in Welfare Recipiency Since 1993." Welfare Reform Information Brief 7, January, Southern Rural Development Center, Mississippi State University. Available at: http://ext.msstate.edu/srdc/publications/reform.htm.

Zimmerman, Julie N., and Lori Garkovich. 1998. "The Bottom Line: Welfare Reform, the Cost of Living, and Earnings in the Rural South." Welfare

Reform Information Brief 2, April, Southern Rural Development Center, Mississippi State University.

Zimmerman, Julie N., and Matthew Renfro-Sargent. 2000. "After Welfare Reform: K-TAP Cases Across Kentucky." Rural Issues Brief 3, December, College of Agriculture, University of Kentucky. Available at: http://ext.msstate.edu/srdc/publications/reform.htm.

Zimmerman, Mary K., and Rodney McAdams. 1999. "What We Say and What We Do: County-Level Public Spending for Health Care." *Journal of Rural Health* 15 (4): 421–30.

Zuniga, Victor, Ruben Hernandez-Leon, Janna Shadduck-Hernandez, and Mario Olivia Villarreal. 2002. "The New Paths of Mexican Immigrants in the United States: Challenges for Education and the Role of Mexican Universities." In *Education in the New Latino Diaspora: Policy and the Politics of Identity*, ed. S. Wortham, E. G. Murillo Jr., and E. T. Hamann, 99–116. Westport, Conn.: Ablex Publishing.

CONTRIBUTORS

LIONEL J. BEAULIEU, Ph.D. Purdue University, is Director of the Southern Rural Development Center and Professor at Mississippi State University. His major research activities are directed at human capital, workforce development, and youth educational achievement issues in rural America. He is President Elect of the Rural Sociological Society.

ALESSANDRO BONANNO, Ph.D. University of Kentucky, is Professor and Chair of the Sociology Department at Sam Houston State University. His research focuses on the implications that the globalization of the economy and society in general, and the agro-food sector in particular, have for democracy.

TED K. BRADSHAW, Ph.D. University of California, Berkeley, is Associate Professor in Community Development at the University of California, Davis, and editor of the *Journal of the Community Development Society*. His research is on rural development, local economic development, and complex community organizations, and he is currently writing a book on the California energy crisis.

JOAN M. BREHM, Ph.D. Utah State University, is Associate Professor of Sociology and Anthropology at Illinios State University. Her research focuses on natural resources, community, place attachment, and demography.

JEFFREY C. BRIDGER, Ph.D. Pennsylvania State University, is a Senior Research Associate in the Institute for Policy Research and Evaluation at the Pennsylvania State University. His research focuses on land use and planning, sustainable community development, and environmental conflict.

DAVID L. BROWN, Ph.D. University of Wisconsin, Madison, is Professor of Development Sociology and Director of the Polson Institute for Global Development at Cornell University. His research and teaching focus on migration and population redistribution and the sociology of community in the U.S. and in Eastern and Central Europe. He is a former president of the Rural Sociological Society.

RALPH B. BROWN, Ph.D. University of Missouri, Columbia, is Associate Professor and Graduate Coordinator of Sociology at Brigham Young

University. His research has centered on social change and development in rural communities.

FREDERICK H. BUTTEL, Ph.D. University of Wisconsin, is Professor of Rural Sociology and Environmental Studies, Co-Director of the Program on Agricultural Technology Studies, and a Senior Fellow in the Center for World Affairs and the Global Economy at the University of Wisconsin, Madison. His research focuses on the environment, technology, and agriculture in a global perspective.

DENNIS J. CONDRON, M.A. Ohio State University, is a doctoral student in the Department of Sociology at the Ohio State University. His research focuses on class and racial stratification in the educational process.

DOUGLAS H. CONSTANCE, Ph.D. University of Missouri, is Assistant Professor of Sociology at Sam Houston State University. His research interests focus on the impact on community of the globalization of the agro-food sector.

STEVEN E. DANIELS, Ph.D. Duke University, is Director of the Western Rural Development Center and Professor in the Department of Sociology, Social Work, and Anthropology and the Department of Environment and Society at Utah State University. His research focuses on natural resource conflict management.

LYNN ENGLAND, Ph.D. University of Pittsburgh, is Professor of Sociology at Brigham Young University. His research is centered on rural communities and Latin America.

WILLIAM W. FALK, Ph.D. Texas A&M University, is Professor and Chair of the Department of Sociology at the University of Maryland, College Park. He is the author, co-author, or co-editor of six books and over seventy articles, chapters, reviews, and essays. He is a former editor of *Rural Sociology,* and in 2001 he received the Rural Sociological Society's highest award, Distinguished Rural Sociologist.

CORNELIA BUTLER FLORA, Ph.D. Cornell University, is Charles F. Curtiss Distinguished Professor of Agriculture and Sociology at Iowa State University and Director of the North Central Regional Center for Rural Development. She is a former president of the Rural Sociological Society.

JAN L. FLORA, Ph.D. Cornell University, is Professor of Sociology and Extension Community Sociologist at Iowa State University. His current research analyzes the relationship of community social capital to economic, community, and sustainable development in the United States and Latin America. He is a former president of the Rural Sociological Society.

GLENN V. FUGUITT, Ph.D. University of Wisconsin, Madison, is Professor Emeritus of Rural Sociology and Sociology at the University of Wisconsin, Madison. His research has concentrated on migration and population redistribution, particularly as they relate to nonmetropolitan areas of the United States, demographic aspects of the American rural village, and commuting and rural/urban relationships. He is a former president of the Rural Sociological Society.

NINA GLASGOW, Ph.D. University of Illinois, Urbana, is Senior Research Associate in the Department of Development Sociology, Cornell University. Her research focuses on rural aging, rural health, and retirement migration.

LELAND GLENNA, Ph.D. University of Missouri, Columbia, holds a Master's degree in biblical theology from the Harvard University School of Divinity. He has worked for the Lutheran Church and as a postdoctoral associate and a lecturer in the Department of Rural Sociology at Cornell University, and now is studying university/industry partnerships in regard to agricultural biotechnology at the University of California, Davis.

ANGELA A. GONZALES, Ph.D. Harvard University, is Assistant Professor of Development Sociology at Cornell University. She is an enrolled member of the Hopi Tribe of Arizona and former director of the tribe's Grants and Scholarship Program. Her current research focuses on the impact of tribal gaming development in New York.

GARY PAUL GREEN, Ph.D. University of Missouri, Columbia, is Professor and Chair of Rural Sociology at the University of Wisconsin, Madison. His research focuses on community, economic, and workforce development issues.

ROSALIND P. HARRIS, Ph.D. Pennsylvania State University, holds a research position in the Department of Community and Leadership Development and a teaching appointment in the Department of Sociology at the University of Kentucky. She conducts sociohistorical research on poverty policy discourse as it relates to the rural South and its implications for children and youth.

DEBRA A. HENDERSON, Ph.D. Washington State University, is Assistant Professor of Sociology at Ohio University, where she teaches courses on family sociology and social inequality. Her research focuses on the effects of structured inequality on culturally diverse families, poverty and family resilience in rural Appalachia, and the impact of racism and inequality in sports.

THOMAS A. HIRSCHL, Ph.D. University of Wisconsin, Madison, is Professor of Development Sociology at Cornell University. His research and teaching interests concern social stratification over the life course, public policy, and demography.

GLENN D. ISRAEL, Ph.D. Pennsylvania State University, is Professor of Agricultural Education and Communication at the University of Florida. His research focuses on community, education, and evaluation methodology.

DOUGLAS B. JACKSON-SMITH, Ph.D. University of Wisconsin, Madison, is Assistant Professor of Sociology at Utah State University. His research focuses on the social and economic dynamics of rural and agricultural change in the United States and their impact on rural families, communities, and the environment.

LEIF JENSEN, Ph.D. University of Wisconsin, Madison, is Professor of Rural Sociology and Demography at the Pennsylvania State University. He studies issues of poverty, inequality, and employment both domestically and internationally.

KENNETH M. JOHNSON, Ph.D. University of North Carolina, Chapel Hill, is a demographer and Professor of Sociology at Loyola University, Chicago. He has written extensively on U.S. population redistribution trends focusing on nonmetropolitan areas, based on research funded by the USDA.

RICHARD S. KRANNICH, Ph.D. Pennsylvania State University, is Professor of Sociology at Utah State University. His research focuses on the social consequences of natural resource utilization and management for rural communities, with a particular emphasis on the western United States.

DANIEL T. LICHTER, Ph.D. University of Wisconsin, Madison, is Professor of Sociology and the Lazarus Chair in Population Studies at the Ohio State University. His current research focuses on poverty and welfare reform, changing patterns of marriage and family formation, and spatial inequality.

LINDA M. LOBAO, Ph.D. North Carolina State University, is Professor of Rural Sociology, Sociology, and Geography at the Ohio State University. Her research focuses on spatial inequality, rural development, agricultural change, and gender. She serves as president of the Rural Sociological Society for 2002–03.

A. E. LULOFF, Ph.D. Pennsylvania State University, is Professor of Rural Sociology in the Department of Agricultural Economics and Rural Sociology, and Senior Scientist at the Institute for Policy Research and Evaluation, at the Pennsylvania State University. His work examines the impact of rapid social change, as a result of demographic shifts, on the natural and human resource bases of the community.

THOMAS A. LYSON, Ph.D. Michigan State University, is Liberty Hyde Bailey Professor of Rural Sociology at Cornell University. His research focuses on community development, agriculture and food systems, and population health.

KATHERINE MACTAVISH, Ph.D. University of Illinois, Champaign-Urbana, is Professor of Human Development and Family Studies at Oregon State University. Her research focuses on child development and family well-being in the context of rural communities.

DAVID A. MCGRANAHAN, Ph.D. University of Wisconsin, Madison, is Senior Economist at the Economic Research Service, U.S. Department of Agriculture, where his research focuses on rural industrial change and the role of natural amenities in rural development.

DIANE K. MCLAUGHLIN, Ph.D. Pennsylvania State University, is Associate Professor of Development Sociology and Demography at the Pennsylvania State University. Her research focuses on rural poverty, inequality, and community development in the U. S.

PHILIP MCMICHAEL, Ph.D. State University of New York, Binghamton, is Professor and Chair of Development Sociology, Cornell University. His research focuses on development, social movements, global political economy, and the world food order.

LOIS WRIGHT MORTON, Ph.D. Cornell University, is Assistant Professor of Sociology at Iowa State University. Her research focuses on population health, civil society and civic structure and their effect on community health, watershed management, and community food security in the United States.

DOMENICO M. PARISI, Ph.D. Pennsylvania State University, is Assistant Professor of Rural Sociology at Mississippi State University. His research focuses on issues related to community development, rural spatial inequality, and natural resource management.

PEGGY PETRZELKA, Ph.D. Iowa State University, is Assistant Professor of Sociology at Utah State University. Her research focuses on the social impacts of national monument consideration and designations for gateway rural communities, particularly the impact on perceptions of community and place identity.

KENNETH E. PIGG, Ph.D. Cornell University, is Associate Professor and Extension Specialist in Rural Sociology at the University of Missouri, Columbia. His work focuses on research related to the deployment of information and communication technologies for rural community development purposes, and on evaluation of extension programs in community development.

VINCENT J. ROSCIGNO, Ph.D. North Carolina State University, is Associate Professor of Sociology at the Ohio State University. His current research focuses on spatial and institutional inequalities in education, adolescent well-being, and inequality and diffusion processes pertaining to historical and contemporary labor mobilization.

ROGELIO SAENZ, Ph.D. Iowa State University, is Professor and Department Head of Sociology at Texas A&M University. His research focuses on the migration, social inequality, and sociology of Latina/os.

SONYA SALAMON, Ph.D. University of Illinois, Champaign-Urbana, is Professor of Community Studies at the University of Illinois. Her research interests include families and community, families and the environment, family farming, and qualitative methods. She is a former president of the Rural Sociological Society.

JEFFREY S. SHARP, Ph.D. Iowa State University, is Assistant Professor of Rural Sociology at the Ohio State University. His research focuses on topics related to community, rural development, agriculture, and the rural/urban interface in the U.S.

TIM SLACK, M.S. Pennsylvania State University, is a Ph.D. candidate in Rural Sociology at the Pennsylvania State University. His dissertation research explores the economic strategies used by low-income rural families, with particular emphasis on the intersection of formal and informal economic activities.

LOUIS E. SWANSON, Ph.D. Pennsylvania State University, is Professor and Chair of Sociology at Colorado State University. Dr. Swanson researches and teaches in the areas of the sociology of agriculture, rural community, and policy studies on the agricultural environment and rural development. He is a former president of the Rural Sociological Society and has served as Chair of the Experiment Station Committee on Operations and Policy (ESCOP) Social Science Committee.

ANN R. TICKAMYER, Ph.D. University of North Carolina, Chapel Hill, is Professor of Sociology and Director of Development Studies at Ohio University and a past editor of *Rural Sociology*. Her research interests are gender and work, rural poverty, inequality, and labor markets in the U.S. and Indonesia. She is a former president of the Rural Sociological Society.

LEANNE M. TIGGES, Ph.D. University of Missouri, Columbia, is Professor of Rural Sociology at the University of Wisconsin. Her research focuses on dimensions of local labor markets and economic restructuring, particularly as they affect women and minorities.

CHARLES M. TOLBERT, Ph.D. University of Georgia, is Professor and Chair of the Department of Sociology and Anthropology, Baylor University. His research interests include social stratification, rural development, and social demography.

CRUZ C. TORRES, Ph.D. Texas A&M University, is Associate Professor of Rural Sociology at Texas A&M University. Her research focuses on health and aging, organizations, community, and sociology of Latina/os.

MILDRED E. WARNER, Ph.D. Cornell University, is Assistant Professor in the Department of City and Regional Planning at Cornell University. Her research focuses on economic development and the restructuring of local government service delivery through decentralization and privatization.

RONALD C. WIMBERLEY, Ph.D. University of Tennessee, is William Neal Reynolds Distinguished Professor of Sociology at North Carolina State University. His research deals primarily with the impoverishment of the Black Belt South. He is a former president of the Rural Sociological Society.

DREAMAL WORTHEN holds a research and teaching position in the College of Agriculture at Florida Agricultural and Mechanical University in Tallahassee, Florida. She conducts research on rural poverty and its impact on the elderly and disabled.

JULIE N. ZIMMERMAN, Ph.D. Cornell University, is Assistant Professor of Rural Sociology at the University of Kentucky, where she works in both research and Cooperative Extension. Her interests include poverty and inequality, public policy, and rural development.

INDEX

Page numbers in *italics* represent figures and tables.